ANNUAL EDITIONS

Comparative Politics

Twenty-Sixth Edition

08/09

Editor

Christian Søe
California State University, Long Beach

Christian Søe was born in Denmark, studied at the Universities of British Columbia (Vancouver), Michigan (Ann Arbor), and the Free University of Berlin, where he received his doctoral degree in political science. As professor (now *professor emeritus*) in political science at California State University in Long Beach, he has taught a variety of courses in comparative politics and contemporary political theory. His research continues to deal primarily with political developments in contemporary Germany. He visits that country regularly, as part of an effort to keep up with the continuities and shifts in German politics. He also maintains a strong interest in the impact of Germany as a relative giant on its many smaller—mostly much smaller—neighbors like Denmark, a topic he first explored in a book co-edited with Dirk Verheyen, *The Germans and Their Neighbors*. His more recent publications include a book co-edited with Mary N. Hampton, *Between Bonn and Berlin: German Politics Adrift?* It examines the last years of Helmut Kohl's center-right government. The milestone election of 1998 is the subject of another book, *Power Shift in Germany*, co-edited with David Conradt and Gerald R. Kleinfeld. The same team brought out a more recent volume on the 2002 Bundestag election, *A Precarious Victory: Schröder and the German Elections of 2002*. In many earlier publications or conference papers he has examined German coalition politics going back to the early 1960s. Dr. Søe has been editor of the twenty-six volumes of *Annual Editions: Comparative Politics* since the beginning of this series in 1983.

Boston   Burr Ridge, IL   Dubuque, IA   New York   San Francisco   St. Louis
Bangkok   Bogotá   Caracas   Kuala Lumpur   Lisbon   London   Madrid   Mexico City
Milan   Montreal   New Delhi   Santiago   Seoul   Singapore   Sydney   Taipei   Toronto

ANNUAL EDITIONS: COMPARATIVE POLITICS, TWENTY-SIXTH EDITION

1 2 3 4 5 6 7 8 9 0 QPD/QPD 0 9 8

ISBN 978–0–07–339766–5
MHID 0–07–339766–0
ISSN 0741–7233

Managing Editor: *Larry Loeppke*
Managing Editor : *Faye Schilling*
Developmental Editor: *Jade Benedict*
Editorial Assistant: *Nancy Meissner*
Production Service Assistant: *Rita Hingtgen*
Permissions Coordinator: *Shirley Lanners*
Senior Marketing Manager: *Julie Keck*
Marketing Communications Specialist: *Mary Klein*
Marketing Coordinator: *Alice Link*
Project Manager: *Jean Smith*
Design Specialist: *Tara McDermott*
Senior Administrative Assistant: *DeAnna Dausener*
Senior Production Supervisor: *Laura Fuller*
Cover Graphics: *Kristine Jubeck*

Compositor: Laserwords Private Limited
Cover Images: IMS Communications Ltd./Capstone Design/Flat Earth Images and Philip Coblentz/Brand X Pictures/Picture Quest

Library in Congress Cataloging-in-Publication Data
Main entry under title: Annual Editions: Comparative Politics. 2008/2009.
 1. Comparative Politics—Periodicals. I. Periodicals. I. Søe, Christian, *comp*. II. Title: Comparative Politics.
658'.05

www.mhhe.com

Editors/Advisory Board

Members of the Advisory Board are instrumental in the final selection of articles for each edition of ANNUAL EDITIONS. Their review of articles for content, level, currentness, and appropriateness provides critical direction to the editor and staff. We think that you will find their careful consideration well reflected in this volume.

Preface

In publishing ANNUAL EDITIONS we recognize the enormous role played by the magazines, newspapers, and journals of the public press in providing current, first-rate educational information in a broad spectrum of interest areas. Many of these articles are appropriate for students, researchers, and professionals seeking accurate, current material to help bridge the gap between principles and theories and the real world. These articles, however, become more useful for study when those of lasting value are carefully collected, organized, indexed, and reproduced in a low-cost format, which provides easy and permanent access when the material is needed. That is the role played by ANNUAL EDITIONS.

One expects to find differences in style, language and approach in articles culled from a variety of publications that range from daily newspapers to academic journals. What brings these writings together is their **shared interest in exploring patterns of governance and politics in different settings.** The articles have been chosen because they serve to promote **a comparative perspective on politics.**

This year the volume has been reorganized, but much of the familiar lay-out has been retained. Each of the six units contains a handful of articles that explore a set of related topics. They are introduced by overviews that give some background and commentary to the readings that follow.

Unit One introduces **comparative politics** as a vigorous and important subfield in political science. It goes on to discuss different systems of governance in the modern world, both democratic and undemocratic. Special attention is directed to the **"Index of Democracy,"** which ranks 167 countries in today's world in terms of the democratic quality of their governance. Only 27 countries are listed as "full" democracies, with the United States ranked in the 17th place, ahead of Britain and France, but trailing countries like Germany, Ireland, Switzerland, and Canada as well as all the Scandinavian countries that together with the Netherlands occupy the top six places.

The "Index of Democracy" gives some perspective on the way systems of government differ. Its inclusion of a section on "methodology" makes it easy to disaggregate a country's overall score and rank. Students are encouraged to think critically about the manner in which such an index is constructed and applied. Soft data and subjective judgment can easily enter into the process of assessment.

The reputation of democracy increased markedly in the last quarter of the twentieth century. This **rise in status** accompanied a huge forward leap that came to be known as the "third wave of democratization." Some of the change was cosmetic: Thomas Caruthers and Marina Ottaway point to the frequent gap between a democratic rhetoric of self presentation and a still largely undemocratic reality. In articles that are widely regarded as among the best on the subject, Robert Dahl as well as Phillipe Schmitter and Terry Lynn Karl discuss the essential features of a representative democracy. Even the "old," "full" or "established" democracies fall short of meeting these criteria completely.

Unit Three covers a number of institutional aspects of modern democracy—political parties and interest groups, judicial review, and the so-called "new politics" with its search for alternative modes of political expression. There is also a comparative discussion of the slow and uneven advance of women into high public office. It requires political will and organization to make real advances toward gender equality, but some institutions like proportional representation (PR) will make it easier to approach that goal. The importance of institutions also underlies Christopher Allen's proposal for an American switch to a parliamentary form of government with a multiparty system based on PR electoral rules.

Units Two, Four and Five contain a total of **ten country** and **four area studies.** The leading industrial countries and established pluralist democracies are presented in **Unit Two—Britain, France, Germany, and Japan.** These four countries have all gone through recent changes in leadership. **Unit Four** brings a juxtaposition of the **European Union, Russia, and China.** These three giants have very little in common apart from their large size and different kinds and levels of "democratic deficits." A case can be made for bringing such very different systems together for comparative purposes, and Robert Dahl has frequently pointed to "the size of the unit" as a factor that ought to be considered in our comparative political studies. **Unit Five** adds four more countries, this time from the developing world—**India, Iran, Nigeria, and Mexico** as well as the **three larger regions of Latin America, the Middle East, and sub-Saharan Africa.**

Unit Six completes the volume by considering three major trends in contemporary politics from a comparative perspective. First, the most recent "wave of democratization" appears to have come to a halt, but it is likely to have left permanent changes in the political process in many countries that previously knew only authoritarian rule. Yet reversals do occur. Some recent "authoritarian rebounds" remind us that there is no simple or guaranteed way to construct a stable democracy anywhere—least of all in countries that are troubled by deep ethnic, economic, religious and similar divisions.

Second, beginning in the early 1980s or sometimes even earlier, a major neoliberal shift took place in economic policy toward greater reliance on private enterprise and markets. There was a corresponding reduction in state ownership and regulation in much of the world, including

China, Soviet Russia, and more recently India. Here too there have been counter-trends in the form of political reactions against the inequalities, dislocations, and uncertainties associated with an unfettered market economy. That has not meant a return to the old status quo, but a new willingness to try "third way" approaches that promise to strive for both efficiency and social justice.

Third, many parts of the world have seen a surge of what has been called "identity politics." This trend has brought group identities more strongly into play when differences are being defined, played out, and resolved in the political arena. Amy Chua and Benjamin Barber warn in different ways about the potential costs of an intense form of such a politics that defines who is "in" and who is "out."

This is an important time to study comparative politics. The past few years have brought changes in the political landscape of many countries along with generational shifts in leadership. Even in a time of political transformation, however, there will often be significant patterns of continuity as well.

Let me add a special word of thanks to the many students who have taken my classes in comparative politics at California State University, Long Beach since my arrival for what was planned as a short period of teaching before "moving on." The students have been wonderfully inquisitive and their reactions to the annual edition have helped keep me posted on matters that must be addressed in such a publication. Some have helped me with suggestions for new materials.

As always, I am particularly grateful to Susan B. Mason, who received her master's degree in political science from Cal State Long Beach more than fifteen years ago. She has continued every year since then, from a distance of some three thousand miles, to volunteer as a research assistant. Over the years, many other former students have left an imprint on the series. It is impossible to name them all, but four names stand out: Linda Wohlman, Mike Petri, Erika Reinhart, and Ali Taghavi. It has been a great joy to work with young people who show a contagious enthusiasm for the project. It seemed like a vote of confidence to learn that Mike Petri's recently published American Government textbook, *Democracy and Action,* includes a series of short comparative sections that draw on his work with me.

To meet the annual deadlines, I have been able to rely on the ready assistance of my two sons, Nils and Erik, who practically grew up with this project. As professor in a very different field, Louise Soe has many academic obligations of her own, but she always finds time to enjoy with me the world we share beyond the paper jungle. Thanks also to Rowena Moore and Margaret Dennis for their cheerful assistance in critical moments. As always, I am indebted to my colleagues and members of the advisory board and McGraw-Hill/Contemporary Learning Series. Finally I wish to thank the many readers who have made useful comments on past selections and suggested new ones. I ask you all to help improve future editions by keeping me informed of your reactions and suggestions for change. Please complete and return the article rating form in the back of the book.

Christian Søe
Editor

Contents

UNIT 1
Patterns of Democratic and Non-Democratic Governance

The concepts in bold italics are developed in the article. For further expansion, please refer to the Topic Guide.

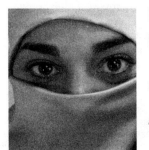

UNIT 2
Pluralist Democracies: Four Country Studies

The concepts in bold italics are developed in the article. For further expansion, please refer to the Topic Guide.

The concepts in bold italics are developed in the article. For further expansion, please refer to the Topic Guide.

UNIT 3
Factors in the Political Process

The concepts in bold italics are developed in the article. For further expansion, please refer to the Topic Guide.

UNIT 4
Three Very Different Giants: Europe, Russia, China

The concepts in bold italics are developed in the article. For further expansion, please refer to the Topic Guide.

UNIT 5
Political Diversity in the Developing World: Country Studies

The concepts in bold italics are developed in the article. For further expansion, please refer to the Topic Guide.

UNIT 6
Major Trends and Continuing Challenges

The concepts in bold italics are developed in the article. For further expansion, please refer to the Topic Guide.

The concepts in bold italics are developed in the article. For further expansion, please refer to the Topic Guide.

Correlation Guide

The *Annual Editions* series provides students with convenient, inexpensive access to current, carefully selected articles from the public press. **Annual Editions: Comparative Politics 08/09** is an easy-to-use reader that presents articles on important topics in the field of comparative politics. For more information on *Annual Editions* and other *McGraw-Hill Contemporary Learning Series* titles, visit www.mhcls.com.

This convenient guide matches the units in **Annual Editions: Comparative Politics 08/09** with the corresponding chapters in one of our best-selling McGraw-Hill Political Science textbooks by Sodaro.

Annual Editions: Comparative Politics 08/09	**Comparative Politics, 3/e by Sodaro**
Unit 1: Patterns of Democratic and Non-Democratic Governance	**Chapter 1:** Comparative Politics: What Is It? Why Study It?
	Chapter 5: The State and Its Institutions
	Chapter 6: States and Nations
	Chapter 7: Democracy: What Is It?
Unit 2: Pluralist Democracies: Four Country Studies	**Chapter 16:** The United Kingdom of Great Britain and Northern Ireland
	Chapter 17: France
	Chapter 18: Germany
	Chapter 19: Japan
Unit 3: Factors in the Political Process	**Chapter 8:** Democracy: How Does It Work?
	Chapter 9: Democracy: What Does It Take?
	Chapter 12: Political Culture
	Chapter 13: Ideology
Unit 4: Three Very Different Giants: Europe, Russia, China	**Chapter 14:** Political Economy
	Chapter 20: Russia
	Chapter 21: China
Unit 5: Political Diversity in the Developing World: Country Studies	**Chapter 10:** Conditions for Democracy In Afghanistan and Iraq
	Chapter 15: The Politics of Development
	Chapter 22: Mexico and Brazil
	Chapter 23: Nigeria and South Africa
Unit 6: Major Trends and Continuing Challenges	**Chapter 2:** Major Topics of Comparative Politics
	Chapter 11: People and Politics: Participation in Democracies and Nondemocracies

Topic Guide

This topic guide suggests how the selections in this book relate to the subjects covered in your course. You may want to use the topics listed on these pages to search the Web more easily.

On the following pages a number of Web sites have been gathered specifically for this book. They are arranged to reflect the units of this *Annual Edition*. You can link to these sites by going to the student online support site at *http://www.mhcls.com/online/*.

ALL THE ARTICLES THAT RELATE TO EACH TOPIC ARE LISTED BELOW THE BOLD-FACED TERM.

African society and politics
1. The Economist Intelligence Unit's Index of Democracy
2. The Failed States Index 2007
3. Democracy's Sobering State
4. Facing the Challenge of Semi-Authoritarian States
5. What Political Institutions Does Large-Scale Democracy Require?
6. What Democracy Is . . . and Is Not
20. Let Women Rule
21. The True Clash of Civilizations
35. Will Africa Ever Get It Right?
36. Africa's Crises of Democracy
43. Cultural Explanations
45. Jihad vs. McWorld

American Democracy in Comparative Perspective
1. The Economist Intelligence Unit's Index of Democracy
2. The Failed States Index 2007
3. Democracy's Sobering State
4. Facing the Challenge of Semi-Authoritarian States
5. What Political Institutions Does Large-Scale Democracy Require?
6. What Democracy Is . . . and Is Not
7. Public Opinion: Is There a Crisis?
8. Advanced Democracies and the New Politics
20. Let Women Rule
21. The True Clash of Civilizations
23. Referendums: The People's Voice
25. The Case for a Multi-Party U.S. Parliament?
40. Iran's Conservative Revival
41. Anti-Americanisms
42. Capitalism and Democracy
43. Cultural Explanations

British politics and society
1. The Economist Intelligence Unit's Index of Democracy
7. Public Opinion: Is There a Crisis?
8. Advanced Democracies and the New Politics
9. British Constitutional Change
10. The Historic Legacy of Tony Blair
11. Muslim's Veils Test Limits of Britain's Tolerance
18. Political Parties: Empty Vessels?
19. Interest Groups: Ex Uno, Plures
20. Let Women Rule
21. The True Clash of Civilizations
22. Judicial Review: The Gavel and the Robe
23. Referendums: The People's Voice
25. The Case for a Multi-Party U.S. Parliament?
27. A Venture at a Standstill

Central and Eastern Europe
1. The Economist Intelligence Unit's Index of Democracy
2. The Failed States Index 2007

Chinese politics and society
1. The Economist Intelligence Unit's Index of Democracy
3. Democracy's Sobering State
4. Facing the Challenge of Semi-Authoritarian States
31. China: The Quiet Revolution
32. In China, Talk of Democracy Is Simply That
33. China to Join Top 3 Economies
42. Capitalism and Democracy
43. Cultural Explanations
44. An Explosive Combination

Conservative and Neo-Liberal Parties
9. British Constitutional Change
10. The Historic Legacy of Tony Blair
12. The Gaullist Revolutionary
14. Angela Merkel's Germany
16. Japanese Spirit, Western Things
17. Come Together: How to Avoid a Twisted Diet
18. Political Parties: Empty Vessels?
19. Interest Groups: Ex Uno, Plures
20. Let Women Rule
21. The True Clash of Civilizations
27. A Venture at a Standstill
34. How Did We Get Here? Mexican Democracy After the 2006 Elections
40. Iran's Conservative Revival

Democratic politics
2. The Failed States Index 2007
3. Democracy's Sobering State
4. Facing the Challenge of Semi-Authoritarian States
5. What Political Institutions Does Large-Scale Democracy Require?
6. What Democracy Is . . . and Is Not
7. Public Opinion: Is There a Crisis?
8. Advanced Democracies and the New Politics
9. British Constitutional Change
10. The Historic Legacy of Tony Blair
11. Muslim's Veils Test Limits of Britain's Tolerance
14. Angela Merkel's Germany
15. Germans Split over a Mosque and the Role of Islam
17. Come Together: How to Avoid a Twisted Diet
20. Let Women Rule
21. The True Clash of Civilizations
23. Referendums: The People's Voice
25. The Case for a Multi-Party U.S. Parliament?

Internet References

The following Internet sites have been carefully researched and selected to support the articles found in this reader. The easiest way to access these selected sites is to go to our student online support site at *http://www.mhcls.com/online/*.

AE: Comparative Politics 08/09

The following sites were available at the time of publication. Visit our Web site—we update our student online support site regularly to reflect any changes.

General Sources

Central Intelligence Agency
http://www.odci.gov

Use this official home page to get connections to *The CIA Factbook,* which provides extensive statistical and political information about every country in the world.

National Geographic Society
http://www.nationalgeographic.com

This site provides links to National Geographic's archive of maps, articles, and documents. There is a great deal of material related to political cultures around the world.

U.S. Information Agency
http://usinfo.state.gov/

This USIA page provides definitions, related documentation, and discussion of topics on global issues. Many Web links are provided.

UNIT 1: Patterns of Democratic and Non-Democratic Governance

World Bank
http://www.worldbank.org

News (press releases, summaries of new projects, speeches) and coverage of numerous topics regarding development, countries, and regions are provided at this site.

World Wide Web Virtual Library: International Affairs Resources
http://www.etown.edu/vl/

Surf this site and its extensive links to learn about specific countries and regions, to research international organizations, and to study such vital topics as international law, development, the international economy, and human rights.

UNIT 2: Pluralist Democracies: Four Country Studies

France.com
http://www.france.com

The links at this site will lead to extensive information about the French government, politics, history, and culture.

GermNews
http://www.germnews.de/dn/about/

Search this site for German political and economic news covering the years 1995 to the present.

Japan Ministry of Foreign Affairs
http://www.mofa.go.jp

Visit this official site for Japanese foreign policy statements and discussions of regional and global relations.

UNIT 3: Factors in the Political Process

Carnegie Endowment for International Peace
http://www.ceip.org

This organization's goal is to stimulate discussion and learning among both experts and the public at large on a wide range of international issues. The site provides links to the well-respected journal *Foreign Policy,* to the Moscow Center, to descriptions of various programs, and much more.

Inter-American Dialogue (IAD)
http://www.iadialog.org

This is the Web site for IAD, a premier U.S. center for policy analysis, communication, and exchange in Western Hemisphere affairs. The 100-member organization has helped to shape the agenda of issues and choices in hemispheric relations.

The North American Institute (NAMI)
http://www.northamericaninstitute.org

NAMI, a trinational public-affairs organization concerned with the emerging "regional space" of Canada, the United States, and Mexico, provides links for study of trade, the environment, and institutional developments.

UNIT 4: Three Very Different Giants: Europe, Russia, China

Europa: European Union
http://europa.eu.int

This server site of the European Union will lead you to the history of the EU; descriptions of EU policies, institutions, and goals; discussion of monetary union; and documentation of treaties and other materials.

NATO Integrated Data Service (NIDS)
http://www.nato.int/structur/nids/nids.htm

NIDS was created to bring information on security-related matters to the widest possible audience. Check out this Web site to review North Atlantic Treaty Organization documentation of all kinds, to read *NATO Review,* and to explore key issues in the field of European security.

Research and Reference (Library of Congress)
http://lcweb.loc.gov/rr/

This massive research and reference site of the Library of Congress will lead you to invaluable information on the former Soviet Union and other countries attempting the transition to democracy. It provides links to numerous publications, bibliographies, and guides in area studies.

Russian and East European Network Information Center, University of Texas at Austin

http://reenic.utexas.edu

This is *the* Web site for information on Russia and the former Soviet Union.

Inside China Today

http://www.einnews.com/china/

Part of the European Internet Network, this site leads to information on China, including recent news, government, and related sites pertaining to mainland China, Hong Kong, Macao, and Taiwan.

UNIT 5: Political Diversity in the Developing World

Africa News Online

http://allafrica.com/

Open this site for extensive, up-to-date information on all of Africa, with reports from Africa's leading newspapers, magazines, and news agencies. Coverage is country-by-country and regional. Background documents and Internet links are among the resource pages.

ArabNet

http://www.arab.net

This home page of ArabNet, the online resource for the Arab world in the Middle East and North Africa, presents links to 22 Arab countries. Each country Web page classifies information using a standardized system of categories.

Organization for Economic Cooperation and Development

http://www.oecd.org/home/

Explore development, governance, and world trade and investment issues on this OECD site. It provides links to many related topics and addresses global economic issues on a country-by-country basis.

Sun SITE Singapore

http://sunsite.nus.edu.sg/noframe.html

These South East Asia Information pages provide information and point to other online resources about the region's 10 countries, including Vietnam, Indonesia, and Brunei.

UNIT 6: Major Trends and Continuing Challenges

Commission on Global Governance

http://www.sovereignty.net/p/gov/gganalysis.htm

This site provides access to *The Report of the Commission on Global Governance,* produced by an international group of leaders who want to find ways in which the global community can better manage its affairs.

IISDnet

http://www.iisd.org/default.asp

This site of the International Institute for Sustainable Development, a Canadian organization, presents information through links on business and sustainable development, developing ideas, and Hot Topics. Linkages is its multimedia resource for environment and development policy makers.

ISN International Relations and Security Network

http://www.isn.ethz.ch

This site, maintained by the Center for Security Studies and Conflict Research, is a clearinghouse for extensive information on international relations and security policy. Topics are listed by category (Traditional Dimensions of Security, New Dimensions of Security) and by major world regions.

United Nations Environment Program

http://www.unep.ch/

Consult this home page of UNEP for links to critical topics about global issues, including decertification and the impact of trade on the environment. The site leads to useful databases and global resource information.

We highly recommend that you review our Web site for expanded information and our other product lines. We are continually updating and adding links to our Web site in order to offer you the most usable and useful information that will support and expand the value of your Annual Editions. You can reach us at: *http://www.mhcls.com/annualeditions/.*

World Map

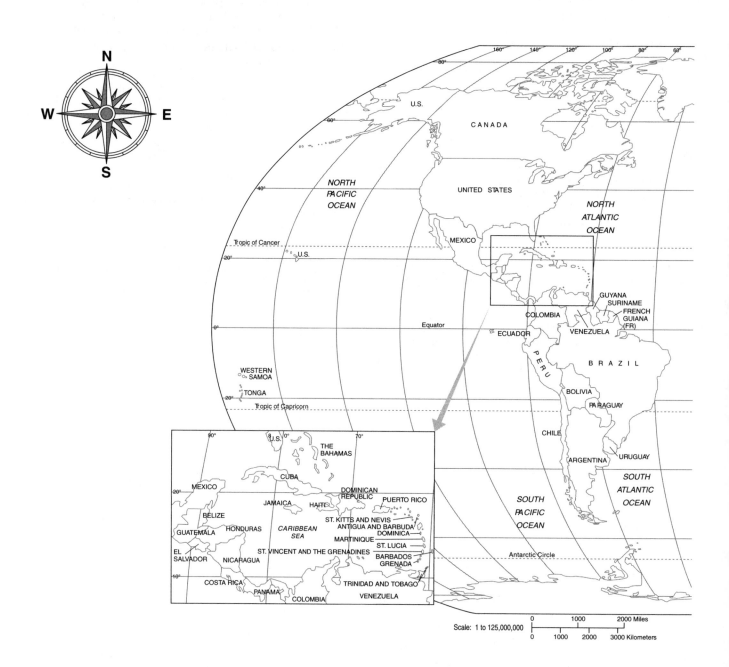

N W E S

160° 140° 120° 100° 80° 60°

80°

U.S.

CANADA

60°

NORTH
PACIFIC
OCEAN

UNITED STATES

NORTH
ATLANTIC
OCEAN

40°

MEXICO

Tropic of Cancer

20°

U.S.

GUYANA
SURINAME
FRENCH
GUIANA
(FR)

COLOMBIA

ECUADOR

VENEZUELA

Equator

0°

P
E
R
U

B R A Z I L

WESTERN
SAMOA

BOLIVIA

TONGA

PARAGUAY

20°

Tropic of Capricorn

CHILE

URUGUAY

ARGENTINA

SOUTH
ATLANTIC
OCEAN

SOUTH
PACIFIC
OCEAN

Antarctic Circle

90° 0° U.S. 70°

THE
BAHAMAS

CUBA

MEXICO

20°

DOMINICAN
REPUBLIC

PUERTO RICO

JAMAICA

HAITI

BELIZE

ST. KITTS AND NEVIS
ANTIGUA AND BARBUDA
DOMINICA

GUATEMALA

HONDURAS

CARIBBEAN
SEA

MARTINIQUE

ST. LUCIA

EL
SALVADOR

NICARAGUA

ST. VINCENT AND THE GRENADINES

BARBADOS
GRENADA

10°

COSTA RICA

TRINIDAD AND TOBAGO

PANAMA

COLOMBIA

VENEZUELA

Scale: 1 to 125,000,000

0   1000   2000 Miles

0   1000   2000   3000 Kilometers

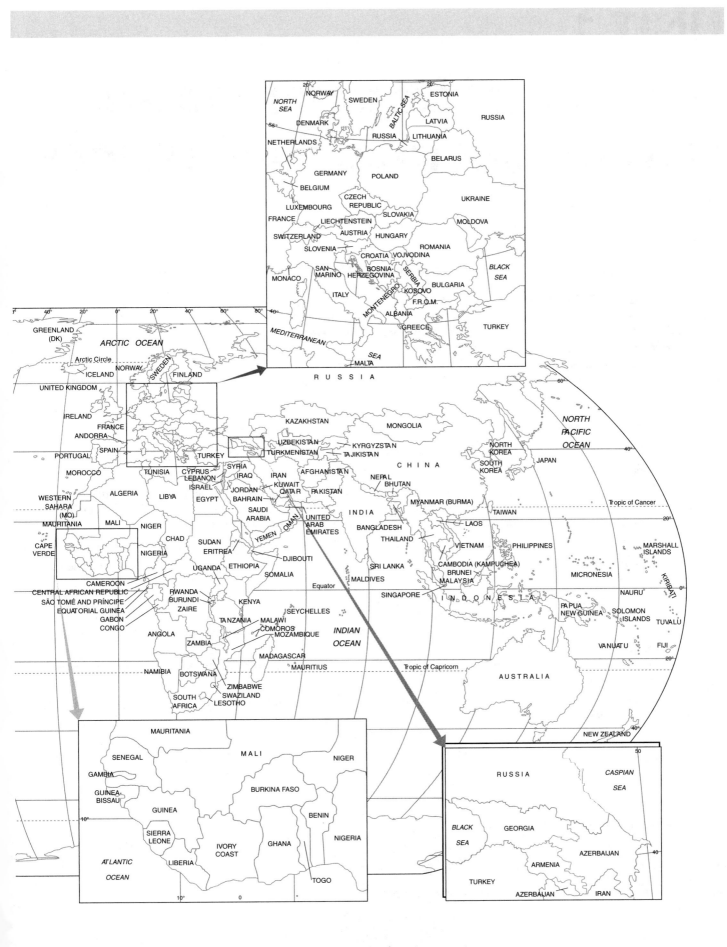

UNIT 1

Patterns of Democratic and Non-Democratic Governance

Unit Selections

Key Points to Consider

- What is the difference between "grand theory" and "middle range theory," and why do most comparativists seem to prefer the latter?

- What is the "index of democracy?" How does it measure a country's score and rank on its democracy scale?

- What does it mean when Laza Kekk points out that when the *Economist Intelligence Unit* constructed its index, it adopted a "*thicker*" concept of democracy than the one developed by Freedom House? And how does this difference largely (but not wholly) explain why there are more countries listed as democracies on the Freedom House scale?

- Why are the United States and Britain ranked relatively low among the 28 "full democracies" on the index?

- Is there a bias in favor of democratic welfare states in such an index? Or how else can the high placement of the Scandinavian countries, the Netherlands, and Canada be explained?

- Why and how do Thomas Carothers and Marina Ottaway question the simple model of democratization that takes place as a three-part process: a fairly short period of liberalization of society and market, followed by the democratic transition to multiparty elections, concluding with a prolonged democratic consolidation and deepening? Explain the distinction between "electoral democracies" and "liberal democracies."

- Is a liberal democracy always more efficient and productive than an authoritarian society? Is a liberal democracy always more affluent and harmonious than an authoritarian one?

- Why and how do Philippe Schmitter and Terry Lynn Karl want to go beyond Joseph Schumpeter's relatively simple definition of democracy? What does Robert Dahl mean by "polyarchy?"

Student Web Site
www.mhcls.com/online

Internet References
Further information regarding these Web sites may be found in this book's preface or online.

World Bank
http://www.worldbank.org
World Wide Web Virtual Library: International Affairs Resources
http://www.etown.edu/vl/

Many comparativists seem to believe they have landed in the most interesting and dynamic subfield of political science. You can sense their scholarly enthusiasm in a series of fascinating interviews collected in a recent book with the well chosen title, *Passion, Craft, and Method in Comparative Politics.*[i] In their reflections on the quest to advance a comparative understanding of government and politics, they "talk of many things." After all, their subject is a multi-faceted one. Yet the underlying theme is invariably their search for significant patterns in the interactions of human beings and institutions that bear on governance in human societies. Nowadays, comparativists tend to shy away from the kind of **grand theory** that once seemed to hold the promise of explaining the basic interrelationships. Instead they are now likely to strive for more modest **middle-range theory** that seeks to explain discrete segments of a complex social reality. Like Isaiah Berlin's **fox,** in the essay "The Hedgehog and the Fox," they are intellectual pluralists who "know many things." They stand in contrast to the monist **hedgehog** who knows "one big thing."

Why take a course in comparative politics? One basic reason would be that this is hardly a time for political illiteracy about the more than six billion other human beings with whom we share this planet. Learning about politics in settings that differ from our own will broaden your intellectual horizon and leave you with a sharpened sense for the importance of **context** or **setting** in politics. Paradoxically, or so it may seem, in your study of other societies and their politics you will end up learning much more about the United States and gain a fresh perspective on our political landscape.

Our Different Institutional Arrangements. Institutions are important building blocks in a country's politics. It turns out that they are not neutral but have an important impact on the political process itself—an insight that underlays James Madison and Alexander Hamilton's reflections on the new U.S. Constitution in *The Federalist Papers*. In your studies, you will soon learn that our "Madisonian" political institutions have not done well as transplants into foreign settings, with some rare exceptions like judicial review. That discovery leads many students to ask a very good question that you may want to think about as the semester proceeds: **Why have the political institutions and practices of the United States, with their more than 200 years of meeting the pragmatic test of performance ("does it work?"), not been widely copied or adapted in the rest of the democratic world? After all, they are not protected by copyright or patent laws!**

In your answer, you might consider the following: There are numerous adaptations of **the parliamentary system,** whether in its British **majoritarian form** or continental **consensus version** (we return to both in Unit Two). More recently, the basic format of **the semi-presidential system** in France's Fifth Republic, with its very strong executive and relatively weak legislature, has found many imitators in the new democracies.

Public Domain

In thinking of an answer, you may also wish apply some critical thinking to the old saw according to which "that government is best which governs least." It is helpful to understand why Francis Fukuyama, in analyzing the founding and maintenance of a well functioning state, makes a key distinction between its **scope** and **strength.** Using the distinction developed in his important book, *State-Building,* he suggests that Americans have a very strong and effective state, but adds that it is one that deliberately from the beginning was given a relatively limited scope of activities. People in the advanced industrial societies of Western Europe and elsewhere have a far higher past experience and future expectation of state intervention into societal life than do Americans. Would the high degree of limitation, fragmentation and dispersion of power in the United States appear to meet the needs of people who are used to a greater scope of state services, as in the provision of some form of national health insurance? You will also soon discover that these other countries share some governing problems and challenges with the United States—but quite often have some distinctive responses of their own. "One size doesn't fit all," as another political saw admonishes us. Yet there may well be room for learning a little from each other about good governance. But even if you end up concluding that—all things considered—the U.S. political system is about "as good as it gets," you will have gained a broader, comparative perspective on government and politics in modern society. Not least, you are likely to understand what a great challenge it is to build and maintain a well functioning political system—especially a flourishing democracy—in the United States or anywhere else. Based on historical experience, there will be a regular need for upkeep and renewal.

What is comparative politics? In common usage, the term refers to both a subfield of political science and a distinctive methodology for the study of politics. Used in the first and broader sense, comparative politics involves the selective and systematic comparison of domestic politics in foreign countries. Its focus is on what Joseph La Palombara once called **Politics Within Nations.** It was an aptly chosen title for his book on comparative politics because of the subtle but important difference from **Politics Among Nations**—the title already used by another scholar, Hans J. Morgenthau, for a major work on international relations. In other words, comparative politics does not focus on the relations **among nation states** but on the patterns of politics **within the domestic arena,** where political parties, interest groups, civil servants, public and published opinion are among the many participants in the political process.

Today, the distinction between these two subfields has become somewhat more blurred. In practice, international relations and comparative politics now overlap more than was the case when Morgenthau and La Palombara wrote their books. The change has been encouraged by such developments as the border-eroding force of globalization and the emergence of transnational institutions like the European Union (EU). If British economic policy becomes more likely to be set in Brussels than in Whitehall, then the comparativists who specialize in political economy will not close up shop but may consider making a shift to a EU reference point.

The second definition of comparative politics identifies it far more stringently with a methodology ("the *how?*" of the analysis) rather than the object of study ("the *what?*" of the analysis).[ii] It emphasizes careful empirical comparison as the way to gain knowledge about the political process. This definition's strict emphasis on establishing comparative politics as the empirical, scientific study of political phenomena serves as a useful reminder to comparativists to be prudent in their scholarship. If seriously applied as a criterion for entry into the subfield, this definition could create havoc. It would result in the exclusion of many an interpretive work and author, including some of the best known and most insightful ones. One of the many victims would likely be the book mentioned at the beginning. Its title would have to drop the reference to "craft" and probably to "passion," retaining only the reference to "method in comparative politics."

Yet the "craft" of comparative politics probably survives and thrives because the scholars involved are rarely quite such strict methodologists in practice as this definition suggests. They tend to be eclectic and pragmatic in their choice of appropriate ways to study different aspects of the political world. Some comparativists seem to do little systematic comparative cross-national comparison. Instead, they work more like country or area specialists. They inevitably make some explicit and implicit comparisons in their work, but they tend to be far less demanding than some of their colleagues. Their work is often rich in descriptive detail and can be very useful to comparativists looking for case studies.

What, then, is a democracy? The concept is a highly contested one, as Laza Kekic pointed out when introducing the 2007 "Index of Democracy."[iii] In his interview, Robert Dahl concurs and specifically expresses his frustration that after years of effort, political scientists have arrived at no generally agreed definition of the concept. His own preference for using the term "polyarchy" for a large representative democracy has

never really caught on outside academe. Joseph Schumpeter gave a frequently cited definition of representative democracy: "the institutional arrangement for arriving at political decisions in which individuals acquire the power to decide by means of a competitive struggle for the people's vote." Terry Karl and Phillipe Schmitter quote these well known phrases, but they are not alone in wanting a "thicker" definition that includes an emphasis on "the accountability of rulers to citizens and the relevance of mechanisms of competition other than elections."[iv]

It makes sense to follow Kekic's advice to **avoid an either/ or proposition** when using the term "democracy"—as in "a country is either democratic or it is not." That makes it possible to quantify and compare **the state of democratization** in two or more countries at the same time (synchronically) as the *Index of Democracy* tries to do. One can also make comparisons through or over time (diachronically) of one country or several as they become more or less democratic or the same country at different times and stages in its development (diachronically).

Avoidance of the either/or dichotomy also makes it possible to accept historically differing standards for a democracy. In that way, it is possible to call some of the **Greek city states** as well as **Alexis de Tocqueville's America** democratic within their historic setting, even though they would not pass muster by today's expectations about broad civic inclusion. Tocqueville regarded the United States as a thriving democracy in the early 1830s, yet by the year 1900 there still was no country—with the possible exception of New Zealand, where women were enfranchised—that would qualify as a democracy by the stricter criteria of today. By using a continuum, it becomes possible to differentiate between varying aspects and degrees of democracy.

Robert Dahl's article brings historical, institutional, and theoretical considerations to bear on our understanding of democracy. He names and explores six "fundamental" institutions that can be seen as essential for reaching a minimum level of modern representative democracy or "polyarchy." Dahl adds a set of further going democratic criteria that today's established democracies generally fall short of meeting. He ends with a normative call for consolidating and further raising the level of democratization everywhere.

In their article, Schmitter and Karl provide another perceptive discussion of democratic governance. They emphasize that democracies differ considerably in their institutional infrastructure, even as they meet some generic criteria that make democracy a unique political system. They add a useful reminder of "what a democracy is not." For example, a democracy does not provide a guarantee of any of the following: freer markets, higher economic growth, greater administrative efficiency, social peace, or ultimate political harmony.

A democratic inventory and ranking. In seeking points of comparison between countries, it is useful to begin with a general inventory of the alternative forms of rule found in the world's nearly 200 states. One such widely used survey has been provided for years by Freedom House. A new assessment, the **index of democracy** developed for 2007 by the *Economist*

Intelligence Unit, has been used here. It is accompanied with an easily accessible explanation of its methodology and is a useful source of comparative information on the state of governance in the world today. Its findings do not differ much from those of Freedom House. If anything, they tend to be a little less generous overall, and particularly in the cases of some countries. The "index of democracy" measures a slightly smaller number of countries than Freedom House—165 independent states and two territories. It excludes 25 micro-states. The index is included as the **first** reading for this Unit. It uses 60 indicators spread across five broad categories for each of the 167 countries, with each country ranked by its overall score. This aggregate score for each country could perhaps be regarded as measuring its "degree of democratization."

Some of the rankings will hardly surprise—above all the occupation of the first six places by the Scandinavian countries and the Netherlands. The relative placements of Germany (13th) and Japan (20th) might raise some eyebrows when compared to the ranking of the United States (17th), the UK (23rd) and France (24th). This may encourage critical reflections regarding some unavoidable subjective choices in the creation of such an index as well as its underlying methodology, and even the empirical data that lie behind the rankings.

The categories are based on a **"thick" or "non-minimalist" definition** of political democracy that includes the following:

- free elections and
- a basic guarantee of political freedoms and civil liberties.
- how well a government functions in implementing its decisions,
- how vigorously the citizenry takes advantage of the opportunities to participate in public life, and
- how supportive the political culture is of such democratic political participation.

In conformity with the dominant liberal democratic tradition, **the index does not include a social or economic component in its definition of political democracy.** In other words, Sweden does not head the list because it is a generous welfare state, but because it scores higher than any other country in the five categories on which the index is based.

In a summary of its findings, the index states that a little more than one-half of the world's population lives in "a democracy of some sort"—often a very imperfect one. Humanity's other half lives in decidedly non-democratic conditions. Using four regime types, the index concludes that:

- fewer than one person in seven (13 percent) lives in one of the 28 countries that it classifies as " **full democracies.**"
- almost three times as many people (38.3 percent) live in one of the 54 " **flawed democracies.**"
- approximately one person in ten (10.5 percent) is found in one of the 30 "**hybrid regimes.**"
- almost four in ten (38.5 percent) live in one of the 55 "**authoritarian regimes.**"

No Global Sweep of Democracy. There is no reason to assume that democratic rule will soon become global or that we can successfully build democracy when and where we choose. After a quarter of a century that recorded a widespread and unexpected advance of democratization, that trend appears to have come to a standstill in the late 1990s. There are signs that a weaker counter-trend of **partial retreat from democratic governance** may have set in—a topic taken up by Thomas Carother's article in this unit's readings.

Cultural and Socio-Economic Context. It would be hard not to be struck by **the very uneven distribution of both democracy** and income in the world of today. Is there a cultural-regional dimension embedded in the data? Even a cursory look at the index reminds one of a **striking regional concentration of regime types.**

- **The Middle East and Sub-Saharan Africa** have by far the highest incidence of authoritarian government and the lowest occurrence of democracy. The single case of "full democracy" among the 64 regimes in these two regions is the tiny island nation of Mauritius. There are 7 "flawed democracies" in sub-Saharan Africa, but only 2 in the Middle East and northern Africa.

- **Eastern Europe, Latin America, Asia, and Australasia** score high in the "flawed democracy" category, which is found in 43 of these regions' 80 countries. In addition, these regions have 14 cases of "hybrid regimes" and 16 "authoritarian regimes," including that of China. There are only seven "full democracies" here—including only a single case in Asia (Japan).

- **Western Europe,** by contrast, has 18 of its 21 countries ranked as "full democracies." Even more striking is the fact that of the world's 28 full democracies, all but two (Mauritius and Japan) lie either in Western Europe (18), in Central Europe (2), or in "overseas" countries that politically were dominated by settlers from Europe and their descendants (6).

Culture and region matter, but they are by no means the whole story. There are also countries within Europe, or settled from there, which have not participated fully in the democratic experience. And it is sobering to remember that the most virulent attacks on democracy in the twentieth century came from European fascists who claimed to represent the political wave of the future.

Strong States—Weak States—Failed States. The modern state, with its highly trained bureaucrats and monopoly of legal violence, is a key reference point in comparative politics. As an institution, it can be traced back thousands of years to the first agricultural societies in China and Mesopotamia. In its modern form, however, it is a European construct with its clearly marked territorial boundaries, within which it claims sovereignty and a monopoly on legal violence.

While the last two decades of the twentieth century were a time of revival of free market economics and a concomitant rollback of interventions by the activist state, comparativists in political science have stressed the need for strong, effective states that have the capacity to provide security and order for their societies. They see a very weak state as one in danger of becoming a failed state. A **strong state** can be defined as one that has the **institutional capacity to carry out its basic functions.** This argument reflects a Hobbesian assumption that without an effective state, human beings could end up in lives that are "solitary, poor, nasty, brutish, and short." The index of failed states provides a list of the 60 states considered to be endangered.

Democracies and Non-Democracies. The transition from some form of autocratic rule to a democratic one turned out to be a major political trend in many countries during the last quarter of the twentieth century. On closer look, the transition to democracy has often been a fragile process and in many cases, not a successful one. We nay need to remind ourselves how remarkable this trend was in the first place. Skeptics on both Right and Left had long raised doubts whether representative government was sufficiently effective and attractive to spread or survive in the modern world.

Samuel Huntington's widely discussed thesis concerning a recent wave of democratization underlies the article by Thomas Carothers. Huntington is not only one of the best-known observers of this trend, but he is also a former skeptic concerning democracy's future prospects. In the 1980s, before the collapse of the communist regimes in Europe, he began to identify a broad but not necessarily deep pattern of democratization. He traced its origins to the mid-1970s, when the three remaining dictatorships in Western Europe came to an almost simultaneous end (in Greece, Portugal, and Spain). In the following decade, democratization spread to most of Latin America. The countries of the Soviet bloc in Central and Eastern Europe followed. The trend also reached some states in East and South Asia like Taiwan and South Korea, as well as some parts of Africa, above all South Africa. Mexico's presidential election in the year 2000, with its transfer of political power after more than seven decades of one-party hegemony, can also be seen in this context.

Three Waves of Democratization. In a widely adopted phrase, Huntington identified this widespread trend as the "third" in a series of successive "waves" of democratization in modern history. The **"first wave"** had been slow to develop but long in its reach. It began in the 1820s and lasted about one century. During this period the United States and 28 other countries established governments based on a broad franchise that eventually came to include women as well as men.

A very short time after the end of the Great War, it was clear the world had not been "made safe for democracy." In the first half of the 1920s, Benito Mussolini installed a fascist dictatorship in Italy, and with it the first wave of democratization was replaced by a reverse wave of severe democratic setbacks—a **first "reverse wave"**—that lasted until the mid-1940s. During those two decades, the number of democracies in the world plunged from 29 by more than half. In the middle of World War II, there were only four full-fledged democratic states left in Europe. Three of them were neutral in a war in which democracy was at stake.

The **"second wave"** of democratization (mid 1940s to early 1960s) started with the Allied victory in World War II and continued during the early postwar years. It lasted until the early 1960s and included the liberated countries in Western Europe that immediately restored their democratic institutions and practices—the Netherlands, Belgium, Luxembourg, Denmark, Norway, France, and also Czechoslovakia. In addition, the major defeated powers, (Western) Germany and Japan, were steered toward democratic politics, while Italy and Finland moved on their own to restore a democratic form of government. There were democratic stirrings in several Latin American countries. Finally, in the process of decolonization, the newly independent countries often started out with a formal democratic framework—one that in many cases turned out to be fragile and sometimes of very short duration. These new states, along with some countries in Latin America, soon became the settings for a politics of authoritarian comebacks—the relatively short **second "reverse wave."** Although it only lasted a little over a decade, some of the new authoritarian regimes (like Chile) held on quite a few years longer. During this second period of setbacks, the total number of democracies fell to 30 and the number of non-democracies rose from 75 to 95, as various former colonies or newly minted democracies fell under authoritarian or dictatorial rule.

The **"third wave" of democratization** (from mid-1970s to mid-1990s turned out to be far more sweeping and universal than its predecessors. Already by the beginning of the 1990s, Huntington counted about 60 democracies in the world. Larry Diamond, another authority on the subject, reported in 2000 that 120 states out of a then-world total of 192 independent states (63 percent) met **at least the minimum requirements** for being classified as electoral democracies. The number was reduced to 71 (or 37 percent) when he applied the stricter standards of **liberal democracy**—which required observation of basic civil rights and liberties, rule of law, political independence and neutrality of the judiciary, an open, pluralist society, and civilian control of the military. His count comes close to that of the "democracy index" made six years later and using a similar (not identical) set of criteria. It lists 82 countries as democracies—but only 28 are counted as "full" democracies while 54 are ranked as "flawed" democracies (among the latter, Italy). The change is impressive, when one considers Robert Dahl's finding that only 22 countries can be identified as **"older democracies,"** in the sense of having a continuous political history as democracies since at least 1950. On the other hand, these findings lend support to the conclusion that democracy's advance in the last two centuries has been at best a "two steps forward, one step back" kind of progress.

Conditions that may have encouraged the third wave. Huntington and some other scholars have tried to identify a cluster of historical factors that would at least partly explain the unexpected third wave of democratization. In their view, one important factor was the widespread perception that the right- and left-wing authoritarian regimes—be they the military in much of Latin America or much of sub-Saharan Africa, the authoritarian oligarchies in parts of Asia and Africa, or the party rulers in the communist countries of Central Europe—all **"had failed to deliver"** on their promises. It was as though they had failed to pass some key test of performance. Another factor, it was suggested, was **the expansion of an urban middle class** with a strong interest in the rule of law and a representative government, at least in some of the countries touched by the third wave. In Latin America, especially, **the influence of a recently more liberal Catholic Church** may have played an important role, as discussed in Unit Five, but there was also a special interest in that two Latin European countries had moved from dictatorships to democracies so quickly. They had received considerable encouragement from the European Community to make the move.

European Community. The United States has promoted such a transition to democracy for other states, although in the Middle East may well have reduced transition to democracy in principle and, has also been suggested that a role was played by various forms of **external influence by the United States and the European Community,** as they have tried, however tentatively and selectively, to promote a human rights agenda. Finally, there was a **"snowballing" effect,** with the successful early transitions to democracy by countries like Spain or Portugal. They came to serve as role models, not least in Latin America. The fall of the Berlin Wall seems to have had almost immediate political repercussions in several of the Soviet bloc countries including Romania and Czechoslovakia.

Will the new democracies endure, stabilize, and become more democratic over time? The question has often been asked and deserves a complex answer. In the early years of the third wave, there was more optimism than later. It has dissipated for a number of reasons. Many of the new democracies have little historical experience with a democratic way of life. Extreme poverty has been recognized as a major obstacle to successful democratization, with Haiti often serving as a warning example. The cultural obstacles to democratization in the Middle East seem formidable—even in an officially secular but in reality highly Muslim country like Turkey. The experience in Iraq has not been kind to any plan to set up a democratic role model there. In his important article, "Democracy's Sobering State," Thomas Carothers puts a damper on the rhetorical enthusiasm for democratization. He emphasizes that it has run into a number of obstacles. Trying to spread it into the Middle East would be difficult and involve some serious trade-offs—possibly also in security. Most of his article deals with several factors that together have brought democratization to a standstill and encouraged reversals. He mentions **"the authoritarian rebound"** that has been made possible by the persistence and revival of authoritarian forces and structures in many countries. This phenomenon is also present in sev-

eral post-Soviet regimes—not least President Putin's Russia. Another widespread factor is democracy's own **"performance problem."** This refers to the unfulfilled high expectations that had originally been associated with the new democracies. They were the victims of a number setbacks resulting from weak state institutions, entrenched and corrupt elites, and poor systems of political representation and accountability. A third factor comes from the revived perception of an **authoritarian bonus** as some countries with authoritarian governments have done quite well socio-economically in recent years. This has led to a partial revival of the old beef that a dictatorship is superior to a democracy in producing economic development. A fourth factor that complicates democratic governance is found in the U.S. war in Iraq, resulting in a **damaged U.S. credibility** as a pro-democratic actor in the region.

The final and most complex issue concerning the advance of democracy in the near future is connected with its **dismal prospects in the Middle East.** Carothers describes this region as "stuck in deeply entrenched patterns of autocratic rule." It is not impossible that the Arab world will over time make some progress toward democracy, but it will not come swiftly and easily. Moreover, free elections the Middle East could lead to results that Washington would not welcome, as the case of Algeria reminds us.

We live in an age in which the concept "democracy" enjoys a high degree of legitimacy throughout most of the world. Few countries would take pride in identifying themselves as non-democratic. That wasn't always so. World War I, fought at least in American eyes to make the world "safe for democracy," played a major role in the rise of communism and fascism. While the former would claim to be a higher form of democracy, it clearly rejected the tradition of "bourgeois" liberal democracy as understood in the West. Fascism pulled no punches about its contempt for democracy and its own anti-democratic, totalitarian commitment.

---

[i] Gerardo L. Munck and Richard Snyder, eds., *Passion, Craft, and Method in Comparative Politics* (the Johns Hopkins University Press, 2007).

[ii] Arend Lijphart, "Comparative Politics and the Comparative Method," *American Political Science Review* (1971) vol. 65, no. 3.

[iii] Laza Kekic, The Economist Intelligence Unit's *Index of Democracy,* reprinted in *Comparative Politics 08/09.*

[iv] See endnote 3 in Phillipe C. Schmitter and Terry Lynn Karl, "What Democracy Is . . . and Is Not" (1991), reprinted in *Comparative Politics 08/09.* The authors include Schumpeter's definition of democracy.

The Economist Intelligence Unit's Index of Democracy

LAZA KEKIC

Defining and Measuring Democracy

There is no consensus on how to measure democracy, definitions of democracy are contested and there is an ongoing lively debate on the subject. The issue is not only of academic interest. For example, although democracy-promotion is high on the list of American foreign-policy priorities, there is no consensus within the American government on what constitutes a democracy. As one observer recently put it, "the world's only superpower is rhetorically and militarily promoting a political system that remains undefined—and it is staking its credibility and treasure on that pursuit" (Horowitz, 2006, p 114).

Although the terms "freedom" and "democracy" are often used interchangeably, the two are not synonymous. Democracy can be seen as a set of practices and principles that institutionalise and thus ultimately protect freedom. Even if a consensus on precise definitions has proved elusive, most observers today would agree that, at a minimum, the fundamental features of a democracy include government based on majority rule and the consent of the governed, the existence of free and fair elections, the protection of minorities and respect for basic human rights. Democracy presupposes equality before the law, due process and political pluralism. Is reference to these basic features sufficient for a satisfactory concept of democracy? As discussed below, there is a question of how far the definition may need to be widened.

Some insist that democracy is necessarily a dichotomous concept—a state is either democratic or not. But most measures now appear to adhere to a continuous concept, with the possibility of varying degrees of democracy. At present, the best-known measure is produced by the US-based Freedom House organisation. The average of its indexes, on a 1 to 7 scale, of political freedom (based on 10 indicators) and of civil liberties (based on 15 indicators) is often taken to be a measure of democracy.

The index is available for all countries, and stretches back to the early 1970s. It has been used heavily in empirical investigations of the relationship between democracy and various economic and social variables. The so-called Polity Project provides, for a smaller number of countries, measures of democracy and regime types, based on rather minimalist definitions, stretching back to the 19th century.

Freedom House also measures a narrower concept, that of "electoral democracy". Democracies in this minimal sense share at least one common, essential characteristic. Positions of political power are filled through regular, free, and fair elections between competing parties, and it is possible for an incumbent government to be turned out of office through elections. Freedom House criteria for an electoral democracy include:

1. A competitive, multiparty political system.
2. Universal adult suffrage.
3. Regularly contested elections conducted on the basis of secret ballots, reasonable ballot security and the absence of massive voter fraud.
4. Significant public access of major political parties to the electorate through the media and through generally open campaigning.

The Freedom House definition of political freedom is somewhat (though not much) more demanding than its criteria for electoral democracy—i.e., it classifies more countries as electoral democracies than as "free" (some "partly free" countries are also categorised as electoral democracies). At the end of 2005, 122 states were classified as electoral democracies; of these, 89 states were classified as free. The Freedom House political-freedom measure covers the electoral process and political pluralism and, to a lesser extent, the functioning of government and a few aspects of participation.

A key difference in the various measures of democracy is between "thin" or minimalist ones and "thick" or wider concepts (Coppedge, 2005). The thin concepts correspond closely to an immensely influential academic definition of democracy, that of Robert Dahl's concept of polyarchy (Dahl, 1970). Polyarchy has eight components, or institutional requirements: almost all adult citizens have the right to vote; almost all adult citizens are eligible for public office; political leaders have the right to compete for votes; elections are free and fair; all citizens are free to form and join political parties and other organisations; all citizens are free to express themselves on all political issues; diverse sources of information about politics exist and are protected by law; and government policies depend on votes and other expressions of preference.

The Freedom House electoral democracy measure is a thin concept. Its measure of democracy based on political rights and civil liberties is thicker than the measure of electoral democracy. Other definitions of democracy have broadened to include aspects of society and political culture in democratic societies.

The Economist Intelligence Unit's Measure of Democracy

The Economist Intelligence Unit's index is based on the view that measures of democracy that reflect the state of political freedoms and civil liberties are not thick enough. They do not encompass sufficiently or at all some features that determine how substantive democracy is or its quality. Freedom is an essential component of democracy, but not sufficient. In existing measures, the elements of political participation and functioning of government are taken into account only in a marginal way.

The Economist Intelligence Unit's democracy index is based on five categories: electoral process and pluralism; civil liberties; the

Table 1 Economist Intelligence Unit Democracy Index 2006

	Rank	Overall Score	I Electoral Process and Pluralism	II Functioning of Government	III Political Participation	IV Political Culture	V Civil Liberties
				Category scores			
Full democracies							
Sweden	1	9.88	10.00	10.00	10.00	9.38	10.00
Iceland	2	9.71	10.00	9.64	8.89	10.00	10.00
Netherlands	3	9.66	9.58	9.29	9.44	10.00	10.00
Norway	4	9.55	10.00	9.64	10.00	8.13	10.00
Denmark	5	9.52	10.00	9.64	8.89	9.38	9.71
Finland	6	9.25	10.00	10.00	7.78	8.75	9.71
Luxembourg	7	9.10	10.00	9.29	7.78	8.75	9.71
Australia	8	9.09	10.00	8.93	7.78	8.75	10.00
Canada	9	9.07	9.17	9.64	7.78	8.75	10.00
Switzerland	10	9.02	9.58	9.29	7.78	8.75	9.71
Ireland	11=	9.01	9.58	8.93	7.78	8.75	10.00
New Zealand	11=	9.01	10.00	8.57	8.33	8.13	10.00
Germany	13	8.82	9.58	8.57	7.78	8.75	9.41
Austria	14	8.69	9.58	8.21	7.78	8.75	9.12
Malta	15	8.39	9.17	8.21	6.11	8.75	9.71
Spain	16	8.34	9.58	7.86	6.11	8.75	9.41
US	17	8.22	8.75	7.86	7.22	8.75	8.53
Czech Republic	18	8.17	9.58	6.79	7.22	8.13	9.12
Portugal	19	8.16	9.58	8.21	6.11	7.50	9.41
Belgium	20=	8.15	9.58	8.21	6.67	6.88	9.41
Japan	20=	8.15	9.17	7.86	5.56	8.75	9.41
Greece	22	8.13	9.58	7.50	6.67	7.50	9.41
UK	23	8.08	9.58	8.57	5.00	8.13	9.12
France	24	8.07	9.58	7.50	6.67	7.50	9.12
Mauritius	25=	8.04	9.17	8.21	5.00	8.13	9.71
Costa Rica	25=	8.04	9.58	8.21	6.11	6.88	9.41
Slovenia	27=	7.96	9.58	7.86	6.67	6.88	8.82
Uruguay	27=	7.96	10.00	8.21	5.00	6.88	9.71
Flawed democracies							
South Africa	29	7.91	8.75	7.86	7.22	6.88	8.82
Chile	30	7.89	9.58	8.93	5.00	6.25	9.71
South Korea	31	7.88	9.58	7.14	7.22	7.50	7.94
Taiwan	32	7.82	9.58	7.50	6.67	5.63	9.71
Estonia	33	7.74	9.58	7.50	5.00	7.50	9.12
Italy	34	7.73	9.17	6.43	6.11	8.13	8.82
India	35	7.68	9.58	8.21	5.56	5.63	9.41
Botswana	36=	7.60	9.17	7.86	5.00	6.88	9.12
Cyprus	36=	7.60	9.17	6.79	6.67	6.25	9.12
Hungary	38	7.53	9.58	6.79	5.00	6.88	9.41
Cape Verde	39=	7.43	9.17	7.86	5.00	6.88	8.24
Lithuania	39=	7.43	9.58	6.43	6.67	5.63	8.82
Slovakia	41	7.40	9.58	7.50	6.11	5.00	8.82
Brazil	42	7.38	9.58	7.86	4.44	5.63	9.41
Latvia	43	7.37	9.58	6.43	6.11	5.63	9.12
Panama	44	7.35	9.58	7.14	5.56	5.63	8.82
Jamaica	45	7.34	9.17	7.14	5.00	6.25	9.12
Poland	46	7.30	9.58	6.07	6.11	5.63	9.12
Israel	47	7.28	9.17	6.64	7.78	7.50	5.29
Trinidad and Tobago	48	7.18	9.17	6.79	6.11	5.63	8.24
Bulgaria	49	7.10	9.58	5.71	6.67	5.00	8.53
Romania	50	7.06	9.58	6.07	6.11	5.00	8.53
Croatia	51	7.04	9.17	6.07	6.11	5.63	8.24

(continued)

Table 1   Economist Intelligence Unit Democracy Index 2006 *(continued)*

	Rank	Overall Score	I Electoral Process and Pluralism	II Functioning of Government	III Political Participation	IV Political Culture	V Civil Liberties
Ukraine	52	6.94	9.58	5.71	5.56	5.63	8.24
Mexico	53	6.67	8.75	6.07	5.00	5.00	8.53
Argentina	54	6.63	8.75	5.00	5.56	5.63	8.24
Serbia	55	6.62	9.17	5.36	5.00	5.63	7.94
Mongolia	56	6.60	9.17	6.07	3.89	5.63	8.24
Sri Lanka	57	6.58	6.92	5.00	5.56	7.50	7.94
Montenegro	58	6.57	9.17	5.71	5.00	5.63	7.35
Namibia	59=	6.54	4.75	4.00	6.67	8.75	8.53
Papua New Guinea	59=	6.54	7.33	6.43	4.44	6.25	8.24
Suriname	61	6.52	9.17	6.07	4.44	5.00	7.94
Moldova	62	6.50	9.17	4.29	6.11	5.00	7.94
Lesotho	63=	6.48	7.92	6.43	4.44	6.25	7.35
Philippines	63=	6.48	9.17	5.36	5.00	3.75	9.12
Indonesia	65=	6.41	6.92	7.14	5.00	6.25	6.76
Timor Leste	65=	6.41	7.00	5.57	5.00	6.25	8.24
Colombia	67	6.40	9.17	4.36	5.00	4.38	9.12
Macedonia	68	6.33	8.25	4.50	7.22	3.75	7.94
Honduras	69	6.25	8.33	6.43	4.44	5.00	7.06
El Salvador	70	6.22	9.17	5.43	3.89	4.38	8.24
Paraguay	71=	6.16	7.92	5.00	5.00	4.38	8.53
Benin	71=	6.16	6.83	6.43	3.89	6.88	6.76
Guyana	73	6.15	8.33	5.36	4.44	4.38	8.24
Dom Rep	74	6.13	9.17	4.29	3.33	5.63	8.24
Bangladesh	75=	6.11	7.42	5.07	4.44	6.25	7.35
Peru	75=	6.11	8.75	3.29	5.56	5.00	7.94
Guatemala	77	6.07	8.75	6.79	2.78	4.38	7.65
Hong Kong	78	6.03	3.50	5.71	5.00	6.25	9.71
Palestine	79	6.01	8.25	2.71	7.78	6.88	4.41
Mali	80	5.99	8.25	5.71	3.89	5.63	6.47
Malaysia	81=	5.98	6.08	5.71	4.44	7.50	6.18
Bolivia	81=	5.98	8.33	5.71	4.44	3.75	7.65
Hybrid regimes							
Albania	83	5.91	7.33	5.07	4.44	5.63	7.06
Singapore	84	5.89	4.33	7.50	2.78	7.50	7.35
Madagascar	85=	5.82	5.67	5.71	5.56	6.88	5.29
Lebanon	85=	5.82	7.92	2.36	6.11	6.25	6.47
Bosnia and Hercegovina	87	5.78	8.25	3.29	4.44	5.00	7.94
Turkey	88	5.70	7.92	6.79	4.44	3.75	5.59
Nicaragua	89	5.68	8.25	5.71	3.33	3.75	7.35
Thailand	90	5.67	4.83	6.43	5.00	5.63	6.47
Fiji	91	5.66	6.50	5.21	3.33	5.00	8.24
Ecuador	92	5.64	7.83	4.29	5.00	3.13	7.94
Venezuela	93	5.42	7.00	3.64	5.56	5.00	5.88
Senegal	94	5.37	7.00	5.00	3.33	5.63	5.88
Ghana	95	5.35	7.42	4.64	4.44	4.38	5.88
Mozambique	96	5.28	5.25	5.71	4.44	6.88	4.12
Zambia	97	5.25	5.25	4.64	3.33	6.25	6.76
Liberia	98	5.22	7.75	2.14	5.00	5.63	5.59
Tanzania	99	5.18	6.00	3.93	5.06	5.63	5.29
Uganda	100	5.14	4.33	3.93	4.44	6.25	6.76
Kenya	101	5.08	4.33	4.29	5.56	6.25	5.00
Russia	102	5.02	7.00	3.21	5.56	3.75	5.59
Malawi	103	4.97	6.00	5.00	3.89	4.38	5.59
Georgia	104	4.90	7.92	1.79	3.33	5.00	6.47

(continued)

Table 1 Economist Intelligence Unit Democracy Index 2006 *(continued)*

	Rank	Overall Score	I Electoral Process and Pluralism	II Functioning of Government	III Political Participation	IV Political Culture	V Civil Liberties
				Category scores			
Cambodia	105	4.77	5.58	6.07	2.78	5.00	4.41
Ethiopia	106	4.72	4.00	3.93	5.00	6.25	4.41
Burundi	107	4.51	4.42	3.29	3.89	6.25	4.71
Gambia	108	4.39	4.00	4.64	4.44	5.63	3.24
Haiti	109	4.19	5.58	3.64	2.78	2.50	6.47
Armenia	110	4.15	4.33	3.21	3.89	3.13	6.18
Kyrgyzstan	111	4.08	5.75	1.86	2.78	5.00	5.00
Iraq	112	4.01	4.75	0.00	5.56	5.63	4.12
Authoritarian regimes							
Pakistan	113=	3.92	4.33	5.36	0.56	4.38	5.00
Jordan	113=	3.92	3.08	3.79	3.89	5.00	3.82
Comoros	115=	3.90	3.00	3.21	4.44	5.63	3.24
Morocco	115=	3.90	3.50	3.79	2.78	5.63	3.82
Egypt	115=	3.90	2.67	3.64	2.78	6.88	3.53
Rwanda	118	3.82	3.00	3.57	2.22	5.00	5.29
Burkina Faso	119	3.72	4.00	1.79	2.78	5.63	4.41
Kazakhstan	120	3.62	2.67	2.14	3.33	4.38	5.59
Sierra Leone	121	3.57	5.25	2.21	2.22	3.75	4.41
Niger	122	3.54	5.25	1.14	1.67	3.75	5.88
Bahrain	123	3.53	3.50	2.57	2.78	5.00	3.82
Cuba	124=	3.52	1.75	4.64	3.89	4.38	2.94
Nigeria	124=	3.52	3.08	1.86	4.44	4.38	3.82
Nepal	126	3.42	0.08	3.57	2.22	5.63	5.59
Côte d'Ivoire	127	3.38	1.25	2.86	3.33	5.63	3.82
Belarus	128	3.34	2.58	2.86	3.33	4.38	3.53
Azerbaijan	129	3.31	3.08	0.79	3.33	3.75	5.59
Cameroon	130	3.27	0.92	3.21	2.78	5.63	3.82
Congo Brazzaville	131	3.19	1.42	2.86	2.22	5.63	3.82
Algeria	132	3.17	2.25	2.21	2.22	5.63	3.53
Mauritania	133	3.12	1.83	4.29	2.22	3.13	4.12
Kuwait	134	3.09	1.33	4.14	1.11	5.63	3.24
Afghanistan	135=	3.06	6.17	0.00	2.22	2.50	4.41
Tunisia	135=	3.06	0.00	2.36	2.22	6.88	3.82
Yemen	137	2.98	2.67	2.71	2.78	4.38	2.35
China	138	2.97	0.00	4.64	2.78	6.25	1.18
Swaziland	139=	2.93	1.75	2.86	2.22	3.13	4.71
Iran	139=	2.93	0.08	3.57	3.89	5.63	1.47
Sudan	141	2.90	2.25	2.36	1.67	5.00	3.24
Qatar	142	2.78	0.00	3.43	1.67	5.00	3.82
Oman	143	2.77	0.00	3.07	1.67	5.00	4.12
Democratic Republic of Congo	144	2.76	4.58	0.36	2.78	3.75	2.35
Vietnam	145	2.75	0.83	4.29	2.78	4.38	1.47
Gabon	146	2.72	0.50	3.21	2.22	5.63	2.06
Bhutan	147=	2.62	0.08	4.64	1.11	3.75	3.53
Zimbabwe	147=	2.62	0.17	0.79	3.89	5.63	2.65
Tajikistan	149	2.45	1.83	0.79	2.22	6.25	1.18
UAE	150	2.42	0.00	3.07	1.11	5.00	2.94
Angola	151	2.41	0.50	2.14	1.11	5.63	2.65
Djibouti	152	2.37	2.50	1.43	0.56	5.00	2.35
Syria	153	2.36	0.00	1.79	1.67	6.88	1.47
Eritrea	154	2.31	0.00	2.14	1.11	6.25	2.06
Laos	155	2.10	0.00	3.21	1.11	5.00	1.18
Equatorial Guinea	156	2.09	0.00	2.86	1.11	5.00	1.47

(continued)

9

Table 1 Economist Intelligence Unit Democracy Index 2006 *(continued)*

			Category scores				
	Rank	Overall Score	I Electoral Process and Pluralism	II Functioning of Government	III Political Participation	IV Political Culture	V Civil Liberties
Guinea	157	2.02	1.00	0.79	2.22	3.75	2.35
Guinea-Bissau	158	2.00	2.08	0.07	3.33	1.88	2.65
Saudi Arabia	159	1.92	0.00	2.36	1.11	4.38	1.76
Uzbekistan	160	1.85	0.08	0.79	2.78	5.00	0.59
Libya	161	1.84	0.00	1.64	1.11	5.00	1.47
Turkmenistan	162	1.83	0.00	0.79	2.78	5.00	0.59
Myanmar	163	1.77	0.00	1.79	0.56	5.63	0.88
Togo	164	1.75	0.00	0.79	0.56	5.63	1.76
Chad	165	1.65	0.00	0.00	0.00	5.00	3.24
Central Africa	166	1.61	0.42	1.43	1.67	1.88	2.65
North Korea	167	1.03	0.83	2.50	0.56	1.25	0.00

functioning of government; political participation; and political culture. The five categories are interrelated and form a coherent conceptual whole. The condition of having **free and fair competitive elections**, and satisfying related aspects of political freedom, is clearly the basic requirement of all definitions.

All modern definitions, except the most minimalist, also consider **civil liberties** to be a vital component of what is often called "liberal democracy". The principle of the protection of basic human rights is widely accepted. It is embodied in constitutions throughout the world as well as in the UN Charter and international agreements such as the Helsinki Final Act. Basic human rights include freedom of speech, expression and the press; freedom of religion; freedom of assembly and association; and the right to due judicial process. All democracies are systems in which citizens freely make political decisions by majority rule. But rule by the majority is not necessarily democratic. In a democracy majority rule must be combined with guarantees of individual human rights and the rights of minorities.

Most measures also include aspects of the minimum quality of **functioning of government**. If democratically based decisions cannot or are not implemented then the concept of democracy is not very meaningful or it becomes an empty shell.

Democracy is more than the sum of its institutions. A democratic **political culture** is also crucial for the legitimacy, smooth functioning and ultimately the sustainability of democracy. A culture of passivity and apathy, an obedient and docile citizenry, are not consistent with democracy. The electoral process periodically divides the population into winners and losers. A successful democratic political culture implies that the losing parties and their supporters accept the judgment of the voters, and allow for the peaceful transfer of power.

Participation is also a necessary component, as apathy and abstention are inimical to democracy. Even measures that focus predominantly on the processes of representative, liberal democracy include (although inadequately or insufficiently) some aspects of participation. In a democracy, government is only one element in a social fabric of many and varied institutions, political organisations and associations. Citizens cannot be required to take part in the political process, and they are free to express their dissatisfaction by not participating. However, a healthy democracy requires the active, freely chosen participation of citizens in public life. Democracies flourish when citizens are willing to take part in public debate, elect representatives and join political parties. Without this broad, sustaining participation, democracy begins to wither and become the preserve of small, select groups.

Table 2 Democracy Index 2006 by Regime Type

	Countries	% of Countries	% of World Population
Full democracies	28	16.8	13.0
Flawed democracies	54	32.3	38.3
Hybrid regimes	30	18.0	10.5
Authoritarian regimes	55	32.9	38.2

"World" population refers to total population of the 167 countries that are covered. Since this excludes only micro states this is nearly equal to the entire actual estimated world population in 2006.
Source: Economist Intelligence Unit; CIA World Factbook

At the same time, even our thicker, more inclusive and wider measure of democracy does not include other aspects—which some authors argue are also crucial components of democracy—such as levels of economic and social wellbeing. Thus our index respects the dominant tradition that holds that a variety of social and economic outcomes can be consistent with political democracy.

The Economist Intelligence Unit's index provides a snapshot of the current state of democracy worldwide for 165 independent states and two territories. This covers almost the entire population of the world and the vast majority of the world's 192 independent states (27 micro-states are excluded).

Several things stand out. Although almost half of the world's countries can be considered to be democracies, the number of "full democracies" is relatively low (only 28). Almost twice as many (54) are rated as "flawed democracies". Of the remaining 85 states, 55 are authoritarian and 30 are considered to be "hybrid regimes". As could be expected, the developed OECD countries (with the notable exception of Italy) dominate among full democracies, although there are two Latin American, two central European and one African country, which means that the level of development is not a binding constraint. Only one Asian country, Japan, makes the grade.

More than half of the world's population lives in a democracy of some sort, although only some 13% reside in full democracies. Despite

2007 Watchlist

Positive Watch

Hong Kong: further improvements in civil liberties and democratic political practices after Donald Tsang's election as chief executive in March 2007.

Negative Watch

Taiwan: risk of a no-confidence vote in the government that could trigger a constitutional crisis; increased pressures in the runup to the 2007 parliamentary elections.

Bangladesh: caretaker government will oversee general elections in early 2007. An unclear or disputed election result could trigger political crisis and rollback of democracy.

Armenia: parliamentary election in May 2007 could be highly flawed, tipping the country into an outright authoritarian regime.

Russia: at present a hybrid regime, with a trend towards curtailment of media and other civil liberties. A potentially highly flawed parliamentary election at the end of 2007 would reflect a further intensification of the country's apparent slide in an authoritarian direction.

Nigeria: a disputed April 2007 election to be followed by political turbulence and the possible installation of a military-backed interim government.

Burundi: president and government intensify crackdown on opponents. The country could slide from a hybrid regime to authoritarianism.

Guinea and Guinea-Bissau are already rated as authoritarian, but things could get even worse in 2007 as there is a high risk of military coups in both. In Guinea there is a risk of a military takeover in 2007 if ailing President Lansana Conte dies. In Guinea-Bissau rising discontent in the army increases the risk of a coup.

Mauritania: the country is undergoing a democratic transition following a military coup in August 2005. But there is a high risk of a backlash, especially as the move from military to civilian rule has potentially destabilising inter-ethnic implications. Hopes of democratisation are unlikely to be fulfilled.

the advances in democracy in recent decades, almost 40% of the world's population still lives under authoritarian rule (with a large share of these being, of course, in China). Given the most recent trends, that are tantamount to a retreat from democracy as discussed in our article in *The World in 2007*, it is unlikely that this proportion will decrease significantly soon. On our ten-country watchlist for likely significant changes in 2007 (see box below) only one country is on positive watch and nine are on negative watch.

The relationship between the level of development (income per head) and democracy is not clear-cut. There is an apparent association, although even in the full democracy category there are a few that are not rich OECD countries. The simple correlation between our democracy index and GDP per head ($ at PPP) in 2006 is 0.6. This may look surprisingly low—it implies that in a simple two-variable regression of the democracy index on income per head, less than 40% of the intercountry variation in democracy is explained by income levels. If we also control for oil wealth (with a so-called dummy variable that takes a value of 1 for major oil exporting countries and 0 otherwise), the explanatory power of the regression rises sharply to almost two-thirds of the intercountry variation in the democracy index. Although this still leaves more than one-third of the variation unexplained, it illustrates the often-observed strong negative impact on democratic development of a reliance on oil.

However, the direction of causality between democracy and income is debatable. The standard modernisation hypothesis that economic development leads to—and is a necessary pre-condition for—democracy, is no longer universally accepted. Instead it has been

argued that the primary direction of causation runs from democracy to income (Rigobon and Rodrik, 2005; Acemoglu et al, 2005).

One advantage of our index compared with others is that it provides for considerable differentiation of scores, including among developed countries. The "near-perfect" democracy is Sweden, the country with the highest score. The other Nordic countries also have high ranks. By contrast, the United States and Britain are near the bottom of the full democracy category, but for somewhat different reasons. America falls down on some aspects of governance and civil liberties. Despite low election turnouts, political participation in the United States is comparatively high. In Britain low political participation (the lowest in the developed world) is a major problem, and to a lesser extent, for now, so are eroding civil liberties. The rating for France is also comparatively low as a result of modest scores for the functioning of government, political participation and political culture. Italy performs even worse, and falls in the flawed democracies category—as a result of problems in functioning of government and the electoral process, as well as weaknesses in the political culture.

These results seem to highlight the interesting hypothesis that large countries, other things being equal, tend to be less democratic. But this appears to be the case only among the developed countries. It does not hold across the whole sample—there is no significant relationship between the value of the democracy index and the size of population for the entire 167-country sample.

Looking at the regional distribution of regime types, flawed democracies are concentrated in Latin America and eastern Europe, and to a lesser extent in Asia. Despite progress in Latin American democratisation in

Table 3 Democracy Across the Regions

	Democracy Index Average	Number of Countries	Full Democracies	Flawed Democracies	Hybrid Regimes	Authoritarian Regimes
North America	8.64	2	2	0	0	0
West Europe	8.60	21	18	2	1	0
Eastern Europe	5.76	28	2	14	6	6
Latin America & the Caribbean	6.37	24	2	17	4	1
Asia & Australasia	5.44	28	3	12	4	9
Middle East & North Africa	3.53	20	0	2	2	16
Sub-Saharan Africa	4.24	44	1	7	13	23
Total	5.52	167	28	54	30	55

recent decades, many countries in the region remain fragile democracies. Levels of political participation are generally very low and democratic cultures are weak (with the caudillismo phenomenon still widespread according to opinion surveys). There has also been significant backsliding in recent years in some areas such as media freedoms.

Much of eastern Europe illustrates the difference between formal and substantive democracy. The new EU members from the region have pretty much equal levels of political freedoms and civil liberties as the old developed EU, but lag significantly in political participation and political culture—a reflection of widespread anomie and weaknesses of democratic development. Only two countries from the region—the Czech Republic and Slovenia (just)—are in the full democracy category. Hybrid and authoritarian regimes dominate heavily in the countries of the former Soviet Union, as the momentum towards "colour revolutions" has appeared to peter out.

Most of the world's authoritarian regimes are to be found in the Middle East and Africa, although there is also a fair number in Asia. The dearth of democratic regimes in the Middle East and North Africa is a well-known phenomenon, with much debate about the causes. In the statistical relationship between democracy and income discussed above, a dummy variable for Middle East and North Africa is negative and highly significant statistically even when oil wealth is controlled for in our 167-country sample—that is, Middle East and North Africa has much lower levels of democratisation than could be inferred on the basis of income levels. A similar variable for Asia is also negative, although at lower levels of statistical significance. And there is some evidence that western Europe's average democracy levels are higher than even its high income levels would suggest. For other regions—Sub-Saharan Africa, eastern Europe and Latin America—average level of democratic development correspond to what would be expected on the basis of average income levels.

Methodology

The Economist Intelligence Unit's index of democracy, on a 0 to 10 scale, is based on the ratings for 60 indicators grouped in five categories: electoral process and pluralism; civil liberties; the functioning of government; political participation; and political culture. Each category has a rating on a 0 to 10 scale, and the overall index of democracy is the simple average of the five category indexes.

The category indexes are based on the sum of the indicator scores in the category, converted to a scale of 0 to 10. Adjustments to the category scores are made if countries do not score a 1 in the following critical areas for democracy:

1. Whether national elections are free and fair;
2. The security of voters;
3. The influence of foreign powers on government;
4. The capability of the civil service to implement policies.

If the scores for the first three questions are 0 (or 0.5), one point (0.5 point) is deducted from the index in the relevant category (either the electoral process and pluralism or the functioning of government). If the score for 4 is 0, one point is deducted from the functioning-of-government category index.

The index values are used to place countries within one of four types of regimes:

1. Full democracies—scores of 8–10.
2. Flawed democracies—scores of 6 to 7.9.
3. Hybrid regimes—scores of 4 to 5.9.
4. Authoritarian regimes—scores below 4.

Threshold points for regime types depend on overall scores that are rounded to one decimal point.

The Scoring System

We use a combination of a dichotomous and a three-point scoring system for the 60 indicators. A dichotomous 1-0 scoring system (1 for a yes and 0 for a no answer) is not without problems, but it has several distinct advantages over more refined scoring scales (such as the often-used 1-5 or 1-7). For many indicators, the possibility of a 0.5 score is introduced, to capture "grey areas" where a simple yes (1) or no (0) is problematic, with guidelines as to when that should be used. Thus for many indicators there is a three-point scoring system, which represents a compromise between simple dichotomous scoring and the use of finer scales.

The problems of 1-5 or 1-7 scoring scales are numerous. For most indicators under such a system, it is extremely difficult to define meaningful and comparable criteria or guidelines for each score. This can lead to arbitrary, spurious and non-comparable scorings. For example, a score of 2 for one country may be scored a 3 in another and so on. Or one expert might score an indicator for a particular country in a different way to another expert. This contravenes a basic principle of measurement, that of so-called reliability—the degree to which a measurement procedure produces the same measurements every time, regardless of who is performing it. Two- and three-point systems do not guarantee reliability, but make it more likely.

Second, comparability between indicator scores and aggregation into a multi-dimensional index appears more valid with a two- or three-point scale for each indicator (the dimensions being aggregated are similar across indicators). By contrast, with a 1-5 system, the scores are more likely to mean different things across the indicators (for example a 2 for one indicator may be more comparable to a 3 or 4 for another indicator, rather than a 2 for that indicator). The problems of a 1-5 or 1-7 system are magnified when attempting to extend the index to many regions and countries.

Some Features of the Economist Intelligence Unit's Index
Public Opinion Surveys

A crucial, differentiating aspect of our measure is that in addition to experts' assessments we use, where available, public opinion surveys—mainly the World Values Survey. Indicators based on the surveys predominate heavily in the political participation and political culture categories, and a few are used in the civil liberties and functioning of government categories.

In addition to the World Values Survey, other sources that can be leveraged include the Eurobarometer surveys, Gallup polls, Latin American Barometer, and national surveys. In the case of countries for which survey results are missing, survey results for similar countries and expert assessment are used to fill in gaps.

Participation and Voter Turnout

After increasing for many decades, there has been a trend of decreasing voter turnout in most established democracies since the 1960s. Low turnout may be due to disenchantment, but it can also be a sign of contentment. Many, however, see low turnout as undesirable, and there is much debate over the factors that affect turnout and how to increase it.

A high turnout is generally seen as evidence of the legitimacy of the current system. Contrary to widespread belief, there is in fact a close correlation between turnout and overall measures of democracy—i.e., developed, consolidated democracies have, with very few exceptions, higher turnout (generally above 70%) than less established democracies.

The Legislative and Executive Branches

The appropriate balance between these is much-disputed in political theory. In our model the clear predominance of the legislature is rated positively as there is a very strong correlation between legislative dominance and measures of overall democracy.

The Model
I Electoral Process and Pluralism

1. Are elections for the national legislature and head of government free? Consider whether elections are competitive in that electors are free to vote and are offered a range of choices.
1: Essentially unrestricted conditions for the presentation of candidates (for example, no bans on major parties)
0.5: There are some restrictions on the electoral process
0: A single-party system or major impediments exist (for example, bans on a major party or candidate)
2. Are elections for the national legislature and head of government fair?
1: No major irregularities in the voting process
0.5: Significant irregularities occur (intimidation, fraud), but do not affect significantly the overall outcome

0: Major irregularities occur and affect the outcome
Score 0 if score for question 1 is 0.
3. Are municipal elections both free and fair?
1: Are free and fair
0.5: Are free but not fair
0: Are neither free nor fair
4. Is there universal suffrage for all adults?
Bar generally accepted exclusions (for example, non-nationals; criminals; members of armed forces in some countries).
1: Yes
0: No
5. Can citizens cast their vote free of significant threats to their security from state or non-state bodies?
1: Yes
0: No
6. Do laws provide for broadly equal campaigning opportunities?
1: Yes
0.5: Yes formally, but in practice opportunities are limited for some candidates
0: No
7. Is the process of financing political parties transparent and generally accepted?
1: Yes
0.5: Not fully transparent
0: No
8. Following elections, are the constitutional mechanisms for the orderly transfer of power from one government to another clear, established and accepted?
1: All three criteria are fulfilled
0.5: Two of the three criteria are fulfilled
0: Only one or none of the criteria is satisfied
9. Are citizens free to form political parties that are independent of the government?
1. Yes
0.5: There are some restrictions
0: No
10. Do opposition parties have a realistic prospect of achieving government?
1: Yes
0.5: There is a dominant two-party system in which other political forces never have any effective chance of taking part in national government
0: No
11. Is potential access to public office open to all citizens?
1: Yes
0.5: Formally unrestricted, but in practice restricted for some groups, or for citizens from some parts of the country
0: No
12. Are citizens free to form political and civic organisations, free of state interference and surveillance?
1: Yes
0.5: Officially free, but subject to some restrictions or interference
0: No

II Functioning of Government

13. Do freely elected representatives determine government policy?
1: Yes
0.5: Exercise some meaningful influence
0: No

14. Is the legislature the supreme political body, with a clear supremacy over other branches of government?
1: Yes
0: No

15. Is there an effective system of checks and balances on the exercise of government authority?
1: Yes
0.5: Yes, but there are some serious flaws
0: No

16. Government is free of undue influence by the military or the security services.
1: Yes
0.5: Influence is low, but the defence minister is not a civilian. If the current risk of a military coup is extremely low, but the country has a recent history of military rule or coups
0: No

17. Foreign powers do not determine important government functions or policies.
1: Yes
0.5: Some features of a protectorate
0: No (significant presence of foreign troops; important decisions taken by foreign power; country is a protectorate)

18. Special economic, religious or other powerful domestic groups do not exercise significant political power, parallel to democratic institutions?
1: Yes
0.5: Exercise some meaningful influence
0: No

19. Are sufficient mechanisms and institutions in place for assuring government accountability to the electorate in between elections?
1: Yes
0.5: Yes, but serious flaws exist
0: No

20. Does the government's authority extend over the full territory of the country?
1: Yes
0: No

21. Is the functioning of government open and transparent, with sufficient public access to information?
1: Yes
0.5: Yes, but serious flaws exist
0: No

22. How pervasive is corruption?
1: Corruption is not a major problem
0.5: Corruption is a significant issue
0: Pervasive corruption exists

23. Is the civil service willing and capable of implementing government policy?
1: Yes
0.5: Yes, but serious flaws exist
0: No

24. Popular perceptions of the extent to which they have free choice and control over their lives
1: High
0.5: Moderate
0: Low
If available, from World Values Survey
% of people who think that they have a great deal of choice/control

1: if more than 70%
0.5: if 50–70%
0: if less than 50%

25. Public confidence in government.
1: High
0.5: Moderate
0: Low
If available, from World Values Survey
% of people who have a "great deal" or "quite a lot" of confidence in government
1: if more than 40%
0.5: if 25–40%
0: if less than 25%

26. Public confidence in political parties.
1: High
0.5: Moderate
0: Low
If available, from World Values Survey
% of people who have a "great deal" or "quite a lot" of confidence
1: if more than 40%
0.5: if 25–40%
0: if less than 25%

III Political Participation

27. Voter participation/turnout for national elections.
(average turnout in parliamentary and/or presidential elections since 2000. Turnout as proportion of population of voting age).
1: if consistently above 70%
0.5: if between 50% and 70%
0: if below 50%
If voting is obligatory, score 0. Score 0 if scores for questions 1 or 2 is 0.

28. Do ethnic, religious and other minorities have a reasonable degree of autonomy and voice in the political process?
1: Yes
0.5: Yes, but serious flaws exist
0: No

29. Women in parliament.
% of members of parliament who are women
1: if more than 20% of seats
0.5: if 10–20%
0: if less than 10%

30. Extent of political participation. Membership of political parties and political non-governmental organisations.
1: if over 7% of population for either
0.5: if 4% to 7%
0: if under 4%.
If participation is forced, score 0.

31. Citizens' engagement with politics.
1: High
0.5: Moderate
0: Low
If available, from World Values Survey
% of people who are very or somewhat interested in politics
1: if over 60%
0.5: if 40% to 60%
0: if less than 40%

32. The preparedness of population to take part in lawful demonstrations.
1:   High
0.5: Moderate
0:   Low

If available, from World Values Survey

% of people who have taken part in or would consider attending lawful demonstrations
1:   if over 40%
0.5: if 30% to 40%
0:   if less than 30%

33. Adult literacy.
1:   if over 90%
0.5: if 70% to 90%
0:   if less than 70%

34. Extent to which adult population shows an interest in and follows politics in the news.
1:   High
0.5: Moderate
0:   Low

If available, from World Values Survey

% of population that follows politics in the news media (print, TV or radio) every day
1:   if over 50%
0.5: if 30% to 50%
0:   if less than 30%

35. The authorities make a serious effort to promote political participation.
1:   Yes
0.5: Some attempts
0:   No

Consider the role of the education system, and other promotional efforts. Consider measures to facilitate voting by members of the diaspora.
If participation is forced, score 0.

IV Democratic Political Culture

36. Is there a sufficient degree of societal consensus and cohesion to underpin a stable, functioning democracy?
1:   Yes
0.5: Yes, but some serious doubts and risks
0:   No

37. Perceptions of leadership; proportion of the population that desires a strong leader who bypasses parliament and elections.
1:   Low
0.5: Moderate
0:   High

If available, from World Values Survey

% of people who think it would be good or fairly good to have a strong leader who does not bother with parliament and elections
1:   if less than 30%
0.5: if 30% to 50%
0:   if more than 50%

38. Perceptions of military rule; proportion of the population that would prefer military.
1:   Low
0.5: Moderate
0:   High

If available, from World Values Survey
% of people who think it would be very or fairly good to have army rule
1:   if less than 10%
0.5: if 10% to 30%
0:   if more than 30%

39. Perceptions of rule by experts or technocratic government; proportion of the population that would prefer rule by experts or technocrats.
1:   Low
0.5: Moderate
0:   High

If available, from World Values Survey

% of people who think it would be very or fairly good to have experts, not government, make decisions for the country
1:   if less than 50%
0.5: if 50% to 70%
0:   if more than 70%

40. Perception of democracy and public order; proportion of the population that believes that democracies are not good at maintaining public order.
1:   Low
0.5: Moderate
0:   High

If available, from World Values Survey

% of people who disagree with the view that democracies are not good at maintaining order
1:   if more than 70%
0.5: if 50% to 70%
0:   if less than 50%

41. Perception of democracy and the economic system; proportion of the population that believes that democracy benefits economic performance.

If available, from World Values Survey

% of people who disagree with the view that the economic system runs badly in democracies
1:   if more than 80%
0.5: if 60% to 80%
0:   if less than 60%

42. Degree of popular support for democracy.
1:   High
0.5: Moderate
0:   Low

If available, from World Values Survey

% of people who agree or strongly agree that democracy is better than any other form of government
1:   if more than 90%
0.5: if 75% to 90%
0:   if less than 75%

43. There is a strong tradition of the separation of church and state.
1:   Yes
0.5: Some residual influence of church on state
0:   No

V Civil Liberties

44. Is there a free electronic media?
1:   Yes

0.5: Pluralistic, but state-controlled media are heavily favoured. One or two private owners dominate the media

0: No

45. Is there a free print media?

1: Yes

0.5: Pluralistic, but state-controlled media are heavily favoured. There is high degree of concentration of private ownership of national newspapers

0: No

46. Is there freedom of expression and protest (bar only generally accepted restrictions such as banning advocacy of violence)?

1: Yes

0.5: Minority viewpoints are subject to some official harassment. Libel laws restrict heavily scope for free expression

0: No

47. Is media coverage robust? Is there open and free discussion of public issues, with a reasonable diversity of opinions?

1: Yes

0.5: There is formal freedom, but high degree of conformity of opinion, including through self-censorship, or discouragement of minority or marginal views

0: No

48. Are there political restrictions on access to the internet?

1: No

0.5: Some moderate restrictions

0: Yes

49. Are citizens free to form professional organisations and trade unions?

1: Yes

0.5: Officially free, but subject to some restrictions

0: No

50. Do institutions provide citizens with the opportunity to successfully petition government to redress grievances?

1: Yes

0.5: Some opportunities

0: No

51. The use of torture by the state

1: Torture is not used

0: Torture is used

52. The degree to which the judiciary is independent of government influence.

Consider the views of international legal and judicial watchdogs. Have the courts ever issued an important judgment against the government, or a senior government official?

1: High

0.5: Moderate

0: Low

53. The degree of religious tolerance and freedom of religious expression.

Are all religions permitted to operate freely, or are some restricted? Is the right to worship permitted both publicly and privately? Do some religious groups feel intimidated by others, even if the law requires equality and protection?

1: High

0.5: Moderate

0: Low

54. The degree to which citizens are treated equally under the law. Consider whether favoured members of groups are spared prosecution under the law.

1: High

0.5: Moderate

0: Low

55. Do citizens enjoy basic security?

1: Yes

0.5: Crime is so pervasive as to endanger security for large segments

0: No

56. Extent to which private property rights protected and private business is free from undue government influence.

1: High

0.5: Moderate

0: Low

57. Extent to which citizens enjoy personal freedoms. Consider gender equality, right to travel, choice of work and study.

1: High

0.5: Moderate

0: Low

58. Popular perceptions on human rights protection; proportion of the population that think that basic human rights are well-protected.

1: High

0.5: Moderate

0: Low

If available, from World Values Survey

% of people who think that human rights are respected in their country

1: if more than 70%

0.5: if 50% to 70%

0: if less than 50%

59. There is no significant discrimination on the basis of people's race, colour or creed.

1: Yes

0.5: Yes, but some significant exceptions

0: No

60. Extent to which the government invokes new risks and threats as an excuse for curbing civil liberties.

1: Low

0.5: Moderate

0: High

References

Acemoglu, Daron, Simon Johnson, James A. Robinson, and Pierre Yared (2005), "Income and democracy", NBER Working Paper No. 11205, March.

Coppedge, Michael (2005), "Defining and measuring democracy", Working paper, International Political Science Association, April.

Dahl, Robert A (1970), "Polyarchy", New Haven, Yale University Press.

Freedom House, various, www.freedomhouse.org.

Horowitz, Irving Louis (2006) "The struggle for democracy", National Interest, spring.

Rigobon, Roberto and Dani Rodrik (2005), "Rule of law, democracy, openness, and income: estimating the interrelationships", Economics of Transition, Volume 13 (3).

The Failed States Index 2007

The world's weakest states aren't just a danger to themselves. They can threaten the progress and stability of countries half a world away. In the third annual Failed States Index, Foreign Policy and The Fund for Peace rank the countries where the risk of failure is running high.

It is an accepted axiom of the modern age that distance no longer matters. Sectarian carnage can sway stock markets on the other side of the planet. Anarchic cities that host open-air arms bazaars imperil the security of the world's superpower. A hermit leader's erratic behavior not only makes life miserable for the impoverished millions he rules but also upends the world's nuclear nonproliferation regime. The threats of weak states, in other words, ripple far beyond their borders and endanger the development and security of nations that are their political and economic opposites.

Few encouraging signs emerged in 2006 to suggest the world is on a path to greater peace and stability. The year began with violent protests that erupted from Indonesia to Nigeria over the publication of cartoons depicting the Prophet Mohammed. February brought the destruction of Samarra's golden-domed mosque, one of Shiite Islam's holiest shrines, unleashing a convulsion of violence across Iraq that continues unabated. After Hezbollah kidnapped two Israeli soldiers last July, southern Lebanon was bombarded for a month by air strikes, sending hundreds of thousands of refugees fleeing into neighboring states. And in October, the repressive North Korean regime stormed its way into the world's nuclear club.

What makes these alarming headlines all the more troubling is that their origins lie in weak and failing states. World leaders and the heads of multilateral institutions routinely take to lecterns to reiterate their commitment to pulling vulnerable states back from the brink, but it can be difficult to translate damage control into viable, long-term solutions that correct state weaknesses. Aid is often misspent. Reforms are too many or too few. Security needs overwhelm international peacekeepers, or chaos reigns in their absence.

The complex phenomenon of state failure may be much discussed, but it remains little understood. The problems that plague failing states are generally all too similar: rampant corruption, predatory elites who have long monopolized power, an absence of the rule of law, and severe ethnic or religious divisions. But that does not mean that the responses to their problems should be cut from the same cloth.

Few encouraging signs emerged in 2006 to suggest the world is on a path to greater peace and stability.

Failing states are a diverse lot. Burma and Haiti are two of the most corrupt countries in the world, according to Transparency International, and yet Burma's repressive junta persecutes ethnic minorities and subjects its population to forced resettlement, while Haiti is wracked by extreme poverty, lawlessness, and urban violence. For a decade, Equatorial Guinea has posted some of the highest economic growth in sub-Saharan Africa, yet its riches have padded the bank accounts of an elite few. And in the Democratic Republic of the Congo, the inability of the government to police its borders effectively or manage its vast mineral wealth has left the country dependent on foreign aid.

To provide a clearer picture of the world's weakest states, the Fund for Peace, an independent research organization, and FOREIGN POLICY present the third annual Failed States Index. Using 12 social, economic, political, and military indicators, we ranked 177 states in order of their vulnerability to violent internal conflict and societal deterioration. The index scores are based on data from more than 12,000 publicly available sources collected from May to December 2006. The 60 most vulnerable states are listed in the rankings, and full results are available at www.ForeignPolicy.com and www.fundforpeace.org.

For the second year in a row, Sudan tops the rankings as the state most at risk of failure. The primary cause of its instability, violence in the country's western region of Darfur, is as well known as it is tragic. At least 200,000 people—and perhaps as many as 400,000—have been killed in the past four years by janjaweed militias armed by the government, and 2 to 3 million people have fled their torched villages for squalid camps as the violence has spilled into the Central African Republic and Chad. These countries were hardly pictures of stability prior to the influx of refugees and rebels across their borders; the Central African Republic plays host to a modern-day slave trade,

The Rankings

The columns highlight the 12 political, economic, military, and social indicators of instability. For each indicator, the highest score (greater instability) is in **bold**; the lowest score (less instability) is in ***bold and italic***.

Indicators of Instability

Rank	Total	Country	Demographic Pressures	Refugees and Displaced Persons	Group Grievance	Human Flight	Uneven Development	Economy	Delegitimization of State	Public Services	Human Rights	Security Apparatus	Factionalized Elites	External Intervention
1	113.7	Sudan	9.2	**9.8**	**10.0**	9.0	9.1	7.7	**10.0**	9.5	**10.0**	9.9	9.7	9.8
2	111.4	Iraq	9.0	9.0	**10.0**	9.5	8.5	8.0	9.4	8.5	9.7	**10.0**	9.8	**10.0**
3	111.1	Somalia	9.2	9.0	8.5	8.0	7.5	9.2	**10.0**	**10.0**	9.7	**10.0**	**10.0**	**10.0**
4	110.1	Zimbabwe	**9.7**	8.7	8.8	9.1	9.5	**10.0**	9.5	9.6	9.7	9.5	9.0	7.0
5	108.8	Chad	9.1	8.9	9.5	7.9	9.0	8.3	9.5	9.1	9.2	9.6	9.7	9.0
6	107.3	Ivory Coast	8.6	8.3	9.8	8.4	8.0	8.9	9.5	7.9	9.2	9.6	9.3	9.8
7	105.5	Dem. Rep. of the Congo	9.4	8.9	8.8	7.6	9.1	8.0	8.3	8.7	8.9	9.6	8.6	9.6
8	102.3	Afghanistan	8.5	8.9	9.1	7.0	8.0	8.3	8.8	8.0	8.2	9.0	8.5	10.0
9	101.3	Guinea	7.8	7.4	8.1	8.3	8.5	8.5	9.6	8.9	8.6	8.1	9.0	8.5
10	101.0	Central African Republic	8.9	8.4	8.8	5.5	8.6	8.4	9.0	8.0	8.2	8.9	9.3	9.0
11	100.9	Haiti	8.6	4.2	8.0	8.0	8.2	8.4	9.2	9.0	9.1	9.3	9.3	9.6
12	100.1	Pakistan	8.2	8.5	9.0	8.1	8.5	5.8	8.7	7.1	8.7	9.5	9.5	8.5
13	97.7	North Korea	8.0	6.0	7.2	***5.0***	8.8	9.6	9.8	9.5	9.7	8.3	7.9	7.9
14	97.0	Burma	8.5	8.5	9.1	6.0	8.9	7.6	9.1	8.3	9.8	9.0	8.2	***4.0***
15	96.4	Uganda	8.1	9.4	8.5	6.0	8.5	7.5	8.5	8.2	8.2	8.3	7.8	7.4
16	95.9	Bangladesh	8.6	5.8	9.6	8.4	9.0	6.9	9.0	7.4	7.8	8.0	9.5	5.9
17	95.6	Nigeria	8.2	5.6	9.5	8.5	9.1	5.4	9.1	8.7	7.1	9.2	9.5	5.7
18	95.3	Ethiopia	9.0	7.9	7.8	7.5	8.6	8.0	7.9	7.0	8.5	7.5	8.9	6.7
19	95.2	Burundi	9.1	8.9	6.7	6.7	8.8	8.2	7.1	8.9	7.5	6.8	7.5	9.0
20	94.9	Timor-Leste	8.1	8.5	7.1	5.3	6.5	8.5	9.5	7.9	6.9	9.0	8.8	8.8
21	93.6	Nepal	8.1	5.2	8.9	6.1	9.2	8.2	8.5	6.6	8.8	8.3	8.5	7.2
22	93.5	Uzbekistan	7.7	5.4	7.1	7.1	8.6	7.5	9.2	6.8	9.0	8.9	9.2	7.0
23	93.4	Sierra Leone	8.6	7.4	7.1	8.7	8.7	8.7	8.0	8.0	7.0	6.5	7.7	7.0
24	93.2	Yemen	8.0	6.7	7.3	7.2	8.7	8.0	7.8	8.1	7.2	8.0	9.0	7.2
25	93.1	Sri Lanka	7.0	8.6	9.5	6.9	8.2	6.0	8.9	6.5	7.5	8.7	9.2	6.1
26	93.0	Republic of the Congo	8.7	7.3	6.8	6.1	8.1	8.3	8.5	8.8	7.9	7.9	7.2	7.4
27	92.9	Liberia	8.1	8.5	6.5	6.8	8.3	8.4	7.0	8.6	6.7	6.9	8.1	9.0
28	92.4	Lebanon	6.9	8.6	9.0	7.0	7.1	6.3	7.3	6.4	7.0	9.0	8.8	9.0
29	92.2	Malawi	9.0	6.0	6.0	8.0	8.8	9.2	7.9	9.0	8.0	5.4	7.5	7.4
30	92.0	Solomon Islands	8.5	4.8	8.0	5.1	8.0	8.0	8.5	8.5	7.1	7.7	8.8	9.0

(continued)

18

The Rankings *(continued)*

Rank	Total	Country	Demographic Pressures	Refugees and Displaced Persons	Group Grievance	Human Flight	Uneven Development	Economy	Delegitimization of State	Public Services	Human Rights	Security Apparatus	Factionalized Elites	External Intervention
									Indicators of Instability					
31	91.3	Kenya	8.4	8.0	6.9	8.0	8.1	7.0	8.0	7.4	7.0	7.1	8.2	7.2
32	91.2	Niger	9.2	5.9	8.9	6.0	7.2	9.2	8.2	8.8	7.1	6.7	6.0	8.0
33	89.7	Colombia	6.8	9.5	7.4	8.4	8.4	3.8	8.2	6.0	7.4	8.3	8.5	7.0
33	89.7	Burkina Faso	8.6	5.6	6.4	6.6	8.9	8.2	7.6	8.9	6.6	7.6	7.7	7.0
35	89.4	Cameroon	7.0	6.8	7.0	7.9	8.7	6.1	8.5	7.5	7.2	7.7	8.0	7.0
36	89.2	Egypt	7.7	6.5	7.8	6.2	7.8	7.0	9.0	6.7	8.5	6.1	8.3	7.6
36	89.2	Rwanda	9.1	7.0	8.7	7.6	7.1	7.5	8.5	6.9	7.4	*4.6*	8.2	6.6
38	88.8	Guinea-Bissau	7.6	6.5	*5.4*	7.0	8.6	8.0	7.2	8.5	8.0	8.0	6.8	7.2
39	88.7	Tajikistan	7.7	6.1	6.3	6.4	7.3	7.3	9.0	7.3	8.6	7.8	8.8	6.1
40	88.6	Syria	6.5	8.9	8.0	6.8	8.1	6.8	8.5	*5.3*	8.5	7.4	7.5	6.3
41	88.2	Equatorial Guinea	8.0	*2.0*	7.0	7.4	9.0	4.0	9.4	8.6	9.4	8.9	8.5	6.0
41	88.2	Kirgizstan	7.5	6.2	6.8	7.4	8.0	7.5	8.2	6.3	7.9	7.9	7.5	7.0
43	87.5	Turkmenistan	7.0	4.5	6.2	5.6	7.3	7.4	9.0	7.7	9.6	8.5	8.2	6.5
44	87.2	Laos	8.0	5.5	6.5	6.6	*5.7*	7.1	7.9	8.0	8.5	8.2	8.6	6.6
45	86.7	Mauritania	8.7	6.2	8.0	5.0	7.0	7.8	6.8	8.1	7.1	7.4	7.9	6.7
46	86.6	Togo	7.5	5.4	6.0	6.5	7.5	8.2	7.7	8.0	7.8	7.8	7.6	6.6
47	86.4	Bhutan	6.5	7.5	7.0	6.7	8.7	7.9	8.0	6.5	8.5	*4.6*	8.0	6.5
48	85.7	Cambodia	7.6	5.9	7.3	8.0	7.2	6.4	8.5	7.6	7.1	6.2	7.5	6.4
48	85.7	Moldova	7.0	4.7	7.3	8.4	7.5	7.5	7.9	7.1	6.8	6.3	7.5	7.7
50	85.5	Eritrea	8.1	7.1	*5.4*	6.0	5.9	8.4	8.3	7.7	7.4	7.5	7.2	6.5
51	85.2	Belarus	8.0	4.6	6.5	*5.0*	7.5	6.8	9.1	6.9	8.5	6.7	8.5	7.1
52	85.1	Papua New Guinea	7.5	3.5	8.0	7.9	9.0	7.3	7.8	7.8	6.1	7.0	6.7	6.5
53	84.9	Angola	8.5	7.5	5.9	*5.0*	8.7	4.2	8.6	7.7	7.5	6.2	7.5	7.6
54	84.5	Bosnia	*6.1*	8.0	8.3	6.0	7.2	6.0	7.6	5.6	5.3	7.3	8.3	8.8
55	84.4	Indonesia	7.0	7.5	6.0	7.5	8.0	6.5	*6.5*	7.0	7.0	7.3	7.2	6.9
56	83.2	Philippines	7.0	5.7	7.2	6.7	7.6	5.8	8.2	5.9	6.8	7.6	7.8	6.9
57	82.8	Iran	6.2	8.6	7.1	*5.0*	7.2	*3.3*	7.8	5.7	8.7	8.3	8.9	6.0
58	82.3	Georgia	6.3	6.8	7.6	5.7	7.0	5.7	7.9	6.1	5.4	7.8	7.8	8.2
59	82.0	Bolivia	7.4	3.7	7.0	7.0	8.5	6.4	7.2	7.4	7.0	6.2	8.3	5.9
60	81.4	Guatemala	7.0	6.0	7.1	6.7	8.0	7.0	7.4	6.6	7.1	7.3	*5.9*	5.3

Failing the Faithful

The world's weakest states are also the most religiously intolerant. Countries with a poor freedom of religion score are often most likely to meet their maker.

Freedom of worship may be a cornerstone of democracy, but it may also be a key indicator of stability. Vulnerable states display a greater degree of religious intolerance, according to scores calculated by the Hudson Institute's Center for Religious Freedom. Persecution of religious minorities in Bangladesh, Burma, Iran, and Uzbekistan has deprived millions of faithful of the freedom to follow their beliefs. But religious repression is often nothing more than a thinly veiled attempt to muzzle the country's civil society. In Zimbabwe, religious leaders were targeted recently as some of the last remaining outspoken voices of opposition in the country. And in Belarus, President Aleksandr Lukashenko has severely curtailed religious freedom in order to quash movements he deems bearers of foreign political influence. It seems the leaders of many failing states distrust any higher power that may be greater than their own.

and rebels attacked Chad's capital in April 2006 in a failed coup attempt. But the spillover effects from Sudan have a great deal to do with the countries' tumble in the rankings, demonstrating that the dangers of failing states often bleed across borders. That is especially worrying for a few select regions. This year, eight of the world's 10 most vulnerable states are in sub-Saharan Africa, up from six last year and seven in 2005.

That is not to say that all failing states suffer from international neglect. Iraq and Afghanistan, the two main fronts in the global war on terror, both suffered over the past year. Their experiences show that billions of dollars in development and security aid may be futile unless accompanied by a functioning government, trustworthy leaders, and realistic plans to keep the peace and develop the economy. Just as there are many paths to success, there are many paths to failure for states on the edge.

The year wasn't all bad news, though. Two vulnerable giants, China and Russia, improved their scores sufficiently to move out of the 60 worst states. That is in part due to the fact that 31 additional countries were assessed this year. But some credit must be paid to the countries themselves. China's economic engine continues to propel the country forward at a breakneck pace, but the growing divide between urban and rural, as well as continued protests in the countryside, reveals pockets of frailty that the

The Best and the Worst

This year, several vulnerable states took a step back from the brink.

No question, 2006 was a lousy year for Iraq." It was an odd statement to come from a normally upbeat U.S. President George W. Bush, but few would disagree. An ever worsening spiral of violence in Iraq, and bloody conflicts in Afghanistan, East Timor, and Somalia ensured that 2006 could understandably go down in the history books as a lousy year for many countries, not least Iraq.

But amid these poor performers, a few bright spots emerged. Several failing states made impressive gains, often thanks to historic turns at the ballot box. The first direct elections were held in December in Indonesia's Aceh Province, host to a three-decade-long separatist war that ended in a truce in 2005. Former rebel leader Irwandi Yusuf, who escaped from jail after his prison was destroyed by the December 2004 tsunami, was elected governor, sidelining former elites who had long monopolized power. And in the Democratic Republic of the Congo, the first multiparty elections in more than 40 years helped improve the state's legitimacy in the eyes of its impoverished populace, though the country remains vulnerable to militia violence.

But Liberia wins the honor of the year's most improved, gaining six points over last year's index score. There, too, a November 2005 election, held after more than a decade of civil war, can be credited with bringing much-needed stability to the country and laying the ground for last year's notable progress. Although 14,000 U.N. peacekeepers remain in Liberia, its economy is growing at 7 percent, militias have been demobilized, and President Ellen Johnson-Sirleaf has led efforts to combat endemic corruption, including the arrests of high-ranking government officials for graft.

Liberia's neighbor in the rankings, however, took this year's largest tumble. Lebanon dropped nearly 12 points in the index, giving it a total score just a hair shy of Liberia's. The war in Lebanon last year reversed much of the progress made since the end of its own civil war in 1990. Israeli air strikes drove more than 700,000 Lebanese from their homes and did an estimated $2.8 billion in damage to the country's infrastructure. A political crisis has the current government deadlocked and the country's economy remains weak. It shows that two states with similar ratings can be on vastly different trajectories, one headed toward stability and one backsliding toward failure.

Country	Change*
Better	
Liberia	+6.1
Indonesia	+4.8
Dem. Rep. of the Congo	+4.6
Bosnia	+4.0
Worse	
Lebanon	−11.9
Somalia	−5.2
Equatorial Guinea	−4.2
Niger	−4.2

*As measured in index points

Nature vs. Nurture

As the world warms, states at risk face severe threats to their groundwater, agriculture, and ecosystems, factors that can rapidly undo political and economic gains. This year's index found a strong correlation between stability and environmental sustainability, a country's ability to avoid environmental disas-ter and deterioration. That means that in poorly performing states on the edge, including Bangladesh, Egypt, and Indonesia, the risks of flooding, drought, and deforestation have little chance of being properly managed. And that suggests storms are brewing on the horizon for the world's most vulnerable.

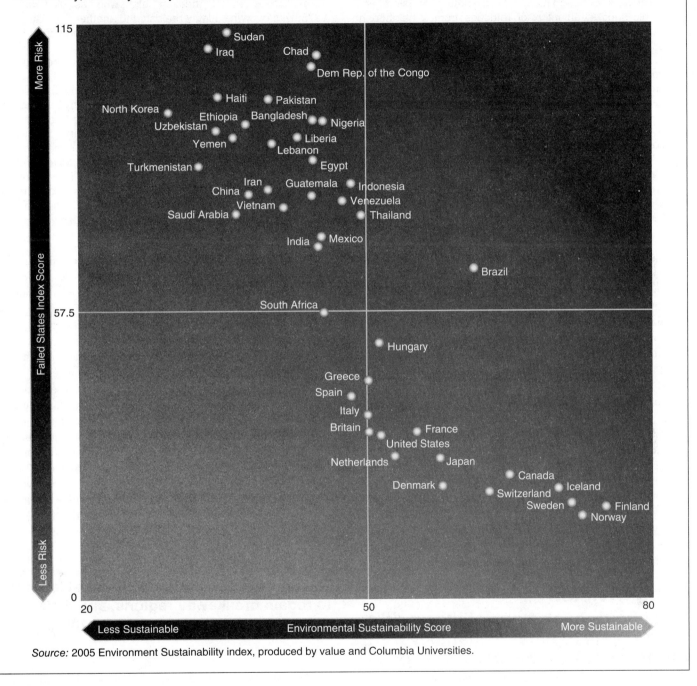

Source: 2005 Environment Sustainability index, produced by value and Columbia Universities.

central government is only just beginning to address. Russia's growing economy and a lull in the violence in Chechnya have had stabilizing effects, despite fresh concerns about the country's democratic future.

The vast majority of the states listed in the index have not yet failed; they exhibit severe weaknesses that leave them vulner-able, especially to shocks such as natural disasters, war, and economic deprivation. The power of such events should not be underestimated. The war in Lebanon last summer helped undo nearly two decades of economic and political progress. But Leb-anon was vulnerable because its political and security structures lacked integrity and remained tensely divided by factionalized

21

Leading the Way to the Bottom

Many states must endure poverty, corruption, and natural disasters. But, for the weak, there is nothing more costly than a strongman calling the shots.

History is full of brutal leaders who have plunged their lands into poverty and war through greed, corruption, and violence. And though many events—natural disasters, economic shocks, an influx of refugees from a neighboring country—can lead to state failure, few are as decisive or as deadly as bad leadership.

This year's index reveals that while failing states like Iraq and Somalia may suffer from poor governance, they are kept company by a number of countries ruled by long-serving strongmen who have presided over their nations' collapse. Three of the five worst performing states—Chad, Sudan, and Zimbabwe—have leaders who have been in power for more than 15 years.

But the problem is not restricted to sub-Saharan Africa. Uzbekistan's President Islam Karimov, who has continued a brutal crackdown on dissent since the massacre of hundreds of unarmed protesters in May 2005, has been in power since 1991. Egyptian President Hosni Mubarak, who has clung to power for the past quarter century, is now orchestrating his own succession, with his son as the heir apparent. And Yemen's President Ali Abdullah Saleh, who has ruled since 1978, was overwhelmingly reelected to another seven-year term last September in an election roundly condemned by the opposition as fraudulent.

Likewise, effective leadership can pull a state back from the brink. Indonesia's first directly elected president, Susilo Bambang Yudhoyono, has helped steer the country, long marred by endemic corruption and devastated by the 2004 tsunami, toward greater stability since coming into office three years ago. He has initiated reform of the country's crooked security sector, negotiated a peace agree-ment with rebels in Aceh Province, and made moderate improvements in government services. These efforts haven't necessarily made him popular. But then, such leadership is exactly what more failing states need: a head of state who chooses continued reforms over his own power and recognition.

---

elites. Those vulnerabilities not only helped turn the clock back on the country's development, but they reverberated across the region—into Israel, Jordan, and Syria. It shows again that a country's problems are never simply its own.

That conclusion becomes especially worrisome when the weak states in question possess nuclear weapons. Today, two countries among the world's 15 most vulnerable, North Korea and Pakistan, are members of the nuclear club. Their profiles could hardly be less similar: The former faces the very real prospect of economic collapse, followed by massive human flight, while the latter presides over a lawless frontier country and a disenchanted Islamist opposition whose ranks grow by the day.

But while these states' failings may be frequent fodder for headlines around the world, it is obvious that there are few easy answers to their troubles. In highlighting which states are at the greatest risk of failure, we can only hope that more effective and long-term solutions emerge over time as we compare the index from year to year. In that way, positive reversals of fortune can occur for the world's most vulnerable nations and, in the process, improve the security and prosperity of everyone.

Long Division
What holds back many of the world's most fragile regimes is that they were never truly in charge in the first place.

When it comes to assessing state failure, some countries emerge with split personalities. That is, states may be the picture of stability, peace, and economic growth in some areas, yet no-go zones in others. A dozen countries among the 60 most vulnerable contain "virtual states," areas that are essentially self-governing, but claimed by the central government.

In the former Soviet republic of Georgia, the two breakaway regions of Abkhazia and South Ossetia have built parallel govern-ing structures. Both regions, heavily supported by Russian security forces and economic aid, continue to reject Tbilisi's authority. In Colombia, the narcoterrorist insurgency movement farc controls a large swath of territory and is known to provide both basic social services and security to the people living outside of Bogotá's reach. And the former British protectorate of Somaliland declared independence from Mogadishu in 1991, despite falling within the internationally recognized borders of the Somali state.

Governments will often go to great lengths to regain such breakaway regions, and their efforts can be tremendously costly. A brutal 2002 civil war aimed at retaking the rebel-held northern half of the Ivory Coast split the country in two, blunting its otherwise impressive economic growth and leaving thousands of U.N. forces to keep the peace. In Pakistan, government efforts to crack down on suspected al Qaeda operatives in the restive border regions have led to violent protests. And attempts by the Sri Lankan government to regain territory from the Tamil Tigers last year sparked some of the worst violence in the country in years.

Governments will often go to great lengths to regain breakaway regions, and their efforts can be tremendously costly.

Ultimately, some countries, such as Slovakia and the Czech Republic, have found greater stability and prosperity as separate entities. Serbia and Montenegro split peacefully in June 2006, unusual in a region where separation usually comes at the cost of bloodshed. But for the split-personality states that appear on this year's index, the decision to go separate ways seems remote. And that may make their hopes for stability equally unlikely.

There Goes the Neighborhood

In some of the world's most dangerous regions, failure doesn't stop at the border's edge. It's contagious.

It is no coincidence that many of the world's failing states tend to cluster together. Porous borders, cultural affinity, and widespread underdevelopment often bind populations. And when some live in a failing state, their woes can quickly spill over into a neighbor's backyard.

Nowhere to Run

The violence in Darfur has created the most extreme ripple effect. The Sudanese government has been accused of backing rebel groups in both Chad and the Central African Republic, creating hundreds of thousands of additional refugees. Vast camps throughout the region are vulnerable to the violent, marauding militias that have terrorized Darfur for the past four years.

States of Disorder

Somalia, hostage to factional fighting be-tween warlords for more than 15 years, convulsed with violence in 2006, when short-lived stability installed by the Union of Islamic Courts was upended by the invasion of Ethiopian troops in favor of an interim government. Over the years, refugees from the fighting have spilled into Ethiopia, Eritrea, and Kenya, destabilizing a large portion of the Horn of Africa.

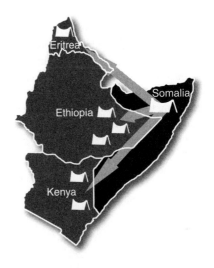

Sowing Instability

Fighting by a resurgent Taliban in Afghanistan and in the lawless Northwest Frontier Province of Pakistan has the potential to spread instability across Central Asia. Pakistan and Uzbekistan have shown only marginal gains in their index scores during the past year and are at risk not only from spillover but from growing internal dissent. But it is Afghanistan's record poppy yield that has neighboring states most concerned. Drug trafficking routes, fueled by underground heroin factories, cut swaths through the former Soviet republics to the north, bringing crime, addiction, and HIV/AIDS in their wake.

From *Foreign Policy,* July/August 2007, pp. 55–63. Copyright © 2007 by the Carnegie Endowment for International Peace. Reprinted with permission. www.foreignpolicy.com

Democracy's Sobering State

**"Democracy still occupies the high ground in the world. . . .
Yet, just a few years into the new century, the grand hope that
it will prove the age of democracy's global triumph appears far
more tenuous than it seemed just 10 or 15 years ago."**

THOMAS CAROTHERS

What Samuel Huntington called the "third wave" of democracy—the multitude of democratic openings that began in southern Europe in the mid-1970s and then spread during the next two decades throughout Latin America, Asia, the former Soviet bloc, and sub-Saharan Africa—has come to a standstill. According to Freedom House, an organization that tracks democratization around the world, there were 118 electoral democracies in 1996. Today, eight years later, there are 117. The relative proportions of countries that Freedom House rates as free, partly free, or not free have been largely static since the end of the 1990s.

Politics
The World, 2005

Of course, good news about democracy around the globe can still be found. Indonesians, for example, are making impressive strides in building democracy in the world's most populous Muslim country and have just inaugurated their first democratically elected president. A year ago Georgians threw off the decaying rule of President Eduard Shevardnadze and embarked on a bold effort to breathe new life into their country's shaky democratic experiment. South Africans recently celebrated the tenth anniversary of their postapartheid democracy, a democracy that is holding together despite myriad challenges. Tens of millions of Central and Eastern Europeans are now citizens of both democratic states and the European Union. And millions of Afghans took part in successful presidential elections in Afghanistan in October. More generally, key prodemocratic values, like government accountability and citizen empowerment, continue to spark interest and activism on every continent. And the community of people, organizations, and governments committed to advancing democracy's fortunes worldwide continues to grow.

Still, the grand hopes that energized some of democracy's most ardent optimists in the heady peak years of the third wave have not been realized. The former Soviet Union has gone from democratic frontier to democratic wasteland in just over a decade.

South America is facing a crisis of democracy marked by political instability, rising conflict, and declining public belief in democratic institutions. Significant parts of East Asia, including China, North Korea, Vietnam, Burma, Laos, and Singapore, remain under authoritarian rule, with little sign of change in sight. Dozens of African countries have seen once-promising democratic openings deliver only weak pluralism at best, or destructive civil conflict at worst. And, the US occupation of Iraq notwithstanding, the Arab world remains a democracy-free zone—despite increased international pressure for reform and some mild efforts by Arab rulers to move a few steps away from long-established patterns of autocracy.

Behind these signs of trouble in different regions lies a diverse set of factors that are coalescing in the first decade of this century to blunt democracy's global advance. No one of the factors is determinative in and of itself, but when combined they present a daunting new context. Understanding this context is vital to shaping an effective response.

The Authoritarian Rebound

The first factor inhibiting democratization is the persistence and even rejuvenation of authoritarian forces and structures in many countries that appeared, at least for a short time, to be experiencing democratic openings. Authoritarian forces were able to lie low or become dormant during the initial period of political change, even as dictatorial regimes fell. The apparent democratic transitions often turned out to be relatively shallow, despite their grand early moments and the high hopes they spawned. Dramatic first-time elections were held, new constitutions written, civil society unleashed, and government reforms announced. But the process of change in many cases did not penetrate the resilient, adaptable institutions behind the day-to-day screen of pluralistic politics—institutions that often harbored authoritarian mindsets, legacies, and actors such as domestic security services, militaries, and crony-dominated, state-owned businesses. In an unfortunately large number of cases, nondemocratic forces have been able to reassert themselves, taking advantage of the often fractious or feckless character of fledgling democratic governments. The rising economic and personal insecurity that many nascent democracies have produced for average citizens has eased the task of resurgent authoritarians since these conditions render citizens susceptible to the argument that a strong hand can set daily life back on track.

> **There is a significant gap between the soaring rhetoric about freedom in the Middle East and actual Western policy in most of the region.**

This phenomenon has been vividly present in the former Soviet Union as well as in parts of sub-Saharan Africa. Post-Soviet authoritarians have gained a grip throughout a region that in the early 1990s seemed to be opening itself to genuine political change. Pluralism is hanging on in a few former Soviet republics, such as Ukraine, Georgia, Kyrgyzstan, and Moldova. But most have become mired again in authoritarian or semi-authoritarian rule.

Russia's authoritarian slide under President Vladimir Putin has been especially damaging and dispiriting. Putin has methodically hollowed out or co-opted every major institution—including the national broadcast media, the Russian Duma, political parties, and regional governorships—that had achieved any real degree of independence. The systematic disassembling of his country's nascent democratic system has been a textbook case of dedemocratization that will be studied, unfortunately, by both political scientists and would-be autocrats for years to come. With Russia's democratic experiment at least alive, albeit troubled, throughout the 1990s, the overall political direction of the region appeared to be still up for grabs, despite bad news out of Central Asia and the Caucasus. But Russia's recent turn, although not necessarily permanent, throws the weight of regional political life firmly in the wrong corner, where it is likely to stay for years.

Adding to the disappointment of the post-Soviet political record is the fact that neither the United States nor Europe really has done much to try to slow or reverse the backsliding. Western governments are comfortable doing business with strongmen leaders as long as access to oil and gas continues uninterrupted, and because these leaders remain helpful on Western counterterrorism concerns.

Although sub-Saharan Africa generally has made substantial progress toward greater political pluralism and openness in the past 15 years, a discouraging number of countries continue to suffer persistent authoritarian rule, especially in francophone Africa, but in other parts of the region as well, including Sudan, Zimbabwe, Eritrea, and Equatorial Guinea. In some cases, such as Ivory Coast and Zimbabwe, authoritarian rule has returned after what looked like an encouraging political opening. In most of the others, authoritarian leaders or parties that may have learned to say a few of the right things about democracy in the early 1990s have reverted fully to type.

The Performance Problem

Although a troubling number of countries that were initially counted as part of the third wave have experienced a reassertion of authoritarian forces, quite a few others have managed to go from initial democratic openings to the establishment of reasonably open pluralistic systems. Many of these countries, however, are facing a different challenge to the consolidation of democracy: they are not succeeding in providing better lives for their citizens socially or economically. The economic reform measures that many new democracies adopt, though helping to reduce government deficits and stabilize currencies, have often produced only tepid growth. Citizens of these countries face higher prices for basic goods, an increased threat of unemployment, and stagnant incomes. Moreover, they are often beset with heightened social problems, especially rising crime and a breakdown of the traditional social safety net.

This overall problem, which has come to be known as the problem of democratic performance, can be debilitating to struggling democracies. It may not be fair in some philosophical sense for people to judge democracy on the basis of the socioeconomic performance of a given weak democratic regime. Democracy is in a strict sense about political values, choices, and processes; it does not per se provide answers to economic and social problems. Yet, fair or not, this is what citizens of new democracies (and for that matter, established ones as well) do. And when the performance is poor over time, the effects can be negative. In many new democracies, citizens are seriously disenchanted with their governments. This disenchantment is turning into a larger loss of belief in democracy itself and, in some more aggravated cases, into instability and political conflict.

> **The war on terrorism has hurt America's status as a model of democracy and weakened America's credibility as a prodemocratic actor.**

South America has been sharply afflicted with this problem, although the challenge of democratic performance has also dogged various countries in Central America, southeastern Europe, South Asia, and Southeast Asia as well. In South America, unlike in the former Soviet Union and some other regions, authoritarians were largely overcome or at least sent back to the barracks after democratic openings occurred. Almost all South American countries achieved flawed but real democratic systems, with most of the main institutional and procedural forms of democracy. Yet, in the past three or four years, the region has experienced what many South Americans and external observers increasingly view as a crisis of democracy. Argentina hit a frightening bump in its political road in 2001 when an economic crisis (itself partly caused by deficiencies in the political system, above all low levels of elite accountability) produced a period of vertiginous political instability; during one three-week spell the country went through five presidents. Venezuela has been suffering serious political polarization and conflict since the 1998 election of Hugo Chávez, a populist strongman with dubious fidelity to democratic norms who survived a recall referendum this year. Peru is undergoing a period of deep political malaise, marked by a hollow party system and the collapse of support for President Alejandro Toledo, whose election in 2001 was heralded as a rebirth of Peruvian democracy after the authoritarian reign of Alberto Fujimori. Bolivia and Ecuador have both experienced the ouster of presidents and the rise of serious new political fissures and tensions. Alongside these punishing developments are two longstanding political problems: the deeply corrupted dominant-power rule by the Colorado Party in Paraguay and the continuing civil war in Colombia.

South America's democratic woes derive from many causes and vary in nature from place to place. They are discouraging precisely because they highlight that democracy can corrode in so many different ways. But the problem of democratic performance—rooted in weak state institutions, entrenched, corrupted political elites, and poor systems of political representation and accountability—plays a role in much of the region. Fifteen to twenty years after the return of democracy, many South Americans do not feel that greater political freedom and choice have improved their lives very much, or at all, especially in terms of economic well-being and personal security. Given the high expectations that many people in the region had for what the end of dictatorship would bring, frustration over poor democratic performance turns easily into bitterness. The result has been a rising tide of cynicism, anger, and hostile actions against political parties, legislatures, governments, and even democracy itself.

Doing Well Under Dictators

A third factor contributing to a newly challenging environment for global democracy is the sense that quite a few authoritarian countries have been doing well economically in recent years, giving new life to the old idea that dictatorship is better than democracy at producing socioeconomic development. This idea was popular in the 1960s and 1970s, both in the West and in developing countries. In the West it was an article of faith among economists worried about populist-oriented policy making and a convenient excuse by diplomats for supporting friendly tyrants who were useful on security issues. In developing countries, ruling elites found it a handy justification for their repressive grip on power. The idea lost some steam in the 1980s, weakened by the accumulated socioeconomic failures of dictatorial regimes in many developing countries, especially in sub-Saharan Africa. Across the 1990s the opposite idea gained considerable ground in international development circles—that democracy and economic development go hand in hand—or even more strongly, that democracy, with its presumably better systems of representation and accountable governance, actually facilitates economic development. The experience in the 1990s of much of the postcommunist world—where for a time progress on political reform and economic growth correlated strongly—added weight to the new view.

China's extraordinary economic success has presented a serious problem for those arguing that democracy is necessary for development or that dictatorial regimes cannot produce sustained economic development. In the current context, in which citizens of many developing countries are dissatisfied with the socioeconomic performance of their new democratic regimes, China's continued very rapid growth and its increasing economic

muscle on the world stage have made it an increasingly powerful example. Talk of the "China model" has become much more common around the developing world than 10 years ago, both among ruling elites and average citizens. Magnifying this effect in the past several years are other authoritarian or semi-authoritarian countries, including Russia, Ukraine, Kazakhstan, and Vietnam, that have also been turning in high growth rates. Indeed, of the ten fastest-growing economies in the developing world between 1999 and 2002, only one—Albania—was led by a (somewhat) democratic government. This trend can be explained in part by the high price of oil, which has buoyed the economies of a number of oil-rich autocracies. Nevertheless, the trend fuels the belief in the developing world that a strong hand is best for development. And it undercuts the efforts of the international development community to make the case for a democracy-development link.

The War on Terrorism

A fourth complicating element for democracy in today's international context is the US war on terrorism. The ouster of the Taliban regime in Afghanistan and of Saddam Hussein in Iraq have opened the possibility, still far from being realized, of establishing stable, peaceful, democratic rule in these countries. President George W. Bush has also made a declared push for democratic transformation of the Middle East a part of his antiterrorism campaign, although this has been problematic in implementation. Other elements of the war on terrorism, however, have hurt democracy's cause. The US government's strongly felt need for closer counterterrorism cooperation with governments in many parts of the world has led it to warm relations with various autocratic regimes, such as those in Pakistan and Uzbekistan, and to go easy on the democratic backsliding of others, such as Russia.

In addition, the war on terrorism has hurt America's status as a model of democracy and weakened America's credibility as a prodemocratic actor. The world has watched closely, and often with disappointment, America's troubled effort to balance heightened law enforcement concerns with domestic political and civil rights, above all for Muslim citizens or residents of the United States. And the abusive treatment of detainees in US-run prisons or detention facilities in Iraq, Afghanistan, and Guantánamo has badly tarnished America's standing as a defender of human rights. Americans may have largely moved on past the stories and images that emerged from the Abu Ghraib prison outside Baghdad, but in many other parts of the world the negative emotions produced by those events are still strongly felt. A further negative consequence of the war on terrorism for global democracy has been the tendency of governments in the Middle East and many parts of Asia to use the antiterrorism banner as an excuse to crack down on political opponents, a tendency the United States has protested too little.

And Now for the Hard Part

The most pressing as well as complex and difficult issue concerning the advance of democracy over the next decade and beyond is the question of whether the Middle East can make any significant democratic progress. Policy makers in Washington and other Western capitals advance the idea that the arrival of democracy in the Middle East is necessary to eliminate the roots of radical Islamist terrorism. Although this proposition is badly oversimplified and potentially misleading as a policy credo, it has raised to an unprecedented degree the level of international attention paid to the Arab world's democratic deficit.

The Bush administration's push for democracy in the Middle East has consisted of both a massive military-led effort to reconstruct Iraqi politics on a democratic template and an interrelated series of much less intrusive measures in the rest of the region, including new aid programs, multilevel diplomatic steps like the Broader Middle East and North Africa Initiative, and some high-level jawboning of Arab leaders by top US officials. The region's skeptical and recalcitrant response to the new push has demonstrated how hard a prodemocratic policy toward the Middle East will be in practice. The political reconstruction of Iraq has been much more difficult and costly (in financial, human, and diplomatic terms) than those in charge of the intervention ever thought it would be. Certainly, many of the political forces in post-Saddam Iraq support some kind of pluralistic outcome, yet the road to achieving it remains littered with daunting obstacles. And although Iraq is less repressive today than it was under Saddam, it has not yet proved a positive model for the region. Arabs largely view Iraq as a violent, chaotic, frightening place, one where thousands of Arabs have died as a direct or indirect result of a foreign invasion and occupation and whose political life is still controlled, deep down, by the United States.

The new international attention to the absence of democracy in the Arab world, including the various US and European initiatives to encourage or stimulate positive movement, has helped engender more discussion in Arab countries about the need for political reform and democracy. A few governments, most notably perhaps that of Morocco, have continued along paths of reform that have led to some real pluralism, albeit still within a monarchical framework. And some of the more authoritarian Arab governments, such as those in Egypt and Saudi Arabia, have announced minor new reform steps, both to respond to these internal debates and to win some international favor.

But in general the region remains stuck in deeply entrenched patterns of autocratic rule. Arab states are willing to engage in limited off-again, on-again political reforms, but more as a liberalizing strategy to avoid democracy rather than to achieve it. Arab ruling elites do not share the new Western view that democratic change is necessary to combat Islamist extremism. In fact, they hold the opposite view: that democracy would likely unleash radical forces that could be harmful to both the region and the West. Pressure from below for democratic change is weak at best throughout the region, despite the stepped-up activities of some civic groups and others speaking out on behalf of reform. Those who advocate for democracy (usually secular Western-oriented intellectuals) lack organized constituencies behind them. And the groups that do have mass-based constituencies—Islamist organizations—often do not frame their political objectives in terms of democracy and are placed under strict limits by regimes nervous about any mass-based processes of political change.

It is by no means impossible that the Arab world will over time make progress toward democracy. But the process is likely to be much slower than the current fervor for reform in Washington and other Western capitals might imply, not to mention more conflictive and unsettling to Western interests than the new policy credo suggests. Despite the rhetoric coming from the White House, in practice US and other Western policy makers are not at all sure that opening up Arab political systems to popular choice would actually serve Western economic and security interests overall. In some cases, dangerous instability or even civil conflict might result. Other Arab societies might choose Islamist leaders who are not inclined to be helpful on the Israeli-Palestinian conflict or other important issues. There is a significant gap between the soaring rhetoric about freedom in the Middle East and actual Western policy in most of the region. Policies more cautious in deeds than in words are likely to persist.

Getting Serious

The state of democracy in the world is sobering. Democracy still occupies the high ground across the world both as the only political ideology to command widespread legitimacy and as the political system of most of the world's wealthy or powerful countries. Yet, only a few years into the new century, the grand hope that it will prove the age of democracy's global triumph appears far more tenuous than it seemed just 10 or 15 years ago.

American policy makers determined to make democracy promotion a major element of US foreign policy will have to do better than rely on attractive but superficial slogans like "freedom is on the march." It is necessary to move away from the mindset that a democratic trend is advancing in the world and that US policy should aim to support it. The challenges now are more fundamental: how to stimulate democracy in regions where authoritarianism has bested the democratic trend, and how to support democracy where it is under siege because of poor performance. Responding to these challenges will require a greater willingness to pressure authoritarian leaders who offer short-term economic and security benefits to the United States but spell long-term trouble, especially in the former Soviet Union and the Middle East. And it will require the United States to construct more effective partnerships with South America and other regions where democracy is under siege. Democracy promotion is a convenient, even easy rhetorical framework for a global policy, especially in the context of the war on terrorism. Making it work in practice is neither convenient nor easy, and the state of democracy in the world is only getting more complex and demanding with each passing year.

THOMAS CAROTHERS is director of the Democracy and Rule of Law Project at the Carnegie Endowment for International Peace. He is coeditor with Marina Ottaway of *Uncharted Journey: Democracy Promotion in the Middle East* (Carnegie Endowment, forthcoming January 2005).

Facing the Challenge of Semi-Authoritarian States

Marina Ottaway

The last decade of the 20th century saw the rise of a great number of regimes that cannot be easily classified as either authoritarian or democratic but display some characteristics of both—in short, they are *semi-authoritarian.* They are ambiguous systems that combine rhetorical acceptance of liberal democracy, the existence of some formal democratic institutions, and respect for a limited sphere of civil and political liberties with essentially illiberal or even authoritarian traits. That ambiguous Character, furthermore, is deliberate. Semi-authoritarian systems are not imperfect democracies struggling toward improvement and consolidation but regimes determined to maintain the appearance of democracy without exposing themselves to the political risks that free competition entails.

Political hybrids, semi-authoritarian regimes allow little real competition for power, thus reducing government accountability. However, they leave enough political space for political parties and organizations of civil society to form, for an independent press to function to some extent, and for some political debate to take place. Such regimes abound in the Soviet successor states: In countries like Kazakhstan and Azerbaijan, for example, former Communist Party bosses have transformed themselves into elected presidents, but in reality remain strongmen whose power is barely checked by weak democratic institutions.

Semi-authoritarian regimes are also numerous in sub-Saharan Africa, where most of the multiparty elections of the 1990s failed to produce working parliaments or other institutions capable of holding the executive even remotely accountable. In the Arab world, tentative political openings in Algeria, Morocco, and Yemen appear to be leading to the modernization of semi-authoritarianism rather than to democracy, in keeping with a pattern first established by Egypt. In the Balkans, the Communist regimes have disappeared, but despite much international support most governments are semi-authoritarian, with only Slovenia and—more recently and tentatively—Croatia moving toward democracy.

Even more worrisome is the case of Latin America, where economic crises and sharply unequal distribution of income create the risk of popular disenchantment with incumbent democratic governments, and even with democratic institutions.

Already in two countries, first Peru and then Venezuela, steady progress toward democracy has been interrupted by the emergence of semi-authoritarian regimes. In Asia, formal democratic processes are accompanied by strong authoritarian features in countries such as Pakistan, Singapore, and Malaysia, putting them in the realm of semi-authoritarianism.

Semi-authoritarianism is not a new phenomenon—many past regimes have paid lip service to democracy while frequently violating its basic tenets. But the number of such regimes was limited because until the end of the cold war many governments, often supported by their countries' leading intellectuals, rejected liberal democracy outright. They did so in the name of people's democracy (that is, socialism), or in the name of communal cultural traditions that precluded the egoistic individualism on which, they claimed, liberal democracy is based. Since the end of the cold war, few governments and even fewer intellectuals are willing to mount an ideological defense of nondemocratic systems of government; most feel they have to at least pretend adherence to the concept of democracy. On the other hand, the number of governments willing to accept the strict limitations on the extent and duration of their power imposed by democratic rule remains small. As a result, semi-authoritarian regimes have become more numerous.

The number of such regimes is likely to increase even further. In many countries that have experienced a political transition since the early 1990s, unfavorable conditions—including weak democratic institutions and political organizations, persistent authoritarian traditions, major socioeconomic problems, and ethnic and religious conflicts—create formidable obstacles to the establishment and, above all, the consolidation of democracy. Nevertheless, citizens everywhere have shown their disillusionment with authoritarian regimes, and a widespread return to the unabashedly top-down forms of government so common in the past is improbable. These conditions, unfavorable to both genuine democracy and overt authoritarianism, further enhance the prospects for the spread of semi-authoritarianism.

With their combination of positive and negative traits, semi-authoritarian regimes pose a considerable challenge to U.S. policy makers. Such regimes often represent a significant improvement over their predecessors or appear to provide a measure of stability that is welcome in troubled regions. But that superficial stability usually masks a host of severe problems and unsatisfied demands that need to be dealt with lest they lead to crises in the future. Despite their growing importance, however, semi-authoritarian regimes have not received systematic attention.

It is tempting to dismiss the problems created by the proliferation of semi-authoritarian regimes with the argument that, all things considered, they are not that bad and should be accepted as yet-imperfect democracies that will eventually mature into the real thing. For instance, compared to the old Communist Yugoslavia, or to a deeply divided Bosnia suffering from the aftermath of civil war and ethnic cleansing, or to a Serbia in a state of economic collapse but still defiant, Croatia under Franjo Tudjman did not appear too badly off; nor did it create insurmountable problems for the international community. Similarly, the semi-authoritarianism of President Heydar Aliyev in oil-rich Azerbaijan poses fewer immediate problems for policy makers and for oil companies than would a protracted power struggle with uncertain outcome. The widespread discontent in at least some semi-authoritarian states, however, suggests that further change is inevitable and that it is not in the interest of the United States to ignore the problem until crises erupt.

Promoting the democratization of semi-authoritarian regimes is a frustrating undertaking, since they are resistant to the arsenal of reform programs on which the United States and other donor countries usually rely. Semi-authoritarian regimes already do much of what the most widely used democratization projects encourage: They hold regular multiparty elections, allow parliaments to function, and recognize, within limits, the rights of citizens to form associations and of an independent press to operate. Indeed, many countries with semi-authoritarian regimes are beehives of civil-society activity, with hundreds of nongovernmental organizations, or NGO's, operating with foreign support. Many have a very outspoken, even outrageously libelous, independent press. Nevertheless, incumbent governments and parties are in no danger of losing their hold on power, not because they are popular but because they know how to play the democracy game and still retain control. Imposing sanctions on these regimes is usually ineffective, and the political and economic costs it entails, both for those who impose the measures and for the citizens of the targeted country, do not appear justified under the circumstances.

If sticks are in short supply for donors seeking to address the problem of semi-authoritarian regimes, carrots are even scarcer: There is little the international community can offer to a stable regime to entice it to risk losing power. The deepening of democracy is in the long-run interest of these countries, but it is definitely not in the short-term interest of the leaders who stand to lose power if their country becomes more democratic. Going down in history as an enlightened leader appears to be less attractive to most politicians than maintaining their power intact.

Such regimes challenge the assumption, dominant since the end of the cold war, that the failure of the socialist regimes means the triumph of democracy. This "end of history" argument, encapsulated in a book by Francis Fukuyama, of the Johns Hopkins University, puts too much emphasis on the importance of ideologies. It accurately notes that socialism, viewed for the best part of the 20th century as the ideological alternative to democracy, lost its appeal with the collapse of the Communist regimes of the Soviet Union anti Eastern Europe. As a result, the particular type of naked, institutionalized authoritarianism associated with socialism, with its massive single party and complex ideological apparatus, has become exceedingly rare. But relatively few governments, propelled by the genuine pluralism of their society and by an economic system capable of supporting such pluralism, have embraced democracy. Many have devised less heavy-handed, more nimble, and in a sense more imaginative systems that combine authoritarian and liberal traits.

The deliberate character of semi-authoritarian regimes also forces a reconsideration of the visually appealing image of countries that fail to democratize because they are caught in a "reverse wave." This idea, set forth and popularized by Samuel Huntington, of Harvard University, is that in a particular period many countries embrace democracy—figuratively, a wave propels them forward. Some of these countries safely ride the wave to dry land and prosper as democracies. Others are sucked back into the nondemocratic sea as the wave recedes, hopefully to be pushed back toward land by the next wave some decades in the future. It is an enticing idea, but it is not entirely accurate. It assumes that the leaders of all the countries supposedly being caught in a reverse wave intended to reach the shore, but in many cases they did not, and probably neither did many of these countries' citizens. Most countries that fail to reach the shore are not failed democracies caught in the wave's reflux; on the contrary, many are successful semi-authoritarian states that rode the wave as far as they wanted and managed to stop.

Another widespread idea challenged by the proliferation of semi-authoritarian regimes is that liberalization is a step toward democracy because it unleashes the democratic forces of a country. Liberalization undoubtedly allows all types of previously repressed ideas and political forces to bubble up. What actually surfaces depends on what was there. If a strong substratum of democratic ideas and, above all, of democratic organizations existed in the country, then liberalization indeed leads to greater democracy. But it can also lead to an outburst of ethnic nationalism, as in Yugoslavia, or of religious fundamentalism, as in Egypt.

How should such regimes be dealt with? Should the United States try to force democratization programs on Egypt, an important U.S. ally in the Middle East, although the Egyptian government would resist and the programs might even prove destabilizing? How should the international community react to Heydar Aliyev's plan to anoint his son as his successor as president of Azerbaijan, as if the country were a monarchy rather than a republic? What action is warranted when Venezuela starts slipping back from democracy to a semi-authoritarian populism? How can donors facilitate Croatia's second transition, the one from semi-authoritarianism?

But there is another layer of issues raised by semi-authoritarian regimes, which may appear abstract when first formulated but are actually very important to the outcome of democracy-promotion policies. Generally, these issues can be organized under the question, Why do semi-authoritarian regimes come into existence? Is it because of bad leaders (support efforts to vote them out of office), weak institutions (set up a capacity-building program), or a disorganized civil society incapable of holding the government accountable (finance and train nongovernmental organizations)? Or is it because there are underlying conditions that seriously undermine the prospects for democracy (and what can be done about underlying conditions)? Even more fundamentally, does the proliferation of semi-authoritarian regimes indicate that the assumptions about democratic transitions that undergird assistance programs need rethinking?

Democracy-assistance programs are based a lot on theory and relatively little on concrete evidence. That's not strange. Democratization is a complicated and little-understood process. In part, that is because the number of well-established democracies is relatively small, making it difficult to detect regular patterns. In part, it is because studies of democratization vary widely in their approaches and methodologies, yielding noncomparable conclusions. As a result, we understand much better how democratic systems function than why and how they emerged in the first place.

In the course of more than a decade of democracy-promotion efforts, policy makers in the United States and other countries have developed their own model of democratic transitions. That model is based in part on a highly selective reading of the literature on democratization and in part on the operational requirements of agencies that need to show results within a fairly short time frame—in the world of democracy promotion, 10 years already qualifies as long-term, although many studies of democratization highlight processes unfolding over many decades and even centuries. Inevitably, historical studies of democratization that point to the long process of socioeconomic transformation underlying the emergence of democracy have been ignored. There is little policy guidance to be derived from learning that the social capital that made democratic development possible in Northern Italy after World War II started to be built up in the 15th century, or that the rise of the gentry in the 17th century contributed to the democratic evolution of Britain. As a result, the studies with the greatest impact on democracy promotion have been those that looked narrowly at the final phase of democratic transitions, without asking too many questions about what had happened earlier or what kind of conditions had made the democratic outcome possible.

Furthermore, sophisticated studies are often given simplistic interpretations when they become a tool to justify policy choices. For example, among the most influential works often cited by democracy promoters are the studies of transitions from authoritarian rule in Latin America and Southern Europe carried out in the 1980s by a team of investigators, with Philippe Schmitter, now an emeritus professor at Stanford, and Guillermo O'Donnell, of the University of Notre Dame, drawing the overall conclusions. These conclusions were highly preliminary, as Schmitter and O'Donnell made clear with the final volume's subtitle: *Tentative Conclusions about Uncertain Democracies*. As is often the case with successful works, these highly qualified conclusions took on a life of their own, losing their nuances and turning into outright policy prescriptions. In the midst of the transition from apartheid in South Africa in the early 1990s, I heard many political commentators invoke O'Donnell and Schmitter in support of their favorite policies, ignoring the two authors' careful qualifications of their conclusions. A similar fate has befallen Robert Putnam, of Harvard, whose concept of social capital has been transformed to denote not a culture of trust and cooperation developed over centuries, but something that could be quickly created by financing NGO's and training them in the techniques of lobbying the government, administering funds, and reporting to donors.

Through this process of distilling the complex lessons of history into policy prescriptions capable of implementation, donors have developed a simple model of democratization as a three-phase process: liberalization, lasting at most a few years, but preferably much less; the transition proper, accomplished through the holding of a multiparty election; and consolidation, a protracted process of strengthening institutions and deepening a democratic culture. The tools used to facilitate this project are also fairly simple: in the liberalization phase, support for civil society and the independent press; during the transition, support for elections, including voter education, training of NGO's for observing elections, and, more rarely, training of all political parties in the techniques of organizing and campaigning; and in the consolidation phase, new programs to build democratic institutions and the rule of law, as well as the continuation of activities to further strengthen civil society and the media, educate citizens, or train parties.

Semi-authoritarian regimes call into question the model's validity. First, these regimes show that liberalization and transitional elections can constitute the end of the process rather than its initial phases, creating governments determined to prevent further change rather than imperfect but still-evolving democracies. Furthermore, this outcome is not necessarily a failure of democratization, but the result of a deliberate decision to prevent democratization on the part of the elites controlling the process.

Second, an analysis of the workings of semi-authoritarian regimes shows that all sorts of conditions—for example, stagnant economies or ethnic polarization—matter, and matter a great deal at that. The semi-authoritarian outcome is not always something imposed by autocratic leaders on a population that wanted something quite different, but is often accepted and even desired by the population. In many countries—Venezuela, for example—people willingly, even enthusiastically, reject democracy at least for a time. The problem cannot be explained away by arguing that what people reject in such cases was not true democracy to begin with. The reality is more complicated. Conditions affect citizens' priorities and the way they perceive democracy.

Third, semi-authoritarian regimes also challenge the view that democracy can be promoted by an elite of true believers.

Democracy promoters extol in theory the virtue and necessity of broad citizen participation beyond the vote, and innumerable projects target the strengthening of civil society. But civil society as defined by donors is much more part of the elite than of the society at large. Donors favor professional-advocacy NGO's, which speak the language of democracy and easily relate to the international community. For understandable reasons, donors are leery of mass movements, which can easily slip into radical postures and can get out of hand politically. But a problem strikingly common to all countries with semi-authoritarian regimes is that the political elite, whether in the government, opposition parties, or even civil-society organizations, has great difficulty reaching the rest of the society. In the end, that situation plays into the hands of semi-authoritarian regimes.

Dealing with semi-authoritarian regimes thus requires going beyond blaming leaders for nondemocratic outcomes of once-promising democratization processes, no matter how tempting that is. To be sure, leaders with authoritarian tendencies are a real obstacle to democratic transformation. It was pointless to hope for real democratization in Serbia as long as Slobodan Milosevic was in power, and Azerbaijan will likely never be a democratic country under the leadership of Heydar Aliyev. Hugo Chavez is not the man who will restore and revitalize Venezuela's now-shaky democracy. But the problem goes well beyond personalities. Countries do not necessarily deserve the leaders they get, but they do get the leaders whose rise conditions facilitate. If the leader is removed, the conditions remain. For democracy promoters that is an unpleasant thought, because it is easier to demonize individuals and even to oust them from power than to alter the conditions that propel those leaders to the fore.

Marina Ottaway is senior associate in the Democracy and Rule of Law Project at the Carnegie Endowment for International Peace. This is an excerpt from her new book, *Democracy Challenged: The Rise of Semi-Authoritarianism* (Carnegie Endowment).

As seen in *Chronicle of Higher Education,* February 7, 2003. Reprinted by permission of the publisher from *The Rise of Semi-Authoritarianism,* by Marina Ottaway, pp. 3–14 (Washington, DC; Carnegie Endowment for International Peace, 2003). Copyright © 2003 by Marina Ottaway. www.carnegieendowment.org

What Political Institutions Does Large-Scale Democracy Require?

Robert A. Dahl

What does it mean to say that a country is governed democratically? Here, we will focus on the political institutions of *democracy on a large scale*, that is, the political institutions necessary for a *democratic country*. We are not concerned here, then, with what democracy in a very small group might require, as in a committee. We also need to keep in mind that every actual democracy has always fallen short of democratic criteria. Finally, we should be aware that in ordinary language, we use the word *democracy* to refer both to a goal or ideal and to an actuality that is only a partial attainment of the goal. For the time being, therefore, I'll count on the reader to make the necessary distinctions when I use the words *democracy, democratically, democratic government, democratic country*, and so on.[1]

How Can We Know?

How can we reasonably determine what political institutions are necessary for large-scale democracy? We might examine the history of countries that have changed their political institutions in response, at least in part, to demands for broader popular inclusion and effective participation in government and political life. Although in earlier times those who sought to gain inclusion and participation were not necessarily inspired by democratic ideas, from about the eighteenth century onward they tended to justify their demands by appealing to democratic and republican ideas. What political institutions did they seek, and what were actually adopted in these countries?

Alternatively, we could examine countries where the government is generally referred to as democratic by most of the people in that country, by many persons in other countries, and by scholars, journalists, and the like. In other words, in ordinary speech and scholarly discussion the country is called a democracy.

Third, we could reflect on a specific country or group of countries, or perhaps even a hypothetical country, in order to imagine, as realistically as possible, what political institutions would be required in order to achieve democratic goals to a substantial degree. We would undertake a mental experiment, so to speak, in which we would reflect carefully on human experiences, tendencies, possibilities, and limitations and design a set of political institutions that would be necessary for large-scale democracy to exist and yet feasible and attainable within the limits of human capacities.

Fortunately, all three methods converge on the same set of democratic political institutions. These, then, are minimal requirements for a democratic country (Figure 1).

Figure 1

What Political Institutions Does Large-Scale Democracy Require?

Large-scale democracy requires:

1. Elected officials
2. Free, fair, and frequent elections
3. Freedom of expression
4. Alternative sources of information
5. Associational autonomy
6. Inclusive citizenship

The Political Institutions of Modern Representative Democracy

Briefly, the political institutions of modern representative democratic government are

- *Elected officials.* Control over government decisions about policy is constitutionally vested in officials elected by citizens. Thus modern, large-scale democratic governments are *representative*.
- *Free, fair and frequent elections.* Elected officials are chosen in frequent and fairly conducted elections in which coercion is comparatively uncommon.

- *Freedom of expression.* Citizens have a right to express themselves without danger of severe punishment on political matters broadly defined, including criticism of officials, the government, the regime, the socioeconomic order, and the prevailing ideology.
- *Access to alternative sources of information.* Citizens have a right to seek out alternative and independent sources of information from other citizens, experts, newspapers, magazines, books, telecommunications, and the like. Moreover, alternative sources of information actually exist that are not under the control of the government or any other single political group attempting to influence public political beliefs and attitudes, and these alternative sources are effectively protected by law.
- *Associational autonomy.* To achieve their various rights, including those required for the effective operation of democratic political institutions, citizens also have a right to form relatively independent associations or organizations, including independent political parties and interest groups.
- *Inclusive citizenship.* No adult permanently residing in the country and subject to its laws can be denied the rights that are available to others and are necessary to the five political institutions just listed. These include the right to vote in the election of officials in free and fair elections; to run for elective office; to free expression; to form and participate in independent political organizations; to have access to independent sources of information; and rights to other liberties and opportunities that may be necessary to the effective operation of the political institutions of large-scale democracy.

The Political Institutions in Perspective

Ordinarily these institutions do not arrive in a country all at once; the last two are distinctly latecomers. Until the twentieth century, universal suffrage was denied in both the theory and practice of democratic and republican government. More than any other single feature, universal suffrage distinguishes modern representative democracy from earlier forms of democracy.

The time of arrival and the sequence in which the institutions have been introduced have varied tremendously. In countries where the full set of democratic institutions arrived earliest and have endured to the present day, the "older" democracies, elements of a common pattern emerge. Elections to a legislature arrived early on—in Britain as early as the thirteenth century, in the United States during its colonial period in the seventeenth and eighteenth centuries. The practice of electing higher lawmaking officials was followed by a gradual expansion of the rights of citizens to express themselves on political matters and to seek out and exchange information. The right to form associations with explicit political goals tended to follow

still later. Political "factions" and partisan organization were generally viewed as dangerous, divisive, subversive of political order and stability, and injurious to the public good. Yet because political associations could not be suppressed without a degree of coercion that an increasingly large and influential number of citizens regarded as intolerable, they were often able to exist as more or less clandestine associations until they emerged from the shadows into the full light of day. In the legislative bodies, what once were "factions" became political parties. The "ins" who served in the government of the day were opposed by the "outs," or what in Britain came to be officially styled His (or Her) Majesty's Loyal Opposition. In eighteenth-century Britain, the faction supporting the monarch and the opposing faction supported by much of the gentry in the "country" were gradually transformed into Tories and Whigs. During that same century in Sweden, partisan adversaries in Parliament somewhat facetiously called themselves the Hats and the Caps.[2]

During the final years of the eighteenth century in the newly formed republic of the United States, Thomas Jefferson, the vice president, and James Madison, leader of the House of Representatives, organized their followers in Congress to oppose the policies of the Federalist president, John Adams, and his secretary of the treasury, Alexander Hamilton. To succeed in their opposition, they soon realized that they would have to do more than oppose the Federalists in the Congress and the cabinet: they would need to remove their opponents from office. To do that, they had to win national elections, and to win national elections they had to organize their followers throughout the country. In less than a decade, Jefferson, Madison, and others sympathetic with their views created a political party that was organized all the way down to the smallest voting precincts, districts, and municipalities, an organization that would reinforce the loyalty of their followers between and during election campaigns and make sure they came to the polls. Their Republican Party (soon renamed Democratic Republican and, a generation later, Democratic) became the first popularly based *electoral* party in the world. As a result, one of the most fundamental and distinctive political institutions of modern democracy, the political party, had burst beyond its confines in parliaments and legislatures in order to organize the citizens themselves and mobilize party supporters in national elections.

By the time the young French aristocrat Alexis de Tocqueville visited the United States in the 1830s, the first five democratic political institutions described above had already arrived in America. The institutions seemed to him so deeply planted and pervasive that he had no hesitation in referring to the United States as a democracy. In that country, he said, the people were sovereign, "society governs itself for itself," and the power of the majority was unlimited.[3] He was astounded by the multiplicity of associations into which Americans organized themselves, for every purpose, it seemed. And towering among these associations were the two major political parties. In the United States, it appeared to Tocqueville, democracy was about as complete as one could imagine it ever becoming.

During the century that followed, all five of the basic democratic institutions Tocqueville observed during his visit to America were consolidated in more than a dozen other countries. Many observers in Europe and the United States concluded that any country that aspired to be civilized and progressive would necessarily have to adopt a democratic form of government.

Yet everywhere, the sixth fundamental institution—inclusive citizenship—was missing. Although Tocqueville affirmed that "the state of Maryland, which had been founded by men of rank, was the first to proclaim universal suffrage," like almost all other men (and many women) of his time he tacitly assumed that "universal" did not include women.[4] Nor, indeed, some men. Maryland's "universal suffrage," it so happened, also excluded most African Americans. Elsewhere, in countries that were otherwise more or less democratic, as in America, a full half of all adults were completely excluded from national political life simply because they were women; in addition, large numbers of men were denied suffrage because they could not meet literacy or property requirements, an exclusion supported by many people who considered themselves advocates of democratic or republican government. Although New Zealand extended suffrage to women in national elections in 1893 and Australia in 1902, in countries otherwise democratic, women did not gain suffrage in national elections until about 1920; in Belgium, France, and Switzerland, countries that most people would have called highly democratic, women could not vote until after World War II.

Because it is difficult for many today to grasp what "democracy" meant to our predecessors, let me reemphasize the difference: in all democracies and republics throughout twenty-five centuries, the rights to engage fully in political life were restricted to a minority of adults. "Democratic" government was government by males only—and not all of them. It was not until the twentieth century that in both theory and practice democracy came to require that the rights to engage fully in political life must be extended, with very few if any exceptions, to the entire population of adults permanently residing in a country.

Taken in their entirety, then, these six political institutions constitute not only a new type of political system but a new kind of popular government, a type of "democracy" that had never existed throughout the twenty-five centuries of experience since the inauguration of "democracy" in Athens and a "republic" in Rome. Because the institutions of modern representative democratic government, taken in their entirety, are historically unique, it is convenient to give them their own name. This modern type of large-scale democratic government is sometimes called *polyarchal* democracy.

Although other factors were often at work, the six political institutions of polyarchal democracy came about, in part at least, in response to demands for inclusion and participation in political life. In countries that are widely referred to as democracies today, all six exist. Yet you might well ask: Are some of these institutions no more than past products of historical struggles? Are they no longer necessary for democratic government? And if they are still necessary today, why?[5]

The Factor of Size

Before answering these questions, I need to call attention to an important qualification. We are considering institutions necessary for the government of a democratic country. Why "country"? *Because all the institutions necessary for a democratic country would not always be required for a unit much smaller than a country.*

Consider a democratically governed committee, or a club, or a very small town. Although equality in voting would seem to be necessary, small units like these might manage without many elected officials: perhaps a moderator to preside over meetings, a secretary-treasurer to keep minutes and accounts. The participants themselves could decide just about everything directly during their meetings, leaving details to the secretary-treasurer. Governments of small organizations would not have to be full-fledged *representative* governments in which citizens elect representatives charged with enacting laws and policies. Yet these governments could be democratic, perhaps highly democratic. So, too, even though they lacked political parties or other independent political associations, they might be highly democratic. In fact, we might concur with the classical democratic and republican view that in small associations, organized "factions" are not only unnecessary but downright harmful. Instead of conflicts exacerbated by factionalism, caucuses, political parties, and so on, we might prefer unity, consensus, agreement achieved by discussion and mutual respect.

The political institutions strictly required for democratic government depend, then, on the size of the unit. The six institutions listed above developed because they are necessary for governing *countries*, not smaller units. Polyarchal democracy is democratic government on the large scale of the nation-state or country.

To return to our questions: Are the political institutions of polyarchal democracy actually necessary for democracy on the large scale of a country? If so, why? To answer these twin questions, let us recall what a democratic process requires (Figure 2).

Why (and When) Does Democracy Require Elected Representatives?

As the focus of democratic government shifted to large-scale units like nations or countries, the question arose: How can citizens *participate effectively* when the number of citizens becomes too numerous or too widely dispersed geographically (or both, as in the case of a country) for them to participate conveniently in making laws by assembling in one place? And how can they make sure that matters with which they are most concerned are adequately considered by officials—that is, how can citizens *control the agenda of* government decisions?

How best to meet these democratic requirements in a political unit as large as a country is, of course, enormously difficult, indeed to some extent unachievable. Yet just as with

Figure 2

Why the Institutions Are Necessary

In a unit as large as a country, these political institutions of polyarchal democracy. . .	are necessary to satisfy the following democratic criteria:
1. Elected representatives. . .	Effective participation Control of the agenda
2. Free, fair and frequent elections. . .	Voting equality Control of the agenda
3. Freedom of expression. . .	Effective participation Enlightened understanding Control of the agenda
4. Alternative information. . .	Effective participation Enlightened understanding Control of the agenda
5. Associational autonomy. . .	Effective participation Enlightened understanding Control of the agenda
6. Inclusive citizenship. . .	Full inclusion

the other highly demanding democratic criteria, this, too, can serve as a standard for evaluating alternative possibilities and solutions. Clearly the requirements could not be met if the top officials of the government could set the agenda and adopt policies independently of the wishes of citizens. The only feasible solution, though it is highly imperfect, is for citizens to elect their top officials and hold them more or less accountable through elections by dismissing them, so to speak, in subsequent elections.

To us that solution seems obvious. But what may appear self-evident to us was not at all obvious to our predecessors.

Until fairly recently the possibility that citizens could, by means of elections, choose and reject representatives with the authority to make laws remained largely foreign to both the theory and practice of democracy. The election of representatives mainly developed during the Middle Ages, when monarchs realized that in order to impose taxes, raise armies, and make laws, they needed to win the consent of the nobility, the higher clergy, and a few not-so-common commoners in the larger towns and cities.

Until the eighteenth century, then, the standard view was that democratic or republican government meant rule by the people, and if the people were to rule, they had to assemble in one place and vote on decrees, laws, or policies. Democracy would have to be town meeting democracy; representative democracy was a contradiction in terms. By implication, whether explicit or implicit, a republic or a democracy could actually exist only in a small unit, like a town or city. Writers who held this view, such as Montesquieu and Jean-Jacques Rousseau, were perfectly

aware of the disadvantages of a small state, particularly when it confronted the military superiority of a much larger state, and were therefore extremely pessimistic about the future prospects for genuine democracy.

Yet the standard view was swiftly overpowered and swept aside by the onrushing force of the national state. Rousseau himself clearly understood that for a government of a country as large as Poland (for which he proposed a constitution), representation would be necessary. And shortly thereafter, the standard view was driven off the stage of history by the arrival of democracy in America.

As late as 1787, when the Constitutional Convention met in Philadelphia to design a constitution appropriate for a large country with an ever-increasing population, the delegates were acutely aware of the historical tradition. Could a republic possibly exist on the huge scale the United States had already attained, not to mention the even grander scale the delegates foresaw?[6] Yet no one questioned that if a republic were to exist in America, it would have to take the form of a *representative* republic. Because of the lengthy experience with representation in colonial and state legislatures and in the Continental Congress, the feasibility of representative government was practically beyond debate.

By the middle of the nineteenth century, the traditional view was ignored, forgotten, or, if remembered at all, treated as irrelevant. "It is evident," John Stuart Mill wrote in 1861

that the only government which can fully satisfy all the exigencies of the social state is one in which the whole people participate; that any participation, even in the smallest public function, is useful; that the participation should everywhere be as great as the general degree of improvement of the community will allow; and that nothing less can be ultimately desirable than the admission of all to share in the sovereign power of the state. But since all cannot, in a community exceeding a single small town, participate personally in any but some very minor portions of the public business, it follows that the ideal type of a perfect government must be representative.[7]

Why Does Democracy Require Free, Fair, and Frequent Elections?

As we have seen, if we accept the desirability of political equality, then every citizen must have an *equal and effective opportunity to vote, and all votes must be counted as equal*. If equality in voting is to be implemented, then clearly, elections must be free and fair. To be free means that citizens can go to the polls without fear of reprisal; and if they are to be fair, then all votes must be counted as equal. Yet free and fair elections are not enough. Imagine electing representatives for a term of, say, twenty years! If citizens are to retain *final control over the agenda*, then elections must also be frequent.

How best to implement free and fair elections is not obvious. In the late nineteenth century, the secret ballot began to replace a public show of hands. Although open voting still has a few defenders, secrecy has become the general standard; a country in which it is widely violated would be judged as lacking free and fair elections. But debate continues as to the kind of voting system that best meets standards of fairness. Is a system of proportional representation (PR), like that employed in most democratic countries, fairer than the first-past-the-post system used in Great Britain and the United States? Reasonable arguments can be made for both. In discussions about different voting systems, however, the need for a fair system is assumed; how best to achieve fairness and other reasonable objectives is simply a technical question.

How frequent should elections be? Judging from twentieth-century practices in democratic countries, a rough answer might be that annual elections for legislative representatives would be a bit too frequent and anything more than five years would be too long. Obviously, however, democrats can reasonably disagree about the specific interval and how it might vary with different offices and different traditional practices. The point is that without frequent elections, citizens would lose a substantial degree of control over their elected officials.

Why Does Democracy Require Free Expression?

To begin with, freedom of expression is required in order for citizens to *participate* effectively in political life. How can citizens make their views known and persuade their fellow citizens and representatives to adopt them unless they can express themselves freely about all matters bearing on the conduct of the government? And if they are to take the views of others into account,

they must be able to hear what others have to say. Free expression means not just that you have a right to be heard. It also means that you have a right to hear what others have to say.

To acquire an *enlightened understanding* of possible government actions and policies also requires freedom of expression. To acquire civic competence, citizens need opportunities to express their own views; learn from one another; engage in discussion and deliberation; read, hear, and question experts, political candidates, and persons whose judgments they trust; and learn in other ways that depend on freedom of expression.

Finally, without freedom of expression, citizens would soon lose their capacity to influence *the agenda* of government decisions. Silent citizens may be perfect subjects for an authoritarian ruler; they would be a disaster for a democracy.

Why Does Democracy Require the Availability of Alternative and Independent Sources of Information?

Like freedom of expression, the availability of alternative and relatively independent sources of information is required by several of the basic democratic criteria. Consider the need for *enlightened understanding*. How can citizens acquire the information they need in order to understand the issue if the government controls all the important sources of information? Or, for that matter, if any single group enjoys a monopoly in providing information? Citizens must have access, then, to alternative sources of information that are not under the control of the government or dominated by any other group or point of view.

Or think about *effective participation* and influencing the *public agenda*. How could citizens participate effectively in political life if all the information they could acquire were provided by a single source, say the government, or, for that matter, a single party, faction, or interest?

Why Does Democracy Require Independent Associations?

It took a radical turnabout in ways of thinking to accept the need for political associations—interest groups, lobbying organizations, political parties. Yet if a large republic requires that representatives be elected, then how are elections to be contested? Forming an organization, such as a political party, gives a group an obvious electoral advantage. And if one group seeks to gain that advantage, will not others who disagree with their policies? And why should political activity cease between elections? Legislators can be influenced; causes can be advanced, policies promoted, appointments sought. So, unlike a small city or town, the large scale of democracy in a country makes political associations both necessary and desirable. In any case, how can they be prevented without impairing the fundamental right of citizens to participate effectively in governing? In a large republic, then, they are not only necessary and desirable but inevitable. Independent associations are also a source of *civic education and enlightenment*. They provide citizens not only with information but also with opportunities for discussion, deliberation, and the acquisition of political skills.

Why Does Democracy Require Inclusive Citizenship?

We can view the political institutions summarized in Figure 1 in several ways. For a country that lacks one or more of the institutions, and is to that extent not yet sufficiently democratized, knowledge of the basic political institutions can help us to design a strategy for making a full *transition* to modern representative democracy. For a country that has only recently made the transition, that knowledge can help inform us about the crucial institutions that need to be *strengthened, deepened, and consolidated.* Because they are all necessary for modern representative democracy (polyarchal democracy), we can also view them as establishing a *minimum level for democratization.*

Those of us who live in the older democracies, where the transition to democracy occurred some generations ago and the political institutions listed in Figure 1 are by now solidly established, face a different and equally difficult challenge. For even if the institutions are necessary to democratization, they are definitely not *sufficient* for achieving fully the democratic criteria listed in Figure 1. Are we not then at liberty, and indeed obligated, to appraise our democratic institutions against these criteria? It seems obvious to me, as to many others, that judged against democratic criteria, our existing political institutions display many shortcomings.

Consequently, just as we need strategies for bringing about a transition to democracy in nondemocratic countries and for consolidating democratic institutions in newly democratized countries, so in the older democratic countries, we need to consider whether and how to move beyond our existing level of democracy.

Let me put it this way. In many countries, the task is to achieve democratization up to the level of polyarchal democracy. But the challenge to citizens in the older democracies is to discover how they might achieve a level of democratization *beyond* polyarchal democracy.

Notes

1. Political *arrangements* sound as if they might be rather provisional, which they could well be in a country that has just moved away from nondemocratic rule. We tend to think of *practices* as more habitual and therefore more durable. We usually think of *institutions* as having settled in for the long haul, passed on from one generation to the next. As a country moves from a nondemocratic to a democratic government, the early democratic *arrangements* gradually become *practices,* which in due time turn into settled *institutions.* Helpful though these distinction may be, however, for our purposes it will be more convenient if we put them aside and settle for *institutions.*

2. "The Hats assumed their name for being like the dashing fellows in the tricorne of the day. . . . The Caps were nicknamed because of the charge that they were like timid old ladies in nightcaps." Franklin D. Scott, *Sweden: The Nation's History* (Minneapolis: University of Minnesota Press, 1977), 243.

3. Alexis de Tocqueville, *Democracy in America,* vol. 1 (New York: Schocken Books, 1961), 51.

4. Tocqueville, *Democracy in America,* 50.

5. Polyarchy is derived from Greek words meaning "many" and "rule," thus "rule by the many," as distinguished from rule by the one, or monarchy, and rule by the few, oligarchy or aristocracy. Although the term had been rarely used, a colleague and I introduced it in 1953 as a handy way of referring to a modern representative democracy with universal suffrage. Hereafter I shall use it in that sense. More precisely, a polyarchal democracy is a political system with the six democratic institutions listed above. Polyarchal democracy, then, is different from representative democracy with restricted suffrage, as in the nineteenth century. It is also different from older democracies and republics that not only had a restricted suffrage but lacked many of the other crucial characteristics of polyarchal democracy, such as political parties, rights to form political organizations to influence or oppose the existing government, organized interest groups, and so on. It is different, too, from the democratic practices in units so small that members can assemble directly and make (or recommend) policies or laws.

6. A few delegates daringly forecast that the United States might ultimately have as many as one hundred million inhabitants. This number was reached in 1915.

7. John Stuart Mill, *Considerations on Representative Government* [1861] (New York: Liberal Arts Press, 1958), 55.

ROBERT A. DAHL is Sterling Professor Emeritus of Political Science, Yale University. He has published many books on democratic theory and practice, including *A Preface to Democratic Theory* (1956) and *Democracy and Its Critics* (1989). This article was adapted from his recent book, *On Democracy,* Yale University Press.

From ON DEMOCRACY by Robert A. Dahl, (As seen in *Political Science Quarterly,* vol. 120, no. 2, pp. 187–197). Copyright © 2005 by Yale University Press. Reprinted by permission.

What Democracy Is . . . and Is Not

Philippe C. Schmitter and Terry Lynn Karl

For some time, the word democracy has been circulating as a debased currency in the political marketplace. Politicians with a wide range of convictions and practices strove to appropriate the label and attach it to their actions. Scholars, conversely, hesitated to use it—without adding qualifying adjectives—because of the ambiguity that surrounds it. The distinguished American political theorist Robert Dahl even tried to introduce a new term, "polyarchy," in its stead in the (vain) hope of gaining a greater measure of conceptual precision. But for better or worse, we are "stuck" with democracy as the catchword of contemporary political discourse. It is the word that resonates in people's minds and springs from their lips as they struggle for freedom and a better way of life; it is the word whose meaning we must discern if it is to be of any use in guiding political analysis and practice.

The wave of transitions away from autocratic rule that began with Portugal's "Revolution of the Carnations" in 1974 and seems to have crested with the collapse of communist regimes across Eastern Europe in 1989 has produced a welcome convergence toward [a] common definition of democracy.[1] Everywhere there has been a silent abandonment of dubious adjectives like "popular," "guided," "bourgeois," and "formal" to modify "democracy." At the same time, a remarkable consensus has emerged concerning the minimal conditions that polities must meet in order to merit the prestigious appellation of "democratic." Moreover, a number of international organizations now monitor how well these standards are met; indeed, some countries even consider them when formulating foreign policy.[2]

What Democracy Is

Let us begin by broadly defining democracy and the generic *concepts* that distinguish it as a unique system for organizing relations between rulers and the ruled. We will then briefly review *procedures*, the rules and arrangements that are needed if democracy is to endure. Finally, we will discuss two operative *principles* that make democracy work. They are not expressly included among the generic concepts or formal procedures, but the prospect for democracy is grim if their underlying conditioning effects are not present.

One of the major themes of this essay is that democracy does not consist of a single unique set of institutions. There are many types of democracy, and their diverse practices produce a similarly varied set of effects. The specific form democracy takes is contingent upon a country's socioeconomic conditions as well as its entrenched state structures and policy practices.

Modern political democracy is a system of governance in which rulers are held accountable for their actions in the public realm by citizens, acting indirectly through the competition and cooperation of their elected representatives.[3]

A *regime or system of governance* is an ensemble of patterns that determines the methods of access to the principal public offices; the characteristics of the actors admitted to or excluded from such access; the strategies that actors may use to gain access; and the rules that are followed in the making of publicly binding decisions. To work properly, the ensemble must be institutionalized—that is to say, the various patterns must be habitually known, practiced, and accepted by most, if not all, actors. Increasingly, the preferred mechanism of institutionalization is a written body of laws undergirded by a written constitution, though many enduring political norms can have an informal, prudential, or traditional basis.[4]

For the sake of economy and comparison, these forms, characteristics, and rules are usually bundled together and given a generic label. Democratic is one; others are autocratic, authoritarian, despotic, dictatorial, tyrannical, totalitarian, absolutist, traditional, monarchic, obligarchic, plutocratic, aristocratic, and sultanistic.[5] Each of these regime forms may in turn be broken down into subtypes.

Like all regimes, democracies depend upon the presence of *rulers*, persons who occupy specialized authority roles and can give legitimate commands to others. What distinguishes democratic rulers from nondemocratic ones are the norms that condition how the former come to power and the practices that hold them accountable for their actions.

> "However central to democracy, elections occur intermittently and only allow citizens to choose between the highly aggregated alternatives offered by political parties . . . "

The *public realm* encompasses the making of collective norms and choices that are binding on the society and backed by state coercion. Its content can vary a great deal across democracies, depending upon preexisting distinctions between the public and the private, state and society, legitimate coercion and voluntary exchange, and collective needs and individual preferences. The liberal conception of democracy advocates circumscribing the public realm as narrowly as possible, while the socialist or social-democratic approach would extend that realm through regulation, subsidization, and, in some cases, collective ownership of property. Neither is intrinsically more democratic than the other—just *differently* democratic. This implies that measures aimed at "developing the private sector" are no more democratic than those aimed at "developing the public sector." Both, if carried to extremes, could undermine the practice of democracy, the former by destroying the basis for satisfying collective needs and exercising legitimate authority; the latter by destroying the basis for satisfying individual preferences and controlling illegitimate government actions. Differences of opinion over the optimal mix of the two provide much of the substantive content of political conflict within established democracies.

Citizens are the most distinctive element in democracies. All regimes have rulers and a public realm, but only to the extent that they are democratic do they have citizens. Historically, severe restrictions on citizenship were imposed in most emerging or partial democracies according to criteria of age, gender, class, race, literacy, property ownership, tax-paying status, and so on. Only a small part of the total population was eligible to vote or run for office. Only restricted social categories were allowed to form, join, or support political associations. After protracted struggle—in some cases involving violent domestic upheaval or international war—most of these restrictions were lifted. Today, the criteria for inclusion are fairly standard. All native-born adults are eligible, although somewhat higher age limits may still be imposed upon candidates for certain offices. Unlike the early American and European democracies of the nineteenth century, none of the recent democracies in southern Europe, Latin America, Asia, or Eastern Europe has even attempted to impose formal restrictions on the franchise or eligibility to office. When it comes to informal restrictions on the effective exercise of citizenship rights, however, the story can be quite different. This explains the central importance (discussed below) of procedures.

Competition has not always been considered an essential defining condition of democracy. "Classic" democracies presumed decision making based on direct participation leading to consensus. The assembled citizenry was expected to agree on a common course of action after listening to the alternatives and weighing their respective merits and demerits. A tradition of hostility to "faction," and "particular interests" persists in democratic thought, but at least since *The Federalist Papers* it has become widely accepted that competition among factions is a necessary evil in democracies that operate on a more-than-local scale. Since, as James Madison argued, "the latent causes of faction are sown into the nature of man," and the possible remedies for "the mischief of faction" are worse than the disease, the best course is to recognize them and to attempt to control their effects.[6] Yet while democrats may agree on the inevitability of factions, they tend to disagree about the best forms and rules for governing factional competition. Indeed,

differences over the preferred modes and boundaries of competition contribute most to distinguishing one subtype of democracy from another.

The most popular definition of democracy equates it with regular *elections*, fairly conducted and honestly counted. Some even consider the mere fact of elections—even ones from which specific parties or candidates are excluded, or in which substantial portions of the population cannot freely participate—as a sufficient condition for the existence of democracy. This fallacy has been called "electoralism" or "the faith that merely holding elections will channel political action into peaceful contests among elites and accord public legitimacy to the winners"—no matter how they are conducted or what else constrains those who win them.[7] However central to democracy, elections occur intermittently and only allow citizens to choose between the highly aggregated alternatives offered by political parties, which can, especially in the early stages of a democratic transition, proliferate in a bewildering variety. During the intervals between elections, citizens can seek to influence public policy through a wide variety of other intermediaries: interest associations, social movements, locality groupings, clientelistic arrangements, and so forth. *Modern democracy, in other words, offers a variety of competitive processes and channels for the expression of interests and values—associational as well as partisan, functional as well as territorial, collective as well as individual. All are integral to its practice.*

Another commonly accepted image of democracy identifies it with *majority rule*. Any governing body that makes decisions by combining the votes of more than half of those eligible and present is said to be democratic, whether that majority emerges within an electorate, a parliament, a committee, a city council, or a party caucus. For exceptional purposes (e.g., amending the constitution or expelling a member), "qualified majorities" of more than 50 percent may be required, but few would deny that democracy must involve some means of aggregating the equal preferences of individuals.

A problem arises, however, when *numbers* meet *intensities*. What happens when a properly assembled majority (especially a stable, self-perpetuating one) regularly makes decisions that harm some minority (especially a threatened cultural or ethnic group)? In these circumstances, successful democracies tend to qualify the central principle of majority rule in order to protect minority rights. Such qualifications can take the form of constitutional provisions that place certain matters beyond the reach of majorities (bills of rights); requirements for concurrent majorities in several different constituencies (confederalism); guarantees securing the autonomy of local or regional governments against the demands of the central authority (federalism); grand coalition governments that incorporate all parties (consociationalism); or the negotiation of social pacts between major social groups like business and labor (neocorporatism). The most common and effective way of protecting minorities, however, lies in the everyday operation of interest associations and social movements. These reflect (some would say, amplify) the different intensities of preference that exist in the population and bring them to bear on democratically elected decision makers. Another way of putting this intrinsic tension between numbers and intensities would be to say that "in modern democracies, votes may be counted, but influences alone are weighted."

Cooperation has always been a central feature of democracy. Actors must voluntarily make collective decisions binding on the polity as a whole. They must cooperate in order to compete. They must be capable of acting collectively through parties, associations, and movements in order to select candidates, articulate preferences, petition authorities, and influence policies.

But democracy's freedoms should also encourage citizens to deliberate among themselves, to discover their common needs, and to resolve their differences without relying on some supreme central authority. Classical democracy emphasized these qualities, and they are by no means extinct, despite repeated efforts by contemporary theorists to stress the analogy with behavior in the economic marketplace and to reduce all of democracy's operations to competitive interest maximization. Alexis de Tocqueville best described the importance of independent groups for democracy in his *Democracy in America*, a work which remains a major source of inspiration for all those who persist in viewing democracy as something more than a struggle for election and re-election among competing candidates.[8]

In contemporary political discourse, this phenomenon of cooperation and deliberation via autonomous group activity goes under the rubric of "civil society." The diverse units of social identity and interest, by remaining independent of the state (and perhaps even of parties), not only can restrain the arbitrary actions of rulers, but can also contribute to forming better citizens who are more aware of the preferences of others, more self-confident in their actions, and more civic-minded in their willingness to sacrifice for the common good. At its best, civil society provides an intermediate layer of governance between the individual and the state that is capable of resolving conflicts and controlling the behavior of members without public coercion. Rather than overloading decision makers with increased demands and making the system ungovernable,[9] a viable civil society can mitigate conflicts and improve the quality of citizenship—without relying exclusively on the privatism of the marketplace.

Representatives—whether directly or indirectly elected—do most of the real work in modern democracies. Most are professional politicians who orient their careers around the desire to fill key offices. It is doubtful that any democracy could survive without such people. The central question, therefore, is not whether or not there will be a political elite or even a professional political class, but how these representatives are chosen and then held accountable for their actions.

As noted above, there are many channels of representation in modern democracy. The electoral one, based on territorial constituencies, is the most visible and public. It culminates in a parliament or a presidency that is periodically accountable to the citizenry as a whole. Yet the sheer growth of government (in large part as a byproduct of popular demand) has increased the number, variety, and power of agencies charged with making public decisions and not subject to elections. Around these agencies there has developed a vast apparatus of specialized representation based largely on functional interests, not territorial constituencies. These interest associations, and not political parties, have become the primary expression of civil society in most stable democracies, supplemented by the more sporadic interventions of social movements.

The new and fragile democracies that have sprung up since 1974 must live in "compressed time." They will not resemble the European democracies of the nineteenth and early twentieth centuries, and they cannot expect to acquire the multiple channels of representation in gradual historical progression as did most of their predecessors. A bewildering array of parties, interests, and movements will all simultaneously seek political influence in them, creating challenges to the polity that did not exist in earlier processes of democratization.

Procedures that Make Democracy Possible

The defining components of democracy are necessarily abstract, and may give rise to a considerable variety of institutions and subtypes of democracy. For democracy to thrive, however, specific procedural norms must be followed and civic rights must be respected. Any polity that fails to impose such restrictions upon itself, that fails to follow the "rule of law" with regard to its own procedures, should not be considered democratic. These procedures alone do not define democracy, but their presence is indispensable to its persistence. In essence, they are necessary but not sufficient conditions for its existence.

Robert Dahl has offered the most generally accepted listing of what he terms the "procedural minimal" conditions that must be present for modern political democracy (or as he puts it, "polyarchy") to exist:

1. Control over government decisions about policy is constitutionally vested in elected officials.
2. Elected officials are chosen in frequent and fairly conducted elections in which coercion is comparatively uncommon.
3. Practically all adults have the right to vote in the election of officials.
4. Practically all adults have the right to run for elective offices.
5. Citizens have a right to express themselves without the danger of severe punishment on political matters broadly defined. . . .
6. Citizens have a right to seek out alternative sources of information. Moreover, alternative sources of information exist and are protected by law.
7. . . . Citizens also have the right to form relatively independent associations or organizations, including independent political parties and interest groups.[10]

These seven conditions seem to capture the essence of procedural democracy for many theorists, but we propose to add two others. The first might be thought of as a further refinement of item (1), while the second might be called an implicit prior condition to all seven of the above.

1. Popularly elected officials must be able to exercise their constitutional powers without being subjected to overriding (albeit informal) opposition from unelected officials. Democracy is in jeopardy if military officers, entrenched civil servants, or state managers retain the capacity to act independently of elected civilians or even veto decisions made by the people's representatives. Without this additional caveat, the militarized polities of contemporary Central America, where civilian control over the military does not exist, might be classified by many scholars as democracies, just as they have been (with the exception of Sandinista Nicaragua) by U.S. policy makers. The caveat thus guards against what we earlier called "electoralism"—the tendency to focus on the holding of elections while ignoring other political realities.

2. The polity must be self-governing; it must be able to act independently of constraints imposed by some other overarching political system. Dahl and other contemporary democratic theorists probably took this condition for granted since they referred to formally sovereign nation-states. However, with the development of blocs, alliances, spheres of influence, and a variety of "neocolonial" arrangements, the question of autonomy has been a salient one. Is a system really democratic if its elected officials are unable to make binding decisions without the approval of actors outside their territorial domain? This is significant even if the outsiders are relatively free to alter or even end the encompassing arrangement (as in Puerto Rico), but it becomes especially critical if neither condition obtains (as in the Baltic states).

Principles that Make Democracy Feasible

Lists of component processes and procedural norms help us to specify what democracy is, but they do not tell us much about how it actually functions. The simplest answer is "by the consent of the people"; the more complex one is "by the contingent consent of politicians acting under conditions of bounded uncertainty."

In a democracy, representatives must at least informally agree that those who win greater electoral support or influence over policy will not use their temporary superiority to bar the losers from taking office or exerting influence in the future, and that in exchange for this opportunity to keep competing for power and place, momentary losers will respect the winners' right to make binding decisions. Citizens are expected to obey the decisions ensuing from such a process of competition, provided its outcome remains contingent upon their collective preferences as expressed through fair and regular elections or open and repeated negotiations.

The challenge is not so much to find a set of goals that command widespread consensus as to find a set of rules that embody contingent consent. The precise shape of this "democratic bargain," to use Dahl's expression,[11] can vary a good deal from society to society. It depends on social cleavages and such subjective factors as mutual trust, the standard of fairness, and the willingness to compromise. It may even be compatible with a great deal of dissensus on substantive policy issues.

All democracies involve a degree of uncertainty about who will be elected and what policies they will pursue. Even in those polities where one party persists in winning elections or one policy is consistently implemented, the possibility of change through independent collective action still exists, as in Italy, Japan, and the Scandinavian social democracies. If it does not, the system is not democratic, as in Mexico, Senegal, or Indonesia.

But the uncertainty embedded in the core of all democracies is bounded. Not just any actor can get into the competition and raise any issue he or she pleases—there are previously established rules that must be respected. Not just any policy can be adopted—there are conditions that must be met. Democracy institutionalizes "normal," limited political uncertainty. These boundaries vary from country to country. Constitutional guarantees of property, privacy, expression, and other rights are a part of this, but the most effective boundaries are generated by competition among interest groups and cooperation within civil society. Whatever the rhetoric (and some polities appear to offer their citizens more dramatic alternatives than others), once the rules of contingent consent have been agreed upon, the actual variation is likely to stay within a predictable and generally accepted range.

This emphasis on operative guidelines contrasts with a highly persistent, but misleading theme in recent literature on democracy—namely, the emphasis upon "civic culture." The principles we have suggested here rest on rules of prudence, not on deeply ingrained habits of tolerance, moderation, mutual respect, fair play, readiness to compromise, or trust in public authorities. Waiting for such habits to sink deep and lasting roots implies a very slow process of regime consolidation—one that takes generations—and it would probably condemn most contemporary experiences *ex hypothesi* to failure. Our assertion is that contingent consent and bounded uncertainty can emerge from the interaction between antagonistic and mutually suspicious actors and that the far more benevolent and ingrained norms of a civic culture are better thought of as a *product* and not a producer of democracy.

How Democracies Differ

Several concepts have been deliberately excluded from our generic definition of democracy, despite the fact that they have been frequently associated with it in both everyday practice and scholarly work. They are, nevertheless, especially important when it comes to distinguishing subtypes of democracy. Since no single set of actual institutions, practices, or values embodies democracy, polities moving away from authoritarian rule can mix different components to produce different democracies. It is important to recognize that these do not define points along a single continuum of improving performance, but a matrix of potential combinations that are *differently* democratic.

1. *Consensus*: All citizens may not agree on the substantive goals of political action or on the role of the state (although if they did, it would certainly make governing democracies much easier).

2. *Participation*: All citizens may not take an active and equal part in politics, although it must be legally possible for them to do so.

3. *Access*: Rulers may not weigh equally the preferences of all who come before them, although citizenship implies that individuals and groups should have an equal opportunity to express their preferences if they choose to do so.

4. *Responsiveness*: Rulers may not always follow the course of action preferred by the citizenry. But when they deviate from such a policy, say on grounds of "reason of state" or "overriding national interest," they must ultimately be held accountable for their actions through regular and fair processes.

5. *Majority rule*: Positions may not be allocated or rules may not be decided solely on the basis of assembling the most votes, although deviations from this principle usually must be explicitly defended and previously approved.

6. *Parliamentary sovereignty*: The legislature may not be the only body that can make rules or even the one with final authority in deciding which laws are binding, although where executive, judicial, or other public bodies make that ultimate choice, they too must be accountable for their actions.

7. *Party government*: Rulers may not be nominated, promoted, and disciplined in their activities by well-organized and programmatically coherent political parties, although where they are not, it may prove more difficult to form an effective government.

8. *Pluralism*: The political process may not be based on a multiplicity of overlapping, voluntaristic, and autonomous private groups. However, where there are monopolies of representation, hierarchies of association, and obligatory memberships, it is likely that the interests involved will be more closely linked to the state and the separation between the public and private spheres of action will be much less distinct.

9. *Federalism*: The territorial division of authority may not involve multiple levels and local autonomies, least of all ones enshrined in a constitutional document, although some dispersal of power across territorial and/or functional units is characteristic of all democracies.

10. *Presidentialism*: The chief executive officer may not be a single person and he or she may not be directly elected by the citizenry as a whole, although some concentration of authority is present in all democracies, even if it is exercised collectively and only held indirectly accountable to the electorate.

11. *Checks and Balances*: It is not necessary that the different branches of government be systematically pitted against one another, although governments by assembly, by executive concentrations, by judicial command, or even by dictatorial fiat (as in time of war) must be ultimately accountable to the citizenry as a whole.

While each of the above has been named as an essential component of democracy, they should instead be seen either as indicators of this or that type of democracy, or else as useful standards for evaluating the performance of particular regimes. To include them as part of the generic definition of democracy itself would be to mistake the American polity for the universal model of democratic governance. Indeed, the parliamentary, consociational, unitary, corporatist, and concentrated arrangements of continental Europe may have some unique virtues for guiding polities through the uncertain transition from autocratic to democratic rule.[12]

What Democracy is Not

We have attempted to convey the general meaning of modern democracy without identifying it with some particular set of rules and institutions or restricting it to some specific culture or level of development. We have also argued that it cannot be reduced to the regular holding of elections or equated with a particular notion of the role of the state, but we have not said much more about what democracy is not or about what democracy may not be capable of producing.

There is an understandable temptation to load too many expectations on this concept and to imagine that by attaining democracy, a society will have resolved all of its political, social, economic, administrative, and cultural problems. Unfortunately, "all good things do not necessarily go together."

First, democracies are not necessarily more efficient economically than other forms of government. Their rates of aggregate growth, savings, and investment may be no better than those of nondemocracies. This is especially likely during the transition, when propertied groups and administrative elites may respond to real or imagined threats to the "rights" they enjoyed under authoritarian rule by initiating capital flight, disinvestment, or sabotage. In time, depending upon the type of democracy, benevolent long-term effects upon income distribution, aggregate demand, education, productivity, and creativity may eventually combine to improve economic and social performance, but it is certainly too much to expect that these improvements will occur immediately—much less that they will be defining characteristics of democratization.

Second, democracies are not necessarily more efficient administratively. Their capacity to make decisions may even be slower than that of the regimes they replace, if only because more actors must be consulted. The costs of getting things done may be higher, if only because "payoffs" have to be made to a wider and more resourceful set of clients (although one should never underestimate the degree of corruption to be found within autocracies). Popular satisfaction with the new democratic government's performance may not even seem greater, if only because necessary compromises often please no one completely, and because the losers are free to complain.

Third, democracies are not likely to appear more orderly, consensual, stable, or governable than the autocracies they replace. This is partly a byproduct of democratic freedom of expression, but it is also a reflection of the likelihood of continuing disagreement over new rules and institutions. These products of imposition or compromise are often initially quite ambiguous in nature and uncertain in effect until actors have learned how to use them. What is more, they come in the aftermath of serious struggles motivated by high ideals. Groups and individuals with recently acquired autonomy will test certain rules, protest against the actions of certain institutions, and insist on renegotiating their part of the bargain. Thus the presence of antisystem parties should be neither surprising nor seen as a failure of democratic consolidation. What counts is whether such parties are willing, however reluctantly, to play by the general rules of bounded uncertainty and contingent consent.

Governability is a challenge for all regimes, not just democratic ones. Given the political exhaustion and loss of legitimacy that have befallen autocracies from sultanistic Paraguay to totalitarian Albania, it may seem that only democracies can now be expected to govern effectively and legitimately. Experience has shown, however, that democracies too can lose the ability to govern. Mass publics can become disenchanted with their performance. Even more threatening is the temptation for leaders to fiddle with procedures and ultimately undermine the principles of contingent consent and bounded uncertainty. Perhaps the most critical moment comes once the politicians begin to settle into the more predictable roles and relations of a consolidated democracy. Many will find their expectations frustrated; some will discover that the new rules of competition put them at a disadvantage; a few may even feel that their vital interests are threatened by popular majorities.

Finally, democracies will have more open societies and polities than the autocracies they replace, but not necessarily more open economies. Many of today's most successful and well-established democracies have historically resorted to protectionism and closed borders, and have relied extensively upon public institutions to promote economic development. While the long-term compatibility between democracy and capitalism does not seem to be in doubt, despite their continuous tension, it is not clear whether the promotion of such liberal economic goals as the right of individuals to own property and retain profits, the clearing function of markets, the private settlement of disputes, the freedom to produce without government regulation, or the privatization of state-owned enterprises necessarily furthers the consolidation of democracy. After all, democracies do need to levy taxes and regulate certain transactions, especially where private monopolies and oligopolies exist. Citizens or their representatives may decide that it is desirable to protect the rights of collectivities from encroachment by individuals, especially propertied ones, and

they may choose to set aside certain forms of property for public or cooperative ownership. In short, notions of economic liberty that are currently put forward in neoliberal economic models are not synonymous with political freedom—and may even impede it.

Democratization will not necessarily bring in its wake economic growth, social peace, administrative efficiency, political harmony, free markets, or "the end of ideology." Least of all will it bring about "the end of history." No doubt some of these qualities could make the consolidation of democracy easier, but they are neither prerequisites for it nor immediate products of it. Instead, what we should be hoping for is the emergence of political institutions that can peacefully compete to form governments and influence public policy, that can channel social and economic conflicts through regular procedures, and that have sufficient linkages to civil society to represent their constituencies and commit them to collective courses of action. Some types of democracies, especially in developing countries, have been unable to fulfill this promise, perhaps due to the circumstances of their transition from authoritarian rule.[13] The democratic wager is that such a regime, once established, will not only persist by reproducing itself within its initial confining conditions, but will eventually expand beyond them.[14] Unlike authoritarian regimes, democracies have the capacity to modify their rules and institutions consensually in response to changing circumstances. They may not immediately produce all the goods mentioned above, but they stand a better chance of eventually doing so than do autocracies.

Notes

1. For a comparative analysis of the recent regime changes in southern Europe and Latin America, see Guillermo O'Donnell, Philippe C. Schmitter, and Laurence Whitehead, eds., *Transitions from Authoritarian Rule*, 4 vols. (Baltimore: Johns Hopkins University Press, 1986). For another compilation that adopts a more structural approach see Larry Diamond, Juan Linz, and Seymour Martin Lipset, eds., *Democracy in Developing Countries*, vols. 2, 3, and 4 (Boulder, Colo.: Lynne Rienner, 1989).

2. Numerous attempts have been made to codify and quantify the existence of democracy across political systems. The best known is probably Freedom House's *Freedom in the World: Political Rights and Civil Liberties*, published since 1973 by Greenwood Press and since 1988 by University Press of America. Also see Charles Humana, *World Human Rights Guide* (New York: Facts on File, 1986).

3. The definition most commonly used by American social scientists is that of Joseph Schumpeter: "that institutional arrangement for arriving at political decisions in which individuals acquire the power to decide by means of a competitive struggle for the people's vote." *Capitalism, Socialism, and Democracy* (London: George Allen and Unwin, 1943), 269. We accept certain aspects of the classical procedural approach to modern democracy, but differ primarily in our emphasis on the accountability of rulers to citizens and the relevance of mechanisms of competition other than elections.

4. Not only do some countries practice a stable form of democracy without a formal constitution (e.g., Great Britain and Israel), but even more countries have constitutions and legal codes that offer no guarantee of reliable practice. On paper, Stalin's 1936 constitution for the USSR was a virtual model of democratic rights and entitlements.

5. For the most valiant attempt to make some sense out of this thicket of distinctions, see Juan Linz, "Totalitarian and Authoritarian Regimes" in *Handbook of Political Science*, eds. Fred I. Greenstein and Nelson W. Polsby (Reading Mass.: Addison Wesley, 1975), 175–411.

6. "Publius" (Alexander Hamilton, John Jay, and James Madison), *The Federalist Papers* (New York: Anchor Books, 1961). The quote is from Number 10.

7. See Terry Karl, "Imposing Consent? Electoralism versus Democratization in El Salvador," in *Elections and Democratization in Latin America, 1980–1985*, eds. Paul Drake and Eduardo Silva (San Diego: Center for Iberian and Latin American Studies, Center for US/Mexican Studies, University of California, San Diego, 1986), 9–36.

8. Alexis de Tocqueville, *Democracy in America*, 2 vols. (New York: Vintage Books, 1945).

9. This fear of overloaded government and the imminent collapse of democracy is well reflected in the work of Samuel P. Huntington during the 1970s. See especially Michel Crozier, Samuel P. Huntington, and Joji Watanuki, *The Crisis of Democracy* (New York: New York University Press, 1975).

For Huntington's (revised) thoughts about the prospects for democracy, see his "Will More Countries Become Democratic?," *Political Science Quarterly* 99 (Summer 1984): 193–218.

10. Robert Dahl, *Dilemmas of Pluralist Democracy* (New Haven: Yale University Press, 1982), 11.

11. Robert Dahl, *After the Revolution: Authority in a Good Society* (New Haven: Yale University Press, 1970).

12. See Juan Linz, "The Perils of Presidentialism," *Journal of Democracy* 1 (Winter 1990): 51–69, and the ensuing discussion by Donald Horowitz, Seymour Martin Lipset, and Juan Linz in *Journal of Democracy* 1 (Fall 1990): 73–91.

13. Terry Lynn Karl, "Dilemmas of Democratization in Latin America" *Comparative Politics* 23 (October 1990): 1–23.

14. Otto Kirchheimer, "Confining Conditions and Revolutionary Breakthroughs," *American Political Science Review* 59 (1965): 964–974.

PHILIPPE C. SCHMITTER is professor of political science and director of the Center for European Studies at Stanford University. **TERRY LYNN KARL** is associate professor of political science and director of the Center for Latin American Studies at the same institution. The original, longer version of this essay was written at the request of the United States Agency for International Development, which is not responsible for its content.

Public Opinion: Is There a Crisis?

After the collapse of communism, the world saw a surge in the number of new democracies. But why are the citizens of the mature democracies meanwhile losing confidence in their political institutions? This is the first in a series of articles on democracy in transition.

Everyone remembers that Winston Churchill once called democracy the worst form of government—except for all the others. The end of the cold war seemed to prove him right. All but a handful of countries now claim to embrace democratic ideals. Insofar as there is a debate about democracy, much of it now centers on how to help the "emerging" democracies of Asia, Africa, Latin America and Eastern Europe catch up with the established democratic countries of the West and Japan. The new democracies are used to having well-meaning observers from the mature democracies descend on them at election time to ensure that the voting is free and fair. But is political life in these mature democracies as healthy as it should be?

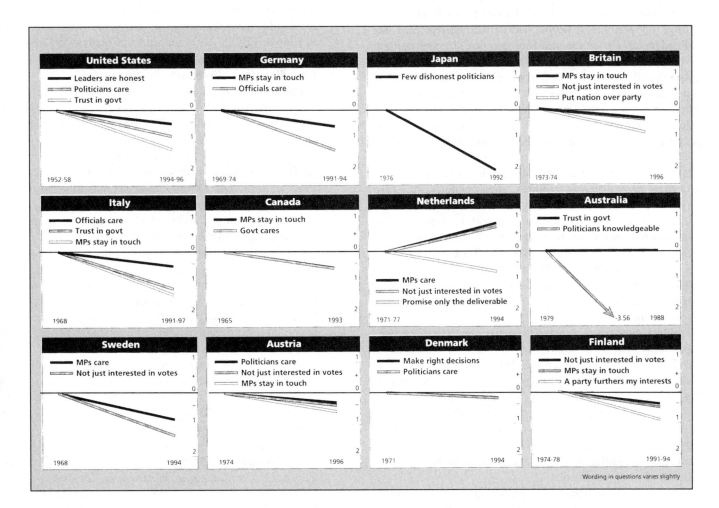

Figure 1   Our Elected Rascals.   Political Confidence, annual % Change

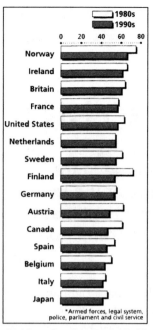

Figure 2 Losing Faith.   Confidence in Political Institutions*, %
Sources: R. Dalton; World Values Surveys

If opinion research is any guide, the mature democracies have troubles of their own. In the United States in particular, the high opinion which people had of their government has declined steadily over the past four decades. Regular opinion surveys carried out as part of a series of national election studies in America show that the slump set in during the 1960s. The civil-rights conflict and the Vietnam war made this an especially turbulent decade for the United States. But public confidence in politicians and government continued to decline over the next quarter-century. Nor (remember the student unrest in Paris and elsewhere in 1968) was this confined to the United States.

It is hard to compare attitudes toward democracy over time, and across many different countries. Most opinion surveys are carried out nation-by-nation: they are conducted at different times and researchers often ask different sorts of questions. But some generalizations can be made. In their introduction to a forthcoming book "What is Troubling the Trilateral Democracies?", Princeton University Press, 2000) three academics—Robert Putnam, Susan Pharr, and Russell Dalton—have done their best to analyze the results of surveys conducted in most of the rich countries.

Figure 1 summarises some of these findings. The downward slopes show how public confidence in politicians seems to be falling, measured by changes in the answers voters give to questions such as "Do you think that politicians are trustworthy?"; "Do members of parliament (MPs) care about voters like you?"; and "How much do you trust governments of any party to place the needs of the nation above their own political party?" In most of the mature democracies, the results show a pattern of disillusionment with politicians. Only in the Netherlands is there clear evidence of rising confidence.

Nor is it only politicians who are losing the public's trust. Surveys suggest that confidence in political institutions is in

decline as well. In 11 out of 14 countries, for example, confidence in parliament has declined, with especially sharp falls in Canada, Germany, Britain, Sweden and the United States. World-wide polls conducted in 1981 and 1990 measured confidence in five institutions: parliament, the armed services, the judiciary, the police and the civil service. Some institutions gained public trust, but on average confidence in them decreased by 6% over the decade (see figure 2). The only countries to score small increases in confidence were Iceland and Denmark.

Other findings summarised by Mr Putnam and his colleagues make uncomfortable reading:

- In the late 1950s and early 1960s **Americans** had a touching faith in government. When asked "How many times can you trust the government in Washington to do what is right?", three out of four answered "most of the time" or "just about always". By 1998, fewer than four out of ten trusted the government to do what was right. In 1964 only 29% of the American electorate agreed that "the government is pretty much run by a few big interests looking after themselves". By 1984, that figure had risen to 55%, and by 1998 to 63%. In the 1960s, two-thirds of Americans rejected the statement "most elected officials don't care what people like me think". In 1998, nearly two-thirds agreed with it. The proportion of Americans who expressed "a great deal of" confidence in the executive branch fell from 42% in 1966 to 12% in 1997; and trust in Congress fell from 42% to 11%.

- **Canadians** have also been losing faith in their politicians. The proportion of Canadians who felt that "the government doesn't care what people like me think" rose from 45% in 1968 to 67% in 1993. The proportion expressing "a great deal of" confidence in political parties fell from 30% in 1979 to 11% in 1999. Confidence in the House of Commons fell from 49% in 1974 to 21% in 1996. By 1992 only 34% of Canadians were satisfied with their system of government, down from 51% in 1986.

- Less information is available about attitudes in **Japan**. But the findings of the few surveys that have been carried out there match the global pattern. Confidence in political institutions rose in the decades following the smashing of the country's old politics in the second world war. Happily for democracy, the proportion of Japanese voters who agree that "in order to make Japan better, it is best to rely on talented politicians, rather than to let the citizens argue among themselves" has been falling for 40 years. However, the proportion who feel that they exert at least "some influence" on national politics through elections or demonstrations also fell steadily between 1973 and 1993.

- Although it is harder to generalize about **Western Europe**, confidence in political institutions is in decline in most countries. In 1985 48% of Britons expressed quite a lot of confidence in the House of Commons. This number had halved by 1995. The proportion of Swedes disagreeing with the statement that "parties are

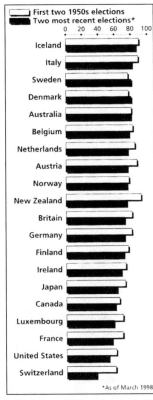

Figure 3   Staying Home.   Voter Turnout, %
Source: Martin P. Wattenberg, University of California, Irvine

only interested in people's votes, not in their opinions" slumped from 51% in 1968 to 28% in 1994. In 1985 51% expressed confidence in the Rikstad (parliament); by 1996 only 19% did. In Germany, the percentage of people who said they trusted their Bundestag deputy to represent their interests rose from 25% in 1951 to 55% in 1978, but had fallen again to 34% by 1992. The percentage of Italians who say that politicians "don't care what people like me think" increased from 68% in 1968 to 84% in 1997.

Such findings are alarming if you take them at face value. But they should be interpreted with care. Democracy may just be a victim of its own success. It could just be that people nowadays expect more from governments, impose new demands on the state, and are therefore more likely to be disappointed. After all, the idea that governments ought to do such things as protect or improve the environment, maintain high employment, arbitrate between moral issues, or ensure the equal treatment of women or minorities, is a relatively modern and still controversial one. Or perhaps the disillusionment is a healthy product of rising educational standards and the scepticism that goes with it. Or maybe it is caused by the media's search-light highlighting failures of government that were previously kept in the dark. Whatever the causes, the popularity of governments or politicians ought not to be the only test of democracy's health.

Moreover, there is encouraging evidence to put beside the discouraging findings. However much confidence in government may be declining, this does not seem to have diminished popular support for democratic principles. On average, surveys show, more than three out of four people in rich countries believe that democracy is the best form of government. Even in countries where the performance of particular governments has been so disappointing as to break up the party system itself (such as Japan and Italy in 1993–95), this has brought no serious threat to fundamental democratic principle. It may seem paradoxical for people to express strong support for democracy even while their confidence in politicians and political institutions crumbles. But it hardly amounts to the "crisis of democracy" which political scientists tend to proclaim from time to time.

Nor, though, is it a ringing endorsement, especially given that the evidence of opinion surveys is reinforced by other trends. These include a decline both in the membership of political parties and in the proportion of people who turn out to vote. Numbers compiled by Martin Wattenberg, also at the University of California, show that in 18 out of 20 of the rich established democracies the proportion of the electorate voting has been lower than it was in the early 1950s (see figure 3), with the median change being a decline of 10%. More controversially, some political scientists see the growth of protest movements since the 1960s as a sign of declining faith in the traditional institutions of representative democracy, and an attempt to bypass them. Others reckon that the most serious threat comes from the increasingly professional pressure groups and lobbying organisations that work behind the scenes to influence government policy and defend special interests, often at the expense of the electorate as a whole.

What is to be done? Those who believe that government has over-reached itself call on governments to become smaller and to promise less. Thus, it is hoped, people will come to do more for themselves. But whatever the appropriate size and reach of governments, there is also scope for making the machinery of democracy work better.

Indeed, some commentators see the public's declining confidence in political institutions as an opportunity for democratic renewal. Pippa Norris, at Harvard University's Kennedy School of Government, hails the advent of a new breed of "critical citizens" (in a book of that name, Oxford University Press, 1999) who see that existing channels of participation fall short of democratic ideals and want to reform them.

There are some signs of this. Countries as different as Italy, Japan, Britain and New Zealand have lately considered or introduced changes in their electoral systems. Countries around the world are making growing use of referendums and other forms of direct democracy. Many are reducing the power of parliaments by giving judges new powers to review the decisions that elected politicians make. And governments everywhere are introducing new rules on the financing of politicians and political parties. The rest of the articles in this series will look at some of these changes and the forces shaping them.

Advanced Democracies and the New Politics

RUSSELL J. DALTON, SUSAN E. SCARROW, AND BRUCE E. CAIN

Over the past quarter-century in advanced industrial democracies, citizens, public interest groups, and political elites have shown decreasing confidence in the institutions and processes of representative government. In most of these nations, electoral turnout and party membership have declined, and citizens are increasingly skeptical of politicians and political institutions.[1]

Along with these trends often go louder demands to expand citizen and interest-group access to politics, and to restructure democratic decision-making processes. Fewer people may be voting, but more are signing petitions, joining lobby groups, and engaging in unconventional forms of political action.[2] Referenda and ballot initiatives are growing in popularity; there is growing interest in processes of deliberative or consultative democracy;[3] and there are regular calls for more reliance on citizen advisory committees for policy formation and administration—especially at the local level, where direct involvement is most feasible. Contemporary democracies are facing popular pressures to grant more access, increase the transparency of governance, and make government more accountable.

Amplifying these trends, a chorus of political experts has been calling for democracies to reform and adapt. Mark Warren writes, "Democracy, once again in favor, is in need of conceptual renewal. While the traditional concerns of democratic theory with state-centered institutions remain importantly crucial and ethically central, they are increasingly subject to the limitations we should expect when nineteenth-century concepts meet twenty-first century realities."[4] U.S. political analyst Dick Morris similarly observes, "The fundamental paradigm that dominates our politics is the shift from representative to direct democracy. Voters want to run the show directly and are impatient with all forms of intermediaries between their opinions and public policy."[5] As Ralf Dahrendorf recently summarized the mood of the times, "Representative government is no longer as compelling a proposition as it once was. Instead, a search for new institutional forms to express conflicts of interest has begun."[6]

Many government officials have echoed these sentiments, and the OECD has examined how its member states could reform their governments to create new connections to their publics.[7] Its report testifies:

> New forms of representation and public participation are emerging in all of our countries. These developments have expanded the avenues for citizens to participate more fully in public policy making, within the overall framework of representative democracy in which parliaments continue to play a central role. Citizens are increasingly demanding more transparency and accountability from their governments, and want greater public participation in shaping policies that affect their lives. Educated and well-informed citizens expect governments to take their views and knowledge into account when making decisions on their behalf. Engaging citizens in policy making allows governments to respond to these expectations and, at the same time, design better policies and improve their implementation.[8]

If the pressures for political reform are having real effects, these should show up in changes to the institutional structures of democratic politics. The most avid proponents of such reforms conclude that we may be experiencing the most fundamental democratic transformation since the beginnings of mass democracy in the early twentieth century. Yet cycles of reform are a recurring theme in democratic history, and pressures for change in one direction often wane as new problems and possibilities come to the fore. What is the general track record for democratic institutional reforms in the advanced industrial democracies over the latter half of the twentieth century? And what are the implications of this record for the future of democracy?

Three Modes of Democracy

In a sense, there is nothing new about the call to inject "more democracy" into the institutions of representative government. The history of modern democracies is punctuated by repeated waves of debate about the nature of the democratic process, some of which have produced major institutional reforms. In the early twentieth century, for example, the populist movement in the United States prompted extensive electoral and governing-process reforms, as well as the introduction of new forms of direct democracy.[9] Parallel institutional changes occurred in Europe. By the end of this democratic-reform period in the late 1920s, most Western democracies had become much more "democratic" in the sense of providing citizens with access to the political process and making governments more accountable.

A new wave of democratic rhetoric and debate emerged in the last third of the twentieth century. The stimulus for this first appeared mainly among university students and young professionals contesting the boundaries of conventional representative democracy. Although their dramatic protests subsequently waned, they stimulated new challenges that affect advanced industrial democracies to this day. Citizen interest groups and other public lobbying organizations, which have proliferated since the 1960s, press for more access to government; expanding mass media delve more deeply into the workings of government; and people demand more from government while trusting it less.

The institutional impact of the reform wave of the late twentieth century can be understood in terms of three different modes of democratic politics. One aims at improving the process of *representative democracy* in which citizens elect elites. Much like the populism of the early twentieth century, reforms of this mode seek to improve electoral processes. Second, there are calls for new types of *direct democracy* that bypass (or complement) the processes of representative democracy. A third mode seeks to expand the means of political participation through a new style of *advocacy democracy,* in which citizens participate in policy deliberation and formation—either directly or through surrogates, such as public interest groups—although the final decisions are still made by elites.

1) Representative democracy. A major example of reform in representative democracy can be seen in changes to processes of electing the U.S. president. In a 30-year span, these elections underwent a dramatic transformation, in which citizen influence grew via the spread of state-level primary elections as a means of nominating candidates. In 1968, the Democratic Party had just 17 presidential primaries while the Republicans had only 16; in 2000 there were Democratic primaries in 40 states and Republican primaries in 43. As well, both parties-first the Democrats, then the Republicans—instituted reforms intended to ensure that convention delegates are more representative of the public at large, such as rules on the representation of women. Meanwhile, legislators introduced and expanded public funding for presidential elections in an effort to limit the influence of money and so promote citizen equality. If the 1948 Republican and Democratic candidates, Thomas E. Dewey and Harry S. Truman, were brought back to observe the modern presidential election process, they would hardly recognize the system as the same that nominated them. More recently, reformers have championed such causes as term limits and campaign-finance reform as remedies for restricting the influence of special interests. In Europe, populist electoral reform has been relatively restrained by institutionalized systems of party government, but even so, there are

parallels to what has occurred in the United States in many European countries. On a limited basis, for example, some European political parties have experimented with, or even adopted, closed primaries to select parliamentary candidates.[10]

In recent decades, changes in both attitudes and formal rules have brought about a greater general reliance on mechanisms of direct democracy within the advanced industrial democracies.

Generally, the mechanisms of representative democracy have maintained, and in places slightly increased, citizen access and influence. It is true that, compared with four decades ago, electoral turnout is generally down by about 10 percent in the established democracies.[11] This partially signifies a decrease in political access (or in citizens' use of elections as a means of political access). But at the same time, the "amount of electing" is up to an equal or greater extent. There has been a pattern of reform increasing the number of electoral choices available to voters by changing appointed positions into elected ones.[12] In Europe, citizens now elect members of Parliament for the European Union; regionalization has increased the number of elected subnational governments; directly elected mayors and directly elected local officials are becoming more common; and suffrage now includes younger voters, aged 18 to 20. Moreover, the number of political parties has increased, while parties have largely become more accountable—and the decisions of party elites more transparent—to their supporters. With the general expansion in electoral choices, citizens are traveling to the polls more often and making more electoral decisions.

2) Direct democracy. Initiatives and referenda are the most common means of direct democracy. These allow citizens to decide government policy without relying on the mediating influence of representation. Ballot initiatives in particular allow nongovernmental actors to control the framing of issues and even the timing of policy debates, further empowering the citizens and groups that take up this mode of action. In recent decades, changes in both attitudes and formal rules have brought about a greater general reliance on mechanisms of direct democracy within the advanced industrial democracies. The Initiative and Referendum Institute calculates, for example, that there were 118 statewide referenda in the United States during the 1950s but 378 such referenda during the 1990s. And a number of other nations have amended laws and constitutions to provide greater opportunities for direct democracy at the national and local levels.[13] Britain had its first national referendum in 1975; Sweden introduced the referendum in a constitutional reform of 1980; and Finland adopted the referendum in 1987. In these and other cases, the referendum won new legitimacy as a basis for national decision making, a norm that runs strongly counter to the ethos of representative democracy. There has also been mounting interest in expanding direct democracy through the innovation of new institutional forms, such as methods of deliberative democracy and citizen juries to advise policy makers.[14]

How fundamental are these changes? On the one hand, the political impact of a given referendum is limited, since only a single policy is being decided, so the channels of direct democracy normally provide less access than do the traditional channels of representative democracy. On the other hand, the increasing use of referenda has influenced political discourse—and the principles of political legitimacy in particular—beyond the policy at stake in any single referendum. With Britain's first referendum on European Community membership in 1975, for instance, parliamentary sovereignty was now no longer absolute, and the concept of popular sovereignty was concomitantly legitimized. Accordingly, the legitimacy of subsequent decisions on devolution required additional referenda, and today contentious issues, such as acceptance of the euro, are pervasively considered as matters that "the public should decide." So even though recourse to direct democracy remains relatively limited in Britain, the expansion of this mode of access represents a significant institutional change—and one that we see occurring across most advanced industrial democracies.

3) Advocacy democracy. In this third mode, citizens or public interest groups interact directly with governments and even participate directly in the policy-formation process, although actual decisions remain in the official hands. One might consider this as a form of traditional lobbying, but it is not. Advocacy democracy involves neither traditional interest groups nor standard channels of informal interest-group persuasion. Rather, it empowers individual citizens, citizen groups, or nongovernmental organizations to participate in advisory hearings; attend open government meetings ("government in the sunshine"); consult ombudsmen to redress grievances; demand information from government agencies; and challenge government actions through the courts.

Evidence for the growth of advocacy democracy is less direct and more difficult to quantify than is evidence for other kinds of institutional change. But the overall expansion of advocacy democracy is undeniable. Administrative reforms, decentralization, the growing political influence of courts, and other factors have created new opportunities for access and influence. During the latter 1960s in the United States, "maximum feasible participation" became a watchword for the social-service reforms of President Lyndon Johnson's "Great Society" programs. Following this model, citizen consultations and public hearings have since been embedded in an extensive range of legislation, giving citizens new points of access to policy formation and administration. Congressional hearings and state-government meetings have become public events, and legislation such as the 1972 Federal Advisory Committee Act even extended open-meeting requirements to advisory committees. While only a handful of nations had freedom-of-information laws in 1970, such laws are now almost universal in OECD countries. And there has been a general diffusion of the ombudsman model across advanced industrial democracies.[15] "Sunshine" provisions reflect a fundamental shift in understanding as to the role that elected representatives should play-one which would make Edmund Burke turn in his grave, and which we might characterize as a move away from the *trustee* toward the *delegate* model.

Reforms in this category also include new legal rights augmenting the influence of individuals and citizen groups. A pattern of judicialization in the policy process throughout most Western democracies, for instance, has enabled citizen groups to launch class-action suits on behalf of the environment, women's rights, or other public interests.[16] Now virtually every public interest can be translated into a rights-based appeal, which provides new avenues for action through the courts. Moreover, especially in European democracies, where direct citizen action was initially quite rare, the expansion of public interest groups, *Bürgerinitiativen,* and other kinds of citizen groups has substantially enlarged the public's repertoire for political action. It is worth noting that "unconventional" forms of political action, such as protests and demonstrations, have also grown substantially over this time span.

Citizens and the Democratic State

If the institutional structure of democracy is changing, how does this affect the democratic process? The answer is far from simple and not always positive, for democratic gains in some areas can be offset by losses in others, as when increased access produces new problems of democratic governability. In the following pages, we limit our attention to how these institutional changes affect the relationship between citizens and the state.

Robert A. Dahl's writings are a touchstone in this matter.[17] Like many democratic theorists, Dahl tends to equate democracy with the institutions and processes of representative democracy, paying much less attention to other forms of citizen participation that may actually represent more important means of citizen influence over political elites. Thus, while we draw from Dahl's *On Democracy* to define the essential criteria for a democratic process, we broaden the framework to include not only representative democracy but direct democracy and advocacy democracy also. Dahl suggests five criteria for a genuinely democratic system:[18]

1. **Inclusion:** With minimal exceptions, all permanent adult residents must have full rights of citizenship.
2. **Political equality:** When decisions about policy are made, every citizen must have an equal and effective opportunity to participate.
3. **Enlightened understanding:** Within reasonable limits, citizens must have equal and effective opportunities to learn about relevant policy alternatives and their likely consequences.
4. **Control of the agenda:** Citizens must have the opportunity to decide which matters are placed on the public agenda, and how.
5. **Effective participation:** Before a policy is adopted, all the citizens must have equal and effective opportunities for making their views known to other citizens.

Robert A. Dahl's Democratic Criteria

Democratic Criteria	Representative Democracy	Direct Democracy	Advocacy Democracy
Inclusion	**Universal suffrage provides inclusion**	**Universal suffrage provides inclusion**	Equal citizen access *(Problems of access to nonelectoral arenas)*
Political Equality	**On person, one vote with high turnout maximizes equality.** *(Problems of low turnout, inequality due to campaign finance issues, etc.)*	**One person, one vote with high turnout maximizes equality** *(Problems of equality with low turnout)*	Equal opportunity *(Problems of very unequal use)*
Enlightened Understanding	*(Problems of information access, voter decision processes)*	*(Problems of greater information and higher decision-making costs)*	**Increased public access to information** *(Problems of even greater information and decision-making demands on citizens)*
Control of the Agenda	*(Problems of control of campaign debate, selecting candidates, etc.)* **Control through responsible parties**	**Citizen initiation provides control of agenda** *(Problems of influence by interest groups)*	**Citizens and groups control the locus and focus of activity**
Effective Participation	*(Principal-agent problems: fair elections, responsible party government, etc.)*	**Direct policy impact ensures effective participation**	**Direct access avoids mediated participation**

Note: Criteria that are well addressed are presented in **bold,** criteria that are at issue are presented in *italics* in the shaded cells.

The first column of the Table lists Dahl's five democratic criteria. The second column summarizes the prevailing view on how well representative democracy fulfills these criteria. For example, advanced industrial democracies have met the *inclusion* criterion by expanding the franchise to all adult citizens (by way of a long and at times painful series of reforms). General success in this regard is illustrated by the bold highlighting of "universal suffrage" in the first cell of this column.

Nearly all advanced industrial democracies now meet the *political equality* criterion by having enacted the principle of "one person, one vote" for elections, which we have highlighted in the second cell. In most nations today, a majority of citizens participate in voting, while labor unions, political parties, and other organizations mobilize participation to achieve high levels of engagement. Indeed, that noted democrat, the late Mayor Richard Daley of Chicago, used to say that electoral politics was the only instrument through which a working-class citizen could ever exercise equal influence with the socially advantaged. At the same time, certain problems of equality remain, as contemporary debates about campaign financing and voter registration illustrate, and full equality in political practice is probably unattainable. We note these problems in the shaded area of the second cell. Nevertheless, overall the principle of

equality is now a consensual value for the electoral processes of representative democracy.

At first glance, it may seem that expanding the number of elections amounts to extending these principles. But increasing the number of times that voters go to the polls and the number of items on ballots actually tends to depress turnout. And when voter turnout is less than 50 percent, as it tends to be in, say, EU parliamentary elections-or less than 25 percent, as it tends to be in local mayoral or school-board elections in the United States-then one must question whether the gap between "equality of access" and "equality of usage" has become so wide that it undermines the basic principle of *political equality.* Moreover, second-order elections tend to mobilize a smaller and more ideological electorate than the public at large, and so more second-order elections tend to mean more distortions in the representativeness of the electoral process.

The tension between Dahl's democratic criteria and democratic practice becomes even more obvious when we turn to the criterion of *enlightened understanding.* Although we are fairly sanguine about voters' abilities to make informed choices when it comes to high-visibility (for instance, presidential or parliamentary) elections, we are less so when it comes to lower-visibility elections. How does a typical resident of Houston,

Texas, make enlightened choices regarding the dozens of judgeship candidates whose names appeared on the November 2002 ballot, to say nothing of other local office seekers and referenda? In such second- and third-order elections, the means of information that voters can use in first-order elections may be insufficient or even altogether lacking. So the expansion of the electoral marketplace may empower the public in a sense, but in another sense may make it hard for voters to exercise meaningful political judgment.

Another criterion is citizen *control of the political agenda.* Recent reforms in representative democracy have gone some way toward broadening access to the political agenda. Increasing the number of elected offices gives citizens more input and presumably more avenues for raising issues, while reforming political finance to equalize campaign access and party support has made for greater openness in political deliberations. More problematic, though, is performance on the *effectiveness of participation* criterion. Do citizens get what they vote for? Often, this principal-agent problem is solved through the mechanism of party government: Voters select a party, and the party ensures the compliance of individual members of parliament and the translation of electoral mandates into policy outcomes.[19] But the impact of recent reforms on the *effectiveness of participation* is complex. On the one hand, more openness and choice in elections should enable people to express their political preferences more extensively and in more policy areas. On the other hand, as the number of office-holders proliferates, it may become more difficult for voters to assign responsibility for policy outcomes. Fragmented decision making, divided government, and the sheer profusion of elected officials may diminish the political responsiveness of each actor.

How much better do the mechanisms of direct democracy fare when measured against Dahl's five criteria (see column 3 of the Table)? Because referenda and initiatives are effectively mass elections, they seek to ensure inclusion and political equality in much the same way as representative elections do. Most referenda and initiatives use universal suffrage to ensure inclusion and the "one person, one vote" rule to ensure political equality. However, whereas turnout in direct-democracy elections is often lower than in comparable elections for public officials, the question of democratic inclusion becomes more complicated than a simple assessment of equal access. For instance, when Proposition 98—which favored altering the California state constitution to mandate that a specific part of the state budget be directed to primary and secondary education—appeared on the 1996 general election ballot, barely half of all voting-age Californians turned out, and only 51 percent voted for the proposition. But as a consequence, the state's constitution was altered, reshaping state spending and public financing in California. Such votes raise questions about the fairness of elections in which a minority of registered voters can make crucial decisions affecting the public welfare. Equality of opportunity clearly does not mean equality of participation.

Moreover, referenda and initiatives place even greater demands for information and understanding on voters. Many of the heuristics that they can use in party elections or candidate elections are less effective in referenda, and the issues them-

selves are often more complex than what citizens are typically called upon to consider in electing office-holders. For instance, did the average voter have enough information to make enlightened choices in Italy's multi-referendum ballot of 1997? This ballot asked voters to make choices concerning television-ownership rules, television-broadcasting policy, the hours during which stores could remain open, the commercial activities which municipalities could pursue, labor-union reform proposals, regulations for administrative elections, and residency rules for mafia members. In referenda, voters can still rely on group heuristics and other cues that they use in electing public officials,[20] but obviously the proliferation of policy choices and especially the introduction of less-salient local issues raise questions about the overall effectiveness of such cue-taking.

The real strengths of direct democracy are highlighted by Dahl's fourth and fifth criteria. Referenda and initiatives shift the focus of agenda-setting from elites toward the public, or at least toward public interest groups. Indeed, processes of direct democracy can bring into the political arena issues that elites tend not to want to address: for example, tax reform or term limits in the United States, abortion-law reform in Italy, or the terms of EU membership in Europe generally. Even when referenda fail to reach the ballot or fail to win a majority, they can nevertheless prompt elites to be more sensitive to public interests. By definition, moreover, direct democracy should solve the problem of effective participation that exists with all methods of representative democracy. Direct democracy is unmediated, and so it ensures that participation is effective. Voters make policy choices with their ballot-to enact a new law, to repeal an existing law, or to reform a constitution. Even in instances where the mechanisms of direct democracy require an elite response in passing a law or a revoting in a later election, the link to policy action is more direct than is the case with the channels of representative democracy. Accordingly, direct democracy seems to fulfill Dahl's democratic criteria of agenda control and effective participation.

But direct democracy raises questions in these areas as well. Interest groups may find it easier to manipulate processes of direct democracy than those of representative democracy.[21] The discretion to place a policy initiative on the ballot can be appealing to interest groups, which then have unmediated access to voters during the subsequent referendum campaign. In addition, decisions made by way of direct democracy are less susceptible to bargaining or the checks and balances that occur within the normal legislative process. Some recent referenda in California may illustrate this style of direct democracy: Wealthy backers pay a consulting firm to collect signatures so as to get a proposal on the ballot, and then bankroll a campaign to support their desired legislation. This is not grassroots democracy at work; it is the representation of wealthy interests by other means.

The expansion of direct democracy has the potential to complement traditional forms of representative democracy. It can expand the democratic process by allowing citizens and public interest groups new access to politics, and new control over political agendas and policy outcomes. But direct democracy also raises new questions about equality of actual influence, if not formal access, and the ability of the public to make fair and reasoned judgments about issues. Perhaps the most important question about direct democracy is not whether it is expanding, but *how* it is expanding: Are there ways to increase access and influence without sacrificing inclusion and equality? We return to this question below.

Formal Access and Actual Use

The final column in our Table considers how new forms of advocacy democracy fulfill Dahl's democratic criteria. These new forms of action provide citizens with significant access to politics, but it is also clear that this access is very unevenly used. Nearly everyone can vote, and most do. But very few citizens file lawsuits, file papers under a freedom-of-information act, attend environmental-impact review hearings, or attend local planning meetings. There is no clear equivalent to "one person, one vote" for advocacy democracy. Accordingly, it raises the question of how to address Dahl's criteria of inclusion, political equality, and enlightened understanding.

"Equality of access" is not adequate if "equality of usage" is grossly uneven. For instance, when Europeans were asked in the 1989 European Election Survey whether they voted in the election immediately preceding the survey, differences in participation according to levels of education were very slight (see the Figure, Social-Status Inequality in Participations). A full 73 percent of those in the "low education" category said they had voted in the previous EU parliamentary election (even though it is a second-order election), and an identical percentage of those in the "high education" category claimed to have voted. Differences in campaign activity according to educational levels are somewhat greater, but still modest in overall terms.

A distinctly larger inequality gap emerges when it comes to participation through forms of direct or advocacy democracy. For instance, only 13 percent of those in the "low education" category had participated in a citizen action group, while nearly three times the percentage of those in the "high education" category had participated. Similarly, there are large inequalities when it comes to such activities as signing a petition or participating in a lawful demonstration.

With respect to the criterion of *enlightened understanding,* advocacy democracy has mixed results. On the one hand, it can enhance citizen understanding and make for greater inclusion. Citizens and public interest groups can increase the amount of information that they have about government activities, especially by taking advantage of freedom-of-information laws, attending administrative hearings, and participating in government policy making. And with the assistance of the press in disseminating this information, citizens and public interest groups can better influence political outcomes. By ensuring that the public receives information in a timely fashion, advocacy democracy allows citizens to make informed judgments and hold governments more accountable. And by eliminating the filtering that governments would otherwise apply, advocacy democracy can help citizens to get more accurate pictures of the influences affecting policy decisions, with fewer cover-ups and self-serving distortions. On the other hand, advocacy democracy makes greater cognitive and resource demands on citizens, and thus may generate some of the same inequalities in participation noted above. It requires much more of the citizen to participate in a public hearing or to petition an official than it does simply to cast a vote. The most insightful evidence on this point comes from Jane Mansbridge's study of collective decision making in New England town meetings.[22] She finds that many participants were unprepared or overwhelmed by the deliberative decision-making processes.

Advocacy democracy fares better when it comes to the remaining two criteria. It gives citizens greater control of the political agenda, in part by increasing their opportunity to press their interests outside of the institutionalized time and format constraints of fixed election cycles. By means of advocacy democracy, citizens can often choose when and where to challenge a government directive or pressure policy makers. Similarly, even though advocacy democracy typically leaves final political decisions in the hands of elites, it nevertheless provides direct access to government. Property owners can participate in a local planning hearing; a public interest group can petition government for information on past policies; and dissatisfied citizens can attend a school board session. Such unmediated participation brings citizens into the decision-making process-which ultimately might not be as effective as the efforts of a skilled representative, but greater direct involvement in the democratic process should improve its accountability and transparency (see the bold entries in these last two cells of the Table).

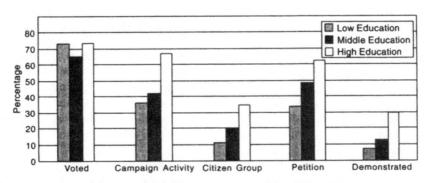

Social-Status Inequality in Participation

Source: Eurobarometers 31 and 31A conducted in connection with the 1989 European Parliament election. Results combine the 12 nations weighted to represent the total EU population.

All in all, advocacy democracy increases the potential for citizen access in important ways. It can give citizens and public interest groups new influence over the agenda-setting process, and it can give them unmediated involvement in the policy-formation process. These are significant extensions of democratic participation. At the same time, advocacy democracy may exacerbate political inequality on account of inequalities in usage. New access points created through advisory panels, consultative hearings, and other institutional reforms empower some citizens to become more involved. But other citizens, relatively lacking in the skills or resources to compete in these new domains, may be left behind. In other words, advocacy democracy may in some ways respond to the strength of the claimants, rather than to the strength of their claims. It can even alter the locus of political expertise. While advocacy democracy values know-how and expertise in the citizenry, it devalues those same characteristics among policy makers.

Environmental policy provides a good illustration of this problem. Here, citizens and public interest groups have gained new rights and new access to the policy process. But these are disproportionately used by relatively affluent and skilled citizens, who are already participating in conventional forms of representative democracy, while the poor, the unskilled, and the otherwise disadvantaged tend to get left behind. So while environmentalism is an example of citizen empowerment, it is also a source of increasing inequality.

No form of democratic action is ideal, each having its advantages and limitations. As democratic practice shifts from a predominant reliance on representation toward a mixed repertoire—including greater use of direct and advocacy democracy—a new balance must be struck among democratic goals. It is possible that new institutional arrangements will maximize the benefits of these new modes while limiting their disadvantages—as, for example, the institutions of representative democracy depend on parties and interest groups. But thus far, the advanced industrialized democracies have not fully recognized the problems generated by the new mixed repertoire of democratic action, and so have yet to find institutional or structural means of addressing them. Democratic reforms create opportunities, but they also create challenges. Our goal should be to ensure that progress on some democratic criteria is not unduly sacrificed for progress on others.

Notes

1. Martin P. Wattenberg, *Where Have All the Voters Gone?* (Cambridge: Harvard University Press, 2002); Susan E. Scarrow, "From Social Integration to Electoral Contestation," in Russell J. Dalton and Martin P. Wattenberg, eds., *Parties Without Partisans: Political Change in Advanced Industrial Democracies* (New York: Oxford University Press, 2000); Russell J. Dalton, *Democratic Challenges, Democratic Choices: The Decline in Political Support in Advanced Industrial Democracies* (Oxford: Oxford University Press, 2004); Susan J. Pharr and Robert D. Putnam, eds., *Disaffected Democracies: What's Troubling the Trilateral Countries?* (Princeton: Princeton University Press, 2000).

2. Russell J. Dalton, *Citizen Politics: Public Opinion and Political Parties in Advanced Industrial Democracies* (New York: Chatham House, 2002), ch. 4; Ronald Inglehart, *Modernization and Postmodernization: Cultural, Economic, and Political Change in 43 Societies* (Princeton: Princeton University Press, 1997); Sidney Verba, Kay Schlozman, and Henry Brady, *Voice and Equality: Civic Volunteerism in American Politics* (Cambridge: Harvard University Press, 1995), 72.

3. James S. Fishkin, *The Voice of the People: Public Opinion and Democracy* (New Haven: Yale University Press, 1995); John Elster, *Deliberative Democracy* (New York: Cambridge University Press, 1998).

4. Mark Warren, *Democracy and Association* (Princeton: Princeton University Press, 2001), 226.

5. Dick Morris, *The New Prince: Machiavelli Updated for the Twenty-First Century* (New York: Renaissance Books, 2000).

6. Ralf Dahrendorf, "Afterword," in Susan J. Pharr and Robert D. Putnam, eds., *Disaffected Democracies: What's Troubling the Trilateral Countries?* 311.

7. OECD, *Government of the Future: Getting from Here to There* (Paris: Organization for Economic Co-operation and Development, 2000).

8. OECD, *Citizens as Partners: OECD Handbook on Information, Consultation and Public Participation in Policy-Making* (Paris: Organization of Economic Cooperation and Development, 2001), 9.

9. Lawrence Goodwyn, *Democratic Promise: The Populist Movement in America* (New York: Oxford University Press, 1976).

10. Susan E. Scarrow, Paul Webb, and David M. Farrell, "From Social Integration to Electoral Contestation," in Russell J. Dalton and Martin P. Wattenberg, eds., *Parties without Partisans: Political Change in Advanced Industrial Democracies;* Jonathan Hopkin, "Bringing the Members Back in: Democratizing Candidate Selection in Britain and Spain," *Party Politics* 7 (May 2001): 343–61.

11. Martin P. Wattenberg, *Where Have All the Voters Gone?*

12. Russell J. Dalton and Mark Gray, "Expanding the Electoral Marketplace," in Bruce E. Cain, Russell J. Dalton, and Susan E. Scarrow, eds., *Democracy Transformed? Expanding Political Opportunities in Advanced Industrial Democracies* (Oxford: Oxford University Press, 2003).

13. Susan E. Scarrow, "Direct Democracy and Institutional Design: A Comparative Investigation," in *Comparative Political Studies* 34 (August 2001): 651–65; also see David Butler and Austin Ranney, eds., *Referenda Around the World* (Washington, D.C.: American Enterprise Institute, 1994); Michael Gallagher and Pier Vincenzo Uleri, eds., *The Referendum Experience in Europe* (Basingstoke: Macmillan, 1996).

14. James S. Fishkin, *The Voice of the People: Public Opinion and Democracy;* Forest David Matthews, *Politics for People: Finding a Responsive Voice,* 2nd ed. (Urbana: University of Illinois Press, 1999).

15. Roy Gregory and Philip Giddings, eds., *Righting Wrongs: The Ombudsman in Six Continents* (Amsterdam: IOS Press, 2000); see also Christopher Ansell and Jane Gingrich, "Reforming the Administrative State," in Bruce E. Cain, Russell J. Dalton, and

Susan E. Scarrow, eds., *Democracy Transformed? Expanding Political Opportunities in Advanced Industrial Democracies.*

16. Alec Stone Sweet, *Governing with Judges: Constitutional Politics in Europe* (New York: Oxford University Press, 2000).

17. Robert A Dahl, *Polyarchy: Participation and Opposition* (New Haven: Yale University Press, 1971); *Democracy and Its Critics* (New Haven: Yale University Press, 1991); *On Democracy* (New Haven: Yale University Press, 1998).

18. Robert A. Dahl, *On Democracy,* 37–38.

19. 1Hans-Dieter Klingemann et al., *Parties, Policies, and Democracy* (Boulder: Westview, 1994).

20. Arthur Lupia, "Shortcuts versus Encyclopedias," *American Political Science Review* 88 (March 1994): 63–76.

21. Elisabeth Gerber, *The Populist Paradox: Interest Group Influence and the Promise of Direct Legislation* (Princeton: Princeton University Press, 1999); see also David S. Broder, *Democracy Derailed: Initiative Campaigns and the Power of Money*

22. Jane Mansbridge, *Beyond Adversary Democracy* (New York: Basic Books, 1980).

RUSSELL J. DALTON is director of the Center for the Study of Democracy at the University of California, Irvine. **SUSAN E. SCARROW** is associate professor of political science at the University of Houston. **BRUCE E. CAIN** is Robson Professor of Political Science at the University of California, Berkeley, and director of the Institute of Governmental Studies. This essay is adapted from their edited volume, *Democracy Transformed? Expanding Political Opportunities in Advanced Industrial Democracies* (2003).

From *Journal of Democracy,* 15:1, January 2004, pp. 124–138. Copyright © 2004 by National Endowment for Democracy and The Johns Hopkins University Press. Reprinted with permission of The Johns Hopkins University Press.

UNIT 2

Pluralist Democracies: Four Country Studies

Unit Selections

Key Points to Consider

• How does the "gini index" measure the income distribution in a society, and how do the United States and Britain compare in this respect to other relatively affluent societies like Germany or the Scandinavian countries?

• What was so new about "new" Labour? Why don't the Liberal Democrats unite with Labour?

• What is cohabitation, and why have the French periodically succumbed to this form of power sharing? Why was the presidential term reduced to five years recently?

• Why have the French, Germans or British been less than successful in their relations with residents of Muslim descent? Why doesn't the French policy of assimilation take care of the problem? Explain laicism and its role in French politics.

• Why might constitutional reform be Tony Blair's most important legacy in British politics? What are the four or five major changes to date?

• Why did Germany's two major parties form a grand coalition to govern the country? What change in electoral behavior has made the traditional "small coalition" impossible for the first time since 1949?

• How does Gordon Brown appear to differ from Tony Blair in his political style?

• What are some distinguishing traits of Angela Merkel as Chancellor, apart from the fact that she is a woman? Why choose the title "the Gaullist revolutionary" for an article about Nicolas Sarkozy?

• Explain the old political joke: "Japan's dominant Liberal Democratic Party is really not Liberal, not Democratic, and not a Party." What is it then?

Student Web Site

www.mhcls.com/online

Internet References

Further information regarding these Web sites may be found in this book's preface or online.

France.com
  http://www.france.com
GermNews
  http://www.germnews.de/dn/about/
Japan Ministry of Foreign Affairs
  http://www.mofa.go.jp

Liquid Library/PictureQuest

Britain, France, Germany, and Japan have been selected as major case studies of pluralist democracy for a number of reasons. After the United States, they are the most populous and economically powerful of the 28 "full democracies," as evaluated by the index of democracy. They are probably somewhat more familiar to most readers than the other countries in the category—and it makes sense to begin with the more familiar and proceed to less familiar territory later. Finally, they offer sufficient political similarities, differences, and contrasts to serve our comparative endeavor.

Our four countries are best approached as real world examples of democracy—"warts and all." It is striking that they all developed from some form of autocratic-oligarchic rule into pluralist democracies with representative forms of government and a prevailing rule of law. None of them is an ideal type or model. Each one of them has democratic shortcomings. Indeed, they all rank relatively low among the full democracies with only Germany making it into the top half—and that only barely, in the 13th rank out of a total of 28. Each has its own peculiarities that invite individual narrative and single case focus. There is a lot to be said for country specialization, but the decisive step into comparative studies is taken when cross-national comparisons are added.

Looking more closely at the political landscape in our four pluralist democracies is a useful way to become more familiar with different forms of democratic expression. All four are examples of **"strong states."** Three of them have a **parliamentary form of government,** with Frances' Fifth Republic being an exception: It provides a **strong executive model** of governance in what has been called a **semi-presidential system** that has later been copied widely in the post-communist countries of Central and Eastern Europe. The exceptionally strong executive should not to be confused with a U.S.-style presidential-congressional system. The topic is addressed by Christopher Allen's article in Unit Three.

They are all members of Robert Dahl's group of "old democracies" the 22 countries that have continuously maintained a representative democratic government since 1950. Yet even our small sample prompts reflections on the fragility of democracy. Of the four case studies of pluralist democracy, the UK was the only one that did not turn away from its democratic heritage at some point during the twentieth century. Italy, Japan, and Germany were the most prominent among several countries that abandoned the democratic road in the period between the two world wars. Official France followed suit after its defeat and partial military occupation by Germany in 1940. After World War II, these countries started out with new democratic constitutions. Representative governments were quickly restored in a number of other European countries where it had collapsed as a result of Nazi invasion and occupation. Only the UK continued to function—as it had for centuries—within an evolving framework of basic laws, rules, and conventions that are often referred to as its "unwritten" or **"uncodified" constitution.**

It is historically ironic that contemporary Britain ranks only 23rd on the democracy index, quite far behind today's Germany (13th). It also trails Japan (20th). Britain's relatively low position can be partly explained by its unusual concentration of power in the political executive, for the index of democracy assumes that a strong legislature is more likely to encourage overall democracy. But the most detrimental impact comes from Britain's very low score on political participation—voter turnout, level of party membership, and willingness to engage in politics. In this category, Britain shares the lowest rating among all the full democracies with Mauritius and Uruguay.

The Modern Nation State. The three West European countries in our sample show the impact of some major developments that are changing the political, social, and economic map of their continent.

The state can be traced back to ancient China and Mesopotamia, but Europe was the birthplace of the modern form, with its claim to sovereignty within the state territory and legal monopoly of force. It is now the location where that basic political construct is undergoing a partial and ambiguous transformation. In principle and practice, all of the member nations of the European Union (EU) have agreed to what is often called a "pooling" or "dilution" of some of their traditional sovereign powers. As a result, some familiar aspects of their political identity, like national borders or distinctive national currencies, have been reduced in importance or entirely replaced. Even then, there are exceptions, for among the older pre-2000 members of the EU, Britain along with Sweden and Denmark has so far stayed out of the euro area and kept their own currencies. None of this signals the end of the modern nation state or its imminent displacement by a United States of Europe. But no student of comparative politics will want to ignore the EU as a novel political formation. It is examined in unit three, along with its constitutional and democratic "deficits."

The Great Economic Compromise. Each of these countries has arrived at some "mixed" form of market capitalism, but the manner and degree of state intervention in the economy show considerable variations. Since the "Thatcher Revolution" of the 1980s, Britain has moved closer to the relatively open market conditions of the United States, while France and Germany have followed a more "organized" and regulated form of capitalism. The highly protected and corporatist Japanese economy is less competitive and sometimes described as neo-mercantilist.

Economic Rankings. When compared in economic strength, the four countries have relatively high and fairly similar rankings. They are all members of the Group of Seven (G 7), where they rank behind the United States among the world's biggest market economies. If China's economy were included, that huge and rapidly developing country would probably take third place in terms of gross domestic product (GDP). On the other hand, if national economies were compared in terms of their GDP per capita, China would fall far behind. By this measure, our four countries would themselves slip somewhat in ranking, as they were passed and separated from each other by a few smaller, high-performing economies.

Saving the Welfare State. Europeans have begun to examine carefully another of their major contributions to contemporary politics, the modern welfare state. In practically every country there are attempts to define a new balance between economic efficiency and social justice, as governments and publics are confronted with the increasing costs of a popular and relatively generous system of welfare and service entitlements. Longer life expectancies and lower birth rates contribute to the funding problem. If the funding problem were merely a cyclical one, it would lend itself more easily to solutions within the existing policy framework. But structural components seem to require a thorough revamping or "reinvention" of the welfare state. Almost everywhere in Europe, this popular social contract has been based on a "pay-as-you-go" formula that in practice involves an inter-generational transfer of wealth. There is much room for creative politics here.

Quality of Life. Each of the four countries records a high performance when it comes to a standard measure of the quality of life. The Human Development Index (HDI) places Japan slightly ahead of equidistant Britain and France, closely followed by Germany. Once again, the aggregate figures are strikingly similar.

Income Disparities. The four countries show some notable differences when compared for disparity in income, as measured by the GINI index. Yet none of them records as big a gap between the highest 10 percent and the lowest 10 percent of the household incomes as the one found in the United States. The income gap is still lowest in Japan and highest in Britain since the "Thatcher Revolution." France used to have an unusually big gap between its highest and lowest income earners, but the GINI index shows a marked reduction of the gap during the past quarter of a century. It seems plausible to link a good part of this development to the delayed political breakthrough by the Left, followed by its dominance in French politics from 1981 to 1986, from 1988 to 1993, and again from 1997 to 2002. Finally, the Scandinavian countries have very low disparities in income, even as they continue to score high on overall GDP per capita, the quality of life index, the perceptions of low corruptibility, the index of democracy, and the advancement of women to high appointed or elected political office. One reasonable conclusion would appear to be that it is not incompatible for a country to maintain the conditions for a vigorous economy even as it also pursues the goal of reducing income disparities—and those additional policy goals that seek to enhance life chances can be added to the public agenda as well.

Ethnic and Cultural Diversity. There are some additional European developments of importance for comparative political studies. For example, much of the continent has experienced difficulties in coping with the growing ethnic and cultural diversity brought about by the arrival of many economic and political immigrants during and after the cold war. Japan remains far more homogeneous, but even this island nation has experienced some ethnic diversification and could one day conceivably conclude that it needs an active immigration policy to offset the aging of the Japanese population. In Western Europe it is widely understood that the influx of newcomers has had stimulating economic and cultural consequences, but it has inevitably brought issues of multicultural co-existence and tolerance back onto the political agenda in a new form.

Politics of Xenophobia. It is remarkable that there appears to be a similar level of potential support for xenophobic populist politics in much of Western Europe. It hovers around 15 percent of the population, sometimes even more. Everywhere these parties seek to explain economic and social problems (crime, unemployment, for example) as largely a result of the newcomers. They demand the closing of the door to new migrants and some system of repatriation for those who have already arrived. Although the electoral results of these extremist parties usually fall far below the 15 percent potential, they have on occasion topped it—as in the French presidential elections of 2002, when the National Front's candidate won close to 20 percent of the vote. In Austria, Jörg Haider's Freedom Party has done even better on several occasions. Still, these parties are at present too weak to win government office by themselves. Apart from the danger that they may grow as a channel for protest, their very presence opens the possibility of political accommodation, especially by some of the more moderate, right-of-center parties that feel an electoral threat from these rivals. An example of this can be seen in Denmark, where a moderately conservative government has tightened immigration laws along lines demanded by the Danish People's Party.

In Germany, there have been occasional regional surges of support for one of Germany's extreme right-wing political parties leading to the capture of a handful of seats in provincial legislatures. But these parties have been fractious and too weak to meet the entry requirements for the federal parliament (Bundestag). There are at present some indications that one of these extreme parties, the National Democrats, is concentrating on establishing a more secure foothold in some eastern states like Saxony, where there is an unusually large reservoir of protest voters. The potential for a revival of right-wing politics in Europe should not be overlooked.

Politics of the Environment and Globalization. Even as West Europeans seek to come to terms with the challenge of greater diversity, their politics has also been affected by a growing awareness of global interdependence. Environmentalists are active in the Green parties. But the other and usually older parties have taken up the ecological theme as well. It is reflected in their widespread support for national and international initiatives to protect the environment, such as the Kyoto Treaty. They are also trying to adjust to the new information technologies and the many challenges of the global market with its opportunities for expansion and its widely perceived threat to job security and economic stability.

Political Terrorism and Civil Liberties. The events of September 11, 2001 and their aftermath have sharply increased the role of organized violence and unpredictability in our political world. The terrorist attacks on the World Trade Towers and the Pentagon were directed at the United States, but the clandestine networks of supporters and sympathizers apparently reach deep into the immigrant communities of several European countries, including the ones we have singled out for special discussion here. Similar strikes have already affected European democracies: the train-bombings in Madrid in the spring of 2004 and in London in the summer of 2005 are the best known examples. There is no transatlantic consensus on the most effective strategy for dealing with the new terrorism. One crucial assumption of the traditional policy of containment seems not to apply to this kind of activity, namely that the desire for self-preservation will restrain potential opponents by making them reluctant to risk severe retaliation. The search for an appropriate and effective response will preoccupy our politics for a long time to come.

The Transatlantic Gap. It is hardly surprising that the transatlantic debate over terrorism has revived the time-honored practice of engaging in public reflections on more fundamental cultural and political differences between continental Europe and the United States. One of the most widely discussed contributions has come from the American political writer, Robert Kagan. He argues that Europe and America are not just separated on the important issue of Iraq. In a widely quoted phrase, Kagan sums up his perception of the difference: "Americans are from Mars and Europeans are from Venus." He points out that Europeans are more likely than Americans to favor multilateral approaches and to prefer a resort to "soft" rather than "hard" power in international relations.

Traditional Values and Secular-Rational Modernity. The transatlantic values gap is illuminated by the world values survey, an ambitious project led by Ronald Inglehart at the University of Michigan. It studies cross-cultural similarities and differences in 81 societies around the world—including the ones discussed in this book. One of its major findings is that while contemporary Americans and West Europeans share some basic values of "self-expression" that are closely associated with political and economic freedoms, Americans tend to be far more traditional, religious, and patriotic in their values than their more "secular-rational" West European contemporaries.

Continuity and Change. This is the point at which to embark on a serial discussion of politics in the four countries that make up our sample. But two suggestions of caution may be in order. First, in our concern to include the most recent changes and newest challenges, we must not lose sight of some equally important if less dramatic elements of continuity or even inertia in political life. In the stable democracies of Western Europe and Japan, the political process is usually defined by a relatively mild blend of change and continuity. Here political agendas are normally modified rather than discarded entirely, and shifts in the balance of power do rarely take the form of revolutionary displacements of a ruling group. Instead, there are occasional changes of government as a result of coalition disagreements or routine elections.

Second, this capacity to adjust and adapt is important, but may not always suffice. Dramatic disruptions of established political systems do sometimes occur, even in "our time" and in democratic contexts. In France, there have been periodic outbreaks of urban and suburban upheavals and riots, massive demonstrations, and politically motivated industrial strikes. In retrospect, it may be possible to reconstruct how the tipping point was reached that led to an unexpected upheaval, but that does not make such upheavals predictable. In the countries we now turn toward, **the unexpected major turns in political development** have included the following: The Thatcher Revolution, "New" Labour, and Blair's support for President Bush's Policy on Iran; President Mitterrand's social and economic reforms, the recurrent periods of cohabitation, the new French party system, the defeat of the EU Constitution, the collapse of the Communist bloc in Europe, Germany and the German unification, and the new German party system after the 1950s and now.

Great Britain

For a long time, Britain has been regarded as the **"mother" of the parliamentary system of government.** In contrast to a presidential system, where the chief executive and legislatures are separately elected by the voters for fixed terms of office, a parliamentary government is often described as based on **a "fusion" of the executive and legislative powers.** This trait is much more pronounced in British parliamentary politics than in most other parliamentary systems. One distinctive trait shared by them all is that the prime minister, as head of government, is in some way "chosen" or "approved" by (and usually from) the popularly elected legislature and remains dependent on its sustained political support or toleration to stay in office. Christopher Allen's article in unit two delivers a sharp institutional comparison between parliamentary and presidential forms of government.

The Westminster Model. In today's British version of parliamentary government, often called the Westminster model, there is almost always one party that wins a majority of the seats in the House of Commons, despite the fact that no party ever wins a majority of the popular vote. The result is **single-party government** and a form of **majoritarian politics** in which the main opposition party of **"outs"** plays the adversary role of an institutionalized critic and rival of the party of **"ins."**

The British Party System. It would be hard to overestimate the importance of the party system in shaping the British political process. Without strong parties and party discipline, the parliamentary system would be chaotic. The requirement that a governing group receives a steady flow of majority support (or, at least, majority toleration) in the Commons would be difficult to meet, and governments would be weak and unstable. France and Italy have in the past exemplified the problems associated with a multiplicity of weak parties.

As in the United States, there was an early development of legislative **caucus parties** in Britain—essentially convenient and mostly informal networks between politicians who followed the same leaders, interests or ideas. The modern party organizations came later as a competitive political response to the sharp increase in the number of voters as the right to vote was extended in a series of reform acts, that began in 1832 and ended almost century later. **Well-developed party organizations** became a practical way to reach the many voters. The two major political parties that existed until the 1920s were the **Conservatives (Tories)** and the **Liberals.** The latter were largely replaced by the new party of **Labour** in the 1920s. In the 1960s, the Liberals had a limited revival. They made an electoral alliance with the new party of Social Democrats in the early 1980s, and eventually the two merged as **Liberal Democrats.** They are now an ever-present alternative to one or both of the two major parties, but their representation in the elected lower chamber is much smaller than their share of the total national vote.

The electoral system (first-past-the-post in single-member districts) is largely responsible for the "two party system" that dominates the House of Commons, even though between 18 and 25 percent of the electorate has supported Liberal Democratic candidates in recent elections. Not surprisingly, the third party supports **electoral reform,** namely a form of **proportional representation (PR).** Its argument emphasizes the "fairness" of outcome that already had attracted John Stuart Mill's support in the 19th century. Over a century later, another liberal philosopher, Karl Popper, countered with a defense of the FPTP system. He argued that its "winner-take-all" provisions were more likely to lead to single-party majorities that could govern effectively and be effectively held to account by the opposition. Popper thought that coalition governments were less effective decision-makers and harder to make accountable to the electorate—concentrated power by a single governing party was effectively paired with concentrated accountability.

Three Major Reform Governments. Since 1945 Britain can be said to have had three reform governments that greatly altered some key features of British society and politics. Each of them also demonstrated the **considerable capacity for decisive governance** that remains a crucial feature of the Westminster model.

The first major reform government after World War II was led by Prime Minister Clement Atlee, who headed a Labour administration from 1945 to 1951. It came to power immediately after World War II, replacing the wartime coalition government led by Winston Churchill. During its first five years in office, Labour established a comprehensive welfare state in Britain, nationalized some key parts of the economy, and took the first major steps to dismantle the large overseas empire by releasing the huge Indian subcontinent.

Toward the end of its time in office, Labour had spent much of its energies and the country had lost some of its appetite for the vision of a **"New Jerusalem"** that originally had energized the reformers. The party narrowly lost its parliamentary majority in 1951 (where it won more votes but fewer seats than the Tories). What some had seen as a **quiet revolution** came to an end, but the six years had changed the UK for ever. There was no major roll back of the reforms, except for some key nationalizations. During the next quarter of a century, the British governmental process seemed to be captured in the phrase **"muddling through."** While the British tradition of adversary rhetoric continued to flourish, the differences between the two major political parties seemed often to have been reduced to relatively minor matters, except for some foreign and defense policy disputes. Labour's return to power between 1964 and 1970 and again from 1974 to 1979 failed to revive the country's sluggish economy or set a new direction.

The Sick Man of Europe? By the mid-1970s, Britain had become obsessed with its governing problems—and this at a time when the ruling Social Democrats in West Germany confidently touted their own *Modell Deutschland,* the German societal model. British debate seemed dominated by a general malaise and a widely shared sense of deterioration. Even serious observers spoke of Britain as "the sick man of Europe." Journalists referred regularly to "the English disease" or **"stagflation"**—a condition that showed up in the coincidence of inflation, economic stagnation, and unemployment along with widespread social squalor and the apparent incapacity of the public authorities to deal effectively with such problems. Academics seriously asked whether the UK suffered **from a "governability** crisis" possibly linked to **"government overload"** or **"overstretch."** It was ironic that this discussion took place less than two decades after an acute American political scientist, Harry Eckstein, had concluded that compared to its major neighbors in Europe, the British form of government showed an unusual structural capacity for effective and responsible action.

Effects on the Party System. The political parties took part in the national debate. In their search for answers, they tended to revisit ideological roots that had been glossed over during what became known as the consensus years. While some Labor intellectuals rediscovered the ideas of a stronger state socialism, there was a revival of market thinking among some Conservatives. Such ideas become important when they influence political elites. Margaret Thatcher became a firm supporter of deregulation, privatization and other central aspects of market economics before she successfully challenged Edward Heath to become Conservative party leader in 1975. She confidently led her party out of the opposition into government in the election of 1979. The hardships of the chaotic "winter of discontents" probably played a bigger role in the defeat of Labour than her economic ideas, but the two were not unconnected. In any case, her neoliberal ideas influenced some important policy shifts during the 1980s.

Once in office, the Conservatives were the political beneficiaries of the continuing divisions among their opponents. Labour's disarray and the rise of a militant left-wing that sought to pull the party away from its centrist course did not sit well with its moderates. Some of the best known members decided to leave the Labour Party and set up a reform-oriented party of their own. Led by the "Gang of Four"—Roy Jenkins, David Owens, William Rodgers, and Shirley Williams—the defectors were encouraged by popular support for the idea of a non-socialist alternative to Thatcherism. Calling themselves **Social Democrats,** the dissidents believed that a loose alliance between the "loony" Left and the "hard" left were taking over the Labour Party. They cooperated with the other "third" party of Liberals and eventually merged with them as **Liberal Democrats.** Their combined share of the vote reached about 25 percent in the 1980s and remained unusually high, at close to 20 percent in the 1990s. They won a much smaller number of parliamentary seats under the British electoral system.

The second major reform government in the UK (1979 to 1990) since World War II was headed by Margaret Thatcher. She saw the new government as an overdue corrective to "consensus politics" pursued by both the major parties since Atlee's earlier reform government. Thatcher prided herself on being a **"conviction politician"** and was determined to replace what she saw as a sluggish socialist torpor with a dynamic entrepreneurial spirit. Her policies were designed to stimulate the private sector, weaken the obstructing trade unions, increase the power of the national government over local authorities, and generally reduce the interventionist role of government. She stood for an assertive British role in Europe, where she resisted the drive toward monetary and greater political union. She practiced a close cooperation with the United States under the leadership of Presidents Ronald Reagan and George Bush.

Thatcher's economic strategy received failing grades from most professional economists, but she could eventually point with pride to some animating effects. Yet even some of those who were impressed by a British **economic revival in the mid-1980s** became disturbed by what they regarded as very **high social and political trade-offs.** The local authorities were reduced in authority, and the "poll tax" was partly designed to guarantee that. The income gap between rich and poor in Britain, as measured by the GINI index, grew precipitously even as neighboring France was moving in the other direction. In foreign affairs, Thatcher gained respect among many voters for her resolute military response in 1982 to the occupation of the Falkland Islands by the junta that ruled Argentina.

Thatcherism Continues. By 1990 Thatcher increasingly came to be regarded as a political liability by her own party. In November 1990, she was challenged as party leader and resigned before she could be defeated in a crucial party vote. Her successor, John Major, continued to support many of her business-friendly reforms and basically consolidated her economic reforms. Some were surprised that the Conservative majority held through the 1992 general election.

Tony Blair and New Labour. Already since the electoral defeat of 1983, the Labour party under Neil Kinnock's leadership had begun to move away from the far left-wing positions announced in its election manifesto of that year—widely lampooned as "the longest suicide note in political history." After taking over the leadership in 1994, Tony Blair succeeded in carrying through a major symbolic reform that removed the famous Clause Four with its demand for socialization from the party's program. Labour became "New Labour," and its hard Left remnants were marginalized. In the public opinion polls, Labour took a commanding lead over the Conservatives. John Major had good reason to delay the next election as long as possible, until May 1997.

The Third Reform Government: Blair's New Labour in Power. Labour's landslide victory in 1997 brought the UK its third reform government since World War II. Unlike Prime Ministers Atlee or Thatcher, however, Tony Blair did not focus primarily on major social and economic policy changes. Since the mid-1990s, the British economy had once again revived well ahead of those on the mainland in Western Europe. A growing number of observers—including Tony Blair and in all probability the Chancellor of the Exchequer and heir apparent as Labour leader, Gordon Brown—willingly conceded that Thatcher's "neo-liberal" policies had played a role in stimulating the U.K. economy. It had become more flexible and dynamic, leading to higher growth rates and lower unemployment. But there were serious tradeoffs that Blair's government could have been expected to give more remedial attention—above all Britain's growing income disparities and the neglected and dilapidated infrastructure of the public service sector, where greater investments were badly needed for maintenance and renewal.

Blair's reform agenda gave prominence to constitutional change, an area to which the Liberals have generally paid more attention. In his important article on this topic, Donley Studlar examines the entire cluster of institutional reforms and reviews their impact untiBlair's departure from office—and beyond. Many of these reforms were implemented relatively quickly. The symbolic change, especially with regard to the House of Lords, has been very great. The political effects vary. Until now, at least, Blair's institutional "modernization" has not brought about a more robust democratic commitment in the country. Political participation is very low. Labour's share of the vote in the 2005 general election was 35 percent in England alone, a little higher in Scotland and Wales—one of the smallest winning results in British history.

In the two most recent general elections, 2001 and 2005, the British voter turnout has reached the lowest level since the early twentieth century. As we have seen, the country ranks relatively low in the index of democracy—it trails both Germany and Japan, and barely comes ahead of France.

New Party Leader: Labour. After the election of 2005, each of the three national parties has come to face a leadership succession. Tony Blair announced his intention to step down and then held on to office until midterm, in the summer of 2007. By then, some Labour dissidents had begun to give vent to their displeasure over his long tenure. His successor as party leader and prime minister, **Gordon Brown,** is intellectually formidable, but he will carry the burden of having supported an increasingly unpopular policy in Iraq. And he may well appear somewhat dour after 10 years of Tony Blair's lively performance.

New Party Leader: The Conservatives. Britain's Conservatives are rarely sentimental about holding on to leaders who don't deliver. After a lost election, they normally sack the leader and look for a new one. In replacing the hapless Michael Howard after the 2005 election, they chose a younger and very different successor: David Cameron. He is often compared to Tony Blair as an unusually articulate and "telegenic" leader. Critics find him somewhat slick and complain that he has more style than substance. It is possible that they underestimate him. He wants to move the Conservatives back toward the center-right and overcome their dull and unattractive public image. His strategy appears to target Liberal Democratic voters. In his first year as leader, the Conservatives climbed to their highest ratings in 20 years before returning to more modest proportions.

New Party Leader: The Liberal Democrats. Under the popular but somewhat chaotic Charles Kennedy, the small party reached its highest parliamentary strength, by winning 62 seats in the general election of 2005. Kennedy stepped down in early 2006 after a controversy connected with his well known personal struggle with alcoholism. The leadership contest was won by Sir Menzies Campbell, who has been the party's foreign policy spokesman.

The third party has thrived when one or both of the major parties departed from centrist positions. It may soon face the danger of being squeezed between the Labour and Conservative parties as both seek to win more voters in the center. There are possible opportunities as well. With the rise in appeal of the Conservatives and the decline of Labour, the Liberal Democrats have again begun to speculate about the possibility of a **"hung" parliament** where no single party has a majority. In such a

situation, the third party could end up holding the balance of power. There could even be a chance to have the electoral law changed toward more proportional representation. Even if this should amount to wishful thinking, the party has learned a lot about conducting successful campaigns in the last couple of decades: it now targets vulnerable districts, so that it wins about three times as many seats with a somewhat smaller share of the total national votes as the Alliance did in its best days.

Brown's policy proposals, both before and after assuming the prime minister's office in the summer of 2007, have so far avoided major U-turns from Blair's positions, while suggesting that Brown has learned from some of his predecessor's public-relations mishaps. An as-yet vaguely defined campaign against corruption may clear the air after the Labour party's recent "cash for honours" scandal, and Brown is at this time walking a line between continuing commitment to the Iraq war and carefully suggesting that its conduct has been less than perfect. It remains to be seen whether Brown will surpass Blair's achievements in policy reform or take a less ambitious path—or whether, of course, some of Labour's supporters find one of the alternative parties more palatable.

France

Has gone through a modern political development that has been far more discontinuous than its British counterpart, with numerous attempts at a fresh start since 1789. For example, historians count between 13 and 17 French constitutions in the first two centuries that followed.

Political Discontinuity with Patterns. In the past, French political discourse often seemed to reflect the sharp ideological cleavages to which the Revolution had given birth. After the Bourbon Restoration in 1815, France built up the energies for intermittent new revolutionary spasms in 1830, 1848, and 1870. After each of these upheavals, France seemed to settle back into a much less exciting political routine, in which the civil service basically administered the country, while governments usually had short life spans (an average of less than one year) with few accomplishments because of the stalling power of parliament.

Third and Fourth Republics. In the **Third Republic** (1870 to 1940) and **Fourth Republic** (1946 to 1958), France was notorious for its multiplicity of undisciplined parties and groupings. They provided a weak and unreliable support for prime ministers and their cabinets, resulting in political paralysis and instability of many short-lived governments. In the frequent absence of responsible political direction and oversight, a well-trained civil service maintained administrative continuity but lacked authority as well as confidence when facing major political issues that required political answers. There developed a risky tradition, known in France as **Bonapartism,** of intermittently calling for strong "political saviors" who were to lead the country out of its recurrent crises. Ironically, it was such a Bonapartist leader who ended up delivering an institutional alternative to such a constitutionally questionable and politically dangerous reliance on a "strong man."

De Gaulle as Bonapartist. The change took place in 1958 when a political emergency caused by the colonial war in

Algeria gave Charles de Gaulle the opportunity to become architect of a new and very different political system. He had already played a Bonapartist role in World War II when he acted as self-designated leader of the Free French and in defiance of the official government of France, headed by a rival Bonapartist leader, Marshal Pétain. After the liberation of France, de Gaulle became interim president before the adoption in 1946—against his strong warnings—of the constitution of the Fourth Republic. It set up a legislative-executive relationship that very much resembled the one that had plagued the Third Republic. Having long viewed the unruly French parties as beyond reform, de Gaulle became convinced that it was necessary to prune their power base in the legislature and greatly empower the political executive. He basically dropped out of French politics for about a decade, until he was asked to resolve the political crisis of 1958.

The new constitution, which practically bears his spirit if not his name, embodies de Gaulle's desire to institutionalize a strong political executive and tame the parliamentary parties. The prime minister remains responsible to the National Assembly but enjoys far more prerogatives and is far less vulnerable to legislative power plays than previously. Above all, de Gaulle strengthened the government by adding a politically powerful president in what became known as a **dual executive.** The president is directly elected and has powers that include the appointment of the prime minister, the dissolution of the National Assembly, and the call for a national referendum on a particular issue rather than leaving a decision to the parliament. The result is often called a semi-presidential system in which the French president played the dominant role for the first quarter of a century. It has found some imitation in the post-Communist political systems set up in Central and Eastern Europe, including Russia.

A Consolidation of the Party System. It is also an unforeseen consequence that the new political framework of the Fifth Republic has become the setting for a consolidation and moderation of the French party system. Almost all of the main parties were started or reconstituted in the first few years after de Gaulle left office in 1969.

Change on the Left. The Communists (PCF) are the main exception. They were once the main party of the Left, receiving about 20 percent of the vote in parliamentary elections until the late 1970s. They were relatively late to join their colleagues elsewhere in Western Europe in the painful withdrawal from their common Leninist and Stalinist heritage. By now they are a marginal force, less than half their former strength, but they have gained a chance to play a role in coalition politics that was previously denied them. After 1981, and again between 1997 and 2002, they were a small partner in the coalition government dominated by the Socialists, who had overtaken them on the Left in 1978.

The Extreme Right. Le Pen's National Front (FN) seemed to be weakened by internal splits and rivalries, before it surprised many by capturing 17 percent of the vote in the first round of the presidential election in 2002. The party continues to find right-wing populist support for its authoritarian and xenophobic rhetoric directed primarily against the country's many residents of Arab origin. In his article, Steven Philip Kramer does not mince words in describing this party as "fascist, racist, xenophobic, and often anti-Semitic, as well as staunchly anti-EU."

The Socialists (PS). Between these peripheral positions, we find the more centrist parties located. On the left of center we find the Socialists (PS), who were revived by François Mitterrand in the early 1970s. It is a social reformist party, with a strong appeal to teachers and white collar workers. The revived Socialist Party is more responsible than any other party for France's welfare state development during the 14-year presidency of Mitterrand and the cohabiting 5-year government during President Chirac's first term.

The Conservatives. On the center-right there is also one leading party that is conservative in a more traditional sense. It is the Rally for the Republic (RPR) that was organized as a neo-Gaullist party. Jacques Chirac played a major role in creating this party during the early 1970s, after de Gaulle's death. It is a neo-Gaullist party—that is, it can be counted on to support measures that will strengthen the armed forces, protect French industry and agriculture, and reinforce law and order. It has taken over some defectors from other parties, notably the UDF (the loosely organized Union for French Democracy, created by Giscard d'Estaing in the 1970s to promote him and his neoliberal views). Since the elections of 2002, the neo-Gaullist party has presented itself as the UMP (Union for a Popular Majority).

Some Political Convergence. One major change is the decline of the previously sharp ideological struggle between the Left and the Right. This seems to have resulted in a sense of loss among some French intellectuals who prefer the political battle to have drama and implications. They apparently find it hard to accept that the grand struggle between Left and Right has been replaced by a more moderate and mundane party politics of competition among groups that tend to cluster fairly close to the center of the political spectrum.

The 2002 Elections. The French faced an electoral marathon in 2002, when there were two-stage elections for both the presidency and the National Assembly. It was expected in advance that the focus of the relatively short presidential campaign would be on the two veteran warhorses, Chirac and Jospin. The big surprise was the elimination of Jospin in the first stage. He ran a close third behind Chirac, who came first, and the far right candidate, Le Pen, who came second. As in 1995, many people on the Left had apparently voted "with their hearts" in the first round. The result was that the Left vote was split among a multiplicity of candidates, none of whom had a chance of making it into the second round. This time, however, the result was the failure of the main candidate of the Left to make it into the second round, since socialist Jospin gathered slightly fewer votes than nationalist Le Pen. In the run-off between Chirac and Le Pen, the incumbent president won an overwhelming victory by attracting moderate votes from both Right and Left.

By now, the Fifth Republic has lasted longer than all other political arrangements in France since 1789, with the notable exception of the crisis-ridden Third Republic (1870–1940). By institutionalizing the strong executive, the Fifth Republic has eliminated any justification for the irregular resort to Bonapartism. The dual executive is clearly more than a custom-made hybrid designed for Charles de Gaulle. It has outlasted him and become a basic model for a number of post-Communist constitutions in Eastern and Central Europe, including Russia. In France, it has given at least the appearance of institutional stability and authority at the price of an enormous concentration of power in the executive. There is at least one important way in which the French electorate can politically reduce the dominant role of the President—by voting in such a way as to make "cohabitation" necessary.

Cohabitation. In politics, this term refers to a French version of divided government. It occurs when the National Assembly has a parliamentary majority of one political orientation (Left or Right) and the President has a different orientation (Left or Right). That did not come about during the first 23 years of the Fifth Republic, when the Right dominated and de Gaulle was followed in the presidency by the Gaullist conservative, Georges Pompidou, and the neoliberal Giscard d'Estaing. In 1981, Socialist François Mitterrand defeated Giscard in the latter's bid for reelection. The new Left-wing president was faced by a Right of center majority in the National Assembly that had been elected for a five-year term in 1978. On winning office in 1981, Mitterrand immediately called parliamentary elections two years early. His calculation that the majority that had just elected him president would carry over into the parliamentary election was vindicated, and Mitterrand was able to preside over the first Socialist government in the Fifth Republic. The new government tackled a major agenda shift that included traditionally socialist reforms, in some ways comparable in its scope to the reform agenda of Clement Atlee's Labour government in 1945.

Mitterrand had effectively postponed the problem of how to deal with a divided government, but it came back to haunt him in a more difficult form in 1986, when the five-year term of the National Assembly came to an end. The Socialist majority had lost public support with some of its economic policies and was voted out of office in the regular parliamentary elections. For the first time in its nearly three decades of existence, the Fifth Republic faced the possibility of divided and possibly gridlocked government—the very problem the Fifth Republic had been designed to deal with effectively. The Socialist president was directly confronted with the question of whether to interpret the electoral defeat of his party as a vote of no confidence and resign early from the presidency. Alternatively, he could stay on and appoint a conservative prime minister who would have the support of the new parliamentary majority. Mitterrand chose the latter option and appointed the neo-Gaullist Jacques Chirac as prime minister.

The resulting co-existence of Left and Right in the dual executive was something new in French politics—and promptly dubbed **"cohabitation."** It only lasted two years, until the end of Mitterrand's seven-year presidential term, but during that time this form of power sharing had a remarkable effect on the balance of power and responsibility between president and prime minister. Mitterrand drew back from the active political role he had played during his first five years and let Prime Minister Chirac dominate the political stage. Chirac's government took advantage of the new relationship. During its two years in office, it in effect rolled back some of Mitterrand's social and economic reforms.

The French have returned to this version of power-sharing in two more recent time periods—from 1993 to 1995 and again between 1997 and 2002. Each time, the same basic pattern could be observed: In domestic politics, the president becomes a less central and less active political figure and the prime minister takes over the leadership in most public matters. One could also say that the system becomes decidedly more parliamentary (or more prime ministerial) and much less presidential in a period of cohabitation.

In the second half of 2005, France was torn by a prolonged series of suburban riots in which young people of North African descent played a major role. Order was eventually restored, but the damage went far beyond the toll of human injuries or the torched cars and buildings. Major politicians seemed to be in a state of shock, and their responses came slowly and unclearly. Sarkozy stood apart by combining an early and unambiguous demand for law and order with suggestions for constructive public policy measures to give more reality to the French promise of integration. The dramatic events drew attention to flaws in the celebrated French policy of full assimilation of immigrants.

A New President. In 2007, France again held both presidential and parliamentary elections. In the presidential race, Sarkozy was chosen by the UMP to face the PS's Ségoléne Royal. There had been female candidates for the French presidency before, but with exotic party labels that doomed them to be "also-rans;" This time, however, the Socialists stirred up the French race with a woman candidate who seemed to be the only politician, male or female, capable of beating Sarkozy. As in all previous presidential elections in the Fifth Republic, it was the second-round runoff between the top two candidates that decided the outcome. In May 2007 Sarkozy was elected with 53 percent of the vote.

It is too early to give an assessment of Sarkozy's impact, but early signs suggest that he is determined to move France's economy in a more entrepreneurial, neo-liberal direction. It seems likely that he will have confrontations with the politically powerful unions that a decade earlier had effectively thwarted similar reforms pursued by President Chirac's first prime minister. There are some indications of a growing support for some form of neo-liberal reform—if pursued skillfully and without embracing the fatal neo-liberal label. Sarkozy appointed a cabinet that included a socialist as foreign minister. He immediately turned toward repair work in the fractured relationship with the United States. His presidency promises to be a busy, interesting and important one.

Germany

In 1990, what had been the eastern German Democratic Republic joined the western Federal Republic of Germany. The event came as one of the big surprises in recent political history, and neither the Germans nor anyone else were ready for the shift. There were no carefully prepared "unification plans" waiting for implementation. Instead, quick judgment and improvisation became the order of the day. Considering such matters as the lack of preparation, the unreliability of the official East

German statistics, and the ideological separation of the political elites in the two states, there was an enormous potential for chaos, conflict or corruption. It is difficult not to be impressed by the fairly low incidence of such problems. On the other hand, the unification has led to an east-west divide in German politics that has attracted the attention of comparativists.

German unification was closely connected to the general weakening and eventual collapse of Communist control in central and eastern Europe. There seem to have been two major preconditions for the rapid transition from authoritarian communism to representative democracy in all of these countries. First, Soviet leader Mikhail Gorbachev had abandoned the so-called **Brezhnev Doctrine** under which the Soviets claimed the right of military intervention on behalf of the communist regimes that had been set up in these countries after World War II. Their rulers were now basically left to fend for themselves. Second, when the test came, these same national leaders turned out to have **lost their will to power**—that is, their determination (and ability) to assert themselves and hold on to power at any cost. Once that became plain, they had lost the game, for none of these regimes had a reservoir of popular legitimacy to back them up. A snowball-like effect set in, and within a year the people's democracies were no longer there. But four decades of communism had left an imprint that would not be removed so readily.

The Federal Republic of Germany and the German Democratic Republic. The two German states had been established in 1949, four years after the total defeat of Adolf Hitler's Third Reich in World War II. During the next 40 years, their rival elites subscribed to the conflicting ideologies and interests of East and West in the cold war. When the two German states began to prepare their separate fortieth anniversaries, the division had lost its provisional character—or so it seemed. National unification was just around the corner, but no leading politician was on record as having foreseen the imminent upheaval. A leading American dictionary published in 1988 reflected the conventional view that the division of Germany was by now a fact of political life, defining it as "a former country in Central Europe."

East Germany comprised the territory of the former Soviet Zone of Occupation in postwar Germany. Here, the rulers established a Communist political system with an economy based on Soviet-style central planning. East Germany lagged behind West Germany in its recovery from the ruinous war, but it gained a reputation for having built one of the most productive economies in the Soviet bloc. The Berlin Wall was erected in August of 1961 to end what for East Germany had become an economically ruinous flight of people to the West. As a result, its population had stabilized at about 16 million by the late 1980s.

East Germany began to unravel in 1989. There were peaceful protest demonstrations in several cities and a dramatic westward flight of thousands of defiant citizens. In effect, these people were "voting with their feet"—and that turned out to be very effective. The confused East German rulers reacted with a mixture of conciliatory and repressive measures that only made the dissidents bolder. After sacking their long-time leader Erich Honecker in October 1989, the Communists elected a new party leadership and adopted a new party name. This **Party of Democratic Socialism (PDS)** also adopted a new program that identified it as a democratic left-wing socialist party. It tried a form of power-sharing with noncommunist groups and agreed to hold a free East German parliamentary election in March 1990.

West Germany and its Basic Law. West Germany comprised the regions that had been the American, British, and French zones of occupation. By the time of unification, it had become a prosperous society of about 62 million people—nearly four times as many as in East Germany. The new West German state had been carefully constructed as a representative democracy that reflected its founders' determination to avoid the political disaster associated with the **Weimar Republic** that had been set up after World War I and in some ways had become a failed state by the time of Adolf Hitler's rise to power. New constitutions often attempt to include remedies for the ills that beset a previous political system. That was very much the case with West Germany's constitution: called the Basic Law, it was replete with **institutional safeguards,** including elaborate **checks and balances.** It set up a **strong federal system,** a very active system of **judicial review,** and gave special emphasis to the importance of a **vigorous system of democratic parties.**

Perhaps the most unusual feature of the Basic Law was that it carried a notice of its own limited shelf life. It foresaw the day when Germans in a united and free country could work out a new constitution. That scenario was not to be; Germany has been united, but the Basic Law (much amended over the years) remains in effect.

West Germany experienced an early, sustained, and impressive economic and political recovery from the postwar disorder. This development stood in sharp contrast to the problems that had beset the first German republic, prior to the Nazi rise to power. Basically, the Weimar Republic in its last years had become a deeply fragmented and politically radicalized society, whereas West Germany started out as a politically exhausted, post-revolutionary society in which individual energies were largely channeled toward the pursuit of economic self-betterment. The new state benefited from an unusually long economic boom that had been triggered by the currency reform of 1948 and was sustained by a fortuitous combination of circumstances but also by skillfully practiced economic policy. By the 1970s, just before some structural problems began to darken the economic horizon, Germany's political class began to refer with new found self-confidence to *Modell Deutschland,* "the German model."

Unification and its Discontents. The March 1990 election in East Germany resulted in a new non-communist coalition government that favored a short, quick route to unification. It was to begin with an early monetary union in the summer and a political union by the fall of 1990. That was indeed the route taken, in tandem with international negotiations that involved the former World War II allies, the United States, the UK, France and the Soviet Union, as well as East and West Germany.

Basically East Germany entered into the existing Federal Republic with its institutional framework. Here some critics saw a missed opportunity to revamp or even "democratize" the Basic Law. Others pointed out that the Basic Law had stood the test of time, by already lasting about three times as long as the Weimar Republic. More technocratic reformers sometimes point out that this would have been an opportune moment to streamline the increasingly cumbersome federal system and consolidate some of the smaller states. The rush to unite Germany would probably have been slowed down by adding such items to the agenda.

Each of the former Communist-ruled countries made its own transition from one-party rule and central planning toward a pluralist democracy and a market economy. The path taken by the eastern part of Germany differed greatly from all the rest, because it alone involved a full merger with a successful (and much larger) non-Communist part of the same nation. As a result, East Germany had the advantage—if advantage it was—of having a prosperous and accomplished West Germany as "sponsor" of its post-communist reconstruction. It became the recipient of generous social programs and some heavy public investments in the infrastructure that were made possible by huge financial transfers from western Germany. It received as well a ready-made and time-tested constitutional, legal and organizational infrastructure as a result of the merger.

At first glance, Germany's unification would appear to have been an unusually friendly and generous takeover. But the projection of West German institutions into East Germany did not transform the East into an easterly extension of the West. Eastern Germany came to depend on "the golden West" to supply public funds and fill vacant leadership positions that required modern business skills or simply to meet consumer demand with Western products.

Some East Germans began to see themselves as partial losers in the unification process—most obviously former elite members who had lost privileged positions and social status, many professionals whose occupational competence did not readily fit into the new order, and the many who for the first time in their lives experienced unemployment. By the late 1990s the jobless approached 4 million in Germany, nearly 10 percent in the West and nearly twice that rate in the East. The parties that had come in from the West—the CDU, SPD, FDP and Greens—often found it difficult to reach many of the voters with such biographies.

The Communist rulers had made great efforts to promote Marxism-Leninism as the new socialist state's official ideology. They do not appear to have had much success in this endeavor, but the experience of life in the GDR nevertheless seems to have left a general ideological residue that still differentiates East from West in Germany more than a decade and a half after their unification. Basically, many easterners seem inclined to prefer a more egalitarian and risk-free order, along with a major role for the state in a kind of collective definition of social justice. By contrast, more westerners seem willing to accept as fair or just an outcome that primarily reflects unequal individual achievements and outcomes in a competitive market context. This resembles a key difference between a socialist and a capitalist orientation, although the difference in "real" life is less sharp-edged than suggested by the ideological contrast. Perhaps one should think in terms of different tendencies rather than dichotomous ("either-or") positions.

The West German "Two-plus-One" Party System. A key role in the West German political success story *before* unification had been the development of the parties and their coalition politics. The Weimar party system had mirrored Weimar society and been highly fragmented and polarized, producing considerable instability.

To avoid the splintering effect attributed to the Weimar system of pure proportional representation (PR), West Germany adopted a modified system of PR that was designed to keep very small parties from gaining seats in the Bundestag. It is a two-ballot system in which the second and most important ballot is cast for a party. Each party wins a share of the total number of Bundestag seats that is approximately equal to its share of the second or party vote—but only parties that win 5 percent or more of the second votes are eligible to participate in this proportional distribution of Bundestag seats. The 5 percent clause will be set aside in the rare case of a small party that has managed to win at least 3 single-member districts on the first ballot.

The 5 Percent Clause and Three Districts Rule. Since they were adopted in the 1950s, these changes in the electoral law have kept very small parties out of the Bundestag. That includes several far right-wing parties that occasionally have managed to gain entry to one of the state parliaments. But the new West German party system could not have been engineered through electoral law alone. Instead, it reflects **the electoral choices** made by voters who were not nearly as deeply divided or ideologically driven as the Weimar population had been. Their votes were based on **moderate or centrist preferences** for parties that largely pursued moderate policies and made centrist appeals. The result was a **simple and amazingly stable party system.** A closer look reveals that it was also a slowly changing one.

The Three Bundestag Parties. During the 1950s, German politics largely concentrated around the two leading parties, the center-right Christian Democrats (CDU or, in Bavaria only, CSU) and the center-left Social Democrats (SPD). Beginning in 1957, these two parties together received well over 80 percent of the vote—and occasionally topped 90 percent. As a result, West Germany ended up with a "two and one-half" or "two plus one" party system in the Bundestag between 1961 and 1983. The business-friendly and liberal Free Democrats (FDP) were the only small Bundestag party to survive the concentration of the party system. Despite their modest share of the vote (an average of 8 to 9 percent), they held the balance of power, and this gave them an opportunity to be kingmakers. In their heyday, the Free Democrats were one of the most successful small parties in Western Europe. One of their last dramatic impacts on West German politics came about in 1982 when they switched coalition partners in midterm. They left the SPD after 13 years of co-governing and joined a new governing coalition led by Helmut Kohl and the CDU/CSU. Here they served for another 16 years, until 1998. By that time, the FDP had been a member of government for a total of 40 years, and less than 10 years in the opposition.

The Greens and the PDS. The role as majority maker and small coalition partner passed to the new Green Party in 1998, fifteen years after they had first entered the Bundestag. With the addition of the Greens, West Germany had in effect gone from a parliamentary "two-plus-one" to a "two-plus-two" party system. A third small party entered the Bundestag in 1990, the year of reunification. It was the post-communist PDS that eventually became strong enough in some parts of former East Germany to win proportional representation in the unusual way of winning three or more individual districts on the first ballot. Germany henceforth has a five party system (two-plus-three) in the Bundestag, although the Greens and PDS have each on occasion failed to win representation and temporarily dropped out of the equation.

In the former East Germany, the one home-grown political party was better positioned for focusing on the grievances of East Germans. The PDS tried without much success to attract new supporters in the populous West. It was, at first, unsuccessful in this endeavor; instead, it became essentially a regional protest party of socialist reformers. There was a high volatility in East German voting behavior, but the total share won by the PDS in the East alone rose from 11.1 percent at the time of unification to hover around 20 percent until 2005, when it rose to 25.3 percent—exactly the same share as the CDU in the East. In effect, the East Germans had created a "three party system" that operated alongside a "two plus two" party system in the West. For in the West, before the addition of the Left Party in 2005, the PDS received only about 1 percent of the vote—even less than the FDP and the Greens received in the East. In an almost evenly balanced Bundestag, the PDS—whether in parliament or not—drew enough votes to act as a spoiler, by either producing a stalemate or tip the election in favor of the Right. The election results from 1994, 2002, and 2005 would all have produced different winners without the PDS.

Small or Big, Two or Three Party Coalitions? In contrast to Britain's single-party tradition, West German governments have all been based on coalitions. They have all been led by one of the two major parties and until 1998 regularly included the small FDP as majority-making junior partner. The only interruption in this pattern of small coalitions was a three-year period in the late 1960s, when the two leading parties came together in a "grand coalition," with the FDP relegated to the role of small opposition party.

In 1998, the German voters finally drove Helmut Kohl's government from office. The next government was similarly based on a small coalition, but now the Greens had replaced the Liberals as majority makers. By deciding that it was time for a change, German voters produced a result that was similar to the turnabouts in Britain and France a year earlier. In Germany the change was also generational: the new government was composed of Germany's first postwar generation in power as well as its first left of center governing coalition.

The Bundestag Election of 2002. This was the closest election in the history of the Federal Republic. Both SPD and CDU/CSU won 38.5 percent of the vote, but a quirk in the two-vote electoral law gave the SPD three more seats than its major rival. At the start, the SPD had a poor stand in the polls. It could hardly claim to have delivered on the promise of an economic turnaround, yet it managed to catch up with an extraordinarily skillful electoral strategy. The recovery was in large part attributable to Chancellor Schröder's campaign, in particular (1) his more impressive performance in the televised debates with the conservative chancellor candidate, Edmund Stoiber, (2) his unusually sharp disavowal of President Bush's strategy toward Iraq, and (3) his well timed appearance as a decisive leader in dealing with the great floods that ravaged parts of eastern Germany in the month before the Bundestag election.

Structural Reforms: Federalism and Agenda 2010. After the 2002 election, German politics turned more seriously toward the task of basic structural reform. The two main topics were the country's federal structure and its socioeconomic model. Federalism is a crucial element not only in the country's governance but also in its self-understanding, as reflected in its official name, the Federal Republic of Germany. The founders of the West German state regarded a strong federal arrangement as a key safeguard against a dangerous concentration and potential abuse of power in the central government. Today there are outspoken reformers who believe that the federal entanglements often impede effective governance in Germany. At the same time, there are powerful vested interests that wish to keep the present arrangements, perhaps with some modifications.

There may be broader agreement about the need for a basic socio-economic reform in Germany. Yet there is no consensus about the specific reform measures themselves. The discussion resembles that carried on in several other advanced industrial and postindustrial societies. It proceeds from the insight that Germany's generous social welfare model will be unsustainable in its present form over the long run. Germany faces not only the familiar demographic shifts of an ageing society and stiff economic competition from abroad. Its problems are compounded by the economic burden of post-communist reconstruction in eastern Germany.

Germans have traditionally favored **a socially more contained form of capitalism** than the untrammeled market version that prevails in Britain or the United States. They are unlikely to accept the kind of massive deregulation that was introduced in the United States and Britain by conservative governments in the 1980s and largely accepted in both countries by their center-left successors in the following decade. Both the political culture and institutional framework of Germany (and much of mainland Europe) lean more toward **corporatist and communitarian solutions than their British and American counterparts.**

At the beginning of 2004, Chancellor Schröder succeeded in mobilizing parliamentary support for a comprehensive structural reform package, Agenda 2010. It ran into protests as Germans began to anticipate the painful rollbacks they were facing. The SPD, as the leading government party, dropped sharply in the polls and experienced an unprecedented loss of voters and dues-paying members.

There was an institutional power shift as well, when victories in several state elections gave the Christian Democrats enough votes in the federal upper chamber (Bundesrat) to have a blocking majority. After the defeat of the SPD-led government in Germany's most populous state, North Rhine Westphalia, for the first time in four decades, Schröder announced his intention to hold the next Bundestag election a year early. He managed to obtain the necessary approval by the Federal President and the Constitutional Court.

The Bundestag Election of 2005. During a short campaign, in which Schröder and the SPD pulled out all the stops, the CDU/CSU managed to lose a more than 10 percent lead and came out only one percentage point ahead of the SPD (35.2 to 34.2 percent). It was the first election since 1949 in which the two major parties had together received less than 70 percent of the vote. That has led to a discussion in Germany whether **the near duopoly by the CDU/CSU and SPD** is coming to an end and will be replaced by a somewhat **more fragmented, pluralized party system.**

The CDU/CSU had expected to form a traditional governing coalition with the FDP. The party leader, Angela Merkel, had been its "chancellor candidate." As detailed in the article by Janes and Szabo, Merkel is notable as an achiever of "firsts" (first woman, former East German, and natural scientist to achieve the chancellorship), but also for the political and diplomatic skill she has exhibited thus far.

The relatively strong performance of the **Left.PDS alliance** determined the outcome of the 2005 election. The Left.PDS brought together the eastern PDS and western socialist dissidents, who had reacted to Schröder's neoliberal reforms by gathering behind the former SPD leader and one-time chancellor candidate, Oskar Lafontaine. Thus, the alliance overcame the weakness of the PDS, which can win between one-fifth and one-fourth of the vote in eastern Germany but not more than 1.2 percent in the West. In 2007, the Left.PDS brought in almost four times as many votes in the West as the PDS had at its best—4.4 percent. The Left still would not have passed the 5 percent barrier by itself, but by adding the result in the eastern states (25.3 percent) the Left.PDS alliance won a combined total of 8.7 percent in Germany as a whole. This may have been a decisive opening of the door to a stronger Left in future elections.

So far, the consequences have been a greater fragmentation of the German party system—until now mostly at the cost of the two major parties, CDU/CSU and SPD—along with a shift in the system's center of gravitation from center-right to center-left. There may be consequences for other small parties, especially for the oldest and, until recently, most successful one—the neoliberal FDP. It can no longer make the most of its role as the sole "majority-maker" in a *"small" two-party coalition* with one of the two major parties (Christian Democrats or Social Democrats). The reason is simple: a parliamentary majority is now possible only by building a *"small" three party coalition* made up of *two* small partners and a major party. The alternative is a **"grand coalition"** of the two major parties, each of them crucially diminished since their heyday. In other words, German politics has become more complex and turned somewhat more leftward overall, even as it has become potentially less stable. The result is seen by some as "the revenge of the GDR" on its West German rival, but it would be a mistake to assume that without reunification the old West German party system would have stayed intact forever. Compared to the Weimar Republic, the Berlin Republic remains a political system that works relatively well and a democracy that is ranked well above Britain, France and the United States by the index of democracy.

The formation of the new government in 2005 illustrated the new political situation very well. The coalition possibilities were greatly restricted because of politics *or* arithmetic, and quite often *both*. Germany has not tried minority government at the national level, and it rarely discusses it as a workable alternative to a governing majority coalition. As we have seen, the **classical German "small coalition"** formed by one major and one small party was *arithmetically* impossible—whether "red-green," "red-yellow," "black-yellow," or "black-green." The PDS was also *politically* impossible as a federal coalition partner. Although the post-communists have entered into governing coalitions at the state level in former East Germany, they are still regarded as political anathema at the federal level. The SPD had special reasons for not getting cozy with the defectors who had joined the renegade, former SPD leader, Oskar Lafontaine. How this will work out in the long run depends on a number of other developments, such as the future electoral strength of the Left in the states of western Germany. But there can be little doubt that Germany is moving toward a politically somewhat more tumultuous future.

Japan

Comparative social scientists have long had a fascination with Japan as a country that began to modernize relatively early, rapidly and thoroughly without abandoning its distinctly non-Western, Japanese identity. Few cultures have shown such a capacity to "assimilate" major borrowings from abroad without losing a considerable part of their own traditional culture. This topic is explored in the article "Japanese Spirit, Western Things."

Like its onetime ally, Germany, Japan's political modernization has traveled a bumpy road. Both countries saw the establishment (or reestablishment) of imperial rule in the late 19th century. Japan did begin to move tentatively toward a semblance of the parliamentary form of government after World War I, but further steps were blocked by a militarist takeover in the early 1930s. Japan's policies were buoyed by extreme nationalism and militarism, but did not include a racial ideology comparable to Germany's radical National Socialism. It has been frequently observed that Adolf Hitler does not seem to have applied his views on racial inferiority of "non-Aryans" to his Japanese allies.

After World War II, Japan also came under military occupation but unlike Germany, however, Japan was occupied by a single power only, the United States. A parliamentary form of representative democracy was installed in Japan under American supervision. This new political system soon acquired **indigenous Japanese characteristics** that set it off from the other major democracies examined here. The adaptation of the representative institutions took place in the context of a prolonged economic boom, which had begun after World War II. In Japan, as in Germany, the new political systems became beneficiaries of this turn of events, gaining legitimacy by meeting the basic pragmatic test (in other words, they "worked").

The party system shows some superficial resemblance to the many weak and internally divided parties of the Third and Fourth Republics. In Japan, however, there are informal but well established, alternative networks for contact and communication between leading politicians and their counterparts as business leaders and top bureaucrats.

Since its creation in 1955, the **Liberal Democratic Party** (LDP) has played a leading role in Japanese party politics. Most of the time, the many opposition parties have been divided and they have provided little effective competition. Yet the LDP could be said to provide its own opposition. According to a standard political joke, the Japanese Liberal Democrats are neither Liberal nor democratic—and they do not really constitute a party either! There is some truth in this remark.

The LDP has essentially performed like a conservative political machine that loosely unites and balances several rival factions, which in turn consists mostly of the personal followers of political bosses who stake out and pursue factional claims to benefits of office.

In Japanese politics, the LDP performs an important coordinating role, and if it were not there, it might have to be invented in order for the parliamentary side of the Japanese system to work. Such a conclusion is supported by the political chaos that resulted during the one year when the LDP was absent from the government.

That was in 1993, when the LDP temporarily lost its parliamentary majority. Thereupon seven different parties, spanning the spectrum from conservative to socialist, formed a fragile coalition government. It was incapable of defining or promoting a coherent policy program and stood helpless as the Japanese economy continued on its course of stagnation. The long postwar economic boom had petered out somewhat later for Japan than in Western Europe, but by the beginning of the 1990s the Japanese economy was on the decline.

One year, two prime ministers and several cabinet reshuffles later, a revived LDP managed by the summer of 1994 to return to the cabinet in coalition with its former rivals, the Socialists. The peculiar alliance was possible because the Socialist leadership took a thoroughly pragmatic view of coalition politics—as did the LDP. By December 1995, the more experienced LDP had recaptured the prime ministerial office for itself.

There followed a rapid succession of short-lived governments headed by LDP factional leaders. When the post once again became open in April 2001, there were a surprising number of willing candidates and an even more surprising victor. The unexpected new leader of the Liberal Democrats and new prime minister of Japan was Junichiro Koizumi. He had unequivocally identified himself as committed to a new course of thorough reform that would go beyond the economy into realms that hitherto had been deemed out of reach for politics.

Once in office, Koizumi immediately took some symbolic steps to show that he meant business. His first cabinet included five women, including the controversial Makiko Tanaka who became head of the foreign ministry. Considered assertive, she quickly became a target for opponents of the new course. She was dismissed as foreign minister in January 2002, but immediately replaced by another prominent woman.

Although he had learned the traditional ways of Japanese party politics before reaching the top, Koizumi soon became widely known for having adopted an unconventional approach. His leadership style brought him media attention and, at times, personal popularity as with no previous prime minister. But he was less successful in turning his popularity into political capital.

He used every opportunity to call for economic reform, and he mastered the language of structural innovation. No previous Japanese prime minister had made such outspoken neoliberal demands for privatization and deregulation. But he worked within a context that was not conducive to reform. His proposals ran into tough resistance from conservative elements in the political class, including factional leaders of his own party and members of the high civil service.

It is remarkable that Japan's prolonged economic stagnation, lasting from the early 1990s for well over a decade—and not yet completely over has not resulted in more political protests or electoral repercussions. A key question has been whether the fragmented parliamentary opposition would one day overcome its divisions and find a way to become a more coherent, alternative force. It is a vision that has brought *The Economist* to speculate about the possible emergence of a two-party system, with the newly emerging Democratic Party of Japan (DPJ) as the clear alternative choice for mainstream voters. So far, this reading of Japanese party politics has failed to pan out. The immediate result of the 2003 parliamentary election was that Koizumi remained prime minister with his coalition intact.

Japanese politics seemed to continue in its well-worn groove. Prime Minister Koizumi continued to run into opposition to his plans for economic liberalization, and much of the resistance came from members of his own party. When his plans to privatize the postal service were rejected by the upper house of parliament in 2005, Koizumi used the occasion to call for early elections. His move resembled the one taken about the same time by the German chancellor in reaction to a political stalemate. The immediate outcome was very different for, in contrast to Gerhard Schröder, Koizumi won a landslide victory.

The Japanese prime minister had used the opportunity to purge his party of some rebels, and in the following parliamentary session the Liberal Democrats acted more as a team and mobilized support to have 82 of 91 proposed bills passed, including the one to privatize the postal services.

The turnabout came in the fifth year of Koizumi's tenure as prime minister—far too late to give him an opportunity to pursue his new course to the end, if that had seriously been his intention. In 2006, following his party's rules on term limits, he stepped down.

Unlike many of his predecessors, Koizumi did not try to pick his own successor. In September 2006, Shinzo Abe was elected to succeed Koizumi as leader of the Liberal Democrats and prime minister of Japan. He seemed to be far less committed to structural reforms than Koizumi. Instead, some observers called attention to the new leader's apparently unrepentant attitude toward his country's war atrocities as likely to have major foreign repercussions. Others found it difficult to believe that Japan would put its hard-won, good relations with China, South Korea, and other neighbors at risk by indulging in a revival of nationalism.

Shinzo Abe lasted only one year as prime minister. He left office in mid-September 2007, in part for health reasons but also because had become a liability for his party. It had lost its majority in the upper house of parliament for the first time in late July. The DJP won a majority there and immediately called for an early election for the lower house as well. It was a difficult moment for the LDP, but it did not really make a clean break with the past in selecting **Yasuo Fukuda** as its next party leader and prime minister. He was a 71-year old veteran politician and son of a former prime minister. Unlike a rival candidate, however, he appeared to have no ties to the Abe administration. His experience in the shadows of party politics could turn out to be an asset or a liability—or a bit of both. Perhaps the best news was that he had a reputation for "competence and common sense." No one expected bold new reform initiatives, as *The Economist* commented: "But slowly, greyly might do it." [i]

---

[i] "Land of the Rising Shadow," *The Economist,* September 27, 2007.

British Constitutional Change: From Blair to Brown and Beyond

DONLEY T. STUDLAR

Commentary on the 2007 retirement of Prime Minister Tony Blair after ten years in office as well as the maiden speech in the House of Commons from new Prime Minister Gordon Brown refocused attention on the Labor government's long-term effects on the British constitution since it assumed office in 1997. The most distinctive policies of the "New Labor" electoral campaign in 1997 were on constitutional reform. From its earliest days in power, Labor promoted its constitutional reform agenda; which included (1) devolution to Scotland and Wales; (2) an elected mayor and council for London and potentially other urban areas; (3) removal of the voting rights of hereditary peers in the House of Lords; (4) incorporation of the European Convention on Human Rights into British law; (5) a *Freedom of Information Act;* and (6) electoral reform at various levels of government, including a referendum on changing the electoral system for Members of Parliament (MPs). This article will consider these reforms, plus others that have arisen: (1) an agreement for governing Northern Ireland; (2) the constitutional implications of membership of the European Union; (3) the question of modernization of the monarchy; (4) the Labor government's recent legislation for a separate Supreme Court; and (5) the Green (discussion) paper of constitutional proposals introduced by Gordon Brown in 2007. The article describes and analyzes Labor's constitutional proposals, including their inspiration, implementation, and potential impact.

Traditional British Constitutional Principles

The United Kingdom as a state in international law is made up of four constituent parts—England, Scotland, Wales, and Northern Ireland—all under the authority of the Queen in Parliament in London. The constitution is the structure of fundamental laws and customary practices that define the authority of state institutions and regulate their interrelationships, including those with citizens of the state. Although in principle very flexible, in practice the "unwritten" British constitution (no single document) is difficult to change. The socialization of political elites in a small country leads to a political culture in which custom and convention make participants reluctant to change practices that brought them to power.

Even though Britain is under the rule of law, all constitutional provisions are subject to change through parliamentary sovereignty. Instead of a written constitution with a complicated amending process, a simple voting majority of the House of Commons can change any law, even over the objections of the House of Lords if necessary. Individual rights are protected by ordinary law and custom, not by a constitutionally entrenched bill of rights.

Officially Britain remains a unitary state, with all constitutional authority belonging to the central government, rather than a federal state with a formal, even if vague, division of powers between the center and a lower level. Some commentators argue that Britain should be considered a "union-state," since the relationship of the four parts to the central government is not uniform. Although limited devolution has been utilized in the past, especially in Northern Ireland, 1921–1972, central government retains the constitutional authority to intervene in lower-level affairs, including local government. A parliamentary general election occurs every four or five years, in which voters effectively are choosing a team of politicians to manage the central government, based on their being able to obtain and retain support of a voting majority in the House of Commons at Westminster. All seats are distributed according to the single member plurality (SMP) electoral system, whereby the candidate with the most votes wins the seat, irrespective of whether that plurality is also a majority of the votes cast. The outcome usually has been a single-party government led by the prime minister and cabinet, based on a plurality of the vote that is transformed by the electoral system into a majority of seats in the Commons. This is a fusion rather than a separation of power between the legislative and executive branches. Referendums have been rare and are only advisory; parliament retains final authority on all legislation. The judiciary seldom makes politically important decisions. If a court finds that the executive has exceeded its lawful authority, such a decision can be overridden by having a parliamentary majority pass an appropriate law, even retrospectively. In the United Kingdom, almost any alteration of the relations among these interlinked political institutions can be considered constitutional in nature.

Constitutional issues were a major subject of party debate during the 1997 election campaign. Labor and the third party, the Liberal Democrats, had developed an agreed agenda for constitutional change. The Conservatives defended traditional British constitutional principles, including the unwritten constitution, no guarantees of civil liberties except through the laws of parliament, maintenance of the unitary state, and a House of Lords composed of hereditary peers and some life peers, the latter appointed by the prime minister.

Other parts of the British constitution also have resisted change. British government has been one of the most secretive among Western democracies, with unauthorized communication of information punishable by law, principally the *Official Secrets Act.* Large cities did not elect their own mayors or even their own metropolitan governing councils. The House of Commons is one of the few remaining democratic legislatures elected by the SMP electoral system, which rewards disproportionate shares of parliamentary seats to larger parties having geographically concentrated voting strength. Thus the membership and organization of the House of Commons has remained largely two-party despite having a multiparty electorate since 1974.

Like the Conservatives, traditionally Labor had embraced the wide-ranging and flexible central executive power that the "elective dictatorship" of British parliamentary government allows. Although Labor sometimes voiced decentralist concerns when in opposition, in government it usually proved to be as centralist as the Conservatives. But that changed in 1997.

Labor's Constitutional Promises

Prior to becoming prime minister, Tony Blair had advocated a more participatory British citizenship. In his book *New Britain,* Blair criticized the traditional Westminster system as too centralized, secretive, and unrepresentative. He argued that since World War I there had been an erosion of consent, self-government, and respect for rights under governments of all parties in Britain. A "New Labor" party true to its own instincts should extend political rights as well as pursuing its recognized goals of economic and social equality.

The most radical part of Labor's 1997 election manifesto was constitutional reform. This program was designed to stimulate the normally passive, relatively deferential British public into becoming more active citizens with a wider range of choices. In addition to parliamentary elections, they would vote more frequently in referendums and for other levels of government with significant authority. In addition, they would have more individual civil rights.

Developing a Program for Constitutional Change

Several events and trends focused Labor's thinking on constitutional reform. Labor had suffered four consecutive general election losses (1979, 1983, 1987, 1992) even though the Conservatives never achieved above 44 percent of the popular vote. Eighteen consecutive years out of government made Labor question whether it could ever return to power as a single-party government. Long-term minority status in a system where having a parliamentary majority confers near-absolute power made the party more receptive to arguments for limiting central authority.

Groups interested in constitutional reform became more numerous. The third party in Britain, the Liberal Democrats, long have advocated several reforms, including decentralization, increased protection for civil liberties, and changing the electoral system. The latter would allow them to have their voting support more proportionally represented in parliament. Since 1988, a nonpartisan lobby group, Charter 88, has proposed a number of reforms, including a written constitution and a bill of rights. Other influential thinkers on the moderate left argued that a precondition for social and economic change in an increasingly middle-class Britain was to encourage citizen involvement by limiting central executive authority. In Scotland, the broadly-based Scottish Constitutional Convention encouraged devolution of power. The Electoral Reform Society has been an active proponent for a more proportional voting system. Eventually Labor and the Liberal Democrats formed a pre-election commission on constitutional matters, which continued after the 1997 election in the form of a special cabinet committee on constitutional reform.

Skeptics have argued that public support for constitutional change is a mile wide and an inch deep. Surveys indicate that the public usually supports constitutional reform proposals in principle without understanding very much about the specifics. Intense elite opinion fueled the discussion. Although constitutional issues featured prominently in discussions of party differences during the 1997 campaign, they did not emerge as a critical voting issue, except perhaps in Scotland.

New Labor had multiple incentives for the development of an agenda for constitutional change. It provided a clear sense of party distinctiveness from the Conservatives, especially important when there were only small differences on social and economic policy. It also helped alleviate threats to Labor by Scottish and Welsh nationalist parties arguing for more autonomy and even independence for their regions. There also was the longer-term prospect of a realignment of the party system through the cooptation of the Liberal Democrats into a more permanent governing alliance of the center, thereby marginalizing the Conservatives and die-hard socialists of the Labor Left wing. The unexpected outcome of the 1997 election, in which Labor obtained a large single-party majority in the House of Commons, did not discourage it from pursuing most of its constitutional reform program, except perhaps on electoral reform for Westminster.

Constitutional Change under Labor

Some commentators have proclaimed that Labor's agenda represents the most fundamental constitutional changes in 400 years. There are now legislatures with devolved powers in Northern Ireland, Scotland, and Wales. All but 92 hereditary peers have been removed from the House of Lords, with the pledge of the eventual elimination of those as well. The European Convention on Human Rights has been incorporated effectively, if controversially, into British law through the Human Rights Act. A *Freedom of Information Act* was passed and implemented. In 1998, Londoners voted favorably for a referendum proposal for the city to be governed by a directly-elected mayor and assembly; these elections were held in 2000 and 2004. Other cities have now adopted this measure through referendums. The judiciary has been separated to a degree from the other branches of government. The major lacuna is the change of electoral system for Westminster although this has been done for lower levels of government. Although a report from the Independent Commission on the Voting System advocated a change in the electoral system for the Commons, no government legislation was proposed.

The Labor government immediately set out to implement more decentralized authority, subject to its acceptance through referendums in the affected regions. The Scottish Parliament has more authority, covering nearly all of domestic policy as well as limited taxation powers while the Welsh Assembly is responsible for implementing legislation after the primary bills have passed through the Westminster but has no taxation powers. Elections in each region in 1999, 2003, and 2007 were held under a combination of the traditional single member district, simple plurality electoral system and party list proportional representation; these yielded no clear majority in either legislature. Instead, coalition and minority governments have been formed. The biggest change occurred in 2007 when the Scottish National Party (SNP), committed to eventual Scottish independence through a referendum, received the largest number of seats and formed a minority government with the support of the Greens.

An organized women's movement took advantage of the opportunity to choose legislators in a new institution without incumbents, leading to high levels of women's representation in both devolved chambers. The Welsh Assembly became the first in the world with a majority of women in 2003.

Perhaps surprisingly, no major disagreements on the constitutional allocation of powers have occurred. The possibility of the Scottish Parliament having differences with the central government now has increased with an SNP-led government. The new coalition government in Wales between Labor and the Welsh Nationalist party, Plaid Cymru, has promised a referendum by 2011 on the Welsh Assembly gaining full lawmaking powers.

Nevertheless, the "West Lothian" question has still not been seriously addressed. This refers to the fact that now Westminster MPs from Scotland and Northern Ireland can still vote on legislation affecting England and Wales even though the devolved Scottish Parliament and Northern Ireland Assembly have authority over the same issue in those parts of the state.

Eighty-five percent of the population of the United Kingdom, however, lives in England, which has been treated as a residual consideration in the plans for devolution. Labor has promised to form devolved governments in "regions with strong identities of their own," as expressed through voting in referendums. However, when the region showing the greatest amount of interest,

the Northeast, was offered limited legislative devolution in 2004, it was rejected overwhelmingly. Nevertheless, with encouragement from the regional aid policies of the European Union, the Northeast does have a considerable amount of administrative devolution. Gordon Brown established ministers for all English regions in his government and has proposed that regional committees in the House of Commons provide oversight.

The Mayor of London is the first modern directly-elected executive in the United Kingdom. The introduction of party primary elections for mayoral candidates led to less central party control over candidates and a more personalized contest. The first mayor, re-elected in 2004, was a dissident leftwing Labor MP and former London official, Ken Livingstone, who has proven to be relatively conciliatory in office but has initiated one important policy change, a financial charge for automobiles entering central London. The 2008 contest is shaping up as a lively one, with Livingstone running for a third term and journalist and MP Boris Johnson contending for the Conservative party nomination.

Northern Ireland is a perennial problem, a hangover of the separation of Ireland from the United Kingdom in 1922. Six counties in the northern part of the island of Ireland, with the majority of the population consisting of Protestants favoring continued union with Great Britain, remained in the United Kingdom. Many Catholics north and south remain convinced that there should be only one country, Ireland, on the island. This fundamental division of opinion over which country should have sovereignty over the territory led to organized violence by proponents of both sides; some 3,600 people have died in sectarian violence since 1968. The provisional Irish Republican Army (IRA) was the main body advocating violence in the cause of a united Ireland.

The Good Friday Agreement of 1998, brokered by the U.S. administration of Bill Clinton, was a peace accord that promised a different future through new institutions. In 1999, devolution of power from the Westminster parliament to the Belfast parliament ushered in a period of what the British call "power sharing," or "consensus democracy." This entailed not only joint authority over internal matters by both Protestants (Unionists) and Catholics (Nationalists) through the requirement of supermajorities in the Northern Ireland Assembly and executive, but also regular consultation between the United Kingdom and Ireland. Both countries pledged that Northern Ireland would remain part of the United Kingdom as long as a majority of the population in the province wishes. The latest census showed Protestants to be in the majority, 53 to 44 percent.

Referendums on the Good Friday Agreement passed overwhelmingly in both Northern Ireland and the Irish Republic; the latter also repealed its constitutional claim over the province. As expected, devolved government in Northern Ireland has been rocky. Groups representing formerly armed adversaries, including Sinn Fein, closely linked to the IRA, assumed ministerial positions in the power-sharing executive, but some dissident factions refused to renounce violence. In 2002 accusations of IRA spying on the government led to the suspension of the Northern Ireland Assembly and government for the fourth time in three years. Direct rule from the central government in London replaced the power-sharing executive. Elections in 2003 resulted in the Democratic Unionist Party (DUP), which had opposed the Good Friday Agreement as a "sell out" to Catholics, becoming the largest Protestant party while Sinn Fein became the largest Catholic party. This further complicated discussions.

Subsequently the IRA moved to decommission it weapons caches and to discourage criminal activities of its members. In September 2006, the Independent Monitoring Commission confirmed the dismantling of most of these internal IRA structures, leading Prime Minister Blair to declare that "the IRA campaign is over," a clear commitment to move from violence to politics. Protestant paramilitary groups also have disarmed. Nevertheless, choosing a new, power-sharing executive was stalled by deep cleavages and lack of trust, which frustrated the hopes of the British and Irish governments for returning devolved authority to the province. In the 2006 St. Andrews Agreement these governments gave the parties in Northern Ireland a deadline to begin reconstituting the power-sharing executive. Sinn Fein had to recognize the authority of the Northern Ireland police (now composed of 20% Catholics), and in return the DUP would have to agree to an executive power-sharing arrangement with Sinn Fein. After a new election that confirmed the leading positions of the DUP and Sinn Fein, the new government assumed office in March 2007. Despite progress in making peace, "normal politics" has not emerged in this most abnormal part of the United Kingdom.

Britain signed the European Convention on Human Rights in 1951. In 1966 it began allowing appeals to the European Court of Human Rights at Strasbourg, where it has lost more cases than any other country. Under New Labor, a law was passed incorporating the European Convention on Human Rights into domestic law. British judges rather than European judges now make the decisions about whether Britain is conforming to the Convention, which enhances the ability of British citizens to raise issues of human rights in domestic courts. Supposedly parliamentary sovereignty is maintained because Westminster retains final authority on whether judicial decisions will be followed. Nevertheless, in practice the British government has lodged appeals against adverse British court decisions with the European Court of Human Rights. Under the *Human Rights Act* suspected terrorists have brought cases against government detention and extradition to countries where they could face persecution. More generally, there has been concern about court decisions favoring human rights over crime and security concerns. The government has rejected a legislative remedy but has urged officials, including judges, to place a higher value on public safety. This has raised controversy about interference with judicial independence. Constitutional scholar Vernon Bogdanor has argued that the *Human Rights Act* is now "fundamental law" beyond the ordinary reach of parliament.

Nevertheless, the combination of a strong, centralized political executive and the struggle against international terrorism can lead to infringements of civil liberties. In recent years several pieces of legislation, notably the *Anti-Terrorism Act* of 2001, have limited individual rights, based on the argument that a state of emergency justified withdrawing from parts of European Convention on Human Rights. A 2007 documentary film,

Taking Liberties, accused the Labor government of reducing the rights of citizens in six ways: (1) the right to protest; (2) the right to freedom of speech; (3) the right to privacy; (4) the right not to be detained without charge; (5) the presumption of innocence until proved guilty; and (6) prohibition from torture. The British government also keeps its citizens under close watch. *A Report on the Surveillance Society,* an independent report in 2006, found the United Kingdom to be "the most surveilled state" among Western democracies.

The first-term Labor government later addressed other measures of constitutional reform—freedom of information, the House of Lords, and the electoral system for the Commons. The *Freedom of Information Act* eventually enacted creates an independent Information Commissioner's Office and allows public access to more government information, but within limits. Applications for information go to the ministry involved, with an Information Commissioner handling appeals. However, department ministers still can overrule decisions of the Information Commissioner. When the act was implemented in 2005, there were both rumors of departments destroying files and revelations of incidents in previous governments, usually based upon inquiries from media organizations. Nevertheless, British governments can still withhold a large amount of information. Overall, the United Kingdom remains one of the most secretive democracies in the world, under the doctrine of executive prerogatives of ministers of the crown. Nevertheless, there now more unprosecuted revelations of government secrets than in the past.

Superficially House of Lords reform appears simple since the *Parliament Act* of 1949 allows a government majority in the House of Commons to override any objections from the Lords. However, the capacity of the Lords to delay legislation makes reform difficult to complete when there is no agreement about new arrangements. New Labor pledged to abolish Lords voting by hereditary peers, leaving only life peers appointed by the prime minister. Life peerages are granted for distinguished service in politics or more broadly in society. Forty percent of life peers are senior political figures who desire a more limited political role after a long career in the Commons. Critics labeled this a plan to make the second chamber one consisting solely of "Tony's Cronies," an entirely patronage-based body. In order to accomplish early reform, Prime Minister Blair in 1999 accepted a temporary arrangement allowing 92 hereditary peers to remain in the House of Lords while eliminating 667 others. Labor also established an independent commission to advise the Prime Minister on non-political Lords appointments, but Blair retained the power to make party political appointments based on recommendations from party leaders. His last year in office was marred by a controversy over "cash for honors." The claim that some peerages were awarded in return for large donations to the Labor party.

There followed a plethora of proposals for the second stage of Lords reform from several official sources. Since proposals ranged from a fully elected to a fully appointed second chamber, agreement has been difficult. Critics have complained that the government's preference for a largely appointed chamber, plus possibly further limits on the power of the Lords to delay legislation, would lead to a weaker second chamber un able to act as a check on the government. In contrast, a body with some elected members would provide greater democratic legitimacy. Both the Conservatives and Liberal Democrats prefer a partially-elected second chamber. Although still committed to eventual elimination of the remaining hereditary peers, the government has agreed to allow a free vote in the Commons on the question of the new composition of the Lords.

A government proposal in early 2007 was for a mixture of 50 percent election and 50 percent appointment, with quotas for women and ethnic minorities, no single party majority (many peers already sit as "cross-benchers," or independents), a reduction in the membership from 746 to 540, an electoral system based on regional list proportional representation with voting on the same day as elections for the European Parliament, electing one third of that allotment every five years, a term limit of 15 years for all members, separating life peerages as an honor from a seat in the Lords, phasing out hereditary and life peers over several years, and renaming the second chamber, possibly calling it the Reformed Chamber. The Commons later voted for nonbinding resolutions that would make the Lords at least 80 percent elected. In contrast, the Lords approved a nonbinding resolution for a 100 percent appointed chamber. The government may propose a new bill in the fall of 2007, but, given the desire for consensus, it is likely to move with "deliberate speed." With the still-yawning gap in preferences among government, Commons, and Lords, it will take a huge amount of political will and parliamentary time to pass legislation. This issue may extend beyond the next general election expected by 2009.

Although Prime Minister Blair indicated that he was not "personally convinced" that a change in the electoral system was needed, he appointed an Independent Commission on the Voting System to consider alternatives to the current electoral system for the House of Commons. In 1998 the Commission recommended what is called "Alternative Vote Plus." The single-member district system would be retained, but instead of casting a vote for one person only, the electorate would rank candidates in order of preference, thus assuring a majority rather than a plurality vote for the winner. There would also be a second vote for a "preferred party." These votes would be distributed regionally, with 15-20 percent of the total seats being awarded to parties based on their proportional share, a favorable development for smaller parties.

Even such a relatively mild reform, however, generated considerable political controversy, as expected when the basis through which legislators gain their seats is challenged. The proposed change was criticized not only by the opposition Conservatives, but by also by Labor members because it might make it more difficult for Labor to obtain a single-party parliamentary majority. With Labor winning 55 percent of the seats in the election of 2005 with only 35 percent of the popular vote (and only 22% of the electorate), there were renewed calls for a new voting system. New Prime Minister Brown has revived this issue for study and consultation in his Green Paper on constitutional reform.

Nevertheless, some change of electoral systems has occurred at lower levels of government. Instead of near-uniform use of the simple plurality electoral system, there are now five differ-

ent systems in operation, including (1) Single Transferable Vote (a form of proportional representation with candidate choice) in Northern Ireland; (2) regional party list proportional representation for European Parliament elections; (3) Alternative Member Systems (a combination of single member district and party list proportional) for the devolved legislatures in Scotland and Wales and the London Assembly; and (4) a popularly elected executive through the Supplementary Vote (voting for two candidates in order of preference) for London. Plurality elections remain the norm only for the House of Commons at Westminster and English local government elections. Gordon Brown has proposed a review of the operation of these different electoral systems.

Until 1997 there had been only four referendums in the entire history of the United Kingdom. In its first year of office, Labor held four additional referendums (in Wales, Scotland, Northern Ireland, and London). Other countrywide ones, however, on the EU constitution, the European single currency, and the Westminster electoral system have been canceled or postponed. There also have been local referendums on elected mayors and potentially others on regional government. Despite these increased opportunities for participation, voting turnout at all elections has plunged, reaching a low of 59 percent in the Westminster parliamentary elections of 2001 and barely increasing in 2005; turnout for the second devolved elections also decreased. To help alleviate this problem, Prime Minister Brown has suggested moving voting day from the traditional Thursdays to the weekend and possibly lowering the voting age to 16.

In 2003 the government decided to move toward greater separation of powers among the executive, legislative, and judicial branches of government. Previously the Lord Chancellor was a member of all three parts—a minister in the cabinet, head of the judiciary (including authority to appoint judges), and also Speaker of the House of Lords. The highest appeals court has been the Appellate Committee of the House of Lords (Law Lords) consisting of the Lord Chancellor, twelve life peers specially appointed for this purpose, and other member of the Lords who have held high judicial office. The Labor government rearranged the duties of the position of Lord Chancellor, retaining the title for court administration and ceremonial functions but creating a new position, Secretary of State for Constitutional Affairs, to deal with areas such as devolution, human rights, and data protection. Nevertheless, under Blair one person occupied both positions. The government also introduced legislation to remove the judiciary from the House of Lords and to designate the highest appellate court as the Supreme Court, with a reformed Judicial Appointments Commission to make recommendations for such positions. Despite controversy, parliament eventually enacted the Constitutional Reform Act, which established the new Supreme Court and is due to take effect by 2008. Some commentators have argued that an independent judiciary could move to establish its ultimate constitutional authority by upholding "the rule of law" even over parliamentary sovereignty, as Supreme Courts in the United States, the European Union, and Israel, among others, have done.

Some analysts argue that the most significant constitutional change in United Kingdom has been brought about not by Labor but by three actions of Conservative governments—joining the European Community (now European Union) in 1972, approving the *Single European Act* (1986), which enshrined qualified-majority voting for passing measures, and signing the *Maastricht Treaty* (1992) providing for greater integration. Lord Denning famously observed that the European Union is an incoming tide that cannot be held back. Within the expanded areas of EU competence, EU law supersedes British law, including judicial review by the European Court of Justice. Almost one half of total annual legislation in the United Kingdom now arises from the European Union, and members of the government, civil service, and even judiciary are in almost daily contact with their counterparts in the EU and in other countries on EU matters. Britain has been wary of increasing EU central authority and promised to subject the proposed EU Constitution to a referendum, which did not occur because prior referendums in the Netherlands and France in 2005 rejected the Constitution. But Prime Minister Brown has refused to submit the substitute plan agreed by chief executives of EU member countries, the European Union amending treaty, to a referendum. If eventually agreed unanimously by all 27 EU member states, it would codify the supremacy of EU law, including a bill of rights.

Britain continues to be a leading member of the "awkward squad" of countries within the EU desiring strong state sovereignty within the organization rather than surrendering more authority to a supranational organization. It remains one of only three long-standing EU members not to join the European Monetary Union (EMU) and its currency, the euro. If Britain were to join the central bank and adopt the euro, then control over monetary policy would effectively pass into the hands of the European Union. The Chancellor of the Exchequer (Treasury Secretary) periodically announces whether economic conditions meet the "five tests" necessary for him to recommend that Britain should converge with euroland. It is the policy of the Labor government that Britain would join the EMU only if supported by the public in a countrywide referendum.

Although not on the Labor party agenda of constitutional change, the role of the monarchy also has come under increased scrutiny in recent years. The Queen's Golden Jubilee Year in 2002, celebrating the first 50 years of her reign, was not a happy one, with two deaths and scandals in the royal family. A resolution of the Scottish Parliament, supported by some MPs and Lords at Westminster, has petitioned the government to allow the monarch or her spouse to be a Roman Catholic, a practice forbidden by the *Act of Settlement* (1701) at the end of a period of religious wars. The heir to the throne, Prince Charles, has proposed removing the monarch's connection to the Church of England in favor of the title of a more general "defender of faith" in what is now, despite appearances, a highly secularized country.

More vaguely, the government has suggested moving toward a "people's monarchy"—a simpler, slimmer, and less ritualized institution, perhaps with a gender-neutral inheritance. This would be more congruent with the lower profile "bicycle monarchs" common in other European countries. For the first time since Queen Victoria, there is substantial, if muted, public expression anti-monarchist (republican) sentiments, largely in elite circles on the Labor Left. However, tampering with this traditional institution, still widely revered by the public, requires extremely careful preparation as many are opposed to change.

Conflicting Views on the Effects of Constitutional Change

Labor's program of constitutional renewal already has brought about some changes in Britain. Broadly, commentators have offered four interpretations of these developments. We might term these the (1) popular social liberalism, (2) lukewarm reform/symbolic politics, (3) radicalism, and (4) constitutional incoherence. These contending explanations exist at least partially because Labor itself has never outlined a comprehensive theory behind its constitutional reforms. Constitutional reform has consisted of a series of *ad hoc* measures rather than a general constitutional convention.

The well-known American analyst of Britain, Samuel H. Beer, has compared Blair's reforms to the popular social liberalism of the early twentieth century Liberal governments, which included restricting the power of the House of Lords and devolving power to Ireland. After the First World War, however, the Conservatives came to dominate Britain electorally as the Left divided between an insurgent Labor Party and the remaining Liberals. In the first term of office for New Labor, social and constitutional reform served as a substitute for a more traditional Labor program of increased government spending. This was important for establishing the long-term political dominance of a revitalized center-left by appealing to the "median voter."

Another constitutional scholar, Philip Norton, has argued that New Labor's proposals are radical in concept but moderate in form and effects, e.g., lukewarm reform. Similarly, Anthony Barnett of Charter 88 claims that the government practices *constitutus interruptus*. Another British academic, Patrick Dunleavy, has suggested that constitutional reform for New Labor represents financially cheap activity at the start of a new Prime Minister's term of office when the government does not want to alienate its middle-class supporters by appearing to be yet another Labor "tax and spend" administration. This amounts to little substantive change, however, until the two critical questions, electoral reform for the House of Commons and Britain's long-term relationship to the EU, are addressed.

Although there has been some grudging acceptance from constitutional conservatives who originally opposed change, they are still fearful of the implications of some reforms. The former editor of *The Times,* William Rees-Mogg, envisions Labor's constitutional changes eroding democracy in the United Kingdom through a semi-permanent Labor-Liberal governing coalition in Westminster, Scotland, and Wales, a House of Lords based on patronage, and a more centralized, bureaucratic European superstate. More sanguinely, *The Economist* foresees a weakening of Westminster's authority through the combined forces of devolution and a more integrated European Union. More recently it has warned that Blair's reform program will be judged a "hypocritical failure" unless it produces a democratically-elected second chamber.

Finally, another prominent British political scientist, Anthony King, has argued that Britain no longer has a coherent set of constitutional principles. Because of the piecemeal constitutional changes over the past quarter century by both Conservative and Labor governments, traditional interpretations of the British constitution no longer adequately describe contemporary practice. But no alternative theory has emerged as a guide. Britain has moved away from its traditional status as a majoritarian democracy (all-powerful single-party governments based on holding a majority of seats in the House of Commons) without becoming a fully-fledged consensus democracy, featuring proportional representation and coalition governments.

Further Constitutional Change on the Horizon?

The second and third Labor terms have consolidated and extended constitutional reforms despite their lack of emphasis in party election manifestos and discussion during election campaigns. In a 2006 White Paper, the Labor government endorsed further, if gradual, reform though elected mayors and more decision making power to local councils in England. The succession of Gordon Brown to the premiership has reinvigorated the constitutional reform agenda.

In his first speech to the House of Commons, Brown set out further constitutional reform proposals, as elaborated in a government Green paper on the topic. Some of these were for immediate action, such as shifting powers from the executive toward parliament in appointments and oversight of the executive, including giving the Commons ultimate decision making power for international treaties and going to war, the latter in response to criticism of Tony Blair taking the country into the Iraq War on bad information. As long as there is a single-party majority in the House of Commons, a government would probably have little to fear from these changes under normal circumstances.

The potentially more radical ones, however, such as a bill of rights, a written constitution, and perhaps even a change in the electoral system for Westminster, were only proposed for study, consultation, and discussion. In Mr. Brown's words, his constitutional reform plan was "a route map" towards change, not a "final blueprint." Furthermore, it explicitly refused to address the West Lothian question, arguing that to have two different sets of MPs with different voting responsibilities would be "the slippery slope towards the breakup of the United Kingdom." Addressing the West Lothian question would, of course, also make it more difficult for Labor to accumulate a majority in the Commons on such votes.

Some commentators have said that Gordon Brown's specifically proposed changes amount to considerably less than Tony Blair's, such as devolution, the near-elimination of hereditary peers, implementation of the European Convention on Human Rights, and the *Freedom of Information Act.* But those proposed for discussion rather than immediate legislation could go far beyond Blair's changes. Thus far Brown only proposes to trim some of the "elective dictatorship" around the edges.

But a bill of rights (and responsibilities), a written constitution, and a change in the voting system could limit the power of the central executive as well as make single-party government less likely. Such changes would shift power toward the citizens of the United Kingdom.

The Conservatives have opposed measures such as an appointed House of Lords, the *Human Rights Act,* further devolution to Wales, and the new Supreme Court, plus, of course, greater European Union authority over member states. They have proposed strengthening the House of Commons against the executive and an elected House of Lords. More recently, party leader David Cameron has proposed a British Bill of Rights as a better-balanced substitute for direct enforcement of general European standards through the *Human Rights Act.* He has established a committee under the chairmanship of former cabinet minister Kenneth Clarke to develop plans for a Conservative policy on the future of democracy. Some form of "English votes for English questions" in parliament (the West Lothian question) will be the focus of that policy.

The Liberal Democrats have the most radical positions on constitutional reform, advocating a written constitution, a bill of rights, and a more proportional voting system. An English Constitutional Convention has been formed to press for self-governing powers for that part of the United Kingdom.

While the Labor government led by Blair engaged in various constitutional innovations for decentralization and individual rights, it has not disturbed the core of the strongly executive-centered Westminster system. In fact, by dominating the cabinet, the extensive use of politically-appointed advisers throughout the executive, attempting, not always successfully, to keep the House of Commons under strong party direction, rarely attending parliamentary debates, and the expressed desire to have a completely appointed House of Lords, Blair's style can be considered more "presidential" than previous prime ministers. British scholar Ross McKibbin has condemned the Blair government for having eviscerated any meaningful constitutional reform, especially changing the electoral system, which would restrain single-party executive authority.

Nevertheless, institutional rearrangements often have unanticipated consequences. Although New Labor legislation on constitutional matters claims not to disturb the principle of parliamentary sovereignty, this constitutional convention has already been compromised. Congruent with the process of decentralization in other European countries, devolution is likely to be entrenched *de facto* if not *de jure.* Some observers have begun calling Britain a "quasi-federal" political system. Although specific powers are granted to each devolved government, disputes over which level has authority over certain policies will eventually arise, especially when governments are led by different parties. Even without a comprehensive bill of rights, incorporation of the European Convention on Human Rights may mean a stronger, more politically active judiciary, a form of creeping judicial review. Lords reform has become so controversial because it is a struggle over how much the second chamber should be allowed to check the Commons and the sitting government. Incorporation of the European Convention on Human Rights, as well as a limited form of joint authority with Ireland over Northern Ireland and possible membership of the European common currency and central bank, suggest that Britain may be moving into new patterns of international shared authority in areas heretofore considered exclusively within the domain of the sovereign state. Regional policies of the European Union even may be helping regions circumvent British central authority and sustaining ethnonationalist demands. If the SNP ever wins a majority in the Scottish Parliament, the United Kingdom will be faced with a "Quebec scenario," whereby control of a subordinate level of government enhances secessionist claims.

The "third way" ideas of Anthony Giddens, influential in the New Labor government, propose a restructuring of government to promote "subsidiarity" (the taking of decisions at the lowest level possible) and correcting the "democratic deficit " through constitutional reform, greater transparency, and more local democracy. Through such a process, Britain would become a more complex polity institutionally. This would demand cultivating habits of conciliation, cooperation, and consent rather than the usual reliance upon single party government, parliamentary laws, and executive orders. This already has occurred through the formation of coalition governments in Scotland and Wales as well as in Northern Ireland. Having additional levels of elected government also has created difficulties for central party organizations attempting to exert control over their parties in these jurisdictions.

Although Prime Minister Brown tried to distance himself in his early days in office from the government of Tony Blair, in constitutional matters he has built on the Blair legacy. Whatever one's view of the desirability and impact of the changes, New Labor has been persistent in pursuing most of its 1997 pledges on constitutional reform. Although delays and retreats have occurred on some issues, the implications of these changes will continue to be felt in British politics for some time to come. The Labor government under Tony Blair has secured a place in history as a constitutional innovator with a long-lasting legacy.

DONLEY T. STUDLAR is Eberly Family Distinguished Professor of Political Science at West Virginia University and served as Executive Secretary of the British Politics Group, 1994 to 2005. The first version of this article appeared in *Harvard International Review*, Spring 1999, and this revision was prepared in September 2007. Professor Studlar recently published an article, "The United Kingdom: From Postwar Collectivist Consensus to 2lst Century Neo-liberalism," in the September 2007 (Vol. 5, No. 3) edition of the online journal *The Forum,* http://www.bepress.com/forum/

The Historic Legacy of Tony Blair

"The public service and constitutional reforms undertaken by the prime minister represent historic achievements, but in recent years these have been overshadowed by the Iraq War. . . . "

VERNON BOGDANOR

Every hero, Emerson once said, becomes a bore at last. The Blair era, an era of unparalleled success for the Labor Party that began so triumphantly in 1997, is now moving, inexorably, toward its close. Electorally, Prime Minister Tony Blair has been by far the most successful leader that Labor has ever had, the only one to have won three consecutive elections, two of them with landslide majorities. In fact, he has had a longer continuous run in office than any prime minister since the Napoleonic wars, with the sole exception of Margaret Thatcher.

Moreover, Blair has led the most successful left-of-center government in Europe. Of the three leaders who shared the new dawn of social democracy in the late 1990s, only he survives; both Lionel Jospin, the former French prime minister, and Gerhard Schröder, the former German chancellor, have departed in ignominy, almost forgotten figures. Yet, despite all this, Blair's current reputation is low, and recent allegations that honors have been given in return for party contributions have not helped. Indeed, survey evidence suggests he is now the most unpopular prime minister since opinion polls began.

This is unlikely to prove the final verdict of history. The twilight of a prime ministership, or of a presidency for that matter, is not the best vantage point from which to analyze its significance. In the United States, for example, the reputations of Harry Truman and Gerald Ford were low when those men left office, but have risen steadily since. Ultimately, Blair's tenure of leadership will be remembered for three things: for his reforms of British public services; for a wide-ranging set of constitutional reforms, most of which occurred between 1997 and 2001; and, finally, for the war in Iraq.

The Third Way Taken

Constitutional reform occupied much of Blair's first term. The second term, which ran from 2001 to 2005, was dominated by public service reform and by the war in Iraq. Both of these involved bold if unpopular decisions. Both alienated Blair from his party. Public service reform, however, is likely to be accepted both by the British people and by the Labor Party—in contrast with the Iraq War, which is in the process of being repudiated by both.

Before coming to office, Blair modernized the Labor Party, much as Bill Clinton did America's Democrats. Blair transformed Old Labor into New Labor, removing the commitment in the party's constitution to the nationalization of the means of production, distribution, and exchange. Indeed, the 1997 general election was the first since Labor became a national party in which nationalization was not an issue. In the place of traditional Labor bromides, Blair touted a "Third Way" between old-fashioned socialism and unfettered capitalism. Tony Giddens, a leading theorist of the Third Way, has argued that Blair was successful because he understood that changes in society, such as the decline of the working class, globalization, and the growth of a knowledge-based economy, had rendered old-style social democracy irrelevant.

Until Blair, Labor had been imprisoned in an old pattern of mind according to which the public sector was inherently good and the private inherently bad. New Labor seeks to escape this crude dichotomy. The essence of New Labor is that public services, if they are to improve, need to use the techniques of private business and the market to increase efficiency. Injections of new money into government programs, therefore, should be dependent on reform.

Moreover, the state should no longer be expected to be the sole provider of public services. Thus, while public schooling and health care under the National Health Service remain free, the business sector is being encouraged to finance new schools—City Academies—for the state sector, particularly in blighted inner cities; and Foundation Hospitals are being allowed, and indeed encouraged, to establish contracts with private bodies to improve their services.

These changes are likely to prove permanent. They go with the grain of British opinion. Most voters are nonideological. They care little whether schools or hospitals are financed privately or publicly so long as their children learn to read and write and medical operations are carried out speedily and effectively.

Thus, while it is possible that the balance between public and private provision will alter with time, no future government of the left is likely to abandon City Academies or Foundation Hospitals. Here, too, there are perhaps parallels with the reforms in America by Clinton and others who sought to modernize the Democratic Party.

Public service issues are, for most British voters, the most important issues, the ones on which they judge the government of the day. The chances of success for the next prime minister, therefore, largely depend on the skill with which he continues public service reforms. But continued reform will be difficult, since public finances will have to be operated on a more stringent basis than has hitherto been the case, because the rate of economic growth is slowing. Moreover, Blair's likely successor, Chancellor of the Exchequer Gordon Brown, is widely thought to be less sympathetic to major public service reform than Blair. (The prime minister has expressed regret with himself for not pressing for more radical change.)

In addition, Brown will face a rejuvenated Conservative Party, under its new leader, David Cameron, who argues that the Conservatives are better equipped to continue the process of reforming public services than is a party of the left that has to struggle to persuade trade unions to accept a role for the private sector. The question of which party is better placed to manage public services will be the key issue of British politics in the post-Blair era.

The New Constitution

Britain now has a new constitution, the result of some very radical reforms implemented since Labor came to power in 1997—and this represents a second enduring achievement of Blair. The reforms include a series of referendums and measures devolving more political authority to Scotland, Wales, and Northern Ireland, in effect putting the non-English parts of the United Kingdom into a quasi-federal relationship with Westminster. Scotland and Wales now have directly elected legislatures. Northern Ireland has one as well, though it is currently in abeyance. Proportional representation in elections has been introduced for these devolved bodies, for a new London authority, and for elections to the European Parliament.

London, for the first time in British history, has a directly elected mayor, following a referendum. Other local authorities have been required to adopt cabinet systems of government, while a few have directly elected mayors following referendums. Today, 5 percent of registered voters can *require* a local authority to hold a referendum on the mayor option. The ballot initiative is a political instrument familiar in the United States, but this is the first statutory provision for its use in Britain.

The Human Rights Act of 1998 requires public bodies to comply with the provisions of the European Convention on Human Rights, allowing judges to declare a British statute incompatible with the Convention and providing a fast-track procedure for Parliament to amend or repeal such a statute. This comes near to providing Britain with a bill of rights. In addition, the Freedom of Information Act of 2000 provides, for the first time in British history, a statutory right to freedom of information, subject to certain important exemptions.

The Political Parties, Elections, and Referendums Act of 2000 requires the registration of parties and places controls on political donations and national campaign expenditures. It also provides for the establishment of an Electoral Commission to oversee elections and to advise on improvements in electoral procedures. This act brings political parties, for the first time, within the framework of British law. Previously, they had been treated, for the purposes of the law, as voluntary organizations, like golf or tennis clubs.

The House of Lords Act of 1999 has removed all but 92 of the hereditary peers from the House of Lords, as the first phase of a wider reform of that body. The Constitutional Reform Act of 2005 has restructured the historic office of Lord Chancellor, establishing a new Supreme Court and removing its judges from the House of Lords. The head of the judiciary will now be the Lord Chief Justice, not the Lord Chancellor, and the Lord Chancellor will no longer be the Speaker of the House of Lords. Instead, the House of Lords chooses its own Lord Speaker. All this goes toward creating a system of separation of powers in Britain. Before this act, the role of the Lord Chancellor was a standing contradiction to the separation of powers, since he was, at the same time, head of the judiciary, Speaker of the Lords, and a cabinet minister. Now the first two of these positions have been devolved to others.

Blair revived a liberal imperialism that owed more to William Gladstone than to traditional Labor doctrine.

Some of the constitutional changes of the past decade (including the Bank of England's new independence in the setting of monetary policy) make the British system of government more like the American—though, of course, they remain fundamentally different, since Britain is still a parliamentary system while the United States has a presidential system. Almost any one of these reforms, taken singly, would constitute a radical change. Taken together, they allow us to label the years since 1997 a historic era of constitutional reform. Indeed, these years bear comparison with two previous periods of constitutional revision in Britain: (1) the 1830s, the era of the Great Reform Act; and (2) the years immediately preceding the First World War, which saw the passage of the Parliament Act of 1911, restricting the powers of the House of Lords; and the abortive Government of Ireland Act of 1914, providing home rule to Ireland; as well as agitation by suffragettes to extend the vote to women, who finally gained the franchise in 1918.

The recent changes, radical though they are, by no means complete the process of constitutional reform. The Blair government is currently holding discussions on reforms of party finance and on further reform of the House of Lords, perhaps including the introduction of an elected element. Moreover, Brown, the likely prime minister-to-be, gives an even higher priority than Blair has done to constitutional reform. Brown is eager to see an elected House of Lords, and has made speeches suggesting that Britain should follow nearly every other democracy in the world and produce a codified constitution.

Since Blair came to office, Britain has been engaged in a process quite unique in the democratic world, that of converting an uncodified constitution into a codified one, but by piecemeal means. There is today neither the political will to do more, nor any consensus on what the final resting-place should be. The British, a member of a public ethics panel recently declared, seem to "like to live in a series of halfway houses." It is beginning to look as if they will need to accustom themselves to living in such halfway houses for rather a long time, at least until the foundations of the new constitution have been fully tested by experience.

Constitutional reform, in short, is an ongoing story in British politics. It is unlikely to come to an end with Blair's resignation. What is already clear, however, is that the constitutional reforms of the Blair government are far-reaching in their implications and almost certainly permanent. They will be remembered long after most current political squabbles are forgotten.

Gladstone Redux

The public service and constitutional reforms undertaken by the prime minister represent historic achievements, but in recent years these have been overshadowed by the Iraq War, a war for which many will never forgive him. Before the invasion of Iraq, more than 40 percent of voters had a favorable opinion of Blair. That figure fell, immediately after the war began, to around 30 percent, and it has hardly risen since. Only 33 percent now think that the invasion was justified, while around two-thirds of those polled believe that Blair either exaggerated the threat from Iraq to justify the war or deliberately deceived the public.

In Iraq, however, survey evidence at the beginning of 2006 indicated that a large majority of Iraqis approved of the ouster of Saddam Hussein. Oddly enough, Blair may have more supporters in Baghdad than in Birmingham, where he is seen as anti-Muslim, even though he might argue that he has liberated more Muslims—in Afghanistan, Kosovo, and Iraq—than any previous British prime minister.

In Britain, it is often suggested that Blair has been George W. Bush's poodle, tamely following the American president. Yet Blair's conception of foreign policy was unveiled well before Bush came to the White House. Speaking in April 1999 in Chicago, Blair said, "We need to enter a new millennium where dictators know that they cannot get away with ethnic cleansing or repress their people with impunity." His next sentence defined his foreign policy. "We are fighting," he said of the war in Kosovo, "not for territory but for values."

The constitutional reforms of the Blair government are far-reaching in their implications and almost certainly permanent.

Blair called for "a new doctrine of international community" that would qualify the principle of noninterference and explicitly recognize the facts of interdependence. Britain, together with other countries that sought to uphold international morality, had a right if not a duty to intervene where necessary to prevent genocide, to deal with "massive flows of refugees" that become "threats to international peace and security," and to combat rogue states. Blair revived a liberal imperialism that owes more to William Gladstone than to traditional Labor doctrine, just as Bush's foreign policy may owe more to Woodrow Wilson than it does to the neoconservatives.

In the past, British foreign policy had been based for the most part on a cool and pragmatic calculation of the national interest. The British had, it was suggested, permanent interests but no permanent allies. The main concern of British foreign policy had been to preserve the balance of power in Europe, whether against Louis XIV, Napoleon, the Kaiser, or Hitler. Moreover, British governments, whether Labor, Conservative, or Liberal, had sought stability and a reduction in international tensions—appeasement in the best sense of that much-abused term.

In the early days of the Labor Party, at the beginning of the twentieth century, there had been much talk of an alternative approach, a "socialist foreign policy," but it was never clear precisely what this meant. In its first election manifesto in 1906, Labor devoted just one half-sentence to foreign policy: "Wars are fought to make the rich richer. . . ." The sentence concluded: " . . . . and school children are still neglected." Keir Hardie, Labor's first leader, felt that foreign policy issues were perfectly straightforward. Indeed, a Labor foreign policy was unnecessary, since the working class in all countries would rise up to prevent the ruling classes from making war. Thus, the coming to power of socialist governments would enable foreign ministries everywhere to shut up shop. Had not Karl Marx insisted that the working class had no country? This illusion died, of course, in 1914.

In 1937, Labor leader Clement Attlee, in his book *The Labor Party in Perspective,* had to confess that his party had "no real constructive foreign policy, but shared the views which were traditional in radical circles." The foreign policy of the first two, minority, Labor governments had not in practice been very different from that of its Liberal predecessors. After World War II, under the foreign secretaryship of Ernest Bevin, from 1945 to 1951, Labor became committed to collective security, and the postwar Labor government played a major role in the setting up of NATO.

All the while, however, there had been an alternative principle of foreign policy on the left, the policy of humanitarian intervention. Gladstone had been its greatest practitioner. He had certainly not equated liberalism with appeasement or nonintervention. When he denounced the Bulgarian Horrors in 1876, he was not suggesting that Britain should disinterest herself in the Balkans. On the contrary, his complaint was that Britain was intervening on the wrong side, supporting the oppressor, Turkey, rather than the victim, Bulgaria. Indeed, wherever there was injustice, Gladstone sometimes seemed inclined to imply, Britain should make her voice felt even if this led to armed conflict. For "However deplorable wars may be," he insisted in one of his Midlothian speeches in 1879, "they are among the necessities of our condition; and there are times when justice, when faith, when the failure of mankind, require a man not to shrink from the responsibility of undertaking them."

So it was that, in 1882, Gladstone inaugurated a humanitarian but "temporary" occupation of Egypt, an occupation that lasted more than 70 years. The one occasion on which President Gamal Abdel Nasser of Egypt met then-Foreign Secretary Anthony Eden, in 1954, was when British troops were at last being removed from Egypt. Nasser was invited to dinner at the British Embassy in Cairo, and said that he would be glad to enter the building from which Egypt had been governed for so long. "Not governed, perhaps," Eden replied, "advised, rather." Perhaps the Americans are saying something similar in Iraq.

It is this Gladstonian foreign policy that Blair has revived. He is perhaps the most Gladstonian prime minister to have occupied 10 Downing Street since the Grand Old Man himself.

The Moral Imperative

The impact of Labor's new foreign policy was first felt in the Balkans. Prime Minister John Major's Conservative government had resisted involvement in the former Yugoslavia, arguing that what happened in the Balkans did not affect British interests. The policy was one of appeasement. Appeasement, however, works best in a community unified by broadly shared values and with some sense of mutual obligations and interests. It had as little to offer in the world of Slobodan Milosevic, Al Qaeda, and Saddam Hussein—the world of ethnic cleansing and the suicide bomber—as it had in the Europe of the 1930s, the Europe of Hitler and Mussolini. In the Balkans, as in Iraq, governments felt little sense of obligation toward their peoples, and there was not even a semblance of community or shared values.

In March 1999, the Blair government committed troops to Kosovo to counter what it regarded as a Serbian threat of genocide against the Albanian Muslim population. Intervention was, Blair believed, a moral duty. The same was true, he believed, in Afghanistan and Iraq. Of course, ministers also insisted that Afghan terrorism and Iraqi weapons of mass destruction constituted a genuine danger to Britain. Indeed, after the attacks of September 11, 2001, on the United States, the definition of British security widened. The war on terror meant that security involved more than mere territorial defense. It meant tackling terrorist networks and financing, and perhaps also removing regimes that promoted or allowed terrorist activity.

Still, this broader definition of security came to be intertwined with humanitarian arguments against the horrible regimes in Kabul and Baghdad. Part at least of the impetus for Blair's foreign policy derives from its moral fervor, not from any careful calculation of British interests. The British went to war in Kosovo, and to some extent in Afghanistan and Iraq also, partly on humanitarian grounds. It would certainly be difficult to pretend that what happened in Kosovo affected British national interests.

And the Blair approach diverged from more than the traditional British focus on narrow national interest. In the past, British foreign policy had also on the whole ignored the internal nature of different regimes. Where it was in Britain's interest to form an alliance with a regime whose internal politics were repugnant to her, as with the Soviet Union in 1941, she would unhesitatingly do so. The twentieth century, however, had seemed to show that the internal nature of a regime could not be divorced from its foreign policy, and that how a country treated its own people might well prove a good indicator of how it would behave in international affairs.

Blair's interventionist foreign policy offended the instincts of many if not most Labor members of Parliament, as it did the social democratic parties of Western Europe. These parties, while being committed to collective security, have been much more hesitant than Blair when it comes to the use of force. Labor was in fact the only social democratic party in Western Europe to support the Iraq War. It is by no means clear, therefore, whether the Blair reorientation of British foreign policy will survive into a new prime ministership.

A Good European?

Blair's foreign policy aligned Britain with the United States rather than with France and Germany, hitherto the leading powers in the European Union. This is at first sight surprising. For whatever President Bush is, he is not a man of the left. He has defined himself as conservative, or perhaps a neoconservative. Classical American conservatism, however, derives from John Quincy Adams's dictum of 1821, according to which America "goes not abroad in search of monsters to destroy." Conservatives in the United States have generally adhered to a "realist" foreign policy, exemplified by former Secretary of State Henry Kissinger, an approach based on hardheaded calculations of the American national interest. It was, by contrast, Woodrow Wilson, a liberal, who had asked a very nonconservative question— How can the world be made safe for democracy?—a question that seemed to gain more relevance after 9-11. And Bush's foreign policy has more in common with that of Wilson than with that of Kissinger. Bush is a Wilsonian, not a conservative, just as Blair is a Gladstonian. Gladstone, after all, would have had far more in common with Wilson than with Kissinger's realism or the principle of *raison d'etat,* another form of realism, which animates Gaullist France.

All the same, Blair's foreign policy alignment with the United States seems paradoxical, since from the time he came to power he had sought to improve relations with the European Union and show himself to be a good European. In the Saint Malo Declaration of 1998, for example, Blair stressed the need for a European defense force. On receiving the Charlemagne prize in May 1999, he insisted that "full use" be made of "the potential Europe has to be a global force for good." His government seemed the first to display a constructive attitude toward Europe since Edward Heath's administration more than 30 years ago.

Blair was successful because he understood that changes in society had rendered old-style social democracy irrelevant.

The paradox, however, is more apparent than real. Blair's ethical foreign policy is incompatible with being a good European only if being a good European is defined in Gaullist terms. In the Iraq crisis, President Jacques Chirac simply proceeded to label the French position "European" and rebuked as *non-communautaire* anyone who could not accept it. Yet Gaullism is not necessarily the same as Europeanism. Indeed, Gaullism may be regarded as but a high-sounding name for the pursuit of the French national interest, a pursuit that has dominated French foreign policy under governments of both left and right since the inauguration of the Fifth Republic in 1958. This is not the same as a European foreign policy.

Gaullism rests on a limited conception of Europe in which Germany remains subordinate while Britain keeps to the sidelines. Enlargement, however, is already causing a diplomatic revolution in Europe. The ex-communist states, as the Iraq crisis shows, are far more likely to accept the Anglo-American position in foreign policy than the Gaullist. (When these states announced that they supported Bush and Blair, President Chirac accused them of being *mal élevé*—badly brought up.) Moreover, the ex-communist states are far more likely to accept the British conception of a loosely organized Europe than the more federalist conceptions of the Germans. Having struggled hard to win the right of national self-determination from Moscow, they are hardly eager to surrender their sovereignty to a supranational organization. The negative outcome of the French referendum on the EU constitution in May 2005 shows that President Chirac's conception of Europe is not shared even by a majority of voters in France, let alone the continent as a whole.

From the time of Charles de Gaulle's veto, in 1963, of Britain's first application to enter the European Community, as it was then called, until the European Union's enlargement during the 1990s, France was the dominant power in Europe, and a Franco-German motor drove the continent. France and Germany set the agenda; Britain was cast in the role of spoiler on the sidelines, the bad boy of Europe. Today, as Prime Minister Blair prepares to leave office, Britain is in a much stronger position in foreign affairs, able to influence both the United States and Europe, as both continents find themselves groping toward a new conception of collective security in a world facing new kinds of threats.

The "International Community"

Of course, the doctrine of humanitarian intervention raises as many questions as it answers, and both Bush and Blair have been struggling to grapple with them. Who is to decide when such intervention is justified? Is humanitarian intervention not in danger of leading to universal war for the sake of universal peace? Where is the "new doctrine of international community" of which Blair spoke at Chicago? One obvious, if flawed, answer to the question of who decides the conditions under which intervention is justified, is that it should be the United Nations. That,

indeed, was the answer given by critics of the war in Iraq, as it had been by critics of the Suez War in 1956.

Woodrow Wilson's conception of the League of Nations had been that of a Parliament of Man. The United Nations, however, is hardly that and perhaps can never be that, since not all of the member states represented there derive legitimacy from the consent of those whom they govern. Perhaps it can be realized only on a more limited basis by those countries whose governments do owe their legitimacy to the citizens whom they govern—that is, the democracies. Perhaps there is a need for the democracies to get together, to form a caucus, a new organization to help secure their interests in an increasingly dangerous international environment.

Blair at least pointed in this direction, as he searched for a middle way between Gaullism and unilateralism. The Gaullists had sought to unite Europe on the basis of an anti-American foreign policy. But such a policy, as the Iraq crisis showed, serves only to divide Europe. It could never unite it. Some in the Bush administration, by contrast, have sought a unilateral approach to problems of international terrorism and rogue states. This, too, has caused a rift in the Atlantic alliance, and it could never form the basis for a stable international order. The "new doctrine of international community" must, therefore, be genuinely multilateralist. Working out precisely what this new doctrine should be constitutes the most important challenge facing Blair's successor as British foreign policy finds itself struggling to adapt the concept of collective security to the conditions of the post–9-11 era.

Is There Anything Left?

The central question raised by Blair's long premiership—and it is highly relevant to the American left as well—is whether there is anything left of social democracy as an ideology. Blair's public service reforms are, in practice, a continuation of those championed by Major, his Conservative predecessor. Blair's constitutional reforms undermine the social democratic principle that benefits and burdens should depend on need and not on geography. For Scotland and Wales are now following principles of state welfare divergent from those of Westminster. In foreign policy, humanitarian interventionism has few roots in Labor's past.

In 1894, a Liberal Chancellor of the Exchequer, Sir William Harcourt, declared, "We are all socialists now." What he meant was that all believed in state intervention. The twentieth century was to be, for much of its duration, the century of state intervention. However, under Margaret Thatcher, the Conservative prime minister from 1979 to 1990, the state began to withdraw from society and the economy. Blair did nothing to reverse this process. Indeed, he could persuade British voters to support Labor only by, in effect, assuring them that "We are none of us socialists now." It is a strange legacy for a prime minister of the left.

VERNON BOGDANOR is a professor of government at Oxford University. His latest book, *The New British Constitution,* will be published by Allen Lane/Penguin next year.

Muslims' Veils Test Limits of Britain's Tolerance

JANE PERLEZ

Increasingly, Muslim women in Britain take their children to school and run errands covered head to toe in flowing black gowns that allow only a slit for their eyes. On a Sunday afternoon in Hyde Park, groups of black-clad Muslim women relaxed on the green baize lawn among the in-line skaters and badminton players.

Their appearance, like little else, has unnerved other Britons, testing the limits of tolerance here and fueling the debate over the role of Muslims in British life.

Many veiled women say they are targets of abuse. Meanwhile, there are growing efforts to place legal curbs on the full-face Muslim veil, known as the niqab.

There have been numerous examples in the past year. A lawyer dressed in a niqab was told by an immigration judge that she could not represent a client because, he said, he could not hear her. A teacher wearing a niqab was dismissed from her school. A student who was barred from wearing a niqab took her case to the courts, and lost. In reaction, the British educational authorities are proposing a ban on the niqab in schools altogether.

A leading Labor Party politician, Jack Straw, scolded women last year for coming to see him in his district office in the niqab. Prime Minister Tony Blair has called the niqab a "mark of separation."

What is unnerving to some is a symbol of identity to others

David Sexton, a columnist for *The Evening Standard,* wrote recently that the niqab was an affront and that Britain had been "too deferential."

"It says that all men are such brutes that if exposed to any more normally clothed women, they cannot be trusted to behave—and that all women who dress any more scantily like that are indecent," Mr. Sexton wrote. "It's abusive, a walking rejection of all our freedoms."

Although the number of women wearing the niqab has increased in the past several years, only a tiny percentage of women among Britain's two million Muslims cover themselves completely. It is impossible to say how many exactly.

Some who wear the niqab, particularly younger women who have taken it up recently, concede that it is a frontal expression of Islamic identity, which they have embraced since Sept. 11, 2001, as a form of rebellion against the policies of the Blair government in Iraq, and at home.

"For me it is not just a piece of clothing, it's an act of faith, it's solidarity," said a 24-year-old program scheduler at a broadcasting company in London, who would allow only her last name, al-Shaikh, to be printed, saying she wanted to protect her privacy. "9/11 was a wake-up call for young Muslims," she said.

At times she receives rude comments, including, Ms. Shaikh said, from a woman at her workplace who told her she had no right to be there. Ms. Shaikh says she plans to file a complaint.

When she is on the street, she often answers back. "A few weeks ago, a lady said, 'I think you look crazy.' I said, 'How dare you go around telling people how to dress,' and walked off. Sometimes I feel I have to reply. Islam does teach you that you must defend your religion."

She started experimenting with the niqab at Brunel University in West London, a campus of intense Islamic activism. She hesitated at first because her mother saw it as a "form of extremism, which is understandable," she said, adding that her mother has since come around.

Other Muslims find the practice objectionable, a step backward for a group that is under pressure after the terrorist attack on London's transit system in July 2005.

"After the July 7 attacks, this is not the time to be antagonizing Britain by presenting Muslims as something sinister," said Imran Ahmad, the author of *"Unimagined,"* an autobiography about growing up Muslim in Britain, and the leader of British Muslims for Secular Democracy. "The veil is so steeped in subjugation, I find it so offensive someone would want to create such barriers. It's retrograde."

Since South Asians started coming to Britain in large numbers in the 1960s, a small group of usually older, undereducated women have worn the niqab. It was most often seen as a sign of subjugation.

Many more Muslim women wear the head scarf, called the hijab, covering all or some of their hair. Unlike in France, Turkey and Tunisia, where students in state schools and civil servants are banned from covering their hair, in Britain, Muslim women can wear the head scarf, and indeed the niqab, almost anywhere, for now.

But that tolerance is slowly eroding. Even some who wear the niqab, like Faatema Mayata, a 24-year-old psychology and religious studies teacher, agreed there were limits.

"How can you teach when you are covering your face?" she said, sitting with a cup of tea in her living room in Blackburn, a northern English town, her niqab tucked away because she was within the confines of her home.

She has worn the niqab since she was 12, when she was sent by her parents to an all-girl boarding school. The niqab was not, as many Britons seemed to think, a sign of extremism, she said.

She condemned Britain's involvement in Iraq, and she described the departure of Mr. Blair at the end of this month as "good riddance of bad rubbish." But, she added, "there are many Muslims like this sitting at home having tea, and not taking any interest in jihad."

The niqab, to her, is about identity. "If I dressed in a Western way I could be a Hindu, I could be anything," she said. "This way I feel comfortable in my identity as a Muslim woman."

No one else in her family wears the niqab. Her husband, Ibrahim Boodi, a social worker, was indifferent, she said. "If I took it off today, he wouldn't care."

An article of clothing raises a host of thorny legal, religious and cultural questions.

She drives her old Alfa Romeo to the supermarket, and other drivers take no exception, she said. But when she is walking she is often stopped, she said. "People ask, 'Why do you wear that?' A lot of people assume I'm oppressed, that I don't speak English. I don't care. I've got a brain."

Some British commentators have complained that mosques encourage women to wear the niqab, a practice they have said should be stopped.

At the East London Mosque, one of the largest mosques in the capital, the chief imam, Abdul Qayyum, studied in Saudi Arabia and is trained in the Wahhabi school of Islam. The community relations officer at the mosque, Ehsan Abdullah Hannan, said the imam's daughter wore the niqab.

At Friday Prayer recently, the women were crowded into a small windowless room upstairs, away from the main hall for the men.

A handful of young women wore the niqab, and they spoke effusively about their reasons. "Wearing the niqab means you will get a good grade and go to paradise," said Hodo Muse, 19, a Somali woman. "Every day people are giving me dirty looks for wearing it, but when you wear something for God you get a boost."

One woman, Sajida Khaton, 24, interviewed as she sat discreetly in a Pizza Hut, said she did not wear the veil on the subway, a precaution her husband encourages for safety reasons. Sometimes, she said, she gets a kick out of the mocking.

"'All right gorgeous,'" she said she had heard men say as she walked along the street. "I feel empowered," she said. "They'd like to see, and they can't."

She often comes to the neighborhood restaurant along busy Whitechapel Road in East London for a slice or two, a habit, she said, that shows that even veiled women are well integrated into Britain's daily life.

"I'm in Pizza Hut with my son," said Ms. Khaton, nodding at her 4-year-old and speaking in a soft East London accent that bore no hint of her Bangladeshi heritage. "I was born here, I've never been to Bangladesh. I certainly don't feel Bangladeshi. So when they say, 'Go back home,' where should I go?"

The Gaullist Revolutionary

"The French people have chosen change, and it is change that I will implement." So declared Nicolas Sarkozy in his victory speech on May 6, before wildly cheering supporters in central Paris, shortly after the Gaullist candidate was elected France's new president by a decisive 53% of the vote. As the French prepare for the handover of power from President Jacques Chirac on May 16, their country seethes with a strange mixture of celebration and apprehension. Since Mr Sarkozy is known for his hyperactivity, nobody doubts that he will move fast. But France is also undoubtedly heading for a period of turbulence.

Once again, the French turned out en masse on polling day. At 84%, voter participation was way above the latest comparable elections in Britain (61%) or America (64%). Mr Sarkozy's score was not a landslide. But, fully six points above that of his Socialist opponent, Ségolène Royal, it was the highest for a Gaullist candidate—apart from Mr Chirac's run-off score against the far-right Jean-Marie Le Pen in 2002—since Georges Pompidou in 1969. At 52, Mr Sarkozy will become the first French president born after the second World War; the first Gaullist president never to have served in government under Charles de Gaulle himself; the first Gaullist president since Pompidou not to have graduated from the elite Ecole Nationale d'Administration; and the first president whose father (a Hungarian immigrant) was not French.

It is a particularly remarkable performance. Until a few weeks ago, Mr Sarkozy was a member of an unpopular government under a worn-out president. After 12 years of Mr Chirac, this was the Socialist Party's election to lose. As it turned out, Mr Sarkozy managed to style himself as a fresh force for change, while Ms Royal failed to convince. Her message was incoherent: she had 100 campaign pledges, "99 too many", in the words of one visiting American political strategist. Her strategy was not credible: having denounced the centrists before the first round, she then described an abrupt U-turn to court them during the second. And her television debate performance raised doubts about her character: her explosion of what she called "healthy anger" at Mr Sarkozy seemed as aggressive as it was unprovoked.

Mr Sarkozy, on the other hand, had a clearer sense of purpose. He stuck doggedly to one chief message—France needs to change and the French need to work more—and hardened it with a right-wing law-and-order accent that he kept up even during the second-round quest for the centrist vote. This enabled him both to bag some two-thirds of Mr Le Pen's voters, despite the far-right leader's appeal to his supporters to abstain, and to

secure the same share (40%) of the centrist vote as Ms Royal, despite a declaration by the centrist candidate, François Bayrou, that he would not vote for Mr Sarkozy.

In some parts of France Ms Royal did very well. She came in the top 11 of the 20 arrondissements of Paris, as well as in a large swathe of central and south-western France, and in many of the working-class banlieues. She also won among the under-24s and older working voters aged 45–59, according to Ipsos, a pollster. Most women, however, did not vote for one of their own: Mr Sarkozy secured 52% of the female vote, as well as of the over-60s and the 25–44s. He also managed, spectacularly, to win in the industrial department of Nord, long a Communist and then a Socialist stronghold, even in such working towns as Tourcoing and Valenciennes. All those campaign stops on the factory floor, posing beside muscular men in overalls and hard hats, seem to have paid off.

On election night at the Salle Gaveau, a Paris concert theatre, the atmosphere was electric. Sarkozy supporters packed the hall to await the results, while hundreds more gathered in the street outside. When Mr Sarkozy at last appeared on the stage, picking his way up the steps with uncharacteristic deliberation, his message was clear: he would "break with the ideas, the habits and the behaviour of the past" in order "to get France moving again". His advisers, watching from the wings, were unequivocal. "Nicolas has a clear mandate for change," said Pierre Lellouche, a deputy and a foreign-policy aide, who may be given a national-security job in the Sarkozy administration. "He's an enormously hard worker, and is courageous, so he will implement it."

Le Tourbillon

With unfortunate symbolism, Mr Sarkozy then jetted off to Malta last week—along with Cécilia, his wife, and ten-year-old son—to spend three days aboard a private yacht, courtesy of a French corporate raider. The idea was to take time off to prepare for office. But the outline of his programme, and his team, is already fairly clear. He is expected to name François Fillon, who brought in a contested pension reform and is his jogging partner, as prime minister. He will take Claude Guéant, a steady-minded prefect and long-time chief of staff, with him to that job at the Elysée Palace.

He has promised a small cabinet, of just 15 members, with half the posts going to women. Michèle Alliot-Marie, the defence minister, Rachida Dati, his spokeswoman, Valérie Pécresse, his party's spokeswoman, Christine Lagarde, the trade minister, and Anne Lauvergeon, head of Areva, a nuclear-energy group, are all tipped for jobs. Alain Juppé, a former prime minister and right-hand-man to Mr Chirac who has become a Sarkozy ally, is expected to get a top post. Mr Sarkozy might also make a surprising appointment from the left, finding a job perhaps for Bernard Kouchner, co-founder of Médecins Sans Frontières, or for someone from among France's ethnic minorities.

The first few months will be marked, characteristically, by a tourbillon of activity. Mr Sarkozy is likely to head to Berlin for his first foreign trip, to revive the Franco-German alliance and consolidate his tie to Angela Merkel, Germany's chancellor, whom he congratulated in the familiar tu style as soon as she was elected. He will also drop in on Brussels to show that, after the paralysis of the twilight years of Mr Chirac and the French rejection of the European Union constitution, France "is now back on the scene in Europe". Foreign meetings already crowd his diary: the G8 summit in early June, in Germany; the European Council at the end of the month, in Brussels; Africa, sometime soon.

Mr Sarkozy will mark a distinct break with the Chirac era, not just in tone but in substance. He is more instinctively sympathetic both to Israel and to America than any French leader for 40 years; he wants to take a tougher line towards Russia and Iran, and put an end to France's traditional African policy, "based on personal ties between heads of state", in favour of a more transparent, democratic approach. Mr Sarkozy has called America "the greatest democracy in the world", and looked immensely chuffed last September after a meeting with George Bush in Washington— despite the disapproval it provoked back home. His rapport with Britain's Tony Blair, who called him "a friend" in a congratulatory message he posted—in French—on YouTube, is genuine; Mr Blair was expected to visit him in Paris this week. He knows Gordon Brown, Mr Blair's presumed successor, far less well.

Indeed there is almost a danger that Mr Sarkozy's Atlanticist leanings have raised expectations unrealistically high in Washington and London. The new president will certainly be keen to avoid what he called the "arrogance" of the French threat to veto UN military action in Iraq in 2003. But he nevertheless backed Mr Chirac's opposition to the invasion. He explicitly told the Americans in his victory speech that "friendship means accepting that friends can think differently". Some of Mr Sarkozy's views collide directly with those of America and Britain, including his vehement hostility to Turkish entry to the European Union, his doubts about the continuing presence of French troops in Afghanistan and his industrial protectionism within Europe. President Sarkozy will be an easier transatlantic ally, for sure, but he will still be no walkover.

On the domestic front, say his advisers, Mr Sarkozy intends to use the five-year mandate in three phases. In the first two years, he will implement tough reforms; in the second two years, he will consolidate them; in the fifth year, he will prepare for re-election. His first hurdle is parliamentary elections on June 10 and 17. Early polls suggest that the French, despite their reputation for rebellion, could well hand him a majority: his party would get 35% of the first-round vote, compared with 30% for the Socialists and 15% for the centrists, according to a CSA poll last week. All candidates scoring at least 12.5% in the first round will go through to a run-off.

Wasting no time, Mr Sarkozy intends to call parliament into extraordinary session this summer. He wants laws passed to exempt workers from tax and social-security charges for hours worked above the 35-hour week (thus both encouraging the 35-hour rule to crumble, and rewarding people for working hard). He also wants to let mortgage-interest payments be deducted from income tax; to tighten immigration rules; and to stiffen sentences for young and repeat offenders.

Other reforms he plans to push through early are a guarantee of minimum service on public transport during strikes; a loosening of the legal right of the big five unions to represent all employees in a workplace, whether or not they are union members; the introduction of a single job contract with progressive rights; the reform of unemployment benefit, in order to penalise claimants who refuse two job offers, while improving services for job-seekers. In time, Mr Sarkozy also plans to make 50% the top limit on all personal taxation and social charges; to grant universities more autonomy to set fees and recruit staff and students; to reduce inheritance tax; and to reform the special pension privileges of certain public-sector workers.

Threats of Resistance

Veteran France-watchers say they have heard it all before. Governments have repeatedly tried to trim privileges and benefits in order to rescue the welfare system from collapse, only to be defeated on the street, the favourite theatre of protest for the French. Dominique de Villepin, the outgoing centre-right prime minister, was fatally wounded by street protests and student-led sit-ins against his proposed, less protected job contract for the young. Mr Chirac also backed down in 1995, when Mr Juppé was his prime minister, in the face of crippling national strikes against proposed reforms. Mr Sarkozy, say the sceptics, will lose his reformist zeal once in power, drop his semi-professed liberalism, and ultimately se chiraquiser.

Resistance is certainly likely. Mr Sarkozy inspires both admiration and hostility. He was demonised during the campaign by his opponents, almost absurdly so; yet his hard line on immigration and on criminality lent him an undeniable harshness. On election night 730 cars were burned, and protesters clashed with riot police in central Paris and a few other cities. Ms Royal, having threatened at her last campaign rally that the French would revolt if Mr Sarkozy were elected, left it to François Hollande, the Socialist Party leader (and her partner), to call belatedly for an end to violence and for the verdict of the poll to be respected.

With a nod to those who accused him of divisiveness, Mr Sarkozy announced on election night that his was "not the victory of one France against another" and that he would be "the president of all the French". He will need to be particularly careful to include the country's black and Muslim minorities, at the very least by bringing diversity into his government. Ms Dati, whose parents are north African, would be one symbolic appointment.

The unions, too, could prove difficult. Mr Sarkozy considers his plans for minimum service on trains and buses to be the key to unlocking reform elsewhere. Once it becomes impossible to paralyse cities and stop commuters getting to work, strikes will lose much of their wider political potency. The statutory role of the five largest labour unions to negotiate on behalf of all workers gives them huge clout, and is one reason why Mr Sarkozy also intends to open up first-round elections within companies to representatives outside the dominant five.

Students too, having defeated Mr de Villepin last year, are bracing for a new struggle. Last week, student unions at one of the Sorbonne universities in Paris voted to strike and blockade their campus, in protest at Mr Sarkozy's university-reform plans. Not only does he intend to inject a small element of competition into France's bureaucratic university system, but he laid into the May '68 generation during the campaign, accusing the "inheritors of May '68" of imposing "moral and intellectual relativism" and calling for this heritage to be "liquidated". As a student himself, a few years after the May events, Mr Sarkozy marched against striking students at his own university, calling for classes to resume.

Powers on His Side

Nonetheless, there are grounds to think that President Sarkozy could get further than his predecessors. First, he has a mandate for change. Mr Chirac in 1995 also won a robust majority (52.6%), but campaigned to "mend the social fracture", not to change France. Mr Sarkozy's mandate secures him electoral legitimacy and, at least in the short run, puts public opinion broadly on his side. For those who considered France too restive, conservative or skittish for change, Mr Sarkozy's victory suggests otherwise.

Second, the crushing defeat of the hard-left parties robs the biggest union, the Communist-backed Confédération Générale du Travail (CGT), of some of its force. The CGT has in the past been behind many of France's biggest street protests. Mr Sarkozy's tactic is to bring in the unions for negotiations first, while holding out the threat of legislation if no agreement can be reached with them. This is how he plans to bring about a deal on minimum service on public transport, telling unions and employers that they have until the end of the summer to do a deal; after that, he will start to legislate.

Third, Mr Sarkozy's hallmark is to introduce reforms with well-communicated and plain-spoken appeals to common sense. The style of his presidency is likely to be hands-on, in contrast with the remoter manner of Mr Chirac, with regular press conferences and, he has suggested, even appearances to explain himself before parliament.

The new president is often caricatured as brutal. Yet during the student protests against Mr de Villepin, Mr Sarkozy urged the prime minister to shelve the reform, since it had never been subject to negotiation and had been rushed through parliament by decree. He has long argued the need to build a consensus around reform by laying out the case for it, rather than proceed-

ing by stealth. If anything, Mr Sarkozy is sometimes too ready to cut deals and to use heavy-handed tactics, as he demonstrated when he was finance minister in 2004, threatening to "out" grocery bosses in the press if they did not bring down prices.

The next six months promise to be turbulent. The Socialist Party too will be keen to resist a politician that their candidate called "dangerous"—although the party itself is now in disarray. Like the Labour Party in 1987, after Margaret Thatcher's third Conservative victory, the Socialists now face a total of 17 years without presidential power, after their own third consecutive presidential defeat. The party is deeply split over what conclusions to draw. Dominique Strauss-Kahn, a moderate, argued in a fierce election-night attack on Ms Royal's performance that the party had not modernised itself and offered only "passé solutions". Laurent Fabius, by contrast, on the party's left wing, argued that the Socialists should stay true to their traditions. Rival Socialist bigwigs, Ms Royal and Mr Hollande jostling among them, already have their eyes on the 2012 elections, and will struggle to overcome the party's divisions in time for the June elections.

Arguably, this defeat could be the shock that the Socialist Party needs to force it at last to break its old links to the Communist Party and the hard left, and transform itself instead into a modern, electable party of the left. Even if this shift were to take place, however, the space looks too cramped to accommodate both a modernised Socialist Party and the new centrist party, the Democratic Movement, that Mr Bayrou launched last week. During the campaign Mr Bayrou baffled many of his own deputies by lurching towards the left after the first round, laying into Mr Sarkozy and flirting with Ms Royal. In the end, three-quarters of them came out in support of Mr Sarkozy, arguing that, with their roots in centre-right Christian Democracy, they had little in common with Ms Royal's state-oriented economic programme.

In return, Mr Sarkozy has offered not to run Gaullist candidates against these deputies in June. It remains to be seen whether Mr Bayrou can do a comparable deal with the Socialist Party.

The Socialists may not like the example, but Mr Sarkozy supplies perhaps the best case study in how to grab hold of a political party, against the will of its elders, and use it to secure the presidency. In a handover ceremony on May 16 Mr Sarkozy will receive the keys to the Elysée Palace from Mr Chirac, the veteran politician who gave him his first break in politics when he was a fresh-faced, long-haired 20-year-old student, and whom he let down by backing a rival presidential candidate 20 years later. Mr Sarkozy declared in that first speech, back in 1975, that "to be Gaullist is to be revolutionary". Little can Mr Chirac have known then that the upstart youngster would one day seize the presidency on the promise of a revolutionary break with the era presided over by Mr Chirac himself.

Liberté, Égalité, Laïcité?

OLIVIER ROY

John Bowen's *Why the French Don't Like Headscarves* is, its title notwithstanding, more a book about French political culture write large than about Islam in France. And so it should be: Islam is now intrinsically linked with the definition of what it means to be French in political terms. This is not because Islamic ideas or groups of well-organized Muslims are threatening a well-entrenched French political culture, but because French political culture itself is being shaken by the vicissitudes of current history. A great debate over what defines France as a nation has been triggered in part from above, as the vaunted construction of Europe is weakening the nation-state model, and in part from below, as immigration, globalization and unemployment threaten to unravel the French social fabric. These changes are sufficiently vast as to overwhelm the traditional post-1789 tenets of French *Jacobinism:* the strong central state and the stress on citizenship, rather than sect or race, as the only focus of common political identity. But even if the present crisis does not originate with Muslim immigration, the debate nowadays in France (and not only in France) definitely centers on Islam. [1]

The French conflict over headscarves and other symbols of parochial religious affiliation thus represents both a manifestation of a deeper discontent and an overlay that is profoundly influencing how that discontent is understood and managed. To his credit, Bowen, a professor of anthropology at Washington University in St. Louis, has properly grasped the essence of the matter. This is what enables him to raise and answer the question, almost incomprehensible to most non-French, of how it could possibly be that some few dozen young schoolgirls wanting to wear a Muslim headscarf in the classroom could be seen as a vital threat to the Republic by some 70 percent of French public opinion. How could it be that a few young girls could trigger a full year of national angst, complete with two government-sponsored high-level commissions and a sprawling debate involving hundreds of newspapers articles, heated op-eds, impassioned televised debates and countless documentaries? How could they have driven the adoption in 2004 of a new law banning the headscarf from the schools?

Bowen answers these questions by way of a triptych. In part one, "State and Religion in the Long Run", he establishes the basic historical context of the debate, without which nothing that happened in 2004 makes much sense. In part two, "Publicity and Politics, 1989–2005", he tracks the headscarf controversy in detail, relying on many scores of interviews and a thorough familiarity with the avenues of debate and controversy. And in part three, "Philosophy, Media, Anxiety", he tries to assay where French political culture is headed.

Laïcité for the Un-French

It is not easy to explain the French notion of *laïcité* to Americans, not because it is entirely foreign to the American experience, but because it is close enough to it to give Americans exactly the wrong idea. *Laïcité* is about the separation of church and state, a concept Americans know well. But in America separation was designed to *free* religion from state interference (and vice versa), whereas in France separation evolved to exclude religion from public space and to promote the supremacy of the state over religious organizations. And the historical reasons for the distinction are clear enough. As de Tocqueville observed, the American Founders saw Protestant Christian religion as a support for freedom and civic virtue; French republicans saw the Catholic Church as having been complicit with the worst features of the *ancien régime* and sought to limit its sway over French democracy.

Bowen is therefore wise not to translate *laïcité,* but instead to describe it as the essence of French exceptionalism, as a political and legal secularism—based on the 1905 Law of Separation of Church and State—that has worked among the French Left (and now also among most of the Right) as a quasi-ideological axiom for defining the French political sphere. France is the opposite of a multicultural society, not in the sense that it promotes a "one-culture" model, but in that it defines citizenship wholly apart from cultural identities, communal belongings and sectarian affiliations, asserting instead an abstract *homo politicus*. This is the essence of French universalist ideology; *Laïcité* both defines and protects that ideology. The headscarf affair was so fundamental an issue because it symbolized core assumptions about France's universalist identity colliding head-on with demographic and social trends—notably an undeniable religious assertiveness among second-generation Muslims (and converts)—whose implications are plainly parochial in nature. A rough and fanciful analogy to American life would be a threat by academic post-modernists, having taken control of the U.S. government, to abolish the assertion in the Declaration of Independence that there are self-evident universal truths.

Laïcité is clearly anti-religious in practice, but it is not only or mainly anti-Islamic. Veiled women were long ago expelled from schools in France (by the army, no less): They were Catholic nuns, and it happened in 1904, exactly one hundred years before the law banning the scarf. Indeed, as Bowen explains, in both historical and philosophical terms the present debate on *laïcité* reflects the two–century long struggle between the French Republic and the Catholic Church. It started with the ambition of the French Revolution to control the Church (and to some extent religious beliefs, too), and eventually moved to a separation (the 1905 law) that sometimes amounted to expulsion—of clerics from schools, and of congregations from "metropolitan territory" (the soil of France, but not, interestingly enough, from French colonies, where missionary orders were supported by the secular state as a tool to control and integrate the indigenous population). Over time, *laïcité* itself became a philosophical, political and even an ideological concept that filled the vacuum left by the expulsion of religion from the public sphere. As such, it helped to unite a very divided Republican Left throughout the 20th century: *Laïcité* was the only common identity between center-left *radicaux*, social democrats and communists.

Moreover, the French school system was taken all along to be the battlefield *par excellence* of *laïcité* from 1905 to 2004. Supporters of ideological *laïcité* wanted the state to promote *laïcité* as a value system as well as enforce it as a law. The French republican tradition is deeply suspicious of any public manifestation of religious feeling. Indeed, France has the most restrictive laws among democratic countries as far as religious "cults" are concerned. There is now a debate in the Parliament over whether to rescind the status of Jehovah's Witnesses as a "religion", recently bestowed by the courts, and instead to list them as a "cult."

It is important to realize, however—as Bowen clearly does—that ideological *laïcité* is not really based on the law. In purely legal and constitutional terms, *laïcité* is no more than an extensive definition of the separation between church and state in the public sphere. As law, it has nothing to say about religious belief in the private sphere. It supposes the state to be a neutral actor: It does not define common secular values, and it does not so much ban as seek to regulate the *presence* of religion in the public sphere. It does so in the framework of the "public good" and of the 1905 law of separation, which delineates when church bells may be rung, how processions can interrupt traffic in city streets, how chaplains may serve in the armed forces and prisons, and when and where distinctive religious symbols may be worn.

French courts have a long and still-evolving tradition of solving church-state issues on a case-by-case basis, avoiding any philosophical or theological statements about what religion should say or be. But French politics has been suffused with the conflict for years. While by law the state is not supposed to meddle with "religion" but only, in the name of public order, with "*culte*"—meaning, in French legal terms, "organized religion"—the reality has been a fluctuating test of wills between religious communities and the state. After coming under attack in the early 20th century, the Catholic Church has been able to fight off state control of its institutions (the role of the bishop was acknowledged by the state only in 1923). And in the course of time a settled arrangement has been devised on religious symbols and activities in public spaces, including trivial issues such as where the bishop sits at an official dinner. It has been agreed.

The contradiction between the two approaches to *laïcité*—the legal, as defined by the courts, and the ideological, which

shapes French political identity—is at the core of the 2004 headscarf crisis. When the Parliament enacted the new law banning the veil from schools, it did so precisely because the courts, upheld by the supreme court (*Conseil d'État*), had consistently refused to do so, except in isolated cases where wearing the headscarf was taken to be tantamount to religious proselytism or caused disturbances. The 2004 law thus represented the elevation of ideological over legal *laïcité,* the former now in the process of turning into sheer Islamophobia in the context of broader pan-European political trends and fears.

The new French and European Islamophobia brings together rightist supporters of a Christian European identity, and anti-Europe, anti-religious, anti-globalization leftists. What is happening in France is also happening in many European countries, not least in the Netherlands and Denmark; and what is happening in those and other countries is affecting perceptions in France, as well. Nevertheless, the French dilemma is most acute because of its strongly universalist republican convictions. In this sense France still is, as Marx said, the "political scene" of Europe.

But it is not a serene scene. At the core of France's dilemma is the inability of French political discourse to confront new forms of religiosity emerging in every great Western religion, including Christianity. "Integralism" (a more precise and less misleading term than fundamentalism), the growing discrepancy between "faith communities" and the rest of civil society, extreme individualism, the deculturation of religious practice (in which the "born again" replaces the nominal Christian), moral conservatism, the impulse to engage in politics not to gain power but to force choices on moral values (against abortion and gay marriages, for example)—all of this is new to the traditional French formula, and all of it is a threat to the capacity of that formula to retain relevance. In France, as elsewhere, religious communities and secularists are not fighting to control a common public sphere: They exist in two different social spaces that only sometimes overlap and often clash when they do. This situation so radically alters the context of *laïcité* that it is on the verge of becoming incomprehensible. This has obviously not been caused by a mere headscarf, but it has been provoked by it.

Bowen cleverly and vividly describes for an American audience the French political debate without simplifying or distorting it. He skillfully blends historical background, factual descriptions of events, in-depth analysis and lively discussions with philosophers and politicians, social workers and ordinary people he meets in the street. The sample of opinion he proffers conveys well the full complexity and diversity of the debate, which Bowen makes intelligible for a large audience.

By way of background, Bowen debunks the myth that France's supposed republican consensus has been shaken by the sudden assertiveness of Islam, convincingly showing that French society has been fiercely divided over the fundaments of politics at least since the Revolution. He shows also that the spirit of the 1905 law, if not its letter, has far more often than not been distorted by the state, which has never ceased to interfere with and even attempt to control religion.

Bowen also shows how in recent years Islam has brought a new challenge, not because it has a strong communal dimension—in fact, French Muslims are as individualistic, not to say anarchist, as other Frenchmen—but, on the contrary, because there are no legitimate Islamic institutions, no interlocutors who can discuss matters with the state. In the French tradition, both pre- and post-Revolution, religion is not about individual belief but group influence. The Ministry of Interior is thus in charge of *cultes* ("religious affairs") in contemporary France, and all interior ministers since 1998 have tried to organize the Muslim community under their aegis. They have been trying desperately to push Muslims to unite under the umbrella of a French Council of Muslim Faith. They have (probably unwisely) negotiated with foreign states, whose governments are only too happy to turn French Muslims into hostages in bilateral relations, in order to promote a complacent Islam. As Bowen recounts, French interior ministers have even picked their favorite candidates for election in the council, all pretty much to no avail.

The French crisis of Islam shows the profound but changing ambivalence of *laïcité*. Never intended to represent a strict separation, *Laïcité* has been reified into a new political religion more or less in proportion to the perception of the threat felt from French Muslim demographic and social trends. French authorities, whose experience includes two centuries of dealing with France's Jews as a corporate body, are now trying to "frame" Islam in a similar unitary "national" context. But this solution does not make sense for a Muslim community of diverse origins, and it goes beyond what can reasonably be expected from France's Muslims, most of whom wish to assimilate into French society to one degree or another.

In the central part of his book, Bowen describes in detail the psychodrama surrounding the 2004 debate on the law forbidding the veil. It is certainly the best account of the crisis in any language. He shows how unfair the debate really was. The media was blatantly biased against not only the veiled women, but also against any show of public religiosity from Muslims. (I recall the following comment from a Channel A2 journalist on a British Muslim mayor: "He is a moderate Muslim: He prays only once a day.") Broadcasted debates mainly staged bearded, heavily accented foreign imams. The high-ranking civil servant in charge of organizing the Stasi Commission (which produced the report justifying the law on the veil) selected mainly non-veiled women to testify, many of them being foreigners (albeit perfect French speakers) who had come as political refugees to France and warned of Islamic pressures building in their countries of birth. Media producers and government officials disregarded the French veiled second-generation girls themselves. The resulting image was that the veil is foreign, backward, alienating and a harbinger of terrorism and violence.

In the aftermath of 9/11 the anti-veil campaign was, of course, a success. But Bowen shows how modern, individualist, educated and integrated most of the veiled schoolgirls actually are. They did not and do not fight in the name of a separate community and culture, but as individuals who want to be recognized as both citizens *and* believers. They see no clash of values or cultures, only an overextension of the principle of separation between religion and state—with which they agree in essence—to the public manifestation of personal faith. To the dismay of most French feminists, the veil girls even adopt the language of modern feminism—"My body is *my* business."

Bowen is clearly sympathetic to both French political culture and the pro-veil schoolgirls. He thinks that the campaign against the veil was blown way out of proportion. Indeed, he is one of the few American scholars who seem to understand in depth the nature of France's over-whelming hostility to the veil. But at the end of the book, after Bowen has carefully analyzed all sides of the story, he still wonders: "Why don't the French like headscarves?" It is as if, after understanding the French down to the nth degree of nuance, he still can't quite believe that they think and act as they do. In this, Bowen is himself a kind of virtual Frenchman. After all, Americans aren't the only ones who seek self-understanding and sometimes fail to find it.

It is clear that multiculturalism is dying in western Europe. From Denmark to Great Britain it has been accused, wrongly or rightly, of fueling separateness and radicalism. Even in very tolerant Great Britain, where women police officers are permitted to wear the veil, high ministers are now calling into question the wearing of the *burqa* or *jiljab* (that is, a veil covering also the face). If tolerance is generally wearing thin in much of Europe, in France there is now specifically too much rigidity in *laïcité*. The issue of the veiled schoolgirls surely could have been handled without a law and in a less passionate atmosphere.

At the same time, a sharp debate is growing on the discrepancy between the two basic European conceptions of integration: one based on abstract political qualities of citizenship, the other on concrete attributes expressed in multiculturalism. That debate is motivated by the recognition that neither model is working very well with European Muslims, and officials all across Europe are at wits end trying to figure out what to try next. Apartheid, exclusion and racism are clearly unacceptable options on the extreme end of an ethno-racial definition of national belonging. But, at the other extreme, defining citizenship as merely holding a passport or an identity card is not enough. At least in the liberal understanding of the concept, citizenship means participating in a common social venture. To exclude from that venture the yearnings of faith, and the healthy exercise of learning to tolerate different expressions of faith, was never a good idea. Today it has become an impossible one.

Note

1. The best in-depth survey of Muslims in France is Jonathan Laurence and Justin Vaisse, *Integrating Islam: Political and Religious Challenges in Contemporary France* (Brookings Institution Press, 2006).

OLIVIER ROY is the author of *Globalized Islam* (Columbia University Press, 2004)

Angela Merkel's Germany

"In part because of deadlock within the government on domestic policy, the chancellor has turned to foreign policy as her main stage."

JACKSON JANES AND STEPHEN SZABO

Angela Merkel, whom *The Economist* has called a "world star," is the most prominent of a new generation of leaders emerging in Europe. She is in charge of Europe's pivotal country at a time of great challenges to the EU as it seeks to come out of its constitutional and enlargement crises. Germany has the presidency of the EU and of the Group of Eight industrial nations in 2007, but Merkel and her country will be central to Europe's evolution long beyond this spring.

With Tony Blair in Britain and Jacques Chirac in France serving as lame ducks, and with many other European countries locked in political stalemates, much of Europe today is experiencing a vacuum of leadership. Thus, both George W. Bush and his successor as US president will look to the German chancellor as America's most important partner in Europe for years to come. Understanding Merkel and the political and economic context in which she operates is, consequently, important for anticipating what to expect from her chancellorship—in its impact both on Germany and on the future direction of the continent.

The Pragmatist

A number of Merkel's personal characteristics influence her approach to leadership and policy making. First, as a natural scientist, having studied and practiced physics, she is a highly rational person, without a strong ideological bent or approach. A problem solver and an incrementalist, Merkel favors a trial-and-error approach to policy and is able to make quick adjustments when they are needed. As she put it, "Many will say, 'This government takes a lot of small steps but not one decisive one.' And I reply, 'Yes. That is precisely what we are doing. Because this is the modern way to do things.'" Merkel lacks a big, unifying vision, and in this respect resembles her predecessor as chancellor, Gerhard Schröder. Unlike Schröder, however, she avoids personalizing political relationships and prefers a businesslike and interest-based approach in policy making.

Second, Merkel is a political latecomer and an outsider to German politics. An East German, she did not become active in politics until after the fall of the Berlin Wall, when she was well into her 30s. She is, consequently, not anchored in her party,

the Christian Democratic Union (CDU), and has not been able to take advantage of an extensive political network—a problem aggravated by her gender in a male-dominated party. She has begun to change this by creating her own network, both within and outside the party, but she still faces many rivals and lacks a deep regional base, something that is normally essential in German politics.

Third, her East German upbringing has made her a very private person who reveals very little about herself or what she is thinking. She is not a social animal or backslapper and is always in control of her emotions.

Finally, Merkel is not among the so-called '68ers, the generation of Schröder and his Green foreign minister, Joschka Fischer, who cut their political teeth in the late 1960s partly in resistance to the American role in the world. Merkel, born in 1954 and raised in East Germany, is the first of a new generation of leaders who were never among the 1960s rebels nor among the Atlanticist generation of her mentor, Helmut Kohl. Although she came of age during the end of the cold war, her political career was shaped in the post–Berlin Wall era of a unified Germany.

Merkel will be joined in power soon by others of her generation in France and the United Kingdom—people like Ségolène Royal or Nicolas Sarkozy in France, and David Cameron or Gordon Brown in Britain—as well as José Manuel Barroso in the EU. This group is pragmatic regarding both Europe, which is no longer seen as the great peace project of the Kohl-Mitterrand era, and the United States, which is neither the model it was for the postwar leaders who shaped Europe nor the anti-model it was for many of the '68ers.

Squabbling in the Ranks

Merkel was sworn in as chancellor on November 22, 2005. The first year of her tenure was marked by uncertainty over whether her political coalition (the "grand coalition"), which includes both Merkel's CDU and the Social Democratic Party (SPD), would have the stamina to hold together for another three years. The SPD holds almost as many seats in the Bundestag (parliament) as does Merkel's own CDU—making the coalition far more challenging to manage than was Schröder's coalition, which consisted of the SPD and the smaller, ideologically kindred Green party.

The German people's skepticism regarding domestic reforms is compounded by a policy making system that discourages strong leadership.

Despite current tensions between the parties in Merkel's coalition, however, there is at present no real alternative to this political equation in Germany. Speculation about the need for new elections remains exactly that, primarily because the voters would lose even more confidence in the political leadership if it declared bankruptcy so soon after taking over. Neither the Greens nor the Free Democrats can offer a viable alternative by themselves. And the idea of creating a red, green, and yellow mixture (SPD, Greens, and Free Democrats) or a black, green, and yellow coalition (CDU, Greens, and Free Democrats) is not in the cards. There is still a great deal of political baggage left over from the September 2005 elections that will prevent any such reconfiguring from happening very soon.

Merkel enjoys a solid level of personal popularity among Germans, but confidence in the two large political partners, the CDU and SPD—which between them have close to three-quarters of the Bundestag under their control—has waned. After all, voters ask, if there is no viable opposition to stop them, why can they not get more done in the way of reforms instead of making so much noise about why they cannot agree on such reforms? Even the CDU and its conservative Bavarian partner, the Christian Social Union, are increasingly bickering over the issue of health care reform.

All this wrangling comes during a continuing slide in membership in the SPD and the CDU. The Social Democrats have lost over 40 percent of their members from a high of more than 1 million in 1980, while the Christian Democrats in the same period have lost 14 percent of their members. Currently, the two parties are virtually tied in membership, at around 600,000 each. The smaller parties have lost ground in the past eight years as well, and the number of citizens choosing not to vote has been increasing steadily.

This frustration is causing a backlash that has allowed a right-wing party, the National Party of Germany (NPD), to squeeze into two state parliaments in eastern Germany. Many of the NPD votes have come from Germans under 30 years old who are beleaguered by high unemployment rates and see dim prospects for their future.

Still, the general loss of confidence among voters and the cross-party bickering that has contributed to it should come as no surprise. Domestic political battles were destined to throw sand into the machine of the CDU-SPD coalition. After all, the domestic policy realm is where the full forces of particular interests meet in battle. Health care reform legislation is the best, or worst,

example, and not only in Germany. It remains a dangerous area for the coalition's future. Indeed, one can also see the wreckage of health care reform efforts in the United States going back many years, not to speak of social security reform efforts more recently. These are the deadly third rails for all politicians.

Pressures for Reform

Merkel has been able to push through important reforms that have toughened up policies dealing with pensions. And corporate tax rates are set to come down significantly. As Germany's export machine continues to hum along at record levels, the economy in 2007 looks to be as strong as it was last year.

In general, though, reform efforts so far have produced a mix of some change but also continued stalemate. Germans are struggling to finance the social systems they have built up over the past five decades, and are trying to redistribute the load. This is not unique to Germany—Sweden, Denmark, and the Netherlands have been struggling with these problems as well. Yet Germany seems to be uncertain about the scope and pace of change. A question being newly framed amid today's global competition is how much of the acclaimed "social market economy" that was developed after World War II should be accounted for by "market" and how much by "social."

The very fact that the 2005 elections resulted in a so-called grand coalition of the two major political blocs was a reflection of the voters' uncertainty in the face of rising pressures to reform social and labor protections. The challenge any government faces is proposing realistic goals and then maintaining support for reaching them, even when changes pinch people where it hurts. It is precisely then when a government must be persuasive in explaining to the public why the goal is worth the pain and the adjustments needed to reach the goal.

On EU enlargement, Germany has moved from being the great promoter to being a skeptic.

This has proved difficult in Germany. For example, the government's decision in November 2006 to raise the statutory retirement age from 65 to 67 was vital to maintaining the viability of the social security system, but it requires a major adjustment in the national psyche. Likewise, reducing unemployment insurance is crucial in encouraging people to search for new jobs, but it violates long-entrenched expectations of the unemployed.

The German people's skepticism regarding domestic reforms is compounded by a policy-making system that is designed for consensus politics and discourages strong leadership. Suspicion of strong leaders is a legacy of Hitler's Third Reich, with its concentration of power at the top. In contrast to Japan, for example, contemporary Germany has a weak state and a strong civil society. This makes unpopular reforms very difficult to achieve.

On top of this, Germany's parliament is one of the largest in the world, with 614 representatives. And Germany has a federal system with powerful state governments. Wrestling with serious problems that involve so many actors, in a 24-7 media environment no less, is not a formula for smooth decision-making.

Berlin's coalition partners are stuck with each other for the moment, whether they like it or not. But they should not be stuck in political mud when it comes to implementing their agenda. Bringing down the national debt and encouraging job growth by deregulating the labor market can generate some confidence in the future. Yet Germany also faces formidable structural problems in the business and banking sectors, and it continues to pay a high cost for the reintegration of (less affluent) eastern Germany. The coalition partners need to look like they are focused on confronting the country's problems, rather than themselves, if they are to bring the voters along with them. This seems to work better with foreign policy than it does at home.

Balancing with Bush

In part because of deadlock within the government on domestic policy, the chancellor has turned to foreign policy as her main stage. Schröder had centralized policy making in the chancellery and marginalized the role of the foreign office and the parliament—since his Social Democrats were in a coalition with the small Green party, this was relatively easy to accomplish. Merkel, on the other hand, is in a much more challenging coalition. In contrast to Fischer, who was Schröder's foreign minister, Merkel must contend with a Social Democrat, Frank Walter Steinmeier, as foreign minister. This means there are far greater checks on Merkel's power than on any chancellor over the past three decades.

This has not stopped her from forming an effective foreign policy team. Merkel generally values analytical thinkers over party politicians in the chancellery. As her chief of staff, Thomas De Mazière, told the German weekly *Die Zeit,* "A clear head can learn about compromises and contacts better than a political tactician can learn clear thinking." Thus, Merkel has tended to hire technocrats or specialists in foreign policy positions. A good example is her key foreign policy adviser, Christoph Heusgen, a thorough Europeanist who served six years in Brussels working for the EU foreign policy chief, Javier Solana.

Merkel entered office believing that the Schröder foreign policy had lost the traditional German balance between France and the United States. She has made the US relationship her primary responsibility and priority, with the goal of reestablishing a constructive and balanced relationship with Washington after the *Sturm und Drang* of the Schröder years. Her East German experience left her with a very positive image of America, which she associates not only with freedom but also with innovation and flexibility.

Nevertheless, Merkel is a politician who understands the deep suspicion toward George W. Bush among the German public and media. This reflects in part the new sense of sovereignty and status of a unified Germany that is no longer as dependent on the United States as it was during the cold war. Merkel understands that she needs to be regarded as a reliable partner in Washington while not being seen as Bush's dachshund back home.

Ever the realist, the German chancellor understands that it is in the national interest to have a good working relationship with the world's dominant power, and that trying to use Europe as a counterweight to America only ends up splitting Europe and isolating Germany. On the other hand, drawing too close to Bush and to America carries its own dangers, as the case of Britain's Blair demonstrates. Thus, the Merkel approach toward the United States combines a close personal relationship between Merkel and Bush with a continuing, critical distance from unilateral aspects of Bush's foreign policy. In many ways she is rebuilding some bridges while waiting for the next American administration, which she hopes will be more user-friendly for Europe.

This approach is apparent in a number of policy areas. On NATO, the Merkel government has emphasized a NATO-first approach, giving the alliance priority in the security realm over the European Union's Security and Defense Policy. The new German Defense White Book, issued in November 2006, underlines a shift in German defense strategy away from the old territorial-defense focus of the cold war to a crisis-intervention rationale with light, mobile forces. Merkel intends to maintain the important German contribution to NATO peace-keeping forces in Afghanistan, without widening its mandate or increasing that commitment. She has also deployed German peacekeepers to Congo and Lebanon, and a German commander now heads the EU force in Bosnia. Along with France and Britain, Germany is working closely with the us administration to forge a unified approach toward thwarting Iran's nuclear ambitions.

In foreign economic policy, the chancellor is interested in maintaining some momentum in trade liberalization despite the likely failure of the Doha round of global trade negotiations. In particular, she has put forward new proposals for a transatlantic free trade area. Merkel has also moved to reduce the German fiscal deficit by raising the value-added tax, thus restoring Germany's reputation for fiscal responsibility in hopes of serving as an example to other EU deficit states. The German leadership remains concerned about the impact that US trade and fiscal deficits will have on the international financial system. As the world's largest exporter, German business worries about the impact of a falling dollar on its foreign markets.

Enlargement Fatigue

Merkel is now on center stage in Europe. Germany will hold the EU presidency during the first half of 2007. In this capacity, Merkel will have a chance to help restore some momentum to the European project, which has been staggering since the rejection of the EU constitutional treaty by French and Dutch voters in 2006. Because of the current leadership vacuum in Europe and the impending French presidential election this spring, the German role is likely to be limited to finding some ground for action in the future regarding the constitutional treaty. So no dramatic breakthroughs should be expected during the German term.

On the other important dimension of the European project, EU enlargement, Germany has moved from being the great promoter to being a skeptic. Past German governments supported the "big bang" enlargement of 2004, which brought in 10 member states, mostly from East-Central Europe. The Merkel government reluctantly went along with the entry of Bulgaria and Romania on January 1, 2007, but seems to have reached its limit regarding future enlargement. The Schröder government supported the entry of Turkey, but the Christian Democrats are opposed, and the governing coalition remains deeply divided on this key issue.

Germany's enlargement fatigue results in part from a fear of immigration and the cheap labor that it brings. Although immigration into Germany has been curtailed by legislation, the foreign population of the country stands at 7.3 million, or about 9 percent of the population. This is a larger proportion of the population than is the case in the United States. Of this group, 1.8 million have Turkish origins, with about one-third having been born in Germany. Another half-million of Turkish origin have been naturalized and are now German citizens. Germans are struggling to deal with the issue of how to define citizenship, which has traditionally been based on German heritage. Although citizenship laws have been liberalized somewhat, Germany is still a long way from becoming a multicultural society, and demands for German language competence for new immigrants have been increasing.

Germany's growing skepticism about enlargement is also the result of strained federal budgets, themselves a consequence of years of slow economic growth and high unemployment. Berlin in the past financed the union's enlargement through its contributions to the EU budget. But Germany is no longer willing or able to serve as Europe's pay-master. This marks an important shift in German foreign policy and implies that the EU is probably approaching its final borders.

Realism on Russia

The German-Russian relationship is once again a central issue in the European political equation. During the cold war, when Germany was divided, it depended on American security guarantees for its territorial integrity. This situation, and the Soviet occupation of East Germany and East-Central Europe, limited Germany's options and flexibility in dealing with the Soviet Union, although the German policy of détente (known as *Ostpolitik*) did develop an independent German approach toward the East.

She needs to be regarded as a reliable partner in Washington while not being seen as Bush's dachshund back home.

After the cold war, the German-Russian relationship regained dynamism. Chancellor Kohl ensured that Russian interests were taken into account during NATO's enlargement to the east. But Schröder took the relationship to a new level by siding with Russia and France against the Bush administration during the lead-up to the Iraq War. He forged an unusually close personal relationship with Russian President Vladimir Putin. He signed the important Baltic Sea gas pipeline agreement with Russia just before leaving office and then, after leaving office, joined the board of Russia's state-controlled energy giant Gazprom.

Merkel came into office resolved to change the tenor of this relationship. She has depersonalized the relationship with Putin, and in her first visit to Moscow as chancellor openly showed her support for human rights groups. Her suspicion of Russian power has been deepened by Russia's use of its energy resources as a foreign policy tool in its relations with Ukraine, Belarus, and Georgia. She is also aware of the suspicions that the close Schröder-Putin relationship raised in the Baltic states and Central Europe, especially in Poland, and wants to repair Germany's relationships with these states.

Merkel has made a priority of improving the Polish-German relationship, but has met resistance from the Polish government, led by the Kaczynski brothers. The German government's decision to establish a Center for Refugees and Expellees, possibly in Berlin, has raised concerns in Poland about potential German property claims for land taken from Germans who lived in Poland before the end of World War II. More generally, the Law and Justice Party of the twins is suspicious of Europe and of Germany in particular. A deeply parochial and nationalist grouping, it has questioned attempts by Poles to reconcile with Germany and is deeply suspicious of Germany's close relationship with Russia.

Yet Merkel the realist has continued to talk about a "strategic partnership" with Russia. Whatever this might mean, it implies that energy dependence and the close economic ties between the two countries remain paramount in German policy. Russia is Germany's largest natural-gas provider, currently providing 40 percent of Germany's natural gas, and this dependence is due to rise above 60 percent once the Baltic pipeline is completed. While Merkel would like to find alternative sources of energy, and is looking at a combination of liquefied natural gas, Central Asian gas, and nuclear power, her options are severely limited. She and her successors are faced with no real alternatives to substantial dependence on Russian natural gas during the coming decades. Moreover, although Russia has used energy as a lever against its former republics, it has never done so with Germany. For its part, Russia has no real alternatives to the EU market for its gas in the medium term. Half of Russia's energy trade is with the EU.

Germany is likely to remain Russia's most important advocate in the EU. The Merkel government continues to resist a common EU energy policy, and thus has made it easier for Russia to play off one EU state against another. In addition, Merkel's foreign minister was a key architect of the close German-Russian relationship when he was Schröder's chief of staff. His presence in the Merkel government is seen as a guarantee of continuity in this policy area.

A New Role in the World

A key change in German foreign policy since the end of the cold war is its increasingly global perspective. While the transatlantic and European relationships remain central to Berlin's view of the world, the Middle East and Asia have increased in importance. This reflects the end of a Western-centric world order and the need for Germany to adapt to the rise of new economic and military powers as well as to its vulnerabilities in the Middle East.

China and India have emerged both as important economic partners and as competitors for scarce sources of energy and raw materials. Germany's role in negotiations with Iran over its nuclear program, its participation in a peacekeeping force in Lebanon, and its efforts to engage Syria in a constructive relationship with the West are further indications of an expanding sense of German interests and responsibilities. As Germany's role in the world expands, it sees itself as deserving more international recognition. This includes a desire to have a seat as a permanent member of the UN Security Council. While Merkel has been less vocal in her pursuit of this goal than was her predecessor, it remains a key objective.

The agenda for the European Union is going to be a difficult one for Merkel to steer. Apart from the uncertain outcome of leadership changes in Great Britain and France, achieving consensus on anything among the union's now-27 members is a challenge at any time and on any issue one picks. Merkel has sent a clear signal that she intends to exercise leadership this year in shaping the still-fragile framework of the EU foreign policy agenda. But merely pushing forward the next phase of the EU constitutional process will give her a full plate, and keeping her fellow member states in line on everything from the Balkans to the Middle East will be a tall order.

The longer-term issues of further EU expansion, particularly with regard to Turkey, will consume Merkel's energies well after this leadership year for Berlin. Here there is a clear division between the views of the chancellor and her party and those of her coalition partners, the Social Democrats. The CDU is opposed to Turkish membership in the EU, favoring a "privileged partnership" instead, while the SPD continues to strongly advocate Turkish membership.

Since becoming chancellor, Merkel has felt confident in the international arena. As with many politicians facing domestic troubles—her coalition with the SPD continues to be a noisy and uncomfortable one—the opportunity to shine as a world leader offers advantages. Despite low poll numbers on domestic issues during the past year, both Merkel and her foreign minister, Steinmeier, top the popularity scales among the German public. The year ahead therefore offers unique opportunities to make progress on the foreign policy front.

Of course, the opportunities will be shadowed by risks. Keeping political squabbles from affecting the foreign policy agenda will not be easy, either at home or within the EU. Still, Merkel has the baton now in Berlin and in Brussels. We will have to wait to see how well the orchestras can perform.

JACKSON JANES is executive director of the American Institute for Contemporary German Studies at Johns Hopkins University. **STEPHEN SZABO** is research director at the institute and a professor of European Studies at Johns Hopkins's School of Advanced International Studies.

Germans Split over a Mosque and the Role of Islam

Mark Landler

In a city with the greatest Gothic cathedral in Germany and no fewer than a dozen Romanesque churches, adding a pair of slender fluted minarets would scarcely alter the skyline. Yet plans for a new mosque are rattling this ancient city to its foundations.

Cologne's Muslim population, largely Turkish, is pushing for approval to build what would be one of Germany's largest mosques, in a working-class district across town from the cathedral's mighty spires.

Predictably, an extreme-right local political party has waged a noisy, xenophobic protest campaign, drumming up support from its far-right allies in Austria and Belgium.

But the proposal has also drawn fierce criticism from a respected German-Jewish writer, Ralph Giordano, who said the mosque would be "an expression of the creeping Islamization of our land." And he does not want to see women shrouded in veils on German streets, he said.

Mr. Giordano's charged remarks, first made at a recent public forum here, have catapulted this local dispute into a national debate in Germany over how a secular society, with Christian roots, should accommodate the religious yearnings of its growing Muslim minority.

Mosques have risen in recent years in Berlin, Mannheim and Duisburg, each time provoking some hand-wringing among residents. But the dispute in Cologne, a city Pope Benedict XVI once called the Rome of the north, seems deeper and more far-reaching.

When Turkey itself is debating the role of Islam in its political life, Germans are starting to ask how—or even if—the 2.7 million people of Turkish descent here can square their religious and cultural beliefs with a pluralistic society that enshrines the rights of women.

Mr. Giordano, a Holocaust survivor, has been sharply criticized, by fellow Jews, among others, and has even received death threats. But others say he is giving voice to Germans, who for reasons of their past, are reluctant to express misgivings about the rise of Islam in their midst.

"We have a common historical background that makes us overly cautious in dealing with these issues," said the mayor of Cologne, Fritz Schramma, who supports the mosque but is not without his qualms.

"For me, it is self-evident that the Muslims need to have a prestigious place of worship," said Mr. Schramma, who belongs to the center-right Christian Democratic Union. "But it bothers me when people have lived here for 35 years and they don't speak a single word of German."

Cologne's Roman Catholic leader, Cardinal Joachim Meisner, is similarly ambivalent. Asked in a radio interview if he was afraid of the mosque, he said, "I don't want to say I'm afraid, but I have an uneasy feeling."

These statements rankle German-Turkish leaders, who have been working with the city since 2001 to build a mosque on the site of a converted drug factory, which now houses a far smaller mosque, a community center and the offices of the Turkish-Islamic Union for Religious Affairs.

"The 120,000 Muslims of Cologne don't have a single place they can point to with pride as the symbol of our faith," said Bekir Alboga, leader of interreligious dialogue at the union, which is known as Ditib. "Christians have their churches, Jews have their synagogues."

Mr. Alboga, a 44-year-old Turkish imam who immigrated here at 18 and speaks rapid-fire German, said the mosque would be a "crowning moment for religious tolerance." Given Germany's dark history, he added, "German politicians need to be careful about what they say."

Mr. Alboga said he was particularly dismayed by Cardinal Meisner, because the Catholic Church, along with Germany's Protestant churches, has long supported the mosque. Ditib, he said, is a moderate organization that acts as a "bulwark against radicalism and terrorism." It plans to finance the project, which will cost more than $20 million, entirely through donations.

The group must obtain a building permit before it can break ground, but Mr. Alboga said he was confident the mosque would not be blocked. Ditib has agreed to various stipulations, including a ban on broadcasting the call to prayer over loudspeakers outside the building.

Public opinion about the project seems guardedly supportive, with a majority of residents saying they favor it, though more than a quarter want its size to be reduced. The polls, taken for a local newspaper, use small samples, 500 people, limiting their usefulness as a gauge of popular sentiment in a city of one million.

How to fit the goals of a Muslim minority into a secular culture?

Cologne, with one of the largest Muslim populations of any German city, already has nearly 30 mosques. Most are in converted factories or warehouses, often tucked away in hidden courtyards, which has contributed to a sense that Muslims in Germany can worship only furtively.

The new mosque would put Islam in plain sight—all the more so because the design calls for a domed building with glass walls. Showing off a model designed by a German architect who specializes in churches, Mr. Alboga said, "Our hearts are open, our doors are open, our mosque is open."

In some ways, the mosque seems calculated to avoid touching nerves. It would not be built near a church or loom over its neighbors, like the new mosque in Duisburg. It would be flanked by multistory office buildings and a giant television tower, which would dwarf its minarets. At 180 feet tall, they would be only one-third the height of the cathedral's spires.

Yet the Turkish community has run into fervent and organized opposition. The far-right party Pro Cologne, which holds 5 of the 90 seats in the city council, collected 23,000 signatures on a petition demanding the halting of the project. The city says only 15,000 of them were genuine.

On June 16, Pro Cologne mobilized 200 people at a rally to protest the mosque. Among those on hand were the leaders of Austria's Freedom Party, which was founded by Jorg Haider, and the extremist party Vlaams Belang, or Flemish Interest, from Antwerp. Both advocate the deportation of immigrants.

Cologne's deputy mayor, Elfi Scho-Antwerpes, a Social Democrat, appeared with Turkish leaders at a counterdemonstration across the street. Mayor Schramma, she noted, did not attend.

Manfred Rouhs, a leader of Pro Cologne, said the mosque would reinforce the development of a parallel Muslim society, and encourage the subjugation of women, which he said was embedded in Islam. "This is not a social model that has any place in the middle of Europe," he said.

In this, he has found common ground with Mr. Giordano, an 84-year-old Jew who eluded the Nazis in World War II by hiding in a cellar. Mr. Giordano, who dismisses Pro Cologne as a "local chapter of contemporary National Socialists," nonetheless agrees that the mosque is a threat.

"There are people who say this mosque could be a step toward integration," Mr. Giordano said in an interview. "I say, 'No, no, and three times no.' Mosques are a symbol of a parallel world."

Mr. Giordano said Germany needed to face the fact that, after three generations of Turkish immigration, efforts to integrate the Turkish minority had failed. Immigrants, he said, sought the privileges of membership in German society but refused to bear the obligations.

Germany's "false tolerance," he said, enabled the Sept. 11 hijackers to use Hamburg as a haven in which to hatch their terrorist plot. Cologne, too, has struggled with radical Islamic figures, most notably Metin Kaplan, a militant Turkish cleric known as the caliph of Cologne.

"I don't want to see women on the street wearing burqas," said Mr. Giordano, a nattily dressed man with the flowing white hair of an 18th-century German romantic. "I'm insulted by that—not by the women themselves, but by the people who turned them into human penguins."

Such blunt language troubles other German Jews, who say a victim of religious persecution should not take a swipe at another religious minority. Henryk M. Broder, a Jewish journalist who is a friend of Mr. Giordano's, said he should have avoided the phrase "human penguins."

But Mr. Broder said that his underlying message was valid, and that his stature as a writer gave him the standing to say it. "A mosque is more than a church or a synagogue," he said. "It is a political statement."

For Mr. Alboga, though, the line between frank debate and racist demagoguery is not so clear. "This is like thinking from the Middle Ages," he said, "and it is sending the racists to the barricades."

Correction—An article on Thursday about a German backlash against plans for a mosque in Cologne, known for its Gothic cathedral, referred incorrectly to the size of polls taken for a local newspaper there, assessing the popularity of the mosque. The sample of 500 people was sufficient for a scientific poll; that sample was not "small," nor did its size limit the poll's "usefulness as a gauge of popular sentiment in a city of one million."

Japanese Spirit, Western Things

When America's black ships forced open Japan, nobody could have predicted that the two nations would become the world's great economic powers

Open up. With that simple demand, Commodore Matthew Perry steamed into Japan's Edo (now Tokyo) Bay with his "black ships of evil mien" 150 years ago this week. Before the black ships arrived on July 8th 1853, the Tokugawa shoguns had run Japan for 250 years as a reclusive feudal state. Carrying a letter from America's president, Millard Fillmore, and punctuating his message with cannon fire, Commodore Perry ordered Japan's rulers to drop their barriers and open the country to trade. Over the next century and a half, Japan emerged as one of history's great economic success stories. It is now the largest creditor to the world that it previously shunned. Attempts to dissect this economic "miracle" often focus intently on the aftermath of the second world war. Japan's occupation by the Americans, who set out to rebuild the country as a pacifist liberal democracy, helped to set the stage for four decades of jaw-dropping growth. Yet the origins of the miracle—and of the continual tensions it has created inside Japan and out—stretch further back. When General Douglas MacArthur accepted Japan's surrender in 1945 aboard the battleship Missouri, the Americans made sure to hang Commodore Perry's flag from 1853 over the ship's rear turret. They had not only ended a brutal war and avenged the attack on Pearl Harbour—they had also, they thought, won an argument with Japan that was by then nearly a century old.

America's enduring frustration—in the decades after 1853, in 1945, and even today—has not been so much that Japan is closed, but that it long ago mastered the art of opening up on its own terms. Before and after those black ships steamed into Edo Bay, after all, plenty of other countries were opened to trade by western cannon. What set Japan apart—perhaps aided by America's lack of colonial ambition—was its ability to decide for itself how to make the process of opening suit its own aims.

One consequence of this is that Japan's trading partners, especially America, have never tired of complaining about its economic practices. Japan-bashing reached its most recent peak in the 1980s, when American politicians and businessmen blamed "unfair" competition for Japan's large trade surpluses. But similar complaints could be heard within a few decades of Commodore Perry's mission. The attitude was summed up by "Mr Dooley", a character created by Peter Finley Dunne, an American satirist, at the close of the 19th century: "Th' trouble is whin the gallant Commodore kicked opn th' door, we didn't go in. They come out."

Nowadays, although poor countries still want Japan (along with America and the European Union) to free up trade in farm goods, most rich-country complaints about Japan are aimed at its approach to macroeconomics and finance, rather than its trade policies. Japan's insistence on protecting bad banks and worthless companies, say its many critics, and its reluctance to let foreign investors help fix the economy, have prevented Japanese demand from recovering for far too long. Once again, the refrain goes, Japan is unfairly taking what it can get from the world economy—exports and overseas profits have been its only source of comfort for years—without giving anything back.

While these complaints have always had some merit, they have all too often been made in a way that misses a crucial point: Japan's economic miracle, though at times paired with policies ranging from protectionist to xenophobic, has nevertheless proved a huge blessing to the rest of the world as well. The "structural impediments" that shut out imports in the 1980s did indeed keep Japanese consumers and foreign exporters from enjoying some of the fruits of that miracle; but its export prowess allowed western consumers to enjoy better and cheaper cars and electronics even as Japanese households grew richer. Similarly, Japan's resistance to inward investment is indefensible, not least because it allows salvageable Japanese companies to wither; but its outward investment has helped to transform much of East Asia into a thriving economic region, putting a huge dent in global poverty. Indeed, one of the most impressive aspects of Japan's economic miracle is that, even while reaping only half the potential gains from free trade and investment, it has still managed to do the world so much good over the past half-century.

Setting an Example

Arguably, however, Japan's other big effect on the world has been even more important. It has shown clearly that you do not have to embrace "western" culture in order to modernise your economy and prosper. From the very beginning, Japan set out to have one without the other, an approach encapsulated by the saying "Japanese spirit, western things". How did Japan pull it off? In part, because the historical combination of having once been wide open, and then rapidly slamming shut, taught Japan how to control the aperture through which new ideas and practices streamed in. After eagerly absorbing Chinese culture, philosophy, writing and technology for roughly a millennium, Japan followed this with 250 years of near-total isolation. Christianity was outlawed, and overseas travel was punishable by death. Although some Japanese scholars were aware of developments in Europe—which went under the broad heading of "Dutch studies"—the shoguns strictly limited their ability to put any of that knowledge to use. They confined all economic and other exchanges with Europeans to a tiny man-made island in the south-western port of Nagasaki. When the Americans arrived in 1853, the Japanese told them to go to Nagasaki and obey the rules. Commodore Perry refused, and Japan concluded that the only way to "expel the barbarians" in future would be to embrace their technology and grow stronger.

But once the door was ajar, the Japanese appetite for "western things" grew unbounded. A modern guidebook entry on the port city of Yokohama, near Tokyo, notes that within two decades of the black ships' arrival it boasted the country's first bakery (1860), photo shop (1862), telephone (1869), beer brewery (1869), cinema (1870), daily newspaper (1870), and public lavatory (1871). Yet, at the same time, Japan's rulers also managed to frustrate many of the westerners' wishes. The constant tension between Japan's desire to measure up to the West—economically, diplomatically, socially and, until 1945, militarily—and its resistance to cultural change has played out in countless ways, good and bad, to this day. Much of it has reflected a healthy wish to hang on to local traditions. This is far more than just a matter of bowing and sleeping on futons and tatami, or of old women continuing to wear kimonos. The Japanese have also clung to distinct ways of speaking, interacting in the workplace, and showing each other respect, all of which have helped people to maintain harmony in many aspects of everyday life. Unfortunately, however, ever since they first opened to the West, anti-liberal Japanese leaders have preferred another interpretation of "Japanese spirit, western things". Instead of simply trying to preserve small cultural traditions, Japan's power-brokers tried to absorb western technology in a way that would shield them from political competition and protect their interests. Imitators still abound in Japan and elsewhere. In East Asia alone, Malaysia's Mahathir Mohamad, Thailand's Thaksin Shinawatra, and even the Chinese Communist Party all see Japan as proof that there is a way to join the rich-country club without making national leaders or their friends accountable. These disciples of Japan's brand of modernisation often use talk of local culture to resist economic and political threats to their power. But they are careful to find ways to do this without undermining all trade and investment, since growth is the only thing propping them up.

Japan's first attempt to pursue this strategy, it must never be forgotten, grew increasingly horrific as its inconsistencies mounted. In 1868, while western writers were admiring those bakeries and cinemas, Japan's nationalist leaders were "restoring" the emperor's significance to that of an imaginary golden age. The trouble, as Ian Buruma describes in his new book, "Inventing Japan" (scc article), is that the "Japanese spirit" they valued was a concoction that mixed in several bad western ideas: German theories on racial purity, European excuses for colonialism, and the observation from Christianity that a single overarching deity (in Japan's case the newly restored emperor) could motivate soldiers better than a loose contingent of Shinto gods. This combination would eventually whip countless young Japanese into a murderous xenophobic frenzy and foster rapacious colonial aggression.

It also led Japan into a head-on collision with the United States, since colonialism directly contradicted America's reasons for sending Commodore Perry. In "The Clash", a 1998 book on the history of American-Japanese relations, Walter LaFeber argues that America's main goal in opening Japan was not so much to trade bilaterally, as to enlist Japan's support in creating a global marketplace including, in particular, China. At first, the United States opened Japan because it was on the way to China and had coal for American steamships. Later, as Japan gained industrial and military might, America sought to use it as a counterweight to European colonial powers that wanted to divide China among their empires. America grew steadily more furious, therefore, as Japan turned to colonialism and tried to carve up China on its own. The irony for America was that at its very moment of triumph, after nearly a century of struggling with European powers and then Japan to keep China united and open, it ended up losing it to communism.

A half-century later, however, and with a great deal of help from Japan, America has achieved almost exactly what it set out to do as a brash young power in the 1850s, when it had barely tamed its own continent and was less than a decade away from civil war. Mainland China is whole. It has joined the World Trade Organisation and is rapidly integrating itself into the global economy. It is part of a vast East Asian trade network that nevertheless carries out more than half of its trade outside the region. And this is all backed up by an array of American security guarantees in the Pacific. The resemblance to what America set out to do in 1853 is striking.

For both Japan and America, therefore, the difficult 150-year relationship has brought impressive results. They are now the world's two biggest economies, and have driven most of the world's technological advances over the past half-century. America has helped Japan by opening it up, destroying its militarists and rebuilding the country afterwards, and, for the last 50 years, providing security and market access while Japan became an advanced export dynamo. Japan has helped America by improving on many of its technologies, teaching it new manufacturing techniques, spurring on American firms with its competition, and venturing into East Asia to trade and invest.

And Now?

What, then, will the continuing tension between Japanese spirit and western things bring in the decades ahead? For America, though it will no doubt keep complaining, Japan's resistance to change is not the real worry. Instead, the same two Asian challenges that America has taken on ever since Commodore Perry sailed in will remain the most worrying risks: potential rivalries, and the desire by some leaders to form exclusive regional economic blocks. America still needs Japan, its chief Asian ally, to combat these dangers. Japan's failure to reform, however, could slowly sap its usefulness.

For Japan, the challenges are far more daunting. Many of them stem from the increasing toll that Japan's old ways are taking on the economy. Chief among these is Japan's hostility towards competition in many aspects of economic life. Although competitive private firms have driven much of its innovation and growth, especially in export-intensive industries, Japan's political system continues to hobble competition and private enterprise in many domestic sectors.

In farming, health care and education, for example, recent efforts to allow private companies a role have been swatted down by co-operatives, workers, politicians and civil servants. In other inefficient sectors, such as construction and distribution, would-be losers continue to be propped up by government policy. Now that Japan is no longer growing rapidly, it is harder for competitive forces to function without allowing some of those losers to fail.

Japan's foreign critics are correct, moreover, that its macroeconomic and financial policies are a disgrace. The central bank, the finance ministry, the bank regulators, the prime minister and the ruling-party politicians all blame each other for failing to deal with the problems. All the while, Japan continues to limp along, growing far below its potential as its liabilities mount. Its public-sector debt, for instance, is a terrifying 140% of GDP.

Lately, there has been much talk about employing more western things to help lift Japan out of its mess. The prime minister, Junichiro Koizumi, talks about deregulatory measures that have been tried in North America, Europe and elsewhere. Western auditing and corporate governance techniques—applied in a Japanese way, of course—are also lauded as potential fixes. Even inward foreign direct investment is held out by Mr Koizumi as part of the solution: he has pledged to double it over the next five years. The trouble with all of these ideas, however, is that nobody in Japan is accountable for implementing them. Moreover, most of the politicians and bureaucrats who pre-

vent competitive pressures from driving change are themselves protected from political competition. It is undeniable that real change in Japan would bring unwelcome pain for many workers and small-business owners. Still, Japan's leaders continue to use these cultural excuses, as they have for 150 years, to mask their own efforts to cling to power and prestige. The ugly, undemocratic and illiberal aspects of Japanese traditionalism continue to lurk behind its admirable elements. One reason they can do so is because Japan's nationalists have succeeded completely in one of their original goals: financial independence. The desire to avoid relying on foreign capital has underlain Japan's economic policies from the time it opened up to trade. Those policies have worked. More than 90% of government bonds are in the hands of domestic investors, and savings accounts run by the postal service play a huge role in propping up the system.

Paradoxically, financial self-reliance has thus become Japan's curse. There are worse curses to have, of course: compare Japan with the countless countries that have wrecked their economies by overexposing themselves to volatile international capital markets. Nevertheless, Japan's financial insularity further protects its politicians, who do not have to compete with other countries to get funding.

Theories abound as to how all of this might change. Its history ought to remind anyone that, however long it takes, Japan usually moves rapidly once a consensus takes shape. Potential pressures for change could come from the reversal of its trade surpluses, an erosion of support from all those placid postal savers, or the unwinding of ties that allow bad banks and bad companies to protect each other from investors. The current political stalemate could also give way to a coherent plan, either because one political or bureaucratic faction defeats the others or because a strong leader emerges who can force them to co-operate. The past 150 years suggest, however, that one important question is impossible to answer in advance: will it be liberalism or its enemies who turn such changes to their advantage? Too often, Japan's conservative and nationalist leaders have managed to spot the forces of change more quickly than their liberal domestic counterparts, and have used those changes to seize the advantage and preserve their power. Just as in the past, East Asia's fortunes still greatly depend on the outcome of the struggle between these perennial Japanese contenders.

Come Together
How to Avoid a Twisted Diet

A great deal of wailing from the commenting class has accompanied Japan's political functions of late. Recall that in the summer the Liberal Democratic Party (LDP), which heads the ruling coalition, lost its majority in the upper house of the Diet (parliament) for the first time in a long and domineering history; that the huge defeat added to the strains of the prime minister, Shinzo Abe, who suffered a physical and nervous breakdown and who resigned last month after less than a year in office; and that the new prime minister, Yasuo Fukuda, chosen in a hurry by the LDP for his seniority and competence, is seen even by his warmest admirers as little more than a caretaker.

For now the opposition Democratic Party of Japan (DPJ) is eager to use its new upper-house majority to frustrate Mr Fukuda, forcing him to resign and call a general (ie, lower-house) election. While the constitution does not mandate such an election before September 2009, most commentators expect one to be called as early as December, and probably no later than next summer.

The government's first test comes in extending the Japanese navy's refuelling presence in American-led operations in the Indian Ocean. The DPJ's leader, Ichiro Ozawa, who believes only a United Nations mandate should authorise Japanese military operations abroad, vows to oppose the move.

A general election in most countries might be expected to clear the air, but in Japan the next one almost certainly will not. That is because, although the LDP will assuredly lose an embarrassing number of seats, the opposition—for all its wishful thinking—does not look strong enough to grab control of the lower house, which appoints the prime minister.

In the upper house, meanwhile, only half the seats are contested every three years; it is scarcely imaginable that the LDP could win back its majority in fewer than six years. So years of what commentators call a "twisted" Diet beckon—or what perhaps can more earthily be translated as an arsy-versy one. And for a country used to its politics served up in straight, predictable and soothing form, this prospect of division, discord and even chaos is shockingly grim.

But is this analysis right? Late last week, Junichiro Koizumi made waves by turning it on its head. Mr Koizumi, the only true iconoclast in Japan's post-war political history, became LDP party leader and prime minister six years ago, challenging his party's machine politics, in which factions competed for money and influence, and arguing for measures to revitalise the economy. In 2005, when he met resistance to reforms from his own party, Mr Koizumi went over its head by calling a snap election. Voters delivered the two-thirds majority that the ruling coalition enjoys today. A year later, the maverick stepped down. Mr Abe stepped up, and the party self-destructed.

Mr Koizumi addressed what was once seen as a rebel faction but is now the LDP's biggest, the "Machimura" faction, which has produced the last four prime ministers. The arsy-versy Diet, Mr Koizumi told members, should not be seen as reflecting ideological clashes: both parties, after all, are essentially free-market and internationalist, while the DPJ's leaders built their political careers within the LDP's mainstream.

Rather, party differences that have sharpened since the upper-house result should be thought of as akin to those fierce policy disputes that used to flare among LDP factions with every leadership contest. On those occasions, as MTC, a blogger on Japanese politics, puts it: "Once the elections were over or a new prime minister was voted into office, factions allowed these seemingly life-or-death differences to fade. Instead, what became important was finding the means to co-operate on passing legislation and equitably dividing the political spoils."

Mr Koizumi's advice to his audience was straightforward. Just as the Machimura faction was once the challenger to the LDP mainstream, so the DPJ now has that role vis-à-vis the LDP. And just as the LDP factions soon settled back into a routine of co-operation and mutual favours, so the LDP should co-operate with, or even co-opt, the DPJ. The comforting genius of this formulation is that LDP members can feel as if they've been here before.

Whether the opposition will choose to play along is another matter. The battle over the Indian Ocean operations, which begins in earnest next week, will be the first test.

UNIT 3

Factors in the Political Process

Unit Selections

Key Points to Consider

- Explain the terms "Left" and "Right" in European politics. Why have the terms "center-left" and "center-right" come into use? Which is the major party on the center-left and center-right, respectively, in Germany, France, and Britain?

- An English political scientist addressing American students, once described the political parties as the "alpha and omega" of British politics. Why do political scientists emphasize the role of parties in democratic politics? Why is party discipline important for government stability and effectiveness?

- Why are women so poorly represented in Parliament and other positions of political leadership? How can this be changed? Name some of the countries that have led in going well beyond the 30 percent mark—often regarded as a "critical mass" among specialists on the subject. Why does the United States rank so low (currently 66th) on such a scale? And why have U.S. women made greater breakthroughs to leadership positions in the economic and business sphere as well as in higher education than is true for some of the countries that lead in the political sphere?

- What are some major arguments made in favor of the parliamentary system of government? Do all parliamentary systems function as well in reality?

- What are some key differences between the United States and Germany in their practice of judicial review? How does Britain handle such matters? And what about France?

- Why do you think de Gaulle added the national referendum to the Constitution of the Fifth Republic? Can you explain its use until now?

Student Web Site

www.mhcls.com/online

Internet References

Further information regarding these Web sites may be found in this book's preface or online.

Carnegie Endowment for International Peace
  http://www.ceip.org
Inter-American Dialogue (IAD)
  http://www.iadialog.org
The North American Institute (NAMI)
  http://www.northamericaninstitute.org

Observers of contemporary Western societies frequently refer to the emergence of a **"new politics"** during the last third of a century. There is no complete agreement on what is novel in the democratic political process and why it is significant. Yet three keen observers, Russell Dalton, Susan Scarrow, and Bruce Cain have concluded that we may be experiencing "the most **fundamental democratic transformation** since the beginning of mass democracy in the early twentieth century." They refer to the old and established democracies of Europe and North America, where there has been a shift away from a—sometimes exclusive—reliance on institutions of representative government, in which the citizens elect decision-making elites. The shift has opened more opportunities for direct **democracy,** where citizens decide on some policy issues themselves and also engage in forms of **direct advocacy,** as the three authors emphasize in their important article, "Advanced Democracies and the New Politics" which is included in this reader.

In two important lines of inquiry, political comparativists have examined two other significant changes (1) the rise and spread of a new set of **"postmaterial" values,** primarily in the "old" democracies and, more recently (2) the growing signs of **political disaffection with political leaders and institutions** in both older and newer democracies (see Thomas Carothers, Democracy's Sobering State). The articles in this and other units also explore some other trends with major impacts on contemporary politics. Very high on the list are the uneven advancement of **women in politics,** especially into high elective and appoint-

ive public office, and the recent **wave of democratization**—the uneven, incomplete, and unstable but nevertheless remarkable spread of democratic forms of governance to many countries during the last three decades. The latter topic was discussed in Unit One, where the distinction between **electoral democracy** and **liberal democracy** was also introduced.

Since the early 1970s, political scientists have followed Ronald Inglehart and others who first noted a marked increase in what they called **post-material values,** especially among younger and more highly educated people in Western Europe. Such voters showed less interest in **traditional material values** of economic well being and security, instead stressing participatory and environmental concerns in politics as a way of improving democracy and the general "quality of life." Studies of post-materialism form a very important addition to our ongoing attempt to interpret and explain not only the so-called **youth revolt of the late 1960s and early 1970s** but also some more lasting **changes in lifestyles and political priorities.** This shift towards a post-material direction has not been complete, nor is it necessarily permanent: note the apparent revival of material concerns among some younger people, as economic prosperity and security seem to have become far less certain. Political reform activities also seem to evoke considerably less interest and commitment than they did a generation or two ago.

A return to the political patterns of the past is highly unlikely. Instead, we may be witnessing the emergence of a **new mix of material and postmaterial orientations,** along with "old" and "new" forms of **political self-expression** by the citizenry. Established political parties appear to be in somewhat of a quandary: the traditional bonding of many voters to one or another party has become weaker, a phenomenon also known as **dealignment.** Some observers perceive a condition of political malaise in advanced industrial countries, suggesting that the decline of confidence in public officials and government shows up not only in opinion polls but also in voting behavior.

Political Parties and Interest Groups. The two briefs that present a comparative perspective on the widespread public disillusionment with politics—reflected in a weakening of the political parties, a decline in party membership and in voter turnout, and an apparent growth of special interest lobbying. Most established parties seem to have developed an ability to adjust to change, even as the balance of power within each party system shifts over time. Occasionally a successful newcomer is admitted to the club—or a failed member is excluded from it. But in a country like Germany, one is struck with the stability and continuity in the party landscape. Each country's system remains uniquely shaped by its political history, electoral laws, and unique cleavages, but it is possible to delineate some very general patterns of recent development. One frequently observed trend is toward a **narrowing of the ideological distance between the moderate Left and Right** in many European countries. Because of this partial **political convergence,** it now often makes more sense to speak of the **Center-Left** and **Center-Right.** Even where such a shift toward the center is observable, there are still some important ideological and practical differences between the two basic orientations.

The Right is usually far more ready to accept as "normal" or "inevitable" the existence of social or economic inequalities, and normally favors lower taxes and the promotion of market forces—with some very important exceptions intended to protect the nation as a whole (national defense and internal security) as well as certain favored values and interest groups (clienteles). In general, the Right sees the state as an instrument that should provide security, order, and protection for an established way of life.

The Left, by contrast, traditionally emphasizes that government has an important task in opening greater opportunities or "life chances" for everyone, delivering affordable public services, and generally reducing social inequality.

Even as the ideological distance between mainstream Left and Right narrows, there are also signs of some political differentiation within each camp. On the Center-Right side of the party spectrum in European politics, **economic neo-liberals** must be clearly distinguished from **social conservatives.** As we have seen in the case of Britain, France and Germany, European liberalism has its roots in a tradition that favors civil liberties and tolerance but that also emphasizes the importance of individual achievement and laissez-faire economics. For **neo-liberals,** the state has an important but limited role to play in providing an institutional framework within which individuals and social groups pursue their interests (or "happiness," as Jefferson put it) without much government intervention. The Liberal Democrats of Britain are somewhat more "social" than their counterparts in Germany or France.

Traditional **social conservatives** don't share the liberal distrust of the state. Instead, they emphasize its key role in maintaining social stability and continuity. They not only value the strong state as an instrument of order, but many of them also show a paternalist or pragmatic appreciation for welfare state programs that will help keep the **social fabric** from tearing apart. They may find themselves supporting welfare state measures, but they will not be motivated by an egalitarian ideology like the Left—instead by the sentiment of *noblesse oblige.* That is how Edwin Heath's wing of the Conservative Party in Britain could support maintaining the welfare state until Margaret Thatcher defeated him in a leadership contest and led the party on a business-friendly course. This kind of conservatism is less well known in the United States, but a few years ago, a campaign for **"compassionate conservatism"** tried to capture some of the gist of it.

On the Left, **democratic socialists** and **ecologists** stress that the sorry record of communist-ruled states in no way diminishes or invalidates their own commitment to social justice and environmental protection in modern industrial society. For them, capitalism will continue to produce acute social problems and dissatisfactions that require politically directed redress. Today, many on the Left show a pragmatic acceptance of the modified market economy as an arena within which to promote their goals of redistribution. **Social Democrats** in Scandinavia and Germany have long been known for taking such positions. In recent years their colleagues in Britain, Spain, and, to a lesser degree, France have followed suit by abandoning some traditional symbols and goals, such as major programs of nationalization.

Some other West European parties, originally further to the Left, have also moved in the centrist direction in recent years. Two striking examples of this shift can be found among the **Greens** in Germany and in what used to be the Communist Party of Italy. The German Greens are by no means an establishment party, but they have served as a coalition partner with the Social Democrats in several state governments and for seven years in the federal government. They have gained respect for their mixture of practical competence and idealism. They now appear to have become a firmly established small party with a distinctive program and a solid record in coalition politics. **The Italian Communists** have traversed an even longer road from a revolutionary past to reach their present Center-Left position, abandoning the Leninist revolutionary tradition and adopting reformist goals and strategies that seem increasingly similar to those identified with social democratic parties elsewhere in Western Europe. Renamed the Left Democrats (DS), they joined Center-Left coalition governments in 1998 and again in 2006, after a five-year interlude under Berlusconi's right-of-center government. When Juan Linz emphasizes the collapse of the old Italian party system in the early 1990s, it could be added that some major political tendencies remained and found expression in a reconstituted party system that continued the Left-Right tradition.

Both Center-Left and Center-Right moderates in Europe face a challenge from the populist tendency on the **Far Right** that usually seeks to curtail, halt, or even reverse immigration, sometimes with a separate neo-fascist appeal. (A charismatic leader like Jörg Haider of the Austrian Freedom Party can speak to both orientations.) The electoral revival of the far-Right parties can be linked in considerable part to anxieties and tensions that affect some socially and economically insecure groups in the lower-middle and working classes. These parties typically eschew a complex explanation of the structural and cyclical problems that beset the European economies, instead blaming external scapegoats, namely immigrants and refugees from Eastern Europe as well as developing countries in Africa and Asia. Nowhere are these parties in control of a national government, but they represent a potential threat to the established parties, which have in some cases responded by adopting an appeasement policy that makes concessions on immigration and refugee policy.

Women in politics are the concern of the second section in this unit. As Swanee Hunt's survey indicates, there continues to be a strong pattern of under-representation of women in positions of political and economic leadership practically everywhere. Still, there are some notable differences from country to country and party to party. Generally speaking, the **parties of the Left** have been far more ready to place women in positions of authority, with some remarkable exceptions (Margaret Thatcher in Britain, Angela Merkel in Germany, and Simone Weil in France). Right-wing parties tend to draw markedly less support from female voters, but at least one of them is led by a woman: Pia Kjaersgaard founded and still heads the People's Party of Denmark. In structural terms, **proportional representation** systems give parties both a tool and an added incentive to run female candidates. But here too, there can be exceptions; there must also be **an organized will and a strategy** among decision makers to use the available tool for the purpose of such a clearly defined reform.

Where the political will exists, **affirmative action** can become such a strategy for promoting change. Such a breakthrough has happened in the Scandinavian countries, which have a markedly higher representation of women in parliament and in party leadership. In each of these five countries, the political center of gravity falls somewhat to the Left, and proportional representation makes it possible to set up **party candidate lists** that are more representative of the population as a whole. It usually does not take long for the more centrist or moderately conservative parties to adopt the new concern of gender equality, and these parties may even move toward the forefront. Even a decidedly non-feminist politician like Germany's Angela Merkel can benefit from reforms that have a feminist origin. Outside Scandinavia, signs of the growing political prominence of women can be seen in traditionally conservative countries such as the Republic of Ireland, Switzerland, and Japan.

Changes that erode gender inequality have already occurred in areas other than representation in government. For example, in many countries, including the United States, the **gender gap in voter turnout** has been practically eliminated in recent decades. Furthermore, younger women in the United States and elsewhere in modernized societies show a more liberal orientation than formerly in their foreign and social policy preferences. These are aggregate differences, of course—women, like men, do not present a monolithic bloc in political attitudes and behavior but are divided by a variety of interests and priorities. One generalization seems to hold across the board—there is much less inclination among women to support parties or candidates that have a decidedly "radical" image.

While European women still tend to be employed at lower wages and in lower-skilled jobs than their male counterparts, the **socioeconomic status of women** in other parts of the world is often far worse. According to reports of the UN Development Program, there have been some rapid advances for women in the field of education and health opportunities, but the doors to economic opportunities are barely ajar. In the field of political leadership, the picture is more varied, as the UN reports indicate, but women generally hold few positions of importance in national politics. Rwanda is an exception. The recent genocide in that country has left women, now nearly two-thirds of the country's population, in positions of leadership. Another notable exception is Costa Rica, the only "older democracy" located in Latin America.

The third section of this unit returns to the institutional framework of a democracy that is the subject of several articles in Unit One and additional ones here. The two briefly examine institutions that are located at opposite ends of a representative government's central location—one examines judicial review and the other looks at the use of national and regional referendums, both of which reduce in very different ways and degrees the power of the representative government. In judicial review, the representative part of government is superseded by a judicial umpire, who interprets and applies the law to individual cases of legal conflict. As for direct democracy, it is the citizens themselves. In the case of direct democracy, it is the citizens themselves who make decisions rather than their elected representatives. In a pluralistic democracy that values checks and balances, such a dispersion of power does not seem illogical, but it can make it a little more difficult to govern.

Finally, Christopher S. Allen brings **U.S. political institutions** into our comparative framework. His article can be seen as part of a long tradition of American interest in the **parliamentary form of government** and, to a lesser degree, in **a multiparty system.** Allen organizes his argument as a mental experiment in institutional transplantation, in order to explore how **a multiparty parliamentary system** would be likely to change the American political process. His intriguing rearrangement of our main political institutions is bound to lead to discussion and debate.

Political Parties: Empty Vessels?

Alexis de Tocqueville called political parties an evil inherent in free governments. The second of our briefs on the mature democracies in transition asks whether parties are in decline

What would democracy look like if there were no political parties? It is almost impossible to imagine. In every democracy worth the name, the contest to win the allegiance of the electorate and form a government takes place through political parties. Without them, voters would be hard put to work out what individual candidates stood for or intended to do once elected. If parties did not "aggregate" people's interests, politics might degenerate into a fight between tiny factions, each promoting its narrow self-interest. But for the past 30 years, political scientists have been asking whether parties are "in decline". Are they? And if so, does it matter?

Generalising about political parties is difficult. Their shape depends on a country's history, constitution and much else. For example, America's federal structure and separation of powers make Republicans and Democrats amorphous groupings whose main purpose is to put their man in the White House. British parties behave quite differently because members of Parliament must toe the party line to keep their man in Downing Street. An American president is safe once elected, so congressmen behave like local representatives rather than members of a national organisation bearing collective responsibility for government. Countries which, unlike Britain and America, hold elections under proportional representation are different again: they tend to produce multi-party systems and coalition governments.

Despite these differences, some trends common to almost all advanced democracies appear to be changing the nature of parties and, on one view, making them less influential. Those who buy this thesis of decline point to the following changes:

People's behaviour is becoming more **private**. Why join a political party when you can go fly fishing or surf the web? Back in the 1950s, clubs affiliated to the Labour Party were places for Britain's working people to meet, play and study. The Conservative Party was, among other things, a marriage bureau for the better-off. Today, belonging to a British political party is more like being a supporter of some charity: you may pay a membership fee, but will not necessarily attend meetings or help to turn out the vote at election time.

Running Out of Ideas

Politics is becoming more **secular**. Before the 1960s, political struggles had an almost religious intensity: in much of Western Europe this took the form of communists versus Catholics, or workers versus bosses. But ideological differences were narrowing by the 1960s and became smaller still after the collapse of Soviet communism. Nowadays, politics seems to be more often about policies than values, about the competence of leaders rather than the beliefs of the led. As education grows and class distinctions blur, voters discard old loyalties. In America in 1960, two out of five voters saw themselves as "strong" Democrats or "strong" Republicans. By 1996 less than one in three saw themselves that way. The proportion of British voters expressing a "very strong" affinity with one party slumped from 44% to 16% between 1964 and 1997. This process of **"partisan de-alignment"** has been witnessed in most mature democracies.

The erosion of loyalty is said to have pushed parties towards the **ideological centre.** The political extremes have not gone away. But mainstream parties which used to offer a straight choice between socialists and conservatives are no longer so easy to label. In the late 1950s Germany's Social Democrats (SPD) snipped off their Marxist roots in order to recast themselves is a *Volkspartei* appealing to all the people. "New" Labour no longer portrays itself as the political arm of the British working class or trade-union movement. Bill Clinton, before he became president, helped to shift the Democratic Party towards an appreciation of business and free trade. Neat ideological labels have become harder to pin on parties since they have had to contend with the emergence of what some commentators call **post-material issues** (such as the environment, personal morality and consumer rights) which do not slot elegantly into the old left-right framework.

The **mass media** have taken over many of the information functions that parties once performed for themselves. "Just as radio and television have largely killed off the door-to-door salesman," says Anthony King, of Britain's Essex University, "so they have largely killed off the old-fashioned party worker." In 1878 the German SPD had nearly 50 of its own newspapers. Today the mass media enable politicians to communicate directly with voters without owning printing presses or needing party workers to knock on doors. In many other ways, the business of winning elections has become more capital-intensive and less labour-intensive, making political donors matter more and political activists less.

Another apparent threat to the parties is the growth of **interest and pressure groups.** Why should voters care about the broad sweep of policy promoted during elections by a party when other organisations will lobby all year round for their special interest, whether this is protection of the environment, opposition to abortion, or the defence of some subsidy? Some academics also claim that parties are playing a smaller role, and **think tanks** a bigger one, in making policy. Although parties continue to draw up election manifestos, they are wary of being too specific. Some hate leaving policymaking to party activists, who may be more extreme than voters at large and so put them off. Better to keep the message vague. Or why not let the tough choices be taken by **referendums**, as so often in Switzerland?

Academics have found these trends easier to describe than to evaluate. Most agree that the age of the "mass party" has passed and that its place is being taken by the "electoral-professional" or "catch-all" party. Although still staffed by politicians holding genuine beliefs and values, these modern parties are inclined to see their main objective as winning elections rather than forming large membership organisations or social movements, as was once the case.

Is this a bad thing? Perhaps, if it reduces participation in politics. One of the traditional roles of political parties has been to get out the vote, and in 18 out of 20 rich countries, recent turnout figures have been lower than they were in the 1950s. Although it is hard to pin down the reasons, Martin Wattenberg, of the University of California at Irvine, points out that turnout has fallen most sharply in countries where parties are weak: Switzerland (thanks to

those referendums), America and France (where presidential elections have become increasingly candidate- rather than party-centred), and Japan (where political loyalties revolve around ties to internal factions rather than the party itself). In Scandinavia, by contrast, where class-based parties are still relatively strong, turnout has held up much better since the 1950s.

Running Out of Members

It is not only voters who are turned off. Party membership is falling too, and even the most strenuous attempts to reverse the decline have faltered. Germany is a case in point. The Social Democrats there increased membership rapidly in the 1960s and 1970s, and the Christian Democrats responded by doubling their own membership numbers. But since the end of the 1980s membership has been falling, especially among the young. In 1964 Britain's Labour Party had about 830,000 members and the Conservatives about 2m. By 1997 they had 420,000 and 400,000 respectively. The fall is sharper in some countries than others, but research by Susan Scarrow of the University of Houston suggests that the trend is common to most democracies (see figure 1). With their membership falling, ideological differences blurring, and fewer people turning out to vote, the decline thesis looks hard to refute.

Or does it? The case for party decline has some big holes in it. For a start, some academics question whether political parties ever really enjoyed the golden age which other academics hark back to. Essex University's Mr King points out that a lot of the evidence for decline is drawn from a handful of parties—Britain's two main ones, the German SPD, the French and Italian Communists—which did indeed once promote clear ideologies, enjoy mass memberships, and organise local branches and social activities. But neither of America's parties, nor Canada's, nor many of the bourgeois parties of Western Europe, were ever mass parties of that sort. Moreover, in spite of their supposed decline, parties continue to keep an iron grip on many aspects of politics.

In most places, for example, parties still control **nomination for public office**. In almost all of the mature democracies, it is rare for independent candidates to be elected to federal or state legislatures, and even in local government the proportion of independents has declined sharply since the early 1970s. When state and local parties select candidates, they usually favour people who have worked hard within the party. German parties, for example, are often conduits to jobs in the public sector, with a say over appointments to top jobs in the civil service and to the boards of publicly owned utilities or media organisations. Even in America, where independent candidates are more common in local elections, the parties still run city, county and state "machines" in which most politicians start their careers.

Naturally, there are some exceptions. In 1994 Silvio Berlusconi, a media tycoon, was able to make himself prime minister at the head of Forza Italia, a right-wing movement drawing heavily on his personal fortune and the resources of his television empire. Ross Perot, a wealthy third-party candidate, won a respectable 19% vote in his 1992 bid for the American presidency. The party declinists claim these examples as evidence for their case. But it is notable that in the end Mr Perot could not compete against the two formidable campaigning and money-raising machines ranged against him.

This suggests that a decline in the membership of parties need not make them weaker in **money and organisation**. In fact, many have enriched themselves simply by passing laws that give them public money. In Germany, campaign subsidies to the federal parties more than trebled between 1970 and 1990, and parties now receive between 20% and 40% of their income from public funds. In America, the paid professionals who have taken over from party activists tend to do their job more efficiently. Moreover, other kinds of political activity—such as donating money to a party or interest group, or attending meetings and rallies—have become more common in America. Groups campaigning for particular causes or candidates (the pro-Republican Christian Coalition, say, or the pro-Democrat National Education Association) may not be formally affiliated with the major party organisations, but are frequently allied with them.

The role of the mass media deserves a closer look as well. It is true that they have weakened the parties' traditional methods of communicating with members. But parties have invested heavily in managing relations with journalists, and making use of new media to reach both members and wider audiences. In Britain, the dwindling of local activists has gone hand-in-hand with a more professional approach to communications. Margaret Thatcher caused a stir by using an advertising firm, Saatchi & Saatchi, to push the Tory cause in the 1979 election. By the time of Britain's 1997 election, the New Labour media operation run from Millbank Tower in London was even slicker.

Another way to gauge the influence of parties is by their **reach**—that is, their power, once in office, to take control of the governmental apparatus. This is a power they have retained. Most governments tend to be unambiguously under the control of people who represent a party, and who would not be in government if they did not belong to such organisations. The French presidential system may appear ideal for independent candidates, but except—arguably—for Charles de Gaulle, who claimed to rise above party, none has ever been elected without party support.

The Fire Next Time

Given the cautions that must be applied to other parts of the case for party decline, what can be said about one of the declinists' key exhibits, the erosion of ideological differences? At first sight, this is borne out by the recent movement to the centre of left-leaning parties such as America's Democrats, New Labour in Britain, and the SPD under Gerhard Schröder. In America, Newt Gingrich stoked up some fire amongst Republicans in 1994, but it has flickered out. The most popular Republican presidential hopefuls, and especially George W. Bush, the frontrunner, are once again stressing the gentler side of their conservatism.

Still, the claim of ideological convergence can be exaggerated. It is not much more than a decade since Ronald Reagan and Mrs Thatcher ran successful parties with strong ideologies. And the anecdotal assumption that parties are growing less distinct is challenged by longer-term academic studies. A look at the experience of ten western democracies since 1945 ("Parties, Policies and Democracy", Westview Press, 1994) concluded that the leading left and right parties continued to keep their distance and maintain their identity, rather than clustering around the median voter in the centre. Paul Webb of Britain's Brunel University concludes in a forthcoming book ("Political Parties in Advanced Industrial Democracies", Oxford University Press) that although partisan sentiment is weaker than it was, and voters more cynical, parties have in general adapted well to changing circumstances.

Besides, even if party differences are narrowing at present, why expect that trend to continue? In Western Europe, the ending of the cold war has snuffed out one source of ideological conflict, but new sparks might catch fire. Battered right-wing parties may try to revive their fortunes by pushing the nationalist cause against the encroachments of the European Union. In some places where ideas are dividing parties less, geography is dividing them more.

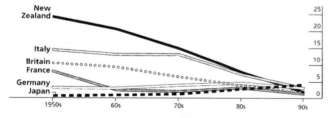

Figure 1   The Few Not the Many.   Party members as % of electorate

Source: Susan E. Scarrow, Centre for German and European Studies Working Paper 2.59, University of California, Berkeley

Politics in Germany and Britain has acquired an increasingly regional flavour: Labour and the Social Democrats respectively dominate the north, Conservatives and Christian Democrats the south. Disaffected *Ossis* are flocking to the Party of Democratic Socialism in eastern Germany. Britain, Italy, Canada and Spain have strong separatist parties.

So there is life in the party system yet. But the declinists are on to something. The Germans have a word for it. One reason given for the rise of Germany's Greens in the 1980s and America's Mr Perot in 1992 was *Parteienverdrossenheit*—disillusionment with mainstream parties that seemed to have abandoned their core beliefs and no longer offered meaningful choices. A "new politics" of citizens' protests appeared to be displacing conventional politics.

In the end, far from undermining the domination of the parties, the German Greens ended up by turning themselves into one and joining the government in an uneasy coalition with the SPD. The balance of evidence from around the world is that despite all the things that are changing them, parties continue to dominate democratic politics.

Indeed, there are grounds for wondering whether their continuing survival is more of a worry than their supposed decline. Is it so very comforting that parties can lose members, worry less about ideas, become detached from broader social movements, attract fewer voters and still retain an iron grip on politics? If they are so unanchored, will they not fall prey to special-interest groups? If they rely on state funding instead of member contributions, will they not turn into creatures of the state? The role of money in politics will be the subject of another brief.

Interest Groups: Ex Uno, Plures

The last article in our series on the mature democracies asks whether they are in danger of being strangled by lobbyists and single-issue pressure groups

Previous briefs in this series have looked at the imperfections in democracy as it is currently practised in the rich countries, and at some of the efforts that different countries are making to overcome them. Evidence that all is not well includes declining public confidence in politicians, falling membership of political parties and smaller turnouts for elections. Ideas for improvement range from making greater use of referendums and other forms of direct democracy, to giving more power to courts to check the power of politicians. This article asks a different question: far from being too powerful, are elected politicians in modern democracies too weak?

When Alexis de Tocqueville visited the United States in the 19th century, he was impressed by the enthusiasm of Americans for joining associations. This, he felt, spread power away from the centre and fostered the emergence of democratic habits and a civil society. Until quite recently, most political scientists shared De Tocqueville's view. Lately, however, and especially in America, doubts have set in. At a certain point, say the doubters, the cumulative power of pressure groups, each promoting its own special interests, can grow so strong that it prevents elected politicians from adopting policies that are in the interest of the electorate as a whole.

A Hitchhiker's Guide

A key text for such critics was a short book published in 1965 by Mancur Olson, an American economist. Called "The Logic of Collective Action", this took issue with the traditional idea that the health of democracy was served by vigorous competition between pressure groups, with governments acting as a sort of referee, able to choose the best policy once the debate between the contending groups was over. The traditional view, Olson argued, wrongly assumed that pressure groups were more or less equal. In fact, for a reason known to economists as the free-rider problem, they weren't.

Why? Take the example of five car firms, which form a lobbying group in the hope of raising the price of cars. If they succeed, each stands to reap a fifth of the gains. This makes forming the group and working for its success well worth each firm's investment of time and money. If the car makers succeed, of course, motorists will suffer. But organising millions of individual motorists to fight their corner is a great deal harder because it involves co-ordinating millions of people and because the potential gain for each motorist will be relatively small. Individual motorists will be tempted to reason that, with millions of other people involved, they do not need to do anything themselves, but can instead hitch a "free ride" on the efforts of everyone else.

This simple insight has powerful implications. Indeed, in a later book Olson went on to argue that his theory helped to explain why some nations flourish and others decline. As pressure groups multiply over time, they tend to choke a nation's vitality by impairing the government's ability to act in the wider interest. That, he argued, is why countries such as Germany and Japan—whose interest groups had been cleared away by a traumatic defeat—had fared better after the second world war than Britain, whose institutions had survived intact. With its long record of stability, said Olson, "British society has acquired so many strong organisations and collusions that it suffers from an institutional sclerosis that slows its adaptation to changing circumstances and changing technologies."

Olson's ideas have not gone unchallenged. But they have had a big impact on contemporary thinking about what ails American democracy. In "Demosclerosis" (Times Books, 1994), Jonathan Rauch, a populariser of Olson's work, says that America is afflicted by "hyperpluralism". With at least seven out of ten Americans belonging to at least one such association, the whole society, not just "special" parts of it, is now involved in influence peddling.

The result is that elected politicians find it almost impossible to act solely in the wider public interest. Bill Clinton wants to reform the health system? The health-insurance industry blocks him. China's membership in the World Trade Organisation would benefit America's consumers? America's producers of textiles and steel stand in the way. Jimmy Carter complained when he left the presidency that Americans were increasingly drawn to single-issue groups to ensure that, whatever else happened, their own private interest would be protected. The trouble is, "the national interest is not always the sum of all our single or special interests".

Pressure groups are especially visible in the United States. As Oxford University's Jeremy Richardson puts it ("Pressure Groups", Oxford University Press, 1993), "pressure groups take account of (and exploit) the multiplicity of access points which is so characteristic of the American system of government—the presidency, the bureaucracy, both houses of Congress, the powerful congressional committees, the judiciary and state and local government."

Nevertheless pressure groups often wield just as much influence in other countries. In those where parliaments exercise tighter control of the executive—Canada, Britain or Germany, say—the government controls the parliamentary timetable and the powers of committees are much weaker. This means that pressure groups adopt different tactics. They have more chance of influencing policy behind closed doors, by bargaining with the executive branch and its civil servants before legislation comes before parliament. In this way pressure groups can sometimes exert more influence than their counterparts in America.

Political Tribes

Many European countries have also buttressed the influence of pressure groups by giving them a semi-official status. In Germany, for example, the executive branch is obliged by law to consult the various big "interest organisations" before drafting legislation. In some German states, leading interest groups (along with political parties) have seats on the supervisory boards of broadcasting firms.

French pressure groups are also powerful, despite the conventional image of a strong French state dominating a relatively weak civil society. It is true that a lot of France's interest groups depend on the state for both money and membership of a network of formal consultative bodies. But a tradition of direct protest compensates for some of this institutional weakness. In France, mass demonstrations, strikes, the blocking of roads and the disruption of public services are seen as a part of normal democratic politics.

In Japan, powerful pressure groups such as the Zenchu (Central Union of Agricultural Co-operatives) have turned large areas of public policy into virtual no-go areas. With more than 9m members (and an electoral system that gives farming communities up to three times the voting weight of urban voters), farmers can usually obstruct any policy that damages their interests. The teachers' union has similarly blocked all attempts at education reform. And almost every sector of Japanese society has its *zoku giin* (political tribes), consisting of Diet members who have made themselves knowledgeable about one industry or another, which pays for their secretaries and provides campaign funds. A Diet member belonging to the transport tribe will work hand-in-glove with senior bureaucrats in the transport ministry and the trucking industry to form what the Japanese call an "iron triangle" consisting of politicians, bureaucrats and big business.

Pressure groups are also increasingly active at a transnational level. Like any bureaucracy, the European Union has spawned a rich network of interest groups. In 1992 the European Commission reckoned that at least 3,000 special-interest groups in Brussels employing some 10,000 people acted as lobbyists. These range from big operations, such as the EU committee of the American Chamber of Commerce, to small firms and individual lobbyists-for-hire. Businesses were the

first to spot the advantages of influencing the EU's law making. But trade unions swiftly followed, often achieving in Brussels breakthroughs (such as regulations on working conditions) that they could not achieve at home.

The Case for the Defense

So pressure groups are ubiquitous. But are they so bad? Although it has been influential, the Olson thesis has not swept all before it. Many political scientists argue that the traditional view that pressure groups create a healthy democratic pluralism is nearer the mark than Olson's thesis.

The case in favour of pressure groups begins with some of the flaws of representative democracy. Elections are infrequent and, as a previous brief in this series noted, political parties can be vague about their governing intentions. Pressure groups help people to take part in politics between elections, and to influence a government's policy in areas that they care and know about. Pressure groups also check excessive central power and give governments expert advice. Although some groups may flourish at the expense of the common weal, this danger can be guarded against if there are many groups and if all have the same freedom to organise and to put their case to government.

Critics of Olson's ideas also point out that, contrary to his prediction, many broad-based groups have in fact managed to flourish in circumstances where individual members stand to make little personal gain and should therefore fall foul of his "free-rider" problem. Clearly, some people join pressure groups for apparently altruistic reasons—perhaps simply to express their values or to be part of an organisation in which they meet like-minded people. Some consumer and environmental movements have flourished in rich countries, even though Olson's theory suggests that firms and polluters should have a strong organisational advantage over consumers and inhalers of dirty air.

Moreover, despite "demosclerosis", well-organised pressure groups can sometimes ease the task of government, not just throw sand into its wheels. The common European practice of giving pressure groups a formal status, and often a legal right to be consulted, minimises conflict by ensuring that powerful groups put their case to governments before laws are introduced. Mr Richardson argues in a forthcoming book ("Developments in the European Union", Macmillan, 1999) that even the pressure groups clustering around the institutions of the EU perform a valuable function. The European Commission, concerned with the detail of regulation, is an eager consumer of their specialist knowledge. As the powers of the European Parliament have grown, it too has attracted a growing band of lobbyists. The parliament has created scores of "intergroups" whose members gain expertise in specific sectors, such as pharmaceuticals, from industry and consumer lobbies.

Governments can learn from pressure groups, and can work through them to gain consent for their policies. At some point, however, the relationship becomes excessively cosy. If pressure groups grow too strong, they can deter governments from pursuing policies which are in the wider public interest. The temptation of governments to support protectionist trade policies at the behest of producer lobbies and at the expense of consumers is a classic example supporting Olson's theories. But problems also arise when it is governments that are relatively strong, and so able to confer special status on some pressure groups and withhold it from others. This puts less-favoured groups at a disadvantage, which they often seek to redress by finding new and sometimes less democratic ways of making their voices heard.

In Germany, for example, disenchantment with what had come to be seen as an excessively cosy system of bargaining between elite groups helped to spark an explosion of protest movements in the 1980s. In many other countries, too, there is a sense that politics has mutated since the 1960s from an activity organised largely around parties to one organised around specialised interest groups on the one hand (such as America's gun lobby) and broader protest and social movements on the other (such as the women's movement, environmentalism and consumerism). One reason for the change is clearly the growth in the size and scope of government. Now that it touches virtually every aspect of people's lives, a bewildering array of groups has sprung up around it.

Many of Olson's disciples blame pressure groups for making government grow. As each special group wins new favours from the state, it makes the state bigger and clumsier, undermining the authority of elected parties, loading excessive demands on government in general, and preventing any particular government from acting in the interest of the relatively disorganised majority of people. By encouraging governments to do too much, say critics on the right, pressure groups prevent governments from doing anything well. Their solution is for governments to do less. Critics on the left are more inclined to complain that pressure groups exaggerate inequalities by giving those better-organised (ie, the rich and powerful) an influence out of all proportion to their actual numbers.

So what is to be done? A lot could be, but little is likely to be. There is precious little evidence from recent elections to suggest that the citizens of the rich countries want to see a radical cut in the size or scope of the state. As for political inequality, even this has its defenders. John Mueller, of America's University of Rochester, argues that democracy has had a good, if imperfect, record of dealing with minority issues, particularly when compared with other forms of government. But he claims that this is less because democratic majorities are tolerant of minorities and more because democracy gives minorities the opportunity

to increase their effective political weight—to become more equal, more important, than their arithmetical size would imply—on issues that concern them. This holds even for groups held in contempt by the majority, like homosexuals. Moreover, the fact that most people most of the time pay little attention to politics—the phenomenon of political apathy—helps interested minorities to protect their rights and to assert their interests.

Adaptability

This series of briefs has highlighted some of the defects in the practice of democracy, and some of the changes that the mature democracies are making in order to improve matters. But the defects need to be kept in perspective.

One famous critic of democracy claimed that for most people it did nothing more than allow them "once every few years, to decide which particular representatives of the oppressing class should be in parliament to represent and oppress them". When Marx wrote those words in the 19th century, they contained an element of truth. Tragically, Lenin treated this view as an eternal verity, with calamitous results for millions of people. What they both ignored was democracy's ability to evolve, which is perhaps its key virtue. Every mature democracy continues to evolve today. As a result, violent revolution in those countries where democracy has taken deepest root looks less attractive, and more remote, than ever.

Let Women Rule

Missing Out

SWANEE HUNT

Women have made significant strides in most socie- ties over the last century, but the trend line has not been straight. In recent interviews with hundreds of female leaders in over 30 countries, I have discovered that where women have taken leadership roles, it has been as social reform- ers and entrepreneurs, not as politicians or government officials. This is unfortunate, because the world needs women's perspec- tives and particular talents in top positions. In 1998, Francis Fukuyama wrote in Foreign Affairs that women's political lead- ership would bring about a more cooperative and less conflict- prone world ("Women and the Evolution of World Politics," September/October 1998). That promise has yet to be fulfilled.

Granted, a few women are breaking through traditional bar- riers and becoming presidents, prime ministers, cabinet mem- bers, and legislators. But even as the media spotlight falls on the 11 female heads of government around the world, another significant fact goes unreported: most of the best and the bright- est women eschew politics. Women are much more likely to wield influence from a nongovernmental organization (NGO) than from public office.

Women are still severely underrepresented in governments worldwide. A recent World Economic Forum report covering 115 countries notes that women have closed over 90 percent of the gender gap in education and in health but only 15 percent of it when it comes to political empowerment at the highest levels. Although 97 countries have some sort of gender quota system for government positions, according to the Inter-Parliamentary Union, an organization that fosters exchange among parlia- ments, women fill only 17 percent of parliamentary seats world- wide and 14 percent of ministerial-level positions—and most of those are related to family, youth, the disabled, and the elderly. At NGOs, the story is very different: women are consistently overrepresented at the top levels.

This pattern also holds for the United States, where 16 of 100 members of the Senate and 71 of 435 members of the House of Representatives are women. The United States ranks 68 out of 189 countries, behind a dozen in Latin America, in terms of the number of women in the legislature. Those low numbers are consistent with Capitol Hill's historic antipathy toward females. Women were denied the vote for 133 years, refused an equal rights amendment, and shut out of government-funded health research for decades. At the same time, American women have gravitated en masse toward NGOs, where they have found fewer barriers to leadership. The 230 NGOs in the National Coun- cil of Women's Organizations represent ten million American women, and women lead many of the country's largest phil- anthropic organizations, including the Bill and Melinda Gates Foundation and the Ford Foundation. As for academia, Harvard, MIT, and Princeton currently have women at the helm.

Most other countries follow a similar pattern. The number of NGOs in the former Soviet republics grew exponentially after the fall of the Iron Curtain, and women formed the backbone of this new civil society, but the percentage of women in eastern European parliaments plummeted. In Lithuania, that percentage declined from approximately 33 percent during the communist era to 17.5 percent in 1997 and 10.6 percent in 2004. According to a group of journalists in Kyrgyzstan, women head 90 percent of NGOs but hold not a single seat in parliament, even though they made up 33 percent of the legislature at the end of the Soviet era. In China, the Communist Party-controlled All-China Women's Fed- eration functions much as an NGO does, engaging women across the country on community issues, but despite the government's claims of equality, Chinese women have rarely held positions of political power. Likewise, in South Korea, women run some 80 percent of the country's NGOs but occupy less than 14 percent of the seats in the National Assembly. The story is the same in Africa. According to Robert Rotberg, director of the Program on Intrastate Conflict and Conflict Resolution at Harvard's Kennedy School of Government, "African women, who traditionally do the hard work of cultivation and all of the family rearing, also nurture NGOs and motivate civic initiatives. But they are widely expected to leave politics—and corruption and conflict—to men."

Women may thrive in NGOs. The world, however, needs them to take that experience into the political sphere. As the Sierra Leonean activist and former presidential candidate Zai- nab Bangura points out, "The real power isn't in civil society; it's in policymaking."

A Woman's View

Greater female political participation would bring significant rewards. Research sponsored by the World Bank has shown that countries with a high number of *women* in parliament enjoy lower levels of corruption. Another World Bank-sponsored study concludes that *women* are less likely to be involved in bribery and that corruption is less severe where *women* make up a large share of senior government officials as well as the labor force. A survey of research by Rachel Croson, of the Wharton School, and Uri Gneezy, of the University of California, San Diego, similarly concluded that *women* are more trustworthy than men. Consider Nigeria. The watchdog group Transparency International ranked it as the most corrupt country in the world in 2003. But that year, Ngozi Okonjo-Iweala left her job as a vice president at the World Bank to become the country's finance minister, and by 2005 Transparency International was hailing Nigeria as one of 21 most improved states. Change came thanks to the indictment of corrupt officials, as well as to reform in banking, insurance, the foreign exchange market, pensions, and income taxation. Similarly, in Liberia, international policymakers have been heartened to see President Ellen Johnson-Sirleaf prioritize the eradication of corruption. Knowing that foreign investment would flow only after a crackdown on the plundering culture of her predecessors, Johnson-Sirleaf fired the entire Finance Ministry staff and brought in *women* for the positions of finance minister, chief of police, commerce minister, and justice minister, among others.

Electing and appointing women to positions of political leadership turns out to be good for the broader economy as well. There is a correlation between women holding political office and the overall economic competitiveness of a nation. Augusto Lopez-Claros, chief economist and director of the World Economic Forum's Global Competitiveness Network, argues that "the Nordic countries seem to have understood the economic incentive behind empowering women: countries that do not fully capitalize on one-half of their human resources are clearly undermining their competitive potential. "The high percentage of women in parliament in countries such as Rwanda (almost 49 percent of members in the lower house), Costa Rica (40 percent), and Mozambique (35 percent) suggests that it is not simply a nation's affluence that causes more women to assume leadership positions. If that were the case, the relatively prosperous United States should be in the top ranks of countries sending women to Congress instead of lagging behind countries such as El Salvador, Nepal, and Tajikistan.

In 2000, an Inter-Parliamentary Union poll of 187 female politicians in 65 countries found that 80 percent of the respondents believed that increased representation of women renews public trust in government, which in turn helps economic welfare. The politicians cited examples from countries as varied as El Salvador, Ethiopia, New Zealand, and Russia in which political activism by women led to "tangible improvements" in social services, the environment, the safety of women and children, and gender equality.

Worldwide, female legislators as a group tend to concentrate on helping marginalized citizens. In the United States, for example, Democratic and moderate Republican congresswomen are more likely than men to focus on socially conscious legislation. Perhaps female politicians take such concerns to heart because they have often honed their skills in the NGO arena. Chilean President Michelle Bachelet, for instance, returned from exile in 1979 to work with children of people who were tortured or who disappeared during the dictatorship of Augusto Pinochet. South Korean Prime Minister Han Myeong Sook was a social activist (and political prisoner) during her country's military dictatorship.

The lessons women learn while leading civil society may also explain why they have "higher moral or ethical standards than their male counterparts," according to the International NGO Training and Research Center. Hannah Riley Bowles, professor of public policy at Harvard's Kennedy School of Government, found that when negotiating for jobs, American women asked for 15 percent less than men did, but when negotiating on behalf of others, women's demands increased substantially. (No such difference was found among male negotiators.) Carrying that tendency into the political sphere, "women may hold back when promoting their own candidacy or securing the resources they need to rise to the fore," argues Bowles. But they can be "fabulous advocates for their constituents."

Given these qualities, it is no surprise that women's involvement in political negotiations tends to solidify conflict resolution. "If we put women in leadership, they have a degree of tolerance, an understanding that allows them to persist even when things seem to be very bad," notes Pumla Gobodo-Madikizela, a South African clinical psychologist who worked in grass-roots NGOs during apartheid and helped establish the Truth and Reconciliation Commission. Unlike men, she continues, "women have the power and emotional inclination to hold onto hope when it comes to negotiating with former enemies." As documented by the Initiative for Inclusive Security, in numerous settings, women have joined forces across party lines to shape peace agreements, sponsor legislation, and influence the drafting of constitutions.

They also come to the table with a different perspective on conflict resolution. Women are more likely to adopt a broad definition of security that includes key social and economic issues that would otherwise be ignored, such as safe food and clean water and protection from gender-based violence. This sentiment was expressed to me by South Korea's Song Young Sun, the National Assembly's military watchdog. Most of the men she serves with define security as protecting South Korea's territory against North Korea, she said; she believes that security considerations should also include "everything from economics to culture, environment, health, and food."

A Man's World

If having women wield political power is so beneficial, why are there not more female leaders? A fundamental reason is that women themselves are not eager or willing to stand for political office. Women view politics as a dirty game, and their loftier standards may keep them away from the grit and grind of it. More than 200 public officials and NGO leaders throughout Kyrgyzstan responded to a 2004 United Nations Development Program poll by saying women would bring transparency, "a strong sense of responsibility," and "fair attitudes" to politics. But Nurgul Djanaeva, who heads a coalition of 88 Kyrgyz women's groups, bemoaned the situation: "The only way for me to feed my family, while working in government, is to be corrupt, so I'd rather work for an NGO and have a living wage."

It does not help that politics has traditionally been a man's world, and that many men—and some women—want to keep it that way. A woman may be considered "too soft" for political leadership—or "unfeminine" if she runs. Often, however, it is women themselves who doubt their own leadership abilities. According to the 2000 World Values Survey, women comprised 21 percent of respondents in Chile and 45 percent of respondents in Mexico who agreed strongly with the statement that men make better political leaders than women do. This distinct lack of self-assurance persists across cultures. According to research by the political scientists Richard Lawless and Jennifer Fox, authors of It Takes a Candidate: Why Women Don't Run for Office, American women were twice as likely as men to describe themselves as "not at all qualified to run for office," even when their credentials were equivalent. Only 25 percent of the women saw themselves as likely or very likely winners, compared with 37 percent of the men.

The traditional role society expects women to play does not spur them on to political leadership either. Reconciling political life with family commitments was the primary concern of the female politicians surveyed in 2000 by the Inter-Parliamentary Union. Women usually believe that their obligations to family members—including parents and in-laws—as the primary caregiver are incompatible with holding public office. Rebeca Grynspan, former vice president of Costa Rica, voices the dilemma: "Society doesn't provide conditions under which we can do our jobs with tranquility and leave our children home with peace of mind, even if we can count on stable, supportive partners." The pressures for women to stay home and tend to their families are compounded by conservative religious doctrines. A fundamentalist interpretation of Islam threatens women's nascent political hopes in countries such as Kuwait, where women gained the right to vote and run for office in the 2006 elections but did not win any parliamentary seats. Similarly, Afghanistan and Iraq, where new constitutions reserve a quarter of parliamentary seats for women, are in danger of backsliding into a collision with resurgent extremism. In the West, the Catholic Church in such countries as Croatia urges women to focus on family rather than public life. Likewise, most women in U.S. politics find their views incompatible with the religious right: in 2004, only two of the 14 female senators, compared with 48 of the 86 male senators, voted consistently with the Christian Coalition.

Even when women want to run for political office, they encounter roadblocks. In most countries, male political party gatekeepers determine candidate lists, and the ordering of candidates on the lists is a fundamental factor in determining who goes to parliament. It takes more than affirmative-action measures, such as quotas or reserved seats, to ensure women's places on those lists; it takes parties' will. According to the Harvard political scientist Pippa Norris, who analyzed the 1997 British elections, the Labour Party showed rare resolve in setting aside for women half of the seats from which members of parliament were retiring and half of those considered "most winnable." That move doubled the total percentage of women in parliament from 9.2 to 18.2 percent of all seats. More typical, however, is the complaint of a Bosnian politician who told me wryly that her place on her party's candidate list dropped precipitously, thanks to backroom hacks and men muscling their way to the top.

Money constitutes another barrier for women. Coming up with fees to file as a candidate or run a campaign can be daunting. Few countries have emulated the creation of organizations such as EMILY's List ("EMILY" stands for "Early Money Is Like Yeast"), which raises contributions across the United States for Democratic pro-choice women.

The financial squeeze can be further compounded by the threat of physical harm. According to Phoebe Asiyo, a prominent Kenyan member of parliament for more than a quarter century, the greatest expense for women running for parliament in Kenya is around-the-clock security, which is necessary because of the danger of rape, a common intimidation tactic. Mary Okumu, a Stanford-educated Kenyan public health expert, was beaten up when she stood for election in 2002. Okumu says that she and other candidates routinely carried concealed knives and wore two sets of tights under their dresses in order to buy more time to scream during an attempted rape. Male opponents were also at risk of physical attack, but Okumu says that "for women political aspirants the violence also includes foul verbal abuse, beatings, abduction, and death threats."

Given prevailing social norms and the numerous barriers to entry to the political arena, as well as women's own perception of politics as a dirty game, it is unsurprising that many women turn away from elected office, believing that they have a better chance of achieving results in the NGO realm. In 1991, as a child, Ala Noori Talabani fled on foot from Saddam Hussein's army. Fourteen years later, she was elected to the interim Iraqi National Assembly. She seemed a model legislator—a well-educated, articulate former diplomat equally comfortable among villagers in Kirkuk, politicians in Baghdad, and policy analysts in Washington. Yet in 2006, she left politics in frustration to work with an NGO SO that she could focus on the problems she cares about most: honor killings, domestic violence, and rape.

What is to be Done?

The forces excluding women from political leadership are so strong that only a serious and comprehensive effort can bring about change. Fortunately, governments, foreign-aid organizations, think tanks, and academic institutions can stimulate both the supply of and the demand for women in the political arena.

At the most basic level, national governments should implement "family-friendly" policies, including straightforward measures such as easier access to daycare, flexible office hours, and limits to evening meetings. But in some countries, to be effective, policies will have to be designed according to more progressive interpretations of religious doctrine regarding gender roles. In 2004, Moroccan King Muhammad VI personally backed a new version of family law that was compatible with sharia and that gave women equal rights. His support of gender-sensitive legislation also increased women's political representation (from two in 2001 to 35 in 2002 of the 325 seats in parliament's lower house) and made Morocco one of the most socially progressive countries in the Muslim world. In May 2006, thanks to another of the king's initiatives, the first class of 50 female imams graduated from an academy in Rabat. They are expected to do everything male imams do except lead Friday prayers in a mosque.

NGOs and governments have an important role to play in equipping women with the confidence and skills necessary to run for office. Grass-roots programs could help recruit and train women across the political spectrum. The Cambodian organization Women for Prosperity, for instance, has prepared more than 5,500 female candidates for elections in Cambodia. Embassies abroad could encourage established female officials to mentor new candidates, learning from the Forum of Rwandan Women Parliamentarians. In 2006, Rwanda's female parliamentarians returned to their districts to rally women to run for local office, increasing the proportion of female mayors and deputy mayors in the country from 24 to 44 percent in one election. Outsiders ought to boost the profile of Liberia's Johnson-Sirleaf, the only elected African female head of state, who recently urged female officeholders, "Don't stop with parliament. Join me. I'm lonely." The Initiative for Inclusive Security, which has brokered relationships between hundreds of female leaders in conflict regions and thousands of policymakers, is a creative and strong model of an external player working to encourage women's political participation. And governments should look to replicate innovative political-party reforms that ensure gender equality, such as those promoted by Michal Yudin's group in Israel—WE (Women's Electoral) Power—which has pressured Knesset members to increase funding for parties that exceed the quota for women's participation.

Supporting transparent and equitable campaign-finance *rules* would also help women in the political arena. Women told me that when they have to choose between their children's school fees or their own campaign, their children win. Government campaign subsidies spread across political parties help level the field. Governments should go further by rewarding parties that boost the representation of women on their candidate lists and penalizing those that do not.

Female politicians also need to be protected. In Afghanistan, where women running for parliament in 2005 were attacked, local and international organizations asked governors, chiefs of police, tribal elders, and other community leaders to provide security details. At least one candidate who reported threats had police protection 24 hours a day. Security measures reassured women that state and community leaders backed their right to engage in politics.

Finally, and most important, governments ought to support quotas for women at all levels of government. In systems with proportional representation, "zippering," requiring that a woman be in every second or third slot on a ballot, has helped raise women's numbers; still, women rarely appear in the top two ballot slots. Although quotas may initially result in female members of parliament being taken less seriously, the upside far outweighs the downside, since quotas propel women into politics. Sixteen of the 19 countries—including Cuba, Iceland, South Africa, Spain, and Sweden—that have parliaments in which at least 30 percent of the members are women have implemented either legislative or party quotas.

Less Swagger, More Sway

Women's community-based wisdom, fresh ideas, and commitment to the social good may be the best news in domestic policy today. They have much to contribute to decisions regarding the environment, security, health care, finance, and education. In foreign policy as well, the world could use more sway and less swagger.

A critical mass of female leaders will change norms; that may be why President Bachelet appointed ten women alongside the ten men in her cabinet. Of course, there are exceptions, but generally speaking, stereotypical "feminine" qualities (such as the tendency to nurture, compromise, and collaborate) have been confirmed by social science research. The world needs those traits. With so many intractable conflicts, conventional strategies—economic sanctions, boycotts, or military intervention—have clearly proved inadequate. Women's voices would provide a call/row arms.

None of these benefits to domestic and foreign policy, however, will be realized if just a few women reach positions of leadership. The few women who now make it to the top of a predominantly male hierarchy, and who do not come out of a women's movement, usually have attributes more similar to those of most men. Indira Gandhi, Margaret Thatcher, and Golda Meir had more "masculine" qualities than many of the men they bested, and they pushed little of the social agenda commonly of interest to women in politics. General wisdom about critical mass would predict that approximately 30 percent of officeholders have to be female for a significant effect to be felt on policy. As Anita Gradin remarked to me about her experience as a member of Sweden's parliament, the same group of women who were once in a small minority in the legislature talked, acted, and voted differently when their proportion increased significantly.

The more women shift from civil society into government, the more political culture will change for the better, and the more other women will follow. Advocates of women's leadership need to stop their handwringing over whether gender differences exist and appreciate the advantages women have over men's brawny style of governance, whether because of biology, social roles, or a cascading combination of the two. In the meantime, however, they will have to put up with some paternalistic responses, such as the one I received from a colonel at the Pentagon shortly after the United States' "shock and awe" attack on Iraq in 2003. When I urged him to broaden his search for the future leaders of Iraq, which had yielded hundreds of men and only seven women, he responded, "Ambassador Hunt, we'll address women's issues after we get the place secure." I wondered what "women's issues" he meant. I was talking about security.

SWANEE HUNT is Director of the Women and Public Policy Program at Harvard University's Kennedy School of Government and Chair of the Initiative for Inclusive Security. She was U.S. Ambassador to Austria from 1993 to 1997 and is the author of *This Was Not Our War: Bosnian Women Reclaiming the Peace*.

The True Clash of Civilizations

Samuel Huntington was only half right. The cultural fault line that divides the West and the Muslim world is not about democracy but sex. According to a new survey, Muslims and their Western counterparts want democracy, yet they are worlds apart when it comes to attitudes toward divorce, abortion, gender equality, and gay rights—which may not bode well for democracy's future in the Middle East.

RONALD INGLEHART AND PIPPA NORRIS

Democracy promotion in Islamic countries is now one of the Bush administration's most popular talking points. "We reject the condescending notion that freedom will not grow in the Middle East," Secretary of State Colin Powell declared last December as he unveiled the White House's new Middle East Partnership Initiative to encourage political and economic reform in Arab countries. Likewise, Condoleezza Rice, President George W. Bush's national security advisor, promised last September that the United States is committed to "the march of freedom in the Muslim world."

> **Republican Rep. Christopher Shays of Connecticut: "Why doesn't democracy grab hold in the Middle East? What is there about the culture and the people and so on where democracy just doesn't seem to be something they strive for and work for?"**

But does the Muslim world march to the beat of a different drummer? Despite Bush's optimistic pronouncement that there is "no clash of civilizations" when it comes to "the common rights and needs of men and women," others are not so sure. Samuel Huntington's controversial 1993 thesis—that the cultural division between "Western Christianity" and "Orthodox Christianity and Islam" is the new fault line for conflict—resonates more loudly than ever since September 11. Echoing Huntington, columnist Polly Toynbee argued in the British *Guardian* last November, "What binds together a globalized force of some extremists from many continents is a united hatred of Western values that seems to them to spring

from Judeo-Christianity." Meanwhile, on the other side of the Atlantic, Republican Rep. Christopher Shays of Connecticut, after sitting through hours of testimony on U.S.-Islamic relations on Capitol Hill last October, testily blurted, "Why doesn't democracy grab hold in the Middle East? What is there about the culture and the people and so on where democracy just doesn't seem to be something they strive for and work for?"

Huntington's response would be that the Muslim world lacks the core political values that gave birth to representative democracy in Western civilization: separation of religious and secular authority, rule of law and social pluralism, parliamentary institutions of representative government, and protection of individual rights and civil liberties as the buffer between citizens and the power of the state. This claim seems all too plausible given the failure of electoral democracy to take root throughout the Middle East and North Africa. According to the latest Freedom House rankings, almost two thirds of the 192 countries around the world are now electoral democracies. But among the 47 countries with a Muslim majority, only one fourth are electoral democracies—and none of the core Arabic-speaking societies falls into this category.

> **. . . the real fault line between the West and Islam. . . concerns gender equality and sexual liberation. . . the values separating the two cultures have much more to do with eros than demos.**

Yet this circumstantial evidence does little to prove Huntington correct, since it reveals nothing about the underlying

The Cultural Divide

Approval of Political and Social Values in Western and Muslim Societies

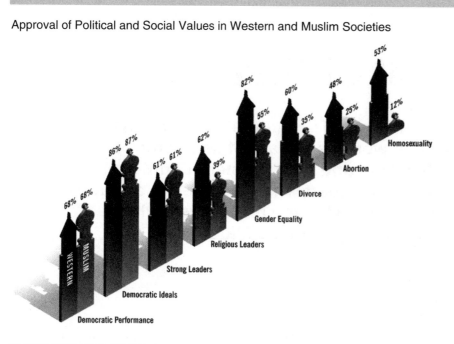

SOURCE: WORLD VALUES SURVEY, POOLED SAMPLE 1995-2001; CHARTS (3) BY JARED
SCHNEIDMAN FOR FP

The chart above draws on responses to various political and social issues in the World Values Survey. The percentages indicate the extent to which respondents agree/disagree with or approved/disapproved of the following statements and questions:

Democratic Performance

- Democracies are indecisive and have too much quibbling. (Strongly disagree.)
- Democracies aren't good at maintaining order. (Strongly disagree.)

Democratic Ideals

- Democracy may have problems, but it's better than any other form of government. (Strongly agree.)
- Approve of having a democratic political system. (Strongly agree.)

Strong Leaders

- Approve of having experts, not government, make decisions according to what they think is best for the country. (Strongly disagree.)
- Approve of having a strong leader who does not have to bother with parliament and elections. (Strongly disagree.)

Religious Leaders

- Politicians who do not believe in God are unfit for public office. (Strongly disagree.)
- It would be better for [this country] if more people with strong religious beliefs held public office. (Strongly disagree.)

Gender Equality

- On the whole, men make better political leaders than women do. (Strongly disagree.)
- When jobs are scarce, men should have more right to a job than women. (Strongly disagree.)
- A university education is more important for a boy than for a girl. (Strongly disagree.)
- A woman has to have children in order to be fulfilled. (Strongly disagree.)
- If a woman wants to have a child as a single parent but she doesn't want to have a stable relationship with a man, do you approve or disapprove? (Strongly approve.)

Divorce

- Divorce can always be justified, never be justified, or something in between. (High level of tolerance for divorce.)

Abortion

- Abortion can always be justified, never be justified, or something in between. (High level of tolerance for abortion.)

Homosexuality

- Homosexuality can always be justified, never be justified, or something in between. (High level of tolerance for homosexuality.)

beliefs of Muslim publics. Indeed, there has been scant empirical evidence whether Western and Muslim societies exhibit deeply divergent values—that is, until now. The cumulative results of the two most recent waves of the World Values Survey (wvs), conducted in 1995–96 and 2000–2002, provide an extensive body of relevant evidence. Based on questionnaires that explore values and beliefs in more than 70 countries, the wvs is an investigation of sociocultural and political change that encompasses over 80 percent of the world's population.

A comparison of the data yielded by these surveys in Muslim and non-Muslim societies around the globe confirms the first claim in Huntington's thesis: Culture does matter—indeed, it matters a lot. Historical religious traditions have left an enduring imprint on contemporary values. However, Huntington is mistaken in assuming that the core clash between the West and Islam is over political values. At this point in history, societies throughout the world (Muslim and Judeo-Christian alike) see democracy as the best form of government. Instead, the real fault line between the West and Islam, which Huntington's theory completely overlooks, concerns gender equality and sexual liberalization. In other words, the values separating the two cultures have much more to do with eros than demos. As younger generations in the West have gradually become more liberal on these issues, Muslim nations have remained the most traditional societies in the world.

This gap in values mirrors the widening economic divide between the West and the Muslim world. Commenting on the disenfranchisement of women throughout the Middle East, the United Nations Development Programme observed last summer that "no society can achieve the desired state of well-being and human development, or compete in a globalizing world, if half its people remain marginalized and disempowered." But this "sexual clash of civilizations" taps into far deeper issues than how Muslim countries treat women. A society's commitment to gender equality and sexual liberalization proves time and again to be the most reliable indicator of how strongly that society supports principles of tolerance and egalitarianism. Thus, the people of the Muslim world overwhelmingly want democracy, but democracy may not be sustainable in their societies.

Testing Huntington

Huntington argues that "ideas of individualism, liberalism, constitutionalism, human rights, equality, liberty, the rule of law, democracy, free markets, [and] the separation of church and state" often have little resonance outside the West. Moreover, he holds that Western efforts to promote these ideas provoke a violent backlash against "human rights imperialism." To test these propositions, we categorized the countries included in the wvs according to the nine major contemporary civilizations, based largely on the historical religious legacy of each society. The survey includes 22 countries representing Western Christianity (a West European culture that also encompasses North America, Australia, and New Zealand), 10 Central European nations (sharing a Western Christian heritage, but which also lived under Communist rule), 11 societies with a Muslim majority (Albania, Algeria, Azerbaijan, Bangladesh, Egypt, Indonesia, Iran, Jordan, Morocco, Pakistan, and Turkey), 12 traditionally Orthodox societies (such as Russia and Greece), 11 predominately Catholic Latin American countries, 4 East Asian societies shaped by Sino-Confucian values, 5 sub-Saharan Africa countries, plus Japan and India.

Despite Huntington's claim of a clash of civilizations between the West and the rest, the wvs reveals that, at this point in history, democracy has an overwhelmingly positive image throughout the world. In country after country, a clear majority of the population describes "having a democratic political system" as either "good" or "very good." These results represent a dramatic change from the 1930s and 1940s, when fascist regimes won overwhelming mass approval in many societies; and for many decades, Communist regimes had widespread support. But in the last decade, democracy became virtually the only political model with global appeal, no matter what the culture. With the exception of Pakistan, most of the Muslim countries surveyed think highly of democracy: In Albania, Egypt, Bangladesh, Azerbaijan, Indonesia, Morocco, and Turkey, 92 to 99 percent of the public endorsed democratic institutions—a higher proportion than in the United States (89 percent).

Yet, as heartening as these results may be, paying lip service to democracy does not necessarily prove that people genuinely support basic democratic norms—or that their leaders will allow them to have democratic institutions. Although constitutions of authoritarian states such as China profess to embrace democratic ideals such as freedom of religion, the rulers deny it in practice. In Iran's 2000 elections, reformist candidates captured nearly three quarters of the seats in parliament, but a theocratic elite still holds the reins of power. Certainly, it's a step in the right direction if most people in a country endorse the idea of democracy. But this sentiment needs to be complemented by deeper underlying attitudes such as interpersonal trust and tolerance of unpopular groups—and these values must ultimately be accepted by those who control the army and secret police.

The wvs reveals that, even after taking into account differences in economic and political development, support for democratic institutions is just as strong among those living in Muslim societies as in Western (or other) societies [see box, The Cultural Divide]. For instance, a solid majority of people living in Western and Muslim countries gives democracy high marks as the most efficient form of government, with 68 percent disagreeing with assertions that "democracies are indecisive" and "democracies aren't good at maintaining order." (All other cultural regions and countries, except East Asia and Japan, are far more critical.) And an equal number of respondents on both sides of the civilizational divide (61 percent) firmly reject authoritarian governance, expressing disapproval of "strong leaders" who do not "bother with parliament and elections." Muslim societies display greater support for religious authorities playing an active societal role than do Western societies. Yet this preference for religious authorities is less a cultural division between the West and Islam than it is a gap between the West and many other less secular societies around the

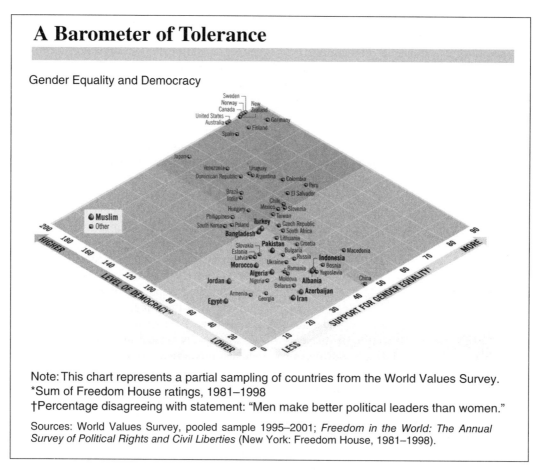

A Barometer of Tolerance

Gender Equality and Democracy

Note: This chart represents a partial sampling of countries from the World Values Survey.
*Sum of Freedom House ratings, 1981–1998
†Percentage disagreeing with statement: "Men make better political leaders than women."

Sources: World Values Survey, pooled sample 1995–2001; *Freedom in the World: The Annual Survey of Political Rights and Civil Liberties* (New York: Freedom House, 1981–1998).

globe, especially in sub-Saharan Africa and Latin America. For instance, citizens in some Muslim societies agree overwhelmingly with the statement that "politicians who do not believe in God are unfit for public office" (88 percent in Egypt, 83 percent in Iran, and 71 percent in Bangladesh), but this statement also garners strong support in the Philippines (71 percent), Uganda (60 percent), and Venezuela (52 percent). Even in the United States, about two fifths of the public believes that atheists are unfit for public office.

Today, relatively few people express overt hostility toward other classes, races, or religions, but rejection of homosexuals is widespread. About half of the world's populations say that homosexuality is "never" justifiable.

However, when it comes to attitudes toward gender equality and sexual liberalization, the cultural gap between Islam and the West widens into a chasm. On the matter of equal rights and opportunities for women—measured by such questions as whether men make better political leaders than women or whether university education is more important for boys than for girls—Western and Muslim countries score 82 percent and

55 percent, respectively. Muslim societies are also distinctively less permissive toward homosexuality, abortion, and divorce.

These issues are part of a broader syndrome of tolerance, trust, political activism, and emphasis on individual autonomy that constitutes "self-expression values." The extent to which a society emphasizes these self-expression values has a surprisingly strong bearing on the emergence and survival of democratic institutions. Among all the countries included in the wvs, support for gender equality—a key indicator of tolerance and personal freedom—is closely linked with a society's level of democracy [see box, A Barometer of Tolerance].

Muslim societies are neither uniquely nor monolithically low on tolerance toward sexual orientation and gender equality. . . . However, on the whole, Muslim countries not only lag behind the West but behind all other societies as well.

In every stable democracy, a majority of the public disagrees with the statement that "men make better political leaders than women." None of the societies in which less than 30 percent of the public rejects this statement (such as Jordan, Nigeria, and Belarus) is a true democracy. In China, one of the world's least

A Widening Generation Gap

Support for Gender Equality, by Age and Type of Society

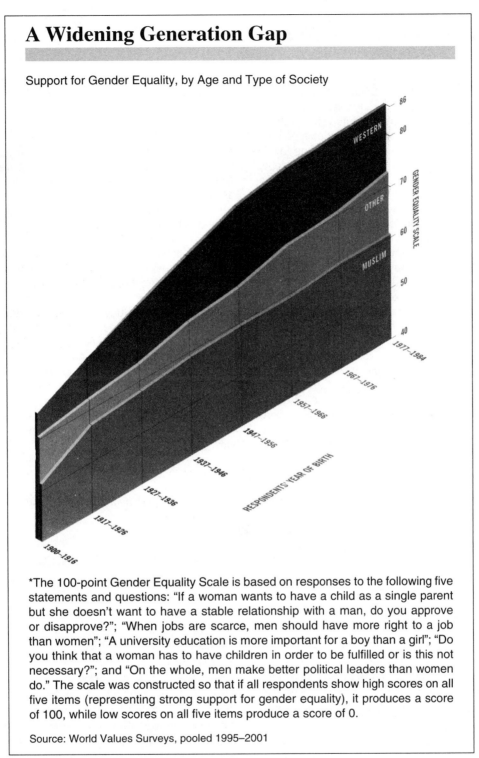

*The 100-point Gender Equality Scale is based on responses to the following five statements and questions: "If a woman wants to have a child as a single parent but she doesn't want to have a stable relationship with a man, do you approve or disapprove?"; "When jobs are scarce, men should have more right to a job than women"; "A university education is more important for a boy than a girl"; "Do you think that a woman has to have children in order to be fulfilled or is this not necessary?"; and "On the whole, men make better political leaders than women do." The scale was constructed so that if all respondents show high scores on all five items (representing strong support for gender equality), it produces a score of 100, while low scores on all five items produce a score of 0.

Source: World Values Surveys, pooled 1995–2001

democratic countries, a majority of the public agrees that men make better political leaders than women, despite a party line that has long emphasized gender equality (Mao Zedong once declared, "women hold up half the sky"). In practice, Chinese women occupy few positions of real power and face widespread discrimination in the workplace. India is a borderline case. The country is a long-standing parliamentary democracy with an independent judiciary and civilian control of the armed forces, yet it is also marred by a weak rule of law, arbitrary arrests, and

extra-judicial killings. The status of Indian women reflects this duality. Women's rights are guaranteed in the constitution, and Indira Gandhi led the nation for 15 years. Yet domestic violence and forced prostitution remain prevalent throughout the country, and, according to the wvs, almost 50 percent of the Indian populace believes only men should run the government.

The way a society views homosexuality constitutes another good litmus test of its commitment to equality. Tolerance of well-liked groups is never a problem. But if someone wants

Want to Know More?

Samuel Huntington expanded his controversial 1993 article into a book, *The Clash of Civilizations and the Remaking of World Order* (New York: Simon and Schuster, 1996). Among the authors who have disputed Huntington's claim that Islam is incompatible with democratic values are Edward Said, who decries the clash of civilizations thesis as an attempt to revive the "good vs. evil" world dichotomy prevalent during the Cold War ("**A Clash of Ignorance,**" *The Nation*, October 22, 2001); John Voll and John Esposito, who argue that "The Muslim heritage. . . contains concepts that provide a foundation for contemporary Muslims to develop authentically Muslim programs of democracy" ("**Islam's Democratic Essence,**" *Middle East Quarterly*, September 1994); and Ray Takeyh, who recounts the efforts of contemporary Muslim scholars to legitimize democratic concepts through the reinterpretation of Muslim texts and traditions ("**Faith-Based Initiatives,**" FOREIGN POLICY, November/December 2001).

An overview of the Bush administration's **Middle East Partnership Initiative**, including the complete transcript of Secretary of State Colin Powell's speech on political and economic reform in the Arab world, can be found on the Web site of the U.S. Department of State. Marina Ottaway, Thomas Carothers, Amy Hawthorne, and Daniel Brumberg offer a stinging critique of those who believe that toppling the Iraqi regime could unleash a democratic tsunami in the Arab world in "**Democratic Mirage in the Middle East**" (Washington: Carnegie Endowment for International Peace, 2002).

In a poll of nearly 4,000 Arabs, James Zogby found that the issue of "civil and personal rights" earned the overall highest score when people were asked to rank their personal priorities (*What Arabs Think: Values, Beliefs and Concerns*, Washington: Zogby International, 2002). A poll available on the Web site of the Pew Research Center for the People and the Press ("**Among Wealthy Nations . . . U.S. Stands Alone in Its Embrace of Religion,**" December 19, 2002) reveals that Americans' views on religion and faith are closer to those living in developing nations than in developed countries.

The Web site of the **World Values Survey** (WVS) provides considerable information on the survey, including background on methodology, key findings, and the text of the questionnaires. The second iteration of the A.T. Kearney/ FOREIGN POLICY Magazine Globalization Index ("**Globalization's Last Hurrah?**" FOREIGN POLICY, January/February 2002) found a strong correlation between the WVS measure of "subjective well-being" and a society's level of global integration.

For links to relevant Web sites, access to the FP Archive, and a comprehensive index of related FOREIGN POLICY articles, go to www.foreignpolicy.com.

to gauge how tolerant a nation really is, find out which group is the most disliked, and then ask whether members of that group should be allowed to hold public meetings, teach in schools, and work in government. Today, relatively few people express overt hostility toward other classes, races, or religions, but rejection of homosexuals is widespread. In response to a WVS question about whether homosexuality is justifiable, about half of the world's population say "never." But, as is the case with gender equality, this attitude is directly proportional to a country's level of democracy. Among authoritarian and quasi-democratic states, rejection of homosexuality is deeply entrenched: 99 percent in both Egypt and Bangladesh, 94 percent in Iran, 92 percent in China, and 71 percent in India. By contrast, these figures are much lower among respondents in stable democracies: 32 percent in the United States, 26 percent in Canada, 25 percent in Britain, and 19 percent in Germany.

Muslim societies are neither uniquely nor monolithically low on tolerance toward sexual orientation and gender equality. Many of the Soviet successor states rank as low as most Muslim societies. However, on the whole, Muslim countries not only lag behind the West but behind all other societies as well [see box, A Widening Generation Gap]. Perhaps more significant, the figures reveal the gap between the West and Islam is even wider among younger age groups. This pattern suggests that the younger generations in Western societies have become progressively more egalitarian than their elders, but the younger generations in Muslim societies have remained almost as tradi-

tional as their parents and grandparents, producing an expanding cultural gap.

Clash of Conclusions

"The peoples of the Islamic nations want and deserve the same freedoms and opportunities as people in every nation," President Bush declared in a commencement speech at West Point last summer. He's right. Any claim of a "clash of civilizations" based on fundamentally different political goals held by Western and Muslim societies represents an oversimplification of the evidence. Support for the goal of democracy is surprisingly widespread among Muslim publics, even among those living in authoritarian societies. Yet Huntington is correct when he argues that cultural differences have taken on a new importance, forming the fault lines for future conflict. Although nearly the entire world pays lip service to democracy, there is still no global consensus on the self-expression values—such as social tolerance, gender equality, freedom of speech, and interpersonal trust—that are crucial to democracy. Today, these divergent values constitute the real clash between Muslim societies and the West.

But economic development generates changed attitudes in virtually any society. In particular, modernization compels systematic, predictable changes in gender roles: Industrialization brings women into the paid work force and dramatically reduces fertility rates. Women become literate and begin to participate in representative government but still have far less power than men. Then, the postindustrial phase brings a shift toward greater gender equality as women move into higher-status economic roles in management and gain political influence within elected and appointed bodies. Thus, relatively industrialized Muslim societies such as Turkey share the same views on gender equality and sexual liberalization as other new democracies.

Even in established democracies, changes in cultural attitudes—and eventually, attitudes toward democracy—seem to be closely linked with modernization. Women did not attain the right to vote in most historically Protestant societies until about 1920, and in much of Roman Catholic Europe until after World War II. In 1945, only 3 percent of the members of parlia-

ments around the world were women. In 1965, the figure rose to 8 percent, in 1985 to 12 percent, and in 2002 to 15 percent.

The United States cannot expect to foster democracy in the Muslim world simply by getting countries to adopt the trappings of democratic governance, such as holding elections and having a parliament. Nor is it realistic to expect that nascent democracies in the Middle East will inspire a wave of reforms reminiscent of the velvet revolutions that swept Eastern Europe in the final days of the Cold War. A real commitment to democratic reform will be measured by the willingness to commit the resources necessary to foster human development in the Muslim world. Culture has a lasting impact on how societies evolve. But culture does not have to be destiny.

Judicial Review: The Gavel and the Robe

Established and emerging democracies display a puzzling taste in common: both have handed increasing amounts of power to unelected judges. Th[is] article examines the remarkable growth and many different forms of judicial review.

To some they are unaccountable elitists, old men (and the rare women) in robes who meddle in politics where they do not belong, thwarting the will of the people. To others they are bulwarks of liberty, champions of the individual against abuses of power by scheming politicians, arrogant bureaucrats and the emotional excesses of transient majorities.

Judges who sit on supreme courts must get used to the vilification as well as the praise. They often deal with the most contentious cases, involving issues which divide the electorate or concern the very rules by which their countries are governed. With so much at stake, losers are bound to question not only judges' particular decisions, but their right to decide at all. This is especially true when judges knock down as unconstitutional a law passed by a democratically elected legislature. How dare they?

Despite continued attacks on the legitimacy of judicial review, it has flourished in the past 50 years. All established democracies now have it in some form, and the standing of constitutional courts has grown almost everywhere. In an age when all political authority is supposed to derive from voters, and every passing mood of the electorate is measured by pollsters, the growing power of judges is a startling development.

The trend in western democracies has been followed by the new democracies of Eastern Europe with enthusiasm. Hungary's constitutional court may be the most active and powerful in the world. There have been failures. After a promising start, Russia's constitutional court was crushed in the conflict between Boris Yeltsin and his parliament. But in some countries where governments have long been riven by ideological divisions or crippled by corruption, such as Israel and India, constitutional courts have filled a political vacuum, coming to embody the legitimacy of the state.

In western democracies the growing role of constitutional review, in which judges rule on the constitutionality of laws and regulations, has been accompanied by a similar growth in what is known as administrative review, in which judges rule on the legality of government actions, usually those of the executive branch. This second type of review has also dragged judges into the political arena, frequently pitting them against elected politicians in controversial cases. But it is less problematic for democratic theorists than constitutional review for a number of reasons.

Democracy's Referees

The expansion of the modern state has seemed to make administrative review inevitable. The reach of government, for good or ill, now extends into every nook and cranny of life. As a result, individuals, groups and businesses all have more reason than ever before to challenge the legality of government decisions or the interpretation of laws. Such challenges naturally end up before the courts.

In France, Germany, Italy and most other European countries, special administrative tribunals, with their own hierarchies of appeal courts, have been established to handle such cases. In the United States, Britain, Canada and Australia, the ordinary courts, which handle criminal cases and private lawsuits, also deal with administrative law cases.

The growth of administrative review can be explained as a reaction to the growth of state power. But the parallel expansion of constitutional review is all the more remarkable in a democratic age because it was resisted for so long in the very name of democracy.

The idea was pioneered by the United States, the first modern democracy with a written constitution. In fact, the American constitution nowhere explicitly gives the Supreme Court the power to rule laws invalid because of their unconstitutionality. The court's right to do this was first asserted in *Marbury v Madison*, an 1803 case, and then quickly became accepted as proper. One reason for such ready acceptance may have been that a Supreme Court veto fitted so well with the whole design and spirit of the constitution itself, whose purpose was as much to control the excesses of popular majorities as to give the people a voice in government decision-making.

In Europe this was the reason why the American precedent was not followed. As the voting franchise was expanded, the will of the voting majority became ever more sacrosanct, at least in theory. Parliamentary sovereignty reigned supreme. European democrats viewed the American experiment with constitutionalism as an unwarranted restraint on the popular will.

Even in the United States, judicial review was of little importance until the late 19th century, when the Supreme Court became more active, first nullifying laws passed after the civil war to give former slaves equal rights and then overturning laws regulating economic activity in the name of contractual and property rights.

After a showdown with Franklin Roosevelt over the New Deal, which the court lost, it abandoned its defence of laissez-faire economics. In the 1950s under Chief Justice Earl Warren it embarked on the active protection and expansion of civil rights. Controversially, this plunged the court into the mainstream of American politics, a position it retains today despite a retreat from Warren-style activism over the past two decades.

Attitudes towards judicial review also changed in Europe. The rise of fascism in the 1920s and 1930s, and then the destruction wrought by the second world war, made many European democrats reconsider the usefulness of judges. Elections alone no longer seemed a reliable obstacle to the rise of dangerously authoritarian governments. Fascist dictators had seized power by manipulating representative institutions.

The violence and oppression of the pre-war and war years also convinced many that individual rights and civil liberties needed special protection. The tyranny of the executive branch of government, acting in the name of the majority, became a real concern. (Britain remained an exception to this trend, sticking exclusively to the doctrine of parliamentary sovereignty. It is only now taking its first tentative steps towards establishing a constitutional court.)

While the goals of constitutional judicial review are similar almost everywhere, its form varies from country to country, reflecting national traditions. Some of the key differences:

• **Appointments.** The most famous method of appointment is that of the United States, largely because of a handful of televised and acrimonious confirmation hearings. The president appoints a Supreme Court judge, subject to Senate approval, whenever one of the court's nine seats falls vacant. Political horsetrading, and conflict, are part of the system. Judges are appointed for life, though very few cling to office to the end.

Other countries may appoint their constitutional judges with more decorum, but politics always plays some part in the process. France is the most explicitly political. The directly elected president and the heads of the Senate and the National Assembly each appoint three of the judges of the Constitutional Council, who serve non-renewable nine-year terms, one-third of them retiring every three years. Former presidents are awarded life membership on the council, although none has yet chosen to take his seat.

Half of the 16 members of Germany's Federal Constitutional Tribunal are chosen by the Bundestag, the lower house of parliament, and half by the Bundesrat, the upper house. Appointments are usually brokered between the two major parties. The procedure is similar in Italy, where one-third of the 15-strong Constitutional Court is chosen by the head of state, one-third by the two houses of parliament and one-third by the professional judiciary.

Senior politicians—both before and after serving in other government posts—have sat on all three constitutional courts, sometimes with unhappy results. In March Roland Dumas, the president of France's Constitutional Council, was forced to step down temporarily because of allegations of corruption during his earlier tenure as foreign minister. The trend in all three countries is towards the appointment of professional judges and legal scholars rather than politicians.

• **Powers.** Most constitutional courts have the power to nullify laws as unconstitutional, but how they do this, and receive cases, varies. Once again, the most anomalous is France's Constitutional Council which rules on the constitutionality of laws only before they go into effect and not, like all other courts, after.

The 1958 constitution of France's Fifth Republic allowed only four authorities to refer cases to the council: the president, the prime minister, and the heads of the two houses of parliament. In 1974, a constitutional amendment authorised 60 deputies or senators to lodge appeals with the council as well. Since then, the council has become more active, and most appeals now come from groups of legislators. Individuals have no right to appeal to the council.

French jurists argue that judicial review before a law goes into effect is simpler and faster than review after a law's promulgation. But it is also more explicitly political, and leaves no room for making a judgment in the light of a law's sometimes unanticipated effect.

No other major country has adopted prior review exclusively, but it is an option in Germany and Italy as well, usually at the request of the national or one of the regional governments. However, most of the work of the constitutional courts in both countries comes from genuine legal disputes, which are referred to them by other courts when a constitutional question is raised.

The Supreme Courts of the United States, Canada and Australia, by contrast, are the final courts of appeal for all cases, not just those dealing with constitutional issues. The United States Supreme Court does not give advisory or abstract opinions about the constitutionality of laws, but only deals with cases involving specific disputes. Moreover, lower courts in the United States can also rule on constitutional issues, although most important cases are appealed eventually to the Supreme Court.

Canada's Supreme Court can be barred from ruling a law unconstitutional if either the national or a provincial legislature has passed it with a special clause declaring that it should survive judicial review "notwithstanding" any breach of the country's Charter of Rights. If passed in this way, the law must be renewed every five years. In practice, this device has rarely been used.

125

• **Judgments.** The French and Italian constitutional courts deliver their judgments unanimously, without dissents. Germany abandoned this method in 1971, adopting the more transparent approach of the common-law supreme courts, which allow a tally of votes cast and dissenting opinions to be published alongside the court's judgment. Advocates of unanimity argue that it reinforces the court's authority and gives finality to the law. Opponents deride it as artificial, and claim that publishing dissents improves the technical quality of judgments, keeps the public better informed, and makes it easier for the law to evolve in the light of changing circumstances.

Also noteworthy is the growth in Europe of supra-national judicial review. The European Court of Justice in Luxembourg is the ultimate legal authority for the European Union. The court's primary task is to interpret the treaties upon which the EU is founded. Because EU law now takes precedence over national law in the 15 member states, the court's influence has grown considerably in recent years. The European Court of Human Rights in Strasbourg, the judicial arm of the 41-member Council of Europe, has, in effect, become the final court of appeal on human-rights issues for most of Europe. The judgments of both European courts carry great weight and have forced many countries to change their laws.

Despite the rapid growth of judicial review in recent decades, it still has plenty of critics. Like all institutions, supreme courts make mistakes, and their decisions are a proper topic of political debate. But some criticisms aimed at them are misconceived.

Unelected Legislators?

To criticise constitutional courts as political meddlers is to misunderstand their role, which is both judicial and political. If constitutions are to play any part in limiting government, then someone must decide when they have been breached and how they should be applied, especially when the relative powers of various branches or levels of government—a frequent issue in federal systems—are in question. When a court interprets a constitution, its decisions are political by definition—though they should not be party political.

Supreme courts also are not unaccountable, as some of their critics claim. Judges can be overruled by constitutional amendment, although this is rare. They must also justify their rulings to the public in written opinions. These are pored over by the media, lawyers, legal scholars and other judges. If unpersuasive, judgments are sometimes evaded by lower courts or legislatures, and the issue eventually returns to the constitutional court to be considered again.

Moreover, the appointment of judges is a political process, and the complexions of courts change as their membership changes, although appointees are sometimes unpredictable once on the bench. Nevertheless, new appointments can result in the reversal of earlier decisions which failed to win public support.

Constitutional courts have no direct power of their own. This is why Alexander Hamilton, who helped write America's constitution, called the judiciary "the least dangerous branch of government." Courts have no vast bureaucracy, revenue-raising ability, army or police force at their command—no way, in fact, to enforce their rulings. If other branches of government ignore them, they can do nothing. Their power and legitimacy, especially when they oppose the executive or legislature, depend largely on their moral authority and credibility.

Senior judges are acutely aware of their courts' limitations. Most tread warily, preferring to mould the law through interpretation of statutes rather than employing the crude instrument of complete nullification. Even the American Supreme Court, among the world's most activist, has ruled only sections of some 135 federal laws unconstitutional in 210 years, although it has struck down many more state laws.

Finally, it is worth remembering that judges are not the only public officials who exercise large amounts of power but do not answer directly to voters. Full-time officials and appointees actually perform most government business, and many of them have enormous discretion about how they do this. Even elected legislators and prime ministers are not perfect transmitters of the popular will, but enjoy great latitude when making decisions on any particular issue. Constitutional courts exist to ensure that everyone stays within the rules. Judges have the delicate, sometimes impossible, task of checking others' power without seeming to claim too much for themselves.

Referendums: The People's Voice

Is the growing use of referendums a threat to democracy or its salvation? The fifth article in our series on changes in mature democracies examines the experience so far, and the arguments for and against letting voters decide political questions directly.

When Winston Churchill proposed a referendum to Clement Attlee in 1945 on whether Britain's wartime coalition should be extended, Attlee growled that the idea was an "instrument of Nazism and fascism". The use by Hitler and Mussolini of bogus referendums to consolidate their power had confirmed the worst fears of sceptics. The most democratic of devices seemed also to be the most dangerous to democracy itself.

Dictators of all stripes have continued to use phony referendums to justify their hold on power. And yet this fact has not stopped a steady growth in the use of genuine referendums, held under free and fair conditions, by both established and aspiring democracies. Referendums have been instrumental in the dismantling of communism and the transition to democracy in countries throughout the former soviet empire. They have also successfully eased democratic transitions in Spain, Greece, South Africa, Brazil and Chile, among other countries.

In most established democracies, direct appeals to voters are now part of the machinery for constitutional change. Their use to resolve the most intractable or divisive public issues has also grown. In the 17 major democracies of Western Europe, only three—Belgium, the Netherlands and Norway—make no provision for referendums in their constitution. Only six major democracies—the Netherlands, the United States, Japan, India, Israel and the Federal Republic of Germany—have never held a nationwide referendum.

The Volatile Voter

Frustrated voters in Italy and New Zealand have in recent years used referendums to force radical changes to voting systems and other political institutions on a reluctant political elite. Referendums have also been used regularly in Australia, where voters go to the polls this November to decide whether to cut their country's formal link with the British crown. In Switzerland and several American states, referendums are a central feature of the political system, rivalling legislatures in significance.

Outside the United States and Switzerland, referendums are most often called by governments only when they are certain of victory, and to win endorsement of a policy they intend to implement in any case. This is how they are currently being used in Britain by Tony Blair's government.

But voters do not always behave as predicted, and they have delivered some notable rebuffs. Charles de Gaulle skillfully used referendums to establish the legitimacy of France's Fifth Republic and to expand his own powers as president, but then felt compelled to resign in 1969 after an unexpected referendum defeat.

Francois Mitterrand's decision to call a referendum on the Maastricht treaty in 1992 brought the European Union to the brink of breakdown when only 51% of those voting backed the treaty. Denmark's voters rejected the same treaty, despite the fact that it was supported by four out of five members of the Danish parliament. The Danish government was able to sign the treaty only after renegotiating its terms and narrowly winning a second referendum. That same year, Canada's government was not so lucky. Canadian voters unexpectedly rejected a painstakingly negotiated constitutional accord designed to placate Quebec.

Referendums come in many different forms. **Advisory referendums** test public opinion on an important issue. Governments or legislators then translate their results into new laws or policies as they see fit. Although advisory referendums can carry great weight in the right circumstances, they are sometimes ignored by politicians. In a 1955 Swedish referendum, 85% of those voting said they wanted to continue driving on the left side of the road. Only 12 years later the government went ahead and made the switch to driving on the right without a second referendum, or much protest.

By contrast, **mandatory referendums** are part of a law-making process or, more commonly, one of the procedures for constitutional amendment.

Both advisory and mandatory referendums can usually be called only by those in office—sometimes by the president, sometimes by parliamentarians, most often by the government of the day. But in a few countries, petitions by voters themselves can put a referendum on the ballot. These are known as **initiatives**. Sometimes these can only repeal an already existing law—so-called "abrogative" initiatives such as those in Italy. Elsewhere, initiatives can also be used to propose and pass new legislation, as in Switzerland and many American states. In this form they can be powerful and unpredictable political tools.

The rules for conducting and winning referendums also vary greatly from country to country. Regulations on the drafting of ballot papers and the financing of Yes and No campaigns are different everywhere, and these exert a great influence over how referendums are used, and how often.

The hurdle required for victory can be a critical feature. A simple majority of those voting is the usual rule. But a low turnout can make such victories seem illegitimate. So a percentage of eligible voters, as well as a majority of those voting, is sometimes required to approve a proposal.

Such hurdles, of course, also make failure more likely. In 1978 Britain's government was forced to abandon plans to set up a Scottish parliament when a referendum victory in Scotland failed to clear a 40% hurdle of eligible voters. Referendums have also failed in Denmark and Italy (most recently in April) because of similar voter-turnout requirements. To ensure a wide geographic consensus, Switzerland and Australia require a "double majority", of individual voters and of cantons or states, for constitutional amendments.

The use of referendums reflects the history and traditions of individual countries. Thus generalising about them is difficult. In some countries referendums have played a central, though peripatetic, role. In others they have been marginal or even irrelevant, despite provisions for their use.

Hot Potatoes

Although referendums (outside Switzerland and the United States) have been most often used to legitimise constitutional change or the redrawing of boundaries, elected politicians have also found them useful for referring to voters those issues they find too hot to handle or which cut across party lines. Often these concern moral or lifestyle choices, such as alcohol prohibition, divorce or abortion. The outcome on such emotive topics can be difficult to predict. In divorce and abortion referendums, for example, Italians have shown themselves more liberal, and the Irish more conservative, than expected.

One of the best single books on referendums—"Referendums Around the World" edited by David Butler and Austin Ranney, published by Macmillan—argues that many assumptions about them are mistaken. They are not usually habit-forming, as those opposed to them claim. Many countries have used them to settle a specific issue, or even engaged in a series of them, and then turned away from referendums for long periods. But this is mostly because politicians decide whether referendums will be held. Where groups of voters can also put initiatives on the ballot, as in Switzerland and the United States, they have become addictive and their use has grown in recent years.

Messrs Butler and Ranney also point out that referendums are not usually vehicles for radical change, as is widely believed. Although they were used in this way in Italy and New Zealand, referendums have more often been used to support

the status quo or to endorse changes already agreed by political parties. Most referendums, even those initiated by voters, fail. In Australia, 34 of 42 proposals to amend the constitution have been rejected by voters. According to an analysis by David Magleby, a professor at Brigham Young University in Utah, 62% of the 1,732 initiatives which reached the ballot in American states between 1898 and 1992 were rejected.

Arguments for and against referendums go to the heart of what is meant by democracy. Proponents of referendums maintain that consulting citizens directly is the only truly democratic way to determine policy. If popular sovereignty is really to mean anything, voters must have the right to set the agenda, discuss the issues and then themselves directly make the final decisions. Delegating these tasks to elected politicians, who have interests of their own, inevitably distorts the wishes of voters.

Referendums, their advocates say, can discipline representatives, and put the stamp of legitimacy on the most important political questions of the day. They also encourage participation by citizens in the governing of their own societies, and political participation is the source of most other civic virtues.

The Case Against

Those sceptical of referendums agree that popular sovereignty, majority rule and consulting voters are the basic building blocks of democracy, but believe that representative democracy achieves these goals much better than referendums. Genuine direct democracy, they say, is feasible only for political groups so small that all citizens can meet face-to-face—a small town perhaps. In large, modern societies, the full participation of every citizen is impossible.

Referendum opponents maintain that representatives, as full-time decision-makers, can weigh conflicting priorities, negotiate compromises among different groups and make well-informed decisions. Citizens voting in single-issue referendums have difficulty in doing any of these things. And as the bluntest of majoritarian devices, referendums encourage voters to brush aside the concerns of minority groups. Finally, the frequent use of referendums can actually undermine democracy by encouraging elected legislators to sidestep difficult issues, thus damaging the prestige and authority of representative institutions, which must continue to perform most of the business of government even if referendums are used frequently.

Testing any of these claims or counter-claims is difficult. Most countries do not, in fact, use referendums regularly enough to bear out either the hopes of proponents or the fears of opponents. The two exceptions are Switzerland and some American states, where citizen initiatives are frequent enough to draw tentative conclusions on some of these points, although both examples fall far short of full-fledged direct democracy.

Voters in both countries seem to believe that referendums do, in fact, lend legitimacy to important decisions. The Swiss are unlikely now to make a big national decision without a referendum. Swiss voters have rejected both UN membership and links with the EU in referendums, against the advice of their political leaders. Similarly, American polls show healthy majorities favouring referendums and believing that they are more likely to produce policies that most people want. Polls also show support for the introduction of referendums on the national level.

The claim that referendums increase citizen participation is more problematic. Some referendum campaigns ignite enormous public interest and media attention. Initiatives also give political outsiders a way to influence the public agenda. But in the United States, much of the activity involved in getting initiatives on the ballot, such as collecting signatures, has been taken over by professional firms, and many referendum campaigns have become slick, expensive affairs far removed from the grassroots (so far, this is much less true in Switzerland). Even more surprising, voter participation in American referendums is well below that of candidate elections, even when these are held at the same time. The average turnout for Swiss referendums has fallen by a third in the past 50 years to about 40%. On big issues, however, turnout can still soar.

Many of the fears of those opposed to referendums have not been realised in either country. Initiatives have not usually been used to oppress minorities. A proposal to limit the number of foreigners allowed to live in Switzerland was rejected by two-thirds of voters in 1988. In 1992 Colorado's voters did approve an initiative overturning local ordinances protecting gays from discrimination, but more extreme anti-gay initiatives in Colorado and California have been defeated by large majorities. Since 1990 voters have consistently upheld certain abortion rights in initiative ballots. Minorities and immigrants have been the targets of initiatives in some states, but voters have generally rejected extreme measures and have often proven themselves no more illiberal than legislators. Most initiatives are, in fact, about tax and economic questions, not civil liberties or social issues, although the latter often gain more attention.

While the frequent use of initiatives has not destroyed representative government, as some feared, it has changed it. Party loyalty among Swiss voters is strong at general elections, but evaporates when it comes to referendum voting. Initiatives, and the threat of mounting one, have become an integral part of the legislative process in Switzerland, as they have in California, Oregon and the other American states where they are most used. Referendums now often set the political agenda in both countries. In the United States they are frequently seen, rightly or wrongly, as a barometer of the national mood. And they can occasionally spark a political revolution. California's Proposition 13, for example, a 1978 initiative lowering local property taxes, set off a tax revolt across America. Elected officials themselves are often active in launching initiatives, and relatively successful in getting their proposals approved, which hardly indicates that voters have lost all faith in their politicians. Initiatives have made legislating more complicated, but also more responsive to the public's concerns.

There is some evidence that American voters, at least, are sometimes overwhelmed by the volume of information coming their way, and cast their vote in ignorance, as critics contend. Mr Magleby cites studies showing that on several ballots, 10–20% of the electorate mistakenly cast their vote the wrong way. Ballot material dropping through the letterboxes of residents in California is now often more than 200 pages long. According to one poll, only one in five Californians believes that the average voter understands most of the propositions put before him. Quite rationally, this has also bred caution. Californians approve only one-third of initiatives.

Hybrid Democracy?

The Swiss and American experience suggests that in the future there is unlikely to be a headlong rush away from representative to direct democracy anywhere, but that, even so, the use of referendums is likely to grow. The Internet and other technological advances have not yet had much impact on referendums, but they should eventually make it easier to hold them, and to inform voters of the issues they are being asked to decide upon.

Representative institutions are likely to survive because of the sheer volume of legislation in modern societies, and the need for full-time officials to run the extensive machinery of government. Nevertheless in an age of mass communication and information, confining the powers of citizens to voting in elections every few years seems a crude approach, a throwback to an earlier era. In a political system based on popular sovereignty, it will become increasingly difficult to justify a failure to consult the voters directly on a wider range of issues.

The Great Divide

Robert Kagan's celebrated analysis of the widening Atlantic—in which he claims that Europe favours peace and negotiation simply out of weakness— is half right. But, as the split over Iraq shows, Europe is a diverse place and wields power in other ways. Vulgar Kaganism is exacerbating division

TIMOTHY GARTON ASH

Anti-Americanism has reached a fevered intensity," Robert Kagan reported from Europe recently in the *Washington Post.* "In London . . . one finds Britain's finest minds propounding, in sophisticated language and melodious Oxbridge accents, the conspiracy theories of Pat Buchanan concerning the 'neoconservative' (read: Jewish) hijacking of US foreign policy. Britain's most gifted scholars sift through American writings about Europe searching for signs of derogatory 'sexual imagery.' "

The last sentence must be a reference to a recent essay I wrote in the *New York Review Books.* Well, thanks for the compliment but no thanks for the implication. If I'm anti-American, then Robert Kagan is a Belgian. Since he and I have never met or conversed in accents melodious or otherwise, I take it that the earlier sentence cannot refer to me; but whoever it does refer to, its innuendo is even more disturbing. That two-word parenthesis " 'neoconservative' (read: Jewish)" can only be taken to imply that this criticism of "neoconservative" views has, at the least, antisemitic overtones. That is a serious charge, which should be substantiated or withdrawn. It illustrates once again how American reports of European anti-Americanism get mixed up with claims, impossible to prove or refute, of antisemitic motivation. I am disturbed to find a writer as sophisticated and knowledgeable as Robert Kagan using such innuendo.

So far as "sexual imagery" is concerned, Kagan seems to have taken offence at a passage in which, discussing the mutual stereotypes of America vs Europe (bullying cowboys vs limp-wristed pansies) I refer to his now famous sentence "Americans are from Mars and Europeans are from Venus," as in "*men* are from Mars and *women* are from Venus." Or perhaps he was irked to find his work discussed under the headline "Anti-Europeanism in America."

So let us start with a necessary clarification: Robert Kagan is no more anti-European than I am anti-American. In his brilliant *Policy Review* article (reprinted in last August's *Prospect*), now expanded into a small book, *Paradise and Power* (Atlantic Books), he gives one of the most penetrating and influential accounts of European-American relations in recent years. It is not yet quite in the Fukuyama *End of History* and Huntington *Clash of Civilisations* class for impact—both of them journal articles later turned into books—but it is heading that way. One reason it has had such an impact is his talent for bold generalisation and provocative overstatement.

"It is time to stop pretending," both article and book begin, "that Europeans and Americans share a common view of the world, or *even that they occupy the same world*" (my italics). He goes on to draw what he admits is a "dual caricature" of Europeans—Venusian, believing in a Kantian "self-contained world of laws and rules and transnational negotiation and cooperation"—and Americans—Martian and martial, knowing that decisive national use of military power is needed in the Hobbesian world beyond Europe's cute little US-protected postmodern paradise. "The reasons for the transatlantic divide," he writes, "are deep, long in development, and likely to endure." The current transatlantic controversy over Iraq, to which more reference is now made in the book, is seen to be representative, even archetypical.

Kagan gives three reasons for this divergence. The main one, to which he returns repeatedly, is European weakness and American power. (The original article was called "Power and Weakness.") By this he means military weakness and military power. Pointing to the growing gulf between US and European military spending and capacity, he argues that when you are weak you tend to favour law, peace, negotiation, and not to see the need for the use of force: "when you don't have a hammer, you don't want anything to look like a nail." Not even Saddam's Iraq. In a vivid simile, he writes that a man walking through a forest armed just with a knife will have a different response to a prowling bear than a man armed with a rifle.

His second reason is that history has led Europeans to a different ideology. Humbled and shocked by our bloody past, we place a higher premium on peace as a value in itself. We aspire, with Immanuel Kant, to a world of perpetual peace. We would like others to imitate our European model of integration. We would rather not hear the growls from the jungle outside. There is a certain tension between these two explanations: do Europeans dislike war because they do not have enough guns, or do they not have enough guns because they dislike war? Kagan favours the former, philosophically materialist view: being determines consciousness. But he also allows for an influence the other way round. Finally, he attributes some of these differences to the fact that, since the end of the cold war, Europeans have sought to define "Europe" as something apart from America, rather than seeking a common definition of "the west."

This is a clever, knowledgeable argument, and there is quite a lot in it. Kagan is right to pour scorn on European pretensions to be a world power, without the military clout or—he might have emphasised this more—the foreign policy unity to deliver. He quotes the Belgian foreign minister saying in December 2001 that the ED military force "should declare itself operational without such a declaration being based on any true capability." I would like to know where this quotation came from—unlike most of the direct quotations in the book version, it is not sourced—but if true, it is classic. We have not advanced very far in the ten years since the Luxembourger Jacques Poos pronounced, over disintegrating Bosnia, his equally ridiculous "the hour of Europe has come."

Kagan is also right to remind us how far the "European miracle" that began with Franco-German reconciliation actually depended on the external American pacifier. Even today, he suggests, the US is "manning the walls of Europe's postmodern order." So Europeans are, in Kipling's famous phrase, making mock of uniforms that guard us while we sleep.

His remedy, so far as he has one, is twofold. First, Europe should stop being a "military pygmy"—in the phrase of George Robertson, Nato secretary-general. This means all of us, and Germany in particular, spending more on defence and getting our militaries together. Second, we should follow Robert Cooper's advice and recognise that, beyond our postmodern world of the EU, there is a modern and a pre-modern world outside. We may be Kantian in our village, but we must be Hobbesian in the jungle around. Saddam Hussein lives by the law of the jungle, so we must threaten him with spears. The two parts of the remedy are connected. Like the man in the forest, once you have a rifle you may start hunting the bear—and if you want to hunt the bear, you will go get a rifle.

There are, however, major problems with the Kagan thesis. One is this: if Europe does not exist as a single, foreign policy actor, then how can you generalise about it? Belgium and Luxembourg are certainly not Martian or martial in Kagan's terms, but Britain and France are. As he acknowledges in two slightly embarrassed asides, it was Blair's Britain that pushed, against the resistance of Clinton's America, for ground troops in Kosovo. This at a time when the martial Americans were still bombing from 15,000 feet in case one of their warrior pilots got his little finger burnt. For three decades, from the end of the Vietnam war to 11th September, Britain and France were more ready to take military casualties abroad than the US was.

Moreover, the controversy over the Iraq war has shown that there is no simple divide between "Europe" and "America." American public opinion is torn and Europeans are divided. Kagan's commentary in the *Washington Post* was occasioned

by the publication of an article by a European "gang of eight" reaffirming transatlantic solidarity against Saddam, as a rebuke to the Franco-German axis. The "gang of eight" included the prime ministers of Britain, Spain, Italy and Poland—that is, Europe's four most important countries after France and Germany—as well as Václav Havel, then still president of the Czech Republic and one of Europe's greatest moral authorities, and the leaders of Portugal, Denmark and Hungary. (Slovakia subsequently joined, to make it nine.) In his commentary, Kagan welcomed the "political and moral courage" of these leaders of what Donald Rumsfeld called "new Europe" as they paid tribute to "American bravery and farsightedness," against the fevered trend of European anti-Americanism. But he might also have written: "whoops, how does this fit my thesis? If Europe's so thoroughly Venusian, as I argue, how come so much of it is cheering for Mars?"

If I wished to be polemical, I would say: where has Kagan been living all these years? The answer, as I understand it, is Brussels—or between Brussels and Washington. And that may be part of the problem. Sitting in Brussels, listening to so much lofty Eurorhetoric matched by so few effective military or diplomatic deeds, one could easily feel as he does. But in the larger EU of 25 member states from 2004—an enlargement that scarcely features in his account the balance of attitudes will be different. Yes, there is a lot of anti-Americanism about, especially in France, Germany, Luxembourg, Belgium. There is also a lot of reasonable, measured scepticism about Bush's policy on Iraq. And then there is a large constituency of the Americanised and the Atlanticist, especially in the new democracies of central and eastern Europe.

In short, Europe's true hallmark is not weakness but *diversity*. It is the sheer diversity of states, nations and views, as much as the popular reluctance to spend on defence, and more than any programmatic Kantianism, that is the main reason for Europe's feebleness in foreign and security policy. If we could just pool and redirect what we already spend on defence, we'd have a formidable European expeditionary force to send to Iraq, or wherever. But we won't, because the French will be French, the British will be British and Belgians will be Belgian.

Kagan stresses military power where Europe is weak and ignores economic and cultural power where it is strong

Another problem with Kagan's book is his emphasis on military power, to the neglect of the two other main dimensions of power: economic and cultural social ("soft power"). He is right to remind Europeans that old-fashioned military power still counts—the postmodern continent is not living in a postmodern world. But he discounts Europe's other forms of power. On a recent trip to the US, I found that what most people are most worried about is not the war on Iraq—it is the state of the US economy. To be sure, there is a two-way interdependence here—Europe cannot be economically strong while America is economically weak, and vice versa—while in the military dimension there is a one-way dependence of Europe on the US. And yes, welfarist complacency, national differences, over-regulation, corporatism, ageing populations and our moral incompetence over immigration are all potential sources of European economic weakness. But the advent of the "Slavonic tigers" will give Europe a shot in the arm. The European economy is already roughly the same size as that of the US. Europe is also growing in a way that America cannot. Its "soft power" is demonstrated by the fact that not only millions of individuals but also whole states want to enter it. Turkey, for example.

Mention of Turkey raises a further difficulty with the Kagan argument: where does the Kantian world end and the Hobbesian begin? Turkey shares a border with Iraq. The frontier runs through the lands of the Kurds, the would-be Kurdistan. Turkey and Iraq have both been hammering their Kurds, on and off, for some time. But the US is urging the EU to take in Turkey, to encourage its adherence to the west by the European process of "conditionality leading finally to accession," while at the same time urging us to join in a war against Saddam. We are being asked to be Kantian-European-postmodern here, but Hobbesian American-pre-modern just a hundred yards across the border. In truth, we need to be both—especially if the democratic reconstruction of postwar Iraq is to succeed. In a now familiar quip: America does the cooking, Europe does the washing-up.

Kagan himself concludes in conciliatory fashion. Unlike his compatriot, Charles A Kupchan, he insists that there is no "clash of civilisations" between Europe and America. Europe should beef up its military and use it a bit more roughly in the jungle, and America, he avers on his last page, should manifest a bit more of what the founding fathers called "a decent respect for the opinion of mankind." America needs Europe, Europe needs America, we both share common western values. I agree. His book is a challenge to make it so, to Europeans especially. But this is not what he said on his first page, which is that Europeans and Americans do not *even occupy the same world*. And that, not his conciliatory conclusion, is what he is being so much quoted for. That, in wider circulation, is "the Kagan thesis."

Of course this is what tends to happen with these "big issue" think pieces turned into books. As once upon a time we had vulgar Marxism, so we now have vulgar Fukuyamaism, vulgar Huntingtonism, and will soon have vulgar Kaganism. Francis Fukuyama can go on insisting until he is purple in the face that what he meant was History not history; people will still snort "well, the end of history, my foot!" Yet usually the author is to some degree complicit, abetted by editors and publishers, in making a bold overstatement to grab attention for his thesis— and to sell. The Hobbesian law of the intellectual jungle leads you, perhaps against your better judgement, to become one of what Jacob Burckhardt called the *terribles simplificateurs*.

The real danger now is that vulgar Kaganism will become popular on both sides of the Atlantic because people either believe Kagan's "dual caricature" or—and I think this is happening—are looking for ways to *emphasive* the gulf. In short, Kagan could have the opposite effect to the one he intends. His conclusion will only be proved right if Americans and Europeans agree that his starting point is wrong.

Timothy Garton Ash is director of the European Studies Centre at St Antony's College, Oxford and a senior fellow at the Hoover Institution, Stanford.

The Case for a Multi-Party U.S. Parliament?
American Politics in Comparative Perspective

This article supports the inclusion of American political institutions within the study of comparative politics. This is a brief on behalf of a multi-party parliamentary system for the United States that can be read as a "what if" experiment in institutional transplantation. It underscores the basic insight that institutions are not neutral but have consequences for the political process itself and encourages American students to think more broadly about the possibilities of reforming the American political system.

CHRISTOPHER S. ALLEN

Introduction

Americans revere the constitution but at the same time also sharply and frequently criticize the government. (Dionne 1991) Yet since the constitution is responsible for the current form of the American government, why not change the constitution to produce better government? After all, the founders of the United States did create the amendment process and we have seen 27 of them in 220 years.

Several recent events prompt a critical look at this reverence for the constitution: unusual developments regarding the institution of the Presidency, including the Clinton impeachment spectacle of 1998–1999; the historic and bizarre 2000 Presidential election that required a Supreme Court decision to resolve; the apparent mandate for fundamental change that President Bush inferred from this exceedingly narrow election; and the increasingly numerous constitutional questions concerning Presidential powers and the conduct of the "war on terror." In the early 21st century, American politics confronted at least three other seemingly intractable problems: significant erosion in political accountability; out of control costs of running for public office; and shamefully low voter turnout. More seriously, none of these four problems is of recent origin, as all four have eroded the functioning of the American government for a period of between 25 and 50 years! The core features of these four problems are:

- Confusion of the roles of head of state and head of government, of which the impeachment issue—from Watergate through Clinton's impeachment and beyond—is merely symptomatic of a much larger problem.
- Eroding political accountability, taking the form of either long periods of divided government, dating back to the "Do Nothing" 80th congress elected in 1946, to the recent "gerrymandering industry" producing a

dearth of competitive elections. The result is millions of "wasted votes" and an inability for voters to assign credit or blame for legislative action.

- Costly and perennial campaigns for all offices producing "the best politicians that money can buy." This problem had its origins with the breakdown of the party caucus system and the growth of primary elections in the 1960s; and
- The world's lowest voter turnout among all of the leading OECD countries, a phenomenon that began in the 1960s and has steadily intensified.

When various American scholars acknowledge these shortcomings, however, there is the occasional, offhand comparison to parliamentary systems which have avoided many of these pathologies. The unstated message is that we don't—or perhaps should never, ever want to—have that here.

Why not? What exactly is the problem with a parliamentary system? In the US, durable trust in government, sense of efficacy, and approval ratings for branches in government have all declined in recent decades. Such phenomena contribute to declining voter turnout and highlight what is arguably a more significant trend toward a crisis in confidence among Americans concerning their governing institutions. So why is institutional redesign off the table?

This article examines these four institutional blockages of the American majoritarian/Presidential system and suggests certain features of parliamentary or consensus systems might overcome these persistent shortcomings of American politics.

Less normatively, the article is framed by three concepts central to understanding and shaping public policy in advanced industrialized states with democratic constitutional structures.

First, is the issue of comparability and 'American Exceptionalism' (Lipset 1996). The article's goal is to initiate a long-delayed dialogue on comparative constitutional structures with scholars of American politics. Second, the article hopes to participate in the active discussion among comparativists on the respective strengths and weaknesses of majoritarian and consensus systems. (Birchfield and Crepaz 1998) Third, scandals surrounding money and politics in a number of democratic states (Barker 1994) should prompt a comparison of parties and party systems and the context within which they function.

This article does not underestimate the quite significant problems associated with "institutional transplantation" (Jacoby 2000) from one country to another. The more modest and realistic goal is to engage American and Comparative scholars in a fruitful debate about political institutions and constitutional design that (finally) includes American politics in a Comparative orbit.

This article is organized in 5 sections that address: 1) the cumbersome tool of impeachment; 2) eroding political accountability due to divided government and safe seats; 3) the costly, never-ending campaign process; 4) the continued deterioration of voter turnout; and 5) the quite formidable obstacles that initiating a parliamentary remedy to these problems would clearly face.

1. Impeachment: Head of State vs Head of Government

The tool of impeachment is merely a symptom of a larger problem. Its more fundamental flaw is that it highlights the constitutional confusion between the two functions of the US presidency: head of state and head of government.

Americanists have delved deeply into the minutiae of the impeachment process during the past thirty years but comparativists would ask a different question. How would other democracies handle similar crises affecting their political leaders? More than two years transpired from the Watergate break-in to Nixon's resignation (1972–74), the Iran-Contra scandal (1986–87) produced no impeachment hearings; and an entire year (1998–99) transpired from the onset of the Clinton-Lewinsky saga to the completion of the impeachment process. Finally, the revelations from 2005–2007 concerning the Bush Administration's clandestine spying on American citizens by the National Security Agency have once again caused some Democrats to mention preliminary impeachment inquiries. Comparativists and citizens of other democratic polities find this astounding, since in a parliamentary system a fundamental challenge to the executive would take the form of a vote of no confidence, (Lijphart 1994) and the issue would be politically resolved within weeks. The executive would either survive and continue or resign.

The portrayal of the Clinton impeachment and trial is characterized as historic. For only the second time in American politics, an American president has been impeached in the House and put on trial in the Senate. Yet, the idea of using impeachment has been much less rare, having been raised three times in the past thirty years; and has only a very slim possibility of being seriously considered in the early 21st century. Basically, impeachment is an extremely blunt tool that has not "worked" at all. It is either not brought to fruition (Watergate), not used when it should have been (Iran-Contra), or completely trivial-

ized (Clinton-Lewinsky) when another path was clearly needed. But impeachment itself isn't the real problem; a larger constitutional design flaw is.

The United States has a constitutional structure based on a separation of powers, while most parliamentary systems have a "fusion" of powers in that the Prime Minister is also the leader of the major party in parliament. However, within the American executive itself, there is a "fusion" of functions, which is the exact opposite of Parliamentary regimes.

The US is the only developed democracy where head of state and head of government are fused in one person. The President is the Head of State and, effectively, the Head of Government. In Parliamentary systems these two functions are performed by two different people. (Linz 1993) Thus impeachment of one person removes two functions in one and likely explained the dichotomy of popular desire for Clinton's retention on the one hand, but also for some form of political censure on the other.

Beyond the impeachment issue, when American presidents undertake some action as head of government for which they are criticized, they then become invariably more remote and inaccessible. For example, Presidents Johnson (Vietnam), Nixon (Watergate), Reagan (Iran/Contra), Clinton (the Lewinsky Affair) and G.W. Bush (Iraq) all reduced their appearances at press conferences as criticism of their policies mounted. In short, when criticized for actions taken in their head of government capacity, they all retreated to the Rose Garden or other "safe" locations and sometimes created the impression that criticizing the President—now wearing the head of state hat (or perhaps, crown)—was somehow unpatriotic. This was especially the case with George W. Bush, who in the post 9/11 and Iraq war periods, has tried to emphasize the commander in chief aspect of the presidency rather than his role as steward of the economy and domestic politics.

Toward a Politically Accountable Prime Minister and a Ceremonial President

A parliamentary system with a separate head of state and head of government would produce two "executive" offices instead of just one. It's odd that the US is so fearful of centralized power yet allows the executive to perform functions that no other leader of an OECD country (France excepted) performs alone. The US Vice President serves many of the functions of heads of state in other countries. But the United States has a comparatively odd way of dividing executive constitutional functions. One office, the Presidency, does everything while the other, the Vice Presidency, does virtually nothing and simply waits until the president can no longer serve (although Vice President Cheney sees this role differently). An American parliamentary system would redefine these 2 offices so that one person (the head of state) would serve as a national symbol and preside over ceremonial functions. The second person (the head of government) would function much like a prime minister does in a parliamentary system, namely as the head of government who could be criticized, censured and held accountable for specific political actions without creating a constitutional crisis.

Thus were it necessary to censure or otherwise take action against the head of government (i.e. prime minister), the solution would be a relatively quick vote of no confidence that would solve the problem and move on and let the country address its political business. (Huber 1996) And unlike impeachment which is the political equivalent of the death penalty, a vote of no confidence does not preclude a politician's making a comeback and returning to lead a party or coalition. Impeachment and removal from office, on the other hand, is much more final.

Prime Ministers, unlike US presidents, are seen much more as active politicians and not remote inaccessible figures. In a parliament, the prime minister as the head of government is required to engage—and be criticized—in the rough-and-tumble world of daily politics. In short, the head of government must be accountable. The British prime minister, for example, is required to participate in a weekly "question time" in which often blunt and direct interrogatories are pressed by the opposition. (Rundquist 1991) There is no equivalent forum for the American president to be formally questioned as a normal part of the political process.

But could such a power be used in a cavalier fashion, perhaps removing the head of government easily after a debilitating scandal? This is unlikely in a well-designed parliamentary system because such cynicism would likely produce a backlash that would constrain partisanship. In fact, the Germans have institutionalized such constraints in the "constructive vote of no confidence" requiring any removal of the head of government to be a simultaneous election of a new one. The context of such a parliamentary system lowers the incentives to engage in the politics of destruction. The political impact of destroying any particular individual in a collective body such as a cabinet or governing party or coalition is much less significant than removing a directly elected president.

A parliamentary head of state is above the kind of criticism generated from no confidence votes and simply serves as an apolitical symbol of national pride. In nation states that have disposed of their monarchies, ceremonial presidents perform many of the same roles as constitutional monarchs such as Queen Elizabeth do, but much less expensively. In fact, many of these ceremonial roles are performed by the American vice president (attending state dinners/funerals, cutting ribbons, presiding over the Senate, etc.) The problem is that the Vice President is often a political afterthought, chosen more for ticket-balancing functions and/or for inoffensive characteristics than for any expected major political contributions. On the other hand, the type of individual usually chosen as a ceremonial president in a parliamentary system is a retired politician from the moderate wing of one of the major parties who has a high degree of stature and can serve as a figure of national unity. In effect, the office of ceremonial president is often a reward or honor for decades of distinguished national service, hardly the characteristics of most American vice presidents.

In retrospect, one might say that President Clinton was impeached not for abusing head of government functions, but for undermining the decorum and respect associated with heads of state. The separation of head of state and head of government would have a salutary effect on this specific point. Scan-dals destroying heads of state would have little real political significance since the head of state would not wield real political power. Similarly, scandals destroying heads of government would have significantly less impact than in the current American system. The head of government role, once separated from the head of state role, would no longer attract monolithic press and public attention or be subject to extraordinarily unrealistic behavioral expectations.

2. Political Accountability: Divided Government & "Safe Seats"

From the "do nothing" 80th Congress elected in 1946 to the 110th elected in 2006, a total of thirty-one Congresses, the United States has experienced divided government for more than two-thirds of this period. In only ten of those thirty-one Congresses has the president's party enjoyed majorities in both houses of Congress. (Fiorina 1992; Center for Voting and Democracy 2007) Some might observe this divided government phenomenon and praise the bipartisan nature of the American system. (Mayhew 1991) But to justify such a conclusion, defenders of bipartisanship would have to demonstrate high public approval of governmental performance, particularly when government was divided. Based on over four decades of declining trust in government, such an argument is increasingly hard to justify.

One explanation for the American preference for divided government is the fear of concentrated political power. (Jacobson 1990) Yet in a search for passivity, the result often turns out to be simply inefficiency.

While the fear of concentrated government power is understandable for historical and ideological reasons, many of the same people who praise divided government also express concern regarding government efficiency. (Thurber 1991) Yet divided government quite likely contributes to the very inefficiencies that voters rightfully lament. Under divided government, when all is well, each of the two parties claims responsibility for the outcome; when economic or political policies turn sour, however, each party blames the other. This condition leads to a fundamental lack of political accountability and the self-fulfilling prophesy that government is inherently inefficient.

Rather than being an accidental occurrence, divided government is much more likely to result due to the American constitutional design. For it is constitutional provisions that are at the heart of divided government; 2 year terms for Congress, 4 year terms for the Presidency, and 6 year terms for the Senate invariably produce divided government.

Were it only for these "accidental" outcomes of divided government, political accountability might be less deleterious. Exacerbating the problem, however, is the decline of parties as institutions. This has caused individuals to have weaker partisan attachments—despite the increased partisan rhetoric of many elected officials since the 1980s—and has thereby intensified the fragmentation of government. (Franklin and Hirczy de Mino 1998) Clearly, divided government is more problematic when partisan conflict between the two parties is greater as the sharper ideological conflict and the increased party line congressional

Table 1   Trust in the Federal Government 1964–2004

	None of the Time	Some of the Time	Most of the Time	Just about Always	Don't Know
1964	0	22	62	14	1
1966	2	28	48	17	4
1968	0	36	54	7	2
1970	0	44	47	6	2
1972	1	44	48	5	2
1974	1	61	34	2	2
1976	1	62	30	13	3
1978	4	64	27	2	3
1980	4	69	23	2	2
1982	3	62	31	2	3
1984	1	53	40	4	2
1986	2	57	35	3	2
1988	2	56	36	4	1
1990	2	69	25	3	1
1992	2	68	26	3	1
1994	1	74	19	2	1
1996	1	66	30	3	0
1998	1	58	36	4	1
2000	1	55	40	4	1
2002	0	44	51	5	0
2004	1	52	43	4	0

Percentage within study year

Source: The National Election Studies (http://www.electionstudies.org/nesguide/toptable/tab5a_1.htm)

Question Text:

"How much of the time do you think you can trust the government in Washington to do what is right—just about always, most of the time or only some of the time?"

Source: The National Election Studies, University of Michigan, 2005

Table 2   The Persistence of Divided Government

Year	President	House	Senate	Divided/ Unified Government
1946	D – Truman	Rep	Rep	D
1948	D – Truman	Dem	Rep	D
1950	D – Truman	Rep	Rep	D
1952	R – Eisenhower	Rep	Rep	U
1954	R – Eisenhower	Dem	Dem	D
1956	R – Eisenhower	Dem	Dem	D
1958	R – Eisenhower	Dem	Dem	D
1960	D – Kennedy	Dem	Dem	U
1962	D – Kennedy	Dem	Dem	U
1964	D – Johnson	Dem	Dem	U
1966	D – Johnson	Dem	Dem	U
1968	R – Nixon	Dem	Dem	D
1970	R – Nixon	Dem	Dem	D
1972	R – Nixon	Dem	Dem	D
1974	R – Ford	Dem	Dem	D
1976	D – Carter	Dem	Dem	U
1978	D – Carter	Dem	Dem	U
1980	R – Reagan	Dem	Rep	D
1982	R – Reagan	Dem	Rep	D
1984	R – Reagan	Dem	Rep	D
1986	R – Reagan	Dem	Dem	D
1988	R – Bush	Dem	Dem	D
1990	R – Bush	Dem	Dem	D
1992	D – Clinton	Dem	Dem	U
1994	D – Clinton	Rep	Rep	D
1996	D – Clinton	Rep	Rep	D
1998	D – Clinton	Rep	Rep	D
2000	R – Bush	Rep	Dem*	D
2002	R – Bush	Rep	Rep	U
2004	R – Bush	Rep	Rep	U
2006	R – Bush	Dem	Dem	D

*After a 50-50 split (with Vice President Cheney as the tiebreaker), Senator Jeffords (I-VT) switched from the Republican Party shortly after the 2000 Election, thereby swinging the Senate to the Democrats.

voting since the mid-1990s would suggest. Under these circumstances, divided government seems to be more problematic, since two highly partisan parties within the American political system seem potentially dangerous. Persistent divided government over time will likely produce a fundamental change in the relationship between Presidents and the Congress. Presidents are unable to bargain effectively with a hostile congress—witness the 1995 government shutdown—leading the former to make appeals over the heads of Congress directly and, hence undermine the legitimacy of the legislative branch. (Kernell 1997) This argument parallels the one made in recent comparative scholarship (Linz 1993) regarding the serious problem of dual legitimacy in presidential systems.

A second component of the political accountability problem is the increasing non-competitiveness of American elections. Accounts of the 2000 Presidential election stressed its historic closeness, settled by only 540,000 popular votes (notwithstanding the Electoral College anomaly). And the narrow Republican majorities in the House and Senate apparently indicated that every congressional or senate seat could be up for grabs each election. The reality is something different. (Center for Voting and Democracy 2007) Out of 435 House seats, only 60 (13.8%)

were competitive, the outcome of most Senate races is known well in advance, and the 2000 and 2004 Presidential races were only competitive in 15 of 50 states. In the remaining 35, the state winners (Bush or Gore; or Bush or Kerry, respectively) were confident enough of the outcome to forgo television advertising in many of them. In essence, voters for candidates who did not win these hundreds of "safe seats" were effectively disenfranchised and unable to hold their representatives politically accountable.

For those who lament the irresponsibility—or perhaps irrelevance—of the two major parties, an institutional design that would force responsibility should be praised. Quite simply, those who praise divided government because it "limits the damage" or see nothing amiss when there are hundreds of safe seats are faced with a dilemma. They can not simultaneously complain about the resulting governmental inefficiency and political cynicism that ultimately follows when accountability is regularly clouded.

Political Accountability and the Fusion of Government

A number of scholars have addressed the deficiencies of divided government, but they suggest that the problem is that the electoral cycle, with its "midterm" elections, intensifies the likelihood of divided government in non-presidential election years. Such advocates propose as a solution the alteration of the electoral cycle so that all congressional elections are on four year terms, concurrent with presidential terms, likely producing a clear majority. (Cutler 1989) Yet this contains a fatal flaw. Because there is no guarantee that this proposal would alleviate the residual tension between competing branches of government, it merely sidesteps the accountability factor strongly discouraging party unity across the executive and legislative branches of government.

This suggestion could also produce the opposite effect from divided government, namely exaggerated majorities common to parliamentary regimes with majoritarian electoral systems such as the UK. The "safe seats" phenomenon would be the culprit just as in the UK. The most familiar examples of this phenomenon were the "stop-go" policies of post-World War II British governments, as each succeeding government tried to overturn the previous election. While creating governing majorities is important for political accountability, the absence of proportional representation creates a different set of problems.

Under a fusion of power system, in which the current presidency would be redefined, the resulting parliamentary system would make the head of the legislative branch the executive, thus eliminating the current separation of powers. Yet if a government should lose its majority between scheduled elections due to defection of its party members or coalition partners, the head of state then would ask the opposition to form a new government and, failing that, call for new elections. This avoids the constitutional crises that the clamor for impeachment seems to engender in the American system.

But what if coalition members try to spread the blame for poor performance to their partners? In theory, the greater the flexibility available in shifting from one governing coalition to another (with a different composition), the greater is the potential for this kind of musical cabinet chairs. The potential for such an outcome is far less than in the American system, however. A century of experience in other parliamentary regimes (Laver and Shepsle 1996) shows that members of such a party

Table 3 Comparative Coalitions

American	Parliamentary
Opaque	Transparent
Issue-by-Issue	Programmatic
Back Room	Open Discussion
Unaccountable	Election Ratifies
Unstable	Generally Stable

capriciously playing games with governing are usually brought to heel at the subsequent election.

In other words, the major advantage to such a parliamentary system is that it heightens the capacity for voters and citizens to evaluate government performance. Of course, many individuals might object to the resulting concentration of power. However, if voters are to judge the accomplishments of elected officials, the latter need time to succeed or fail, and then the voters can make a judgment on their tenure. The most likely outcome would be a governing party or coalition of parties that would have to stay together to accomplish anything, thereby increasing party salience. (Richter 2002) Phrased differently, such an arrangement would likely lead to an increase in responsible government.

Many Americans might react unfavorably at the mention of the word coalition due to its supposed instability. Here we need to make the distinction between transparent and opaque coalitions. Some argue that coalition governments in parliamentary systems have the reputation of increased instability. That, or course, depends on the substance of the coalition agreement and the willingness of parties to produce a stable majority. (Strom et al. 1994) But in most parliamentary systems, these party coalitions are formed transparently before an election so the voters can evaluate and then pass judgment on the possible coalition prior to Election Day. It's not as if there are no coalitions in the US Congress. There they take the opaque form of ad-hoc groups of individual members of Congress on an issue-by-issue basis. The high information costs to American voters in understanding the substance of such layered bargains hardly are an example of political transparency.

Finally, for those concerned that the "fusion" of the executive and legislative branches—on the British majoritarian model—would upset the concept of checks and balances, a multi-party consensus parliamentary system produces them slightly differently. (Lijphart 1984) Majoritarianism concentrates power and makes "checking" difficult, while consensus democracies institutionalize the process in a different and more accountable form. A multi-party parliamentary system would also provide greater minority representation, fewer safe seats, and protection by reducing majoritarianism's excessive concentration of power. A consensus parliamentary system would also address the "tyranny of the majority" problem and allow checking and balancing by the voters in the ballot box since the multiple parties would not likely allow a single party to dominate. Consensus systems thus represent a compromise between the current U.S. system and the sharp concentration of British Westminster systems. Americans who simultaneously favor checks and balances but decry inefficient government need to clarify what they actually want their government to do.

3. Permanent and Expensive Campaigns

The cost to run for political office in the United States dwarfs that spent in any other advanced industrialized democracy. The twin problems are time and money; more specifically a never-ending campaign "season" and the structure of political advertising that depend so heavily on TV money. (Gans 1993) In listening to the debates about "reforming" the American campaign finance system, students of other democratic electoral systems find these discussions bizarre. More than $2 billion was raised and spent (Corrado 1997) by parties, candidates and interest groups in the 1996 campaign, and for 2000 it went up to $3 billion. Finally, the Center for Responsive Politics estimated the total cost for 2004 Presidential and Congressional elections was $3.9 billion (Weiss 2004) and the preliminary estimates for the 2006 midterm elections—in which there was no presidential race—were approximately $3 billion.

The two year congressional cycle forces members of the House of Representatives to literally campaign permanently. The amount of money required to run for a Congressional seat has quadrupled since 1990. Presidential campaigns are several orders of magnitude beyond the House of Representatives or the Senate. By themselves they are more than two years long, frequently longer. Unless a presidential candidate is independently wealthy or willing and able to raise upfront $30–$50 million it is simply impossible to run seriously for this office.

Many of the problems stem from the post-Watergate "reforms" that tried to limit the amount of spending on campaigns which then produced a backlash in the form of a 1976 Supreme Court decision (Buckley vs Valeo) that undermined this reform attempt. In essence, Buckley vs Valeo held that "paid speech" (i.e. campaign spending) has an equivalent legal status as "free speech". (Grant 1998) Consequently, since then all "reform" efforts have been tepid measures that have not been able to get at the root of the problem. As long as "paid speech" retains its protected status, any changes are dead in the water.

At its essence this issue is a fissure between "citizens" and "consumers". What Buckley vs Valeo has done is to equate the citizenship function (campaigning, voting, civic education) with a market-based consumer function (buying and selling consumer goods as commodities). (Brubaker 1998) Unlike the United States, most other OECD democracies consider citizenship a public good and provide funding for parties, candidates and the electoral process as a matter of course. The Buckley vs Valeo decision conflates the concepts of citizen and consumer, the logical extension of which is there are weak limits on campaign funding and no limits on the use of a candidate's own money. We are all equal citizens, yet we are not all equal consumers. Bringing consumer metaphors into the electoral process debases the very concept of citizenship and guarantees that the American political system produces the best politicians money can buy.

Free Television Time and the Return of Political Party Dues

Any broadcaster wishing to transmit to the public is required to obtain a broadcast license because the airways have the legal status of public property. To have access to such property, the government must license these networks, cable channels, and stations to serve the public interest. In return, broadcasters are able to sell airtime to sponsors of various programs. Unfortunately for those concerned with campaign costs, candidates for public office fall into the same category as consumer goods in the eyes of the broadcasters. (Weinberg 1993) What has always seemed odd to observers of other democratic states is that there is no Quid Pro Quo requiring the provision of free public airtime for candidates when running for election.

Any serious reform of campaign finance would require a concession from all broadcasters to provide free time for all representative candidates and parties as a cost of using the public airways. Since the largest share of campaign money is TV money, this reform would solve the problem at its source. Restricting the "window" when these free debates would take place to the last two months before a general election would thus address the time dimension as well. Such practices are standard procedure in all developed parliamentary systems. Very simply, as long as "reform" efforts try to regulate the supply of campaign finance, it will fail. A much more achievable target would be the regulation of demand.

The United States could solve another money problem by borrowing a page from parliamentary systems: changing the political party contribution structure from individual voluntary contributions (almost always from the upper middle class and the wealthy) to a more broad-based dues structure common to parties other developed democracies. This more egalitarian party dues structure would perform the additional salutary task of rebuilding parties as functioning institutions. (Allen 1999) Rather than continuing in their current status as empty shells for independently wealthy candidates, American political parties could become the kind of dynamic membership organizations they were at the turn of the 20th century when they did have a dues structure.

4. Low Voter Turnout?

The leading OECD countries have voter turnout ranging from 70% to 90% of their adult population while the US lags woefully behind.

Among the most commonly raised explanations for the US deficiency are: registration requirements, the role of television, voter discouragement, and voter contentment (although the latter two are clearly mutually exclusive). None are particularly convincing nor do they offer concrete suggestions as to how it might be overcome.

The two party system and the electoral method that produces it: the single member district, first past the post, or winner take all system with its attendant "safe seats" often escapes criticism. The rise of such new organizations as the Libertarian, and Green parties potentially could threaten the hegemony of the Democrats and Republicans. Yet the problem of a third (or fourth) party gaining a sufficient number of votes to actually win seats and challenge the two party system is formidable. The electoral arithmetic would require any third party to win some 25% of the vote on a nationwide basis—or develop a highly-concentrated regional presence—before it would actually gain more than a token number of seats. And failing to actually win seats produces a "wasted

Table 4　Voter Turnout and Type of Electoral System Major Developed Democracies–1945–2005

Country	% Voter Turnout	Type of Electoral System
Italy	91.9	PR
Belgium	84.9	PR
Netherlands	84.8	PR
Australia	84.4	Mixed Member
Denmark	83.6	PR
Sweden	83.3	PR
Germany	80.0	Mixed-PR
Israel	80.0	PR
Norway	79.2	PR
Finland	79.0	PR
Spain	76.4	PR
Ireland	74.9	SMD
UK	73.0	SMD
Japan	68.3	SMD/Mixed
France	67.3	SMD + runoff
Canada	66.9	SMD
USA – Presidential	55.1	SMD
USA – Congress (Midterm)	40.6	SMD

Source: Voter Turnout: A Global Survey (Stockholm: International IDEA, 2005)

Table 5　The Advantages of Proportional Representation

Higher Voter Turnout
No "Wasted" Votes
Few Safe, Uncontested Seats
More Parties
Greater Minority Representation
Greater Gender Diversity in Congress
Greater Ideological Clarity
Parties Rebuilt as Institutions
6% Threshold Assumed
No More Gerrymandered Redistricting

vote" syndrome among party supporters which is devastating for such a party. (Rosenstone et al. 1996) Most voters who become disillusioned with the electoral process refer to the "lesser of two evils" choices they face. In such a circumstance, declining voter turnout is not surprising.

The US is a diverse country with many regional, religious, racial, and class divisions. So why should we expect that two "catch all" parties will do a particularly good job in appealing to the interests of diverse constituencies? The solution to lower voter turnout is a greater number of choices for voters and a different electoral system.

Proportional Representation

Under electoral systems using proportional representation, the percentage of a party's vote is equivalent to the percentage of seats allocated to the party in parliament. Comparative analysis shows that those countries with proportional representation—and the multiple parties that PR systems produce—invariably have higher voter turnout. (Grofman and Lijphart 1986) In other words, PR voting systems provide a wider variety of political choices and a wider variety of political representation.

Eliminating majoritarian single member districts (SMDs) in favor of PR voting would have several immediate effects. First, it would increase the range of choices for voters, since parties would have to develop ideological and programmatic distinctions to make themselves attractive to voters. As examples in other countries have shown, it would lead to formation of several new parties representing long underserved interests.

Such a change would force rebuilding of parties as institutions, since candidates would have to run as members of parties and not as independent entrepreneurs. The so-called Progressive "reforms" at the turn of the 20th century and the 1960s introduction of primaries—plus TV advertising—plus the widespread use of referenda have all had powerful effects in undermining parties as coherent political organizations. (Dwyre et al. 1994) In trying to force market-based individual "consumer choice" in the form of high-priced candidates, the collective institutions that are political parties have been hollowed out and undermined.

There are, of course, a wide range of standard objections to PR voting systems by those favoring retention of majoritarian SMD systems.

The first of these, coalitional instability, was addressed briefly above, but it needs to be restated here. The US has unstable coalitions in the Congress right now, namely issue-by-issue ones, usually formed in the House cloakroom with the "assistance" of lobbyists. Few average voters know with certainty how "their" member of Congress will vote on a given issue. (Gibson 1995) With ideologically coherent parties, they would.

An American parliament with several parties could very effectively produce self-discipline. Clearly there would have to be a coalition government since it is unlikely that any one party would capture 50% of the seats. The practice in almost all other coalition governments in parliamentary systems is that voters prefer a predictable set of political outcomes. Such an arrangement forces parties to both define their programs clearly and transparently, once entering into a coalition, and to do everything possible to keep the coalition together during the course of the legislative term.

The second standard objection to PR is the "too many parties" issue. PR voting has been practiced in parliaments for almost 100 years in many different democratic regimes. There is a long history of practices that work well and practices that don't. (Norris 1997) Two countries are invariably chosen as bad examples of PR, namely Israel and Italy. There is an easy solution to this problem of an unwieldy number of parties, namely an electoral threshold requiring any party to receive a certain minimal percentage to gain seats in the parliament. The significant question is what should this minimal threshold be? The Swedes have a 4% threshold and have 7 parties in their parliament, the Germans have a 5% threshold and have 5 parties represented in the Bundestag.

The third standard objection to PR voting is "who's my representative?" In a society so attuned to individualism, most Americans want a representative from their district. This argument presumes that all Americans have a member of Congress that represents their views. However, a liberal democrat who lived in former House Speaker Tom Delay's district in Texas might genuinely wonder in what way he represented that liberal's interests. By the same token, conservative Republicans living in Vermont had for almost twenty years the independent socialist, Bernard Sanders as the state's lone member of Congress representing "their" interests.

Yet if Americans reformers are still insistent on having individual representatives (Guinier 1994) the phenomenon of "Instant Runoff Voting" (Hill 2003) where voters rank order their preferences could produce proportionality among parties yet retain individual single member districts. It also could be used in Presidential elections and avoid accusations of "spoiler" candidates such as Ralph Nader in 2000.

If there were PR voting in an American parliament, what would the threshold be? The US threshold probably should be at least 6%. The goal is to devise a figure that represents all significant interests yet does not produce instability. The "shake out" of parties would likely produce some strategic "mergers" of weak parties which, as single parties, might not attain the 6% threshold. For example, a separate Latino party and an African-American party might insure always attaining a 6% threshold by forming a so-called "rainbow" party. Similarly the Reform Party and the Libertarian Party might find it electorally safer to merge into one free market party.

There are four primary arguments in favor of PR.

The first is simplicity; the percentage of the votes equals the percentage of the seats. To accomplish this, the more individualistic US could borrow the German hybrid system of "personalized" proportional representation. This system requires citizens to cast two votes on each ballot: the first for an individual candidate; and the second for a list of national/regional candidates grouped by party affiliation. (Allen 2001) This system has the effect of personalizing list voting because voters have their own representative but also can choose among several parties. Yet allocation of seats by party in the Bundestag corresponds strongly with the party's percentage of the popular vote.

The second advantage to PR is diversity. The experience of PR voting in other countries is that it changes the makeup of the legislature by increasing both gender and racial diversity. Obviously, parties representing minority interests who find it difficult to win representation in 2 person races, will more easily be able to win seats under PR. (Rule and Zimmerman 1992) Since candidates would not have to run as individuals—or raise millions of dollars—the parties would be more easily able to include individuals on the party's list of candidates who more accurately represent the demographics of average Americans. What a multi-party list system would do would provide a greater range of interests being represented and broaden the concept of "representation" to go beyond narrow geography to include representation of such things as ideas and positions on policy issues that would be understandable to voters. Moreover, as for geographic representation on a list system, it would be in the self interest of the parties to insure that there was not only gender balance—if this is what the party wanted—on their list, but also other forms of balance including geography, ideology, and ethnicity, among others.

The third advantage is government representativeness. Not only is a consensus-based parliamentary system based on proportional representation more representative of the voting public, it also produces more representative governments. (Birchfield and Crepaz 1998) This study finds that consensus-based, PR systems also produce a high degree of "popular cabinet support," namely the percentage of voters supporting the majority party or coalition.

The fourth advantage to a PR system in the US is that it would eliminate the redistricting circus. Until recently, the decennial census occasioned the excruciating task of micro-managing the drawing of congressional districts. Yet, since the 2002 elections, Republicans in Texas and Georgia have redistricted a second time, creating even "safer" seats by manipulating district lines to their advantage. (Veith et al. 2003) Under PR however, districts would be eliminated. Candidate lists would be organized statewide, in highly populated states, or regionally in the case of smaller states like those in New England. To insure geographical representation, all parties would find it in their own self-interest that the candidate list included geographical diversity starting at the top of the list.

Getting from Here to There: From Academic Debates to Constitutional Reform?

Clearly, none of these four structural reforms will take place soon. But if reformers wanted to start, what would be the initial steps? Of the four proposals, two of them could be accomplished by simple statute: campaign reform and the electoral system. The other two would require constitutional change: head of state/government and divided government. Given the above caveats, it would be easiest to effect campaign reform (the Supreme Court willing) and to alter the electoral system.

The largest obstacles to such a radical change in the American constitutional system are cultural and structural. Culturally, the ethos of American individualism would have difficulty giving up features such as a single all-powerful executive and one's own individual member of congress, no matter how powerful the arguments raised in support of alternatives. Ideology and cultural practice change very slowly. A more serious obstacle would be the existing interests privileged by the current system. All would fight tenaciously to oppose this suggested change.

Finally, specialists in American politics may dismiss this argument as the farfetched "poaching" of a comparativist on a terrain that only Americanists can write about with knowledge and expertise. However, the durability of all four of the above-mentioned problems, stretching back anywhere from 25 to 50 years, suggests that Americanists have no monopoly of wisdom on overcoming these pathologies. More seriously, what this comparativist perceives is a fundamental failure of imagination based largely on the "N of 1" problem that all comparativists struggle to avoid. If a single observed phenomenon—in this case, the American political system—is not examined comparatively, one never knows whether prevailing practice is optimal or suboptimal. In essence, those who do not look at these issues comparatively suffer a failure of imagination because they are unable to examine the full range of electoral and constitutional options.

References

Allen, Christopher S. 1999. *Transformation of the German Political Party System: Institutional Crisis or Democratic Renewal?* New York: Berghahn Books.

———. 2001. "Proportional Representation." In *Oxford Companion to Politics of the World,* ed. J. Krieger. Oxford: Oxford University Press.

Barker, A. 1994. "The Upturned Stone: Political Scandals and their Investigation Processes in 20 Democracies." *Crime Law and Social Change* 24 (1):337–73.

Birchfield, Vicki, and Markus M. L. Crepaz. 1998. "The Impact of Constitutional Structures and Collective and Competitive Veto Points on Income Inequality in Industrialized Democracies." *European Journal of Political Research* 34 (2):175–200.

Brubaker, Stanley C. 1998. "The Limits of U.S. Campaign Spending Limits." *Public Interest* 133:33–54.

Center for Voting and Democracy. *Dubious Democracy 2007,* September 3 2007 [cited. Available from http://www.fairvote.org/?page=1917.

Corrado, Anthony. 1997. *Campaign Finance Reform: A Sourcebook.* Washington, D.C.: Brookings Institution.

Cutler, Lloyd. 1989. "Some Reflections About Divided Government." *Presidential Studies Quarterly* 17:485–92.

Dionne, E. J., Jr. 1991. *Why Americans Hate Politics.* New York: Simon and Schuster.

Dwyre, D., M. O'Gorman, and J. Stonecash. 1994. "Disorganized Politics and the Have-Notes: Politics and Taxes in New York and California." *Polity* 27 (1):25–48.

Fiorina, Morris. 1992. *Divided Government.* New York: Macmillan.

Franklin, Mark N., and Wolfgang P. Hirczy de Mino. 1998. "Separated Powers, Divided Government, and Turnout in U.S. Presidential Elections." *American Journal of Political Science* 42 (1):316–26.

Gans, Curtis. 1993. "Television: Political Participation's Enemy #1." *Spectrum: the Journal of State Government* 66 (2):26–31.

Gibson, Martha L. 1995. "Issues, Coalitions, and Divided Government." *Congress & the Presidency* 22 (2):155–66.

Grant, Alan. 1998. "The Politics of American Campaign Finance." *Parliamentary Affairs* 51 (2):223–40.

Grofman, Bernard, and Arend Lijphart. 1986. *Electoral Laws and Their Consequences.* New York: Agathon Press.

Guinier, Lani. 1994. *The Tyranny of the Majority: Fundamental Fairness in Representative Democracy.* New York: The Free Press.

Hill, Steven. 2003. *Fixing Elections: The Failure of America's Winner Take All Politics.* New York: Routledge.

Huber, John D. 1996. "The Vote of Confidence in Parliamentary Democracies." *American Political Science Review* 90 (2): 269–82.

Jacobson, Gary C. 1990. *The Electoral Origins of Divided Government: Competition in U.S. House Elections, 1946–1988.* Boulder, CO: Westview.

Jacoby, Wade. 2000. *Imitation and Politics: Redesigning Germany.* Ithaca: Cornell University Press.

Kernell, Samuel. 1997. *Going Public: New Strategies of Presidential Leadership.* 3rd ed. Washington, D.C.: CQ Press.

Laver, Michael, and Kenneth A. Shepsle. 1996. *Making and Breaking Governments: Cabinets and Legislatures in Parliamentary Democracies.* New York: Cambridge University Press.

Lijphart, Arend. 1984. *Democracies: Patterns of Majoritarian and Consensus Government in Twenty-One Countries.* New Haven: Yale University Press.

———. 1994. "Democracies: Forms, Performance, and Constitutional Engineering." *European Journal of Political Research* 25 (1):1–17.

Linz, Juan. 1993. "The Perils of Presidentialism." In *The Global Resurgence of Democracy,* ed. L. Diamond and M. Plattner. Baltimore: Johns Hopkins University Press.

Lipset, Seymour Martin. 1996. *American Exceptionalism: A Double-Edged Sword.* New York: Norton.

Mayhew, David. 1991. *Divided We Govern: Party Control, Lawmaking, and Investigations, 1946–1990.* New Haven: Yale University Press.

Norris, Pippa. 1997. "Choosing Electoral Systems: Proportional, Majoritarian and Mixed Systems." *International Political Science Review* 18 (3):297–312.

Richter, Michaela. 2002. "Continuity or Politikwechsel? The First Federal Red-Green Coalition." *German Politics & Society* 20 (1):1–48.

Rosenstone, Steven J. , Roy L. Behr, and Edward H. Lazarus. 1996. *Third Parties in America: Citizen Response to Major Party Failure.* Princeton: Princeton University Press.

Rule, Wilma, and Joseph F. Zimmerman, eds. 1992. *United States Electoral Systems: Their Impact on Women and Minorities.* New York: Praeger.

Rundquist, Paul S. 1991. *The House of Representatives and the House of Commons: A Brief Comparison of American and British Parliamentary Practice.* Washington, DC: Congressional Research Service, Library of Congress.

Strom, Kaare, Ian Budge, and Michael J. Laver. 1994. "Constraints on Cabinet formation in Parliamentary Democracies." *American Journal of Political Science* 38 (2):303–35.

Thurber, James A. 1991. "Representation, Accountability, and Efficiency in Divided Party Control of Government." *PS* 24:653–7.

Veith, Richard, Norma Jean Veith, and Susan Fuery. 2003. "Oral Argument." In *U.S. Supreme Court.* Washington, DC.

Weinberg, Jonathan. 1993. "Broadcasting and Speech." *California Law Review* 81 (5):1101–206.

Weiss, Stephen. 2004. "'04 Elections Expected to Cost Nearly $4 Billion." In *opensecrets.org—Center for Responsive Politics:* http://www.opensecrets.org/pressreleases/2004/04spending.asp.

UNIT 4

Three Very Different Giants: Europe, Russia, China

Unit Selections

Key Points to Consider

- Why did a former President of the European Commission refer to the European Union (EU) as a UPO (Unidentified Political Object)? In order to be a member of the EU, a country must meet some economic and political criteria. If Turkey can meet those criteria, should it be admitted as a full member? What are the main reasons for an affirmative answer, and what are the main reasons raised against full membership?

- What is meant by the phrase "democratic deficit" with regard to the European Union? Why is the voter turnout in elections for the European Parliament so low?

- Compare three Russian leaders in terms of their major contributions to the collapse of the Soviet Union, early hopes for a democratic Russia, and an increasing reliance on authoritarian politics in that country.

- Show how the strong executive model that de Gaulle developed for France has been copied in many countries that were formerly members of the Soviet bloc. Why? How does President Putin apparently plan to retain an important position in the dual executive even after Russian term limits force him to leave the presidential office no later than the spring of 2008?

- How did Russia and China differ in their reform strategies that ended the central planning of their economies? How has China built up a huge industrial infrastructure that produces wealth for the country but also recreates the vast gap in incomes that the communists were going to abolish?

- Does it seem likely that, as China grows more prosperous, there will be greater demands for respect of civil rights and political freedoms, so that the power monopoly of the Communist party will eventually erode?

Student Web Site
www.mhcls.com/online

Internet References
Further information regarding these Web sites may be found in this book's preface or online.

Europa: European Union
  http://europa.eu.int
NATO Integrated Data Service (NIDS)
  http://www.nato.int/structur/nids/nids.htm
Research and Reference (Library of Congress)
  http://lcweb.loc.gov/rr/

The three "giants" in this unit illustrate the diversity of today's political universe. The modern state had forerunners in other parts of the world, but it became the keystone and chief reference point in European politics. Yet the **European Union** has not become a state, nor does it appear likely to become one in the near future, despite its enormous success in overcoming traditional national barriers and building an institutional basis for a supranational entity. Jacques Delors, who served ten years as President of the EU Commission and strove mightily to increase its **authority and scope,** once called it a UPO, or "Unidentified Political Object."

Russia was the dominant member of the now-defunct **Soviet Union.** For most of the twentieth century Russia sat at the center of this huge Marxist-Leninist construct that covered most of the former Czarist empire. It has lost that empire, along with about one-half of the Soviet population of 300 million, which has mostly ended up divided among 15 successor states.

China is in a category of its own: this former empire has retained both its territory and its Marxist ideological foundation by grafting a *de facto* capitalist economy onto its statist political structure.

A. Europe and the European Union

The two articles in this unit present different views of the supranational project now known as the European Union (EU) and its impact on the European countries, both member and non-member states, and their citizens. The present time can be seen as an important turning point for the EU, and also a crucial test of its viability.

Its institutional origins go back to 1951, when France, West Germany, Italy, and the three Benelux countries integrated their coal and steel industries. By 1957 the same six nations founded the European Economic Community (EEC) that later became the European Union. The European Community quickly turned out to be a supranational framework that served to stimulate the economies of the member states. Britain sought to join by the early 1960s, but French President de Gaulle opposed Britain's entry. The EU did not add new members until 1973, when Britain finally entered along with Ireland and Denmark. Thereafter the European Community continued to expand incrementally in sets of three newcomers per decade: three former dictatorships, Greece, Portugal, and Spain, entered during the 1980s, after having established their credentials as well-functioning new democracies and market economies; and in 1995, soon after the end of the Cold War, three neutral countries—Austria, Finland, and Sweden—joined the EU and increased its total membership to fifteen.

In 2004 the EU abandoned this incremental growth in favor of what has been called a great leap forward. In one swoop, the EU expanded its membership by two-thirds, from fifteen to twenty-five countries. This greatly increased the EU's economic, cultural, and political diversity, as its population rose from 375 million to some 450 million people.

Eight of the ten newcomers lie in central or eastern Europe: Poland, Hungary, the Czech Republic, Slovakia, Slovenia, and the three Baltic states, Lithuania, Latvia, and Estonia. They differ from most of the first fifteen members in two major respects. First, they all have had a relatively short recent experience with pluralist democracy. Second, their economies are far less productive than those of the older EU members for reasons stretching back before the years of Communist mismanage-

ment: even before World War II, most of these countries lagged behind the more developed parts of Western Europe. The remaining two in the group of ten newcomers are the small Mediterranean island nations of Malta and Cyprus.

The EU enlargement proceeds, and it is not hard to imagine it as a political conglomerate of thirty or more members. With the admission of two more East European post-Communist states (Romania and Bulgaria) in January 2007, the EU's population rose by another 30 million to between 480 and 490 million.

The case of Turkey is special. The EU members are divided, with some strongly resisting any plans for granting full membership. This country is poorer and less modernized than its close and distant European neighbors, and it has a tainted record on human rights and democracy. Although the state is officially secular, the Turkish population is overwhelmingly Muslim. Opposition is often culturally based, but there are also voices of caution that point out that Turkey's entry would change the balance of power in the EU considerably. They underscore that Turkey now has some 70 million people and presumably will outnumber Germany's 80 million within a decade or two. They tend to portray Turkey as a potential economic dead weight in the EU and as a political, cultural, and demographic threat to the "*acquis communautaire.*" It does not help matters that Turkey has refused to recognize the government of Cyprus and keeps troops on the island to protect the Turkish minority living there.

Supporters of Turkey's entry argue the real hope for a workable model of modernization and democratization in the Middle East may lie in Turkey. They also commend the Turkish government for a series of reforms, including the abolition of the death penalty and a relaxation of its policy toward the Kurdish minority. Given the deep division on this issue, it seems most likely that Turkey will be limited to a close association status—perhaps sweetened to read "privileged partnership"–rather than full membership in the EU. That would resemble a status that would resemble in practice the one chosen voluntarily by Norway and Switzerland. Both of these countries would presumably have no difficulties in attaining full membership, but have decided against it.

The enlargement of the EU, with or without Turkey, will in any case bring changes and challenges. It cannot be ruled out that the larger and more diverse EU will begin (or has already begun) to depart from the founders' idealistic vision of "an ever closer union among the peoples of Europe," as stated in the preamble to the EU's founding document, the Rome Treaty. Although this phrase echoes the preamble to the U.S. Constitution ("a more perfect union"), some observers think the EU will not become a loose-knit United States of Europe.

Within a few days of each other, and only a little more than a year after the latest and greatest expansion of the EU membership, French and Dutch voters rejected a proposed EU constitution. The negative votes, coming from two founding members of the EU, cancelled the plans for completing the constitutional process during 2006.

Even without a constitution, the EU is an impressive political construct that has no close parallel anywhere. It has largely dismantled national barriers to the free movement of people, goods, services, and capital among the member nations. Above all, the EU and its institutions have supranational authority that goes far beyond anything envisaged by NAFTA or other regional free trade arrangements. The appointed executive Commission initiates common policy decisions and oversees their implementation. The independent European Court of Justice makes binding decisions in its adjudication of EU-related disputes. The European Parliament has seen its authority grow over the years, even though it is not a full-blown legislature in the traditional sense. The powerful Council of Ministers remains an intergovernmental body, where the national government of every member nation is represented.

For an American student of the EU, it is interesting that the organization has faced the same basic "big state-small state" problem that gave headaches to the Founders in Philadelphia. The Europeans have sought a solution in an intricate system of differently weighted votes for the member states, related to the size of each nation's population. It lacks some of the rough simplicity of the solution offered by the Connecticut Compromise, but both are attempts to recognize some equality of status among all members without completely ignoring their considerable differences in population. It remains to be seen whether a new system of qualified and double majorities will be more acceptable than weighted votes. It cannot be denied that there is a problem in an association where the population of the smallest member, Malta, has about 400,000 citizens, while the largest member, Germany, has more than 80 million people—a ratio of roughly 1:200.

B. Russia

In countries on both sides of the "old EU-new EU" line, one encounters a debate over the most effective way to stimulate growth and reform the welfare state without introducing what has come to be called "American conditions." A similar debate has been carried out in the former Soviet Union. It could be argued that Mikhail Gorbachev, the last Soviet head of government (1985 to 1991), failed to opt clearly for one or the other approach to economic reform in his program of *perestroika,* or restructuring. In the eyes of some born-again Soviet free-marketers, he remained far too socialist; but Communist hard-liners never forgave him for dismantling a system in which they had enjoyed security and privilege.

Gorbachev appears to have regarded his own demands for democratization and *glasnost* (openness and transparency) as essential counterparts of *perestroika* in his overall program of modernization. He seems to have understood (or become convinced) that a highly developed economy needs a freer flow of information and a more decentralized system of decision-making if its component parts are to be efficient, flexible, and capable of learning and self-correction. In that sense, a market economy has some integral feedback traits that make it incompatible with the traditional Soviet models of a centrally-directed "command economy" and repressive one-party rule. Rather than modernizing the Soviet system, Gorbachev's reforms contributed to its eventual collapse.

One of the greatest vulnerabilities of the Soviet Union turned out to be its multiethnic character. Gorbachev was not alone in having underestimated the potential centrifugal tendencies of a "Union of Soviet Socialist Republics" (USSR) erected on the territory of the old Russian Empire. Many non-Russian minorities retained a territorial identification with their homelands, where they often lived as ethnic majorities, making it easier for them to demand greater autonomy or national independence as the Soviet regime weakened. The first national assertions came from the Baltic peoples in Estonia, Latvia, and Lithuania; soon, others, including the Georgians and Armenians, expressed similar demands through newly open political channels. The death knell sounded for the Soviet Union in 1991, when the Ukrainians, the second largest national group after the Russians, made similar demands for independence.

In August 1991, Communist hard-liners failed in a coup attempt against Gorbachev. The coup was defeated by a popular resistance led by Russian President Boris Yeltsin, a seemingly more committed convert to the reformist agenda. After his restoration to power, Gorbachev became politically dependent on Yeltsin and was increasingly seen as a transitional figure. Quickly, and essentially without armed conflict, the Soviet state was dissolved a week before the end of 1991, to be replaced by the loose union of the Commonwealth of Independent States (CIS).

Many accounts of post-Communist and post-Soviet Russia paint a gloomy picture of a politically exhausted society, with a turn to some form of authoritarian nationalist populism seeming more and more possible. A quick survey of recent parliamentary and presidential elections gives a picture of electoral volatility, growing voter apathy or disgruntlement, and widespread authoritarian leanings. It also illustrates how governmental leaders can favor, manipulate, or even help create "loyal" political parties.

Duma Elections 1993 and 1995. The first election of a new Russian *Duma,* or parliament, after the end of the Soviet Union came after a complete breakdown of relations between President Yeltsin and the parliamentary majority. A vote to impeach Yeltsin was followed by his armed expulsion of the parliamentarians and the banning of some political parties. The 1993 elections returned a fragmented Duma, in which nationalists and Communists occupied key positions and reformers suffered setbacks. A chastened Yeltsin seemed to play a more subdued role, and the new government pursued far more cautious reform policies. Disunity in the reform camp was a large cause of further losses in 1995, though reform factions still held a larger total portion of the vote than either the Communists or nationalists.

Presidential Election 1996. Yeltsin still knew how to win elections, albeit in a run-off, against the Communist presidential leader, Zyuganov. By this time, ill health and heavy drinking had reportedly exacerbated his governing problems. His frequent and seemingly erratic replacements of prime ministers did not improve the situation.

Duma Elections 1999. In the latter half of 1999, Yeltsin selected a stronger figure for what turned out to be his last prime minister. Vladimir Putin, then 47 years old, quickly turned his attention to a tough new military intervention in Chechnya. Within Russia, his strong determination to suppress the breakaway Muslim province generated widespread support, and probably helped reduce the Communist result to 113 seats, or a quarter of the Duma.

Presidential Election 2000. Without warning, but with impeccable timing, President Yeltsin announced his resignation on December 31, 1999, just as the century and millennium came to an end. Putin became the new acting president and easily won the presidential election a few months later. Largely due to a favorable oil market for Soviet exports, the new president inherited a much better fiscal balance and continuing revenues than Yeltsin or Gorbachev before him.

In his first term as President of Russia, Putin aroused popular support with tough measures against organized crime and political terrorism. Also popular were his judicial actions against some of the super-rich **"oligarchs,"** who had made huge fortunes when state-owned enterprises were privatized. Putin's maneuvers had strategic import beyond their populist appeal: some of the oligarchs had used their fortunes to oppose him politically.

Duma Election 2003. In an election marked by lower voter turnout, the Communists and liberal parties lost ground to a new party, called **United Russia,** which performed better than any party since the end of one-party "elections". Outside observers found evidence of fraud and cited media favors toward United Russia, but it seems likely that

144

this party, largely defined by its loyalty to the person of President Putin, would have done well in any case.

Presidential Election 2004. Putin seemed a sure bet to win the presidential election in March 2004. In advance of the contest, he asserted his authority within the dual executive by dismissing the prime minister and appointing a new one. With the dependable backing of a parliamentary majority, supplied by United Russia and a few independents, the institutional and political basis for a strong presidency until 2008 seemed to have been secured. As discussed in Robert Skidelsky's article, "Putin's Patrimony," some Russians wonder whether Putin will step aside, seek to determine his successor (as Yeltsin did), or seek a third term—a move that would require a change in the Russian constitution.

Duma Election 2007. In advance of this election, scheduled for early December 2007, it was widely expected that parties supportive of President Putin and his program, would win handily. Political scientists were curious about the election as a way of studying the impact of a new electoral law that President Putin had promoted as a means of consolidating the Russian party system. It provides that the 450 seats in the lower chamber of the legislature will be distributed among party-list candidates only, using a proportional representation (PR) system modified by a 7 percent eligibility requirement for the parties. Hitherto, only one-half of the lower house (225 members) had been elected in that manner, while the other 225 had won their seats in single-member districts using a simple plurality system (with first-past-the-post rules). The result had been the election in the single-member districts of many independents or minor party candidates in the Duma. In a further attempt to build a system dominated by a few major parties, the threshold for eligibility to win seats was raised from 5 percent to 7 percent of the vote. In a sense, the election could be regarded as a test of the political consequences of these and some other targeted changes in the electoral rules.

There would be other factors at play in the election. The outgoing President Putin was expected to try in other ways to influence the outcome. Less than three months before the December election, Putin accepted the resignation of the prime minister, Mikhail Fradkov, and appointed Viktor Zubkov to replace him.

Presidential Election 2008. The Russian Constituition does not allow a third consecutive term in the presidency. It was thus clear that, bar a formal constitutional change of this provision, Putin would not be a candidate in 2008. It was pointed out that he would be eligible once again after the lapse of four years. On October 1st—just two months shy of December's parliamentary election—Putin announced that he would run for parliament as head of the United Russia party list, hinting that he might try for the prime minister's position if (as seemed likely) his party came out ahead. How he planned to juggle the presidency and a parliamentary seat was not made explicit; some speculate that he plans to appoint a figurehead to the presidency, and continue to exercise executive power from the premier's chair.

In conclusion, pluralist democracy and the open market economy have once again been discredited for many Russians after being tried out under highly imperfect circumstances. Stephen F. Cohen has long argued in favor of a better understanding of Russia by American political leaders. In "The New American Cold War," he explains why he thinks the United States has contributed to the problems besetting post-Soviet Russia.

C. China

China is the homeland of nearly 1.3 billion people, or about one-fifth of the world's population. Here the reform Communists, who took power after Mao Zedong's death in 1976, began, a decade before their Soviet counterparts, to steer the country toward a relatively decontrolled market economy. They also introduced some political relaxation, by ending Mao's ideological campaigns to mobilize the masses.

In their place came domestic tranquility such as China had not known for over half a century. But the regime encountered a basic dilemma: it wished to maintain tight controls over politics and society while simultaneously freeing its economy. When a new openness began to emerge in Chinese society, comparable in some ways to the pluralism encouraged by Gorbachev's *glasnost,* it ran into determined opposition among hard-line Communist leaders. The aging reform leader, Deng Xiaoping, presided over a bloody crackdown on student demonstrations in Beijing's Tiananmen Square in May 1989.

The regime has refused to let up on its tight political controls of society, but it continues to loosen economic controls in the zones designated for such reforms. In recent years, China has experienced a remarkable economic surge, with growth rates unmatched elsewhere in the world. A still unanswered question is whether the emerging market-oriented society can coexist for long with a tightly controlled political system.

In February 1997 Beijing announced the death of Deng Xiaoping, but the leadership since then has not really changed direction. Jiang Zemin, chosen by Deng as his successor in 1989, had been the country's president since 1993. As government and party leader, he appeared determined to continue the relatively pragmatic course adopted by Deng. The regime has revived a hard line in dealing with real, imagined, or potential political dissidence, which includes some forms of religious expression. Moreover, there are familiar signs of social tension, as China's mixed economy leaves both "winners" and "losers" in its wake.

Despite the country's undeniable problems and shortcomings, China's leaders have steered clear of the chaos that has plagued post-Soviet Russia. They seem determined to continue with tight political controls, even as their economy becomes freer and more market-oriented. Some observers believe that the basic economic and political norms will eventually begin to converge, but that remains to be seen. A test case is the movement known as **Falun Gong,** which the ruling Communists see as a threat because of its effective organization and solidarity—qualities that do not characterize the Chinese Communist Party as much as they once did.

Hu Jintao was named party leader in the latter half of 2002. He moved quietly to further consolidate power: in September 2004 he replaced Jiang Zemin as the country's military chief. There had been speculation that Jiang would continue to wield power from behind the scenes, perhaps provoking a succession struggle. But Hu now holds the highest posts in the three centers of state power: the Communist Party of China, the military, and the government itself.

The struggle to retain its own national character in the face of economic development and increased contact with its partners in the global economy will challenge China's leaders for years to come. Issues to watch are the **environment,** which has been severely damaged by rampant industrialization; the **2008 Summer Olympics,** to be held in Beijing, which have already begun to draw greater outside attention to conditions inside China; and free expression and access to information, particularly via the **Internet.** Internet use has exploded in China in the past few years, and the government's response has been to extend the limits placed on other forms of communication into the digital sphere. Still, the rapid pace of technological change seems likely to bring about increased public awareness and communication within China, which could bring increased pressure on the government to reform its policies. But underestimating the Chinese government's ability to exercise social control is no safe bet either.

For Europe, A Moment to Ponder

Roger Cohen

It is not easy to think of Spain as Poland. Stroll around this southern city at dusk, beneath the palms, beside the handsome bridges on the Guadalquivir River, past the chic boutiques and the Häagen-Dazs outlet, the Gothic cathedral and the Moorish palace, and it is scarcely Warsaw that comes to mind.

But, insisted Adam Michnik, the Polish writer, "Poland is the new Spain, absolutely." He continued: "Spain was a poor country when it joined the European Union 21 years ago. It no longer is. We will see the same results in Poland."

If history is prologue, Mr. Michnik is likely to be right. The European Union, which celebrates the 50th anniversary of its founding treaty this weekend, is more often associated with Brussels bureaucrats setting the maximum curvature of cucumbers than with transformational power. But step by step, stipulation by stipulation, Europe has been remade.

What began in limited fashion in 1957 as a drive to remove tariff barriers and promote commercial exchange has ended by banishing war from Europe, enriching it beyond measure, and producing what Mr. Michnik called "the first revolution that has been absolutely positive."

Over five decades, its union remade the continent. The next step might be harder

Asia, still beset by nationalisms and open World War II wounds, can only envy Europe's conjuring away agonizing history, a process that involved a voluntary dilution of national sovereignty unthinkable in the United States.

This achievement will be symbolized as leaders from the 27 member states gather in Berlin—the city that stood at the crux of violent 20th-century European division. They will sign a "Berlin Declaration" celebrating the peace, freedom, wealth and democracy that the Treaty of Rome has now helped spread among almost half a billion Europeans.

But it is a celebration in uncertainty. A bigger union, expanded to include the ex-Communist states of Central Europe, has proved largely ungovernable. A constitution designed to streamline its governance was rejected in 2005. Integration has been a European triumph, but not always of those who are part of large-scale Muslim immigration. "The E.U. is on autopilot, in stalemate, in deep crisis," said Joschka Fischer, the former German foreign minister who seven years ago called for a European federation run by a true European government. The founding treaty, signed by the six founding members on March 25, 1957, rested on creative ambiguity. It called for an "ever closer union among the European peoples"; behind it lay dreams of a United States of Europe. The bold politics nestled inside basic economics—a common market—and was thus rendered unthreatening. A common currency, the euro, emerged in 2002.

Still, the ambiguity persisted; it has proved divisive. Economic power has been built more effectively than political or strategic unity. Military power has lagged. Recent disputes—from Iraq to current American plans to install missile defenses in Poland and the Czech Republic—have shown how hard it is for Europe to speak with one voice or, as Fischer put it, "define what strategic interests it has in common."

Nonetheless, "autopilot" in the union still amounts to a lot.

It will ensure, for example, that over $100 billion is sent to Poland from now to 2013 to upgrade its infrastructure and agriculture, a sum that dwarfs American aid. Similarly, more than $190 billion has been devoted to Spain since it joined the union in 1986, 11 years after the end of Franco's dictatorship.

The result has been Spain's extraordinary transition from a country whose per capita output was 71 percent of the European average in 1985, 90 percent in 2004, and now 100.7 percent of the median of the 27 members. Spain has moved into the club of the well off. Dictatorship seems utterly remote.

Poland under the Kaczynski brothers is far from overcoming the painful legacy of Communist tyranny, but by 2025—its own 21-year membership anniversary—safe to say that healing will be advanced.

"The E.U. slashes political risk," said Chris Huhne, a Liberal Democrat member of the British Parliament. "It also exercises a soft power on its periphery that has far more transformational impact than the American neocon agenda in the Middle East. Countries in the Balkans wanting to come into the European democratic family have to adapt."

That adaptation is economic as well as political. The creation of something approximating an American single market has been powerful in ending cartels and monopolies, introducing competition, pushing privatization and generally promoting the market over heavily managed capitalism.

Which is not to say, of course, that European capitalism is American capitalism. It is less fluid; it creates fewer jobs. It is also less harsh.

Indeed, defense of what is called the European social model, with universal health care and extensive unemployment benefits, has become a tenet of European identity. How far that identity, as opposed to national identities, exists today is a matter of dispute. Only 2 percent of European Union inhabitants of working age live in member states other than their own.

But a survey in the French daily Le Figaro showed that 71 percent of French people now feel some pride in a European identity. The Erasmus program has helped about 1.5 million young Europeans spend a year studying in European universities outside their own countries.

The movie "L'Auberge Espagnole," or "The Spanish Inn," captured the Erasmus experience: jumbled cultures, linguistic and amorous discovery, and the births of new identities from this mingling. Countless Eurocouples have not been the least of the union's achievements.

How this generation will deal with what is often called the question of Europe's final destination remains unclear. The union is open geographically: It could end at the Iranian and Iraqi borders if Turkey joins. It is also open politically: How much of a federation should Europe be?

The union has been upended by Communism's unexpected demise. The European Economic Community, as formed in 1957, did not try to liberate the continent; it tried to ensure that half of it cohered in freedom. "Europe was initially built on accepting—with more or less equanimity—to forget about half of it, including historic centers of European civilization like Prague or Budapest," said Jonathan Eyal, a British analyst. "And the irony is that it is precisely the return of these centers that has thrown the E.U. into existential crisis today."

The Franco-German core is gone, and nobody knows what to put in its place

That crisis is partly procedural: It is not clear how you get things done in a Europe of 27. It is partly of identity: The rapidly cohering Europe with a Franco-German core is gone, and nobody quite knows what to put in its place. And it is partly political: The conception of Europe in post-Communist countries is simply different.

These differences are apparent in recent tensions between *Germany* and Poland, whose reconciliation has been one of the European Union's conspicuous miracles.

Germany has been utterly remade by an integrating Europe to the point that more people worry today about German pacifism than expansionism. But Poland is just entering that transformational process; under Lech Kaczynski's conservative presidency its wariness of the pooling of sovereignty inherent in the union has been clear.

Poland today, said Karl Kaiser, a German political analyst, "looks out and tends to see the old Germany and the old expansionist *Russia;* it has not taken part mentally in the long process of integration."

So Warsaw sees Moscow-Berlin plots of sinister memory when Russia and Germany agree to build a gas pipeline directly between each other, under the Baltic Sea rather than over Poland.

It pushes hard, but unsuccessfully, for references to Europe's Christian roots in the Berlin declaration. It contemplates, as does the Czech Republic, installing part of a new American missile defense system against Iran, and does so despite German unease, Russian fury and the absence of any European or NATO consensus.

Of course, what Poles and Czechs see beyond Germany or Russia is the America that defeated the Soviet Union and freed them: Poles, as Mr. Michnik noted, "tend to be more pro-American than Americans."

Whatever tempering of this sentiment Iraq has brought, Poland and the rest of Central and Eastern Europe remain more pro-American than the Europe of the Treaty of Rome. With Britain they now form a club within the club that sees Europe more as loose alignment than strategic union.

"For Britain, Europe is a convenience rather than a concept," said Karsten Voigt, a German Foreign Ministry official.

This is an intractable division, and the Bush administration has accentuated the split with its ad hoc approach to European alliances. That stance was evident at the time of the Iraq invasion and again today over missile defenses. Coalitions of the willing tend to leave the unwilling bristling.

At a deeper level, Homo europeus, formed over 50 years, now lies at some distance from Homo americanus. Post-heroic Europeans tend to favor procedure, talk, international institutions and incremental measures to resolve issues, where Americans tend to favor resolve backed by force.

Peace is much more of an absolute value today in Europe than in the United States, as are opposition to the death penalty and commitment to reversing global warming. So what? The ties that bind the Atlantic family remain strong. But, unglued by the cold war's end, they are not as strong as they were. Europe sees the United States today more through the prism of Baghdad than Berlin.

Generations pass; memories fade; perceptions change. That is inevitable. The great achievement of the European Union has

147

been to absorb those changes and zigzags within the broader push for unity.

That push, that journey, is incomplete. But Europeans have learned, as Mr. Eyal said, that "traveling can be just as good as arriving." Perpetual difficulty has been the union's perpetual stimulus. A United States of Europe remains a distant, probably unreachable dream. At the same time, continent-wide war has become an unthinkable nightmare.

"The E.U. is an unfinished project, but so what?" Mr. Voigt said. "Why be nervous? We have time."

Time enough even, the 50-year history of the union suggests, for Turkey to become the new Poland.

Roger Cohen writes the Globalist column for *The International Herald Tribune.*

Europe's Future

A Venture at a Standstill

Twelve months after the French and Dutch said no, the European Union has yet to rediscover its purpose

As Chou En-lai observed of the 1789 revolution in France, the full impact of events in that country can take centuries to discern. That may yet prove true of the French no to the European Union's draft constitution, expressed in a referendum on May 29th last year. But there was no doubting the shock, especially when it was amplified three days later by an even bigger no from the Dutch. For the first time since a European common market was set up in 1957, two of the six founders of the club had decisively rejected a step in the long march towards fuller integration.

Ever since, Europe's leaders have been unsure what to do next. The immediate gloom was deepened by one of the EU's periodic budget squabbles, prompting Jean-Claude Juncker to declare that "Europe is not in crisis: it is in a deep crisis." As Luxembourg's prime minister, he spoke with authority: his country was then president of the European Council, the group of national leaders who together are the ultimate decision-makers in the EU. Discombobulated summiteers hurriedly agreed to a "pause for reflection".

A year on, what has the pondering brought forth? There have been speeches galore, by such luminaries as Britain's Tony Blair, France's Jacques Chirac and, most recently, Germany's Angela Merkel. The European Commission, the EU's policy-proposing executive, has produced not a plan B but a plan D (for democracy). Its president, José Manuel Barroso, has issued many papers. Belgium's prime minister, Guy Verhofstadt, has even written a book. And yet, as EU foreign ministers meet to discuss the constitution this weekend, before a summit under the Austrian presidency, the answer to the question is: precious little. The summit will simply extend the pause for reflection for another year.

After such a shock, it was perhaps inevitable that a year would not be enough. But three other problems have increased the EU's paralysis since last May. The first is a familiar lack of leadership, exacerbated by the electoral cycle. After a tight election in September, Ms Merkel replaced Gerhard Schröder as German chancellor only last November. After an almost equally narrow win in April, Romano Prodi has only just become Italy's prime minister in place of Silvio Berlusconi.

Meanwhile France is going through the drawn-out dénouement of Mr Chirac's 11-year-old presidency. He is now so feeble politically that little can be expected in the way of fresh EU initiatives until he leaves office next May.

The second problem is that nobody agrees about the reasons the French and Dutch said no. Eurosceptics were swift to hail the votes as a rejection of the drive towards ever-closer union that had, they said, been foisted on reluctant voters by the European elite for 50 years. Euro-enthusiasts were just as quick with a very different interpretation: that the voters wanted more Europe, to increase social protection and to keep at bay the excesses of free markets. Still others thought the voters were merely taking the chance to bash unpopular national governments.

What seems certain is that the naysayers were not rejecting the EU constitution as such: few could have mastered such a complex text, and fewer still could have grasped how it differed from existing European treaties. Rather they were showing dissatisfaction with the European project in a wider sense. The no campaigns played on fears of globalisation, on slow growth and on high unemployment. These feelings found expression in hostility to the expansion of the union to take in low-wage countries to the east, and to plans for more liberalisation of energy markets and trade in services. Yet none of these was directly linked to the constitution.

Unlike the first two problems, the third was self-inflicted. This was the refusal of many governments to draw the clearest conclusion from the two noes: that the constitutional treaty was dead. Countries that had already ratified it were understandably loth to give it up. Much stranger has been the spectacle of six more countries solemnly ratifying the text even after last May. Luxembourg did it by referendum in July. The others put it through their parliaments. Finland is expected soon to become the 16th of the EU's 25 members to give it final approval:

Any EU treaty has to be ratified by all members before it can come into force. Yet those who still want to press ahead with the constitution point to two previous experiences. In 1992 Denmark's voters turned down the Maastricht treaty; and in 2001 the Irish threw out the Nice treaty. After each rejection the treaty was slightly titivated, with various declarations or opt-outs added, after which the voters were asked to pronounce again—and then they said yes. It was also noted that the constitution itself envisaged that ratification might be difficult in some countries. A declaration attached to the text provided that if, within two years of the treaty's signature, four-fifths of the members had ratified it but some had not, the European Council should meet to consider what to do.

Carry on Regardless

The implication of this declaration, some have argued, was that a rejection by one or two of the EU's members should not deter the others from proceeding. Only after every country had had its say would it be right to discuss the next steps. The unspoken assumption was that, if only one or two had jibbed at the text, some way would be found of getting them to vote again and say yes. To make that look more plausible after the no votes, it was also noted that elections were due in 2007 in both France and the Netherlands.

Yet a moment's consideration shows that dreams of proceeding with the constitution are utterly unrealistic. It contains nothing that could be adjusted to give France or the Netherlands opt-outs. And, anyway, there is something undemocratic about asking electorates to endorse a text and, when they deliver a resounding no, asking them again. No French or Dutch leaders, now or in prospect, have floated the idea of putting the constitution to a fresh vote (though France's Valéry Giscard d'Estaing, who presided over the constitutional convention, has suggested it). Besides, six countries—Britain, Ireland, Sweden, Denmark, Poland and the Czech Republic—have made

% responding "yes", February-March 2006:

Is your country's membership of the European Union a good thing?

Are things in the European Union going in the right direction?

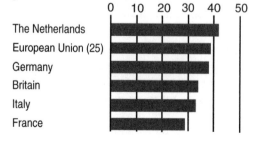

Figure 1 European Blues.

Source: Eurobarometer

clear that, after the French and Dutch votes, they have no plans to ratify the constitution. Most of these had promised referendums.

One sensible thing that next month's summit could do is to agree to forget the present text. That would enable the summiteers to move on to the more fundamental questions that the constitution was supposed, but failed, to answer: how to restore the EU's purpose (and, just as desirable, its popularity), and what institutional changes this might require.

What is wrong with Europe? The main answer is, as it has been for some years, the economy. Especially but not only in the core euro countries of Germany, France and Italy, growth has been sluggish, at best. In many countries unemployment seems both high and stuck. The morosity that underlay the French and Dutch noes was primarily about growth and jobs.

Not surprisingly, the constitution, which was meant to be about the efficiency and organisation of the EU, offered little on the economy. The prime responsibility for getting economies growing again remains national, not European—a point that is obvious when you contrast the performance of Britain and Spain (average growth of 2.6% in 2001–05) with that of France, Germany and Italy (average annual growth of 0.9% in the same period). Some have blamed tight monetary and fiscal policy in the euro zone for holding back growth, but such euro-members as Spain, Ireland and Finland have done well.

As it happens, growth in Europe has picked up in recent months, though a rising euro may slow it down again. The most urgent measures now needed are the further deregulation of labour markets, services, energy and so on. The obstacles to this liberalisation lie largely at national level, although the EU's Lisbon Agenda—the self-imposed measures needed to make Europe "the most dynamic and competitive knowledge-based economy in the world" by 2010—can help to chivvy governments along. So long as the Lisbon Agenda lacks carrots or sticks, it will be up to governments to decide how far to pursue it, and how far to push reform over resistance by unions and other lobbies.

The task of the Brussels commission is to sustain whatever it controls that contributes to Europe's economic growth. This means, above all, safeguarding the single market and its competition rules. A nasty outbreak of economic nationalism struck earlier this year, when several countries started to talk of fostering national energy champions and of protecting their biggest companies from foreign takeover. This must be beaten back. Indeed, much work is needed to bolster all the EU's four freedoms—of goods, services, movement of labour and of capital—each of which has been under attack this year. Once again, the constitution has little directly to do with this. But its demise might be used as an excuse to roll back the single market.

A Pause for Digestion

Similarly, some politicians are using the constitution's troubles to question the EU's expansion to take in new members. At least some of those who voted no may have done so in protest at the recent and future enlargement of their club. The threat of the mythical Polish plumber played strongly in France. The prospect of Turkey joining was a factor in both France and the Netherlands. Indeed, it was partly because of this that Mr Chirac changed the French constitution to provide that any new entrant after Bulgaria, Romania and Croatia must be approved by a referendum in France. Austria has similarly promised a vote on Turkey, and other countries may yet follow suit.

The expansion of the European club is widely touted as its biggest single success. The lure of membership has helped to entrench stability and democracy, first in the southern Mediterranean and now in central Europe. A similar pull is at work in Turkey and the western Balkans, and even as far afield as Ukraine and the Caucasus. Moreover, the economics of enlargement looks good. An exhaustive commission analysis recently concluded that the entry of new countries from central Europe in 2004 had raised economic growth and created jobs not only in the new members but also in existing ones.

The EU should continue to welcome aspirant countries, for its own benefit as much as for theirs. The alternative is distinctly unappealing. Analysts of the western Balkans agree that, if Brussels were to slam the door, these countries could easily slip back into nationalism, drug- and people-smuggling, organised crime and even war—with lots of undesirable consequences for western Europe. Similarly, a Turkey spurned by Europe could soon regress into a sour and militant Islamist mood, right on Europe's front line.

So the question left by the failed constitution should not be: how can we resurrect it? It should be: what changes are needed to ensure that the EU continues to benefit from its single market, to help promote economic reform and to keep the club open to new members?

Pick and Choose

Many different answers have been proffered during the pause for reflection. In some ways, the argument has turned into a new round in the long debate between "institutionalists", who would like a new institutional framework that then produced closer integration; and "incrementalists", who would prefer the club to develop organically, with institutional change coming later.

In this second camp stand, in particular, the British, supported here by Mr Barroso, who thinks further discussion of the EU's institutions should be put off for now. They admit that the current set-up has unsatisfactory features—the six-monthly rotating presidency, a bizarre system of voting, a commission that is too big, a continued muddle over who is in charge of foreign policy. Despite all this, though, the EU is able to function.

Yet it is hardly tenable to suggest that the EU's treaties need no changes at all. Under the Nice treaty, new voting weights and seats in the European Parliament must be fixed for Croatia or any country that joins after it. At that point, too, Nice scraps the rule that gives each country one commissioner in Brussels, though it does not offer a replacement. So some treaty amendment will be needed by 2009 or 2010, when Croatia is likely to join. For that reason a new inter-governmental conference may have to be called to consider treaty changes, perhaps in late 2007, after the French elections.

This gives heart to those who still insist on pursuing the constitution and nothing but the constitution. Even though that looks unrealistic, several governments, including (at least formally) Germany's, stick to it. So does Italy, under Mr Prodi, Luxembourg, Belgium, Spain and some members in central Europe.

A wide variety of ideas lie between the two extremes of no action and the full constitution. Most involve picking the best bits of the constitutional treaty and producing a shorter version, which might even be brought into force without approval by referendum. The trouble with that idea is that few EU members agree on which parts of the document to keep. Typically, big countries want to slim the commission, change the voting system and install a permanent presidency in place of the present six-monthly one. But small countries see most of these changes as steps backward: if they are to accept them, they want something in exchange, such as more majority voting and a stronger European Parliament.

It was the need to balance such widely differing desires that led to such a cumbersome constitutional treaty in the first place. Several leaders have duly given warning against attempts to unpick the compromises that went into the document. Indeed, some countries are no longer willing to honour the concessions they made in the constitution. Poland, for instance, which in 2003 was, with Spain, a fierce opponent of a proposed new "double-majority" voting system, only to give way in the summer of 2004, now says that it wants to stick to the system agreed on in the Nice treaty in 2000.

Besides the practical and political difficulty of resurrecting bits of the treaty, there are two other objections. The first is the democratic one: the people have voted no, which makes it unattractive to bring in any change by the back door, especially if an avowed goal is to avoid consulting the people again. The second is that if, despite that, any new treaty ends up being put to the vote, its odds of passing are small. Around a dozen national referendums have now been held on such EU issues as new treaties and whether to join the euro. As many as six have been lost. In an EU of 25, soon to be 27, in which half the members now choose to put significant constitutional changes to the vote, there is a risk that no treaty will ever be passed.

If cherry-picking does not work, that leaves two other options. One is to put into effect changes that do not require any treaty amendment at all. These could include more openness in the EU's legislative procedures and a bigger role for national parliaments. Such changes could be made at once. The other is to pursue closer European integration within a smaller group. This idea of a hard core that might proceed without the foot-draggers has always appealed to some of the original six. Mr Verhofstadt has proposed basing it on the 12-strong euro group. Mr Chirac has spoken repeatedly of pioneer groups.

The EU is, indeed, turning into a variegated organisation, with clubs such as the members of the euro, a defence grouping, the Schengen passport-free area and the seven-country Prüm group that is pursuing police exchanges and border co-operation. The existing treaties allow "enhanced co-operation" to form such clubs-within-clubs. Yet the notion of a hard core seems unlikely to work. Any such group would have to include France, yet this is now one of the countries most hostile to the European project. As for the euro group, it is destined to expand to take in most central European countries in the next few years. When it has, say, 20 members, it will surely be too big to be a core.

In short, almost any big institutional change is now fraught with difficulty. It is true that some treaty amendments will be necessary when Croatia and, later, others join. Perhaps then, to please the growing band of small countries, a commissioner could after all be retained for each; and the votes in the council might then be reallocated to give a bit more weight to big members. But any such changes will probably have to be kept to a minimum.

If such minor amendments went into the accession treaties rather than a new constitutional treaty, ratification should become easier in most countries. And in one way, such an outcome would be refreshing: it would mean that, instead of the past decade of endless tinkering with new treaties and constitutions, the European Union would have to concentrate on delivering benefits to its members. Now that's a prospect to reflect on.

The EU and Its "Constitution" Public Opinion, Political Elites, and Their International Context

ALBERTA SBRAGIA

The European Union is going about its regular business. It is putting forth proposals to keep the Doha Round alive, continuing to negotiate a major trade agreement with Mercosur in South America, keeping peace-keeping troops in Bosnia and Herzegovina, spending development aid in numerous poor countries, financially supporting the Palestine Authority while giving Israel preferential access to the EU market, investigating Microsoft's business practices, and battling over the reach and scope of an ambitious new legislative attempt to regulate the chemical industry. The EU Greenhouse Trading Scheme, the largest greenhouse emissions trading scheme in the world, is up and running. The European Central Bank is making monetary policy decisions while the euro makes up almost 20% of central banks' foreign currency holdings. The European Medicines Agency (EMEA) has called for suspending the sale of the children's vaccine Hexavac. The European Court of Justice, for its part, has recently declared illegal a high profile Italian law designed to prevent foreign take-over of Italian energy companies. And the commissioner for Health and Consumer Protection is playing a leading role in the EU's response to the threat of a pandemic of avian bird flu.

Meanwhile, EU citizens are enjoying the benefits of the EU in very direct ways—when they fly on a low cost airline, make a phone call which is far cheaper than it otherwise would have been, study abroad while receiving credit back at their home institution, cross national boundaries without passport or customs control, or use the euro in any one of the 12 EU member-states which have adopted it. Although the EU is often characterized as a regulatory rather than a welfare state (Majone 1996), it is responsible for many policy outputs which are generally popular.

The defeat of the EU Constitution[1] in French and Dutch referenda held in mid-2005 has not blocked the EU from carrying out its usual activities. Those are currently subject to the Treaty of Nice as well as the other treaties which have been ratified since 1958 and are still in force. Nor has it affected the kinds of benefits to which EU citizens have become accustomed. While there is angst and confusion about the future direction of the Union among political elites, it is important to note that the institutionalized machinery of governance which has evolved over nearly 50 years is in place and functioning. The fact that the Constitution's defeat did not alter the by now routine operations of policymaking highlights how embedded such policymaking is in the political life of an integrating Europe. The institutions of the European Union—the European Commission, the European Court of Justice, the European Parliament, the Council of Ministers, and the European Central Bank—are in place and doing the kind of substantive work they did before the Constitution was drafted.

Nonetheless, the Constitution's defeat is clearly an important moment in the history of European integration. For the first time, an agreement designed to further integration has been resoundingly defeated in two of the original six founding members of the European Union. Although supporters of the Constitution argue that the use of the referendum is an inappropriate mechanism for the approval of treaties, the referendum does enjoy a legitimacy which is difficult to negate. The impact of the "no" votes has been so great that many analysts argue the days of further integration in Europe are finished.

The medium to long-term impact of the Constitution's rejection, however, is far from clear. Even without the contingency endemic to international affairs, the Constitution's defeat very probably will have unanticipated consequences. And those consequences, in turn, may actually run counter to the predictions of those who argue that the future looks bleak for European integration.

Two basic arguments can be made regarding the implications for European integration of the Constitution's defeat. The first argues that the political context has changed so fundamentally that policymaking and the trajectory of further integration will be affected in irreversible ways. In that sense, the defeat is a strategic defeat for those who wish for Europe to move toward ever greater integration.

The second argues that, by contrast, this defeat will simply encourage Europe's political elites to continue the process of integration through means other than treaties put to a referendum. That process could include a new treaty focused on the institutional changes incorporated in the Constitution which would be submitted to parliamentary ratification only. More interestingly, however, it could also involve moving toward further integration by using the institutional instruments currently available under the Treaty of Nice—in spite of the fact that political elites supported the Constitution because they viewed those instruments as too weak to allow further integration. Both arguments can be justified.

The Constitution

The Constitution was clearly meant to drive integration forward. Although the "Constitution" was actually a constitutional treaty since it had to be ratified unanimously and could only be amended unanimously, it was viewed as the next major agreement which would lead both to more integration among the EU-25 and pave the way for further enlargement. It was written in a less intergovernmental fashion than had been previous treaties. Although national governments negotiating in an intergovernmental forum had the last word, national and (especially) European parliamentarians had an important role in shaping its content and direction.

The comparatively diverse group of participants in the Constitution-drafting process highlighted the Constitution's symbolic value. That symbolic value was in fact far greater than its actual substantive content would have warranted. And the question now stands—how much does its defeat matter?

Much of the EU Constitution was not new. It included "old" treaties which had been approved (at times in referenda in selected countries) and had been in effect for years. Those treaties will remain in effect. The defeat primarily affects proposed new institutional arrangements. Those included increasing the power of the European Parliament, establishing new voting weights for the various member-states, and strengthening the Union's external relations. It may, therefore, become more difficult, at the institutional level, to construct a more cohesive European Union in the global arena. Finally, enlargement will become more problematic, as the proposed institutional changes were designed to accommodate new members.

A Strategic Defeat?

There is no doubt that the defeats have re-framed the process of European integration in the minds of Europe's political class. There is currently a sense of indirection, of confusion, and of doubt as to where the grand project that the Six began with the Treaty of Paris in 1951 is going. The current climate is reminiscent of that which emerged after the Maastricht Treaty was approved by a margin of 1% in France in September 1992 and was only approved by the Danes in a second referendum in May 1993. At that time, too, the Commission was weakened, political elites were shaken, and the process of integration seemed much frailer than it had appeared only a few months earlier. The calls for full EU membership by the post-communist countries undergoing often difficult transitions to democracy added a kind of pressure which national leaders were at times reluctant to accept. Terms such as "a multi-speed Europe," "variable geometry," and

a "Europe a la Carte" entered the political as well as academic discourse about future paths which European integration might follow (Stubb 1996).

Of course, the EU recovered in a spectacular fashion from the Maastricht crisis. Although a great deal was written at the time about the caution that elites would need to demonstrate given the French public's reluctance to whole-heartedly endorse the next stage of integration, the European Union in 2005 looks very different from its pre-Maastricht incarnation. It created the new institutions called for in the Treaty and continued to become more important as a global actor. The European Central Bank was established, the euro was accepted by 12 of the 15 members, and, on the international stage, the EU was critical to the establishment of an important new international institution—the International Criminal Court—as well as to the successful conclusion of the Uruguay Round. It even began developing a European Security and Defense Policy. Thus, the question arises of whether the long-term implications of the Constitution's defeat will be as transient as were those of the narrow margin of victory in France (and the necessity of holding a second referendum in Denmark) during the Maastricht process.

The difference between Maastricht and the Constitution lies in the clear and unequivocal distinction between approval (however slim the margin) and defeat. Maastricht became the treaty in force—with its commitment to a single currency and a more united European Union acting on the global stage. Furthermore, it was a much smaller EU that had to deal with the aftershocks of the Maastricht debate—the then EU-12 could more easily regroup than the current EU-25 (soon to be 27).

The consequences of defeat could in fact be far more damaging than the consequences of a razor-thin ratification. The political momentum which has traditionally been so important for the movement toward further integration could be absent, for political leaders would be unwilling to act against public opinion. The lack of a "permissive consensus" on the part of electorates could lead to a protracted stalemate, paralysis, and a gradual drift away from the kind of goals and aspirations which are traditionally associated with further integration. In particular, the attempt to create a stronger global presence would be stymied, and the move toward bringing ever more policy areas under the EU umbrella would be stopped or even reversed. The role of the so-called Community method—which involves a key policymaking role for the supranational European Commission, the European Parliament, and the European Court of Justice—would be at best frozen. And further enlargement—beyond the accession of Romania and Bulgaria—would become impossible.

In a worst case scenario, the lack of commitment by political leaders to the European Union would gradually infect the EU's institutions, for the latter's effectiveness is in fact anchored in the willingness of national institutions and elites to support the overall project of integration by supporting its supranational institutions.

The view that the defeat of the Constitution will sap the political momentum from the Union privileges the role of public opinion in the process of European integration. It implicitly argues that the hitherto elite-driven process of integration has been fundamentally transformed. The role of a majoritarian representative institution—the national parliament—in ratifying treaties which advance European integration would have been diminished by the expression of voters engaged in direct democracy through the referendum. In fact, given the role of party government and party discipline in national parliamentary systems, the role of political parties would have been diminished.

Since the major political parties in Europe (whether in government or in opposition) have supported treaty ratification since 1958 and supported the ratification of the Constitution, the view that European integration will stall privileges public opinion *vis a vis* the opinions of governmental and party elites. In brief, the key support for integration—elite consensus—would become less powerful as an effective driving force.

The role of public opinion in European integration over the past 50 years has been ambiguous. The scholarly literature has come to varied conclusions, and in general scholars of European integration have focused on the role of elites in driving integration forward. Yet it is fair to ask how such an elite-driven process could sustain itself over so many decades. The liberalization of markets in particular would have been expected to lead to more contentious politics directed specifically against the EU than has been evident (Imig and Tarrow 2001; Gabel 1998; Sbragia 2000). Perhaps the underlying assumption of those who assume that public opinion should be expected to play a central role in the integration process was most pungently expressed by Herbert Morrison, deputy prime minister of Britain at the time when the British Cabinet rejected the invitation to join the European Coal and Steel Community. As Morrison summed up the issue, "It's no good. We can't do it. The Durham miners would never wear it" (cited in Gilbert 2003, 42).

If public opinion were indeed to significantly slow the pace of integration or re-shape its nature in the post-Constitution phase, it would have entered the stage as a significant factor relatively late in the process of integration. Given that elections to the European Parliament have been viewed as "second order elections"—based far more on national issues and political cleavages as opposed to EU-wide political debate—and that elites have enjoyed a "permissive consensus" which they have used to deepen integration, the strengthening of the role of public opinion in determining the course of European integration would represent a major new phase in this project.

The EU: A Geo-Economic/ Political Project?

Europe's political elites, however, may well continue the process of European integration, enlargement, and global integration *even if* key aspects of the Constitution are not ultimately resurrected in some fashion. This argument views the European Union as a key geo-economic/political project as well as a complex variant of a (con) or (semi) or (crypto) federation/federalism-constructing exercise (Sbragia 1993; Majone 2006).

It is quite possible that the EU's international dimension may well override the kinds of constraints imposed by public opinion. If the EU is viewed only or primarily as a domestic political system, the defeat of the Constitution would in fact be a strategic defeat. If the EU is also conceptualized as a geo-economic/political project, however, the defeat might well have unanticipated consequences which are far more conducive to further integration than might be evident in the short-term.

The beginning of the accession negotiations with Turkey in October in the face of widespread public hostility to Turkish membership symbolizes the determination of governments to carry out the promises they have already made to other international actors. Although governments opened the accession negotiations with Turkey after a good deal of conflict with each other and down-to-the-wire negotiations with the Austrian government (which wanted to leave open the possibility of a privileged partnership for Turkey rather than accession), what stands out is the fact that accession negotiations actually went forward as planned. A mere four months after the Constitution's defeat, the EU was not only back in business, but back in a very difficult kind of business. Although many analysts argue that Turkey will never actually join, the very fact of opening negotiations has triggered a process of long-term change within Turkey that makes the outcome less predictable than the skeptics admit.

In a similar vein, the active engagement of the EU in the Doha Round symbolizes the understanding by elites that Europe's economic well-being is nested within a larger—global—economic reality. Although French voters fear economic liberalization of the services sector, it is quite possible that at least some such liberalization will occur due to pressure from the Doha negotiations. The EU is enmeshed in a larger multilateral trading system, and the decisions made at that level affect it in ways which have not been well understood by either publics or political scientists.

I would argue that external challenges, although under-studied in the EU literature, have always been very significant in influencing the evolution of European integration.[2] The Soviet threat and the evolution of the GATT in the 1950s, the impact of de-colonization on states' commercial interests in the 1960s, the changes in economic competitiveness in the 1980s, and the perceived need for greater military and political power during the Balkan crises of the 1990s have all been influential in the process. The dynamics of European integration have been embedded in the larger international environment, and that environment cannot be ignored in explaining the extraordinary depth of European integration.

More specifically, the implementation of the customs union in goods was supported by the GATT negotiations in the Kennedy and Dillon rounds (Langhammer 2005). The Single European Act which brought the single market to the EU was motivated in great part by the sense that European firms were falling behind their Japanese and American counterparts (Sandholtz and Zysman 1992) while the Maastricht Treaty was shaped in significant ways by the fall of the Berlin Wall and the end of the division of Europe. The restructuring of the Common Agricultural Policy was partially driven by the Uruguay Round negotiations (Patterson 1997). The movement toward a European Security and Defense Policy was at least partially a response to pressure from Washington (Howorth 2005) as well as to Europe's failures in addressing the tragedy of the wars in the Balkans.

External economic and security pressures will continue to exert a deep influence. While some of the most immediate pressures have been addressed by extending membership to the EU-15's neighbors, the enlargement process cannot keep meeting that challenge indefinitely. The WTO, the rise of China, changes in American grand strategy, and new security threats on the periphery of the Union will unavoidably push the European project in new directions as elites attempt to deal with emerging situations in world politics.

Some of the most significant institutional changes that the Constitution would have made were in fact designed to help the EU address foreign policy challenges in a more cohesive and effective way. Ironically, public opinion across the EU seems to favor a more unified global posture on the part of Brussels (German Marshall Fund 2005). Europe does not exist in a vacuum, and both elites and publics are aware of that basic fact. A more cohesive Euro-level foreign policy may therefore emerge even in the absence of the institutional changes that the Constitution would have produced. It is very likely that elites can pull mass publics with them in the area of foreign policy. In fact, the effort to strengthen the Union as a global actor can serve to link elites and publics more firmly than have economic policies of liberalization and regulation.

Economic integration, inevitably involving economic liberalization, is not as intuitively attractive as is a "stronger Europe on the world stage." Whether such liberalization can be successfully presented to voters as necessary for the strengthening of the EU as a geo-economic project is unclear, but it is possible that the "twinning" of European economic and foreign policy integration would help make economic liberalization more appealing.

The argument that an elite-driven process of integration—which incorporates party, governmental, and many business elites as well as national parliamentarians—has suffered a disruption but neither a strategic change of direction nor a strategic defeat downplays the role of public opinion as expressed in the defeat of the Constitution. It assumes that elites will in fact be able to move toward further integration. External events will provide support for further integration—such as recent events in the area of energy have demonstrated.

One of the unanticipated consequences of the Constitution's defeat in France and the Netherlands may be that integration will proceed in new ways. Just as the defeat of the European Defence Community in 1954 led to the European Economic Community, so too the need to circumvent public opinion (or at least not consult it directly) may lead to new forms of integration. The American executive, for example, has developed a host of ways to deal with international affairs which essentially circumvent or limit the role of Congress. Executive agreements and "fast track authority" for trade agreements (now known as trade promotion authority) both have been designed to allow the executive to have more flexibility in international than domestic affairs.

Second, cohesion in the foreign policy arena may develop more quickly than it has heretofore. Integration in foreign policy has lagged integration in "domestic" affairs given the member-states' concern with sovereignty. However, elites' desire to continue the process of integration coupled with the need to matter in a world in which not only the U.S. but also such countries as China and India will be important actors may provide the impetus for moving forward in that area. The role that the EU has played since 1958 in the GATT/WTO provides a useful precedent.

The defeat of the Constitution ironically may lead national leaders to move forward, develop new mechanisms to forge agreements without creating a context in which referenda are called, and actually become far more cohesive in foreign policy than would have been expected. One of the motivating forces for the Constitution was the desire on the part of national elites that the European Union should become a more effective global actor. The defeat of the Constitution will not necessarily defeat that desire, and external pressures will continue to entice national leaders to follow that road. Geo-economics and geo-politics have always provided a rationale within domestic politics for the insulation of representative institutions from direct constituency pressures. It is very possible that they will provide the same kind of rationale for the European Union.

If the EU is in fact framed or presented by elites as a geo-economic and geo-political project which will maximize European influence on the world stage and thereby help it respond to external events, it is quite possible that mass publics will become more supportive and that integration will move relatively rapidly in the one area that has been most resistant to Europeanization—that of foreign policy. Furthermore "sensitive" domestic areas clearly subject to external influences, such as energy, will become Europeanized far more quickly than one would expect.

The lack of institutional efficiency which the Constitution was supposed to remedy will undoubtedly make this process messier and more convoluted than the Constitution's backers would have liked. That same inefficiency will, however, allow the new accession states to play a role more similar to that which the EU-15 have played and give them a chance to make their mark in the shaping of the EU-25. If external pressures do indeed allow political elites to move integration forward, convince public opinion that such integration is acceptable, and help integrate the new accession states politically rather than simply institutionally, the defeat of the Constitution may be viewed quite differently 20 years from now than it is at present.

References

Gabel, Matthew J. 1998. *Interest and Integration: Market Liberalization, Public Opinion, and European Union.* Ann Arbor: University of Michigan Press.

German Marshall Fund of the United States et al. 2005. *Transatlantic Trends: Key Findings 2005.* Washington, D.C.: German Marshal Fund of the United States.

Gilbert, Mark. 2003. *Surpassing Realism: The Politics of European Integration since 1945.* New York: Rowman and Littlefield.

Howorth, Jolyon. 2005. "Transatlantic Perspectives on European Security in the Coming Decade." *Yale Journal of International Affairs* (summer/fall): 8–22.

Imig, Doug, and Sidney Tarrow, eds. 2001. *Contentious Europeans: Protest and Politics in the New Europe.* Lanham, MD: Rowman and Littlefield.

Langhammer, Rolf J. 2005. "The EU Offer of Service Trade Liberalization in the Doha Round: Evidence of a Not-Yet-Perfect Customs Union." *Journal of Common Market Studies* 51 (2): 311–325.

Majone, Giandomenico. 1996. *Regulating Europe.* New York: Routledge.

———. 2006. "The Common Sense of European Integration." Presented at the Princeton International Relations Faculty Colloquium, March 13.

Mayhew, David R. 2005. "Wars and American Politics." *Perspectives on Politics* 3 (September): 473–493.

Patterson, Lee Ann. 1997. "Agricultural Policy Reform in the European Community: A Three-Level Game Analysis." *International Organization* 51 (1): 135–165.

Sandholtz, Wayne, and John Zysman. 1989. "1992: Recasting the European Bargain." *World Politics* 42: 95–128.

Sbragia, Alberta. 1993. "The European Community: A Balancing Act." *Publius: The Journal of Federalism* 23 (summer): 23–38.

———. 2000. "Governance, the State, and the Market: What Is Going On?" *Governance* 13 (April): 243–250.

Stubb, Alexander C-G. 1996. "A Categorization of Differentiated Integration." *Journal of Common Market Studies* 13 (2): 283–295.

Notes

1. The "Constitution" was actually a constitutional treaty rather than a constitution as traditionally understood. However, the political debate in most countries used the term "Constitution" rather than "constitutional treaty," and I therefore shall use the term "Constitution" as well.

2. For a similar perspective on American politics, see Mayhew 2005.

ALBERTA SBRAGIA is director of the European Union Center of Excellence and a Jean Monnet Professor of Political Science at the University of Pittsburgh. She has chaired the European Union Studies Association and is particularly interested in EU-U.S. comparisons. Her current work focuses on the role of the EU in the field of commercial diplomacy and the global emergence of economic regionalism.

The Making of a Neo-KGB State

Political power in Russia now lies with the FSB, the KGB's successor

On the evening of August 22nd 1991—16 years ago this week—Alexei Kondaurov, a KGB general, stood by the darkened window of his Moscow office and watched a jubilant crowd moving towards the KGB headquarters in Lubyanka Square. A coup against Mikhail Gorbachev had just been defeated. The head of the KGB who had helped to orchestrate it had been arrested, and Mr Kondaurov was now one of the most senior officers left in the fast-emptying building. For a moment the thronged masses seemed to be heading straight towards him.

Then their anger was diverted to the statue of Felix Dzerzhinsky, the KGB's founding father. A couple of men climbed up and slipped a rope round his neck. Then he was yanked up by a crane. Watching "Iron Felix" sway in mid-air, Mr Kondaurov, who had served in the KGB since 1972, felt betrayed "by Gorbachev, by Yeltsin, by the impotent coup leaders". He remembers thinking, "I will prove to you that your victory will be short-lived."

Those feelings of betrayal and humiliation were shared by 500,000 KGB operatives across Russia and beyond, including Vladimir Putin, whose resignation as a lieutenant-colonel in the service had been accepted only the day before. Eight years later, though, the KGB men seemed poised for revenge. Just before he became president, Mr Putin told his ex-colleagues at the Federal Security Service (FSB), the KGB's successor, "A group of FSB operatives, dispatched under cover to work in the government of the Russian federation, is successfully fulfilling its task." He was only half joking.

Over the two terms of Mr Putin's presidency, that "group of FSB operatives" has consolidated its political power and built a new sort of corporate state in the process. Men from the FSB and its sister organisations control the Kremlin, the government, the media and large parts of the economy—as well as the military and security forces. According to research by Olga Kryshtanovskaya, a sociologist at the Russian Academy of Sciences, a quarter of the country's senior bureaucrats are *siloviki*—a Russian word meaning, roughly, "power guys", which includes members of the armed forces and other security services, not just the FSB. The proportion rises to three-quarters if people simply affiliated to the security services are included. These people represent a psychologically homogeneous group, loyal to roots that go back to the Bolsheviks' first political police, the Cheka. As Mr Putin says repeatedly, "There is no such thing as a former Chekist."

By many indicators, today's security bosses enjoy a combination of power and money without precedent in Russia's history. The Soviet KGB and its pre-revolutionary ancestors did not care much about money; power was what mattered. Influential though it was, the KGB was a "combat division" of the Communist Party, and subordinate to it. As an outfit that was part intelligence organisation, part security agency and part secret political police, it was often better informed, but it could not act on its own authority; it could only make "recommendations". In the 1970s and 1980s it was not even allowed to spy on the party bosses and had to act within Soviet laws, however inhuman.

The KGB provided a crucial service of surveillance and suppression; it was a state within a state. Now, however, it has become the state itself. Apart from Mr Putin, "There is nobody today who can say no to the FSB," says Mr Kondaurov.

All important decisions in Russia, says Ms Kryshtanovskaya, are now taken by a tiny group of men who served alongside Mr Putin in the KGB and who come from his home town of St Petersburg. In the next few months this coterie may well decide the outcome of next year's presidential election. But whoever succeeds Mr Putin, real power is likely to remain in the organisation. Of all the Soviet institutions, the KGB withstood Russia's transformation to capitalism best and emerged strongest. "Communist ideology has gone, but the methods and psychology of its secret police have remained," says Mr Kondaurov, who is now a member of parliament.

Scotched, Not Killed

Mr Putin's ascent to the presidency of Russia was the result of a chain of events that started at least a quarter of a century earlier, when Yuri Andropov, a former head of the KGB, succeeded Leonid Brezhnev as general secretary of the Communist Party. Andropov's attempts to reform the stagnating Soviet economy in order to preserve the Soviet Union and its political system have served as a model for Mr Putin. Early in his presidency Mr Putin unveiled a plaque at the Lubyanka headquarters that paid tribute to Andropov as an "outstanding political figure".

Staffed by highly educated, pragmatic men recruited in the 1960s and 1970s, the KGB was well aware of the dire state of the Soviet economy and the antique state of the party bosses. It was therefore one of the main forces behind *perestroika*, the loose policy of restructuring started by Mr Gorbachev in the

1980s. *Perestroika*'s reforms were meant to give the Soviet Union a new lease of life. When they threatened its existence, the KGB mounted a coup against Mr Gorbachev. Ironically, this precipitated the Soviet collapse.

The defeat of the coup gave Russia an historic chance to liquidate the organisation. "If either Gorbachev or Yeltsin had been bold enough to dismantle the KGB during the autumn of 1991, he would have met little resistance," wrote Yevgenia Albats, a journalist who has courageously covered the grimmest chapters in the KGB's history. Instead, both Mr Gorbachev and Yeltsin tried to reform it.

The "blue blood" of the KGB—the First Chief Directorate, in charge of espionage—was spun off into a separate intelligence service. The rest of the agency was broken into several parts. Then, after a few short months of talk about openness, the doors of the agency slammed shut again and the man charged with trying to reform it, Vadim Bakatin, was ejected. His glum conclusion, delivered at a conference in 1993, was that although the myth about the KGB's invincibility had collapsed, the agency itself was very much alive.

Indeed it was. The newly named Ministry of Security continued to "delegate" the officers of the "active reserve" into state institutions and commercial firms. Soon KGB officers were staffing the tax police and customs services. As Boris Yeltsin himself admitted by the end of 1993, all attempts to reorganise the KGB were "superficial and cosmetic"; in fact, it could not be reformed. "The system of political police has been preserved," he said, "and could be resurrected."

Yet Mr Yeltsin, though he let the agency survive, did not use it as his power base. In fact, the KGB was cut off from the post-Soviet redistribution of assets. Worse still, it was upstaged and outwitted by a tiny group of opportunists, many of them Jews (not a people beloved by the KGB), who became known as the oligarchs. Between them, they grabbed most of the country's natural resources and other privatised assets. KGB officers watched the oligarchs get super-rich while they stayed cash-strapped and sometimes even unpaid.

Some officers did well enough, but only by offering their services to the oligarchs. To protect themselves from rampant crime and racketeering, the oligarchs tried to privatise parts of the KGB. Their large and costly security departments were staffed and run by ex-KGB officers. They also hired senior agency men as "consultants". Fillip Bobkov, the head of the Fifth Directorate (which dealt with dissidents), worked for a media magnate, Vladimir Gusinsky. Mr Kondaurov, a former spokesman for the KGB, worked for Mikhail Khodorkovsky, who ran and largely owned Yukos. "People who stayed in the FSB were B-list," says Mark Galeotti, a British analyst of the Russian special services.

Lower-ranking staff worked as bodyguards to Russia's rich. (Andrei Lugovoi, the chief suspect in the murder in London last year of Alexander Litvinenko, once guarded Boris Berezovsky, an oligarch who, facing arrest in Russia, now lives in Britain.) Hundreds of private security firms sprang up around the country and most of them, though not all, kept their ties to their *alma mater*. According to Igor Goloshchapov, a former KGB special-forces commando who is now a spokesman for almost 800,000 private security men,

In the 1990s we had one objective: to survive and preserve our skills. We did not consider ourselves to be separate from those who stayed in the FSB. We shared everything with them and we saw our work as just another form of serving the interests of the state. We knew that there would come a moment when we would be called upon.

That moment came on New Year's Eve 1999, when Mr Yeltsin resigned and, despite his views about the KGB, handed over the reins of power to Mr Putin, the man he had put in charge of the FSB in 1998 and made prime minister a year later.

The Inner Circle

As the new president saw things, his first task was to restore the management of the country, consolidate political power and neutralise alternative sources of influence: oligarchs, regional governors, the media, parliament, opposition parties and nongovernmental organisations. His KGB buddies helped him with the task.

The most politically active oligarchs, Mr Berezovsky, who had helped Mr Putin come to power, and Mr Gusinsky, were pushed out of the country, and their television channels were taken back into state hands. Mr Khodorkovsky, Russia's richest man, was more stubborn. Despite several warnings, he continued to support opposition parties and NGOs and refused to leave Russia. In 2003 the FSB arrested him and, after a show trial, helped put him in jail.

To deal with unruly regional governors, Mr Putin appointed special envoys with powers of supervision and control. Most of them were KGB veterans. The governors lost their budgets and their seats in the upper house of the Russian parliament. Later the voters lost their right to elect them.

All the strategic decisions, according to Ms Kryshtanovskaya, were and still are made by the small group of people who have formed Mr Putin's informal politburo. They include two deputy heads of the presidential administration: Igor Sechin, who officially controls the flow of documents but also oversees economic matters, and Viktor Ivanov, responsible for personnel in the Kremlin and beyond. Then come Nikolai Patrushev, the head of the FSB, and Sergei Ivanov, a former defence minister and now the first deputy prime minister. All are from St Petersburg, and all served in intelligence or counter-intelligence. Mr Sechin is the only one who does not advertise his background.

That two of the most influential men, Mr Sechin and Viktor Ivanov, hold only fairly modest posts (each is a deputy head) and seldom appear in public is misleading. It was, after all, common Soviet practice to have a deputy, often linked to the KGB, who carried more weight than his notional boss. "These people feel more comfortable when they are in the shadows," explains Ms Kryshtanovskaya.

In any event, each of these KGB veterans has a plethora of followers in other state institutions. One of Mr Patrushev's former deputies, also from the KGB, is the minister of the interior, in charge of the police. Sergei Ivanov still commands authority within the army's headquarters. Mr Sechin has close family ties to the minister of justice. The prosecution service, which in Soviet times at least nominally controlled the KGB's work, has now become its instrument, along with the tax police.

The political clout of these *siloviki* is backed by (or has resulted in) state companies with enormous financial resources. Mr Sechin, for example, is the chairman of Rosneft, Russia's largest state-run oil company. Viktor Ivanov heads the board of directors of Almaz-Antei, the country's main producer of air-defence rockets, and of Aeroflot, the national airline. Sergei Ivanov oversees the military-industrial complex and is in charge of the newly created aircraft-industry monopoly.

But the *siloviki* reach farther, into all areas of Russian life. They can be found not just in the law-enforcement agencies but in the ministries of economy, transport, natural resources, telecoms and culture. Several KGB veterans occupy senior management posts in Gazprom, Russia's biggest company, and its pocket bank, Gazprombank (whose vice-president is the 26-year-old son of Sergei Ivanov).

Alexei Gromov, Mr Putin's trusted press secretary, sits on the board of Channel One, Russia's main television channel. The railway monopoly is headed by Vladimir Yakunin, a former diplomat who served his country at the United Nations in New York and is believed to have held a high rank in the KGB. Sergei Chemezov, Mr Putin's old KGB friend from his days in Dresden (where the president worked from 1985 to 1990), is in charge of Rosoboronexport, a state arms agency that has grown on his watch into a vast conglomerate. The list goes on.

Many officers of the active reserve have been seconded to Russia's big companies, both private and state-controlled, where they draw a salary while also remaining on the FSB payroll. "We must make sure that companies don't make decisions that are not in the interest of the state," one current FSB colonel explains. Being an active-reserve officer in a firm is, says another KGB veteran, a dream job: "You get a huge salary and you get to keep your FSB card." One such active-reserve officer is the 26-year-old son of Mr Patrushev who was last year seconded from the FSB to Rosneft, where he is now advising Mr Sechin. (After seven months at Rosneft, Mr Putin awarded Andrei Patrushev the Order of Honour, citing his professional successes and "many years of conscientious work".) Rosneft was the main recipient of Yukos's assets after the firm was destroyed.

The attack on Yukos, which entered its decisive stage just as Mr Sechin was appointed to Rosneft, was the first and most blatant example of property redistribution towards the *siloviki,* but not the only one. Mikhail Gutseriev, the owner of Russneft, a fast-growing oil company, was this month forced to give up his business after being accused of illegal activities. For a time, he had refused; but, as he explained, "they tightened the screws" and one state agency after another—the general prosecutor's office, the tax police, the interior ministry—began conducting checks on him.

From Oligarchy to Spookocracy

The transfer of financial wealth from the oligarchs to the *siloviki* was perhaps inevitable. It certainly met with no objection from most Russians, who have little sympathy for "robber barons".

It even earned the *siloviki* a certain popularity. But whether they will make a success of managing their newly acquired assets is doubtful. "They know how to break up a company or to confiscate something. But they don't know how to manage a business. They use force simply because they don't know any other method," says an ex-KGB spook who now works in business.

Curiously, the concentration of such power and economic resources in the hands of a small group of *siloviki,* who identify themselves with the state, has not alienated people in the lower ranks of the security services. There is trickle-down of a sort: the salary of an average FSB operative has gone up several times over the past decade, and a bit of freelancing is tolerated. Besides, many Russians inside and outside the ranks believe that the transfer of assets from private hands to the *siloviki* is in the interests of the state. "They are getting their own back and they have the right to do so," says Mr Goloshchapov.

The rights of the *siloviki,* however, have nothing to do with the formal kind that are spelled out in laws or in the constitution. What they are claiming is a special mission to restore the power of the state, save Russia from disintegration and frustrate the enemies that might weaken it. Such idealistic sentiments, says Mr Kondaurov, coexist with an opportunistic and cynical eagerness to seize the situation for personal or institutional gain.

The security servicemen present themselves as a tight brotherhood entitled to break any laws for the sake of their mission. Their high language is laced with profanity, and their nationalism is often combined with contempt for ordinary people. They are, however, loyal to each other.

Competition to enter the service is intense. The KGB picked its recruits carefully. Drawn from various institutes and universities, they then went to special KGB schools. Today the FSB Academy in Moscow attracts the children of senior *siloviki;* a vast new building will double its size. The point, says Mr Galeotti, the British analyst, "is not just what you learn, but who you meet there".

Graduates of the FSB Academy may well agree. "A Chekist is a breed," says a former FSB general. A good KGB heritage— a father or grandfather, say, who worked for the service—is highly valued by today's *siloviki.* Marriages between *siloviki* clans are also encouraged.

Viktor Cherkesov, the head of Russia's drug-control agency, who was still hunting dissidents in the late 1980s, has summed up the FSB psychology in an article that has become the manifesto of the *siloviki* and a call for consolidation.

We [*siloviki*] must understand that we are one whole. History ruled that the weight of supporting the Russian state should fall on our shoulders. I believe in our ability, when we feel danger, to put aside everything petty and to remain faithful to our oath.

As well as invoking secular patriotism, Russia's security bosses can readily find allies among the priesthood. Next to the FSB building in Lubyanka Square stands the 17th-century church of the Holy Wisdom, "restored in August 2001 with zealous help from the FSB," says a plaque. Inside, freshly painted icons gleam with gold. "Thank God there is the FSB. All power is from God and so is theirs," says Father Alexander, who leads the service. A former KGB general agrees: "They really believe that they were chosen and are guided by God and that even the high oil prices they have benefited from are God's will."

Sergei Grigoryants, who has often been interrogated and twice imprisoned (for anti-Soviet propaganda) by the KGB, says the security chiefs believe "that they are the only ones who have the real picture and understanding of the world." At the centre of this picture is an exaggerated sense of the enemy, which justifies their very existence: without enemies, what are they for? "They believe they can see enemies where ordinary people can't," says Ms Kryshtanovskaya.

"A few years ago, we succumbed to the illusion that we don't have enemies and we have paid dearly for that," Mr Putin told the FSB in 1999. It is a view shared by most KGB veterans and their successors. The greatest danger comes from the West, whose aim is supposedly to weaken Russia and create disorder. "They want to make Russia dependent on their technologies," says a current FSB staffer. "They have flooded our market with their goods. Thank God we still have nuclear arms." The siege mentality of the *siloviki* and their anti-Westernism have played well with the Russian public. Mr Goloshchapov, the private agents' spokesman, expresses the mood this way: "In Gorbachev's time Russia was liked by the West and what did we get for it? We have surrendered everything: eastern Europe, Ukraine, Georgia. NATO has moved to our borders."

From this perspective, anyone who plays into the West's hands at home is the internal enemy. In this category are the last free-thinking journalists, the last NGOs sponsored by the West and the few liberal politicians who still share Western values.

To sense the depth of these feelings, consider the response of one FSB officer to the killing of Anna Politkovskaya, a journalist whose books criticising Mr Putin and his brutal war in Chechnya are better known outside than inside Russia. "I don't know who killed her, but her articles were beneficial to the Western press. She deserved what she got." And so, by this token, did Litvinenko, the ex-KGB officer poisoned by polonium in London last year.

In such a climate, the idea that Russia's security services are entitled to deal ruthlessly with enemies of the state, wherever they may be, has gained wide acceptance and is supported by a new set of laws. One, aimed at "extremism", gives the FSB and other agencies ample scope to pursue anyone who acts or speaks against the Kremlin. It has already been invoked against independent analysts and journalists. A lawyer who complained to the Constitutional Court about the FSB's illegal tapping of his client's telephone has been accused of disclosing state secrets. Several scientists who collaborated with foreign firms are in jail for treason.

Despite their loyalty to old Soviet roots, today's security bosses differ from their predecessors. They do not want a return to communist ideology or an end to capitalism, whose fruits they enjoy. They have none of the asceticism of their forebears. Nor do they relish mass repression: in a country where fear runs deep, attacking selected individuals does the job. But the concentration of such power and money in the hands of the security services does not bode well for Russia.

And Not Very Good at their Job

The creation of enemies may smooth over clan disagreements and fuel nationalism, but it does not make the country more secure or prosperous. While the FSB reports on the ever-rising numbers of foreign spies, accuses scientists of treason and hails its "brotherhood", Russia remains one of the most criminalised, corrupt and bureaucratic countries in the world.

During the crisis at a school in Beslan in 2004, the FSB was good at harassing journalists trying to find out the truth. But it could not even cordon off the school in which the hostages were held. Under the governorship of an ex-FSB colleague of Mr Putin, Ingushetia, the republic that borders Chechnya, has descended into a new theatre of war. The army is plagued by crime and bullying. Private businessmen are regularly hassled by law-enforcement agencies. Russia's foreign policy has turned out to be self-fulfilling: by perpetually denouncing enemies on every front, it has helped to turn many countries from potential friends into nervous adversaries.

The rise to power of the KGB veterans should not have been surprising. In many ways, argues Inna Solovyova, a Russian cultural historian, it had to do with the qualities that Russians find appealing in their rulers: firmness, reserve, authority and a degree of mystery. "The KGB fitted this description, or at least knew how to seem to fit it."

But are they doing the country any good? "People who come from the KGB are tacticians. We have never been taught to solve strategic tasks," says Mr Kondaurov. The biggest problem of all, he and a few others say, is the agency's loss of professionalism. He blushes when he talks about the polonium capers in London. "We never sank to this level," he sighs. "What a blow to the country's reputation!"

Putin's Patrimony

Russia's economy is more dependent on natural resources than in Soviet times. This "oil curse" means a brittle economy and an unstable political system based on the fusion of power and property. Watch out for the coming Putin succession crisis.

ROBERT SKIDELSKY

When asked about the effects of the French revolution, Zhou Enlai is famously supposed to have said: "It is too early to tell." After only 15 years, post-communist Russia is still near the start of a film which clearly has a long time to run. Official and editorial commentary from the west takes the form of criticism and exhortation—the attitude of an improving, sometimes despairing, schoolmaster. Recently Russia has had an exceptionally bad press. The expulsion of "illegal" Georgian and other trans-Caucasian, central Asian and Chinese immigrants, the unexplained murders of Anna Politkovskaya and Alexander Litvinenko, the interruption of oil supplies to Belarus, the forced sale to Gazprom of a controlling stake in Royal Dutch Shell's Sakhalin-II project have all been pilloried. These incidents follow a long period of attrition of fledgling democratic institutions and civil society, and the brutal war in Chechnya. Like naughty schoolboys, Russians react to western sermons with a defensive truculence ("double standards") or by changing the subject. Rather than continue this sterile tit for tat, it is more useful to try to understand the structural features of the Russian system that stop Russia doing what the west wants it to do. Two of these stand out: first, the domination of its economy by a monopolised energy sector; second, the fusion of power and property. These two features together have created Putin's system. They are a product both of Russia's history and geography and the way the transition to post-communism was handled in the 1990s. They shed light on the three questions of most interest about Russia today. How solid is its economy? How solid is its political system? And is it a "reliable partner"?

How Solid is Russia's Economy?

As we know, the Russian economy suffered a severe collapse between 1990 and 1996. Official GDP fell by 50 percent. The average standard of living probably fell by much less, but there was a big increase in inequality and in absolute poverty. Growth started in 1997, but there was another collapse following the rouble crisis of 1998. Since 1999, the economy has been growing at an annual average rate of 6.7 percent. Russia is now the tenth largest economy in the world, and its income per head has doubled since 1999 to around $12,000, about the same as Chile's. The stock market has been doing even better: 2006 was the fourth year in which it notched up returns of over 50 percent. Russia runs big annual budget surpluses, it has almost no foreign debt, and has the largest foreign exchange reserves outside Asia. No wonder investors love Putin.

However, Russia is a single-track economy. Its boom is driven by rising energy and commodity prices. The dominance of the energy sector is the result of two factors: the failure of "shock therapy" to restructure the Soviet economy in the 1990s, and the belief that energy—oil, gas, pipelines—keeps Russia in the great power game. Since 2001, energy prices have more than doubled. By 2006, oil and gas made up 40 percent of GDP; energy and minerals accounted for 60 percent of Russian exports, and 40 percent of government revenue. Commodity stocks comprised 80 percent of the stock market. The economy is more dependent on the production and export of natural resources than it was in Soviet times, a unique case of de-industrialisation.

In the short run, Russia has benefited hugely from the energy boom. But the long-run effects are quite possibly dire. This is because of what economists call the "oil curse," or the "natural resource curse." Broadly speaking, a country with poor natural resources has no alternative, if it is to grow, to developing its industry and services. Japan, China and now India have climbed up the economic ladder by exploiting their abundant labour, and keeping it artificially cheap by means of undervalued exchange rates. By contrast, a resource-rich country can become wealthy quickly by exploiting its abundant natural resources, even if it also has cheap labour. But this may be at the cost of its long-term future.

There are several reasons, obvious and not so obvious, for this. First, commodity prices are more volatile than industrial prices, so a country which depends on commodity exports is exceptionally vulnerable to price shocks. Second, large foreign cash inflows from commodity exports destroy the competitiveness of non-oil industry by forcing up the exchange rate. Third, a natural resource economy is more likely to be a politicised economy, as natural resources are viewed as part of the nation's "patrimony," to be kept out of foreign hands and made available for political deployment. Fourth, natural-resource abundance diverts economic and political energy from creating wealth to fighting over its distribution. The wealth is already there: the question is, who will control the "rents" from it? Fifth, it decreases the demand for democratic representation, as governments don't need to rely so much on income tax to finance expenditure. This promotes authoritarianism. Finally, it makes control of territory a central concern of politics. The uneven distribution of resources within a resource-rich country can either encourage resource-rich regions to try to break away, or encourage resource-poor regions to establish control over the whole country by dictatorial means. Both pulls have been evident in Iraq.

These are tendencies rather than inevitable outcomes. They can be offset by good policies. Norway and Holland escaped the oil curse; most of Latin America has succumbed to it. The Soviet Union offered Russia an escape through forced industrialisation. Post-communist Russia has succumbed to it by the speed of industrial collapse and by the failure to introduce the competition which would have enabled a rapid restructuring of the economy.

Three consequences stand out. First, the Russian economy is highly vulnerable to any downturn in oil prices. This is most obvious in its energy-dominated stock market. If the price of crude fell from $60 to $45 a barrel, the stock market could drop by as much as one third. Such a drop would hit the Russian economy through a "wealth effect"—as personal wealth falls, people spend less—while a reduction in the oil price would also hit government revenue through a fall in taxable profits. Both would lead to a fall in aggregate demand, and quite possibly to the collapse of the current real estate boom, buoyed up by oil dollars.

An abundance of oil diverts energy from creating wealth to fighting over its distribution. The wealth is there, it's a matter of who controls the rents from it.

Second, the patrimonial attitude to natural resources has led the Kremlin to restrict foreign investment in them. This makes even the energy sector less productive than it should be. If you have got only one national champion, you might as well make it as efficient as you can.

Third, there is the competitiveness story. Since 2003, the rouble has appreciated 15 percent against the dollar, despite heavy intervention by the central bank. The November OECD policy brief on Russia states baldly that "the main factors underpinning current growth are transitory." By this it means that the gains from the rouble devaluation of 1998 are exhausted, and

that growth due to higher commodity prices will slow as the economy becomes progressively less competitive. One reason for this decline in competitiveness is that the petrodollar inflow has reduced the urgency of reform and innovation, which in turn has produced greater dependence on the energy economy.

Putin's first-term (2000-04) reforming zeal, which saw tax, judicial and land reform, an attempt at social security and education reform, and serious debate about restructuring and privatising the "natural monopolies" (gas, electricity, railways), has dried up. Property rights remain revocable, as the confiscation of the oil giant Yukos in 2005, showed. This did not deter stock market speculators, but it inhibited long-term investment in oil and gas exploration, and production in these areas is stagnant and even falling.

Abundant oil revenues have meant that small and medium-size enterprises (SMEs) have played a much smaller part in Russia's economic growth than in resource-poor countries. Russia's economy is highly monopolised. State ownership of the gas industry covers 90 percent of gas production; in addition, the state monopoly Gazprom owns all the export pipe-lines. State control of the oil industry has grown from 19 percent in 2004 to 34 percent, and will rise to 40 percent with Rosneft's acquisition of Yukos. In the metal industry, there are three non-ferrous giants (Rusal, Sual and Norilsk) and four steel giants (Severstal, MMK, NLMK and Yevraz). By contrast, the SME sector's share of GDP is below 25 percent—the lowest in emerging market economies, where it normally accounts for 35–40 percent (the EU average is 60–65 percent). There has been little incentive for the Kremlin to reduce over-regulation and corruption, which are still formidable barriers to entry. Although foreign banks have now been allowed in, the banking system is still state-dominated and crony-ridden, keeping old businesses going while choking off capital for new ones. The central bank has closed a number of under-capitalised and/or crooked banks—which may well have cost Andrei Kozlov, the reforming deputy chairman, his life (he was shot dead last September). Venture capital has only recently started to grow, from a very low base.

Russia has also been slow to exploit its comparative advantage in human capital. India and China, not Russia, have been favoured locations for outsourcing, despite Russia's favourable combination of cheap labour and superior scientific and technical prowess. Joint partnerships, like that between Boeing and Luxoft, have been rare. The energy economy does nothing to reverse the emigration of skilled personnel, which aggravates the problem of a falling population. The government is now paying more attention to these issues—but too little.

Putin is physically unprepossessing, a hoarder rather than a squanderer of power. One cannot imagine him getting up on a tank as Yeltsin did in 1991.

The economist might well say that a weakening of the oil price is just what Russia needs. A lower exchange rate would help wean the Russian economy off energy by making the non-energy sector more internationally competitive. However, this transition will not be smooth, and it ignores the volatility of the oil market. No one knows what the long-run sustainable oil price is. The budget (and economy) is protected from a cyclical downturn by foreign exchange reserves of more than $300bn and an oil stabilisation fund which now has accrued $90bn; but these very protections are a barrier to restructuring.

So one might say that the Russian economy is prosperous but not stable. The cyclical character of its prosperity is more marked than in resource-poor emerging economies, and certainly than in rich ones.

How Solid is Russia's Political System?

Here the stability is very impressive. There is hardly any political opposition, and Putin enjoys an approval rating of 70 percent—beyond the wildest dreams of any western leader. Stability is a crucial element of the political predictability that investors crave. However, there is a serious problem of the succession. Who or what after Putin? This is a question which will need to be answered before the next presidential election, due in early 2008.

Putin, and his intentions, remain enigmatic. Is he puppet or puppet-master? To Anna Politkovskaya, who paid for her views with her life, he was the epitome of mediocrity: an over-promoted middle-ranking KGB officer with the attitudes of a secret policeman. This is a serious underestimation, but Putin's success has owed much to his being persistently underestimated by cleverer, or more charismatic, figures. He is physically unprepossessing, averse to risk, a hoarder rather than squanderer of power. One cannot imagine him getting up on a tank as Yeltsin did in 1991. But then he is widely admired in Russia for not being Yeltsin, who left office with an approval rating of five percent. He is (relatively) young at 52, healthy and hard-working. He speaks good Russian, laced with coarse jokes, which Russians seem to love. People meeting him are impressed. As one businessman put it: "He was relaxed . . . He looks you in the eye, he has a good sense of humour, he listens intently to questions, and gives thoughtful answers." After three decades of decrepit or erratic leadership, these are formidable pluses. He has also stamped his authority on the government in a way unknown since Stalin, though by consensus rather than terror. He is not a democrat, but neither is he a tyrant. He has imposed as much coherence in policy and decision-making, and in carrying out decisions, as the clash of sectional interests and the confusion over Russia's identity allow, carefully balancing liberals and conservatives. Key members of his government and staff came with him from St Petersburg to Moscow, and he relies heavily on this tribal loyalty—which he reciprocates—not to mess things up for him. The tribe he has promoted most strongly is the KGB (especially KGB officers from St Petersburg), which was discredited but not disbanded under Yeltsin. The security and intelligence apparatus wields greater political power now than it did even in Soviet times, when it was subject to party control. Broadly speaking,

Putin has stuck to his original aim of restoring Russia as a great power by restoring central authority, reviving the economy, and using economic instruments to increase Russia's leverage. Concentration on the energy sector thus has a geopolitical as well as an economic logic to it.

However, to understand why the transition from Putin is likely to be so fraught, it is not enough to focus on his personal qualities. It is important to grasp that power in Russia has always been intimately connected with possession. The two words vlast (power) and *vladenie* (possession, domain, estate) have a common root, both expressing the idea of patrimony. Putin has reconstituted this connection in a particularly striking form.

A former prime minister of Russia, Yegor Gaidar, says of the Russian tradition: "Lose your position—lose your property. Property is the natural prey, and the state is the natural predator, always in pursuit, always redividing and redistributing existing spoils." Gaidar's voucher privatisation programme of 1992 was intended, in his own words, to "cut the umbilical cord between political power and the economy." It failed, handing control of state assets to inside managers. This generated the funds for the notorious "loans for shares" scheme of 1995-97, through which unscrupulous banker oligarchs acquired ownership of the most lucrative state-owned oil companies—Yukos, Surgut Holding, Sidanco, LUKoil, Sibneft—at knockdown prices. This manoeuvre succeeded in getting the Kremlin the cash and media support to secure Yeltsin's re-election in 1996, but had the effect of handing ownership of the commanding heights of the Russian economy, as well as the media, to a handful of billionaires. This created the political headwind for Putin's attack on the oligarchs and his renationalisation programme.

Tsar Paul I is reported to have said: "In Russia, an important person is only the one I am talking to and only as long as I am talking to him." Paul's fantasy is Putin's reality. He set out to restore the vertical system of power (state authority) which he, and most Russians, felt had been fatally weakened in the 1990s. This has meant neutralising independent centres of action or opinion. Like George W Bush, he has used terrorist outrages to create an atmosphere of a state at war. The Chechen war provided plenty of opportunities, and there is no doubt that the Beslan school crisis of September 2004—when Chechen rebels took 1,200 children and parents hostage and hundreds were killed in the subsequent shoot-out—accelerated the slide to soft dictatorship at home and paranoia in foreign policy. Beslan was Russia's 9/11.

Since he became president, Putin has replaced local elections by appointments to governorships and supervision by seven presidential plenipotentiaries. Except for the declining Communists, Russia's political parties are creatures of the Kremlin: fakes. Stephen Holmes has called the Putin system "Potemkin democracy"; Andrew Wilson has called it "virtual politics," in which the Kremlin manages democracy more by controlling inputs (parties, media) than by manipulating outputs (election results). The prime minister, Mikhail Fratkov, is a cipher, and members of Putin's government are important only insofar as they have direct access to the president. He has cut off funding from the political NGOs, secured the loyalty of the Orthodox church by giving it a religious quasi-monopoly, and crippled that other great barrier to unchecked power, the independent media. By these means he has ensured that the political pillar of the vertical structure is subservient to the Kremlin.

In doing this, Putin has created a highly personalised system of rule more like that of the tsars than Communist party general secretaries. This has serious weaknesses. Apart from the fact that the president cannot do everything, Putin has drastically narrowed the base of support and criticism needed to make difficult choices and to correct policy mistakes. His support is personal rather than institutional. The lack of intermediate bodies between the Kremlin and the people makes the Putin consensus skin-deep, despite the president's own popularity. It also explains his rather desperate promotion of groups like Nashi (the youth movement of his United Russia party) to create a simulacrum of populist politics.

The other vertical pillar of power is the economy, dominated by the strategic industries. Putin has replaced the corrupt oligarchic capitalism of the Yeltsin period with a corrupt presidential-administration capitalism, a patrimonial fusion of executive power and material wealth. In his first term he dislodged the three most ambitious magnates—Boris Berezovsky and Vladimir Gusinsky, because they controlled the two independent television channels, and the Yukos boss Mikhail Khodorkovsky, because he was using his wealth to challenge Putin. The others are on notice to do what the Kremlin wants, or face prosecution or dispossession. But Putin's most striking innovation has been to integrate the political and economic pillars into the vertical system of command. A web of Kremlin staffers and government ministers have been put in charge, or on the boards, of the largest state-controlled companies. Five Kremlin officials chair companies controlling at least a third of GDP, while continuing with their day jobs on the president's staff.

> **The constitution does not allow Putin to stay on, but the system he has created does not allow him a trouble-free departure. A crisis looms.**

This fusion of power and wealth is key to understanding the modus operandi of the Russian system. By concentrating economic power in this way, Putin has locked up much of the potential for economic growth. There is a massive conflict between treating ownership as an instrument of power and building a broad-based economy which can exploit Russia's comparative advantage in science and technology. As Robert Cottrell, an acute Kremlin-watcher, put it in the *New York Review of Books* three years ago, Putin and his generation are "reconstructing the secretive, centralised, militarised political culture of their youth, reversing much of what was good, and what was bad, about the Yeltsin years." Caught between "his need for economic growth and his need for political control," Putin, Cottrell accurately predicted, will choose political control, because he can get economic growth too as long as oil prices stay high.

One clear result of this development has been the failure to specify and enforce property rights. This is deliberate. Repeated calls by western officials for Russia to remedy this legal defect ignore the fact that it is in the Kremlin's interest to have unclear property rights. Important segments of the economy have to be kept available for distribution and redistribution to the Kremlin power-holders.

This leads back to the problem of the succession to Putin. The transfer of power in such a system involves not just the replacement of one lot of politicians by another but the transfer of property entitlements and patronage. Putin's political appointees face being dispossessed not only of their government offices but their bloated income streams. The obvious way of mitigating this is the hand-picked successor. But this will not be easy. The current front-runner is the deputy prime minister Dmitry Medvedev, who is also backed by members of the old Yeltsin family. This may fail because he is not strong enough. But the alternatives are much less clearly defined.

If the incoming president is to satisfy his own clique, he will either have to seize control of new property or redistribute existing property now under state control. Putin did both, but his "family" will be harder to dislodge than that of Yeltsin, who was sick and discredited when he left office. The constitution does not allow Putin to stay on, but the system he has created does not allow him a trouble-free departure. The added twist is that under the constitution, he can stand for a third term after one interval. He may nominate a fake successor—someone to keep his seat warm for four years or shorter (before resigning on "health" grounds). But then who governs? So the vaunted stability of the Putin system depends on a highly unstable transition from Putin to Putin. In the longer term, as the economy turns down and social tensions grow, the failure of the Putinists to address Russia's needs will be exposed, and there will be a significant risk of turbulence when they eventually lose power. But "eventually," in the view of most observers, looks like a long way off, unless the Kremlin—which has handled every crisis under Putin with conspicuous incompetence, from the Kursk submarine disaster through the orange revolution in Ukraine to the Beslan hostage siege—is subjected to a major internal or external shock. While energy prices stay buoyant, this is unlikely.

The great advantage of democracy is that it allows the orderly transfer of power. An orderly transfer of power, and concomitant security of property rights, is incompatible with the Putin system. There is no way out of the Putin system except through crisis. It is unreformable.

Is Russia a Reliable Partner?

Soviet Russia was called a one-track superpower; post-communist Russia is a one-track great power. It has traded its military-industrial complex for an energy complex. This has stopped the diversification of the economy, but given it more choices in foreign policy. Oil has enabled Russia to avoid defining its national interest, or sorting out its confused identity; oil wealth has drowned the classic debates about its place in the world—whether it is western or eastern, a nation or empire, a partner or a pole. It enables Russia to punch above its weight.

"Geoeconomics," writes Bobo Lo, "has become for Moscow the geopolitics of the new millennium . . ."

Mikhail Gorbachev wanted Russia to "join the world," but the world has changed greatly since the fall of communism. The romance of globalisation has given way to the war on terror, the challenge of climate change, the rise of China, the struggle for scarce natural resources. Putin brilliantly exploited the opportunity opened up by 9/11. Overruling his military, he expressed strong support for America, gave the US access to central Asia, closed Russian bases in Vietnam and Cuba, and acceded to US requests to keep the price of oil lower than Opec wanted it. This might have laid the basis for a long-term partnership with the west to reduce its dependence on Opec oil. Officials from both sides started talking about a "strategic partnership" with the US and an "energy space" uniting Russia and the EU.

Putin invested a lot of political capital in this partnership project; Russia's subsequent retreat from it to purely "functional relationships" has been dictated by its failure. There was some mitigation of western criticism of Russia's Chechen policies, but Russia has not been offered a fast track to WTO membership, meaningful anti-missile agreements, a security role in Nato or the middle east, or even a proper partnership with the EU. Moreover, a series of US-inspired (or at least CIA-financed) "coloured" revolutions in Serbia, Georgia and Ukraine have increased Russia's sense of isolation and paranoia by depriving it of reliable clients. Russia retaliated by joining France in opposing the Iraq war, and has been out of step with the west on Iran and Kosovo. Whatever residue of the originally warm Bush-Putin relationship survives, it was an illusion to suppose that the US could have a partnership with Russia on Iran while rolling back its influence everywhere else. (Putin's latest anti-American outburst, in Munich on 11th February, had the tone of a jilted lover.)

The energy partnership with the EU is hostage to the same struggle for influence. Russia has used its energy power to remind its former territories that their future lies with Russia rather than with the EU. This is the symbolic meaning of the interruptions of supply of gas to Georgia and Ukraine, and oil to Lithuania and Belarus. The end of empire didn't automatically spell the end of Russia's imperial reflexes. There are too many Russian people and resources scattered in these now independent countries for Russians not to entertain a hope of reconstituting at least part of their former empire.

We are back to the oil curse. It is this which makes the economy brittle, the political system unstable, partnership unreliable—while shielding Russia from the full consequences of the failure to reform, the failure to democratise, the failure to embrace a realistic destiny. It produces what the writer Viktor Erofeyev called an "imperial discourse" which is "in principle not translatable into other languages." Erofeyev may be right to think that Russia will need a new generation of leaders to overcome the "image war." More importantly, it will need a lifting of the "curse" to make them think differently about Russia's future.

ROBERT SKIDELSKY'S most recent book is *John Maynard Keynes: Economist, Philosopher, Statesman* (Pan).

China: The Quiet Revolution
The Emergence of Capitalism

Doug Guthrie

When Deng Xiaoping unveiled his vision of economic reform to the Third Plenum of the 11th Central Committee of the Chinese Communist Party in December 1978, the Chinese economy was faltering. Reeling from a decade of stagnation during the Cultural Revolution and already falling short of the projections set forth in the 1976 10-year plan, China needed more than a new plan and the Soviet-style economic vision of Deng's political rival, Hua Guofeng, to improve the economy. Deng's plan was to lead the country down a road of gradual and incremental economic reform, leaving the state apparatus intact, while slowly unleashing market forces. Since that time, the most common image of China, promulgated by members of the US Congress and media, is of an unbending authoritarian regime that has grown economically but seen little substantive change.

There is often a sense that China remains an entrenched and decaying authoritarian government run by corrupt Party officials; extreme accounts depict it as an economy on the verge of collapse. However, this vision simply does not square with reality. While it is true that China remains an authoritarian one-party system, it is also the most successful case of economic reform among communist planned economy in the 20th century. Today, it is fast emerging as one of the most dynamic market economies and has grown to be the world's sixth largest. Understanding how this change has come about requires an examination of three broad changes that have come together to shape China's transition to capitalism: the state's gradual recession from control over the economy, which caused a shift in economic control without privatization; the steady growth of foreign investment; and the gradual emergence of a legal-rational system to support these economic changes.

Reform Without Privatization

During the 1980s and 1990s, economists and institutional advisors from the West advocated a rapid transition to market institutions as the necessary medicine for transforming communist societies. Scholars argued that private property provides the institutional foundation of a market economy and that, therefore, communist societies making the transition to a market economy must privatize industry and other public goods. The radical members of this school argued that rapid privatization—the so-called "shock therapy" or "big bang" approach to economic reforms—was the only way to avoid costly abuses in these transitional systems.

The Chinese path has been very different. While countries like Russia have followed Western advice, such as rapidly constructing market institutions, immediately removing the state from control over the economy, and hastily privatizing property, China has taken its time in implementing institutional change. The state has gradually receded from control over the economy, cautiously experimenting with new institutions and implementing them incrementally within existing institutional arrangements. Through this gradual process of reform, China has achieved in 20 years what many developing states have taken over 50 to accomplish.

The success of gradual reform in China can be attributed to two factors. First, the gradual reforms allowed the government to retain its role as a stabilizing force in the midst of the turbulence accompanying the transition from a planned to a market economy. Institutions such as the "dual-track" system kept large state-owned enterprises partially on the plan and gave them incentives to generate extra income by selling what they could produce above the plan in China's nascent markets. Over time, as market economic practices became more successful, the "plan" part of an enterprise's portfolio was reduced and the "market" part grew. Enterprises were thus given the stability of a continued but gradually diminishing planned economy system as well as the time to learn to set prices, compete for contracts, and produce efficiently. Second, the government has gradually promoted ownership-like control down the government administrative hierarchy to the localities. As a result, the central government was able to give economic control to local administrators without privatization. But with economic control came accountability, and local administrators became very invested in the successful economic reform of the villages, townships, and municipalities under their jurisdictions. In a sense, as Professor Andrew Walder of Stanford University has argued, pushing economic responsibilities onto local administrators created an incentive structure much like those experienced by managers of large industrial firms.

Change from Above

Even as economic reform has proceeded gradually, the cumulative changes over two decades have been nothing short of radical. These reforms have proceeded on four levels: institutional changes instigated by the highest levels of government; firm-level institutions that reflect the legal-rational system emerging at the state level; a budding legal system that allows workers institutional backing outside of the factory and is heavily influenced by relationships with foreign investors; and the emergence of new labor markets, which allow workers the freedom and mobility to find new employment when necessary. The result of these changes has been the emergence of a legal-rational regime of labor, where the economy increasingly rests upon an infrastructure of ordered laws that workers can invoke when necessary.

Under Deng Xiaoping, Zhao Ziyang brought about radical change in China by pushing the country toward constitutionality and the rule of law to create rational economic processes. These changes, set forth ideologically as a package of reforms necessary for economic development, fundamentally altered the role of politics and the Communist Party in Chinese society. The early years of reform not only gave a great deal of autonomy to enterprise managers and small-scale entrepreneurs, but also emphasized the legal reforms that would undergird this process of change. However, by creating a body of civil and economic law, such as the 1994 Labor Law and Company Law and the 1995 National Compensation Law upon which the transforming economy would be based, the Party elites held themselves to the standards of these legal changes. Thus the rationalization of the economy led to a decline in the Party's ability to rule over the working population.

In recent years, this process has been continued by global integration and the tendency to adopt the norms of the international community. While championing global integration and the Rule of Law, Zhu Rongji also brought about broader political and social change, just as Zhao Ziyang did in China's first decade of economic reform.

Zhu's strategy has been to ignore questions of political reform and concentrate instead on the need to adopt economic and legal systems that will allow the country to integrate smoothly into the international community. From rhetoric on "linking up with the international community" to laws such as the 2000 Patent Law to institutions such as the State Intellectual Property Office and the Chinese International Economic Trade and Arbitration Commission, this phase of reform has been oriented toward enforcing the standards and norms of the international investment community. Thus, Zhu's objective is to deepen all of the reforms that have been discussed above, while holding these changes to the standards of the international community.

After two decades of transition, the architects of the reforms have established about 700 new national laws and more than 2,000 new local laws. These legal changes, added regulations, and experiments with new economic institutions have driven the reform process. A number of laws and policies in the 1980s laid the groundwork for a new set of policies that would redefine labor relations in fundamental ways. For example, the policies that set in motion the emergence of labor contracts in China were first introduced in an experimental way in 1983, further codified in 1986, and eventually institutionalized with the Labor Law in 1994. While there are economic incentives behind Chinese firms' willingness to embrace labor contracts, including the end of lifetime employment, these institutional changes have gradually rationalized the labor relationship, eventually providing a guarantee of due process in the event of unfair treatment and placing workers' rights at the center of the labor relationship. Incremental changes such as these have been crucial to the evolution of individual rights in China.

The obvious and most common response to these changes is that they are symbolic rather than substantive, that a changing legal and policy framework has little meaning when an authoritarian government still sits at the helm. Yet the scholarship that has looked extensively at the impact of these legal changes largely belies this view. Workers and managers take the new institutions seriously and recognize that the institutions have had a dramatic impact on the structure of authority relations and on the conception of rights within the workplace.

Other research shows that legal and policy changes that emphasize individual civil liberties are also significant. In the most systematic and exhaustive study to date of the prison system, research shows that changes in the treatment of prisoners have indeed resulted in the wake of the Prison Reform Law. And although no scholarship has been completed on the National Compensation Law, it is noteworthy that 97,569 suits were filed under this law against the government in 1999, a proportional increase of over 12,000 percent since the beginning of the economic reforms. These institutions guarantee that, for the first time in the history of the People's Republic of China, individuals can have their day in court, even at the government's expense.

The 1994 Labor Law and the Labor Arbitration Commission (LAC), which has branches in every urban district, work hand-in-hand to guarantee workers their individual rights as laborers. Chapter 10 of the Labor Law, entitled "Labor Disputes," is specifically devoted to articulating due process, which laborers are legally guaranteed, should a dispute arise in the workplace. The law explicitly explains the rights of the worker to take disputes to outside arbitration (the district's LAC) should the resolution in the workplace be unsatisfactory to the worker. Further, many state-owned enterprises have placed all of their workers on fixed-term labor contracts, which significantly rationalize the labor relationships beyond the personalized labor relations of the past. This bundle of changes has fundamentally altered the nature of the labor relationship and the mechanisms through which authority can be challenged. For more than a decade, it has been possible for workers to file grievances against superiors and have those grievances heard at the LACs. In 1999, 52 percent of the 120,191 labor disputes settled by arbitration or mediation were decided wholly in favor of the workers filing the suits. These are official statistics from the Chinese government, and therefore should be viewed skeptically. However, even if the magnitude is incorrect, these numbers illuminate an important trend toward legal activity regarding workers' rights.

Many of these changes in labor practices were not originally adopted with workers' rights in mind, but the unintended consequence of the changes has been the construction of a regime of labor relations that emphasizes the rights of workers. For instance, extending the example of labor contracts that were being experimented with as early as 1983, these were originally intended as a form of economic protection for ailing enterprises, allowing a formal method of ending lifetime employment. However, workers began using the terms of employment codified in the contracts as the vehicle for filing grievances when contractual agreements were not honored. With the emergence of the LACs in the late 1980s and the further codification of these institutions in the Labor Law, the changes that were in progress became formalized in a set of institutions that ultimately benefited workers in the realm of rights. In a similar way, workers' representative committees were formed in the state's interest, but became an institution workers claimed as their own. These institutions, which many managers refer to as "our own little democracy," were adopted early in the reforms to co-opt the agitation for independent labor unions. These committees do not have the same power or status as independent labor unions in the West, but workers have made them much more significant in factories today than they were originally intended to be.

Foreign Investment's Impact

At the firm level, there is a process of rationalization in which firms are adopting a number of rational bureaucratic systems, such as grievance filing procedures, mediation

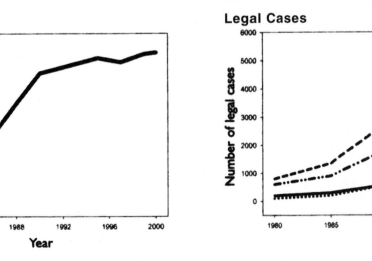

2002 Statistical Yearbook of China

Figure 1 An Age of Jurisprudence.

The above graphs depict two recent trends in China: a growing body of lawyers and an increasing number of legal cases. As the graph at left indicates, the number of lawyers in China has increased dramatically in the past 20 years, rising from fewer than 10,000 in 1980 to over 100,000 in 2000. The graph at right shows the growth in various types of legal cases over the same period. In particular, there have been significant increases in civil, economic, and first-trial cases.

committees, and formal organizational processes, that are more often found in Western organizations. In my own work on these issues, I have found that joint venture relationships encourage foreign joint ventures to push their partner organizations to adopt stable legal-rational structures and systems in their organizations. These stable, legal-rational systems are adopted to attract foreign investors, but have radical implications for the structure of authority relations and the lives of individual Chinese citizens. Chinese factories that have formal relationships with foreign, and particularly Western, firms are significantly more likely to have institutionalized formal organizational rules, 20 times more likely to have formal grievance filing procedures, five times more likely to have worker representative committee meetings, and about two times more likely to have institutionalized formal hiring procedures. They also pay about 50 percent higher wages than other factories and are more likely to adopt China's new Company Law, which binds them to abide by the norms of the international community and to respect international legal institutions such as the Chinese International Economic Arbitration and Trade Commission. Many managers openly acknowledge that the changes they have set in place have little to do with their own ideas of efficient business practices and much more to do with pressure brought on them by their foreign partners. Thus, there is strong evidence that foreign investment matters for on-the-ground change in China.

Foreign investors and Chinese firms are not interested in human rights per se, but the negotiations in the marketplace lead to transformed workplaces, which affect millions of Chinese citizens on a daily basis.

Given the common image of multinational corporations seeking weak institutional environments to capitalize on cheap labor, why would joint venture relationships with Western multinationals have a more positive impact in the Chinese case? The answer has to do with the complex reasons for foreign investment there. Corporations are rarely the leading advocates of civil liberties and labor reform, but many foreign investors in China are more interested in long-term investments that position them to capture market share than they are in cheap labor. They generally seek Chinese partners that are predictable, stable, and knowledgeable about Western-style business practices and negotiations. Chinese factories desperately want to land

these partnerships and position themselves as suitable investment partners by adopting a number of the practices that Western partners will recognize as stable and reform-minded. Among the basic reforms they adopt to show their fitness for "linking up" with the international community are labor reforms. Thus, the signaling of a commitment to stable Western-style business practices through commitments to labor reform has led to fundamental changes in Chinese workplace labor relations. Foreign investors and Chinese firms are not interested in human rights per se, but the negotiations in the marketplace lead to transformed workplaces, which affect millions of Chinese citizens on a daily basis.

However, changes at the firm level are not meaningful if they lack the legal infrastructure upon which a legal-rational system of labor is built. The construction of a legal system is a process that takes time; it requires the training of lawyers and judges, and the emergence of a culture in which individuals who are part of the legal system come to process claims. This process of change is difficult to assess because it relies on soft variables about the reform process, such as, for example, how judges think about suits and whether a legal-rational culture is emerging. But we can look at some aspects of fundamental shifts in society. All of these changes, in turn, rest upon a legal-rational system that is slowly but surely emerging in China.

Finally, beyond the legal and institutional changes that have begun to transform Chinese society fundamentally, workers are no longer tied to workplaces in the way that they once were. In the pre-reform system, there was very little mobility of labor, because workers were generally bound to their "work units" for life. The system created a great deal of stability for workers, but it also became one of the primary means through which citizens were controlled. Individuals were members of their work units, which they were dependent on for a variety of fundamental goods and services.

This manufactured dependence was one of the basic ways that the Party exercised control over the population. Writing about the social uprisings that occurred in 1989, Walder points out that the erosion of this system is what allowed citizens to protest with impunity on a scale never before observed in communist China: "[W]hat changed in these regimes in the last decade was not their economic difficulties, widespread cynicism or corruption, but that the institutional mechanisms that served to promote order in the past—despite these long-standing problems—lost their capacity to do so." It is precisely because labor markets have opened up that workers are no longer absolutely dependent upon the government for job placements; they now have much more leverage to assert the importance of their own rights in the workplace. And while the private sector was nonexistent when the economic reforms began, the country has seen this sector, which includes both private enterprises and household businesses, grow to more than 30 million individuals. With the growth of the private sector, there is much greater movement and autonomy among laborers in the economy. This change has afforded workers alternative paths to status attainment, paths that were once solely controlled by the government.

Quiet Revolution

Much like the advocates of rapid economic reform, those demanding immediate political and social reform often take for granted the learning that must occur in the face of new institutions. The assumption most often seems that, given certain institutional arrangements, individuals will naturally know how to carry out the practices of capitalism. Yet these assumptions reflect a neoclassical view of human nature in which rational man will thrive in his natural environment—free markets. Completely absent from this view are the roles of history, culture, and pre-existing institutions; it is a vision that is far too simplistic to comprehend the challenge of making rational economic and legal systems work in the absence of stable institutions and a history to which they can be linked. The transition from a command economy to a market economy can be a wrenching experience, not only at the institutional level but also at the level of individual practice. Individuals must learn the rules of the market and new institutions must be in place long enough to gain stability and legitimacy.

The PRC government's methodical experimentation with different institutional forms and the Party's gradual relinquishing of control over the economy has brought about a "quiet revolution." It is impossible to create a history of a legal-rational economic system in a dramatic moment of institutional change. The architects of China's transition to capitalism have had success in reforming the economy because they have recognized that the transition to a radically different type of economic system must occur gradually, allowing for the maximum possible institutional stability as economic actors slowly learn the rules of capitalism. Capitalism has indeed arrived in China, and it has done so via gradual institutional reform under the communist mantle.

Doug Guthrie is Associate Professor of Sociology at New York University.

In China, Talk of Democracy Is Simply That

JOSEPH KAHN

Like the spring showers that give the parched landscape a veneer of green, China's authoritarian leaders, approaching the end of their five-year terms in office, have suggested that they would like to see their country become more democratic.

Communist Party journals and the state-run news media have published a stream of commentaries by retired officials and academics on "political system reform" and the need for "socialist democracy," including a bold-sounding call for China to mimic Switzerland's worker-friendly democratic governing style.

Top leaders have authorized the publication of the pro-democratic political reflections of Lu Dingyi, a Long March veteran who advocated political change before his death a decade ago, two party officials said. Prime Minister Wen Jiabao spoke at length about the value of democracy in a nationally televised news conference last month, and promised steps toward political openness on a recent trip to Japan and South Korea.

China is not embracing Western-style democracy, even in theory. But by permitting a relatively open round of political discussion, President Hu Jintao and other top leaders have sought to cast themselves publicly as progressives who are open-minded about ways to improve government practices and reduce corruption, party officials and political experts say.

Mr. Hu may also be trying to rally support among younger party members and intellectuals ahead of an important party congress in the fall. At that time, the five-year terms of the most senior officials expire, and top leaders have begun lobbying internally for the personnel and the ideological positions they favor.

Those who advocate faster political change say they hope that Mr. Hu, who is expected to serve a second five-year term as China's Communist Party chief, will broaden the use of elections rather than rely almost exclusively on top-down appointments inside the party structure.

But even that limited step toward devolving power remains a highly delicate one. China's leaders claim that the one-party state has long practiced democracy, in the sense of governing on behalf of the people, and they show no signs of preparing to cede any political power.

Even some top Chinese intellectuals who favor more political pluralism tend to define democracy in instrumental terms—as a force that can help party leaders stay in touch with the people and provide a popular check on corruption—rather than as the core of a new political system in which people choose their leaders in free elections.

In an internal party document issued last year, Mr. Hu sharply criticized the Communist government of Vietnam for moving too rashly toward so-called inner-party democracy. He argued that the Chinese party had to maintain tight discipline to prevent the promotion of a figure like the former Soviet leader Mikhail S. Gorbachev, whom Chinese Communists consider a traitor to socialism, party officials who read Mr. Hu's comments on the subject said.

Still, some other leading officials, including Mr. Hu's most influential colleague within the party structure, Vice President Zeng Qinghong, have been pushing to increase the number of senior officials who participate in the selection of a successor to Mr. Hu, who is expected to retire in 2012.

At a minimum, the recent flurry of articles suggests that the terms democracy and freedom have lost the taboo they had after the bloody crackdown on pro-democracy protests in 1989, after which Deng Xiaoping squelched talk of any democratic-style political change.

"What we're seeing is a repudiation of Deng Xiaoping's edict that the party should focus exclusively on economic development," said Lu De, an influential economist who has pushed for greater political pluralism.

Mr. Lu, known as a princeling because of his family ties to the party elite, is the son of Lu Dingyi, a propaganda chief and vice premier under Mao who fell out of political favor during the Cultural Revolution and spent 13 years in custody. Lu Dingyi's thoughts on democracy and freedom, as recorded by Lu De before his father's death in 1996, were published this week in the party journal Yanhuang Chunqiu after an extended review by top party leaders.

"I think that Hu Jintao and Wen Jiabao have caught up with the thinking of party leaders from an earlier era, who understood that political change and economic change had to proceed hand in hand," said Mr. Lu, an economic policy adviser to China's State Council, which functions as a cabinet. "Of course, they must move step by step. It will not be one big leap and we're there."

Many political analysts are more guarded. Big political events like party congresses, which are held once every five years, can sometimes give rise to relatively unfettered debate that officials stop tolerating after the congress settles on a new slate of leaders. Mr. Hu stirred up expectations of imminent political change around the time he became Communist Party chief in 2002. But since then, they say, he has pursued repeated crackdowns on journalists, lawyers and rights advocates, leading many to conclude that the space for divergent political views in China has shrunk on his watch.

The state-run news media's newly prolific references to democracy to describe a range of prosaic political actions—like setting up an e-mail address so that the public can comment on pending legislation—so devalue the term that critics of the leadership suspect that Mr. Hu's goal may be to strip democracy of meaning.

"They want democracy to belong to the party, not to belong to people who oppose the party," said one retired party official who declined to be identified because top leaders sometimes punish people for discussing elite politics. "If the party can define what democracy is, then it will not be as dangerous."

The essays in party journals do not endorse multiparty democracy. Most of the authors argue that democracy can be functionally consistent with single-party rule. But they say it is necessary to enliven intellectual life and creativity, and to curtail official corruption.

Lu Dingyi argued that the party should embrace democracy and freedom because intellectuals favored those ideas and the party needed the support of intellectuals. He said people in the sciences and the arts must be allowed broad latitude to express themselves as they saw fit, provided they did not contest the party's political leadership.

He also said the party must also move toward some form of open elections.

"If we're going to have democracy, the most important thing is elections," Mr. Lu is quoted as saying in the article.

He adds that the party cannot continue to act as both "player and referee" when it comes to corruption. The referee role belongs to the public, he said, and is "a basic function of democracy."

Similar sentiments, though from less historically influential figures, were expressed in a series of commentaries in Study Times, a newspaper devoted to issues facing the ruling party, and some popular media as well.

One of the most passionate calls came from another party elder, Xie Tao, a former vice dean of People's University in Beijing, who suggested that China follow what he described as a Swiss model of "socialist democracy." Writing in Yanhuang Chunqiu in February, Mr. Xie warned that unless the party embraced democracy, it was headed for defeat.

"If we pursue only economic reform, to say it straight, we're headed toward the path of bureaucratic capitalism that destroyed Chiang Kai-shek's rule on the mainland," he said. Chiang Kai-shek's Nationalist Party was overthrown by the Communists in 1949.

Mr. Wen, the prime minister, largely endorsed such thinking, though in more cautious language, when he held his annual news conference in mid-March. Like Mr. Lu, he argued that socialists should welcome the ideas associated with liberal thinking in the West.

"Democracy, rule of law, freedom, human rights, equality and fraternity do not belong solely to capitalism," Mr. Wen said.

Diplomats and human rights groups say such statements have not been accompanied by any notable expansion of political participation or the development of an independent judiciary. The question remains whether the talk foreshadows a faster pace of political change or just amounts to a hollow propaganda offensive.

Mr. Hu has tried to cast the Communist Party as more responsive to the concerns of the Chinese people, hundreds of millions of whom have not seen their fortunes rise as fast as those of the urban elite during the years of China's robust but highly unbalanced economic growth.

His catch phrase, "harmonious society," has become the ideological umbrella under which China has taken the first steps toward developing a redistributive welfare program. Mr. Hu has also encouraged broader discussion of Confucianism, the political and social philosophy of ancient China, which treats harmony as a core virtue.

Democracy is seen domestically as another benevolent concept that hints vaguely at inclusiveness and consultation. Mr. Hu could well see it as useful at a time when riots among peasants and migrant workers have become a commonplace feature of political life, political commentators say.

Whatever Mr. Hu's motives, China is not in the process of overhauling its political system, but rather preparing to engage in its contentious and secretive ritual of succession.

The party will decide sometime in the fall which of the current senior leaders will stay on for new terms and who among their proteges will enter the Politburo Standing Committee, one of whom seems likely to replace Mr. Hu in 2012.

Many analysts contend that the talk of democracy cannot be viewed outside the context of the congress.

"This could signal differences at the top, or pressure from a particular group that wants to seize an opportunity to get its views out on the eve of the congress," said Bonnie S. Glaser, a China expert at the Center for Security and International Studies in Washington. "It could also simply be part of the jockeying for political position."

She said she did not view the flurry of articles as a sign that China was about to become measurably more democratic, at least in the way that term is understood in the West.

"I'm not convinced that it means political reform is on the agenda," Ms. Glaser said.

China to Join Top 3 Economies

**The Asian giant is poised to overtake Germany this year
as its growth soars. But challenges await.**

DON LEE

China's economy grew at an extraordinary rate of 11.9% in the second quarter, the fastest clip in more than 12 years and a pace that puts the nation on track to overtake Germany this year as the world's third-largest economy.

For the last 35 years, the United States, Japan and Germany have ranked 1-2-3 in gross domestic product, but as growth in those mature economies has slowed, China's has accelerated, powered by foreign investments and trade amid a global shift in production activity to the Far East.

Just 12 years ago, China's economy ranked No. 8, behind Brazil's, and was less than one-third the size of Germany's.

But figures released in a report by China's government Thursday show increasing challenges ahead for Beijing: surging inflation, breakneck investments in factories and a dramatic jump in exports that is stoking tensions between China and its major trading partners, particularly the United States.

For the first half of the year, China's trade surplus with the rest of the world reached $115 billion, up 85% from a year ago.

In recent months, the U.S., Japan and Mexico have filed or joined complaints with the World Trade Organization that accused China of illegally subsidizing exporters.

Washington has also taken China to the WTO over piracy issues, and members of Congress are threatening to impose hefty tariffs on Chinese imports if Beijing doesn't change its currency policy, which some believe gives China an unfair advantage in global markets.

While China's economic transformation has lifted millions out of poverty, its 1.3 billion people have a long way to go before their standard of living catches up with those of the other top economies.

The government's intense focus on economic growth has led to environmental degradation and violent clashes as farmland is appropriated for development.

Shoddy manufacturing and tainted food products from China have recently damaged its reputation worldwide.

Ordinary Chinese were incredulous at the notion that China's economy, by any measure, could surpass Germany's.

"It's impossible," said a 42-year-old Shanghai merchant named Wang. "There is no way that China can compare with Germany.

For example, I have an electric shaver my friend bought for me from Germany, and I have been using it for many years and it is still working well. But for domestic ones, no matter how many I buy, each one breaks soon."

Analysts said the latest statistics signaled an overheating Chinese economy that would probably prompt the government to raise interest rates and take other measures to slow growth. But rate hikes in the past and other top-down controls have had little effect.

In the second quarter, China's gross domestic product, or total value of goods and services generated, expanded by 11.9% from a year earlier, far higher than expectations and ahead of the 11.1% increase for all of last year.

By China's calculations, its GDP in 2006 was about $2.7 trillion. Germany's was $2.9 trillion, based on International Monetary Fund data, but its economy, like those of the U.S. and Japan, has been growing at a fraction of the rate China's has. The U.S. remains far ahead of the rest of the world in GDP, with $13.2 trillion in 2006.

Chinese leaders often have said they want more balanced and sustainable growth.

But at the local level, many officials seem to strive for the highest numbers they can achieve, seeing them as a key basis for their job evaluation and promotion. So they approve new plants and projects, sometimes indiscriminately, in an effort to boost tax dollars, employment and overall growth figures.

Through June of this year, investments in factories, roads and other real estate projects climbed by 26% from a year earlier. The new construction is soaking up more energy and adding to the pollution that is filling China's air and waters, and sometimes spreading beyond its borders.

In a report released this week, the Organization for Economic Cooperation and Development said Beijing had been ineffective in countering the negative effects of its rapid economic development and industrialization.

China's "air pollution levels in some cities are among the worst in the world, one-third of water courses are severely polluted, and illnesses and injuries are associated with poor environmental and occupational conditions," the report said, adding that China was poised to overtake the U.S. as the top emitter of greenhouse gases.

Rising inflation is another worry. Consumer prices jumped by 4.4% in June from a year earlier after moderate increases of about 2% last year.

Food prices have soared, largely a result of higher grain costs, a shortage of pork in the wake of a disease outbreak on pig farms, and greater demand by consumers for meat. Government statistics showed meat and poultry prices in June were up 20% from a year ago, and egg prices were 28% higher.

In the last two decades, economists said, almost every inflationary crisis began with food price hikes. And it is starting to pinch consumers.

"It's not like food prices suddenly rose, but little by little," said Qu Xilin, 25, a newspaper vendor in Shanghai who said he earned almost $400 a month but spent less than $1.25 a day on meals. "But what can I do? I have to eat every day."

It isn't just food. The cost of textiles, home appliances and services such as education and medical care are moving a bit too fast as well, said Zhu Baoliang, chief economist for the State Information Center Economy Forecast Department, a government-affiliated group.

"There is excessive demand . . . we should be wary of such a trend," he said.

Beijing has taken steps to keep inflation in check, discouraging certain investments and bank-lending through a variety of measures. The government this month cut or abolished a variety of rebates for exporters.

The United States, China's largest trading partner, reported a $232.5-billion trade deficit with China in 2006, and this year's figure was expected to be higher.

That has led to sharp calls from some American business groups and politicians to step up pressure on China to revalue its currency, the yuan, which it allows to trade only in a narrow range. The yuan has risen about 7.5% against the dollar in the last two years, but critics say it is undervalued by as much as 30%, giving Chinese exporters an advantage in global markets.

Beijing has insisted on maintaining its currency strategy, not wanting to jolt exporters and risk the loss of jobs and rising incomes.

Despite China's overall size and growing clout in the global economy, Chinese officials and scholars say the country is still developing and grappling with critical issues of lifting millions out of poverty and reducing the widening income gap between the city and countryside, where most Chinese live.

The figures released Thursday showed retail sales in the first half of the year jumped by 15% from a year earlier. Average incomes after taxes also rose briskly during the period. For the first six months, average disposable income for urban dwellers rose 14% to $921. For rural residents, it rose 13% to about $276, the government said.

"Being the world's third-largest is not that significant," said economist Zhu. "It's the quality of life."

UNIT 5

Political Diversity in the Developing World: Country Studies

Unit Selections

Key Points to Consider

• What have developing countries have in common, and how are they diverse?

• How did PRI maintain its dominance in Mexican politics for such a long time?

• Give a couple of major reasons why some initial supporters of President Fox eventually became disillusioned by his leadership. What obstacles did he face?

• What does it mean to speak of a new "left turn" in Latin American politics, and what are the two main forms the Latin American Left tends to take?

• Why do economic development and representative democracy run into such difficulties in both Latin America and Africa?

• Is Nigeria a "failed state?" How would you assess Nigeria's likelihood of finally realizing a widely shared, modest prosperity that its rich natural and human resources could sustain under the right leadership?

• How do you explain the apparent resiliency of Indian democracy? And how has the recent economic boom affected life in India?

• What are some of the most common obstacles to the installation of a functioning democracy in a country like Iraq or Afghanistan?

• Iran a few years ago seemed ready to pursue a more secular and moderate foreign and domestic policy. Who were the moderates, and what happened to them? Is it still possible that in another turn of events they—or people like them—will end up in power?

Student Web Site
www.mhcls.com/online

Internet References
Further information regarding these Web sites may be found in this book's preface or online.

Africa News Online
   http://allafrica.com/
ArabNet
   http://www.arab.net
Organization for Economic Cooperation and Development
   http://www.oecd.org/home/
Sun SITE Singapore
   http://sunsite.nus.edu.sg/noframe.html

The **Third World** was, for many years, a widely used umbrella term for a disparate group of states now more frequently called **developing countries.** The common thread was that they had, at best, taken only modest steps toward becoming modernized. In other words, they were latecomers in a world that was rapidly moving towards a self-sustaining process of economic growth resting on modern science, technology and organization.

Both terms are ambiguous, and there is no consensus as to exactly where or why to draw the boundaries for inclusion. There are critics who plausibly argue that the terms have little or no analytic value as long as they remain residual categories in a classification that otherwise has no place for them.

Many, but by no means all, of the developing nations have been burdened with the problems of **widespread poverty** and **rapid population growth.** Their present economic situation and potential for development vary considerably, as shown by the juxtaposition of countries such as Saudi Arabia, Chad and Bangladesh, or Brazil, Nigeria and Haiti—not to mention India or Indonesia. Some have in recent years become strong candidates for economic advancement, while others seem to be doomed to stagnation.

An additional element of confusion is linked to the original use of the term "The Third World," continued to be used to refer to countries—many of them recently freed former colonies—which had chosen to remain nonaligned in the Cold War confrontation between the so-called **First World** (or Western bloc) and the **Second World** (or Communist bloc). Neither of these latter terms became widely used outside the textbooks and syllabi in comparative politics courses, where the so-called **"three worlds"** approach served as a convenient organizing principle.

There were always enormous differences of political and economic prospects among these countries. An additional term, "the **fourth world,**" found favor for a while as a category reserved for countries which were so desperately lacking in comparative advantages that they appeared to have little, if any, prospects of improving their lot through greater contact with the outside world. As could be expected, there was even another category for the seemingly hopeless basket cases.

All along, these countries have varied hugely in their socio-cultural, economic, and political characteristics. Their governmental forms are overwhelmingly ranked by the democracy index as **authoritarian** or **semi-authoritarian**—indeed, they include nearly all of the 85 countries listed in those two categories. In addition, they include several of the 54 countries classified as **"flawed democracies,"** including South Africa, Mexico and Brazil. None of the 28 members of the "full democracy" category would appear to be what we now call a developing country, with the possible exceptions of Uruguay or the island nation of Mauritius. On the other hand, the **"failed" states** would *all* fall in the category of developing countries.

In studying attempts by developing countries to promote their socio-economic development, it is important not to leave out the international context. Political and intellectual leaders in these countries have often drawn upon some version of what is called **dependency theory** to explain why they remain poor, and sometimes to demand some form of

John Wang/Getty Images

compensation. Dependency theorists were partly influenced by a theory of imperialist exploitation by the richer nations. They concentrated on **external factors** to explain a country's failure to generate self-sustained growth and create wealth. Meanwhile, rival explanations gave greater emphasis to a country's **internal obstacles** to development (whether socio-cultural, political, geographical or a combination of these). Such theoretical disagreements cannot always be dismissed as of merely academic interest: here, ideas can turn out to have real consequences for millions of human beings, because they deliver the intellectual basis for some strikingly different policy conclusions and development strategies in such countries.

Perhaps the most important change was new openness to choose policies and strategies that meet the pragmatic test: "Does it work?" It is exemplified by Deng Xiaoping, the Chinese Communist leader who broke with Maoism.

Indeed, there is an unmistakable recent **leftward turn** in politics, and a questioning of the shift toward free-market solutions. It is too simplistic to explain this phenomenon as a product of impatience alone; the benefits of economic growth do not "trickle down" as freely in practice as they do in economic theory. Instead, there are many instant losers in the economic dislocations that usually attend a liberalization of the economy. If neoliberal policies have themselves failed to meet the pragmatic test, the reasonable reaction would be to replace the purebred, neoliberal cat with one that, even though of "mixed" pedigree, will really catch mice.

It now appears that dependency theory, at least in its simplest and most direct form, has lost some intellectual and political support. In its place we now find a variety of middle-range theories that pay greater attention to the contextual aspects of each case of development (and thereby include elements of dependency theory when and if they appear relevant). This **theoretical eclecticism** can then be carried over into diverse policy responses: strategies of development that work well in one setting may come to naught in a different environment. One size or shape doesn't fit all—as we seem to have to re-learn from time to time.

Latin America and Mexico. The problems of dire poverty and extreme inequality in living conditions afflict much of the developing world. They are socially and politically explosive. Nowhere is the **income gap** between the very rich and the very poor as huge as in large parts of

South America. With its gross inequalities, it is hardly surprising that the region has given rise to a radical political Left, committed to removing the social squalor by radical political reforms. In their fear of revolution and their opposition to meaningful reform, the privileged classes have often resorted to brutal repression as a means of preserving the status quo. During the Cold War, the United States generally supported and became identified with the general goal of keeping the Left from reaching power in Latin America, as popular memory in that region has not forgotten.

The Catholic Church had long been seen as a conservative force in Latin America. Beginning in the 1970s, however, the continuing plight of the poor politicized many laypersons and clergy. These new voices demanded social reform in the name of what was called **liberation theology,** an outlook that drew partly on dependency theory's explanation of the great inequalities in Latin America, partly on the moral message of Christianity's social gospel. It filled a practical ideological function by providing Christian reformers with a relatively simple analytical and moral explanation of an ugly reality and an incentive to do something about it. It was not an easy step to take. This was the time when the security agencies in several military dictatorships of the region pursued a program of selective elimination of individuals who questioned (or were thought to have questioned) the social order.

Today, the political context has changed significantly. The Cold War has entered the history books and the military officers have largely returned to the barracks in Latin America. Liberation theology like dependency theory appears to have been effectively absorbed into more pluralistic outlooks and more pragmatic reformist strategies. But extreme poverty continues to co-exist with extreme wealth. It is hardly surprising that Latin America today has a robust Left, impatient and unhappy with what its supporters see as the failure of the free market policies adopted in the last ten to fifteen years of the twentieth century.

Jorge Castañeda distinguishes between two major orientations of the Left in Latin America—**the populist left,** which he describes as mixing ostentatious egalitarianism with an often anti-American and nationalist stridency, and **the communist-descended left,** which he describes as having become "modern, open-minded, reformist, and internationalist."

Latin America illustrates that establishing stable pluralist democracies in many parts of the developing world is difficult but not impossible. Robert Dahl lists only one "old democracy" in Latin America (Costa Rica) and the democracy index finds only two "full democracies" (but seventeen "flawed democracies") there. Some authors have argued that Latin America's dominant political tradition is basically authoritarian and corporatist rather than competitively pluralist, the result of a "unitary" bias in the political culture. Still, there are other countries with corporatist traditions where democracy has taken roots, and elected governments have replaced one dictatorship after another in Latin America. The demonstration effect of democratic governments in Spain and Portugal, and the negative experience with authoritarian rulers, may have aided their democratic successors.

Mexico. The presidential election in Mexico in the summer of 2000 will be remembered primarily because it ended with defeat for the candidate of the Institutional Revolutionary Party (PRI). The PRI had held power for more than 70 continuous years—longer than the life span of the Soviet Union—but there had been indications that its grip was loosening. Three years earlier, the hegemonic party had lost control of the lower house of congress, and the two main opposition parties had begun to transform the chamber, previously regarded as a rubber stamp, into a political check on the president.

In 2000 the PRI candidate, Francisco Labastida, was defeated by businessman Vicente Fox, the candidate of the center-right National Action Party (PAN), who received about 43 percent of the vote in a three-way race. Although it also became the leading party in Congress, PAN did not win a controlling majority. The political turnover could be seen as a milestone in Mexican politics, but it also demonstrated that the real challenge came in dealing with political gridlock and economic setbacks. The new president's reform agenda soon stalled in the bitterly divided legislature. It did not take long before the high expectations that accompanied a long-awaited transfer of power were followed by grave disappointments.

Nigeria has been called Africa's "**slumbering giant,**" but the metaphor of a raging bull in a china shop may be closer to the truth. It covers a large area with 140 million inhabitants, making it the most populous country in Africa; with over 250 distinct ethnic groups, and a fairly even split between Muslims (50 percent) and Christians (40 percent), Nigeria is also a notable example of diversity on the African continent—and the conflict that can result.

Alternating between civilian and military rule since its independence from British colonial rule in 1960, Nigeria has seen three republican governments (more or less—the third government's presumed president-elect, Mashood Abiola, was never allowed to take office) fall to military *coups d'etat.* The current Fourth Republic, in place since 1999, faces some of the same basic problems as its predecessors: **ethnic and religious conflict,** especially between the predominantly Muslim northern part of the country and Christians and others who dominate the central and southern regions; a **military** that sees itself as an all-too-ready savior, ready to step in and impose discipline in the case of political crisis; and an economy heavily dependent upon its rich **national resources,** especially petroleum, but lacking a coherent economic policy or reliable infrastructure. The combination of valuable resources and an inconsistent governmental and political structure has led to rampant and systemic **corruption;** ironically, while governments have risen and fallen, many of the elites within and without the government **bureaucracy** have remained in place, maintaining their hold on the wealth flowing from Nigeria's natural bounty.

In the most recent round of national elections, held in April 2007, these issues came once again to the forefront; on the balance, the outcome is at least worrisome. On the one hand, this was an achievement for Nigeria: one elected President was succeeded by another, without military intervention. Umaru Yar'Adua, candidate of the ruling People's Democratic Party, was declared winner with approximately 70% of the vote, and assumed office in May 2007. On the other, the election was marred by inter-ethnic violence beforehand, and what other governments have taken to be very credible allegations of **vote-rigging** in the aftermath. That both of the main opposition candidates were also tarnished, by accusations of respectively of corruption and anti-democratic practices, does not make this result more palatable, either to outside observers or Nigerians. As Lydia Polgreen points out in her article, satisfaction with the democratic process has dropped precipitously since the Fourth Republic's inception.

India. Often referred to as a subcontinent, and second only to China in population (and ahead of the continents of Latin America and Africa combined), India is listed as a democracy by our index, albeit a "flawed" one, with its deeply divisive ethnic, religious, and regional differences, including the still-important **caste system** described in Ashutosh Varshney's article. It is a secular state, but tense relations between politicized Hindu extremists and members of the large Muslim minority occasionally erupt in violence. For the vast majority of the huge population, a life of material deprivation has long seemed inescapable.

That may be changing. As detailed in Jo Johnson's article, an important turn toward effective economic development can be traced back to the early 1990s, when the market revolution cautiously touched India. In 1992 the national elections were marred by the assassination of Rajiv Gandhi, a former prime minister. When his Congress party won the election, one of its veteran politicians, P.V. Narasimha Rao, headed the new government. He followed cautiously in the neoliberal steps of other reformers in the developing world at that time, loosening economic planning and controls on international trade and investment. These market-oriented policies brought substantial economic gains but were accompanied by a flurry of corruption scandals that tainted several members of Rao's cabinet. His Congress party was badly defeated in the general election of May 1996.

In the spring of 1998, parliamentary elections produced a result that seemed to promise even more instability for the world's largest democracy. The Bharatiya Janta Party (BJP), dominated by Hindu nationalists, won the most seats, but it was only able to govern in alliance with several smaller parties. The coalition provided a weak parliamentary majority, but it was able to survive just over a year, partly because the BJP leader, Prime Minister Atal Behari Vajpayee, was able to tame the rhetoric of his party's more militant Hindu-nationalist members. As was long expected, the government collapsed in April 1999, when a small coalition defected.

Some 300 million Indian voters took part in the new elections that followed. The result was a clear victory for the incumbent governing coalition, now numbering 24 parties. It was the first time in 27 years that an incumbent prime minister won re-election in India. The once dominant Congress party, which had hoped to revive and return to power, instead suffered its worst defeat since independence. In the elections of 2004, however, it recuperated and returned to power as key member of the United Progressive Alliance. The BJP returned to the opposition.

Iran presents unique issues for the student of comparative politics. Though its national roots stretch back millennia to the ancient Persian Empire, its current system of government is not quite three decades old. Its population of seventy million, while quite ethnically diverse, is mostly of Persian or related descent, in contrast to its mostly Arabic neighbors in the rest of the Persian Gulf region; its mostly Shiite population also creates sectarian differences with its mostly Sunni neighbor-states. And Iran also stands apart for its system of government, simultaneously popular, revolutionary, and rigorously theocratic.

We have seen that a state's democratic (or undemocratic) nature may best be evaluated along a continuum, rather than as an absolute proposition ("a country is either democratic or it is not"). In Unit One, we also saw what some argue are the signs of a recent de-democratizing trend, supporting the conclusion that democratization is neither inevitable nor irreversible. Iran's complex recent history illustrates both of these concepts.

The 1979 revolution that overthrew the autocratic Shah established an **"Islamic republic,"** a curious mix of democratic and undemocratic elements: a popularly elected president and legislature, several semi-elected councils of clerics and advisors, and above it all the Supreme Leader, since 1989 the Grand Ayatollah Ali Khamenei. In keeping with its revolutionary origins, the new Iranian state enshrined principles of mass political participation in general, and notably for women in particular, in its new constitution. But the constitution also requires that all legislation comport with *Sharia,* Islamic law—and the various clerical councils that interpret *Sharia,* not to mention the Supreme Leader himself, have the power to block legislation they deem out-of-bounds. If the clerics choose to exercise this power vigorously, to the point of keeping their ideological opponents off the ballot, this republic-in-theory becomes authoritarian in practice—as Iran's 28th-from-the-bottom ranking on the index of democracy indicates.

By the late 1990s, as the country recovered from a war with neighboring Iraq a decade earlier, many Iranians were impatient with the gap between the revolution's Islamic-democratic principles and the realities of curtailed personal expression and the entrenchment of power in the theocratic councils and their bureaucracies. The election of Mohammad Khatami to the presidency in 1997 signaled the beginning of what many hoped would be a democratic wave throughout Iranian society. With the help of a reformist parliamentary majority elected in 2000, the moderate cleric hoped to reform the electoral laws, which granted the councils right of approval over candidates, and redefine the presidency itself as a more co-equal partner to the other branches of government, capable of blocking or mitigating their excesses. With Khatami's market-oriented economic policies, and his overtures toward normalization of relations with the United States, many Western observers had high hopes that Iran might join the democratic club sooner rather than later.

But the councils, dominated by conservative clerics, used their unique powers to block reform. The reformist press was censored, and Khamenei blocked parliamentary efforts to repeal the restrictive press laws. In the 2004 parliamentary elections the Council of Guardians banned candidates from the reformist bloc *en masse,* leading to historically low voter turnout and a conservative majority. As the United States' policy toward Iran re-hardened after the September 2001 terrorist attacks, public opinion also began to swing toward the hard-liners. In 2005, Mahmoud Ahmedinejad was elected president on a populist platform, seeming to signal the end of this most recent reformist wave.

Ahmedinejad has reversed his predecessor's course in crucial areas of policy. Economically, he has espoused a nationalist-populist approach that stresses self-sufficiency over international trade.

Domestically, Ahmedinejad's actions have gotten a mixed response. His economic agenda seems increasingly unpopular, as shorter supplies and wage subsidies have led to high inflation. In what seems to be a bit of a vicious circle, student protests have led to crackdowns on political expression and purges of moderate faculty, which in turn provoke more protests. Meanwhile, his revolutionary populism has drawn fire from conservative elements within the clerical councils, who have vetoed some of his policies (including a plan to allow women to attend sporting events) and criticized his hostile approach toward the outside world. Will popular pressure or entrenched resistance within the government prove to be his downfall, or will increasingly hostile rhetoric from the United States have the consequence of rallying popular opinion behind their president? Or will Iran's situation change in some way we have not anticipated? We must wait and see.

How Did We Get Here? Mexican Democracy after the 2006 Elections

Chappell Lawson

1. Introduction

On July 2, 2006, Mexican voters elected National Action Party (PAN) candidate Felipe Calderón as the next president of Mexico. Calderón's victory was extremely narrow; he won under 36% of the total vote and less that 0.6% more than his leftist rival, Andrés Manuel López Obrador. This potentially problematic situation was aggravated by López Obrador's decision to challenge Calderón's victory, both in the courts and in the streets. López Obrador's protest campaign culminated on September 16, when tens of thousands of his followers gathered in downtown Mexico City to acclaim him "legitimate president" of Mexico. Meanwhile, in the legislature, leaders of López Obrador's Party of the Democratic Revolution (PRD) oscillated between hints that they would collaborate with Calderón's administration and signs that they would adopt a posture of untrammeled hostility.

Post-electoral controversies raised the specter of a Left that had abandoned parliamentary tactics and returned to mass mobilization as its principal political strategy. At worst, they presaged the sort of political upheaval that could threaten Mexico's young democratic institutions. There was certainly no missing the symbolism involved in López Obrador's choice of the date on which he would take the oath of office—November 20, the anniversary of the Mexican Revolution—nor could students of Mexican history fail to recall that a contested election had sparked that decade-long conflagration.

How did Mexico find itself in the middle of such a crisis? Why had the country's vaunted electoral regime, generally regarded as a model for other democracies, failed to produce an outcome that all parties considered legitimate? Were Mexican political institutions so shaky that the actions of a single man could threaten their collapse? And, given the answers to these questions, what does the future hold for Mexico's political system?

Over the last decade, research on Mexican politics has focused on (1) institutional reform, especially in the electoral sphere, and (2) mass behavior, especially voting. Both areas of research are, of course, essential to understanding Mexico's transition from a one-party-dominant regime to a multiparty democracy. How-

ever, scholarly attention to them has tended to understate the importance of political leadership and informal arrangements among elites, topics which were so central to earlier work on democratization (see O'Donnell and Schmitter 1986).

This article argues that the way these elites interact plays a pivotal role in the current situation. It first summarizes Mexico's transition to democracy over the last 15 years. It then addresses the simmering tensions between the PRD and the PAN during the administration of Vicente Fox that boiled over in the 2006 elections. The third section suggests that Mexico's current climate of polarization is a function of elite attitudes and interactions, rather than those of the mass public. The fourth section shows how these same interactions exercise a far greater influence on Mexican politics than do those institutions most often implicated in poor governance. The route out of Mexico's political impasse thus runs through pacting and compromise among members of Mexico's current political class, rather than further institutional tinkering.

2. Incomplete Transition

For close to seven decades, a single party (known today as the Institutional Revolutionary Party, or PRI) won all elections for significant posts. Over time, however, modernization weakened the corporatist and clientelist apparatuses through which the "official" party and the state had ensured social control. The collapse of Mexico's economy in the 1980s further undermined autocratic institutions and provoked mass disaffection with the old regime.

In the face of mounting social unrest, representatives of Mexico's political establishment negotiated a series of reforms with the leaders of the main opposition parties during the 1990s. These elite pacts, most notably the 1996 "Reform of the State," ultimately leveled the electoral playing field. In 1997, the PRI lost control of the Chamber of Deputies, and in 2000 PAN candidate Vicente Fox captured the presidency.

Data from standard measures of democracy nicely capture both the scope and the limitations of Mexico's political transition during the 1990s. In 1991, Mexico scored a zero on the combined Polity IV index; by 2001, it scored an eight.[1] Freedom House scores show a similar trend, with Mexico's score falling from eight in 1991 to four 10 years later.[2] By either measure, this transition left Mexico in the same league as many other new democracies at the beginning of the twenty-first century, such as Argentina, Brazil, Mongolia, South Korea, Taiwan, or Romania. In the prevailing scholarly discourse, Mexico had undergone a gradual transition from a moderately authoritarian regime to an "electoral democracy," but it had not yet become a "liberal democracy" (Diamond 1999).

A closer view of Mexico's political transition reveals the unevenness of democratization across different institutions and spheres of governance. For instance, Mexico's electoral regime and party system were quite well developed (see Todd Eisenstadt's essay in this symposium). As in the old regime, the military and the security services remained small and firmly under civilian control. Finally, despite the domination of broadcast television by two relentlessly commercial networks, Mexico's mass media had become quite open by the time of Fox's election in 2000 (Lawson 2003). By contrast, progress toward reforming the police, the judiciary, the prosecutorial apparatus, and other parts of the bureaucracy remained painfully slow. The PRI remained the country's largest party (until 2006); businessmen with longstanding ties to conservative factions of the regime continued to monopolize most sectors of the economy; and corrupt bosses affiliated with the PRI controlled most labor unions.

As president, Fox presided over modest democratic deepening. Civic groups and opposition parties successfully challenged the PRI's remaining strongholds at the state and local level; independent newspapers sprouted throughout the country; state-level electoral authorities became more independent and professional; prominent PRI figures and organizations began to defect to the opposition; and the passage of a federal Transparency Law exposed government operations to public scrutiny. Although corruption remained a serious problem, especially in the criminal justice system, the administration itself managed to avoid major scandals.

For most Mexicans, the PRI's defeat in 2000 represented the culmination of a long process of democratic transition and the beginning of an equally arduous process of democratic deepening. For the Left, however, alternation in power between the old ruling party and the conservative PAN constituted only partial or cosmetic change. Three episodes during Fox's tenure seemed to confirm their fears.

In 2003, the PAN and the PRI joined forces to name the new leaders of the Federal Electoral Institute (IFE) over the objections of the PRD. In contrast to the previous set of "Citizen Councilors," who included a number of distinguished academics and activists, the new cohort included a number of political unknowns and party hacks. Their selection signaled the breakdown of the partisan consensus that had characterized the political accords of 1996–1997.

Two years later, PAN and PRI legislators voted to impeach López Obrador, then mayor of Mexico City, on the grounds that he had violated a court injunction in a zoning dispute. Had the legal proceedings continued, they would have prevented López Obrador from seeking the presidency. The Fox administration backed down in the face of widespread public opposition, international pressure, and massive demonstrations in Mexico City organized by López Obrador. Most Mexicans saw the affair as an attempt to trump up charges against a popular rival.

A third insult came in the midst of the 2006 presidential race, with the passage of the new broadcasting law (the "Ley Televisa") that was notoriously favorable to Mexico's two main television networks. During the second half of the race, television coverage of Calderón became more favorable, while reporting on López Obrador turned rather sour. In the leftist narrative, all of these events signaled a conspiracy between the government, the PAN, the old ruling party, leading businessmen, and a now-perverted electoral authority to deprive their candidate of victory.

Panistas (PAN partisans), of course, saw matters in an entirely different light. Their party stood for the same Christian Democratic principles that it had represented steadfastly since the late 1930s; by contrast, the PRD represented both the radicalism of the Marxist left and the corruption of the old PRI (from which many of the PRD's founders had come). It was the PRD that had rejected Fox's offer to form something like a government of national unity in 2000, and it was PRD obstructionism that had prevented partisan consensus in the selection of a new set of IFE Councilors.

Despite López Obrador's moderate position on many policy issues, his administration as mayor of Mexico City struck opponents as eerily reminiscent of PRI rule. For instance, López Obrador incorporated whole hog into the PRD apparatus almost two dozen PRI organizations, several with decidedly unsavory reputations. Episodes of corruption among his top aides, some captured on videotape, raised serious questions about financial probity, as did López Obrador's refusal to endorse a local transparency law modeled after the federal statute.

For his opponents, post-electoral controversies only confirmed their instincts: López Obrador was simply unwilling to accept the results of an election that the IFE, the Federal Electoral Court, and most international observers considered free and fair (see Eisenstadt's article). His ad-libbed responses to critics in speeches after the elections—e.g., "to hell with your institutions"—betrayed a casual attitude toward the rule of law that would have imperiled democracy had he won. This perspective contrasted starkly with Calderón's pledges to respect the autonomy of regulatory institutions, insulate the office of the public prosecutor from direct control by the executive, reform the judicial system, and further devolve authority to state and local governments—precisely the steps Mexico needed to overcome its autocratic legacy.

Since 2003, the tactics adopted by Mexican political elites in their partisan disputes have proven more tendentious and incendiary than analysts predicted. For instance, few political observers in 2001 would have anticipated PRI and PAN attempts to prevent López Obrador from contesting the 2006 elections through an act of legal legerdemain. Even fewer would have guessed how far López Obrador was willing to escalate his tactics after July 2, 2006.

3. Elites or Masses?

Do trends at the elite level reflect increasing polarization among ordinary Mexicans? Over the last five decades, support for the PRI in the mass public has declined at a rate of about 3% per election cycle. The weakness of the PRI's presidential candidate in 2006, Roberto Madrazo, only accelerated this process by hastening defections from the old ruling party (see Langston's contribution to this symposium). Because the PRI was ideologically and socially amorphous, its unraveling should theoretically have divided Mexico along lines of class and ideology. Left-Right differences should also become more salient as the issue of democratization faded from the agenda, forcing people to choose between very different political alternatives rather than simply selecting the one that was most likely to defeat the regime.

Nevertheless, the way in which voters have attached themselves to the PRD and the PAN has not seem to followed such a clear logic. Most Mexicans do not base their electoral choices on the policy positions adopted by parties and candidates (see Moreno's and Bruhn and Greene's articles in this collection). Still less do Mexicans vote along class lines (see Moreno). Although indicators of social status—such as living standards, education, skin color, and occupation—influence voting behavior at the margin, for ordinary Mexicans, region is a far more important predictor.[3] Consider, for instance, the "classic" PRD voter in May 2006: a brown-skinned, low-income man with a modest education who never attends church. A person with this demographic profile living in the north of the country had a 20% chance of favoring López Obrador—far lower than his probability of favoring Calderón. If his home was in the center of the country, however, his probability of supporting López Obrador rose to 34%. If he lived in the south, it was 44%, and if he resided in the Mexico City metropolitan area, it was 72%. Even this regional cleavage is muddled by the continued strength of the PRI in many areas of the country (see Klesner's essay in this symposium). In other words, divisions between the PRD and the PAN at the mass level are not simply less pronounced than those at the elite level, the fundamental axis of cleavage is different.

The episodes so central to polarization at the elite level have played out very differently in the electorate. For instance, polling data indicate that there is little support for continued protests by López Obrador; even many of those who voted for him express ambivalence about his tactics.[4] This situation echoes public sentiment during the impeachment of López Obrador: not only did an overwhelming majority of Mexicans oppose attempts to prevent him from running in the 2006 election, so did a majority of *panistas*.[5] These facts lend credence to arguments advanced by Bermeo (2003) and others that political crises are typically the product of elite machinations, rather than of mass preferences.

Acknowledging the truth of this argument, however, tells us little about why elite conflict has become so pronounced. The principal answer to this question lies in the patterns of party-building in Mexico. During the period of one-party rule, the PRI's eclectic nature gave rise to a fragmented opposition. Because opposition politics promised few tangible rewards, it

tended to draw more extreme or ideologically purist members of society, on both the Right and the Left (Greene, forthcoming). Today, PAN and PRD activists come from strikingly different backgrounds. PAN candidates to Congress in 2006 were generally introduced to politics through their ties to the private sector and the Church; PRD candidates came up through labor unions and popular social movements (see the Mexico 2006 Candidate and Party Leader Survey, described in Bruhn and Greene's contribution to this collection). Although many leaders in both parties have attended public school, PAN politicians are far more likely to have attended private or parochial institutions. As a result of these patterns of political recruitment, party elites share relatively few cultural reference points.

Despite steps toward internal democracy in both parties, old guard elements still exercise substantial influence. The PAN remains a "club" party, in the sense that membership is not automatically open to anyone. Rather, those who wish to join must first be accepted as junior members (*miembros adherentes*); after a minimum trial period of six months and participation in various party activities, they may then apply to become full, dues-paying members (*miembros activos*). Both types of members could vote in the 2006 presidential primary, but only full members can vote for candidates for other offices or for party leaders. Not surprisingly, the party's current leadership remains far more conservative than party voters, not to mention ordinary citizens. In the case of the PRD, presidents have exercised rather wide discretion in whom they appoint to the National Executive Committee. Many of the current members were placed there by López Obrador. This fact may help to explain why, despite the steady influx of pragmatic PRI defectors into the PRD, its leadership supported López Obrador's post-electoral protest movement. These party elites are, in turn, the principal source of political polarization in Mexico.

4. Elites or Institutions?

For those political scientists who emphasize the role of institutions, the roots of Mexico's current political predicament lie in a cluster of familiar constitutional rules. First, Mexico's electoral system contains a large component of proportional representation, which in turn encourages multipartism. A multiparty system is not inherently problematic, but it becomes so when paired with a second institution: presidentialism. The combination of these two institutions virtually guarantees divided government. The adverse effects of these arrangements are compounded by the lack of run-off elections for president, which permits the election of non-Condorcet winners, and by the length of the presidential term (six years). Finally, to make matters worse, the prohibition on consecutive reelection renders politicians less accountable.

Dysfunctional institutions, however, cannot account for the most salient features of Mexico's current political topography. Most obviously, they cannot explain why one of the best-designed electoral systems in the world failed to produce a result that party leaders on the losing side would accept. If institutions are the main issue, governance problems should be the product of gridlock, rather than political polarization. Today, the reverse is true: as a result of likely collaboration between the PAN and elements of the PRI, legislative gridlock is now relatively unlikely; on the other hand, alleged electoral irregularities provoked a crisis.

Choice and leadership have more to do with today's situation than do formal institutions. In the case of post-electoral protests, for instance, other men in the same situation would have made different decisions than did López Obrador. In 1988, PRD candidate Cuauhtémoc Cárdenas proved less vigorous in protesting the official results of the election than López Obrador is today, even though the Left had much stronger grounds to do so then. Likewise, had Calderón lost the election, there is no doubt that he would have accepted the result or challenged it through strictly constitutional channels. The problem, then, lies less in how Mexico's president was elected than in how elites reacted to his election.

The simple fact that institutions have played a role in permitting the overrepresentation of extremists at the top of Mexico's main parties does not consign Mexico to crisis. Even fairly doctrinaire politicians can compromise, as the 1996–1997 inter-party negotiations showed. Nothing in the current context compels the PRD's leadership in Congress to adopt a relentlessly obstructionist stance, and the electoral benefits of doing so are at best unclear. Nor do present circumstances prevent Mexico's president-elect from reaching out to the Left.

There is not necessarily anything wrong with further institutional reform in Mexico, of course. But such reform is important as a symptom of agreement among the main political parties, not as its cause. In the end, it is the way particular leaders interact that will propel events toward compromise, or toward crisis.

References

Bermeo, Nancy. 2003. *Ordinary People in Extraordinary Times: The Citizenry and the Breakdown of Democracy*. Princeton: Princeton University Press.

Bruhn, Kathleen, and Kenneth F. Greene. 2007. "Elite Polarization Meets Mass Moderation in Mexico's 2006 Elections." *PS: Political Science and Politics* 40 (January): 33–38.

Diamond, Larry. 1999. *Developing Democracy: Toward Consolidation*. Baltimore: Johns Hopkins University Press.

Eisenstadt, Todd A. 2007. "The Origins and Rationality of the 'Legal versus Legitimate' False Dichotomy Invoked in Mexico's 2006 Post-Electoral Conflict." *PS: Political Science and Politics* 40 (January): 39–43.

Greene, Kenneth F. Forthcoming. *Defeating Dominance: Party Politics and Mexico's Democratization in Comparative Perspective*. Cambridge: Cambridge University Press.

Klesner, Joseph. 2007. "The 2006 Mexican Elections: Manifestation of a Divided Society?" *PS: Political Science and Politics* 40 (January): 27–32.

Langston, Joy. 2007. "The PRI's 2006 Electoral Debacle." *PS: Political Science and Politics* 40 (January): 21–25.

Lawson, Chappell. 2003. *Building the Fourth Estate: Democratization and the Rise of a Free Press in Mexico*. Berkeley: University of California Press.

———. 2006. "Preliminary Findings from the Mexico 2006 Panel Study: Blue States and Yellow States." Unpublished manuscript available at http://web.mit.edu/polisci/research/mexico06/Pres.htm.

Mainwaring, Scott. 1993. "Presidentialism, Multipartism, and Democracy: The Difficult Combination." *Comparative Political Studies* 26 (2): 198–228.

Moreno, Alejandro. 2007. "The 2006 Mexican Presidential Election: The Economy, Oil Revenues, and Ideology." *PS: Political Science and Politics* 40 (January): 15–19.

O'Donnell, Guillermo, and Philippe C. Schmitter. 1986. *Transitions from Authoritarian Rule: Tentative Conclusions about Uncertain Democracies*. Baltimore: Johns Hopkins University Press.

Notes

1. The combined Polity IV score ranges from –10 (utter autocracy) to 10 (full democracy). A score of zero indicates that autocratic features of the regime evenly balance.

2. Freedom House scores range from 2–14; higher scores indicate *less* freedom.

3. Results are based on simulations from a multinomial logit model of vote choice, in which the dependent variable took on one of four values (Calderón, López Obrador, Madrazo, or none/undecided). Independent variables included: age, gender, living standards (as measured by an index of material possessions, education, church attendance, region, political engagement, skin color, and urban or rural residence). Data are taken from the Mexico 2006 Panel Study, Wave 2. For full results, see Lawson 2006, available at: http://web.mit.edu/polisci/research/mexico06/Pres.htm.

4. Mexico 2006 Panel Study, Wave 3 and accompanying cross-section; Consulta Mitovsky, National Household Survey, August 2006.

5. Parametría, "El desafuero de López Obrador," National Household Survey, August 2004; Consulta Mitovsky, Household Survey in the Federal District, September 2004; Consulta Mitovsky, National Household Survey, January 2005; Consulta Mitovsky, National Telephone Survey and National Household Survey, April 2005; Consulta Mitovsky, Household Survey in the Federal District, February 2005.

Will Africa Ever Get It Right?

Nigeria's latest shameful and rigged election does not mean that all of Africa is hopeless

If Nigeria, Africa's most populous country, is anything to go by, the sub-Saharan continent of some 800m people may be doomed to spend another generation or so in misery. Nigeria's recent bout of elections has been a fiasco (see pages 68–70). The country is rich in resources—the United States may soon be getting a tenth of its oil from it—but most of its 140m-odd people languish in poverty. And yet their rotten leaders presume they have some kind of right, by virtue of their country's size and natural wealth, to strut the global stage as leaders of the continent. How wrong they are. Nigeria's new president, Umaru Yar'Adua, is tainted from the start. The elections at all levels should be held again—but of course they won't be. Any notion that Nigeria should be taken seriously as a continental spokesman, let alone a model, should be laughed out of court.

But is Nigeria typical of Africa? And does its dismal performance as a would-be democracy cast a blight across the rest of Africa? The answer to both questions is no. Nigeria is not Africa. Over the past decade or so, the rest of the continent has on the whole been taking modest, belated but encouraging steps towards greater prosperity, security and democracy.

To be sure, there is a very long way to go. The African backdrop is still fairly bleak. Many features of this latest Nigerian farce, namely corruption and mismanagement, still scar many other parts of Africa. The post-colonial continent has hitherto been a colossal flop. The killer comparison is with Asia, where many countries suffered from the same colonial humiliations and rapacity that independent Africa customarily blamed for its early failings. According to the World Bank, real income per head in the 48 countries of sub-Saharan Africa between 1960 and 2005 rose on average by 25%, while it leapt 34 times faster in East Asia; countries like South Korea and Malaysia were once as poor as Ghana and Kenya. The excuse of colonialism wore out at least a generation ago—and Africans know it.

But many lessons have been learnt, even—believe it or not—in Nigeria, where the macroeconomic picture is actually not too bad. On Africa's economic front, the deadening left-wing nostrums of the early days, dressed up in the verbiage of "African socialism", have long since been discarded. Private enterprise and freer markets have been given more of a head.

In politics, the once-predominant belief in a one-party system has faded, if not fizzled completely. Remember, it was only in 1991 that, for the first time since independence, the leader of any African country (not counting the Indian Ocean state of Mauritius) was peacefully voted out of office—in Benin, as it happens. Since then, many African countries have followed suit. Multi-party elections, though often very messy, have become far commoner.

It's Not All Bad

This month the IMF's latest figures give further cause for hope. For the third year in a row, sub-Saharan African countries grew on average by around 6% and may soon hit the 7% mark predicated by the UN in its call to halve Africa's poverty rate by 2015. True, this comes on the back of high oil and other commodity prices. But non-oil African countries are recording similar rates of growth. Such figures are modest by Asian standards. But they are going the right way—and quite fast.

The horrors of Africa still, of course, persist. It hosts most of the world's worst wars and disasters. Congo, its second biggest country in land mass, is fraught with tension and violence. The government of Africa's biggest country, Sudan, is still behaving appallingly in Darfur. Somalia (see page 66) is a failed state whose latest spasm of civil war could infect the Horn of Africa. Robert Mugabe's Zimbabwe is a wart on the face of southern Africa—and deters many who might invest in the surrounding region.

An abiding failure of Africa is the reluctance of relatively decent leaders to club together to shame the really bad ones out of office. Zimbabwe's case is the most egregious, disgracing the countries nearby, especially South Africa, whose leaders hide behind a misguided sense of past comradeship and racial solidarity. In Nigeria's case, the African Union should waste no time in denouncing the election as fraudulent—and freezing Nigeria's incoming government out of Africa's leading councils. Alas, that is unlikely to happen. Nigeria may seem too big, its peacekeepers too badly needed, for the rest of Africa to cold-shoulder it.

How can the outside world help Africa? There is no easy answer. Western countries, vital donors of aid, should make it clear they will give more help to countries whose governments are relatively clean and efficient—and hold fair elections. The latest aid-givers' consensus is to identify "good" countries, still quite a small bunch, and let them spend the cash as they see fit. Yet time and again, good guys—most recently, Ethiopia's Meles Zenawi and Uganda's Yoweri Museveni—slip back into old despotic ways, putting aid-givers into a quandary. By punishing governments, are they not hurting the innocent poor? In the end, Africa must help itself, just as Asia has. Then the outsiders will pile in, with investment that is better than aid at creating wealth. Even into Nigeria.

Africa's Crisis of Democracy

LYDIA POLGREEN

Kano, Nigeria: Nigeria's troubled presidential election, which came under fire on Sunday from local and international observers and was rejected by two leading opposition candidates, represents a significant setback for democracy in sub-Saharan Africa at a time when voters in countries across the continent are becoming more disillusioned with the way democracy is practiced.

Analysts said the Nigerian vote was the starkest example of a worrying trend—even as African countries hold more elections, many of their citizens are steadily losing confidence in their democracies.

"The picture in Africa is really mixed," said Peter Lewis, director of the African Studies program at Johns Hopkins University, who was among the researchers who conducted the Afrobarometer survey of African public opinion. "Some countries have vibrant political scenes, while other countries go through routine of elections but governance doesn't seem to improve."

African voters are losing patience with faulty elections that often exclude popular candidates and are marred by serious irregularities, according to the Afrobarometer survey, published last year, which sampled voters in 18 countries, based on interviews with 1,200 to 2,400 people per country. While 6 in 10 Africans said democracy was preferable to any other form of government, according to the survey, satisfaction with democracy dipped to 45 percent from 58 percent in 2001.

The threat to Nigeria's fragile democracy was underscored on Sunday by government officials, who dropped dark hints warning of a possible coup attempt, and said election critics were welcoming a military putsch by inciting violence.

Twenty-five candidates vied to replace the departing president in the Saturday vote, the first time in Nigeria's history that power will be transferred between two civilian administrations. But the election was marred by chaos, violence and fraud. Results are not expected until Monday at the earliest.

Election officials gave themselves high marks on Sunday for the handling of the polls, but their comments were in sharp contrast to assessments of international observers. Madeleine Albright, the former Secretary of State, who observed the election for the National Democratic Institute, said that "in a number of places and in a number of ways, the election process failed the Nigerian people." The International Republican Institute said that the election fell "below acceptable standards."

Such observations represent a stunning turnabout for Nigeria, Africa's most populous and second richest country, and reflect the deep frustrations of millions of Nigerians. In 2000, in the euphoric aftermath of Nigeria's transition from a long spell of military rule to democracy, 84 percent of Nigerians said that they were satisfied with democracy as practiced in Nigeria, according to the Afrobarometer survey.

By 2005 that number had plummeted to 25 percent, lower than all the countries surveyed save Zimbabwe. Almost 70 percent of Nigerians did not believe elections would allow them to remove objectionable leaders, the survey found.

Freedom House, an organization that monitors the spread of democracy and free speech, said in a report last year that the overall trends for African democracy were mixed. "Sub-Saharan Africa in 2006 presents at the same time some of the most promising examples of new democracies," the report said. It also has "some of the most disheartening examples of political stagnation, democratic backsliding, and state failure."

For every successful election, like those held this year in once-troubled countries like Mauritania and Democratic Republic of Congo, there have been elections in countries that seemed on the road to consolidating democracy but then swerved, like the Gambia, Uganda, Ethiopia and Zambia. There are also countries that hold regular elections, but they are so flawed they cannot really be called democratic, like those in Guinea, Zimbabwe and Gabon.

In 1976, according to Freedom House, just three countries in Africa were listed as "free," while the vast majority, 25, were "not free." Thirty years later, the not-free category had shrunk to 14 states, and the bulk of Africa now falls into the "partly free" category.

In the middle of that group is Nigeria, a nation of 140 million people divided among 250 ethnic groups and two major religions, Islam and Christianity, all of whom live in a space twice the size of California. It is rich in oil, exporting about two million barrels a day, but the riches that oil brings have not translated into meaningful development.

In Kano, a once vibrant manufacturing center, the contradictions of Nigeria's eight-year-old experiment with elected government are vividly on display. Far from building a unified country aimed at the greatest good for all, Nigeria has instead become an every-man-for-himself nation. In Kano's Government Residential Area, where the wealthy live, each household is its own power and water company. Plastic water tanks on spidery legs tower over the tiled roofs, each fed by an electric pump sucking water from a private well. The electric company provides light just a few hours a day, so the air is thick with the belching diesel smoke of a thousand generators, clattering away in miserable, endless unison.

The poor must manage however they can. With the decline of manufacturing and few formal jobs, many residents make a meager living off one another's misery. Idriss Abdoulaye sells water from a pushcart for 20 naira a jerry can, about 15 cents, to people like himself, too poor to have wells. He makes about $2 a day, and cannot afford to send his sons to school. Instead they go to a Koranic school, where they learn the Koran by rote. He said he worries they will end up as poor, illiterate traders like him. "There is no future for the poor man in this country," he said.

The government was supposed to make improving the nation's infrastructure a priority—President Olusegun Obasanjo, elected in 1999 and stepping down next month after two terms in office, campaigned on the promise of more electricity. Despite billions spent on the problem, all that changed was the name of the state power company. Once known as NEPA—which Nigerians joked stood for Never Expect Power Again—it is now called Power Holding Company. The improvement in service has been so minimal that a new joke has taken hold—Please Hold Candle.

But when Saidu Dattijo Adhama laughs about Nigeria's troubles, it is through gritted teeth. He is a textile manufacturer in Kano, and his factory used to produce 3,000 cotton jersey garments a day. Six years ago he was forced to shut down because paying for private generator power to spin his knitters and spinners and pump water for his bleaching and dyeing machines left him unable to compete with cheap imports flooding the country in the wake of trade liberalization. "The reason I went out of business is simple," he said. "It is the Nigerian factor. No light. No water. No reliable suppliers. How can I compete with someone in China who opens the tap and sees water? Who taps a switch and sees light?"

Adhama used to employ 330 workers in his workshops in the 1980s, but now he has just 24 employees as he tries to restart his business. He said the blame for the country's dilapidated condition lay with its leaders. Corrupt officials have plundered an estimated $380 billion from Nigeria's treasury since it won independence from Britain in 1960.

"We are not a poor country," Adhama said. "We have oil, we have resources. But it is the management of those resources that has been lacking. They have been hijacked. And then when we come to vote them out of office for their misdeeds, they hijack that as well." He said life now was in many ways worse than it was under military rule—there was more crime, less order. The one real improvement is the ability to freely speak his mind, Adhama said. "But even that is worthless," he said. "What is the point of talking if no one is listening?"

Adhama said he had no nostalgia for military rule, but some Nigerians do. For them, the names Sani Abacha, Muhammadu Buhari and Ibrahim Babangida, fearsome military rulers from Nigeria's past, signify security and decisive leadership, not autocracy and corruption.

In Malumfashi, a small town in southern Katsina state, men and boys not yet born when Buhari, now the candidate of a popular opposition party, was ruler, torched tires, threw stones and trashed billboards in a rampage to express their anger that they had not been able to vote. The ballot boxes in their town, an opposition stronghold, had been snatched by thugs loyal to the governing party, they said. "We need Buhari, only Buhari," the young men shouted, wild-eyed as they encircled a foreign journalist and photographer, half menacing and half embracing, as they pressed their grievances.

"No job!"
"No food!"
"No light!"
"No freedom!"
"No election!"

A Confident New Country

JO JOHNSON

In the 60 years since India won its independence, it has confounded dire predictions made for its future. Winston Churchill once famously described the country as a mere "geographical expression", a land that was "no more a united nation than the Equator".

He warned that "to abandon India to the rule of the Brahmins would be an act of cruel and wicked negligence". If the British left, he predicted, India would "fall back quite rapidly through the centuries into the barbarism and privations of the Middle Ages", a fear that the massacre of an estimated 1m refugees during the partition of the subcontinent in 1947 seemed at first to confirm.

Self-government, let alone good government, colonialists said, could never be possible in a country with such ethnic, religious, linguistic, climatic and developmental diversity. With more than 35 languages—and each one of them spoken by 1m people—and with profound cleavages along caste and communal lines, India seemed destined to fragment within a few years of the British departure. Post-independence history has been "peppered with forecasts of imminent dissolution, or of its descent into anarchy or authoritarian rule", notes Ramachandra Guha, a leading historian. That India could sustain democracy seemed in 1947 highly improbable.

Only by the late 1970s—after the country rejected Indira Gandhi's authoritarian tendencies—did fears for democracy start to recede. But doubts persisted that the country would ever attain the great power status coveted by its elites. India seemed "destined always to be 'emerging' but never actually arriving", a country fated to be forever "lodged in the second rank of international politics", as Stephen P Cohen of the Brookings Institution put it.* With its economy growing at just 3 or per cent a year until the 1980s—a pace disparagingly termed the "Hindu rate of growth"—there seemed little prospect that India would ever rise in the hierarchy of states.

Churchill claimed that India was 'no more a united nation than the Equator'

The pessimists were wrong. Now, 60 years on, India has consolidated a vibrant and competitive form of democracy; banished famine; more than halved its absolute poverty rate; dramatically improved literacy and health conditions; achieved global competitiveness in information technology, business process outsourcing, telecommunications and pharmaceuticals; acquired de facto membership of the elite club of acknowledged nuclear powers; created more billionaires than any other country in Asia; and became one of the world's most dynamic and fastest growing economies, ranked the world's fourth largest in purchasing power parity terms.

Over the past decade, India has acquired a new geo-strategic importance. The US National Intelligence Council's "Mapping the Global Future" project argued that the emergence of China and India would transform the geopolitical landscape with an impact comparable with the rise of Germany in the 19th century and that of the US in the early 20th century. Between the two Asian powers, there is little doubt where US affinities lie. An India that can emerge as a "geopolitical counterweight" to China and buttress of the Pax Americana is a persistent private theme of administration officials. George W Bush regularly notes that New Delhi's "commitment to secular government and religious pluralism" makes India a natural partner for the US.

The most telling indication of this new stature and perceived value as an ally came in March 2005, when Condoleezza Rice, secretary of state, formally proclaimed the US's determination to support India's emergence as global power. The second Bush administration has worked tirelessly to construct a deep strategic partnership with India, from which it had been estranged during the cold war. Pivotal to this has been an agreement to resume civil nuclear co-operation, abruptly suspended following India's test of a nuclear device in 1974. The deal, now awaiting approval by the US Congress and the International Atomic Energy Agency, promises to end three decades of isolation for the Indian scientific establishment.

"India is a rising global power with a rapidly growing economy," says Nicholas Burns, US under-secretary of state for political affairs, who has led the two-year negotiations on the nuclear deal. "Within the first quarter of this century, it is likely to be included among the world's five largest economies. It will soon be the world's most populous nation and it has a demographic distribution that bequeaths it a huge, skilled and youthful workforce. India's military forces will continue to be large, capable and increasingly sophisticated." That consciousness of India's significance is echoed in the American private sector. Membership of the US India Business Council, a 32-year-old lobby group, has soared from 90 companies at the start of 2005 to more than 250.

Nothing more clearly illustrates the new confidence than the spate of cross-border takeovers involving Indian companies.

Tata Steel's $11bn acquisition of Corus, the Anglo-Dutch steel group, and Vodafone's $11bn purchase of a controlling interest in Hutchison Essar, the fourth-largest Indian mobile operator, have only smashed existing records for mergers and acquisitions involving Indian companies, both as predators and prey, but also mark what many see as a new era of India-centric corporate activity. At the heart of this trend is a reappraisal of the country's economic potential after decades of miserly growth. Over the past three years, growth in gross domestic product has expanded at an unprecedented pace. It touched 9.4 per cent last year, making India's the second-fastest growing economy in Asia.

Even though higher interest rates may trigger a slowdown this year, with Morgan Stanley predicting GDP growth will fall to 7.7 per cent, India's Planning Commission expects the economy to grow by 9 per cent during the 11th five-year plan period (2008-2012). India is now growing nearly as fast as China and globalising almost as rapidly. Whether measured in terms of trade as a share of GDP, the number of Indian companies seeking overseas listings and acquisitions, or the global ambitions of its resurgent manufacturers, India is intertwining with the world as never before.

Decades of socialist experimentation with import substitution, high tariffs and industrial licensing left India a minnow in world trade at the start of the 1990s. Today it accounts for a smaller share of global merchandise exports than in 1947 and its economy remains far less trade-intensive than China's. This is starting to change. Kamal Nath, the commerce minister, hopes the country will exports goods worth $160bn this year despite the sharp appreciation of the rupee, an increase of 28 per cent over 2006-7.

Many challenges still face even this confident new India. One of the most worrying is that its highly competitive democracy has been increasingly unable to provide voters with a means of holding governments accountable for the delivery of core public services. As incomes rise and media penetration boosts awareness of inequalities, there is mounting frustration at the state's failure to provide decent water, sanitation, power, education, policing, roads and healthcare. Progress has been made in getting more children into primary school but the education imparted remains of an abysmally low standard.

Although population growth has fallen below 2 per cent a year, many of the country's human development indicators still flash red. In some states, malnutrition rates have been rising in recent years.

In the excitement about the "new" India, it is often forgotten that it has a child malnutrition rate higher than sub-Saharan Africa—at 45.9 per cent of children aged under three, a rate that reflects "negligible improvement" over the past five years, according to Unicef, the United Nations children's agency.

Above all, India faces the challenge of making growth more inclusive. Senior Congress party leaders are worried that the United Progressive Alliance government, which has lost a series of state elections in recent months and suffered from a backlash against its promotion of special economic zones, has neglected the "aam admi" (common man) in pursuit of economic growth.

Substantial disparities persist. The World Bank notes that, in a marked departure from previous decades, the reforms of the 1990s were accompanied by a visible increase in income inequality. Although this continues to be relatively low by global standards—on the Gini index, where 0 represents perfect equality and 100 absolute inequality, India measures 32.5 and China 44.7—disparities between urban and rural areas, prosperous and lagging states, skilled and low-skilled workers are growing. Evidence of social unrest in some disadvantaged regions is alarming, with an extreme leftist revolutionary movement, known as Naxalism, now affecting more than a quarter of the country's 600 or so districts.

Slow agricultural growth—at just 2.7 per cent, it is far below the government's 4 per cent target—is perhaps the single greatest worry for policymakers concerned at the prospect of uncontrollable migration to the cities. The World Bank believes that current agricultural practices are neither economically nor environmentally sustainable. Poorly maintained irrigation systems, inadequate roads, over-regulation and lack of access to formal sources of finance are all factors that hamper farmers' access to markets.

Rural indebtedness to money-lenders has resulted in a politically explosive wave of suicides among small, marginal and tenant farmers. With yields for many agricultural commodities low and falling, India has been forced to start importing wheat and other essential foodstuffs.

While the services sector booms with promising job opportunities for skilled workers, 90 per cent of India's labour force remains trapped in low productivity informal sector jobs.

Sixty years ago, on the eve of independence, Jawaharlal Nehru, the country's first prime minister, in a famous speech to parliament, evoked India's "tryst with destiny" and called on his then 340m fellow countrymen to help him "build the noble mansion of free India where all her children may dwell. There is no resting for any one of us till we redeem our pledge in full, till we make all the people of India what destiny intended them to be".

With one in four Indians still living in absolute poverty, Nehru's promise remains unfulfilled for more than 260m people. Confronted by a population set to expand from 1.1bn to perhaps 1.5bn by the time it stabilises in the middle of the century, with more than half of this increase in five of the poorest states, there will be no rest for India's leaders for years to come.

It is forgotten that India has a child malnutrition rate higher than sub-Saharan Africa

India: Emerging Power, STEPHEN P COHEN, Oxford University Press, 2001.

Caste Battle Only Half Won as North Lags South

ASHUTOSH VARSHNEY

Like race in the US, caste is the dark underbelly of Indian politics and society. Skin colour is not its primary basis, but the caste system resembles racial stratification in several other ways. Traditionally, castes were birth-based groups organised in a vertical hierarchy. The upper castes had the higher professions; the lower castes—now called the "other backward classes" (OBCs)—were peasants and servants; and the Dalits, placed at the bottom of the social scale, were restricted to menial jobs. Upward mobility in the caste system was highly limited. Tradition was supported by coercion, if violated.

When India became independent, its leaders wanted to attack the centuries-old caste system. They developed a two-track strategy. Universal franchise was the first pillar of the strategy. The underlying assumption was that, since the OBCs and Dalits constituted a majority of the population, universal franchise would end up addressing the concerns of the plebian orders. Affirmative action was the second pillar. Seats were reserved for Dalits in the legislature, bureaucracy and educational institutions. Centuries of degradation had produced collective guilt in the upper tiers of the polity and so spurred corrective public action.

The same guilt, however, did not mark the attitude of leaders, mostly upper caste, towards the OBCs. The dominant view was that the OBCs were never subjected to the extreme deprivations that the Dalits experienced. Moreover, the OBCs constituted a large proportion of the overall Indian population, much larger than the Dalits. Such large numbers did not need government protection; the power of their vote could forcefully express their preferences.

An all-India policy for the OBCs, thus, could not be formulated. It was left to state governments to decide which policies would be appropriate. In southern India, OBCs had already been mobilised into social movements during the last decades of British rule. In the 1950s and 1960s, they rose in politics as well. As a consequence, southern state governments ended up reserving a large number of government jobs and positions in higher education. By the late 1960s, in some southern states, 65 per cent of the public sector jobs and nearly 70 per cent of seats in colleges of science and engineering were reserved for Dalits

and OBCs. In the north, there were no OBC movements at the time of independence. As a result, northern state governments felt no pressure to follow southern strategies. It was only in the 1990s that the north moved in the same direction as the south.

Southern state governments ended up reserving a large number of government jobs

Has India's democracy—after 60 years—finally undermined its traditional caste order? What have been the political and economic consequences of democracy's interaction with caste?

By the late 1960s, all over southern India, upper caste hegemony was undermined, leading to a new political equilibrium in the 1970s in which the OBCs held the upper hand and the upper castes accepted their junior role. In the north, such political reversal is under way in two of the largest states, Uttar Pradesh and Bihar. Politics in these two states have begun to resemble what happened in the south four to five decades back. On caste issues, the north is roughly half a century behind.

Southern India has also surged ahead on human development indicators. The south is considerably more literate and healthy than the north. But a remarkable contrast, not yet sufficiently analysed, is economic.

Between 1960 and 1980, the growth rates of all four southern states were below the national average. The same was true of the Hindi-speaking north. Since 1980, however, a clear contrast has emerged. Southern states, with the exception of Kerala, have grown at a rate higher than the national average, whereas the northern states have continued to fall below it. If current growth rates continue for the next 20 years, southern India will begin to look like southern Europe, and the north will at best resemble north Africa.

The rise of the south since 1980 has generated two standard explanations in policy circles: better governance and higher literacy. It has not been asked whether the remarkable weakening of the southern caste system has anything to do with it. After all, southern states did not do well in the first three decades of

Indian independence. It is only with the emergence of a new political order, with lower castes in command by the 1970s, that the economic turnaround took place after 1980.

If the north can follow in the footsteps of the south, India's social revolution will be more comprehensive. That the two biggest states of northern India are finally showing southern patterns gives reason for hope.

ASHUTOSH VARSHNEY is professor of political science, at the University of Michigan, Ann Arbor, US.

Bin Laden, the Arab "Street," and the Middle East's Democracy Deficit

"Bin Laden speaks in the vivid language of popular Islamic preachers, and builds on a deep and widespread resentment against the West and local ruling elites identified with it. The lack of formal outlets to express opinion on public concerns has created [a] democracy deficit in much of the Arab world, and this makes it easier for terrorists such as bin Laden, asserting that they act in the name of religion, to hijack the Arab street."

DALE F. EICKELMAN

In the years ahead, the role of public diplomacy and open communications will play an increasingly significant role in countering the image that the Al Qaeda terrorist network and Osama bin Laden assert for themselves as guardians of Islamic values. In the fight against terrorism for which bin Laden is the photogenic icon, the first step is to recognize that he is as thoroughly a part of the modern world as was Cambodia's French-educated Pol Pot. Bin Laden's videotaped presentation of self intends to convey a traditional Islamic warrior brought up-to-date, but this sense of the past is a completely invented one. The language and content of his videotaped appeals convey more of his participation in the modern world than his camouflage jacket, Kalashnikov, and Timex watch.

Take the two-hour Al Qaeda recruitment videotape in Arabic that has made its way to many Middle Eastern video shops and Western news media.[1] It is a skillful production, as fast paced and gripping as any Hindu fundamentalist video justifying the destruction in 1992 of the Ayodhya mosque in India, or the political attack videos so heavily used in American presidential campaigning. The 1988 "Willie Horton" campaign video of Republican presidential candidate George H. W. Bush—in which an off-screen announcer portrayed Democratic presidential candidate Michael Dukakis as "soft" on crime while showing a mug shot of a convicted African-American rapist who had committed a second rape during a weekend furlough from a Massachusetts prison—was a propaganda masterpiece that combined an explicit although conventional message with a menacing, underlying one intended to motivate undecided voters. The Al Qaeda video, directed at a different audience—presumably alienated Arab youth, unemployed and often living in desperate conditions—shows an equal mastery of modern propaganda.

The Al Qaeda producers could have graduated from one of the best film schools in the United States or Europe. The fast-moving recruitment video begins with the bombing of the USS *Cole* in Yemen, but then shows a montage implying a seemingly coordinated worldwide aggression against Muslims in Palestine, Jerusalem, Lebanon, Chechnya, Kashmir, and Indonesia (but not Muslim violence against Christians and Chinese in the last). It also shows United States generals received by Saudi princes, intimating the collusion of local regimes with the West and challenging the legitimacy of many regimes, including Saudi Arabia. The sufferings of the Iraqi people are attributed to American brutality against Muslims, but Saddam Hussein is assimilated to the category of infidel ruler.

Osama bin Laden . . . is thoroughly imbued with the values of the modern world, even if only to reject them.

Many of the images are taken from the daily staple of Western video news—the BBC and CNN logos add to the videos' authenticity, just as Qatar's al-Jazeera satellite television logo rebroadcast by CNN and the BBC has added authenticity to Western coverage of Osama bin Laden.

Alternating with these scenes of devastation and oppression of Muslims are images of Osama bin Laden: posing in front of bookshelves or seated on the ground like a religious scholar, holding the Koran in his hand. Bin Laden radiates charismatic authority and control as he narrates the Prophet Mohammed's flight from Mecca to Medina, when the early Islamic movement was threatened by the idolaters, but returning to conquer them. Bin Laden also stresses the need for jihad, or struggle for the cause of Islam, against the "crusaders" and "Zionists." Later images show military training in Afghanistan (including target practice at a poster of Bill Clinton), and a final sequence—the word "solution" flashes across the screen—captures an Israeli soldier in full riot gear retreating from a Palestinian boy throwing stones, and a reading of the Koran.

The Thoroughly Modern Islamist

Osama bin Laden, like many of his associates, is imbued with the values of the modern world, even if only to reject them. A 1971 photograph shows him on family holiday in Oxford at the age of 14, posing with two of his half-brothers and Spanish girls their own age. English was their common language of communication. Bin Laden studied English at a private school in Jidda, and English was also useful for his civil engineering courses at Jidda's King Abdul Aziz University. Unlike many of his estranged half-brothers, educated in Saudi Arabia, Europe, and the United States, Osama's education was only in Saudi Arabia, but he was also familiar with Arab and European society.

The organizational skills he learned in Saudi Arabia came in to play when he joined the mujahideen (guerrilla) struggle against the 1979 Soviet invasion of Afghanistan. He may not have directly met United States intelligence officers in the field, but they, like their Saudi and Pakistani counterparts, were delighted to have him participate in their fight against Soviet troops and recruit willing Arab fighters. Likewise, his many business enterprises flourished under highly adverse conditions. Bin Laden skillfully sustained a flexible multinational organization in the face of enemies, especially state authorities, moving cash, people, and supplies almost undetected across international frontiers.

The organizational skills of bin Laden and his associates were never underestimated. Neither should be their skills in conveying a message that appeals to some Muslims. Bin Laden lacks the credentials of an established Islamic scholar, but this does not diminish his appeal. As Sudan's Sorbonne-educated Hasan al-Turabi, the leader of his country's Muslim Brotherhood and its former attorney general and speaker of parliament, explained two decades ago, "Because all knowledge is divine and religious, a chemist, an engineer, an economist, or a jurist" are all men of learning.[2] Civil engineer bin Laden exemplifies Turabi's point. His audience judges him not by his ability to cite authoritative texts, but by his apparent skill in applying generally accepted religious tenets to current political and social issues.

The Message on the Arab "Street"

Bin Laden's lectures circulate in book form in the Arab world, but video is the main vehicle of communication. The use of CNN-like "zippers"—the ribbons of words that stream beneath the images in many newscasts and documentaries—shows that Al Qaeda takes the Arab world's rising levels of education for granted. Increasingly, this audience is also saturated with both conventional media and new media, such as the Internet.[3] The Middle East has entered an era of mass education and this also implies an Arabic lingua franca. In Morocco in the early 1970s, rural people sometimes asked me to "translate" newscasts from the standard transnational Arabic of the state radio into collo-

quial Arabic. Today this is no longer required. Mass education and new communications technologies enable large numbers of Arabs to hear—and see—Al Qaeda's message directly.

Bin Laden's message does not depend on religious themes alone. Like the Ayatollah Ruhollah Khomeini, his message contains many secular elements. Khomeini often alluded to the "wretched of the earth." At least for a time, his language appealed equally to Iran's religiously minded and to the secular left. For bin Laden, the equivalent themes are the oppression and corruption of many Arab governments, and he lays the blame for the violence and oppression in Palestine, Kashmir, Chechnya, and elsewhere at the door of the West. One need not be religious to rally to some of these themes. A poll taken in Morocco in late September 2001 showed that a majority of Moroccans condemned the September 11 bombings, but 41 percent sympathized with bin Laden's message. A British poll taken at about the same time showed similar results.

Osama bin Laden and the Al Qaeda terrorist movement are thus reaching at least part of the Arab "street." Earlier this year, before the September terrorist attacks, United States policymakers considered this "street" a "new phenomenon of public accountability, which we have seldom had to factor into our projections of Arab behavior in the past. The information revolution, and particularly the daily dose of uncensored television coming out of local TV stations like al-Jazeera and international coverage by CNN and others, is shaping public opinion, which, in turn, is pushing Arab governments to respond. We don't know, and the leaders themselves don't know, how that pressure will impact on Arab policy in the future."[4]

Director of Central Intelligence George J. Tenet was even more cautionary on the nature of the "Arab street." In testimony before the Senate Select Committee on Intelligence in February 2001, he explained that the "right catalyst—such as the outbreak of Israeli-Palestinian violence—can move people to act. Through access to the Internet and other means of communication, a restive public is increasingly capable of taking action without any identifiable leadership or organizational structure."

Because many governments in the Middle East are deeply suspicious of an open press, nongovernmental organizations, and open expression, it is no surprise that the "restive" public, increasingly educated and influenced by hard-to-censor new media, can take action "without any identifiable leadership or organized structure." The Middle East in general has a democracy deficit, in which "unauthorized" leaders or critics, such as Egyptian academic Saad Eddin Ibrahim—founder and director of the Ibn Khaldun Center for Development Studies, a nongovernmental organization that promotes democracy in Egypt—suffer harassment or prison terms.

One consequence of this democracy deficit is to magnify the power of the street in the Arab world. Bin Laden speaks in the vivid language of popular Islamic preachers, and builds on a deep and widespread resentment against the West and local ruling elites identified with it. The lack of formal outlets to express opinion on public concerns has created the democracy deficit in much of the Arab world, and this makes it easier for terrorists such as bin Ladin, asserting that they act in the name of religion, to hijack the Arab street.

The immediate response is to learn to speak directly to this street. This task has already begun. Obscure to all except specialists until September 11, Qatar's al-Jazeera satellite television is a premier source in the Arab world for uncensored news and opinion. It is more, however, than the Arab equivalent of CNN. Uncensored news and opinions increasingly shape "public opinion"—a term without the pejorative overtones of "the street"—even in places like Damascus and Algiers. This public opinion in turn pushes Arab governments to be more responsive to their citizens, or at least to say that they are.

Rather than seek to censor al-Jazeera or limit Al Qaeda's access to the Western media—an unfortunate first response of the United States government after the September terror attacks—we should avoid censorship. Al Qaeda statements should be treated with the same caution as any other news source. Replacing Sinn Fein leader Gerry Adams' voice and image in the British media in the 1980s with an Irish-accented actor appearing in silhouette only highlighted what he had to say, and it is unlikely that the British public would tolerate the same restrictions on the media today.

Ironically, at almost the same time that national security adviser Condoleezza Rice asked the American television networks not to air Al Qaeda videos unedited, a former senior CIA officer, Graham Fuller, was explaining in Arabic on al-Jazeera how United States policymaking works. His appearance on al-Jazeera made a significant impact, as did Secretary of State Colin Powell's presence on a later al-Jazeera program and former United States Ambassador Christopher Ross, who speaks fluent Arabic. Likewise, the timing and content of British Prime Minister Tony Blair's response to an earlier bin Laden tape suggests how to take the emerging Arab public seriously. The day after al-Jazeera broadcast the bin Laden tape, Blair asked for and received an opportunity to respond. In his reply, Blair—in a first for a Western leader—directly addressed the Arab public through the Arab media, explaining coalition goals in attacking Al Qaeda and the Taliban and challenging bin Laden's claim to speak in the name of Islam.

Putting Public Diplomacy to Work

Such appearances enhance the West's ability to communicate a primary message: that the war against terrorism is not that of one civilization against another, but against terrorism and fanaticism in all societies. Western policies and actions are subject to public scrutiny and will often be misunderstood. Public diplomacy can significantly diminish this misapprehension. It may, however, involve some uncomfortable policy decisions. For instance, America may be forced to exert more diplomatic pressure on Israel to alter its methods of dealing with Palestinians.

Western public diplomacy in the Middle East also involves uncharted waters. As Oxford University social linguist Clive Holes has noted, the linguistic genius who thought up the first name for the campaign to oust the Taliban, "Operation Infinite Justice," did a major disservice to the Western goal. The expres-

sion was literally and accurately translated into Arabic as *adala ghayr mutanahiya,* implying that an earthly power arrogated to itself the task of divine retribution. Likewise, President George W. Bush's inadvertent and unscripted use of the word "crusade" gave Al Qaeda spokesmen an opportunity to attack Bush and Western intentions.

Mistakes will be made, but information and arguments that reach the Arab street, including on al-Jazeera, will eventually have an impact. Some Westerners might condemn al-Jazeera as biased, and it may well be in terms of making assumptions about its audience. However, it has broken a taboo by regularly inviting official Israeli spokespersons to comment live on current issues. Muslim religious scholars, both in the Middle East and in the West, have already spoken out against Al Qaeda's claim to act in the name of Islam. Other courageous voices, such as Egyptian playwright Ali Salem, have even employed humor for the same purpose.[5]

We must recognize that the best way to mitigate the continuing threat of terrorism is to encourage Middle Eastern states to be more responsive to participatory demands, and to aid local nongovernmental organizations working toward this goal. As with the case of Egypt's Saad Eddin Ibrahim, some countries may see such activities as subversive. Whether Arab states like it or not, increasing levels of education, greater ease of travel, and the rise of new communications media are turning the Arab street into a public sphere in which greater numbers of people, and not just a political and economic elite, will have a say in governance and public issues.

Notes

1. It is now available on-line with explanatory notes in English. See <http://www.ciaonet.org/cbr/cbr00/video/excerpts_index.html>.

2. Hasan al-Turabi, "The Islamic State," in *Voices of Resurgent Islam,* John L. Esposito, ed. (New York: Oxford University Press, 1983), p. 245.

3. On the importance of rising levels of education and the new media, see Dale F. Eickelman, "The Coming Transformation in the Muslim World," *Current History,* January 2000.

4. Edward S. Walker, "The New US Administration's Middle East Policy Speech," *Middle East Economic Survey,* vol. 44, no. 26 (June 25, 2001). Available at <http://www.mees.com/news/a44n26d01.htm>.

5. See his article in Arabic, "I Want to Start a Kindergarten for Extremism," *Al-Hayat* (London), November 5, 2001. This is translated into English by the Middle East Media Research Institute as Special Dispatch no. 298, Jihad and Terrorism Studies, November 8, 2001, at <http://www.memri.org>.

DALE F. EICKELMAN is Ralph and Richard Lazarus Professor of Anthropology and Human Relations at Dartmouth College. His most recent book is *The Middle East and Central Asia: An Anthropological Approach,* 4th ed. (Englewood Cliffs, N. J.: Prentice Hall, 2002). An earlier version of this article appeared as "The West Should Speak to the Arab in the Street," *Daily Telegraph* (London), October 27, 2001.

Iran's Conservative Revival

"No one has benefited more from American blunders in the Middle East than the conservatives in Iran who now control all the power centers. . . . "

BAHMAN BAKTIARI

The rise to the Iranian presidency of ultra-conservative Mahmoud Ahmadinejad reflects how much Iran has changed in recent years. Today it is Ahmadinejad, in the eyes of the world, who embodies Iran's increasing hard-line assertiveness. In light of this, how should we assess Ahmadinejad's impact on Iranian politics? And how have recent developments in Iraq and elsewhere in the region affected Iran?

Iranian officials remember the 2002 speech by President George W. Bush in which he labeled the Islamic Republic of Iran part of an "axis of evil." Coming at a time when Iran's own politics was characterized by rivalry between reformists and conservatives, and hot on the heels of the American invasion of Iran's neighbor Afghanistan, that speech was interpreted by many Iranians as a signal that the United States intended to topple the ruling theocracy. This conviction hardened after America's seemingly effortless dislodging of another neighboring ruler, Saddam Hussein.

Indeed, during the us invasion of Iraq, Iran put out feelers to explore the possibility of détente. Iranians wrote a letter in April 2003 to their American counterparts offering to discuss the mutual interests of the two countries, including the suspension of uranium enrichment, accepting a two-state solution for Palestinians and Israelis, and helping the United States to secure post-Hussein Iraq. The Americans, high on their "mission accomplished" in Iraq, chose to ignore the letter.

Much has changed since then. Just as the United States felt strong enough then to spurn Iran's overture, the Iranians have now rejected incentives that the Americans and others proffered in the summer of 2006 to tempt the Iranian regime to give up its ambition to make the country an industrial producer of nuclear fuel. Now it is the Iranian government's turn to enjoy the Americans' failure, which the regime vicariously considers its own success. If history is any guide, the Iranian government will overplay its hand, and the absurd hostility between the United States and Iran will continue beyond 2007.

With Iran's regional position stronger than ever and its coffers bulging with oil receipts, hubris alone might seem to threaten the country's good fortunes. Inside the country, however, economic mismanagement, human rights abuses, and popular resentment are as prevalent as ever. Ahmadinejad's administration has launched crackdowns on independent journalists and human rights activists since he became president. In September 2006, he urged conservative, pro-regime students to push for a purge of liberal and secular teachers from universities, a reflection of his determination to create an Islamic revival in the country.

But for most of Iran's defeated reformers, it is Bush's policies, not the clergy's inspired leadership, that have put the Iranian regime in its present strong position. No one has benefited more from American blunders in the Middle East than the conservatives in Iran who now control all the power centers: the presidency, the parliament, the judiciary, the security forces, and the office of the supreme leader.

Ahmadinejad's Ascent

Iranian politics is a complicated affair, involving such institutions as the Expediency Council (which mediates between the parliament and an unelected high chamber called the Council of Guardians), and the Assembly of Experts (an 86-member body whose job is to select the country's supreme leader). The Islamic Republic has always followed a limited system of electoral politics; both the parliament and the president are elected, though candidates who stand for office must be approved by the conservatives. This system has helped the Islamic Republic to survive, but it also prevents the national political discourse from moving forward.

Ahmadinejad came to power in 2005 on a platform of piety, honesty, and the redistribution of wealth, a set of principles reminiscent of the 1979 Islamic revolution that displaced the shah and brought to power Ayatollah Ruhollah Khomeini. Ahmadinejad was born the son of a blacksmith in 1956 in Garmsar, near Tehran. He earned a Ph.D. in traffic and transportation from Tehran's University of Science and Technology and served for four years as the governor of the northwestern towns of Maku and Khoy. In 1993, he was appointed the cultural adviser for Ali Larijani—then Minister of Islamic Culture and Guidance and currently the head of the Supreme National Security

Council and the country's chief nuclear negotiator. A few months later, Ahmadinejad was appointed governor of the newly created Ardebil province. In 2003, the Tehran Municipal Council, which is controlled by conservatives, appointed him mayor of Tehran. When he announced his candidacy for president, he received barely any attention from either reformist or conservative news outlets.

After the first round of voting for president, support for the reformist and conservative camps appeared evenly split. The independent centrist Hashemi Rafsanjani led the voting with over 6 million votes. Ahmadinejad came in second with something under 6 million. An additional 6 million votes were split between conservatives Mohammad Baqer Qalibaf and Larijani—which meant that conservative candidates received about 12 million votes combined. Approximately 11 million votes were won by reformists, including third-place finisher Mehdi Karroubi, a cleric who received more than 5 million votes, along with Mostafa Moin and Mohsen Mehr-alizadeh. If at that point reformist voters had united behind Rafsanjani, the centrist would have coasted to victory with about 17 million votes.

But reformists did not unite behind Rafsanjani because they did not approve of his record. When he had served as president from 1989 to 1997, his administration, though it practiced some socioeconomic liberalization early on, failed to reform Iran's bureaucracy and attract foreign investment. Rafsanjani had also failed to engage the Clinton administration when it made quiet overtures to restore diplomatic ties. When Rafsanjani left the presidency, all member states of the European Union had recalled their ambassadors from Iran because Iranian agents had allegedly assassinated dissidents abroad.

Because Rafsanjani could not easily run on his record, he organized his campaign around the policies that he would pursue if elected again. He also cast himself as a veteran of government who could draw on his long experience in Iran's factional politics to re-energize the economy, bring Iran's nuclear dispute with foreign powers to a close, and normalize diplomatic relations with the United States. In the end, however, Ahmadinejad in a runoff trounced Rafsanjani, by 17.3 million votes to 10 million, a far bigger margin than anyone had predicted.

Ahmadinejad's election resulted partly from his manipulation of the electoral process, partly from his personal drive and determination, and partly from the deficiencies of the other candidates. He managed to qualify for the runoff election to begin with, after the first round in which five of seven candidates were eliminated, partly because of illegal canvassing on his behalf by a nationwide militia of religious vigilantes known as *basijis*. And according to the Interior Ministry, which was then controlled by the reformist government of President Muhammad Khatami, the runoff election itself was tarnished by "unprecedented irregularities."

A Surprising Alliance

In analyzing the reasons why a populist like Ahmadinejad won election in 2005, Iranian intellectuals draw parallels with the period before the revolution of 1979, a time characterized, like today, by oil riches, high inflation, and social upheaval. Between 2004 and 2005, Iran's imports increased by 26 percent, and the wealthy areas of its cities were full of Western items that most Iranians could not afford. Meanwhile, one-third of Iranians in their 20s were unemployed, and the country's infrastructure could not accommodate the huge demographic group that was reaching adulthood. Some 1.4 million young people took the university entrance exams in the summer of 2005, competing for just 200,000 spots.

Conservative Iranians, including the pious poor, were attracted to Ahmadinejad's apparent honesty and his modest lifestyle, along with the insular vision of the world that he projected. He drew on popular resentment against Iran's elite classes, which are widely viewed as enriching themselves through corruption. Rafsanjani, who was seen as the face of that elite, argued that the way forward for Iran should include better relations with the United States and increased foreign investment in Iran. Ahmadinejad saw no need for improved relations with "the Great Satan."

After the election it appeared to many that Rafsanjani's political career was finished. Yet, a year and a half later, Rafsanjani remained a potent force, vying for the speakership of the Assembly of Experts in elections slated for December of 2006, and aspiring ultimately to become supreme leader when the current holder of that position, Ayatollah Ali Khamenei, leaves office. Rafsanjani's bid for power sets him up against Ayatollah Mohammed Taghi Mesbah-Yazdi, an archconservative and a mentor of Ahmadinejad. Mesbah-Yazdi is believed to want the supreme leader's job for himself, and he lined up support among hard-line clerics for his own candidacy for the speakership of the Assembly of Experts.

This dynamic has produced a surprising new alliance between the reformists and Rafsanjani. The same bloc that once treated the former president with scorn is now supporting him for fear that the alternative would be worse. The reformists, comprised mainly of educated urbanites who recoil from the populism of Ahmadinejad, are alarmed by Mesbah-Yazdi's support for violent measures against political opponents and his connections to intelligence personnel, who have in the past been involved in the killing of dissidents. Reformists were strongly put off by language in a May 2006 magazine published by Mesbah-Yazdi that characterized Rafsanjani, along with the reformist former president Khatami and the former chief nuclear negotiator Hassan Rowhani, as "traitors to Islam and Iran" who should not be allowed to hold office.

Ayatollah Khamenei is now firmly in the camp of the hardliners, welcoming the election of Ahmadinejad after apparently having tried to dissuade Rafsanjani from running at all.

The Sputtering Economy

"Serving the Iranian people," Ahmadinejad says, "is more worthy than lording it over the world." But despite the conservative president's rhetoric about improving living conditions for the impoverished and making the country even more Islamic, Ahmadinejad so far has not brought much change to Iran, a country facing serious demographic and economic challenges.

Iran has 70 million inhabitants, of whom one-third are under 14 and another one-third under 35. The country registered 6 percent gdp growth in 2005, but that was not enough to meet the growing population's need for jobs. Unemployment has been running above 15 percent, and the real rate may be higher than reported in official figures. Inflation is about 17 percent, outstripping wage increases. Although the government heavily subsidizes staple foods among other items, the urban poor live in a discouraging economic environment.

In 2006, Iran's per capita income was projected to rise to $3,465, which would be $700 higher than in the previous year. Yet the Iranian Social Security Organization reports that 30 percent of Iranians live in poverty. Meanwhile, the wealthiest 20 percent of Iran's citizens account for 50 percent of national income and 80 percent of total wealth. Ahmadinejad came into office pledging to address this situation, saying he would deliver "oil revenues to people's dinner tables," and that he would not ignore poverty as his predecessors had done. "My whole family voted for Ahmadinejad because he promised to improve our lives," said a 67-year-old pensioner quoted in the *Asia Times*. "He said oil money belonged to the people. I haven't seen any of the oil money in my house yet, but I have to deal with the ever-increasing prices anyway."

Under Ahmadinejad, conservative forces are determined to make the Islamic Republic more Islamic than republican.

Iran's economic problems are numerous. The country has suffered a large decline in the value of its stock market, and low interest rates have left some banks on the verge of bankruptcy. The government's budget deficit amounts to about $8 billion a year. Highly subsidized and highly dependent on oil revenues, the Iranian economy now faces inflation and stagnation simultaneously. Although it is OPEC's second-largest producer of oil, Iran actually faces a shortage of refining capacity and has had to consider rationing gasoline.

High oil revenues have helped the public sector grow—in February 2006, for instance, the government increased the budget of the state broadcasting monopoly by 46 percent and that of the Institute for Islamic Propagation by 96 percent. The private sector on the other hand is falling behind, and the government has aggravated the situation by granting large contracts to military entities without going through tendering processes. Over the past few months, the Islamic Revolutionary Guards Corps has received government contracts amounting to $8 billion.

Ahmadinejad has been president for more than a year, yet Iran's economy is as inefficient as it was when Khatami was president. It also depends as much as ever on oil revenues. Indeed, the key parts of Ahmadinejad's program for populist uplift, including the government's increased control over the economy, seem less intended to stoke economic activity than to fix in place the state of affairs that existed before attempts were made at reform. Already, the government's populist economic policies have provoked criticism from some former allies of Ahmadinejad, including Ahmad Tavakkoli and Mahmoud Khoshchehreh, both hard-line members of parliament.

For these reasons and others, Ahmadinejad's grip on power must be seen as somewhat tenuous. Some reckon that only about 15 percent of Iranians strongly support Ahmadinejad's fundamentalism and the political factions that back it. His official powers are subject to constitutional and other constraints. And, despite ongoing efforts to make the country yet more Islamic, Iranian society continues to become more secularized in the cities. At some point, political upheaval could result from the dismal outcomes of the high expectations that the new government has created. Most Iranians identify their primary problems as economic ones, and Ahmadinejad has failed so far to improve the people's economic lot.

International Isolation

Compounding Ahmadinejad's political problems is his tendency to anger many in the international community with his verbal attacks against the West and particularly Israel, including his expressions of doubt that the Holocaust occurred. In October 2005, at a conference for students organized by the government and called "World Without Zionism," Ahmadinejad alarmed many by suggesting that Israel should be "wiped off the map." In July 2006, while Israel and Lebanon were engaged in conflict, he likened Israel's offensive to Adolf Hitler's aggression. In August, he said that "the main solution" to tensions in the Middle East would be "the elimination of the Zionist regime."

Opposition to Israel is written into Iran's constitution, but the country's approach to the Israeli-Palestinian issue has never been as cut-and-dried as might be inferred from listening to the public comments of Iranian officials. In the 1980s, for example, although Iran's Revolutionary Guards were providing assistance to Syria in setting up the Hezbollah militia in Lebanon, the Iranian government was buying American arms through Israel for its war against Iraq. Khatami, the reformist president, gave indications during his term that he would not rule out a two-state solution for the Israelis and Palestinians—and Khatami has since criticized Ahmadinejad's anti-Israel remarks.

At times, when state control over media content and intellectual discourse has been reduced, discussions have taken place as to whether Israel has a right to exist. Although Israel certainly views Iran's nuclear program as a threat to its existence, the threat is probably not imminent or severe. The CIA believes that Iran is still five to ten years away from being able to manufacture nuclear weapons. And Iran's nuclear ambitions may be driven more by the regime's desire to ensure its own survival than by any desire to destroy Israel. Indeed, any attack against Israel might invite a massive response that could very well cause the end of the Islamic Republic.

Still, Ahmadinejad's comments on the Holocaust and Israel have not benefited Iran. They have only served to increase tensions, and have also made it easier for Israel and the United States to portray Iran as a threat that must be confronted.

Nuclear Nationalism

Western nations have suspected for a number of years that Iran has been attempting to develop nuclear weapons. Iran has only made the suspicions stronger with its tough negotiating tactics and its willingness to lie about its nuclear programs. Although Ahmadinejad's election heralded a further assertiveness in Iran's positions regarding the nuclear programs, the president himself does not determine his country's foreign or nuclear policies. These remain the province of the supreme leader, Ayatollah Khamenei, and Larijani of the Supreme National Security Council.

That said, Ahmadinejad has done all he can to become the face of Iran's nuclear programs and ambitions. This is because, as both a populist and a politician whose fate ultimately rests in the hands of voters, he benefits from fomenting nationalist fervor. This may be why he chose to announce personally that Iran had succeeded in enriching small amounts of uranium, and to later state publicly that "Iran is a nuclear country. It has the full gamut of nuclear technology at its disposal."

Ahmadinejad has been able to project such assertiveness in part because of high oil prices, which paradoxically enough have stayed at high levels in part because of world oil markets' concerns about Iran. Oil revenues in Iran for the year ending in March 2006 came in at about $50 billion, almost double the amount from two years before. Moreover, as long as oil prices stay high, Iranian leaders know that they face little danger of an international oil embargo, because such an action would cause oil prices to go still higher.

Officials in Iran are thus able to cultivate the idea that international actions cannot hurt them. They assert that no embargo will take place, and that sanctions short of an embargo would have no tangible effect. They also suggest that any interruption in the flow of imports from Europe could be circumvented by increasing imports from China and other Asian countries, many of which are perfectly willing to continue doing business with Iran.

Although the nuclear powers China and Russia would prefer not to see Iran join the nuclear club, in part because this might prompt other Middle Eastern countries such as Turkey and Saudi Arabia to develop nuclear weapons of their own, both powers are wrapped up in Iran's energy sector. China is aggressively pinning down future sources of energy around the world, and Russia is assisting Iran in its construction of a civilian nuclear reactor in Bushehr. Therefore, it seems unlikely that China or Russia, both permanent members of the United Nations Security Council, would support meaningful sanctions against Iran. This in turn allows Iran more maneuvering room as it faces down the United States and the European Union.

The Iranian public's views on the nuclear program are generally positive, even if many Iranians doubt the official claim that the program's purposes are peaceful. In fact, according to public opinion research conducted by the InterMedia Survey Institute, 41 percent of Iranians strongly support the development of nuclear weapons. Among those who support the development of these weapons, 84 percent would be willing to face UN sanctions, and 75 percent would risk hostilities with the United States in order to develop them.

Iranians tend to support the nuclear program as a matter of national pride, something that is not likely to change as long as they do not believe the program threatens their security or impinges on their standard of living. Approval of the program is also stoked by anger over what Iranians see as a double standard in international attitudes toward other countries that have joined the nuclear club—Pakistan and Israel, for example.

Through the state media, Iran's leadership has popularized the idea that the nation's nuclear program is about much more than nuclear weapons. Government propaganda about nuclear activities is intended to reinforce the public's pride, and the nuclear program is cast as a way to force Western countries to recognize the Iranian revolution as legitimate. The program is also portrayed as a remedy to Iranians' historical dissatisfactions and as a source of hope for the future.

Iran's leaders suggest the nuclear problem will be solved when the United States and countries in the EU realize that they will have to deal with Iran as an equal. Thus, the conservatives in Iran's government are successfully using the nuclear issue as a means to cement their own power through nationalist fervor. In this, they have been unwittingly assisted by President Bush.

In this sensitive political environment, nothing is more counterproductive than talking of a military strike against Iran. Israeli Prime Minister Ehud Olmert has said that Iran must not have nuclear weapons "under any circumstances." The head of the Israeli air force, asked how far he would go to stop the development of nuclear weapons in Iran, joked "two thousand kilometers." In fact, any air strikes against Iran's nuclear facilities would be extremely risky, prompting Iran to retaliate through terrorist activities in Israel, Iraq, and Afghanistan. Moreover, air strikes in all likelihood would only slow Iran's program, not stop it, since nuclear facilities are probably spread throughout the country.

If history is any guide, the Iranian government will overplay its hand, and the absurd hostility between the United States and Iran will continue beyond 2007.

Hedging on Iraq

The Middle East has been undergoing great change since the US invasion of Iraq, and one of the effects, not intended by the United States, is Iran's growing power in the region. When Tehran was presented with Hussein's removal and the resulting power vacuum, it could not pass up the chance to pursue its desire for greater regional influence. For years Iranian leaders had promoted Islamic interests ahead of national interests; since the Iraq invasion they have gone back to the nationalist approach employed 30 years ago by Mohammad Reza Shah.

The US removal of Hussein eliminated Iran's main regional rival. Elections in Iraq have given power to that country's Shiite majority, among whom Shiite Iran retains influence. Weakened by violent chaos, Iraq has now come to see Iran as the more powerful player in the two countries' relationship. Iran's top interest in Iraq is to ensure that Iraq cannot emerge again as a military, political, or ideological threat.

Potential threats to Iran could be posed by Iraq's success— that is, if the country manages to succeed as a democracy or as a workable state arranged on religious lines different from Iran's. Threats might also be posed by Iraq's failure—that is, if Iraq falls into all-out civil war, or if it allows an independent Kurdistan to come into being (which Iran does not wish to see because of its own Kurdish minority).

Iran does not wish to see Iraq partitioned. It does not want full-scale instability or civil war. Rather, it would like to see a friendly Shiite government rule Iraq, and would also like for the United States to remain preoccupied with that country so that it cannot turn its attention to Iran. To achieve these aims, Tehran has pursued a three-part strategy. First, it has encouraged democracy as a way to achieve Shiite rule. Second, it has worked to promote disorder, while taking care to ensure that such disorder does not spin out of control entirely. Third, it has backed a wide variety of protagonists in Iraq to make sure that it has a working relationship with whatever faction finally gains control of the country.

Worried that the United States intends to bring Iran's nuclear ambitions to a halt through the use of force, Tehran has sought to build large networks of pro-Iranian actors within Iraq. These include special-forces units called the Quds Brigade, which could carry out attacks against US troops in Iraq in the event of American military action against Iran. Such elements in Iraq, combined with the threat that Iran poses to Israel through Hezbollah in Lebanon, provide leverage for Iran against possible US hostile action.

The worsening violence in Iraq, however, is causing strategy to change in Tehran as much as it is in Washington. The Iranian leadership was initially gleeful about Hussein's removal. But now this joy has been overwhelmed by the realization that if Iraq tears apart completely along ethnic and religious lines, and if the United States retreats hastily as a result, Iranian interests in the region would be gravely threatened. These threats would include the possibility of chaos leaping the border into Iran and provoking unrest among Iran's minorities. Therefore, Iran is working vigorously to prevent utter collapse from taking place.

Any end to US involvement in Iraq will have to include cooperation from Iran, the most powerful player in the area because of its links to Iraq's majority Shiites, to power centers in the Iraqi government, and to militias. In exchange for its cooperation, Iran will want a guarantee of its own security— incidentally, the same thing it wants in exchange for ending the conflict over its nuclear programs. Iran would also like to see the end of trade restrictions against it, and progress toward diplomatic normalization with the United States. The Americans in turn would expect Iran to exercise maximum possible restraint with its allies within Iraq.

Prospects for Change

Under Ahmadinejad, conservative forces are determined to make the Islamic Republic more Islamic than republican. Whether they will succeed is another matter. Power in Iran is a complicated matter, and various factions exist even among conservatives, who run the gamut from hard-liners to pragmatists. Some among Iran's leadership would accept accommodation with the West in exchange for economic and strategic concessions, while others are content to accept isolation from the West. Others favor a "Chinese model," which in Iran would mean opening the economy to international investment while maintaining the clergy's dominance. It is these complex internal forces that will decide the future of Iranian politics.

For now, not much optimism can be attached to the notion that sanctions and similar measures will cause regime change in Tehran. Nor is military action, short of full-scale invasion, likely to bring about regime change, since a limited attack by either the United States or Israel would only cause Iranians to throw more support behind the government.

BAHMAN BAKTIARI is the director of research and academic programming at the University of Maine's William S. Cohen Center for International Policy and Commerce.

UNIT 6

Major Trends and Continuing Challenges

Unit Selections

Key Points to Consider

- Why is it important to the authors that the unusual plural form of their subject, anti-Americanisms, be used in the title and the body of their discussion of this topic?

- Distinguish between anti-Americanism when it is rooted in a persistent cultural bias and when it is rooted in differences of opinion. What difference does it make?

- What do the authors mean by their reference to the United States as a *"polyvalent"* society? Why is such a society, especially when very powerful, diverse and influential like the United States, unlikely to be admired and respected everywhere and at all times?

- What is meant by three major trends that, along with counter-trends, have done much to change the shape of our political landscape in recent years?

- Why is neo-liberalism likely to meet with resistance to its ideological promotion of deregulation, privatization, and free trade—even though such measures have resulted in some substantial economic improvements in countries like India and China?

- What are some main problems and dilemmas of old and new democracies?

- Market capitalism and liberal democracy can both support and subvert each other, according to Gabriel Almond, at one and the same time. Explain this apparent paradox, and indicate why Almond considered some form of liberal social democracy as the most promising resolution.

- How does Amy Chua's article, "Explosive Combination," remind us of the dangerous situations that can arise for market-dominating minorities when authoritarian patterns of governance are suddenly cast off?

- How does the article with the intriguing title "The Man in the Baghdad Café" cast doubt on some current cultural explanations in social science?

- What does Benjamin Barber mean when he warns that democracy is threatened by both globalism and tribalism?

Student Web Site

www.mhcls.com/online

Internet References

Further information regarding these Web sites may be found in this book's preface or online.

Commission on Global Governance
http://www.sovereignty.net/p/gov/gganalysis.htm

IISDnet
http://www.iisd.org/default.asp

ISN International Relations and Security Network
http://www.isn.ethz.ch

United Nations Environment Program
http://www.unep.ch/

Today's comparativists tend to approach grand theory skeptically. Yet they will tackle big topics and engage in generalizations about trends or tendencies, as long as they are backed by empirical evidence and open to modification or correction. In this final unit, we will try to connect several readings to three major political trends or patterns of development that have been observed in much of the contemporary world. It is important to stress at the outset that, with the possible exception of Benjamin Barber, none of the authors predict some form of global convergence in which all political systems would become alike in major respects. On closer examination, even Barber turns out to propose no end to history. He argues that a strong tendency toward global homogenization is offset by a concurrent tendency toward intensified group differentiation and fragmentation.

The trends or patterns discussed may be widespread, but they are neither unidirectional nor universal. They reflect the situations in which they arise. On occasion they have turned out to be reversible. One major trend—democratization—has apparently come to a halt, but its far-reaching consequences can be seen in the greatly altered political landscape left behind.

Each has resulted in what could be called a countervailing trend. Moreover, the three trends (with counter-trends) do not necessarily reinforce one another. Their varying forms of development are the very stuff of comparative politics.

Democratization. We have already discussed at length the democratization that without advance warning swept through much of the world during the last quarter of the twentieth century. It took form as a variety of **demands for popularly chosen, accessible, and accountable government officials,** often to replace rule by some kind of authoritarian oligarchy or dictatorship. We saw that it did not always succeed, and that in some cases a democratic façade was installed to hide continuing or returning authoritarian or semi-authoritarian realities. The country rankings established by the index of democracy, like those made by Freedom House, try to assess the real political situation.

Although there never was a global rush to democratization, it came closer than any "realist" would have anticipated, and it changed the political balance in much of our world. Now that a decade has passed since the third wave petered out, we need to remind ourselves how remarkable—and unexpected—this development was in the first place. It swept away many repressive authoritarian regimes, even though the new democracies did not always prove to be exemplary or viable. The index of "failed states" gives an unsentimental report on the need to establish robust states that have the power to carry out the fundamental promise of the social contract—namely to provide and maintain a setting in which a civil society can prosper. Not all of the new democracies can meet that basic performance test.

Sometimes using different criteria and data, skeptics on both Right and Left for a long time raised doubt if representative government was sufficiently effective or attractive to spread or survive in the modern world. Samuel Huntington expressed such misgivings in the mid-1970s in his contribution to a book with the suggestive title, *The Democratic Distemper*, in which he warned against an "excess of democracy." A few years later, in 1984, he concluded an article "Will More Countries Become Democratic?" by basically saying no: "...with few exceptions, the limits of democratic development in the world may well have been reached."[1]

Similar skepticism has resurfaced in recent years. In different parts of the world, there are again people who wonder about the viability of the democratic version of government. Democracy is evidently "not the only game in town," as the authors of a study of political preferences among Eastern and Southern Asians conclude.

Despite some very real setbacks, the democratic label still appears to have retained an **honorific status** in much of the world. As long as that is the case, we may expect more politics of pretending to be democratic, as in some of the hybrid regimes. But it is also conceivable that a non-democratic counter model may gain favor. The third wave of democratization almost completely missed **the Arab and Muslim worlds.** If meaningful elections were permitted there, the result could well be some very illiberal governments. They would probably reflect a popular embrace of theocratic governance in these countries, analogous to Iran's "Islamic Republic." Another notable alternative to our democratic experience is the **Chinese strategy** of combining market capitalism with continued authoritarian rule—perhaps in the future further softened by an elaborate pretense of consulting the people, even as they remain deprived of the right to choose their rulers.

Russia's present leadership seems to be searching for an effective, top-down way of maintaining basic security in this vast country. There can no longer be much doubt about the survival of strong authoritarian tendencies at both elite and mass levels in Russia. But the country may well have gone so far in its sudden, unexpected and chaotic democratization that it will be difficult to turn back the clock in this country.

Finally, there is a **populist form of authoritarian rule,** a system for which some countries in Latin America have shown a weakness. It can support leaders who find latent anti-Americanism a cheap political resource in a world where the international as well as domestic differences in the distribution of wealth are crass, visible and growing. Indirectly, the old question of whether a market economy is compatible with an authoritarian regime has already been answered—and the answer from

historical and present-day developments is surely affirmative. Even while we keep looking for signs that modest prosperity will be followed by a turn in a more democratic direction, there is good reason to remember the skeptic Missourian position: "First show me!"

A second major trend has been a significant shift toward a **liberalization of the economy** and greater reliance on private enterprise, the profit motive, and relatively **free markets.** It involves a concurrent move away from strong regulation, central planning, and state ownership. Without the market-friendly reforms, we would not have experienced **globalization** and its supportive ideology, **globalism.** For that reason this trend is sometimes called the "**market revival,**" or "**neoliberalism.**" Because of their crucial role in introducing these changes, the terms "**Thatcherism**" or "**Reaganomics**" also crop up. It is not so much a particular economic model that is being advocated as an approach to the economy which—so advocates claim—will encourage economic growth.

This trend also came without advance warning. It was intellectually sustained by economic theories that were associated with the pre-Keynesian economic ideas of a bygone era, but it found supporters in some strategic quarters. What's more, it often seemed to "deliver" in the form of economic growth. In Asian Communist-ruled countries, above all China, we have become used to seeing once self-proclaimed revolutionary socialists introduce and encourage forms of capitalist practice in their formerly centrally-planned economies. It is historically ironic that capitalism is being established in China by the courtesy of leaders who not so long ago were counted among its most fervent ideological opponents. In Russia, leading reformers were for a while also enthusiastic free marketers. More recently, as we saw in Unit Five, similar market- and business-friendly changes have been brought to India with similar consequences.

Not everyone shares the enthusiasm of the neoliberal reformers for deregulation and what opponents deem to be a "**dismantling**" of the welfare state. In fact, one widely shared challenge to many governments today is the **growing economic inequality** in society, as reflected in the **gini index** that measures the distance between the top 10 percent and the bottom 10 percent of household incomes. There are other problems. Although they could point to areas of success, the neoliberals did not always deliver what were thought to have been the promised goods. While their ideas produced initial enthusiasm in some quarters, they often became a test of patience in the face of disappointments, whether these resulted from unwarranted promises or naïve expectations of quick, if not instant, prosperity for all.

Above all, however, it has been shown that even if a market economy is more efficient than a centrally planned economy—and it may well be, *ceteris paribus*—it has rarely earned a reputation for ensuring social justice. For better or worse, capitalism is fundamentally associated with highly **unequal rewards** and considerable **economic insecurity,** and it has been remarkably poor in stating **a compelling moral case for itself.** It could be that this moral obtuseness stems from a more general lack of interest in moral issues per se, given the neoliberal assumption that egoism will have positive, but not really intended, social consequences in a market setting.

The Ambivalence About Markets. In an article that grew out of a speech given to a Soviet audience during the Gorbachev reform era, Gabriel Almond explored the complex and ambiguous connections between capitalism and democracy. His systematic discussion draws upon both theory and empirical studies. It shows that there are ways in which capitalism and democracy support each other, but also ways in which they tend to undermine each other. Is it possible to have the best of both? Almond answers at length that there is a non-utopian manner in which capitalism and democracy can be reconciled, namely in **democratic welfare capitalism.**

Rival Forms of Capitalism. Almond's discussion can be linked to a theme emphasized by some contemporary political economists. They point out that the economic competition between capitalism and socialism is effectively over. The central question now is which form of market economy will be more successful and acceptable. A similar argument has been made by the French theorist, Michel Albert, who distinguished between the **British-American** or "Anglo-Saxon" and the continental **"Rhineland" models of capitalism.** The former is more individualistic, more likely to resist governmental intervention, and characterized by such traits as high employee turnovers and short-term profit maximizing. It differs considerably from what the Germans call their "social market economy." The latter is more team-oriented, emphasizes cooperation between management and organized labor, and leaves a considerable role for government in the setting of general economic strategy, the training of an educated labor force, and the provision of social welfare services.

These different conceptions of capitalism can be linked to different histories. While Britain and the United States experienced a head start in their industrial revolutions and felt no great need for deliberate government efforts to encourage growth, Germany and Japan both played the role of relative latecomers, who looked to government in their attempts to catch up. The emergence of a kind of "social capitalism" in other continental countries of Europe suggests that cultural and institutional factors also played major roles in this development. We should continue to expect very differently mixed market economies, because one economic model or size is unlikely to fit all.

A crucial question is whether the relative prosperity and social security associated with this kind of mixed economy can be maintained in a time of technological breakthroughs and global competition. In 1999, Gerhard Schröder and Tony Blair attempted to formulate an answer: the two European leaders reaffirmed their commitment to a **"third way" strategy of reform** and made a potentially important distinction between a **"market economy"** and a **"market society."** Their outspoken support for the market economy was based on their conclusion that a strong economy was a fundamental precondition for maintaining the public services, public goods, and entitlements of the modern welfare state. Their rejection of a "market society" was rooted in their conviction that the criteria of a good society should not be determined primarily by the market's criteria of efficiency and profitability.

The Politics of Group Identity. The third major trend could be called the revival and intensification of **ethnic or cultural identity politics.** This refers to a growing emphasis on some form of an exclusive group identity as the primary basis for political expression. In modern times, it has been common for a group to identify itself by its special ethnic, religious, linguistic, or other cultural traits, and to make this identity the basis for a claim to special recognition and, sometimes, even to rule by and for itself. Multiculturalism and assimilation have been the two best-known attempts to deal with newcomer minorities. Britain and Canada are examples of a **multicultural response** and France has an official commitment to **assimilation** that is not always honored in practice. A third option is to ignore that there is a problem at all: this seems to have been the main course followed in Germany for years, but that country now recognizes the need to face the challenge of its many refugees and immigrants. We should not overlook that some poor countries bear the brunt of this problem. There are large numbers of political refugees and economic migrants in countries like Jordan, Lebanon, and Pakistan, and other countries close to regions of turmoil and failed states.

Relatively few observers seem to have foreseen that identity politics would play such a divisive role in the contemporary world. There were some early indications, such as the ethno-nationalist stirrings in the late 1960s and early 1970s, sometimes in peripheral areas of such countries as Britain, Canada, or Spain. Identity politics also lay behind many of the conflicts in the newly independent countries of the developing world. But most Western leaders—like their Soviet counterparts—seem to have missed have misread the signals of what was to come. As a result they were unprepared for the politicized resurgence of religious, ethnic, or other cultural forces.

The politicization of religion in many parts of the world falls into this development of a "politics of identity." In recent years, religious groups in parts of North America, Asia, the Middle East, sub-Saharan Africa, Asia, and Southern Europe have set out on the political road in the name of their faith. As Max Weber warned in a classic lecture shortly before his death, it can be dangerous to seek "the salvation of souls" along the path of politics. The coexistence of people of divergent faiths is possible only because religious conviction need not fully determine or direct a person's (or a group's) politics. When absolute and fervent convictions take over, they make it difficult to compromise pragmatically and live harmoniously with people who believe differently. Pluralist democracy requires an element of tolerance, which for many takes the form of a casual "live and let live" attitude.

There is an important debate among political scientists concerning the sources and scope of politics based on ethnic, religious, and cultural differences. Samuel Huntington has concluded that the most important and dangerous future conflicts will be based on **clashes of civilizations,** above all those of the Christian and Muslim worlds. In his view, they will be far more difficult to resolve than those rooted in socioeconomic or even ideological differences, because "the soul" is somehow at stake. His critics argue that Huntington distorts the differences among civilizations and trivializes the differences within civilizations.

Others have pointed out that ethnic conflicts are in fact often the result of political choices made by elites, implying that such conflicts are avoidable with better political choices. In her article,

Amy Chua reminds us that markets have short-run impacts that can be devastating for multi-ethnic societies. This is the case whenever ethnic minorities turn out to be "market-dominant" and become viewed as outside exploiters, as has happened to Chinese minorities in South East Asia on a number of occasions (Asian Indians, Jews, Lebanese, Armenians are among other groups in a similar position).

It seems appropriate to include an article on "Anti-Americanisms" by Peter Katzenstein and Robert Keohane in this book of readings in comparative politics and to place it in a section on identity politics. The authors cast much light on the widespread tendency around the world to hold negative views of the United States and American society in general. They give a differentiated analysis of this complex phenomenon that touches closely on American sensibilities. There are in reality a great **variety of "anti-Americanisms,"** hence the unusual use of the plural. Several of them are presented. The article makes a basic distinction between anti-Americanisms that are based on (1) **unfavorable opinion of an American policy or action** along with openness to new information that could change one's view, and (2) **a bias** leading to a **distortion of** information processing and resulting in a willingness to believe negative reports on the United States and to discount positive ones. The authors reject what they call "a grand explanation for anti-Americanism" and suggest several particular ones instead. At present it seems likely that anti-American bias will spread and harden, especially in the Middle East, in the wake of the Iraq War. Even without this conflict, however, the sources of anti-Americanism would not dry up. As an essentially polyvalent society, a powerful America that embodies a multiplicity of different values, the United States will probably always annoy somebody, somewhere. The authors have much more to say about this phenomenon but end on a note similar to the one we started this book with: Namely, that one can learn much about oneself and one's own society by studying how other human beings and societies work—and how they see us.

In his widely discussed article, Benjamin Barber brings a broad perspective to the discussion of identity politics in the contemporary world. He sees two major tendencies that threaten democracy. One is the force of globalism, brought about by modern technology, communications, and commerce. Its logical end station is what he calls a "McWorld," in which human diversity, individuality, and meaningful identity are erased. The second tendency works in the opposite direction: tribalism, which drives human beings to exacerbate their group differences and engage in holy wars or "jihads" against each other. Barber argues that globalism is at best indifferent to liberal democracy, while militant tribalism is deeply antithetical to it. He argues in favor of seeking a confederal solution, based on democratic civil societies, which could provide human beings with a nonmilitant, parochial communitarianism as well as a framework that suits the global market economy fairly well.

---

[1]See Samuel Huntington, "Will More Countries Become Democratic?," in Christian Søe, ed., *Comparative Politics 85/86,* pp. 148–161. The quoted passages are found in the conclusion, p. 160.

Anti-Americanisms

Biases as Diverse as the Country Itself

PETER J. KATZENSTEIN AND ROBERT O. KEOHANE

Arab reactions to American support for Israel in its recent conflict with Hezbollah have put anti-Americanism in the headlines once again. Around the world, not just in the Middle East, when bad things happen there is a widespread tendency to blame America for its sins, either of commission or omission. When its Belgrade embassy is bombed, Chinese people believe it was a deliberate act of the United States government; terror plots by native British subjects are viewed as reflecting British support for American policy; when AIDS devastates much of Africa, the United States is faulted for not doing enough to stop it.

These outbursts of anti-Americanism can be seen simply as a way of protesting American foreign policy. Is "anti-Americanism" really just a common phrase for such opposition, or does it go deeper? If anti-American expressions were simply ways to protest policies of the hegemonic power, only the label would be new. Before World War I Americans reacted to British hegemony by opposing "John Bull." Yet there is a widespread feeling that anti-Americanism is more than simply opposition to what the United States *does,* but extends to opposition to what the United States *is*—what it stands for. Critiques of the United States often extend far beyond its foreign policy: to its social and economic practices, including the public role of women; to its social policies, including the death penalty; and to its popular culture, including the flaunting of sex. Globalization is often seen as Americanization and resented as such. Furthermore, in France, which has had long-standing relations with the United States, anti-Americanism extends to the decades before the founding of the American republic.

With several colleagues we recently completed a book, *Anti-Americanisms in World Politics,*[1] exploring these issues, and in this short article we discuss four of its themes. First, we distinguish between anti-Americanisms that are rooted in opinion or bias. Second, as our book's title suggests, there are many varieties of anti-Americanism. The beginning of wisdom is to recognize that what is called anti-Americanism varies, depending on who is reacting to America. In our book, we describe several different types of anti-Americanism and indicate where each type is concentrated. The variety of anti-Americanism helps us to see, third, the futility of grand explanations for anti-Americanism. It is accounted for better as the result of particular sets of forces.

Finally, the persistence of anti-Americanism, as well as the great variety of forms that it takes, reflects what we call the *polyvalence* of a complex and kaleidoscopic American society in which observers can find whatever they don't like—from Protestantism to porn. The complexity of anti-Americanism reflects the polyvalence of America itself.

Opinion and Bias

Basic to our argument is a distinction between *opinion* and *bias.* Some expressions of unfavorable attitudes merely reflect opinion: unfavorable judgments about the United States or its policies. Others, however, reflect *bias:* a predisposition to believe negative reports about the United States and to discount positive ones. Bias implies a distortion of information processing, while adverse opinion is consistent with maintaining openness to new information that will change one's views. The long-term consequences of bias for American foreign policy are much greater than the consequences of opinion.

The distinction between opinion and bias has implications for policy, and particularly for the debate between left and right on its significance. Indeed, our findings suggest that the positions on anti-Americanism of both left and right are internally inconsistent. Broadly speaking, the American left focuses on opinion rather than bias—opposition, in the left's view largely justified, to American foreign policy. The left also frequently suggests that anti-Americanism poses a serious long-term problem for U.S. diplomacy. Yet insofar as anti-Americanism reflects ephemeral opinion, why should it have long-lasting effects? Policy changes would remove the basis for criticism and solve the problem. Conversely, the American right argues that anti-Americanism reflects a deep bias against the United States: People who hate freedom hate us for what we are. Yet the right also tends to argue that anti-Americanism can be ignored: If the United States follows effective policies, views will follow. But the essence of bias is the rejection of information inconsistent with one's prior view: Biased people do not change their views in response to new information. Hence, if bias is the problem, it poses a major long-term problem for the United States. Both left and right need to rethink their positions.

The view we take in the volume is that much of what is called anti-Americanism, especially outside of the Middle East, indeed is largely opinion. As such, it is volatile and would diminish in response to different policies, as it has in the past. The left is correct on this score, while the right overestimates resentment toward American power and hatred of American values. If the right were correct, anti-Americanism would have been high at the beginning of the new millennium. To the contrary, 2002 Pew polls show that outside the Middle East and Argentina, pluralities in every country polled were favorably disposed toward the United States. Yet with respect to the consequences of anti-American views, the right seems to be on stronger ground. It is difficult to identify big problems for American foreign policy created by anti-Americanism as such, as opposed to American policy. This should perhaps not be surprising, since prior to the Iraq war public opinion toward the United States was largely favorable. The right is therefore broadly on target in its claim that much anti-Americanism—reflecting criticisms of what the United States does rather than what it is—does not pose serious short-term problems for American foreign policy. However, if opinion were to harden into bias, as may be occurring in the Middle East, the consequences for the United States would be much more severe.

Anti-Americanisms

Since we are interested in attitudes that go beyond negative opinions of American foreign policy, we define anti-Americanism as *a psychological tendency to hold negative views of the United States and of American society in general.* Such negative views, which can be more or less intense, can be classified into four major types of anti-Americanism, based on the identities and values of the observers. From least to most intense, we designate these types of anti-Americanism as liberal, social, sovereign-nationalist, and radical. Other forms of anti-Americanism are more historically specific. We discuss them under a separate rubric.

Liberal anti-Americanism. Liberals often criticize the United States bitterly for not living up to its own ideals. A country dedicated to democracy and self-determination supported dictatorships around the world during the Cold War and continued to do so in the Middle East after the Cold War had ended. The war against terrorism has led the United States to begin supporting a variety of otherwise unattractive, even repugnant, regimes and political practices. On economic issues, the United States claims to favor freedom of trade but protects its own agriculture from competition stemming from developing countries and seeks extensive patent and copyright protection for American drug firms and owners of intellectual property. Such behavior opens the United States to charges of hypocrisy from people who share its professed ideals but lament its actions.

Liberal anti-Americanism is prevalent in the liberal societies of advanced industrialized countries, especially those colonized or influenced by Great Britain. No liberal anti-American ever detonated a bomb against Americans or planned an attack on the United States. The potential impact of liberal anti-Americanism would be not to generate attacks on the United States but to reduce support for American policy. The more the United States

is seen as a self-interested power parading under the banners of democracy and human rights rather than as a true proponent of those values, the less willing other liberals may be to defend it with words or deeds.

Since liberal anti-Americanism feeds on perceptions of hypocrisy, a less hypocritical set of United States policies could presumably reduce it. Hypocrisy, however, is inherent in the situation of a superpower that professes universalistic ideals. It afflicted the Soviet Union even more than the United States. Furthermore, a prominent feature of pluralist democracy is that its leaders find it necessary to claim that they are acting consistently with democratic ideals while they have to respond to groups seeking to pursue their own self-interests, usually narrowly defined. When the interests of politically strong groups imply policies that do not reflect democratic ideals, the ideals are typically compromised. Hypocrisy routinely results. It is criticized not only in liberal but also in nonliberal states: for instance, Chinese public discourse overwhelmingly associates the United States with adherence to a double standard in its foreign policy in general and in its conduct of the war on terror specifically.

Hypocrisy in American foreign policy is not so much the result of the ethical failings of American leaders as a byproduct of the role played by the United States in world politics and of democratic politics at home.

It will not, therefore, be eradicated. As long as political hypocrisy persists, abundant material will be available for liberal anti-Americanism.

Social anti-Americanism. Since democracy comes in many stripes, we are wrong to mistake the American tree for the democratic forest. Many democratic societies do not share the peculiar combination of respect for individual liberty, reliance on personal responsibility, and distrust of government characteristic of the United States. People in other democratic societies may therefore react negatively to America's political institutions and its social and political arrangements that rely heavily on market processes. They favor deeper state involvement in social programs than is politically feasible or socially acceptable in the United States. Social democratic welfare states in Scandinavia, Christian democratic welfare states on the European continent, and developmental industrial states in Asia, such as Japan, are prime examples of democracies whose institutions and practices contrast in many ways with those of the United States.

Social anti-Americanism is based on value conflicts that reflect relevant differences in many spheres of life that are touching on "life, liberty and the pursuit of happiness." The injustice embedded in American policies that favor the rich over the poor is often decried. The sting is different here than for liberals who resent American hypocrisy. Genuine value conflicts exist on issues such as the death penalty, the desirability of generous social protections, preference for multilateral approaches over unilateral ones, and the sanctity of international treaties. Still, these value conflicts are smaller than those with radical anti-Americanism, since social anti-Americanism shares in core American values.

Sovereign-nationalist anti-Americanism. A third form of anti-Americanism focuses not on correcting domestic market outcomes but on political power. Sovereign nationalists focus on two values: the importance of not losing control over the terms by which polities are inserted in world politics and the inherent importance and value of collective national identities. These identities often embody values that are at odds with America's. State sovereignty thus becomes a shield against unwanted intrusions from America.

The emphasis placed by different sovereign nationalists can vary in three ways. First, it can be on *nationalism:* on collective national identities that offer a source of positive identification. National identity is one of the most important political values in contemporary world politics, and there is little evidence suggesting that this is about to change. Such identities create the potential for anti-Americanism, both when they are strong (since they provide positive countervalues) and when they are weak (since anti-Americanism can become a substitute for the absence of positive values).

Second, sovereign nationalists can emphasize *sovereignty.* In the many parts of Asia, the Middle East, and Africa where state sovereignty came only after hard-fought wars of national liberation, sovereignty is a much-cherished good that is to be defended. And in Latin America, with its very different history, the unquestioned preeminence of the U.S. has reinforced the perceived value of sovereignty. Anti-Americanism rooted in sovereignty is less common in Europe than in other parts of the world for one simple reason: European politics over the past half-century has been devoted to a common project—the partial pooling of sovereignty in an emerging European polity.

A third variant of sovereign-nationalist anti-Americanism appears where people see their states as potential great powers. Such societies may define their own situations partly in opposition to dominant states. Some Germans came to strongly dislike Britain before World War I as blocking what they believed was Germany's rightful "place in the sun." The British-German rivalry before the First World War was particularly striking in view of the similarities between these highly industrialized and partially democratic societies and the fact that their royal families were related by blood ties. Their political rivalry was systemic, pitting the dominant naval power of the nineteenth century against a rapidly rising land power. Rivalry bred animosity rather than vice versa.

Sovereign-nationalist anti-Americanism resonates well in polities that have strong state traditions. Encroachments on state sovereignty are particularly resented when the state has the capacity and a tradition of directing domestic affairs. This is true in particular of the states of East Asia. The issues of "respect" and saving "face" in international politics can make anti-Americanism especially virulent, since they stir nationalist passions in a way that social anti-Americanism rarely does.

China is particularly interesting for this category, since all three elements of sovereign-nationalist anti-Americanism are present there. The Chinese elites and public are highly nationalistic and very sensitive to threats to Chinese sovereignty. Furthermore, China is already a great power and has aspirations to become more powerful. Yet it is still weaker than the United States. Hence, the superior military capacity of the United States and its expressed willingness to use that capacity (for instance, against an attack

by China on Taiwan) create latent anti-Americanism. When the United States attacks China (as it did with the bombing of the Chinese embassy in Belgrade in 1999) or seems to threaten it (as in the episode of the EC–3 spy plane in 2001), explicit anti-Americanism appears quickly.

Radical anti-Americanism. We characterize a fourth form of anti-Americanism as radical. It is built around the belief that America's identity, as reflected in the internal economic and political power relations and institutional practices of the United States, ensures that its actions will be hostile to the furtherance of good values, practices, and institutions elsewhere in the world. For progress toward a better world to take place, the American economy and society will have to be transformed, either from within or from without.

Radical anti-Americanism was characteristic of Marxist-Leninist states such as the Soviet Union until its last few years and is still defining Cuba and North Korea today. When Marxist revolutionary zeal was great, radical anti-Americanism was associated with violent revolution against U.S.-sponsored regimes, if not the United States itself. Its Marxist-Leninist adherents are now so weak, however, that it is mostly confined to the realm of rhetoric. For the United States to satisfy adherents of this brand of radical anti-Americanism, it would need to change the nature of its political-economic system.

The most extreme form of contemporary radical anti-Americanism holds that Western values are so abhorrent that people holding them should be destroyed. The United States is the leading state of the West and therefore the central source of evil. This perceived evil may take various forms, from equality for women, to public displays of the human body, to belief in the superiority of Christianity. For those holding extreme versions of Occidentalist ideas, the central conclusion is that the West, and the United States in particular, are so incorrigibly bad that they must be destroyed. And since the people who live in these societies have renounced the path of righteousness and truth, they must be attacked and exterminated.

Religiously inspired and secular radical anti-Americanism argue for the weakening, destruction, or transformation of the political and economic institutions of the United States. The distinctive mark of both strands of anti-Americanism is the demand for revolutionary changes in the nature of American society.

It should be clear that these four different types of anti-Americanism are not simply variants of the same schema, emotions, or set of norms with only slight variations at the margin. On the contrary, adherents of different types of anti-Americanism can express antithetical attitudes. Radical Muslims oppose a popular culture that commercializes sex and portrays women as liberated from the control of men and are also critical of secular liberal values. Social and Christian democratic Europeans, by contrast, may love American popular culture but criticize the United States for the death penalty and for not living up to secular values they share with liberals. Liberal anti-Americanism exists because its proponents regard the United States as failing to live up to its professed values—which are entirely opposed to those of religious radicals and are largely embraced by liberals. Secular radical anti-Americans may oppose the American embrace of capitalism but may accept scientific rationalism, gender egalitarianism, and secularism—as Marxists have done. Anti-Americanism can be fostered by Islamic fundamentalism, idealistic liberalism, or Marxism. And it can be embraced by people who, not accepting any of these sets of beliefs, fear the practices or deplore the policies of the United States.

Historically Specific Anti-Americanisms

Two other forms of anti-Americanism, which do not fit within our general typology, are both historically sensitive and particularistic: elitist anti-Americanism and legacy anti-Americanism.

Elitist anti-Americanism arises in countries in which the elite has a long history of looking down on American culture. In France, for example, discussions of anti-Americanism date back to the eighteenth century, when some European writers held that everything in the Americas was degenerate.[2] The climate was enervating; plants and animals did not grow to the same size; people were uncouth. In France and in much of Western Europe, the tradition of disparaging America has continued ever since. Americans are often seen as uncultured materialists seeking individual personal advancement without concern for the arts, music, or other finer things of life. Or they are viewed as excessively religious and therefore insufficiently rational. French intellectuals are the European epicenter of anti-Americanism, and some of their disdain spills over to the public. However, as our book shows, French anti-Americanism is largely an elite phenomenon. Indeed, polls of the French public between the 1960s and 2002 indicated majority pro-Americanism in France, with favorable ratings that were only somewhat lower than levels observed elsewhere in Europe.

Legacy anti-Americanism stems from resentment of past wrongs committed by the United States toward another society. Mexican anti-Americanism is prompted by the experiences of U.S. military attack and various forms of imperialism during the past 200 years. The Iranian revolution of 1979 and the subsequent hostage crisis were fueled by memories of American intervention in Iranian politics in the 1950s, and Iranian hostility to the United States now reflects the hostile relations between the countries during the revolution and hostage crisis. Between the late 1960s and the end of the twentieth century, the highest levels of anti-Americanism recorded in Western Europe were found in Spain and especially Greece—both countries that had experienced civil wars; in the case of Spain the United States supported for decades a repressive dictator. Legacy anti-Americanism can be explosive, but it is not unalterable. As the Philippines and Vietnam—both highly pro-American countries today—show, history can ameliorate or reverse negative views of the United States as well as reinforce them.

The Futility of Grand Explanations

Often Anti-Americanism is explained as the result of some master set of forces—for example, of hegemony or globalization. The United States is hated because it is "Mr. Big" or because

of its neoliberalism. However, all of these broad explanations founder on the variety of anti-Americanisms.

Consider first the "Mr. Big" hypothesis. Since the end of the Cold War, the United States has been by far the most powerful state in the world, without any serious rivals. The collapse of the Soviet bloc means that countries formerly requiring American protection from the Soviet Union no longer need such support, so their publics feel free to be more critical. In this view, it is no accident that American political power is at its zenith while American standing is at its nadir. Resentment at the negative effects of others' exercise of power is hardly surprising. Yet this explanation runs up against some inconvenient facts. If it were correct, anti-Americanism would have increased sharply during the 1990s; but we have seen that outside the Middle East, the United States was almost universally popular as late as 2002. The Mr. Big hypothesis could help account for certain forms of liberal and sovereign-nationalist anti-Americanism: Liberals criticize the United States for hypocrisy (and sometimes for being too reluctant to intervene to right wrongs), while sovereign nationalists fear the imposition of American power on their own societies. But it could hardly account for social, radical, elitist, or legacy anti-Americanism, each of which reacts to features of American society, or its behavior in the past, that are quite distinct from contemporary hegemony.

A second overarching explanation focuses on *globalization backlash.* The expansion of capitalism—often labeled globalization—generates what Joseph Schumpeter called "creative destruction." Those who are adversely affected can be expected to resist such change. In Benjamin Barber's clever phrase, the spread of American practices and popular culture creates "McWorld," which is widely resented even by people who find some aspects of it very attractive.[3] The anti-Americanism generated by McWorld is diffuse and widely distributed in world politics. But some societies most affected by economic globalization—such as India—are among the most pro-American. Even among the Chinese, whose reactions to the United States are decidedly mixed, America's wealth and its role in globalization are not objects of distrust or resentment as much as of envy and emulation. In terms of our typology, only social anti-Americanism and some forms of sovereign-nationalist anti-Americanism could be generated by the role of the United States in economic globalization—not the liberal, radical, elitist, or legacy forms.

A third argument ascribes anti-Americanism to cultural and religious identities that are antithetical to the values being generated and exported by American culture—from Christianity to the commercialization of sex. The globalization of the media has made sexual images not only available to but also unavoidable for people around the world. One reaction is admiration and emulation, captured by Joseph Nye's concept of soft power. But another reaction is antipathy and resistance. The products of secular mass culture are a source of international value conflict. They bring images of sexual freedom and decadence, female emancipation, and equality among the sexes into the homes of patriarchal and authoritarian communities, Muslim and otherwise. For others, it is American religiosity, not its sex-oriented commercialized culture, that generates negative reactions. Like the other arguments, the cultural identity argument has some resonance, but only for certain audiences. It may provide an explanation of some aspects of social, radical, and elitist anti-Americanism, but does not explain the liberal, sovereign-nationalist, or legacy varieties.

Each of the grand explanations probably contains at least a grain of truth, but none constitutes a general explanation of anti-Americanism.

The Polyvalence of American Society

American symbols are *polyvalent.* They embody a variety of values with different meanings to different people and indeed even to the same individual. Elites and ordinary folks abroad are deeply ambivalent about the United States. Visitors, such as Bernard-Henri Lévy, are impressed, repelled, and fascinated in about equal measure. Lévy dislikes what he calls America's "obesity"—in shopping malls, churches, and automobiles—and its marginalization of the poor; but he is impressed by its openness, vitality, and patriotism.[4] As David Laitin has noted, the World Trade Center was a symbol not only of capitalism and America but of New York's cosmopolitan culture, so often scorned by middle America. The Statue of Liberty symbolizes not only America and its conception of freedom. A gift of France, it has become an American symbol of welcome to the world's "huddled masses" that expresses a basic belief in America as a land of unlimited opportunity.

The United States has a vigorous and expressive popular culture, which is enormously appealing both to Americans and to many people elsewhere in the world. This popular culture is quite hedonistic, oriented toward material possessions and sensual pleasure. At the same time, however, the U.S. is today much more religious than most other societies. One important root of America's polyvalence is the tension between these two characteristics. Furthermore, both American popular culture and American religious practices are subject to rapid change, expanding further the varieties of expression in the society and continually opening new options. The dynamism and heterogeneity of American society create a vast set of choices: of values, institutions, and practices.

America's openness to the rest of the world is reflected in its food and popular culture. The American fast-food industry has imported its products from France (fries), Germany (hamburgers and frankfurters) and Italy (pizza). What it added was brilliant marketing and efficient distribution. In many ways the same is true also for the American movie industry, especially in the past two decades. Hollywood is a brand name held by Americans and non-Americans alike. In the 1990s only three of the seven major Hollywood studios were controlled by U.S. corporations. Many of Hollywood's most celebrated directors and actors are non-American. And many of Hollywood's movies about America, both admiring and critical, are made by non-Americans. Like the United Nations, Hollywood is both in America and of the world. And so is America itself—a product of the rest of the world as well as of its own internal characteristics.

"Americanization," therefore, does not describe a simple extension of American products and processes to other parts of the world. On the contrary, it refers to the selective appropriation of American symbols and values by individuals and groups in other societies—symbols and values that may well have had their origins elsewhere. Americanization thus is a profoundly interactive process between America and all parts of the world. And, we argue here, it is deeply intertwined with anti-American views. The interactions that generate Americanization may involve markets, informal networks, or the exercise of corporate or governmental power—often in various combinations. They reflect and reinforce the polyvalent nature of American society as expressed in the activities of Americans, who freely export and import products and practices. But they also reflect the variations in attitudes and interests of people in other societies, seeking to use, resist, and recast symbols that are associated with the United States. Similar patterns of interaction generate pro-Americanism and anti-Americanism, since both pro- and anti-Americanism provide an idiom to debate American and local concerns. Anti- and pro-Americanism have as much to do with the conceptual lenses through which individuals living in very different societies view America as with America itself. In our volume, Iain Johnston and Dani Stockmann report that when residents of Beijing in 1999 were asked simply to compare on an identity-difference scale their perceptions of Americans with their views of Chinese, they placed them very far apart. But when, in the following year, Japanese, the antithesis of the Chinese, were added to the comparison, respondents reduced the perceived identity difference between Americans and Chinese. In other parts of the world, bilateral perceptions of regional enemies can also displace, to some extent, negative evaluations of the United States. For instance, in sharp contrast to the European continent, the British press and public continue to view Germany and Germans primarily through the lens of German militarism, Nazi Germany, and World War II.

Because there is so much in America to dislike as well as to admire, polyvalence makes anti-Americanism persistent. American society is both extremely secular and deeply religious. This is played out in the tensions between blue "metro" and red "retro" America and the strong overtones of self-righteousness and moralism this conflict helps generate. If a society veers toward secularism, as much of Europe has, American religiosity is likely to become salient—odd, disturbing, and, due to American power, vaguely threatening. How can a people who believe more strongly in the Virgin Birth than in the theory of evolution be trusted to lead an alliance of liberal societies? If a society adopts more fervently Islamic religious doctrine and practices, as has occurred throughout much of the Islamic world during the past quarter-century, the prominence of women in American society and the vulgarity and emphasis on sexuality that pervades much of American popular culture are likely to evoke loathing, even fear. Thus, anti-Americanism is closely linked to the polyvalence of American society.

In 1941 Henry Luce wrote a prescient article on "the American Century." The American Century—at least its first 65 years—created enormous changes, some sought by the United States and others unsought and unanticipated. Resentment and anti-Americanism were among the undesired results of American power and engagement with the world. Our own cacophony projects itself onto others and can be amplified as it reverberates, via other societies, around the world.

Perhaps the most puzzling thing about anti-Americanism is that we Americans seem to care so much about it. Americans want to know about anti-Americanism: to understand ourselves better and, perhaps above all, to be reassured. This is one of our enduring traits. Americans' reaction to anti-Americanism in the twenty-first century thus is not very different from what Alexis de Tocqueville encountered in 1835:

The Americans, in their intercourse with strangers, appear impatient of the smallest censure and insatiable of praise. . . . They unceasingly harass you to extort praise, and if you resist their entreaties they fall to praising themselves. It would seem as if, doubting their own merit, they wished to have it constantly exhibited before their eyes.[5]

Perhaps we care because we lack self-confidence, because we are uncertain whether to be proud of our role in the world or dismayed by it. Like people in many other societies, we look outside, as if into a mirror, in order to see our own reflections with a better perspective than we can provide on our own. Anti-Americanism is important for what it tells us about United States foreign policy and America's impact on the world. It is also important for what it tells us about ourselves.

Notes

1. Peter J. Katzenstein and Robert O. Keohane, eds., *Anti-Americanisms in World Politics* (Cornell University Press, 2007).

2. Philippe Roger, *The American Enemy: The History of French Anti-Americanism* (University of Chicago Press, 2005).

3. Benjamin Barber, *Jihad vs. McWorld* (Crown, 1995).

4. Bernard-Henri Lévy, *American Vertigo: Traveling America in the Footsteps of Tocqueville* (Random House, 2006).

5. Alexis de Tocqueville, *Democracy in America* (1835), 1965 edition, 252.

Capitalism and Democracy*

GABRIEL A. ALMOND

Joseph Schumpeter, a great economist and social scientist of the last generation, whose career was almost equally divided between Central European and American universities, and who lived close to the crises of the 1930s and '40s, published a book in 1942 under the title, *Capitalism, Socialism, and Democracy*. The book has had great influence, and can be read today with profit. It was written in the aftergloom of the great depression, during the early triumphs of Fascism and Nazism in 1940 and 1941, when the future of capitalism, socialism, and democracy all were in doubt. Schumpeter projected a future of declining capitalism, and rising socialism. He thought that democracy under socialism might be no more impaired and problematic than it was under capitalism.

He wrote a concluding chapter in the second edition which appeared in 1946, and which took into account the political-economic situation at the end of the war, with the Soviet Union then astride a devastated Europe. In this last chapter he argues that we should not identify the future of socialism with that of the Soviet Union, that what we had observed and were observing in the first three decades of Soviet existence was not a necessary expression of socialism. There was a lot of Czarist Russia in the mix. If Schumpeter were writing today, I don't believe he would argue that socialism has a brighter future than capitalism. The relationship between the two has turned out to be a good deal more complex and intertwined than Schumpeter anticipated. But I am sure that he would still urge us to separate the future of socialism from that of Soviet and Eastern European Communism.

Unlike Schumpeter I do not include Socialism in my title, since its future as a distinct ideology and program of action is unclear at best. Western Marxism and the moderate socialist movements seem to have settled for social democratic solutions, for adaptations of both capitalism and democracy producing acceptable mixes of market competition, political pluralism, participation, and welfare. I deal with these modifications of capitalism, as a consequence of the impact of democracy on capitalism in the last half century.

At the time that Adam Smith wrote *The Wealth of Nations*, the world of government, politics and the state that he knew—pre-Reform Act England, the French government of Louis XV and XVI—was riddled with special privileges, monopolies, interferences with trade. With my tongue only half way in my check

I believe the discipline of economics may have been traumatized by this condition of political life at its birth. Typically, economists speak of the state and government instrumentally, as a kind of secondary service mechanism.

I do not believe that politics can be treated in this purely instrumental and reductive way without losing our analytic grip on the social and historical process. The economy and the polity are the main problem solving mechanisms of human society. They each have their distinctive means, and they each have their "goods" or ends. They necessarily interact with each other, and transform each other in the process. Democracy in particular generates goals and programs. You cannot give people the suffrage, and let them form organizations, run for office, and the like, without their developing all kinds of ideas as to how to improve things. And sometimes some of these ideas are adopted, implemented and are productive, and improve our lives, although many economists are reluctant to concede this much to the state.

My lecture deals with this interaction of politics and economics in the Western World in the course of the last couple of centuries, in the era during which capitalism and democracy emerged as the dominant problem solving institutions of modern civilization. I am going to discuss some of the theoretical and empirical literature dealing with the themes of the positive and negative interaction between capitalism and democracy. There are those who say that capitalism supports democracy, and those who say that capitalism subverts democracy. And there are those who say that democracy subverts capitalism, and those who say that it supports it.

The relation between capitalism and democracy dominates the political theory of the last two centuries. All the logically possible points of view are represented in a rich literature. It is this ambivalence and dialectic, this tension between the two major problem solving sectors of modern society—the political and the economic—that is the topic of my lecture.

Capitalism Supports Democracy

Let me begin with the argument that capitalism is positively linked with democracy, shares its values and culture, and facilitates its development. This case has been made in historical, logical, and statistical terms.

* Lecture presented at Seminar on the Market, sponsored by the Ford Foundation and the Research Institute on International Change of Columbia University, Moscow, October 29—November 2.

Albert Hirschman in his *Rival Views of Market Society* (1986) examines the values, manners and morals of capitalism, and their effects on the larger society and culture as these have been described by the philosophers of the 17th, 18th, and 19th centuries. He shows how the interpretation of the impact of capitalism has changed from the enlightenment view of Montesquieu, Condorcet, Adam Smith and others, who stressed the *douceur* of commerce, its "gentling," civilizing effect on behavior and interpersonal relations, to that of the 19th and 20th century conservative and radical writers who described the culture of capitalism as crassly materialistic, destructively competitive, corrosive of morality, and hence self-destructive. This sharp almost 180-degree shift in point of view among political theorists is partly explained by the transformation from the commerce and small-scale industry of early capitalism, to the smoke blackened industrial districts, the demonic and exploitive entrepreneurs, and exploited laboring classes of the second half of the nineteenth century. Unfortunately for our purposes, Hirschman doesn't deal explicitly with the capitalism–democracy connection, but rather with culture and with manners. His argument, however, implies an early positive connection and a later negative one.

Joseph Schumpeter in *Capitalism, Socialism, and Democracy* (1942) states flatly, "History clearly confirms . . . [that] . . . modern democracy rose along with capitalism, and in causal connection with it . . . modern democracy is a product of the capitalist process." He has a whole chapter entitled "The Civilization of Capitalism," democracy being a part of that civilization. Schumpeter also makes the point that democracy was historically supportive of capitalism. He states, ". . . the bourgeoisie reshaped, and from its own point of view rationalized, the social and political structure that preceded its ascendancy . . ." (that is to say, feudalism). "The democratic method was the political tool of that reconstruction." According to Schumpeter capitalism and democracy were mutually causal historically, mutually supportive parts of a rising modern civilization, although as we shall show below, he also recognized their antagonisms.

Barrington Moore's historical investigation (1966) with its long title, *The Social Origins of Dictatorship and Democracy; Lord and Peasant in the Making of the Modern World*, argues that there have been three historical routes to industrial modernization. The first of these followed by Britain, France, and the United States, involved the subordination and transformation of the agricultural sector by the rising commercial bourgeoisie, producing the democratic capitalism of the 19th and 20th centuries. The second route followed by Germany and Japan, where the landed aristocracy was able to contain and dominate the rising commercial classes, produced an authoritarian and fascist version of industrial modernization, a system of capitalism encased in a feudal authoritarian framework, dominated by a military aristocracy, and an authoritarian monarchy. The third route, followed in Russia where the commercial bourgeoisie was too weak to give content and direction to the modernizing process, took the form of a revolutionary process drawing on the frustration and resources of the peasantry, and created a mobilized authoritarian Communist regime along with a state-controlled industrialized economy. Successful capitalism dominating and transforming the rural agricultural sector, according

to Barrington Moore, is the creator and sustainer of the emerging democracies of the nineteenth century.

Robert A. Dahl, the leading American democratic theorist, in the new edition of his book (1990) *After the Revolution? Authority in a Good Society*, has included a new chapter entitled "Democracy and Markets." In the opening paragraph of that chapter, he says:

> It is an historical fact that modern democratic institutions . . . have existed only in countries with predominantly privately owned, market-oriented economies, or capitalism if you prefer that name. It is also a fact that all "socialist" countries with predominantly state-owned centrally directed economic orders—command economies—have not enjoyed democratic governments, but have in fact been ruled by authoritarian dictatorships. It is also an historical fact that some "capitalist" countries have also been, and are, ruled by authoritarian dictatorships.

> To put it more formally, it looks to be the case that market-oriented economies are necessary (in the logical sense) to democratic institutions, though they are certainly not sufficient. And it looks to be the case that state-owned centrally directed economic orders are strictly associated with authoritarian regimes, though authoritarianism definitely does not require them. We have something very much like an historical experiment, so it would appear, that leaves these conclusions in no great doubt. (Dahl 1990)

Peter Berger in his book *The Capitalist Revolution* (1986) presents four propositions on the relation between capitalism and democracy:

> Capitalism is a necessary but not sufficient condition of democracy under modern conditions.

> If a capitalist economy is subjected to increasing degrees of state control, a point (not precisely specifiable at this time) will be reached at which democratic governance becomes impossible.

> If a socialist economy is opened up to increasing degrees of market forces, a point (not precisely specifiable at this time) will be reached at which democratic governance becomes a possibility.

> If capitalist development is successful in generating economic growth from which a sizable proportion of the population benefits, pressures toward democracy are likely to appear.

This positive relationship between capitalism and democracy has also been sustained by statistical studies. The "Social Mobilization" theorists of the 1950s and 1960s which included Daniel Lerner (1958), Karl Deutsch (1961), S. M. Lipset (1959) among others, demonstrated a strong statistical association between GNP per capita and democratic political institutions. This is more than simple statistical association. There is a logic in the relation between level of economic development and democratic institutions. Level of economic development has been shown to be associated with education and literacy, exposure to mass media, and democratic psychological propensities such as subjective efficacy, participatory aspirations and skills. In a major investigation of the social psychology of industrialization and modernization, a research team led by the sociologist Alex Inkeles (1974) interviewed several thousand workers in the modern industrial and the traditional economic sectors of six countries of differing culture. Inkeles found empathetic, efficacious, participatory and activist propensities much more frequently among the modern industrial workers, and to a much lesser extent in the traditional sector in each one of these countries regardless of cultural differences.

The historical, the logical, and the statistical evidence for this positive relation between capitalism and democracy is quite persuasive.

Capitalism Subverts Democracy

But the opposite case is also made, that capitalism subverts or undermines democracy. Already in John Stuart Mill (1848) we encounter a view of existing systems of private property as unjust, and of the free market as destructively competitive—aesthetically and morally repugnant. The case he was making was a normative rather than a political one. He wanted a less competitive society, ultimately socialist, which would still respect individuality. He advocated limitations on the inheritance of property and the improvement of the property system so that everyone shared in its benefits, the limitation of population growth, and the improvement of the quality of the labor force through the provision of high quality education for all by the state. On the eve of the emergence of the modern democratic capitalist order John Staurt Mill wanted to control the excesses of both the market economy and the majoritarian polity, by the education of consumers and producers, citizens and politicians, in the interest of producing morally improved free market and democratic orders. But in contrast to Marx, he did not thoroughly discount the possibilities of improving the capitalist and democratic order.

Marx argued that as long as capitalism and private property existed there could be no genuine democracy, that democracy under capitalism was bourgeois democracy, which is to say not democracy at all. While it would be in the interest of the working classes to enter a coalition with the bourgeoisie in supporting this form of democracy in order to eliminate feudalism, this would be a tactical maneuver. Capitalist democracy could only result in the increasing exploitation of the working classes. Only the elimination of capitalism and private property could result in the emancipation of the working classes and the attainment of true democracy. Once socialism was attained the basic political problems of humanity would have been solved through the elimination of classes. Under socialism there would be no distinctive democratic organization, no need for institutions to resolve conflicts, since there would be no conflicts. There is not much democratic or political theory to be found in Marx's writings. The basic reality is the mode of economic production and the consequent class structure from which other institutions follow.

For the followers of Marx up to the present day there continues to be a negative tension between capitalism, however reformed, and democracy. But the integral Marxist and Leninist rejection of the possibility of an autonomous, bourgeois democratic state has been left behind for most Western Marxists. In the thinking of Poulantzas, Offe, Bobbio, Habermas and others, the bourgeois democratic state is now viewed as a class struggle state, rather than an unambiguously bourgeois state. The working class has access to it; it can struggle for its interests, and can attain partial benefits from it. The state is now viewed as autonomous, or as relatively autonomous, and it can be reformed in a progressive direction by working class and other popular movements. The bourgeois democratic state can be moved in the direction of a socialist state by political action short of violence and institutional destruction.

Schumpeter (1942) appreciated the tension between capitalism and democracy. While he saw a causal connection between competition in the economic and the political order, he points out ". . . that there are some deviations from the principle of democracy which link up with the presence of organized capitalist interests. . . . [T]he statement is true both from the standpoint of the classical and from the standpoint of our own theory of democracy. From the first standpoint, the result reads that the means at the disposal of private interests are often used in order to thwart the will of the people. From the second standpoint, the result reads that those private means are often used in order to interfere with the working of the mechanism of competitive leadership." He refers to some countries and situations in which ". . . political life all but resolved itself into a struggle of pressure groups and in many cases practices that failed to conform to the spirit of the democratic method." But he rejects the notion that there cannot be political democracy in a capitalist society. For Schumpeter full democracy in the sense of the informed participation of all adults in the selection of political leaders and consequently the making of public policy, was an impossibility because of the number and complexity of the issues confronting modern electorates. The democracy which was realistically possible was one in which people could choose among competing leaders, and consequently exercise some direction over political decisions. This kind of democracy was possible in a capitalist society, though some of its propensities impaired its performance. Writing in the early years of World War II, when the future of democracy and of capitalism were uncertain, he leaves unresolved the questions of ". . . Whether or not democracy is one of those products of capitalism which are to die out with it . . ." or ". . . how well or ill capitalist society qualifies for the task of working the democratic method it evolved."

Non-Marxist political theorists have contributed to this questioning of the reconcilability of capitalism and democracy. Robert A. Dahl, who makes the point that capitalism historically has been a necessary precondition of democracy, views contemporary democracy in the United States as seriously compromised, impaired by the inequality in resources among the citizens. But Dahl stresses the variety in distributive patterns, and in politico-economic relations among contemporary democracies. "The category of capitalist democracies" he writes, "includes an extraordinary variety . . . from nineteenth century, laissez faire, early industrial systems to twentieth century, highly regulated, social welfare, late or postindustrial systems. Even late twentieth century 'welfare state' orders vary all the way from the Scandinavian systems, which are redistributive, heavily taxed, comprehensive in their social security, and neocorporatist in their collective bargaining arrangements to the faintly redistributive, moderately taxed, limited social security, weak collective bargaining systems of the United States and Japan" (1989).

In *Democracy and Its Critics* (1989) Dahl argues that the normative growth of democracy to what he calls its "third transformation" (the first being the direct city-state democracy of classic times, and the second, the indirect, representative inegalitarian democracy of the contemporary world) will require democratization of the economic order. In other words, modern corporate capitalism needs to be transformed. Since government control and/or ownership of the economy would be destructive of the pluralism which is an essential requirement of democracy, his preferred solution to the problem of the mega-corporation is employee control of corporate industry. An economy so organized, according to Dahl, would improve the distribution of political resources without at the same time destroying the pluralism which democratic competition requires. To those who question the realism of Dahl's solution to the problem of inequality, he replies that history is full of surprises.

Charles E. Lindblom in his book, *Politics and Markets* (1977), concludes his comparative analysis of the political economy of modern capitalism and socialism, with an essentially pessimistic conclusion about contemporary market-oriented democracy. He says

> We therefore come back to the corporation. It is possible that the rise of the corporation has offset or more than offset the decline of class as an instrument of indoctrination. . . . That it creates a new core of wealth and power for a newly constructed upper class, as well as an overpowering loud voice, is also reasonably clear. The executive of the large corporation is, on many counts, the contemporary counterpart to the landed gentry of an earlier era, his voice amplified by the technology of mass communication. . . . [T]he major institutional barrier to fuller democracy may therefore be the autonomy of the private corporation.

Lindblom concludes, "The large private corporation fits oddly into democratic theory and vision. Indeed it does not fit.

There is then a widely shared agreement, from the Marxists and neo-Marxists, to Schumpeter, Dahl, Lindblom, and other liberal political theorists, that modern capitalism with the dominance of the large corporation, produces a defective or an impaired form of democracy.

Democracy Subverts Capitalism

If we change our perspective now and look at the way democracy is said to affect capitalism, one of the dominant traditions of economics from Adam Smith until the present day stresses the importance for productivity and welfare of an economy that is relatively free of intervention by the state. In this doctrine of minimal government there is still a place for a framework of rules and services essential to the productive and efficient performance of the economy. In part the government has to protect the market from itself. Left to their own devices, according to

Smith, businessmen were prone to corner the market in order to exact the highest possible price. And according to Smith businessmen were prone to bribe public officials in order to gain special privileges, and legal monopolies. For Smith good capitalism was competitive capitalism, and good government provided just those goods and services which the market needed to flourish, could not itself provide, or would not provide. A good government according to Adam Smith was a minimal government, providing for the national defense, and domestic order. Particularly important for the economy were the rules pertaining to commercial life such as the regulation of weights and measures, setting and enforcing building standards, providing for the protection of persons and property, and the like.

For Milton Friedman (1961, 1981), the leading contemporary advocate of the free market and free government, and of the interdependence of the two, the principal threat to the survival of capitalism and democracy is the assumption of the responsibility for welfare on the part of the modern democratic state. He lays down a set of functions appropriate to government in the positive interplay between economy and polity, and then enumerates many of the ways in which the modern welfare, regulatory state has deviated from these criteria.

A good Friedmanesque, democratic government would be one ". . . which maintained law and order, defended property rights, served as a means whereby we could modify property rights and other rules of the economic game, adjudicated disputes about the interpretation of the rules, enforced contracts, promoted competition, provided a monetary framework, engaged in activities to counter technical monopolies and to overcome neighborhood effects widely regarded as sufficiently important to justify government intervention, and which supplemented private charity and the private family in protecting the irresponsible, whether madman or child. . . ." Against this list of proper activities for a free government, Friedman pinpointed more than a dozen activities of contemporary democratic governments which might better be performed through the private sector, or not at all. These included setting and maintaining price supports, tariffs, import and export quotas and controls, rents, interest rates, wage rates, and the like, regulating industries and banking, radio and television, licensing professions and occupations, providing social security and medical care programs, providing public housing, national parks, guaranteeing mortgages, and much else.

Friedman concludes that this steady encroachment on the private sector has been slowly but surely converting our free government and market system into a collective monster, compromising both freedom and productivity in the outcome. The tax and expenditure revolts and regulatory rebellions of the 1980s have temporarily stemmed this trend, but the threat continues. "It is the internal threat coming from men of good intentions and good will who wish to reform us. Impatient with the slowness of persuasion and example to achieve the great social changes they envision, they are anxious to use the power of the state to achieve their ends, and confident of their own ability to do so." The threat to political and economic freedom, according to Milton Friedman and others who argue the same position, arises out of democratic politics. It may only be defeated by political action.

In the last decades a school, or rather several schools, of economists and political scientists have turned the theoretical models of economics to use in analyzing political processes. Variously called public choice theorists, rational choice theorists, or positive political theorists, and employing such models as market exchange and bargaining, rational self interest, game theory, and the like, these theorists have produced a substantial literature throwing new and often controversial light on democratic political phenomena such as elections, decisions of political party leaders, interest group behavior, legislative and committee decisions, bureaucratic, and judicial behavior, lobbying activity, and substantive public policy areas such as constitutional arrangements, health and environment policy, regulatory policy, national security and foreign policy, and the like. Hardly a field of politics and public policy has been left untouched by this inventive and productive group of scholars.

The institutions and names with which this movement is associated in the United States include Virginia State University, the University of Virginia, the George Mason University, the University of Rochester, the University of Chicago, the California Institute of Technology, the Carnegie Mellon University, among others. And the most prominent names are those of the leaders of the two principal schools: James Buchanan, the Nobel Laureate leader of the Virginia "Public Choice" school, and William Riker, the leader of the Rochester "Positive Theory" school. Other prominent scholars associated with this work are Gary Becker of the University of Chicago, Kenneth Shepsle and Morris Fiorina of Harvard, John Ferejohn of Stanford, Charles Plott of the California Institute of Technology, and many others.

One writer summarizing the ideological bent of much of this work, but by no means all of it (William Mitchell of the University of Washington), describes it as fiscally conservative, sharing a conviction that the ". . . private economy is far more robust, efficient, and perhaps, equitable than other economies, and much more successful than political processes in efficiently allocating resources. . . ." Much of what has been produced ". . . by James Buchanan and the leaders of this school can best be described as contributions to a theory of the failure of political processes." These failures of political performance are said to be inherent properties of the democratic political process. "Inequity, inefficiency, and coercion are the most general results of democratic policy formation." In a democracy the demand for publicly provided services seems to be insatiable. It ultimately turns into a special interest, "rent seeking" society. Their remedies take the form of proposed constitutional limits on spending power and checks and balances to limit legislative majorities.

One of the most visible products of this pessimistic economic analysis of democratic politics is the book by Mancur Olson, *The Rise and Decline of Nations* (1982). He makes a strong argument for the negative democracy–capitalism connection. His thesis is that the behavior of individuals and firms in stable societies inevitably leads to the formation of dense networks of collusive, cartelistic, and lobbying organizations that make economies less efficient and dynamic and polities less governable. "The longer a society goes without an upheaval, the more powerful such organizations become and the more they slow

down economic expansion. Societies in which these narrow interest groups have been destroyed, by war or revolution, for example, enjoy the greatest gains in growth." His prize cases are Britain on the one hand and Germany and Japan on the other.

> The logic of the argument implies that countries that have had democratic freedom of organization without upheaval or invasion the longest will suffer the most from growth-repressing organizations and combinations. This helps explain why Great Britain, the major nation with the longest immunity from dictatorship, invasion, and revolution, has had in this century a lower rate of growth than other large, developed democracies. Britain has precisely the powerful network of special interest organization that the argument developed here would lead us to expect in a country with its record of military security and democratic stability. The number and power of its trade unions need no description. The venerability and power of its professional associations is also striking. . . . In short, with age British society has acquired so many strong organizations and collusions that it suffers from an institutional sclerosis that slows its adaptation to changing circumstances and technologies. (Olson 1982)

By contrast, post-World War II Germany and Japan started organizationally from scratch. The organizations that led them to defeat were all dissolved, and under the occupation inclusive organizations like the general trade union movement and general organizations of the industrial and commercial community were first formed. These inclusive organizations had more regard for the general national interest and exercised some discipline on the narrower interest organizations. And both countries in the post-war decades experienced "miracles" of economic growth under democratic conditions.

The Olson theory of the subversion of capitalism through the propensities of democratic societies to foster special interest groups has not gone without challenge. There can be little question that there is logic in his argument. But empirical research testing this pressure group hypothesis thus far has produced mixed findings. Olson has hopes that a public educated to the harmful consequences of special interests to economic growth, full employment, coherent government, equal opportunity, and social mobility will resist special interest behavior, and enact legislation imposing anti-trust, and anti-monopoly controls to mitigate and contain these threats. It is somewhat of an irony that the solution to this special interest disease of democracy, according to Olson, is a democratic state with sufficient regulatory authority to control the growth of special interest organizations.

Democracy Fosters Capitalism

My fourth theme, democracy as fostering and sustaining capitalism, is not as straightforward as the first three. Historically there can be little doubt that as the suffrage was extended in the last century, and as mass political parties developed, democratic development impinged significantly on capitalist institutions and practices. Since successful capitalism requires risk-taking entrepreneurs with access to investment capital, the democratic propensity for redistributive and regulative policy tends to reduce the incentives and the resources available for risk-taking and creativity. Thus it can be argued that propensities inevitably resulting from democratic politics, as Friedman, Olson and many others argue, tend to reduce productivity, and hence welfare.

But precisely the opposite argument can be made on the basis of the historical experience of literally all of the advanced capitalist democracies in existence. All of them without exception are now welfare states with some form and degree of social insurance, health and welfare nets, and regulatory frameworks designed to mitigate the harmful impacts and shortfalls of capitalism. Indeed, the welfare state is accepted all across the political spectrum. Controversy takes place around the edges. One might make the argument that had capitalism not been modified in this welfare direction, it is doubtful that it would have survived.

This history of the interplay between democracy and capitalism is clearly laid out in a major study involving European and American scholars, entitled *The Development of Welfare States in Western Europe and America* (Flora and Heidenheimer 1981). The book lays out the relationship between the development and spread of capitalist industry, democratization in the sense of an expanding suffrage and the emergence of trade unions and left-wing political parties, and the gradual introduction of the institutions and practices of the welfare state. The early adoption of the institutions of the welfare state in Bismarck Germany, Sweden, and Great Britain were all associated with the rise of trade unions and socialist parties in those countries. The decisions made by the upper and middle class leaders and political movements to introduce welfare measures such as accident, old age, and unemployment insurance, were strategic decisions. They were increasingly confronted by trade union movements with the capacity of bringing industrial production to a halt, and by political parties with growing parliamentary representation favoring fundamental modifications in, or the abolition of capitalism. As the calculations of the upper and middle class leaders led them to conclude that the costs of suppression exceeded the costs of concession, the various parts of the welfare state began to be put in place—accident, sickness, unemployment insurance, old age insurance, and the like. The problem of maintaining the loyalty of the working classes through two world wars resulted in additional concessions to working class demands: the filling out of the social security system, free public education to higher levels, family allowances, housing benefits, and the like.

Social conditions, historical factors, political processes and decisions produced different versions of the welfare state. In the United States, manhood suffrage came quite early, the later bargaining process emphasized free land and free education to the secondary level, an equality of opportunity version of the welfare state. The Disraeli bargain in Britain resulted in relatively early manhood suffrage and the full attainment of parliamentary government, while the Lloyd George bargain on the eve of World War I brought the beginnings of a welfare system to Britain. The Bismarck bargain in Germany produced an early welfare state, a postponement of electoral equality and parliamentary government. While there were all of these differences in historical encounters with democratization and "welfarization," the important outcome was that little more than a century after the process began all of the advanced capitalist democracies had similar versions of the welfare state, smaller in scale in the case of the United States and Japan, more substantial in Britain and the continental European countries.

We can consequently make out a strong case for the argument that democracy has been supportive of capitalism in this strategic sense. Without this welfare adaptation it is doubtful that capitalism would have survived, or rather, its survival, "unwelfarized," would have required a substantial repressive apparatus. The choice then would seem to have been between democratic welfare capitalism, and repressive undemocratic capitalism. I am inclined to believe that capitalism as such thrives more with the democratic welfare adaptation than with the repressive one. It is in that sense that we can argue that there is a clear positive impact of democracy on capitalism.

We have to recognize, in conclusion, that democracy and capitalism are both positively and negatively related, that they both support and subvert each other. My colleague, Moses Abramovitz, described this dialectic more surely than most in his presidential address to the American Economic Association in 1980, on the eve of the "Reagan Revolution." Noting the decline in productivity in the American economy during the latter 1960s and '70s, and recognizing that this decline might in part be attributable to the "tax, transfer, and regulatory" tendencies of the welfare state, he observes,

> The rationale supporting the development of our mixed economy sees it as a pragmatic compromise between the competing virtues and defects of decentralized market capitalism and encompassing socialism. Its goal is to obtain a measure of distributive justice, security, and social guidance of economic life without losing too much of the allocative efficiency and dynamism of private enterprise and market organization. And it is a pragmatic compromise in another sense. It seeks to retain for most people that measure of personal protection from the state which private property and a private job market confer, while obtaining for the disadvantaged minority of people through the state that measure of support without which their lack of property or personal endowment would amount to a denial of individual freedom and capacity to function as full members of the community. (Abramovitz 1981)

Democratic welfare capitalism produces that reconciliation of opposing and complementary elements which makes possible the survival, even enhancement of both of these sets of institutions. It is not a static accommodation, but rather one which fluctuates over time, with capitalism being compromised by the tax-transfer-regulatory action of the state at one point, and then correcting in the direction of the reduction of the intervention of the state at another point, and with a learning process over time that may reduce the amplitude of the curves.

The case for this resolution of the capitalism-democracy quandary is made quite movingly by Jacob Viner who is quoted in the concluding paragraph of Abramovitz's paper, ". . . If . . . I nevertheless conclude that I believe that the welfare state, like old Siwash, is really worth fighting for and even dying for as compared to any rival system, it is because, despite its imperfection in theory and practice, in the aggregate it provides more promise of preserving and enlarging human freedoms, temporal prosperity, the extinction of mass misery, and the dignity of man and his moral improvement than any other social system which has previously prevailed, which prevails elsewhere today or which outside Utopia, the mind of man has been able to provide a blueprint for" (Abramovitz 1981).

References

Abramovitz, Moses. 1981. "Welfare Quandaries and Productivity Concerns." *American Economic Review*, March.

Berger, Peter. 1986. *The Capitalist Revolution*. New York: Basic Books.

Dahl, Robert A. 1989. *Democracy and Its Critics*. New Haven: Yale University Press.

_____. 1990. *After the Revolution: Authority in a Good Society*. New Haven: Yale University Press.

Deutsch, Karl. 1961. "Social Mobilization and Political Development." *American Political Science Review*, 55 (Sept.).

Flora, Peter, and Arnold Heidenheimer. 1981. *The Development of Welfare States in Western Europe and America*. New Brunswick, NJ: Transaction Press.

Friedman, Milton. 1981. *Capitalism and Freedom*. Chicago: University of Chicago Press.

Hirschman, Albert. 1986. *Rival Views of Market Society*. New York: Viking.

Inkeles, Alex, and David Smith. 1974. *Becoming Modern: Individual Change in Six Developing Countries*. Cambridge, MA: Harvard University Press.

Lerner, Daniel. 1958. *The Passing of Traditional Society*. New York: Free Press.

Lindblom, Charles E. 1977. *Politics and Markets*. New York: Basic Books.

Lipset, Seymour M. 1959. "Some Social Requisites of Democracy." *American Political Science Review*, 53 (September).

Mill, John Stuart. 1848, 1965. *Principles of Political Economy*, 2 vols. Toronto: University of Toronto Press.

Mitchell, William. 1988. "Virginia, Rochester, and Bloomington: Twenty-Five Years of Public Choice and Political Science." *Public Choice*, 56: 101–119.

Moore, Barrington. 1966. *The Social Origins of Dictatorship and Democracy*. New York: Beacon Press.

Olson, Mancur. 1982. *The Rise and Decline of Nations*. New Haven: Yale University Press.

Schumpeter, Joseph. 1946. *Capitalism, Socialism, and Democracy*. New York: Harper.

GABRIEL A. ALMOND, professor of political science emeritus at Stanford University, is a former president of the American Political Science Association.

From *PS: Political Science and Politics,* by Gabriel A. Almond, September 1991, pp. 467–474. Copyright © 1991 by American Political Science Association. Reprinted by permission.

Cultural Explanations
The Man in the Baghdad Café

Which "civilisation" you belong to matters less than you might think

Goering, it was said, growled that every time he heard the word culture he reached for his revolver. His hand would ache today. Since the end of the cold war, "culture" has been everywhere—not the opera-house or gallery kind, but the sort that claims to be the basic driving force behind human behaviour. All over the world, scholars and politicians seek to explain economics, politics and diplomacy in terms of "culture-areas" rather than, say, policies or ideas, economic interests, personalities or plain cock-ups.

Perhaps the best-known example is the notion that "Asian values" explain the success of the tiger economies of South-East Asia. Other accounts have it that international conflict is—or will be—caused by a clash of civilisations; or that different sorts of business organisation can be explained by how much people in different countries trust one [an]other. These four pages review the varying types of cultural explanation. They conclude that culture is so imprecise and changeable a phenomenon that it explains less than most people realise.

To see how complex the issue is, begin by considering the telling image with which Bernard Lewis opens his history of the Middle East. A man sits at a table in a coffee house in some Middle Eastern city, "drinking a cup of coffee or tea, perhaps smoking a cigarette, reading a newspaper, playing a board game, and listening with half an ear to whatever is coming out of the radio or the television installed in the corner." Undoubtedly Arab, almost certainly Muslim, the man would clearly identify himself as a member of these cultural groups. He would also, if asked, be likely to say that "western culture" was alien, even hostile to them.

Look closer, though, and the cultural contrasts blur. This coffee-house man probably wears western-style clothes—sneakers, jeans, a T-shirt. The chair and table at which he sits, the coffee he drinks, the tobacco he smokes, the newspaper he reads, all are western imports. The radio and television are western inventions. If our relaxing friend is a member of his nation's army, he probably operates western or Soviet weapons and trains according to western standards; if he belongs to the government, both his bureaucratic surroundings and the constitutional trappings of his regime may owe their origins to western influence.

The upshot, for Mr Lewis, is clear enough. "In modern times," he writes, "the dominating factor in the consciousness of most Middle Easterners has been the impact of Europe, later

of the West more generally, and the transformation—some would say dislocation—which it has brought." Mr Lewis has put his finger on the most important and least studied aspect of cultural identity: how it changes. It would be wise to keep that in mind during the upsurge of debate about culture that is likely to follow the publication of Samuel Huntington's new book, "The Clash of Civilisations and the Remaking of World Order".

The Clash of Civilisations

A professor of international politics at Harvard and the chairman of Harvard's Institute for Strategic Planning, Mr Huntington published in 1993, in *Foreign Affairs*, an essay which that quarterly's editors said generated more discussion than any since George Kennan's article (under the by-line "x") which argued in July 1947 for the need to contain the Soviet threat. Henry Kissinger, a former secretary of state, called Mr Huntington's book-length version of the article "one of the most important books . . . since the end of the cold war."

The article, "The Clash of Civilisation?", belied the question-mark in its title by predicting wars of culture. "It is my hypothesis", Mr Huntington wrote, "that the fundamental source of conflict in this new world will not be primarily ideological or primarily economic. The great division among humankind and the dominating source of conflict will be cultural."

After the cold war, ideology seemed less important as an organising principle of foreign policy. Culture seemed a plausible candidate to fill the gap. So future wars, Mr Huntington claimed, would occur "between nations and groups of different civilisations"—western, Confucian, Japanese, Islamic, Hindu, Orthodox and Latin American, perhaps African and Buddhist. Their disputes would "dominate global politics" and the battle-lines of the future would follow the fault-lines between these cultures.

No mincing words there, and equally few in his new book:

Culture and cultural identities . . . are shaping the patterns of cohesion, disintegration and conflict in the post-cold war world . . . Global politics is being reconfigured along cultural lines.

Mr Huntington is only one of an increasing number of writers placing stress on the importance of cultural values and institutions in the confusion left in the wake of the cold war. He looked at the influence of culture on international conflict. Three other schools of thought find cultural influences at work in different ways.

- **Culture and the economy**. Perhaps the oldest school holds that cultural values and norms equip people—and, by extension, countries—either poorly or well for economic success. The archetypal modern pronouncement of this view was Max Weber's investigation of the Protestant work ethic. This, he claimed, was the reason why the Protestant parts of Germany and Switzerland were more successful economically than the Catholic areas. In the recent upsurge of interest in issues cultural, a handful of writers have returned to the theme.

It is "values and attitudes—culture", claims Lawrence Harrison, that are "mainly responsible for such phenomena as Latin America's persistent instability and inequity, Taiwan's and Korea's economic 'miracles', and the achievements of the Japanese." Thomas Sowell offers other examples in "Race and Culture: A World View". "A disdain for commerce and industry", he argues, "has . . . been common for centuries among the Hispanic elite, both in Spain and in Latin America." Academics, though, have played a relatively small part in this debate: the best-known exponent of the thesis that "Asian values"—a kind of Confucian work ethic—aid economic development has been Singapore's former prime minister, Lee Kuan Yew.

- **Culture as social blueprint**. A second group of analysts has looked at the connections between cultural factors and political systems. Robert Putnam, another Harvard professor, traced Italy's social and political institutions to its "civic culture", or lack thereof. He claimed that, even today, the parts of Italy where democratic institutions are most fully developed are similar to the areas which first began to generate these institutions in the 14th century. His conclusion is that democracy is not something that can be put on like a coat; it is part of a country's social fabric and takes decades, even centuries, to develop.

Francis Fukuyama, of George Mason University, takes a slightly different approach. In a recent book which is not about the end of history, he focuses on one particular social trait, "trust". "A nation's well-being, as well as its ability to compete, is conditioned by a single, pervasive cultural characteristic: the level of trust inherent in the society," he says. Mr Fukuyama argues that "low-trust" societies such as China, France and Italy—where close relations between people do not extend much beyond the family—are poor at generating large, complex social institutions like multinational corporations; so they are at a competitive disadvantage compared with "high-trust" nations such as Germany, Japan and the United States.

- **Culture and decision-making**. The final group of scholars has looked at the way in which cultural assumptions act like blinkers. Politicians from different

countries see the same issue in different ways because of their differing cultural backgrounds. Their electorates or nations do, too. As a result, they claim, culture acts as an international barrier. As Ole Elgstrom puts it: "When a Japanese prime minister says that he will 'do his best' to implement a certain policy," Americans applaud a victory but "what the prime minister really meant was 'no'." There are dozens of examples of misperception in international relations, ranging from Japanese-American trade disputes to the misreading of Saddam Hussein's intentions in the weeks before he attacked Kuwait.

What Are They Talking About?

All of this is intriguing, and much of it is provocative. It has certainly provoked a host of arguments. For example, is Mr Huntington right to lump together all European countries into one culture, though they speak different languages, while separating Spain and Mexico, which speak the same one? Is the Catholic Philippines western or Asian? Or: if it is true (as Mr Fukuyama claims) that the ability to produce multinational firms is vital to economic success, why has "low-trust" China, which has few such companies, grown so fast? And why has yet-more successful "low-trust" South Korea been able to create big firms?

This is nit-picking, of course. But such questions of detail matter because behind them lurks the first of two fundamental doubts that plague all these cultural explanations: how do you define what a culture is?

In their attempts to define what cultures are (and hence what they are talking about), most "culture" writers rely partly on self definition: cultures are what people think of themselves as part of. In Mr Hungtington's words, civilisation "is the broadest level of identification with which [a person] intensely identifies."

The trouble is that relatively few people identify "intensely" with broad cultural groups. They tend to identify with something narrower: nations or ethnic groups. Europe is a case in point. A poll done last year for the European Commission found that half the people of Britain, Portugal and Greece thought of themselves in purely national terms; so did a third of the Germans, Spaniards and Dutch. And this was in a part of the world where there is an institution—the EU itself—explicitly devoted to the encouragement of "Europeanness".

The same poll found that in every EU country, 70% or more thought of themselves either purely in national terms, or primarily as part of a nation and only secondly as Europeans. Clearly, national loyalty can coexist with wider cultural identification. But, even then, the narrower loyalty can blunt the wider one because national characteristics often are—or at least are often thought to be—peculiar or unique. Seymour Martin Lipset, a sociologist who recently published a book about national characteristics in the United States, called it "American Exceptionalism". David Willetts, a British Conservative member of Parliament, recently claimed that the policies espoused by the opposition Labour Party would go against the grain of "English exceptionalism". And these are the two components of western culture supposedly most like one another.

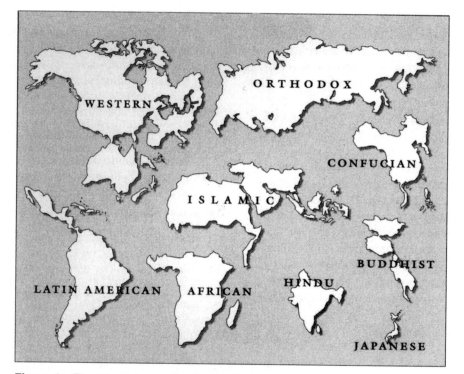

Figure 1 The World According to Huntington.

Source: Adapted by The Economist from "The Clash of Civilisations and the Remaking of World Order" by Samuel Huntington

In Islamic countries, the balance between cultural and national identification may be tilted towards the culture. But even here the sense of, say, Egyptian or Iraqi or Palestinian nationhood remains strong. (Consider the competing national feelings unleashed during the Iran-Iraq war.) In other cultures, national loyalty seems preeminent: in Mr Huntington's classification, Thailand, Tibet and Mongolia all count as "Buddhist". It is hard to imagine that a Thai, a Tibetan and a Mongolian really have that much in common.

So the test of subjective identification is hard to apply. That apart, the writers define a culture in the usual terms: language, religion, history, customs and institutions and so on. Such multiple definitions ring true. As Bernard Lewis's man in the Levantine café suggests, cultures are not singular things: they are bundles of characteristics.

The trouble is that such characteristics are highly ambiguous. Some push one way, some another.

Culture as Muddle

Islamic values, for instance, are routinely assumed to be the antithesis of modernising western ones. In Islam, tradition is good; departure from tradition is presumed to be bad until proven otherwise. Yet, at the same time, Islam is also a monotheistic religion which encourages rationalism and science. Some historians have plausibly argued that it was the Islamic universities of medieval Spain that kept science and rationalism alive during Europe's Dark Ages, and that Islam was a vital medieval link between the ancient world of Greece and Rome and the Renaissance. The scientific-rationalist aspect of Islam could well come to the fore again.

If you doubt it, consider the case of China and the "Confucian tradition" (a sort of proxy for Asian values). China has been at various times the world's most prosperous country and also one of its poorest. It has had periods of great scientific innovation and times of technological backwardness and isolation. Accounts of the Confucian tradition have tracked this path. Nowadays, what seems important about the tradition is its encouragement of hard work, savings and investment for the future, plus its emphasis on co-operation towards a single end. All these features have been adduced to explain why the tradition has helped Asian growth.

To Max Weber, however, the same tradition seemed entirely different. He argued that the Confucian insistence on obedience to parental authority discouraged competition and innovation and hence inhibited economic success. And China is not the only country to have been systematically misdiagnosed in this way. In countries as varied as Japan, India, Ghana and South Korea, notions of cultural determination of economic performance have been proved routinely wrong (in 1945, India and Ghana were expected to do best of the four—partly because of their supposed cultural inheritance).

If you take an extreme position, you could argue from this that cultures are so complicated that they can never be used to explain behaviour accurately. Even if you do not go that far, the lesson must be that the same culture embraces such conflicting features that it can produce wholly different effects at different times.

That is hard enough for the schools of culture to get to grips with. But there is worse to come. For cultures never operate in isolation. When affecting how people behave, they are always part of a wider mix. That mix includes government policies, personal leadership, technological or economic change and so on. For any one effect, there are always multiple causes. Which raises the second fundamental doubt about cultural explanations: how do you know whether it is culture—and not something else—that has caused some effect? You cannot. The problem of causation seems insoluble. The best you can do is work out whether, within the mix, culture is becoming more or less important.

Culture as Passenger

Of the many alternative explanations for events, three stand out: the influence of ideas, of government and what might be called the "knowledge era" (shorthand for globalisation, the growth of service-based industries and so forth). Of these, the influence of ideas as a giant organising principle is clearly not what it was when the cold war divided the world between communists and capitalists. We are all capitalists now. To that extent, it is fair to say that the ideological part of the mix has become somewhat less important—though not, as a few people have suggested, insignificant.

As for the government, it is a central thesis of the cultural writers that its influence is falling while that of culture is rising: cultures are in some ways replacing states. To quote Mr Huntington again "peoples and countries with similar cultures are coming together. Peoples and countries with different cultures are coming apart."

In several respects, that is counter-intuitive. Governments still control what is usually the single most powerful force in any country, the army. And, in all but the poorest places, governments tax and spend a large chunk of GDP—indeed, a larger chunk, in most places, than 50 years ago.

Hardly surprising, then, that governments influence cultures as much as the other way around. To take a couple of examples. Why does South Korea (a low-trust culture, remember) have so many internationally competitive large firms? The answer is that the government decided that it should. Or another case: since 1945 German politicians of every stripe have been insisting that they want to "save Germany from itself"—an attempt to assert political control over cultural identity.

South Korea and Germany are examples of governments acting positively to create something new. But governments can act upon cultures negatively: ie, they can destroy a culture when they collapse. Robert Kaplan, of an American magazine *Atlantic Monthly*, begins his book, "The Ends of the Earth", in Sierra Leone: "I had assumed that the random crime and social chaos of West Africa were the result of an already-fragile cultural base." Yet by the time he reaches Cambodia at the end of what he calls "a journey at the dawn of the 21st century" he is forced to reconsider that assumption:

Here I was . . . in a land where the written script was one thousand two hundred years old, and every surrounding country was in some stage of impressive economic growth. Yet Cambodia was eerily similar to Sierra Leone: with random crime, mosquito-borne disease, a government army that was more like a mob and a countryside that was ungovernable.

His conclusion is that "The effect of culture was more a mystery to me near the end of my planetary journey than at its beginning." He might have gone further: the collapse of governments causes cultural turbulence just as much as cultural turbulence causes the collapse of governments.

Culture as Processed Data

Then there is the "knowledge era". Here is a powerful and growing phenomenon. The culture writers do not claim anything different. Like the Industrial Revolution before it, the knowledge era—in which the creation, storage and use of knowledge becomes the basic economic activity—is generating huge change. Emphasising as it does rapid, even chaotic, transformation, it is anti-traditional and anti-authoritarian.

Yet the cultural exponents still claim that, even in the knowledge era, culture remains a primary engine of change. They do so for two quite different reasons. Some claim that the new era has the makings of a world culture. There is a universal language, English. There are the beginnings of an international professional class that cuts across cultural and national boundaries: increasingly, bankers, computer programmers, executives, even military officers are said to have as much in common with their opposite numbers in other countries as with their next-door neighbors. As Mr Fukuyama wrote in his more famous book: the "unfolding of modern natural science . . . guarantees an increasing homogenisation of all human societies." Others doubt that technology and the rest of it are producing a genuinely new world order. To them, all this is just modern western culture.

Either way, the notion that modernity is set on a collision course with culture lies near the heart of several of the culture writers' books. Summing them up is the title of Benjamin Barber's "Jihad versus McWorld". In other words, he argues that the main conflicts now and in future will be between tribal, local "cultural" values (Jihad) and a McWorld of technology and democracy.

It would be pointless to deny that globalisation is causing large changes in every society. It is also clear that such influences act on different cultures differently, enforcing a kind of natural selection between those cultures which rise to the challenge and those which do not.

But it is more doubtful that these powerful forces are primarily cultural or even western. Of course, they have a cultural component: the artefacts of American culture are usually the first things to come along in the wake of a new road, or new television networks. But the disruptive force itself is primarily economic and has been adopted as enthusiastically in Japan, Singapore and China as in America. The world market is not a cultural concept.

Moreover, to suggest that trade, globalisation and the rest of it tend to cause conflict, and then leave the argument there, is not enough. When you boil the argument down, much of it seems to be saying that the more countries trade with each other, the more likely they are to go to war. That seems implausible. Trade—indeed, any sort of link—is just as likely to reduce the potential for violent conflict as to increase it. The same goes for the spread of democracy, another feature which is supposed to encourage civilisations to clash with each other. This might well cause ructions within countries. It might well provoke complaints from dictators about "outside interference". But serious international conflict is a different matter. And if democracy really did spread round the world, it might tend to reduce violence; wealthy democracies, at any rate, are usually reluctant to go to war (though poor or angrily nationalist ones may, as history has shown, be much less reluctant).

In short, the "knowledge era" is spreading economic ideas. And these ideas have three cultural effects, not one. They make cultures rub against each other, causing international friction. They also tie different cultures closer together, which offsets the first effect. And they may well increase tensions within a culture-area as some groups accommodate themselves to the new world while others turn their back on it. And all this can be true at the same time because cultures are so varied and ambiguous that they are capable of virtually any transformation.

The conclusion must be that while culture will continue to exercise an important influence on both countries and individuals, it has not suddenly become more important than, say, governments or impersonal economic forces. Nor does it play the all-embracing defining role that ideology played during the cold war. Much of its influence is secondary, ie, it comes about partly as a reaction to the "knowledge era". And within the overall mix of what influences people's behaviour, culture's role may well be declining, rather than rising, squeezed between the greedy expansion of the government on one side, and globalisation on the other.

The books mentioned in this article are:

Benjamin Barber. Jihad versus McWorld (Random House; 1995; 400 pages; $12.95).

Francis Fukuyama. The End of History and the Last Man (Free Press; 1992; 419 pages; $24.95. Hamish Hamilton; £20.) and Trust: The Social Virtues and the Creation of Prosperity (Free Press; 1995; 480 pages; $25. Hamish Hamilton; £25).

Lawrence E. Harrison. Who Prospers? How Cultural Values Shape Economic and Political Success (Basic Books; 1992; 288 pages; $14).

Samuel Huntington. The Clash of Civilisations? *Foreign Affairs* Vol. 72 (Summer 1993) and The Clash of Civilisations and the Remaking of World Order (Simon & Schuster; 1996; 367 pages; $26).

Robert Kaplan. The Ends of the Earth (Random House; 1996; 475 pages; $27.50. Papermac; £10).

Bernard Lewis. The Middle East (Wiedenfeld & Nicolson; 1995; 433 pages; £20. Simon & Schuster; $29.50).

Seymour Martin Lipset. American Exceptionalism (Norton; 1996; 352 pages; $27.50 and £19.95).

Robert Putnam. Making Democracy Work: Civic Traditions in Modern Italy (Princeton; 1993; 288 pages; $24.95 and £18.95).

Thomas Sowell. Race and Culture: A World View (Basic Books; 1994; 331 pages; $14).

An Explosive Combination

Capitalism, democracy don't always go together as planned

AMY CHUA

In May 1998, Indonesian mobs swarmed the streets of Jakarta, looting and torching more than 5,000 ethnic Chinese shops and homes. One hundred and fifty Chinese women were gang-raped, and more than 2,000 people died.

In the months that followed, anti-Chinese hate-mongering and violence spread throughout Indonesia's cities. The explosion of rage can be traced to an unlikely source: the rapid combination of democracy and free markets—the very prescription wealthy democracies have promoted for healing the ills of underdevelopment.

How did things go so wrong?

During the 1980s and 1990s, Indonesia's aggressive shift to unrestrained free-market policies allow the country's Chinese minority, just 3 percent of the population, to take control of 70 percent of the private economy.

When Indonesians ousted President General Suharto in 1998, the country's poor majority rose up in a violent backlash against the Chinese minority and against markets. The democratic elections that abruptly followed 30 years of autocratic rule, while free and fair, were rife with ethnic scapegoating by indigenous politicians and calls for confiscation of Chinese wealth and a "People's Economy."

Today, the Indonesian government sits on $58 billion worth of nationalized assets, almost all formerly owned by Chinese tycoons. These once-productive assets now lie stagnant, while unemployment and poverty deepen.

What occurred in Indonesia is part of a pattern. It is the rule of unintended—but reasonably predicted—consequences. It is also a lesson for U.S. policy-makers in running postwar Iraq.

The reality is that given the conditions that actually exist now in many postcolonial countries—conditions created by history, colonialism, divide-and-conquer policies, corruption, autocracy—the combination of laissez-faire capitalism and unrestrained majority rule may well have catastrophic consequences.

Roots of Resentment

The notion that market democracy promotes peaceful prosperity has not always held sway. In the 18th and 19th centuries, most leading political philosophers and economists believed that market capitalism and democracy could only coexist in fundamental tension with each another. It is one of history's great surprises that Western nations succeeded so spectacularly in integrating markets and democracy.

Conditions in today's developing world, however, make the combination of markets and democracy much more volatile than was the case when Western nations embarked on their own paths to market democracy.

One reason has to do with scale: The poor are vastly more numerous, and poverty far more entrenched, in the developing world today.

Another has to do with process: Universal suffrage in developing countries is often implemented wholesale and abruptly—a destabilizing approach that is quite removed from the gradual enfranchisement seen during Western democratization.

But the most formidable problem the developing world faces is structural—and it's one that the West has little experience with.

It's the phenomenon of the market-dominant minority, ethnic minorities who tend under market conditions to dominate economically, often to an astounding extent, the impoverished "indigenous" majorities around them.

They're the Chinese in Southeast Asia, Indians in East Africa and the West Indies, Lebanese in West Africa, Kikuyu in Kenya, Ibo in Nigeria, Jews in post-Communist Russia, and whites in Zimbabwe, South Africa, and Bolivia, to name just a few.

It is crucial to recognize that groups can be market-dominant for widely different reasons, ranging from superior entrepreneurialism to a history of apartheid or colonial oppression. If, for example, as with whites in South Africa, a minority uses force to relegate the indigenous majority to inferior education and inhumane conditions for over a century, then that minority is likely to be market-dominant, for reasons that have nothing to do with culture.

In countries with a market-dominant minority, the rich are not just rich but belong to a resented "outsider" ethnic group.

In free-market environments, these minorities, together with foreign investors (who are often their business partners), tend to accumulate starkly disproportionate wealth, fueling ethnic envy and resentment among the poor majorities.

When democratic reforms give voice to this previously silenced majority, opportunistic demagogues can swiftly marshal majoritarian animosity into powerful ethnonationalist movements that can subvert both markets and democracy.

That's what happened in Indonesia and is happening around the world. The same dynamic—in which markets and democracy pit a poor, frustrated majority against a rich "outsider" minority—has produced retaliation, violence, and even mass slaughter of market-dominant minorities, from Croats in the former Yugoslavia to Tutsi in Rwanda.

A Stake in the Game

How can Western nations advance capitalism and democracy in the developing world without encouraging conflagration and bloodshed? They must stop promoting unrestrained, bare-knuckled capitalism (a form of markets that the West, itself, has repudiated) and unrestrained, overnight majority rule (a form of democracy Western nations have also repudiated).

Instead of encouraging a caricature of free-market democracy, they should follow their own successful model and sponsor the gradual introduction of democratic reforms, tailored to local circumstances.

They also should cultivate stabilizing institutions and programs such as social safety nets, tax-and-transfer programs, antitrust laws, philanthropy, constitutionalism and property protections. Most crucially, they must find ways to give the poor majorities of the world an ownership stake in their countries' corporations and capital markets.

In the United States, a solid majority of Americans, even members of the lower middle classes, own shares in major U.S. companies, often through pension funds, and thus have a stake in the U.S. market economy.

This is not the case in the developing world, where corporations are typically owned by single families belonging to a market-dominant minority. In South Africa as of June 2002, for example, blacks, although making up 77 percent of the population, controlled only 2 percent of the Johannesburg Stock Exchange's total capitalization.

Continued global democratization seems inevitable. But in this climate, international businesses, Western investors and market-dominant minorities should heed the lessons from Jakarta. It is an act of enlightened self-interest to launch highly visible local corporate responsibility initiatives and innovative profit-sharing programs.

Consider these models:

- In East Africa, powerful families of Indian descent include Africans in top management positions in their companies and provide education, training, and wealth-sharing schemes for their African employees.
- In Russia, where anti-Semitism is rampant, the Jewish billionaire Roman Abramovich was recently elected governor of Chukotka after spending tens of millions of dollars of his personal fortune to airlift food, medicine, computers and textbooks into the poverty-stricken region.

- In Central America, a few Western companies have started to contribute to local infrastructure development and to offer stock options to local employees.

In these ways, foreign investors and market-dominant minorities can give local populations a stake in their local economy and businesses. This is perhaps the best way to defuse tensions that, history tells us, can sabotage both markets and democracy, the very structures businesses need to thrive.

The Bush administration might consider these lessons as it decides how to rebuild Iraq.

Perhaps because of beliefs in the "melting pot" and America's own relatively successful—though halting and incomplete—history of ethnic assimilation, Americans don't always understand the significance of ethnicity, both in the United States and especially in other countries. Interestingly, British colonial governments were fastidiously conscious of ethnic divisions.

Of course, their ethnic policies are a dangerous model. When it was the British Empire's turn to deal with nation-building and ethnicity, the British engaged in divide-and-conquer policies, not only protecting but favoring ethnic minorities, and simultaneously aggravating ethnic resentments.

Laissez-faire markets and overnight democracy in Iraq could well favor different ethnic or religious groups in the short run, creating enormous instability.

As a result, when the British decamped, the time bombs often exploded, from Africa to India to Southeast Asia. This contrast can be seen in how the United States and Britain looked at the situation in postwar Iraq.

At least before the war, the U.S. government's ethnic policy for Iraq was essentially to have no ethnic policy. Instead, U.S. officials seemed strangely confident that Iraq's ethnic, religious, and tribal divisions would dissipate in the face of democracy and market-generated wealth.

But in countries as deeply divided as Iraq, everything—even freedom and wealth—has ethnic and sectarian ramifications. Who will comprise the police? Who has experience in engineering and oil or the skills to run a stock exchange? Given Saddam Hussein's sadistically unfair and repressive regime, some groups—namely, the Sunni minority, particularly the Ba'athists—will almost certainly have a head start in terms of education, capital, and economic and managerial experience.

Consequently, as is true in so many other non-Western countries, laissez-faire markets and overnight democracy in Iraq could well favor different ethnic or religious groups in the short run, creating enormous instability.

At the same time, because by analogy at the global level, the United States has come to be seen as a kind of global market-dominant minority—wielding wildly disproportionate power relative to our size and numbers—every move we make with respect to Iraq is being closely—and perhaps even unfairly—scrutinized.

Despite Hussein's barbarous gulags, gross human-rights violations and repeated refusals to comply with U.N. requirements, international public opinion was overwhelmingly against the United States going to war with Iraq.

It is important to see that this opposition to U.S. policies was closely bound up with deep feelings of resentment and fear of U.S. power and cynicism about American motives.

Deep ethnic and religious divisions remain in Iraq, but ironically one theme unifying the Iraqi people at the moment is their intensifying opposition to American and British occupation.

Many Americans are bewildered—outraged—at the depth and pervasiveness of anti-Americanism in the world today. "Why do so many people want to come here if we're so terrible?" frustrated Americans demand. "What would France be doing if it were the world's superpower?" "Why do they hate us?" These are reasonable points.

But the fact of the matter is that because the United States is the world's sole superpower, we are going to be held to a higher standard than everyone else—market-dominant minorities always are.

For this reason, it is in the United States' own interest to avoid taking actions that suggest hypocrisy, look glaringly exploitative, or display lack of concern for the rest of the world, including of course the people of Iraq.

It is easy to criticize the United States, just as it is easy to hide behind facile calls for "free-market democracy." With the international community watching, I prefer to view this moment as a critical opportunity for the United States to surprise a skeptical world.

One thing, however, is clear:

The United States cannot simply call for elections and universal suffrage and at the same time support an economic system that is seen as benefiting only a tiny, privileged minority—whether an ethnic or religious minority or U.S. and British companies.

To do so would be a recipe for disaster.

AMY CHUA is a professor of law at Yale University in New Haven, Conn., and the author of *World on Fire: How Exporting Free Market Democracy Breeds Ethnic Hatred and Global Instability* (Doubleday, 2003). Portions of this article previously appeared in the Harvard Business Review.

As seen in *Orlando Sentinel*, September 21, 2003, pp. G1, G4, adapted from *Harvard Business Review* (August 2003). Copyright © 2003 by Harvard Business School Publishing. Reprinted by permission.

Jihad vs. McWorld

The two axial principles of our age—tribalism and globalism—clash at every point except one: they may both be threatening to democracy

BENJAMIN R. BARBER

J ust beyond the horizon of current events lie two possible political figures—both bleak, neither democratic. The first is a retribalization of large swaths of humankind by war and bloodshed: a threatened Lebanonization of national states in which culture is pitted against culture, people against people, tribe against tribe—a Jihad in the name of a hundred narrowly conceived faiths against every kind of interdependence, every kind of artificial social cooperation and civic mutuality. The second is being borne in on us by the onrush of economic and ecological forces that demand integration and uniformity and that mesmerize the world with fast music, fast computers, and fast food—with MTV, Macintosh, and McDonald's, pressing nations into one commercially homogenous global network: one McWorld tied together by technology, ecology, communications, and commerce. The planet is falling precipitantly apart and coming reluctantly together at the very same moment.

These two tendencies are sometimes visible in the same countries at the same instant: thus Yugoslavia, clamoring just recently to join the New Europe, is exploding into fragments; India is trying to live up to its reputation as the world's largest integral democracy while powerful new fundamentalist parties like the Hindu nationalist Bharatiya Janta Party, along with nationalist assassins, are imperiling its hard-won unity. States are breaking up or joining up: the Soviet Union has disappeared almost overnight, its parts forming new unions with one another or with like-minded nationalities in neighboring states. The old interwar national state based on territory and political sovereignty looks to be a mere transitional development.

The tendencies of what I am here calling the forces of Jihad and the forces of McWorld operate with equal strength in opposite directions, the one driven by parochial hatreds, the other by universalizing markets, the one re-creating ancient subnational and ethnic borders from within, the other making national borders porous from without. They have one thing in common: neither offers much hope to citizens looking for practical ways to govern themselves democratically. If the global future is to pit Jihad's centrifugal whirlwind against McWorld's centripetal black hole, the outcome is unlikely to be democratic—or so I will argue.

McWorld, or the Globalization of Politics

Four imperatives make up the dynamic of McWorld: a market imperative, a resource imperative, an information-technology imperative, and an ecological imperative. By shrinking the world and diminishing the salience of national borders, these imperatives have in combination achieved a considerable victory over factiousness and particularism, and not least of all over their most virulent traditional form—nationalism. It is the realists who are now Europeans, the utopians who dream nostalgically of a resurgent England or Germany, perhaps even a resurgent Wales or Saxony. Yesterday's wishful cry for one world has yielded to the reality of McWorld.

The market imperative. Marxist and Leninist theories of imperialism assumed that the quest for ever-expanding markets would in time compel nation-based capitalist economies to push against national boundaries in search of an international economic imperium. Whatever else has happened to the scientistic predictions of Marxism, in this domain they have proved farsighted. All national economies are now vulnerable to the inroads of larger, transnational markets within which trade is free, currencies are convertible, access to banking is open, and contracts are enforceable under law. In Europe, Asia, Africa, the South Pacific, and the Americas such markets are eroding national sovereignty and giving rise to entities—international banks, trade associations, transnational lobbies like OPEC and Greenpeace, world news services like CNN and the BBC, and multinational corporations that increasingly lack a meaningful national identity—that neither reflect nor respect nationhood as an organizing or regulative principle.

The market imperative has also reinforced the quest for international peace and stability, requisites of an efficient international economy. Markets are enemies of parochialism, isolation, fractiousness, war. Market psychology attenuates the psychology of ideological and religious cleavages and assumes a concord among producers and consumers—categories that ill fit narrowly conceived national or religious cultures. Shopping has little tolerance for blue laws, whether dictated by pub-closing British paternalism, Sabbath-observing Jewish Orthodox fundamentalism, or no-Sunday-liquor-sales Massachusetts puritanism. In the context of common markets, international law ceases to be a vision of justice and becomes a workaday framework for getting things done—enforcing contracts, ensuring that governments abide by deals, regulating trade and currency relations, and so forth.

Common markets demand a common language, as well as a common currency, and they produce common behaviors of the kind bred by cosmopolitan city life everywhere. Commercial pilots, computer programmers, international bankers, media specialists, oil riggers, entertainment celebrities, ecology experts, demographers, accountants, professors, athletes—these compose a new breed of men and women for whom religion, culture, and nationality can seem only marginal elements in a working identity. Although sociologists of everyday life will no doubt continue to distinguish a Japanese from an American mode, shopping has a common signature throughout the world. Cynics might even say that some of the recent revolutions in Eastern Europe have had as their true goal not liberty and the right to vote but well-paying jobs and the right to shop (although the vote is proving easier to acquire than consumer goods). The market imperative is, then, plenty powerful; but, notwithstanding some of the claims made for "democratic capitalism," it is not identical with the democratic imperative.

The resource imperative. Democrats once dreamed of societies whose political autonomy rested firmly on economic independence. The Athenians idealized what they called autarky, and tried for a while to create a way of life simple and austere enough to make the polis genuinely self-sufficient. To be free meant to be independent of any other community or polis. Not even the Athenians were able to achieve autarky, however: human nature, it turns out, is dependency. By the time of Pericles, Athenian politics was inextricably bound up with a flowering empire held together by naval power and commerce —an empire that, even as it appeared to enhance Athenian might, ate away at Athenian independence and autarky. Master and slave, it turned out, were bound together by mutual insufficiency.

The dream of autarky briefly engrossed nineteenth-century America as well, for the underpopulated, endlessly bountiful land, the cornucopia of natural resources, and the natural barriers of a continent walled in by two great seas led many to believe that America could be a world unto itself. Given this past, it has been harder for Americans than for most to accept the inevitability of interdependence. But the rapid depletion of resources even in a country like ours, where they once seemed inexhaustible, and the maldistribution of arable soil and mineral resources on the planet, leave even the wealthiest societies ever more resource-dependent and many other nations in permanently desperate straits.

Every nation, it turns out, needs something another nation has; some nations have almost nothing they need.

The information-technology imperative. Enlightenment science and the technologies derived from it are inherently universalizing. They entail a quest for descriptive principles of general application, a search for universal solutions to particular problems, and an unswerving embrace of objectivity and impartiality.

Scientific progress embodies and depends on open communication, a common discourse rooted in rationality, collaboration, and an easy and regular flow and exchange of information. Such ideals can be hypocritical covers for power-mongering by elites, and they may be shown to be wanting in many other ways, but they are entailed by the very idea of science and they make science and globalization practical allies.

Business, banking, and commerce all depend on information flow and are facilitated by new communication technologies. The hardware of these technologies tends to be systemic and integrated—computer, television, cable, satellite, laser, fiber-optic, and microchip technologies combining to create a vast interactive communications and information network that can potentially give every person on earth access to every other person, and make every datum, every byte, available to every set of eyes. If the automobile was, as George Ball once said (when he gave his blessing to a Fiat factory in the Soviet Union during the Cold War), "an ideology on four wheels," then electronic telecommunication and information systems are an ideology at 186,000 miles per second—which makes for a very small planet in a very big hurry. Individual cultures speak particular languages; commerce and science increasingly speak English; the whole world speaks logarithms and binary mathematics.

Moreover, the pursuit of science and technology asks for, even compels, open societies. Satellite footprints do not respect national borders; telephone wires penetrate the most closed societies. With photocopying and then fax machines having infiltrated Soviet universities and *samizdat* literary circles in the eighties, and computer modems having multiplied like rabbits in communism's bureaucratic warrens thereafter, *glasnost* could not be far behind. In their social requisites, secrecy and science are enemies.

The new technology's software is perhaps even more globalizing than its hardware. The information arm of international commerce's sprawling body reaches out and touches distinct nations and parochial cultures, and gives them a common face chiseled in Hollywood, on Madison Avenue, and in Silicon Valley. Throughout the 1980s one of the most-watched television programs in South Africa was *The Cosby Show*. The demise of apartheid was already in production. Exhibitors at the 1991 Cannes film festival expressed growing anxiety over the "homogenization" and "Americanization" of the global film industry when, for the third year running, American films dominated the awards ceremonies. America has dominated the world's popular culture for much longer, and much more decisively. In November of 1991 Switzerland's once insular culture boasted best-seller lists featuring *Terminator 2* as the No. 1 movie, *Scarlett* as the No. 1 book, and Prince's *Diamonds and Pearls* as the No. 1 record album. No wonder the Japanese are buying Hollywood film studios even faster than Americans are buying Japanese television sets. This kind of software supremacy may in the long term be far more important than hardware superiority, because culture has become more potent than armaments. What is the power of the Pentagon compared with Disneyland? Can the Sixth Fleet keep up with CNN? McDonald's in Moscow and Coke in China will do more to create a global culture than military colonization ever could. It is less the goods than the brand names that do the work, for they convey life-style images that alter perception and challenge behavior. They make up the seductive software of McWorld's common (at times much too common) soul.

Yet in all this high-tech commercial world there is nothing that looks particularly democratic. It lends itself to surveillance as well as liberty, to new forms of manipulation and covert control as well as new kinds of participation, to skewed, unjust market outcomes as well as greater productivity. The consumer society and the open society are not quite synonymous. Capitalism and democracy have a relationship, but it is something less than a marriage. An efficient free market after all requires that consumers be free to vote their dollars on competing goods, not that citizens be free to vote their values and beliefs on competing political candidates and programs. The free market flourished in junta-run Chile, in military-governed Taiwan and Korea, and, earlier, in a variety of autocratic European empires as well as their colonial possessions.

The *ecological imperative*. The impact of globalization on ecology is a cliché even to world leaders who ignore it. We know well enough that the German forests can be destroyed by Swiss and Italians driving gas-guzzlers fueled by leaded gas. We also know that the planet can be asphyxiated by greenhouse gases because Brazilian farmers want to be part of the twentieth century and are burning down tropical rain forests to clear a little land to plough, and because Indonesians make a living out of converting their lush jungle into toothpicks for fastidious Japanese diners, upsetting the delicate oxygen balance and in effect puncturing our global lungs. Yet this ecological consciousness has meant not only greater awareness but also greater inequality, as modernized nations try to slam the door behind them, saying to developing nations, "The world cannot afford your modernization; ours has wrung it dry!"

Each of the four imperatives just cited is transnational, transideological, and transcultural. Each applies impartially to Catholics, Jews, Muslims, Hindus, and Buddhists; to democrats and totalitarians; to capitalists and socialists. The Enlightenment dream of a universal rational society has to a remarkable degree been realized—but in a form that is commercialized, homogenized, depoliticized, bureaucratized, and, of course, radically incomplete, for the movement toward McWorld is in competition with forces of global breakdown, national dissolution, and centrifugal corruption. These forces, working in the opposite direction, are the essence of what I call Jihad.

Jihad, or the Lebanonization of the World

OPEC, the World Bank, the United Nations, the International Red Cross, the multinational corporation . . . there are scores of institutions that reflect globalization. But they often appear as ineffective reactors to the world's real actors: national states and, to an ever greater degree, subnational factions in permanent rebellion against uniformity and integration—even the kind represented by universal law and justice. The headlines feature these players regularly: they are cultures, not countries; parts, not wholes; sects, not religions; rebellious factions and dissenting minorities at war not just with globalism but with the traditional nation-state. Kurds, Basques, Puerto Ricans, Ossetians, East Timoreans, Quebecois, the Catholics of Northern Ireland, Abkhasians, Kurile Islander Japanese, the Zulus of Inkatha, Catalonians, Tamils, and, of course, Palestinians—people without countries, inhabiting nations not their own, seeking smaller worlds within borders that will seal them off from modernity.

A powerful irony is at work here. Nationalism was once a force of integration and unification, a movement aimed at bringing together disparate clans, tribes, and cultural fragments under new, assimilationist flags. But as Ortega y Gasset noted more than sixty years ago, having won its victories, nationalism changed its strategy. In the 1920s, and again today, it is more often a reactionary and divisive force, pulverizing the very nations it once helped cement together. The force that creates nations is "inclusive," Ortega wrote in *The Revolt of the Masses*. "In periods of consolidation, nationalism has a positive value, and is a lofty standard. But in Europe everything is more than consolidated, and nationalism is nothing but a mania. . . ."

This mania has left the post-Cold War world smothering with hot wars; the international scene is little more unified than it was at the end of the Great War, in Ortega's own time. There were more than thirty wars in progress last year, most of them ethnic, racial, tribal, or religious in character, and the list of unsafe regions doesn't seem to be getting any shorter. Some new world order!

The aim of many of these small-scale wars is to redraw boundaries, to implode states and resecure parochial identities: to escape McWorld's dully insistent imperatives. The mood is that of Jihad: war not as an instrument of policy but as an emblem of identity, an expression of community, an end in itself. Even where there is no shooting war, there is fractiousness, secession, and the quest for ever smaller communities. Add to the list of dangerous countries those at risk: In Switzerland and Spain, Jurassian and Basque separatists still argue the virtues of ancient identities, sometimes in the language of bombs. Hyperdisintegration in the former Soviet Union may well continue unabated—not just a Ukraine independent from the Soviet Union but a Bessarabian Ukraine independent from the Ukrainian republic; not just Russia severed from the defunct union but Tatarstan severed from Russia. Yugoslavia makes even the disunited, ex-Soviet, nonsocialist republics that were once the Soviet Union look integrated, its sectarian fatherlands springing up within factional motherlands like weeds within weeds within weeds. Kurdish independence would threaten the territorial integrity of four Middle Eastern nations. Well before the current cataclysm Soviet Georgia made a claim for autonomy from the Soviet Union, only to be faced with its Ossetians (164,000 in a republic of 5.5 million) demanding their own self-determination within Georgia. The Abkhasian minority in Georgia has followed suit. Even the good will established by

Canada's once promising Meech Lake protocols is in danger, with Francophone Quebec again threatening the dissolution of the federation. In South Africa the emergence from apartheid was hardly achieved when friction between Inkatha's Zulus and the African National Congress's tribally identified members threatened to replace Europeans' racism with an indigenous tribal war. After thirty years of attempted integration using the colonial language (English) as a unifier, Nigeria is now playing with the idea of linguistic multiculturalism—which could mean the cultural breakup of the nation into hundreds of tribal fragments. Even Saddam Hussein has benefited from the threat of internal Jihad, having used renewed tribal and religious warfare to turn last season's mortal enemies into reluctant allies of an Iraqi nationhood that he nearly destroyed.

The passing of communism has torn away the thin veneer of internationalism (workers of the world unite!) to reveal ethnic prejudices that are not only ugly and deep-seated but increasingly murderous. Europe's old scourge, anti-Semitism, is back with a vengeance, but it is only one of many antagonisms. It appears all too easy to throw the historical gears into reverse and pass from a Communist dictatorship back into a tribal state.

Among the tribes, religion is also a battlefield. ("Jihad" is a rich world whose generic meaning is "struggle"—usually the struggle of the soul to avert evil. Strictly applied to religious war, it is used only in reference to battles where the faith is under assault, or battles against a government that denies the practice of Islam. My use here is rhetorical, but does follow both journalistic practice and history.) Remember the Thirty Years War? Whatever forms of Enlightenment universalism might once have come to grace such historically related forms of monotheism as Judaism, Christianity, and Islam, in many of their modern incarnations they are parochial rather than cosmopolitan, angry rather than loving, proselytizing rather than ecumenical, zealous rather than rationalist, sectarian rather than deistic, ethnocentric rather than universalizing. As a result, like the new forms of hypernationalism, the new expressions of religious fundamentalism are fractious and pulverizing, never integrating. This is religion as the Crusaders knew it: a battle to the death for souls that if not saved will be forever lost.

The atmospherics of Jihad have resulted in a breakdown of civility in the name of identity, of comity in the name of community. International relations have sometimes taken on the aspect of gang war—cultural turf battles featuring tribal factions that were supposed to be sublimated as integral parts of large national, economic, postcolonial, and constitutional entities.

The Darkening Future of Democracy

These rather melodramatic tableaux vivants do not tell the whole story, however. For all their defects, Jihad and McWorld have their attractions. Yet, to repeat and insist, the attractions are unrelated to democracy. Neither McWorld nor Jihad is remotely democratic in impulse. Neither needs democracy; neither promotes democracy.

McWorld does manage to look pretty seductive in a world obsessed with Jihad. It delivers peace, prosperity, and relative unity—if at the cost of independence, community, and identity (which is generally based on difference). The primary political values required by the global market are order and tranquility, and freedom—as in the phrases "free trade," "free press," and "free love." Human rights are needed to a degree, but not citizenship or participation—and no more social justice and equality than are necessary to promote efficient economic production and consumption. Multinational corporations sometimes seem to prefer doing business with local oligarchs, inasmuch as they can take confidence from dealing with the boss on all crucial matters. Despots who slaughter their own populations are no problem, so long as they leave markets in place and refrain from making war on their neighbors (Saddam Hussein's fatal mistake). In trading partners, predictability is of more value than justice.

The Eastern European revolutions that seemed to arise out of concern for global democratic values quickly deteriorated into a stampede in the general direction of free markets and their ubiquitous, television-promoted shopping malls. East Germany's Neues Forum, that courageous gathering of intellectuals, students, and workers which overturned the Stalinist regime in Berlin in 1989, lasted only six months in Germany's mini-version of McWorld. Then it gave way to money and markets and monopolies from the West. By the time of the first all-German elections, it could scarcely manage to secure three percent of the vote. Elsewhere there is growing evidence that *glasnost* will go and *perestroika*—defined as privatization and an opening of markets to Western bidders—will stay. So understandably anxious are the new rulers of Eastern Europe and whatever entities are forged from the residues of the Soviet Union to gain access to credit and markets and technology—McWorld's flourishing new currencies—that they have shown themselves willing to trade away democratic prospects in pursuit of them: not just old totalitarian ideologies and command-economy production models but some possible indigenous experiments with a third way between capitalism and socialism, such as economic cooperatives and employee stock-ownership plans, both of which have their ardent supporters in the East.

Jihad delivers a different set of virtues: a vibrant local identity, a sense of community, solidarity among kinsmen, neighbors, and countrymen, narrowly conceived. But it also guarantees parochialism and is grounded in exclusion. Solidarity is secured through war against outsiders. And solidarity often means obedience to a hierarchy in governance, fanaticism in beliefs, and the obliteration of individual selves in the name of the group. Deference to leaders and intolerance toward outsiders (and toward "enemies within") are hallmarks of tribalism—hardly the attitudes required for the cultivation of new democratic women and men capable of governing themselves. Where new democratic experiments have been conducted in retribalizing societies, in both Europe and the Third World, the result has often been anarchy, repression, persecution, and the coming of new, noncommunist forms of very old kinds of despotism. During the past year, Havel's velvet revolution in Czechoslovakia was imperiled by partisans of "Czechland" and of Slovakia as independent entities. India seemed little less rent by Sikh, Hindu, Muslim, and Tamil infighting than it was immediately after the British pulled out, more than forty years ago.

To the extent that either McWorld or Jihad has a *natural* politics, it has turned out to be more of an antipolitics. For McWorld, it is the antipolitics of globalism: bureaucratic, technocratic, and meritocratic, focused (as Marx predicted it would be) on the administration of things—with people, however, among the chief things to be administered. In its politico-economic imperatives McWorld has been guided by laissez-faire market principles that privilege efficiency, productivity, and beneficence at the expense of civic liberty and self-government.

For Jihad, the antipolitics of tribalization has been explicitly antidemocratic: one-party dictatorship, government by military junta, theocratic fundamentalism—often associated with a version of the *Führerprinzip* that empowers an individual to rule on behalf of a people. Even the government of India, struggling for decades to model democracy for a people who will soon number a billion, longs for great leaders; and for every Mahatma Gandhi, Indira Gandhi, or Rajiv Gandhi taken from them by zealous assassins, the Indians appear to seek a replacement who will deliver them from the lengthy travail of their freedom.

The Confederal Option

How can democracy be secured and spread in a world whose primary tendencies are at best indifferent to it (McWorld) and at worst deeply antithetical to it (Jihad)? My guess is that globalization will eventually vanquish retribalization. The ethos of material "civilization" has not yet encountered an obstacle it has been unable to thrust aside. Ortega may have grasped in the 1920s a clue to our own future in the coming millennium.

> Everyone sees the need of a new principle of life. But as always happens in similar crises—some people attempt to save the situation by an artificial intensification of the very principle which has led to decay. This is the meaning of the "nationalist" outburst of recent years . . . things have always gone that way. The last flare, the longest; the last sigh, the deepest. On the very eve of their disappearance there is an intensification of frontiers—military and economic.

Jihad may be a last deep sigh before the eternal yawn of McWorld. On the other hand, Ortega was not exactly prescient; his prophecy of peace and internationalism came just before blitzkrieg, world war, and the Holocaust tore the old order to bits. Yet democracy is how we remonstrate with reality, the rebuke our aspirations offer to history. And if retribalization is inhospitable to democracy, there is nonetheless a form of democratic government that can accommodate parochialism and communitarianism, one that can even save them from their defects and make them more tolerant and participatory: decentralized participatory democracy. And if McWorld is indifferent to democracy, there is nonetheless a form of democratic government that suits global markets passably well—representative government in its federal or, better still, confederal variation.

With its concern for accountability, the protection of minorities, and the universal rule of law, a confederalized representative system would serve the political needs of McWorld as well as oligarchic bureaucratism or meritocratic elitism is currently doing. As we are already beginning to see, many nations may survive in the long term only as confederations that afford local regions smaller than "nations" extensive jurisdiction. Recommended reading for democrats of the twenty-first century is not the U.S. Constitution or the French Declaration of Rights of Man and Citizen but the Articles of Confederation, that suddenly pertinent document that stitched together the thirteen American colonies into what then seemed a too loose confederation of independent states but now appears a new form of political realism, as veterans of Yeltsin's new Russia and the new Europe created at Maastricht will attest.

By the same token, the participatory and direct form of democracy that engages citizens in civic activity and civic judgment and goes well beyond just voting and accountability—the system I have called "strong democracy"—suits the political needs of decentralized communities as well as theocratic and nationalist party dictatorships have done. Local neighborhoods need not be democratic, but they can be. Real democracy has flourished in diminutive settings: the spirit of liberty, Tocqueville said, is local. Participatory democracy, if not naturally apposite to tribalism, has an undeniable attractiveness under conditions of parochialism.

Democracy in any of these variations will, however, continue to be obstructed by the undemocratic and antidemocratic trends toward uniformitarian globalism and intolerant retribalization which I have portrayed here. For democracy to persist in our brave new McWorld, we will have to commit acts of conscious political will—a possibility, but hardly a probability, under these conditions. Political will requires much more than the quick fix of the transfer of institutions. Like technology transfer, institution transfer rests on foolish assumptions about a uniform world of the kind that once fired the imagination of colonial administrators. Spread English justice to the colonies by exporting wigs. Let an East Indian trading company act as the vanguard to Britain's free parliamentary institutions. Today's well-intentioned quick-fixers in the National Endowment for Democracy and the Kennedy School of Government, in the unions and foundations and universities zealously nurturing contacts in Eastern Europe and the Third World, are hoping to democratize by long distance. Post Bulgaria a parliament by first-class mail. Fed Ex the Bill of Rights to Sri Lanka. Cable Cambodia some common law.

Yet Eastern Europe has already demonstrated that importing free political parties, parliaments, and presses cannot establish a democratic civil society; imposing a free market may even have the opposite effect. Democracy grows from the bottom up and cannot be imposed from the top down. Civil society has to be built from the inside out. The institutional superstructure comes last. Poland may become democratic, but then again it may heed the Pope, and prefer to found its politics on its Catholicism, with uncertain consequences for democracy. Bulgaria may become democratic, but it may prefer tribal war. The former Soviet Union may become a democratic confederation, or it may just

230

grow into an anarchic and weak conglomeration of markets for other nations' goods and services.

Democrats need to seek out indigenous democratic impulses. There is always a desire for self-government, always some expression of participation, accountability, consent, and representation, even in traditional hierarchical societies. These need to be identified, tapped, modified, and incorporated into new democratic practices with an indigenous flavor. The tortoises among the democratizers may ultimately outlive or outpace the hares, for they will have the time and patience to explore conditions along the way, and to adapt their gait to changing circumstances. Tragically, democracy in a hurry often looks something like France in 1794 or China in 1989.

It certainly seems possible that the most attractive democratic ideal in the face of the brutal realities of Jihad and the dull realities of McWorld will be a confederal union of semi-autonomous communities smaller than nation-states, tied together into regional economic associations and markets larger than nation-states—participatory and self-determining in local matters at the bottom, representative and accountable at the top. The nation-state would play a diminished role, and sovereignty would lose some of its political potency. The Green movement adage "Think globally, act locally" would actually come to describe the conduct of politics.

This vision reflects only an ideal, however—one that is not terribly likely to be realized. Freedom, Jean-Jacques Rousseau once wrote, is a food easy to eat but hard to digest. Still, democracy has always played itself out against the odds. And democracy remains both a form of coherence as binding as McWorld and a secular faith potentially as inspiring as Jihad.

Benjamin R. Barber is the Whitman Professor of Political Science at Rutgers University. Barber's most recent books are *Strong Democracy* (1984), *The Conquest of Politics* (1988), and *An Aristocracy of Everyone.*

Test-Your-Knowledge Form

We encourage you to photocopy and use this page as a tool to assess how the articles in *Annual Editions* expand on the information in your textbook. By reflecting on the articles you will gain enhanced text information. You can also access this useful form on a product's book support Web site at *http://www.mhcls.com/online/*.

NAME: DATE:

_____

TITLE AND NUMBER OF ARTICLE:

_____

BRIEFLY STATE THE MAIN IDEA OF THIS ARTICLE:

_____

LIST THREE IMPORTANT FACTS THAT THE AUTHOR USES TO SUPPORT THE MAIN IDEA:

_____

WHAT INFORMATION OR IDEAS DISCUSSED IN THIS ARTICLE ARE ALSO DISCUSSED IN YOUR TEXTBOOK OR OTHER READINGS THAT YOU HAVE DONE? LIST THE TEXTBOOK CHAPTERS AND PAGE NUMBERS:

_____

LIST ANY EXAMPLES OF BIAS OR FAULTY REASONING THAT YOU FOUND IN THE ARTICLE:

_____

LIST ANY NEW TERMS/CONCEPTS THAT WERE DISCUSSED IN THE ARTICLE, AND WRITE A SHORT DEFINITION:

We Want Your Advice

ANNUAL EDITIONS revisions depend on two major opinion sources: one is our Advisory Board, listed in the front of this volume, which works with us in scanning the thousands of articles published in the public press each year; the other is you—the person actually using the book. Please help us and the users of the next edition by completing the prepaid article rating form on this page and returning it to us. Thank you for your help!

ANNUAL EDITIONS: Comparative Politics 08/09

ARTICLE RATING FORM

Here is an opportunity for you to have direct input into the next revision of this volume.
We would like you to rate each of the articles listed below, using the following scale:

1. **Excellent: should definitely be retained**
2. **Above average: should probably be retained**
3. **Below average: should probably be deleted**
4. **Poor: should definitely be deleted**

Your ratings will play a vital part in the next revision.
Please mail this prepaid form to us as soon as possible.
Thanks for your help!

RATING	ARTICLE	RATING	ARTICLE
	1. The Economist Intelligence Unit's Index of Democracy		23. Referendums: The People's Voice
	2. The Failed States Index 2007		24. The Great Divide
	3. Democracy's Sobering State		25. The Case for a Multi-Party U.S. Parliament?
	4. Facing the Challenge of Semi-Authoritarian States		26. For Europe, A Moment to Ponder
	5. What Political Institutions Does Large-Scale Democracy Require?		27. A Venture at a Standstill
	6. What Democracy Is . . . and Is Not		28. The EU and Its "Constitution"
	7. Public Opinion: Is There a Crisis?		29. The Making of a Neo-KGB State
	8. Advanced Democracies and the New Politics		30. Putin's Patrimony
	9. British Constitutional Change		31. China: The Quiet Revolution
	10. The Historic Legacy of Tony Blair		32. In China, Talk of Democracy Is Simply That
	11. Muslim's Veils Test Limits of Britain's Tolerance		33. China to Join Top 3 Economies
	12. The Gaullist Revolutionary		34. How Did We Get Here? Mexican Democracy After the 2006 Elections
	13. Liberté, Égalité, Laïcité?		35. Will Africa Ever Get It Right?
	14. Angela Merkel's Germany		36. Africa's Crises of Democracy
	15. Germans Split over a Mosque and the Role of Islam		37. A Confident New Country
	16. Japanese Spirit, Western Things		38. Cast Battle Only Half Won as North Lags South
	17. Come Together: How to Avoid a Twisted Diet		39. Bin Laden, the Arab "Street," and the Middle East's Democracy Deficit
	18. Political Parties: Empty Vessels?		40. Iran's Conservative Revival
	19. Interest Groups: Ex Uno, Plures		41. Anti-Americanisms
	20. Let Women Rule		42. Capitalism and Democracy
	21. The True Clash of Civilizations		43. Cultural Explanations
	22. Judicial Review: The Gavel and the Robe		44. An Explosive Combination
			45. Jihad vs. McWorld

BUSINESS REPLY MAIL
FIRST CLASS MAIL PERMIT NO. 551 DUBUQUE IA

POSTAGE WILL BE PAID BY ADDRESSEE

McGraw-Hill Contemporary Learning Series
501 BELL STREET
DUBUQUE, IA 52001

ABOUT YOU

Name

Date

Are you a teacher? ☐ A student? ☐
Your school's name

Department

Address   City   State   Zip

School telephone #

YOUR COMMENTS ARE IMPORTANT TO US!

Please fill in the following information:
For which course did you use this book?

Did you use a text with this ANNUAL EDITION? ☐ yes ☐ no
What was the title of the text?

What are your general reactions to the Annual Editions concept?

Have you read any pertinent articles recently that you think should be included in the next edition? Explain.

Are there any articles that you feel should be replaced in the next edition? Why?

Are there any World Wide Web sites that you feel should be included in the next edition? Please annotate.

May we contact you for editorial input? ☐ yes ☐ no
May we quote your comments? ☐ yes ☐ no